1968-2001

Compiled by R M Clarke

A Brooklands Portfolio

BROOKLANDS BOOKS LTD.
P.O. BOX 146, COBHAM,
SURREY, KT11 1LG. UK
sales@brooklands-books.com

Printed in China

Hard Cover Edition

ISBN 185520 5858   Ref: A-MORQPHC

Soft Cover Edition

ISBN 185520 5777   Ref: A-MORQP

ACKNOWLEDGEMENTS

Time flies. It is now well over ten years since we published our Gold Portfolio covering Morgans built between 1968-1989 and nearly two years since it went out of print. Interest in all things Morgan is so strong that we knew that it was necessary to revisit the subject and bring it up to date. What we didn't realise was the wealth of articles that had been written about the marque in recent years and so to do justice to the subject we have produced one of our special 320 page 'portfolios'.

Traditionally, Brooklands Books have drawn on pre-published material for books such as this one. We are again delighted to acknowledge the generosity of the magazine publishers who have allowed us to reproduce the road tests and other stories that appear in this book. The material is drawn from *Auto International, Autocar, Autosport, BMW Car, Car, Car and Driver, Car Australia, Cars & Car Conversions, Classic & Sportscar, Classic Cars, Drive, Fast Car, Fast Lane, Motor, Motor Sport, Motor Trend, Performance Car, Practical Classics, Road & Track, Road & Track Specials, Road Test, Sports Car Graphic, Sports Car International, Sports Car World, Top Gear, What Car?* and the *World Car Guide*.

R. M. Clarke

Morgan's appearances are deceptive to the outsider. In the introduction to Brooklands Morgan Cars Gold Portfolio, 1968-1989, I wrote, "a Morgan tends to be a car which you either love or simply do not understand. Morgan enthusiasts tend to be fanatical; the rest of the world tends to perceive them as eccentric." Nothing has changed there. On the face of it, Morgans have not changed in 30 years or more - but, as this book shows, the Malvern factory has, in fact, produced a variety of models.

Leaving aside the latest Aero 8, which even a non-fanatic can see is radically different whilst embodying the essence of all that is Morgan, just look at the variety of engines featured. It has always been Morgan policy to buy its engines in, and they range from the early carburettor Rover V8, through injected versions to modern 16-valve four-cylinder units. Each one has imparted its own particular character to the cars, which have retained their individuality throughout. 1968 was the year the Plus 8 model was launched, and over the succeeding years this has been well developed to take the more powerful engines available. During this time the 4/4 and Plus 4 have not been forgotten, and as better engines became available the cars were able to keep pace with modern traffic conditions.

The appeal of a raw two-seater roadster, which unashamedly traces its design roots back to the 1930s, and yet is not self consciously "retro", is quite unique. Morgans are, perhaps, an acquired taste, but for the lucky few who own them (and there have always been long waiting lists) nothing else will do.

James Taylor

CONTENTS

CONTENTS - *continued*

Power drifts (note the tyre smoke!) can be enjoyed if you have access to a deserted airfield like we did here

With the hood up the body looks more vertical. Here it is in Belgium for maximum speed runs

AT-A-GLANCE: Rover 3½-litre vee-8 in the familiar Morgan two-seater sports car. Superb performance and very great flexibility. Poor synchromesh on top three gears; precise but stiff gearchange. Fade-free brakes. Hard bumpy ride. Very good smooth surface roadholding, not as good on bad roads. Heavy, accurate steering; poor lock. Great fun.

MANUFACTURER:

Morgan Motor Co., Pickersleigh Road, Malvern Link, Worcestershire.

PRICES

Basic	£1,155 0s 0d
Purchase Tax	£322 18s 4d
Total (in GB)	£1,477 18s 4d

PERFORMANCE SUMMARY

Mean maximum speed	124 mph
Standing start ¼-mile	15.1 sec
0-60 mph	6.7 sec
30-70 mph through gears	6.3 sec
Typical fuel consumption	21 mpg
Miles per tankful	250

IT really all depends on what you mean by "sports car". Defining that term is a favourite after-dinner or saloon bar diversion for many motoring enthusiasts. If it's a comfortable, soft-riding open touring car you want, with a lot of luggage room as well as a good performance and with everything made as convenient as possible, then read no further. If, as many still do, you think that more than 4¼in. of front suspension movement is cissy, that a quickly erected top and winding windows are effete, and that beat-proof synchromesh on all gears is a sign of moral decay, then here is a car for you. Especially if you'd like to get to 60 mph quicker than in any production E-type Jaguar which *Autocar* has ever tested, even though the E-type's better aerodynamics will win after 90 mph.

The Morgan Plus 8 is described on the preceding pages. It is the largest-engined Morgan ever made and the fastest normal production sports car to come from Malvern. The light-aluminium Rover 3.5-litre vee-8 engine goes into the space where the Plus 4's 2.2-litre

Triumph engine used to live. The only modification which might just possibly affect the Rover's normal 160.5 bhp (at 5,200 rpm) is the dent in the top of the air-cleaner, knocked-in a little to clear the central bonnet hinge. Compared with the Plus 4, net bhp is increased by about 54 per cent, net torque by nearly 60 per cent but—and a most important 'but' in any engine swap—kerb weight at 17.7 cwt is only increased by 3.2 per cent. Even that is done with only a 1-per-cent-heavier front end, which ensures that the Plus 8 doesn't unduly suffer in the balance of its roadholding.

Performance is what the Plus 8 is all about. Our best starts on MIRA's timing straights were done letting the heavy clutch in with a bang at nearly 4,000 rpm. With around five yards of slightly smoking wheelspin the car left the line and was doing 90 mph (14.5sec) just before the quarter-mile post (15.1sec) and 110 only 10sec later (25.7sec). Corresponding figures for the open 4.2-litre Jaguar E-type tested last October are respectively 15.1sec, 15.0sec and 23.1sec.

PERFORMANCE

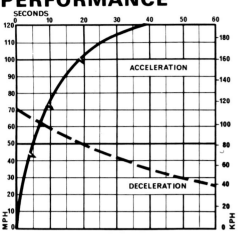

SECONDS

TIME IN SECONDS	2.3	3.5	5.2	6.7	8.6	11.8	14.5	18.4	25.7	42.9

TRUE SPEED MPH	30	40	50	60	70	80	90	100	110	120
INDICATED SPEED	28	38	49	59	69	79	89	100	111	121

Mileage recorder 3.2 per cent fast.   Test distance 1,413 miles.

SPEED RANGE, GEAR RATIOS AND TIME IN SECONDS

mph	Top (3.53)	3rd (4.25)	2nd (6.16)	1st (10.48)
10–30	5.8	4.7	3.2	1.8
20–40	5.0	4.2	2.7	1.9
30–50	4.8	3.8	2.4	– –
40–60	4.6	3.7	2.9	—
50–70	4.5	3.9	3.6	—
60–80	5.2	4.5	—	—
70–90	6.0	5.4	—	—
80–100	7.4	7.2	—	—
90–110	10.9	—	—	—
100–120	13.8	—	—	—

MAXIMUM SPEEDS

Gear	mph	kph	rpm
Top (mean)	124	200	5,640
(best)	125	201	5,690
3rd	105	169	5,750
2nd	72	116	5,750
1st	43	69	5,750

Standing ¼-mile 15.1 sec 92 mph.
Standing Kilometre 27.9 sec 113 mph.

MOTORWAY CRUISING

Error (ind. speed at 70 mph)	69 mph
Engine (rpm at 70 mph)	3,180 rpm
(mean piston speed)	1,485 ft/min
Fuel (mpg at 70 mph)	26.3 mpg
Passing (50–70)	3.4 sec
Noise (per cent silent at 70 mph)	40 per cent (hood down)
	20 per cent (hood up)

CONSUMPTION

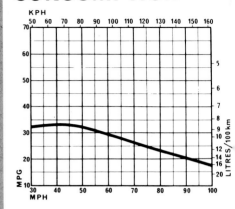

FUEL

At constant speeds—mpg	
30 mph	31.7
40 mph	33.6
50 mph	32.3
60 mph	29.4
70 mph	26.3
80 mph	24.1
90 mph	20.8
100 mph	17.5

Typical mpg . . 21 (13.5 litres/100km)
Calculated (DIN) mpg 23.9 (11.8 litres/100km)
Overall mpg . . 18.3 (15.5 litres/100km)
Grade of fuel: Super Premium, 5-star (min 1CORM)

OIL

Miles per pint (SAE 20/40)   500

HOW THE CAR COMPARES

Maximum speed (mph)

100 110 120 130 140

- Morgan Plus 8
- MGC
- Jaguar 4.2 E-type Roadster
- Triumph TR5
- Lotus Elan Coupe

0-60 mph (sec)

20   10

- Morgan Plus 8
- MGC
- Jaguar 4.2 E-type Roadster
- Triumph TR5
- Lotus Elan Coupe

Standing start ¼-mile (sec)

30   20   10

- Morgan Plus 8
- MGC
- Jaguar 4.2 E-type Roadster
- Triumph TR5
- Lotus Elan Coupe

MPG Overall

10   20   30

- Morgan Plus 8
- MGC
- Jaguar 4.2 E-type Roadster
- Triumph TR5
- Lotus Elan Coupe

PRICES

Morgan Plus 8	£1,478
MG MGC	£1,184
Jaguar E-Type Roadster	£2,117
Triumph TR5	£1,261
Lotus Elan	£1,902

TEST CONDITIONS
Weather: Sunny. Dry. Wind: 0–5 mph. Temperature: 18 deg. C. (64 deg. F.). Barometer: 30.0in. Hg. Humidity: 65 per cent. Surfaces: Dry concrete and asphalt.

WEIGHT
Kerb weight: 17.7cwt (1,979lb-898kg) (with oil, water and half-full fuel tank). Distribution, per cent F, 48.1; R, 51.9. Laden as tested: 21.3cwt (2,392lb-1,086kg).

Figures taken at 4,000 miles by our own staff at the Motor Industry Research Association proving ground at Nuneaton and on the Continent.

TURNING CIRCLES
Between kerbs: L, 39ft 5in.; R, 40ft 5in.
Between walls: L, 40ft 4in.; R, 41ft 4in.

Steering wheel turns, lock to lock: 2.4

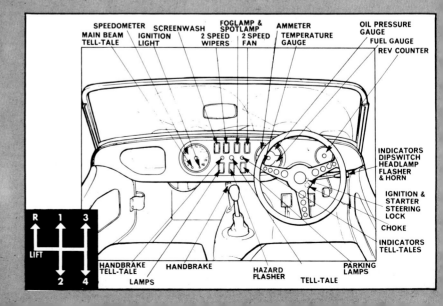

BRAKES

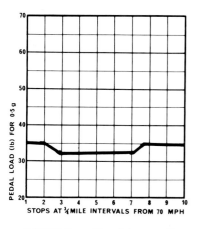

STOPS AT ¾ MILE INTERVALS FROM 70 MPH

BRAKES (from 30 mph in neutral)

ad	g	Distance
b	0.15	200ft
b	0.43	70ft
b	0.75	40ft
b	0.88	34ft
b	0.92	32.8ft
ndbrake	0.30	100ft

x. gradient 1 in 4
tch pedal: 50lb and 4.3in.

FROM 30 MPH IN NEUTRAL

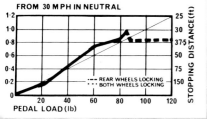

- - - REAR WHEELS LOCKING
····· BOTH WHEELS LOCKING

SPECIFICATION

FRONT ENGINE, REAR WHEEL DRIVE

ENGINE

Cylinders	8, in 90 deg. Vee
Cooling system	Water, pump, thermostat and thermo-statically operated cooling fan
Bore	88.9mm (3.50in.)
Stroke	71.12mm (2.80in.)
Displacement	3,529c.c. (215 cu.in.)
Valve gear	Pushrods and rockers
Compression ratio	10.5-to-1 : Min. octane rating: 100RM
Carburettors	2 SUHS6
Fuel pump	AC mechanical
Oil filter	Full flow, renewable element
Max. power	160.5bhp (net) at 5,200 rpm
Max. torque	210lb.ft (net) at 3,000rpm

TRANSMISSION

Clutch	Borg and Beck, diaphragm spring, 9.5 in.dia.
Gearbox	Moss Gear, 4-speed, synchromesh on Top, 3rd and 2nd.
Gear ratios	Top 1.00
	Third 1.205
	Second 1.745
	First 2.97
	Reverse 2.97
Final drive	Hypoid bevel with Power-Lok limited-slip differential, 3.58-to-1.

CHASSIS and BODY

Construction	Separate steel chassis, ash-framed body panelled in steel

SUSPENSION

Front	Independent, coil springs, sliding pillars, telescopic dampers
Rear	Live axle, half-elliptic leaf springs, lever-type dampers

STEERING

STEERING	Cam Gear worm and nut
Wheel dia.	14.5in.

BRAKES

Make and type	Girling, disc front, drum rear
Servo	Girling vacuum
Dimensions	F. 11.0in. dia discs
	R. 9.0in. dia 1.75in. wide shoes

Swept area	F. 226.4sq.in., R. 98.9sq.in.
	Total 325.3sq.in. (304.5sq.in./ton laden)

WHEELS

Type	Cast magnesium alloy, five stud fixing 5.5in. wide rim.
Tyres—make	Dunlop
—type	SP Sport radial-ply, tubed
—size	185VR—15in.

EQUIPMENT

Battery	12 volt 60-Ah
Alternator	11AC 45amp a.c.
Headlamps	Lucas sealed beam 120/90 watt (total)
Reversing lamp	No provision
Electric fuses	3
Screen wipers	2 speed, self-parking
Screen washer	Standard, electric pump
Interior heater	Standard, recirculating
Heated backlight	No provision
Safety belts	Extra, anchorages built in
Interior trim	Pvc seats, pvc hood
Floor covering	Rubber and carpet
Starting handle	No provision
Jack	Screw pillar
Jacking points	Anywhere under chassis
Windscreen	Laminated
Underbody protection	Painted chassis

MAINTENANCE

Fuel tank	13.5 Imp. gallons (no reserve) (62 litres)
Cooling system	16 pints (including heater)
Engine sump	9 pints (5 litres) SAE 20w
	Change oil every 5,000 miles
	Change filter element every 5,000 miles
Gearbox	2.5 pints SAE 30 Change oil every 10,000 miles
Final drive	1.5 pints SAE 90LS Change oil every 10,000 miles
Grease	4 points every 3,000 miles plus one-shot lubrication daily
Tyre pressures	F. 22 ; R. 22psi (normal driving)
	F. 24-26 ; R. 24-26psi (fast driving)
Max. payload	430lb (195kg)

PERFORMANCE DATA

Top gear mph per 1,000 rpm	22.0
Mean piston speed at max power	2,425ft/min.
Bhp per ton laden	153

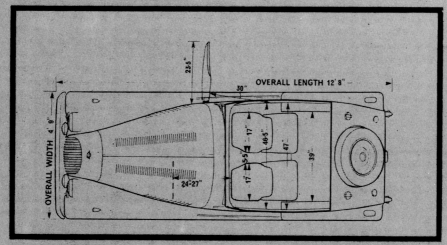

STANDARD GARAGE 16ft x 8ft 6in.

OVERALL LENGTH 12' 8"
OVERALL WIDTH 4' 9"

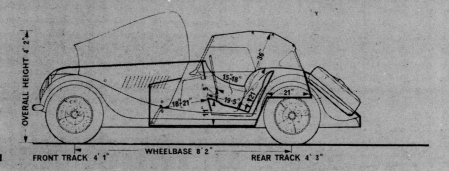

OVERALL HEIGHT 4' 2"

SCALE 0.3in. to 1ft.
Cushions uncompressed

FRONT TRACK 4' 1"   WHEELBASE 8' 2"   REAR TRACK 4' 3"

Autotest

Autotest Number 2204

In a lazy mood, the car's wonderful flexibility tempts one to think that the stubby little lever on the transmission tunnel is the range selector for an automatic. First gear takes you up to 43 mph at the engine's allowed maximum of 5,750 rpm, which sends you way out in front of any 'drag'. Second, with a maximum of 72 mph, copes with all awkward traffic situations, though the 105-mph third picks up nearly as well. Top you can use almost exclusively if feeling very lazy indeed. It will take you most effectively from below 10 mph, accelerating from 10 to 30 more quickly than it does from 70 to 90 (5.8 and 6.0sec in each case). By slipping the clutch up to 6 mph (just below 300 rpm), we still covered a top gear standing $\frac{1}{4}$-mile in 22.9sec—not to be recommended normally but it showed what can be done with a light car and a relatively big, vee-8 engine.

Our overall fuel consumption of 18.3 mpg, as is usual with this sort of model, is the result of consistently hard driving during the test period. An owner should be able to obtain 20 to 22 mpg without any difficulty on a journey.

Maximum speed of 124 mph mean was seen with the hood up. With the hood down this dropped to 118 mph because of the extra drag; there is no fairing of any sort behind the flat screen. Few open cars are pleasant to drive with the hood up and the Plus 8 is no exception, particularly since after the struggle of putting it up one then has a car which seems noisier and, as detailed elsewhere, much more "blind". The majority of Morgan drivers will avoid using the hood, and without it the car is remarkably quiet mechanically. The engine's smoothness and subdued exhaust note are very refined and seem almost out of place in such a harsh car. Only with wheelspin brutally induced —normally traction is very good—will an exhibitionist annoy his neighbours. There is surprisingly little road noise even over rough surfaces. Most noise comes from the gearbox which whines noticeably in the indirects; there are also a few rattles, the most annoying of which is caused by the exhaust pipe touching a frame bolt. Moving the exhaust pipe outwards, away from the frame, is not practicable, as it is already in firm rubbing contact with the left rear tyre when the car is cornered exuberantly on right-handers—this despite judicious flattening of the pipe at this point.

The gearchange takes quite a lot of learning to get the best out of the Plus 8. That delightful little lever is directly on top of the gearbox where one's hand falls straight to it, even though it is almost under the dashboard. There isn't any synchromesh on first and not as much as there should be on the other gears. Movements are absolutely precise and "mechanical" in feel—no question of any rubber-jointed linkage as there isn't ány linkage. Like the bulkhead under the passenger's feet, the lever gets quite hot after any fast driving. Taking acceleration figures, we hauled the lever through the tight little gate as callously as possible, trying to ignore the nasty grunts which this caused. With practice, the synchromesh can be made to work fairly well; it is as much a question of getting the pressure on the lever right as timing the sequence correctly. It is

essential to double de-clutch into first on the move, although there is never really any need to change down below second. Normally one treats gear changing in the vintage manner, timing changes accurately with the left foot keeping double time.

The steering is heavy, high-geared (2.4 turns from lock to lock) and has too large a turning circle for a sports car (40 ft mean between kerbs), mainly because of the big 185-15in. Dunlop SP Sport tyres having to fit inside wheel arches meant for a smaller section. On the test car it felt somewhat stiff and there was also nearly $\frac{3}{4}$in. of play at the leather rim of the handsome black alloy wheel. The manufacturers tell us that this slop and the stiffness are not normal. In any case it is not noticed when driving. The Morgan will hold an accurate line of the driver's choosing perfectly and is one of those cars which makes a keen driver extra conscious of precision in cornering. On rough surfaces, however, there can be quite hefty steering "fight", but this is in no way disconcerting, merely adding to the "vintage" feel of the car.

Steering and handling

Once you have become acclimatized to steering from the elbows again rather than with the fingertips, driving the Morgan through any winding road becomes immense fun. You must also get used to being jolted hard over every little bump in a way that would not have escaped unfavourable comment even before the last war. The ride is decidedly uncomfortable over second-class roads, even though the bucket seats are well padded and fit an average person nicely. Maximum speed runs on a bumpy Belgian *autoroute* were far more exciting at 124 mph in the Morgan than they have been in more modern Grand Touring cars at over 150. And yet one of the puzzling things about this is that it does not make the Plus 8 anywhere near difficult or dangerous on bumpy roads. One would expect it to jump wildly off line when cornering really fast and hitting a bump. There is some bump skid of course, at the rear wheels, but rarely enough to cause concern. Over most surfaces it copes surprisingly well and never behaves treacherously. A characteristic that makes the driver wince is a tendency for the front suspension to "top" noisily on occasions, almost as if there is insufficient rebound damper control. Side winds have little effect on the excellent straight-ahead stability at any speed.

Normally the Morgan understeers slightly and rolls very little even under the hardest cornering. On MIRA's smooth high-friction surfaces it was difficult to break the back wheels away in the dry. On not-so-good roads or in the wet power brings the tail out *pro rata*, though even then it takes a surprising amount of provocation, which says a lot for the tyres. The quick steering makes correction of any indiscretion easy, once an experienced driver is used to it. Brakes are servo-assisted, big and well-cooled enough to completely resist fade during our usual 10 stops from 70 mph.

Braking ratio between front and rear seemed just right on the test car, but one curious effect was noticed. At above 0.5g the front tyres "yelped" rhythmically as though a Dunlop Maxaret was fitted, making retardation jerky. Morgan's say that this is the tread of the SP Sport tyres opening and closing under strain and that it only happens with these covers. At any rate we were unable to achieve better than 0.92g maximum retardation, which is good but below the best standards. The handbrake, a fly-off type which needs a long lean forward to reach, would only hold the car on 1-in-4. Restarting from 1-in-3 was done with contemptuous ease and a little wheelspin.

The driving position is definitely vintage. You sit close to the steering wheel and dashboard but do not feel cramped even if tall. The pedals are a bit high for drivers with small feet. Heel-and-toe changes are easy nevertheless and the simple, time-honoured, roller throttle pedal is a delight to use, being at one end of a very smooth unsnatchy throttle linkage, which is just as well on a car with such a power-to-weight ratio. Another Morgan time-honoured fitting is the floor button where a dipswitch might be; when pressed after starting up each day or every 200 miles or so on a journey, engine oil is bled-off to lubricate the front suspension. Because of this the vee-8's oil consumption is perhaps a little higher than when Rover use it, though still quite acceptable. The padded top of the door cut-away makes a convenient armrest when the hood is down, which is when the Morgan is best to drive, particularly in traffic. The view ahead is of a long louvred bonnet and the tops of the front wings. At night one can see the side lights glim on the paint, so that a bulb failure is immediately obvious. One can reverse with great precision because of the short tail.

With the hood erected, something which takes quite a time and is easier with a passenger's help, it is very different. The three-quarter rear panels are too big and the rear window too small; one must treat road junctions with great care, always lining the car up at right angles in order to see enough on the left. Hood up or down, the mirror isn't much use, as the screen vibrates in sympathy with the suspension.

Over any bump there is a lot of body and scuttle shake, although the car as a whole feels more than strong enough to take the worst that a road can give. At high speed with the hood and sidescreens erected, wind pressure forces the latter to lean outwards beyond the side of the windscreen. Presumably because of the uncompromisingly flat screen, the little wiper blades never lift from the glass even at maximum speed; another advantage of flat glass is that replacements are much cheaper and can be made by any competent glass supplier anywhere. Apart from the seat belts there were no extras on our car; the Lucas spot and foglamps are standard equipment, and with the headlamps give enough light for medium-fast night driving.

Under-bonnet appearance

Engine accessibility is good and Rover are to be congratulated on making a vee-8 engine look really handsome and well finished; the ribbed aluminium rocker covers with the neat filler cap somehow look even more in place in this fierce sports car. We were most impressed with the complete oil-tightness of all engine joints. Morgan use a very compact Wood-Jeffrys electric fan to replace the normal engine-driven one and it proved perfectly capable of cooling the engine adequately under all conditions, being audible only on tick-over.

Summing up the Morgan Plus 8 isn't easy. It owes much to that very fine power unit and becomes a case of new wine in an old bottle. We cannot bring ourselves to disapprove too strongly about the discomforts of the classic style of body (several of us loved this nostalgia as much as anything about this very appealing car) and of course it is one of the reasons for the success of the Morgan, especially in America. One cannot help thinking that even more remarkable results could be achieved with more up-to-date suspension and a bettter gearbox, without losing anything of the car's tremendous character. Perhaps the spontaneous remark made when slowing hard after an acceleration run at MIRA does the job adequately—"There's a lot which could be better, but there's an awful lot right". ☐

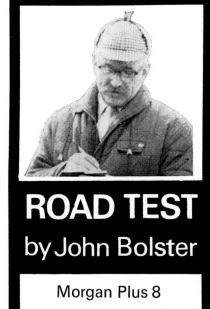

ROAD TEST
by John Bolster

Morgan Plus 8

New from Malvern Link:
The sensational Plus 8

IN the beginning, the Morgan was a three-wheeler called a Runabout. On the wall in the factory at Malvern Link, you can see a large picture of H. F. S. Morgan taking records in one at Brooklands before the first war, and it has the same independent front suspension as the latest production which his son, Peter, is now launching. Indeed, it would not be a Morgan if the front wheels were not on sliding stub axles operating against helical springs.

No car is quite so traditional as the Morgan. The shape of the body is derived from that of the first four-wheelers in the 1930s, and the straight chassis frame, passing beneath the rear axle, is of course retained. There would be a bloody revolution if any of these beloved features were altered, but the construction is very light and strong, while Morgan have for long been unbeatable on a performance for money basis.

The latest model is even more dramatic than those 100 mph JAP-engined three-wheelers, for the V-twin of those days has given place to a V8. The chassis is a couple of inches longer than its predecessor, and there is a similar increase in track. The Girling disc brakes are bigger and have servo assistance, while modern wide tyres are carried on new light-alloy wheels. The chassis now allows a little more rear suspension deflection but the travel is still short both in front and behind.

The engine is the Rover of 3528 cc, developing 184 bhp in standard tune with hydraulic tappets. Since it normally mates with an automatic transmission, it has been necessary to produce a special flywheel to carry the Morgan clutch. As with the previous, Triumph-engined model, the gearbox is remote from the engine but joined to it by a light alloy tubular extension through which the clutch-shaft runs. This brings the box back between the seats, so that a short vertical lever, projecting from its lid, can operate the selectors directly. The gearbox is still the traditional one with no synchromesh on bottom gear and only light synchronisation of the other speeds. However, it gives four close ratios and is commendably light in weight.

Although the body is a comfortably wide two-seater, and nothing has been skimped in its construction, this 3.5-litre car weighs less than 17 cwt. Obviously, the power to weight ratio is something quite out of the ordinary and the performance must be terrific. That is precisely what it turns out to be, the car leaping forward at a touch of the accelerator, almost irrespective of which gear is engaged.

In open form, the Morgan is a delightfully quiet car. The two exhaust manifolds run into a single pipe, which almost completely eliminates the typical V8 beat that is so irritating. The exhaust has a deep note and the sound might almost be that of a straight-eight, while some weight is saved without any measurable loss of power.

It is permissible to run up to 5750 rpm, which gives 42, 70 and 101 mph on the indirect gears. Third is a splendid ratio, giving really vivid acceleration, but even on top gear the car is very lively and will rush up almost any hill. If desired, top gear can be used for hours at a time, even in the heaviest traffic. Any car which can break the 15 secs barrier for the standing quarter-mile is a ball of fire, and the Morgan is of this select company. Such a car is intended for people who heel-and-toe, so I shall not bemoan the absence of Porsche-type synchromesh, but I might mention that during repeated acceleration tests the gearbox tended to tighten up, the change returning to normal when the box had a chance to cool down.

The roadholding of Morgans is famous and this one, with its big tyres on wide rims, has even greater cornering power. Initially it understeers, becoming neutral when pressed, and it is difficult to hang the tail out. The steering is light and responsive, but the width of the tyres has limited the steering lock.

The fine roadholding encourages one to throw the car about and very hard driving can be enjoyed in perfect safety. The

---

SPECIFICATION AND PERFORMANCE DATA

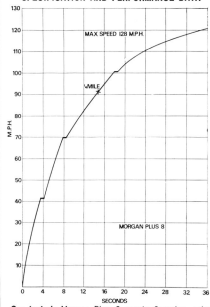

MAX SPEED 128 M.P.H.

¼ MILE

MORGAN PLUS 8

Car tested: Morgan Plus 8 sports 2-seater, price £1475 including PT.

Engine: Eight cylinders, 88.9 mm x 71.12 mm (3528 cc). Pushrod operated overhead valves. Compression ratio 10.5:1 184 bhp at 5200 rpm. Twin SU carburetters.

Transmission: Single dry plate clutch. 4-speed gearbox with synchromesh on upper 3 gears and short central lever. Hypoid rear axle with limited slip differential. Overall ratios 3.53, 4.2, 6.2 and 10.4:1.

Chassis: Straight Z-section steel frame members. Independent front suspension by sliding stub axles and helical springs with telescopic dampers. Worm and lever steering gear. Rear axle on semi-elliptic springs with lever-type dampers. Girling front disc and rear drum brakes with vacuum servo. Bolt-on aluminium wheels with 5½ ins J rims, fitted 185-15 Dunlop VR high-speed radial tyres.

Equipment: 12-volt lighting and starting with alternator and electric radiator fan. Speedometer. Rev counter. Ammeter. Oil pressure, water temperature, and fuel gauges. Heater. Windscreen wipers and washers. Cigar lighter. Flashing direction indicators.

Dimensions: Wheelbase, 8 ft 2 ins; track (front), 4 ft 1 in, (rear), 4 ft 3 ins; overall length, 12 ft 3 ins; width, 4 ft 10 ins; weight, 16 cwt 3 grs.

Performance: Maximum speed, 128 mph. Speeds in gears: third, 101 mph; second, 70 mph; first, 42 mph. Standing quarter-mile: 14.8 s. Acceleration: 0-30 mph, 2.3 s; 0-50 mph, 5.1 s; 0-60 mph, 6.6 s; 0-80 mph, 11.6 s; 0-100 mph, 18.1 s; 0-120 mph, 35 s.

Fuel consumption: 20 to 25 mpg.

brakes are immensely powerful but some front wheel tramp can be provoked by applying them hard on a bumpy road. Curiously enough, this does not cause the car to deviate and there is no apparent loss of braking power.

On very bumpy roads, nobody could pretend that the Morgan is comfortable, but though it pitches and the suspension may bottom, it is all part of the traditional sports car image. On good roads, which abound in England, the ride is comfortable and the suspension does not feel particularly hard.

Although the shape does not look very streamlined, the drag must be fairly low, as the car simply flashes up to 120 mph, whether the hood be up or down. It is only the axle ratio of 3.53:1 which limits the speed, and though the car can just about attain 130 mph, the engine is then revving past its peak. If one lived on the Continent, a higher gear might be pulled with advantage and would probably put the maximum up to 135 mph or so, but for use in England during most of the year, the present ratio is ideal.

To enjoy driving a sports car to the full, the location of the controls is particularly important. In an ordinary saloon, some compromise might be tolerated, but when a car is specifically intended for hard driving, a bad seat, a wrongly positioned steering wheel, or pedals not in their correct relationship, can ruin the pleasure of handling the machine. In the Morgan, everything is just right, and one at once becomes a part of the vehicle, which is essential before driving can become the art that it should be.

The view down the louvred bonnet is a delight and the headlamps permit the maximum speed to be used in the dark under suitable conditions. When the car is parked, the tonneau cover can be quickly buttoned in place to keep the seats dry in case of a shower. This and the hood are made of particularly stout material, as has for years been a Morgan feature. The speedometer is unusually accurate, but it is astonishing how often it swings past the 100 mph mark, even 120 mph coming up in the most unlikely places.

I always enjoy driving Morgans because they are cars built for the owner's pleasure. Some makes appeal because of their novel engineering features but the Morgan endears itself by being predictably the same. With its powerful light-alloy V8 engine and wide tyres, the latest model is perhaps even more typically Morgan than anything that has gone before. This is an exciting sports car with electric acceleration that is glued to the road, at a price which many of us can afford to pay.

The Morgan Plus 8's attractively traditional lines are unchanged, but enhanced by new cast alloy road wheels.

Dash arrangement is neater, with rocking-action switches.

Sixty years young: the Plus 8 still uses sliding pillar front suspension, as on the first Moggie three-wheelers (left). The light-alloy V8 is a snug fit, and is mounted well forward (right).

Quite unique

MOTOR TESTED

Vintage chassis with a modern V-8 engine gives tremendous performance, passable handling and very poor ride: civilized cockpit but primitive hood

SOME cars are good enough to be judged by absolute standards regardless of price; others must be examined in relation to their rivals. The Morgan Plus 8, however, is unique. First, it has no real rivals but occupies its own little niche in the market. Second, by absolute standards it jumps from one extreme to the other—rather like its live rear axle on a bumpy corner. On the credit side, the magnificent Rover V-8 engine gives the car tremendous performance (0-100 m.p.h. in 19 seconds, top speed 125 m.p.h.) and on smooth roads the roadholding is quite good. At the other extreme, on grade two surfaces the ride is so bad that the roadholding suffers even more than do the passengers; moreover, protection from the weather in an otherwise comfortable and civilized cockpit is about as primitive as you can get and the gearbox almost as Vintage as the styling.

A modern chassis with a little more suspension movement and a lot more torsional rigidity would bring the Morgan into line with other two-seater sports cars in terms of handling, performance, accommodation and creature comforts. But of course it would then cost a lot more than £1,500 and would lose most of its Vintage individuality which many customers will interpret as charm. So the makers, probably rightly, have chosen to retain the old Morgan flavour with a new ingredient—performance—that at

some times enhances the car and at others almost spoils it. For instance, long journeys on bumpy roads in heavy rain reveal the car at its most Hyde-like—it rattles and bounces and skips and leaks. Yet on a fine day on good roads the car sheds its Hyde clothing and becomes an exhilerating Jekyll and you waft along with the hood down and the side screens up (paradoxically, this Vintage car is at its best on a motorway). It is perhaps so different from other present-day vehicles that some drivers thoroughly enjoyed the car while others could never quite come to terms with its inherent faults even though conceding that, in the right conditions its rating as a fun car is very high indeed.

Performance and economy

Shoe-horn jobs—the currently fashionable insertion of an oversized engine into a conventional chassis—are not always successful; in some you get a slightly uncomfortable feeling of living next door to the powerhouse which begins to throb and scream as the revs rise. But the Rover engine in its Morgan installation is a remarkably fine marriage; the lightweight V-8 is extremely smooth and it delivers its power in such a subdued and unfussy manner that really high speeds become deceptively effortless. At low speed, it pulls well from less than 500 r.p.m. and the only hint of harshness compared with the Rover installation is at low revs which cannot be used in the Rover because of its automatic transmission. Once in the usual working range, anywhere between 1,500 and 5,000 r.p.m., the unit remains unobtrusive and you have to

PRICE: £1,155 plus £320 equals £1,475. Seat belts £12 2s.9d. extra. Total as tested equals £1,487 2s. 9d. Insurance: AOA Group rating and Lloyds': on application.

Morgan 3½-litre Plus Eight

watch the rev-counter to prevent over revving. Rover's limit is 5,000 r.p.m., but 6,000 r.p.m. is possible—and was used in our acceleration tests without the hydraulic tappets "pumping up".

Starting is simple, with a manual choke mounted alongside the ignition key on top of the steering column which also incorporates a steering lock. The engine pulls so well from cold that you have to remember to take it gently for a mile or so until the water and oil warm up. The choke is set to give fast idling without enrichment for the first part of its movement.

Apart from some trouble with the mechanical fuel pump, which will have an electric pump in series to help it out on production models, the engine was completely untemperamental, and a

Performance

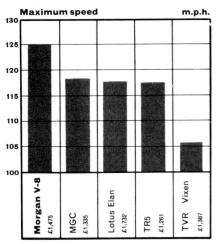

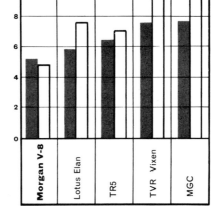

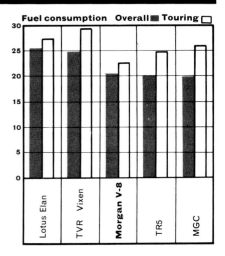

Performance tests carried out by *Motor's* staff at the Motor Industry Research Association proving ground, Lindley.

Test Data; World copyright reserved; no unauthorized reproduction in whole or in part.

Conditions

Weather: Dry, winds up to 12 mph.
Temperature 62°–68°F.
Barometer 29.35–29.30 in. Hg.
Surface: Dry tarmacadam and concrete
Fuel: Super premium 101 octane (RM) 5-star rating.

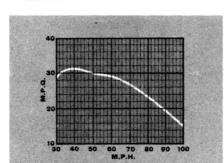

Maximum speeds

	m.p.h.	k.p.h.
Estimated maximum speed	125	202
Direct top gear	122½	197
3rd gear ⎫	101	163
2nd gear ⎬ at 5,750 r.p.m.	70	113
1st gear ⎭	41	66

Acceleration times

m.p.h.		sec.
0–30	. . . .	2.5
0–40	. . . .	3.5
0–50	. . . .	5.1
0–60	. . . .	6.7
0–70	. . . .	8.7
0–80	. . . .	12.1
0–90	. . . .	15.4
0–100	. . . .	19.0
Standing quarter mile	. . . .	15.0

m.p.h.	Top sec.	3rd sec.
10–30	—	4.7
20–40	4.9	4.3
30–50	4.8	3.9
40–60	4.7	3.9
50–70	5.1	4.2
60–80	6.1	4.5
70–90	6.4	5.4
80–100	8.1	7.3

Fuel consumption

Touring (consumption midway between 30 m.p.h. and maximum less 5% allowance for acceleration) . . . . 22.2 m.p.g.
Overall . . . . 20.3 m.p.g.
(= 13.9 litres/100km)
Total test distance . . . . 1,080 miles

Brakes

Pedal pressure, deceleration and equivalent stopping distance from 30 m.p.h.

lb.	g	ft.
25	0.21	143
50	0.51	59
75	0.96	31
Handbrake	0.31	97

Fade test

20 stops at ½g deceleration at 1 min. intervals from a speed midway between 40 m.p.h. and maximum speed (=82½ m.p.h.)

	lb.
Pedal force at beginning	 41
Pedal force at 10th stop	 40
Pedal force at 20th stop	 40

Steering

Turning circle between kerbs:	ft.
Left	37½
Right	38¼
Turns of steering wheel from lock to lock	2.4
Steering wheel deflection for 50ft. diameter circle	0.9 turns

Clutch

Free pedal movement	= 1 in.
Additional movement to disengage clutch completely	= 1½ in.
Maximum pedal load	= 62 lb.

Speedometer

Incorrect head fitted to test car giving mean 10% fast. Production head should be accurate.
Distance recorder . . . . 1% slow

Weight

Kerb weight (unladen with fuel for approximately 50 miles) . . . . 17.2 cwt.
Front/rear distribution 49/51
Weight laden as tested . . . . 21.0 cwt.

Parkability

Gap needed to clear 6 ft. wide obstruction parked in front:

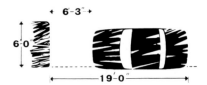

smooth throttle linkage controlled by an old fashioned roller accelerator pedal tames the power well. The strongest pulling range is a little way up the rev scale, as our best 20 m.p.h. step was from 40-60 m.p.h. in top shows; in third, 30-50 m.p.h. and 40-60 m.p.h. took only 3.9 seconds. From 90-100 m.p.h. is quicker in top than in third as this is beyond the peak power of the engine.

The car's standing start figures are fast in any company; it reaches 50 m.p.h. in 5.1 seconds, 60 in 6.7, 70 in 8.7 and 80 m.p.h. in 12.1 seconds, beyond which the drag increases steeply and the E-type Jaguar, for example, which the Morgan can hold to 70 m.p.h., would pull ahead. Even so there is only a handful of other cars, all more expensive, which can reach 100 m.p.h. in under 20 seconds.

Unfortunately we didn't have the opportunity to record the ultimate maximum speed on a straight road so we had to use the speed trap on MIRA's outer banked circuit. Maintaining around 110 m.p.h. on the apex of the banking, at which the Morgan was reassuringly stable despite the bumps (the hands off speed on the banking is about 85 m.p.h.), we recorded 120.8 m.p.h., which past experience suggests is equivalent to an all-out maximum of 125 m.p.h. The best lap, which includes easing for the bankings, was 114 m.p.h.; with the hood down the car is only about 2 m.p.h. slower.

If you enjoy all the performance as we did, the fuel consumption—which the makers say should be of 101-octane petrol although it seemed happy on 98--was 20.3 m.p.g., which gives a range of around 250 miles of hard driving on the 13½-gallon tank. Our touring figure at 22.2 m.p.g. represents more gentle driving, cruising around 75/80 m.p.h. The tank conveniently has two fillers and it helped to open both when filling up to avoid splash back.

Vintage layout with modern equipment—the dashboard sums up the whole car very well.

As it always was—foldaway hood tucked in at the back.

Under the dash—the recirculating heater and pedals sprouting up from the floor.

Morgan 3½-litre Plus Eight

Transmission

The only real objection to the gearbox is its very poor synchromesh. A Moss gearbox similar to that in early Jaguars, it uses the ball and spring system, which is easy to override. The upper three ratios are very close so you don't have to wait long to get a smooth snick-free change; but between the unsynchronised first and second, where the gap is greater, waiting too long will let the engine slow down too much and too short a wait will cause a crunch as the gearbox internals haven't slowed enough. It really helps to double declutch upwards on this change; downwards you have to do it anyway on all the changes, though the pedals are so comfortably spaced for heel and toeing that it is an easy action.

One of the reasons for having the gearbox mounted well back, with a closed shaft between it and the engine, is to obviate the need for a remote control linkage; apart from the increased rotary inertia of the input shaft there is no disadvantage and the short stiff lever is ideally placed. Clumsy hands and feet will initially "make a pig's ear" of the box, but once mastered it is quite satisfying. The clutch was one of the heaviest we have used though the angle of attach on the pedal was comfortable.

The car romped away on a 1-in-4 hill but the trouble with the fuel pump prevented us testing effectively on a 1-in-3; with all that torque it should manage quite comfortably when pulling properly.

With a sliding pinion first gear and what sounds like straight-cut constant mesh gears, there is a lot of gearbox noise in the intermediates, but in top it is quiet and the Salisbury axle is never audible.

Handling and brakes

The chassis has not been changed much over the years (although it has been strengthened) so we did not expect it to be very stiff. It isn't. On bumpy roads there is a lot of scuttle shake as well as some live-axle hop, though re-angling the rear leaf springs and using a limited slip differential prevents any tramping; on our standing start tests the car just rocketed away with about five yards of wheel-spin. At the front, the familiar coil sprung sliding pillars (originally patented in 1912) are retained. Telescopic dampers are separate. As ever, the traditional pillar lubrication is required daily, good lubrication being essential since the pillar is the steering pivot as well as the prime front suspension location. Pressing the button just above the clutch pedal taps the engine oil circuit to give a single high pressure squirt.

Wider tyres, now 185-15 Dunlop SP Sport, with high self-aligning torque make the steering heavier than that of earlier models and we found it rather sticky on tighter corners. It frees up at higher speeds though, and despite a little free play in the box the car runs dead straight; the lock, however, is poor with a 38 ft. turning circle. On dry roads understeer is the predominant characteristic if you are trying hard, even when you ease the throttle. On tighter corners a burst of power can snap the tail round progressively so a skilled driver can steer as much with the throttle as with the wheel. On wet roads the throttle has to be treated with a lot more respect as the tail can leap out quite sharply but the tyres grip very well and they come back into line as soon as the throttle is eased. The limited-slip differential lets you put down a surprising amount of power quite early in a corner, without breaking adhesion.

If you press the car really hard on a track with the standard road tyre pressures of 22 p.s.i. the limit is accompanied by some undamped lurching, as if the chassis were bending under the stresses of cornering power; raising the pressures to 28 p.s.i. controlled the lurching and also lightened the steering quite usefully.

With bigger Girling calipers and a servo the brakes are first class; the pedal pressure is average (about 1 lb. per 0.01g) and progressive in response and our fade and water splash tests had no effect at all. However, braking hard from high speed could set up a low frequency pitching (about 2 cycles per second) which was enough to vary the weight on the front wheels and give the same effect as brake grab. The fly-off handbrake, mounted inconve-

Detachable sidescreens slot into the doors.
*It **must** be a Morgan! Note the wheels as immediate Plus Eight identification points.*

The luggage area behind the seats takes 4.4 cu.ft. of our luggage, all of which is retained in place by the seat backs and it doesn't obscure the view. Tool roll is an extra.

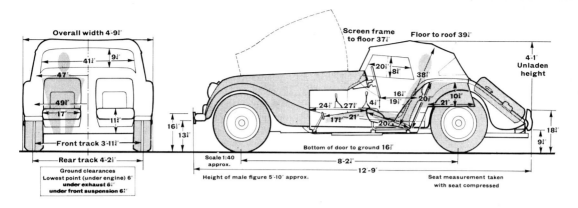

Light alloy 3,530 c.c. V-8 front mounted; live rear axle on leaf springs; steel body on ash frame.

Engine

Block material	Aluminium
Head material	Aluminium
Cylinders	V-8
Cooling system	Water with thermostatic fan
Bore and stroke	89 mm. (3.5 in.) 71 mm. (2.8 in.)
Cubic capacity	3,530 c.c. (215 cu. in.)
Main bearings	Five
Valves	Pushrod o.h.v.
Compression ratio	10.5:1
Carburetters	Twin SU HS6
Fuel pump	AC mechanical
Oil filter	Full flow
Max. power (net)	168 b.h.p. at 5,200 r.p.m.
Max. power (gross)	184 b.h.p. at 5,200 r.p.m.
Max. torque (net)	210 lb. ft. at 2,700 r.p.m.
Max. torque (gross)	226 lb. ft. at 3,000 r.p.m.

Transmission

Clutch	Single plate diaphragm sprung 9.5 in. dia.

Internal gearbox ratios

Top gear	1.00
3rd gear	1.205
2nd gear	1.745
1st gear	2.97
Reverse	2.97
Synchromesh	On 2, 3, and 4
Final drive	Hypoid bevel limited slip 3.58:1

M.p.h. at 1,000 r.p.m. in:—

Top gear	21.3
3rd gear	17.7
2nd gear	12.2
1st gear	7.2

Chassis and body

Construction	Z-section side members with boxed cross members and steel and wood flooring. Steel body on ash frame.

Brakes

Type	Girling hydraulic with servo
Dimensions	11 in. dia. disc, 9 in. dia. drum

Friction areas:

Front	21 sq. in. of lining operating on 124 sq. in. of disc
Rear	59 sq. in. of lining operating on 99 sq. in. of drum

Suspension and steering

Front	Independent with vertical sliding pillars, coil springs
Rear	Live axle with semi-elliptic leaf springs

Shock absorbers:

Front	Telescopic
Rear	Lever arm
Steering type	Cam Gears, cam and peg
Tyres	Dunlop SP Sport 185-15VR
Wheels	Aluminium alloy
Rim size	5½J-15

Coachwork and equipment

Starting handle	None
Tool kit contents	Wheel changing equipment
Jack	Lazy tong
Jacking points	Under chassis
Battery	12 volt negative earth 59 amp hrs capacity
Number of electrical fuses	Four
Headlamps	Lucas sealed beam
Indicators	Self-cancelling flashers
Reversing lamp	No
Screen wipers	3-blade 2-speed electric
Screen washers	Electric
Sun visors	No

Locks:

With ignition key	Steering column lock
With other keys	None
Interior heater	Recirculatory
Upholstery	Ambla
Floor covering	Rubber with carpet for luggage area
Alternative body styles	None
Maximum load	4 cwt
Major extras available	Luggage rack

Maintenance

Fuel tank capacity	13½ galls
Sump	10 pints SAE 10W/30
Gearbox	2.5 pints SAE 20W/30
Rear axle	1.5 pints SAE 90 (hypoy l.s.)
Steering gear	SAE 20W/30
Coolant	15 pints (3 drain taps)
Chassis lubrication	(Foot operated) every 200 miles to 2 points (or daily)
Minimum service interval	3,000 miles
Ignition timing	6°btdc static
Contact breaker gap	0.014-0.016 in.
Sparking plug gap	0.025 in.
Sparking plug type	Champion L87Y
Tappet clearances	Hydraulic

Valve timing:

inlet opens	30°btdc
inlet closes	75°abdc
exhaust opens	68°bbdc
exhaust closes	37°atdc
Rear wheel toe-in	Live axle
Front wheel toe-in	⅛ in.
Camber angle	2°
Castor angle	4°
King pin inclination	2°

Tyre pressures:

Front	24 p.s.i.
Rear	24 p.s.i.

Safety

Steering box position	Behind front suspension
Steering column collapsible	Yes, with UJs and AC Delco collapsible system
Steering wheel boss padded	No
Steering wheel dished	No
Screen type	Laminated
Standard driving mirrors	Framed
Interior mirror collapsible	No
Sun visors	None
Safety belts	Lap and diagonal
Anti-burst doors	No
Child-proof locks	No

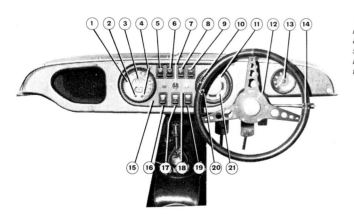

1, speedometer. 2, head light warning beam. 3, trip and total mileage recorders. 4, ignition. 5, washers. 6, wipers. 7, alternator charge tell-tale. 8, fog/spot lights. 9, heater fan. 10, ammeter. 11, oil pressure. 12, ignition/steering column lock. 13, rev. counter. 14, horn/flasher/dipswitch. 15, hand brake warning light. 16, light switch. 17, hazard warning flasher. 18, indicator tell-tale. 19, parking light switch. 20, water temperature. 21, fuel gauge.

Morgan 3½-litre Plus Eight

niently far forward on the left of the transmission tunnel, held the car on a 1-in-4 hill but ran out of adjustment for the stronger requirements of 1-in-3 parking although the potential seemed to be there.

Comfort and controls

Ride comfort was not a feature which greatly concerned the drivers of pre-war sports cars except where it directly involved roadholding on inferior surfaces. Even though the Morgan has this sort of heredity, its ride is better than mediocre Vintage, though in comparison with most modern sports cars it is very poor and one is conscious of steering round the bad bumps and not over them. Badly filled road holes generate loud bonks from the front suspension and a very pitchy ride. Bumps on corners can throw the car out of line, too, but with all that rubber on the road there is little danger of this starting a slide.

Poor surfaces also make the sidescreens rattle; without them (they can be stowed flat behind the seats) the car can be fairly quiet but the slipstream begins to buffet around 70 m.p.h.; if the sidescreens are up without the hood you can maintain almost any speed you like without getting overtaxed by the noise. At first the hood takes a long time to put up, although you improve with practice. First you raise the three permanently attached hoops and then lay the hood on top; poppers and press studs all round hold it fairly taut with the screen effectively providing most of the tension. Up to 80 or 90 m.p.h. the flap isn't too bad but beyond that the sidescreens bow outwards and the noise gets worse. So, most of the time, we kept the hood down as you don't get wet while the car is moving.

With the hood down, visibility is excellent and the view along the long, louvred bonnet, across which can be seen the side light on the opposite wing, provides a splendid aiming sight. Clear plastic panels in the hood give a good rearward view but there is a blind spot to the side. You have to keep the side screens fairly clean because dirty plastic is harder to see through than dirty glass. A framed rear-view mirror is glued to the screen and occasionally gets in the way when you want to look half left. It also needed frequent adjustment when travelling fast as wind pressure changes the angle of the screen.

With new Restall bucket seats, as opposed to the familiar bench, the driving position is quite comfortable and you are well supported for fast cornering. You can't move far enough back to get a long-arm driving position, but then the heavy steering demands a short-arm style anyway. The pedals are well spaced for heel and toeing, but the best place for your left foot is resting on the rocker shaft between the clutch and brake. The separate gearbox allows the direct acting gear lever to be in just the right place and its short movement keeps it within easy reach.

Only a "fug-stirrer" heater is used, mounted down in the passenger's foot well where the driver can barely reach it; a water cock under the bonnet regulates temperature but since there is no ram effect there is no hot air leakage unless the two-speed blower fan is on; thus unless you want cold air in hot weather you leave the cock open all the time—it's quite pleasant to have the heater on on a cool summer evening when the hood is down. It is quite effective as a foot warmer but there is no provision for demisting from the inside, although we found that hot air from the bonnet louvres seemed to heat the screen sufficiently to keep it clear once the worst had been wiped off. Ventilation is, of course, according to taste, but with the hood up and fastened properly the car was reasonably free of draughts and the sliding sidescreens could be used to get a little air in; some water crept under the screen in heavy rain and in our water splash test some came in through the pedal holes.

Our test car was fitted with only two wiper blades leaving an unwiped gap in the middle but later cars will have three, with two speeds; the electric screen washer has a separate switch alongside that for the wipers. The headlights are good, both on main and dipped beam, but the pitchy ride sweeps them through quite a large vertical arc which is more disconcerting to those approaching than to the driver.

Fittings and furniture

The layout of the interior is probably one of the more obvious external signs that the Plus 8 is a new Morgan. The metal facia panel is covered in black leathercloth and padded at the bottom; production models will be padded on the top edge too. Although the car is not destined immediately for the American market, the central panel now incorporates all the rocker type safety switches, and the wiring loom incorporates a hazard warning connection, which flashes front and rear indicators simultaneously. Incidentally, it was difficult to pick out the yellow indicators against the orange car on a bright day. A parking switch is also incorporated which turns out the nearside and tail lights and also isolates the ignition circuit.

With the tonneau cover over the passenger side only, the speedometer is almost completely obscured and you have to remember the relevant revs for the speed limits. The other dial matching the speedometer contains four gauges (fuel, ammeter, water temperature and oil pressure). A multi-position Cortina style stalk controls indicators, flasher, dipswitch and the rather weak horn.

A rubber covering is used for the front floor, leathercloth for the doors and carpet for the luggage well. With the hood up, and the hoops consequently out of the way, we managed to fit 4.4 cu. ft. of our test luggage behind the seats without obscuring the rearward view, and it is all retained by the seat backs. With the hood down there is very little room for any serious luggage.

Servicing and maintenance

The standard tool kit covers wheel changing equipment, but our car had the extra toolkit which fits into the compartment on top of the scuttle under the bonnet; this includes enough for any roadside work, although the plug spanner was too bulky to get into the recesses on the Rover engine. Servicing is required every 3,000 miles covering the usual servicing items which any garage can manage, although obviously a Rover dealer will be that much more familiar with the power unit. Chassis lubrication only involved the sliding pillars which, as we mentioned earlier, required a squirt daily (or every 200 miles) via the foot operated plunger. **M**

1, coil. 2, fuel filter. 3, distributor. 4, radiator filler cap. 5, oil filler cap. 6, dipstick. 7, cylinder block drain tap. 8, washer reservoir. 9, heater cock.

MAKE: Morgan. MODEL: Plus 8. MAKERS: Morgan Motor Company Ltd., Pickersleigh Road, Malvern Link, Worcs.

The 3½-litre MORGAN PLUS-8

125 m.p.h. A standing-start ¼-mile in 15 sec.

A True but Primitive Sports Car

ON TEST IN MID-WALES.—*The Plus-8 at the beginning of the Abergwesyn-Tregaron mountain road, well known to rally drivers.*

SPORTS CARS come and sports cars go but the Morgan has outlived most of them. Just when it seems to have out-dated itself from even the American fanatical and British enthusiast sales-charts, something happens to give the Morgan four-wheeler, basically unchanged down the years, a new lease of life, sustaining the interest of prospective purchasers.

The original Morgan four-wheeler was an attractive little car, but it lacked the flair and sporting appearance of the similar-size M.G.s, which in those days had wire wheels and a trials reputation, against which the Morgan 4/4, had to compete. Pressed-steel wheels and a chassis rather self-consciously aware that is was closely related to a long generation of three-wheelers. But it had independent front suspension and a gear lever most commendably located, due to the employment of a separate gearbox. The 4/4 ran through a succession of engines and then came the exciting news that a Morgan Plus-4, with 2-litre engine, was on the assembly-shop floor at Malvern.

The Plus-4 chassis was a somewhat inflated version of that used for the 4/4, strengthened only where the ingenious Mr. Peter Morgan thought this absolutely essential. It had the appearance and performance of a good vintage or p.v.t. sporting car, and when, later, it was powered with warmed-up 2.2-litre Triumph TR4A engines instead of a single-carburetter Standard Vanguard engine, it really motored most effectively, and was impressive on the Club circuits. That, however, was quite a long time ago and the Plus-4 clearly needed a new lease of life. This has been most effectively accomplished by installing under a somewhat lengthened bonnet (still heavily louvred) a perfectly normal Rover V8 engine, of Buick persuasion, as used by the Rover Company in their 3500 and 3½-litre cars. The potential of these light-alloy General Motors-Oldsmobile and Buick power units was emphasised by racing development, from mild souping for stock-car work to virtual rebuilding for installation in the Formula One Repco Brabhams, so it can be said to have links with racing if not to be actually race developed. It gives 161 (net) b.h.p. at a crankshaft speed of 5,200 r.p.m. This is on a c.r. of 10½ to 1, so that 101-octane petrol is preferable but not essential if only Premium is available. The engine is absolutely standard, as used in the Rover 3500, even to very ordinary exhaust manifolds, and there should be plenty of development to come.

Using this splendid Rover V8 engine so ably adapted to Solihull specification by Peter Wilks has lifted the performance of this Morgan sports two-seater from effective to highly impressive. That is to say, this primitive, certainly old-fashioned, car will now reach a top speed of 125 m.p.h., will devour a s.s. ¼-mile in 15.0 sec. or less, and will out-accelerate a Jaguar E-type up to the legal limit of public-road speed in this go-slow country. It continues to accelerate excitingly beyond 70 m.p.h. (on private roads, of course!). For having got to that pace in well under 9 sec., it requires only another ten seconds to be motoring at 100 m.p.h. This, with a bog-standard 89 × 71 mm. (3,530 c.c.) Rover engine. It is fascinating to think how the Morgan Plus-8 will go when fuel-injection or other performance-enhancers are tried—and I expect one or other of the Peters *will* experiment with them.

Right away, therefore, it seems obvious that if sheer performance, in terms especially of acceleration and a reasonable top speed, appeals—straight-line go, if you like—the Morgan Plus-8 is a formidable motor-car, because it offers this in terms which only very few cars, costing more, can *equal*. Take for instance 0 to 100 m.p.h. in 19 to 20 sec., for a price, including p.t., of £1,487. Those interested in Marque Sports Car Racing should be interested. . . .

Returning to the differences between the Triumph-powered Plus-4 and the new Plus-8, they are quite few in number. For instance, the separate gearbox is retained, coupled to the engine flywheel by a short shaft within a large-diameter tube, and it is the same Moss gearbox used on the Morgan Plus-4 and earlier Jaguars, this apparently being sufficiently rugged to transmit the 226 lb./ft. maximum torque of the Rover engine. The real separate chassis is also retained, although it has been somewhat strengthened. The old wood plank floor—I was intrigued that it was not so much as creosoted—has given place to a welded-steel floor. The coil-spring and pillar i.f.s., which is basically nearly 60 years old, remains, and still necessitates a bronze damper-ring and lubrication bled off the engine supply, for the pillars also form the king-pins of the steering layout. Similarly, at the back the suspension is by ½-elliptic leaf springs, although these are now mounted at a different angle, which has killed tramp, and the movement has been increased, to 4½ in. The steering column now incorporates two universal joints to clear the wide vee engine, is collapsible, and the

Test held up—the Morgan Plus-8 meets ponies on their way to the November auction sales.

box is a Cam Gears' cam-and-peg unit.

The wheelbase has been increased by 2 in., the bonnet is longer, and the body 2 in. wider to accommodate wider wheel rims. The wheels have been changed to imposing Robinson five-stud cast-alloy ones, the same make as those on the Gilbern Genie featured last month, having 5½ in. rims, shod with imposing looking 185×15VR Dunlop SP Sport radial-ply Aquajet-tread tyres. A further concession to the increased and spectacular performance is the use of 16P Girling brake calipers instead of 14P, although the disc/drum sizes are unchanged. There is now a 13½-gallon fuel tank and instrumentation and details have been changed. For instance, for years there was no adjustment, either of cushion or squab, for the bench front seat of the Plus-4. The Plus-8 has sliding Restall bucket seats upholstered in Ambla leather-cloth—a revolutionary mod, for the Malvern *marque*!

The Rover V8 engine installation has necessitated a Woods-Jeffreys thermostatically-controlled electric fan, and the Salisbury back axle has a limited-slip differential and a ratio of 3.58 to 1. The 90° engine goes snugly under the traditional Morgan bonnet with just a slight flattening of the air-cleaner for the two HS6 SU carburetters. Naturally, the clutch (a 9.5 in.-dia. Borg & Beck), flywheel and starter are special to the Plus-8—it seems that Rover may use these components if and when they bring out a manual-gearbox version of their 3500.

Because the engine is not supplied to the Morgan Motor Company—actually they go to Solihull and collect 15 a month—without exhaust anti-pollution equipment the Plus-8 is not yet an export proposition to America, although it has press-button switches for safety, to comply with that aspect of the U.S.A. safety requirements which are costing such a lot of money to incorporate, and which are restrictive to small-output concerns.

The Morgan has frequently been called a vintage car. It is true it has many vintage-style characteristics, and that its specification includes a real chassis frame, hard springing, and a carefully-hand-made body of steel panelling over a wooden framework, which is hand painted. On the other hand, the Morgan is something quite different from those modern versions of classic cars, such as that terrible Giulia-engined open 1750 Alfa Romeo, pseudo front-drive Cord, mock Mercedes-Benz and Bugatti and the like, of which I refuse to take any notice whatsoever. Either you want a vintage car, or you don't; to crave the part-attractions of vintagery providing they come with a load of Mod. Cons. makes a mockery of vintage motoring, and I was glad to see the aforesaid imitation 1750 Alfa Romeo referred to in a weekly contemporary very recently as "degenerate". I would use stronger terms !

The Morgan, however, cannot be classed with these fearful mock-vintage confections, because it is a replica of nothing, has had an unbroken history of production and development, and has been modernised from time to time. The radiator is now cowled in, the headlamps are faired, rather grotesquely, into valanced front wings, the screen won't fold flat, and although the spare wheel is still mounted exposed on the tail—tempting to the wheel and tyre thieves, who are apparently on the increase—it has replaced the twin upright-

mounted spares which were a proud feature of the Morgan Plus-4 I used to drive as Editorial transport.

So, while we mourn the passing of sports cars such as the H.R.G., Singer Le Mans, Frazer Nash and Rapier, the Morgan survives. How does the Plus-8 behave on the road ? Morgan owners need read no further, perhaps—because it behaves just like a Morgan, which is admittedly in a primitive but, in some ways, a fascinatingly unique fashion ! Rather delightfully, the only major extra available is a luggage grid !

Driving the Morgan Plus-8

Apart from its very satisfying measurable performance, 100 m.p.h. possible on quite short straights, so quickly and unobtrusively that only radar would notice it, as emphasised by the previously-quoted figures, the truly striking aspect of the Morgan Plus-8's running is the enormous torque delivered by the engine. Maximum torque is delivered at 3,000 r.p.m. and reaches 210 lb./ft. at 2,700 r.p.m., but the car pulls very smoothly away from a mere 1,000 r.p.m. in top gear, and before 2,000 r.p.m. is reached things are very definitely starting to happen ! This makes the Morgan as docile and one-gear as any big American sedan ! Yet, using the gears, the acceleration is sizzling. The engine runs safely to 5,000 r.p.m. and can be pushed for short periods towards 6,000 r.p.m. Without taking the needle quite to the end of the tachometer scale, this means, apart from bullet-like take-off, maxima in the gears of 40, 70 and just over 100 m.p.h. Running at 30 m.p.h. in towns the Morgan's engine idles over at under 1,400 r.p.m. in top gear. It is possible to accelerate away without making use of the harsh and notchy gear change, and at 70 m.p.h. the engine will be turning over at less than 3,200 r.p.m. Even so, a higher axle ratio could be used with advantage, although as it is, cruising at 100 m.p.h. on the Continent, the Rover V8 is running within 400 r.p.m. of the beginning of the red-sector on the tachometer.

The gear change is by a splendid little central lever just forward of the facia. It is all too easy to brutally over-ride the synchromesh, which doesn't exist on bottom gear anyway, but enthusiastic drivers are unlikely to complain unduly ! Reverse is selected by lifting the rigid little lever beyond the first-gear location. The clutch is very heavy, but not unduly fierce. The gear lever protrudes directly from the Moss gearbox, out of the transmission tunnel. Ahead of it, rather far forward on the left of the tunnel, though an average-height driver sitting close to the steering wheel had no complaints, is the handbrake—and full marks, for it is the good old true fly-off type. It failed to hold the car only on the steepest gradients.

The Morgan Plus-8 is steered by a 14½ in.-dia. wheel mounted very close to the facia, so that one tends to adopt a cranked-arms driving stance. It is an Astrali wheel with three drilled spokes and a thick rim covered with a laced-up leather glove. The steering is heavy for parking, the huge tyres dragging, dead in feel, a bit jerky in action, and not a lot lighter for sudden changes of direction, although in sober town driving it feels light. There is only very mild castor return, and kick-back is less evident than "fight" over bad surfaces, accentuated

The Plus-8 posing for its picture in Tregaron, at the other end of th mountain run.

In scenic country, these views show the virtually unchanged external appearance, apart from new type wheels, of the 3½-litre sports car from Malvern.

by scuttle shake. This is not particularly nice steering, but, at 2.4 turns, lock-to-lock, it is quick and accurate. The big tyres have resulted in a restricted turning circle. The steering pivots require lubrication every day, or every 200 miles—a matter of conscience—which is achieved by prodding a high-set floor button, like a dip-switch. This is hard to press but seems to momentarily drop engine oil pressure by no more than about 10 lb./sq. in. when the lubricant is hot. But it is a crude, messy arrangement and one hopes the strip-steel connections between bronze damper ring and the frame last longer than they used to do, especially as the well-valanced front wings now hide them completely, making inspection impossible and replacement unthinkable.

The ride? Those concerned with modern suspension systems would no doubt cry from anguish or mirth, if driven fast over rough roads in the Plus-8. On really bad going the car seems to have no springs. On less bad roads it just jumps about and rattles. On main roads it floats along nicely. Trying hard on Welsh mountain passes the Morgan felt less safe than the Gilbern and I would think that a competition driver would lose time when the back-end bounced upwards and sideways and by the front-end suddenly going softish. On the other hand, I regard the Morgan as supremely good fun, and very safe, to drive round a race circuit and certainly in ordinary fast road motoring the Dunlop SP Sports refused to breakaway or to protest. The Morgan rides and corners—like a Morgan. Which infers hard springing, negative roll, some understeer. The limited-slip differential and those excellent Dunlops permit lots of throttle to be used out of corners, even on wet roads. Yet although rear-end breakaway is not normal, a dab of throttle helps to balance the cornering by combating the understeer. Over the Aberywesyn-Tregaron mountain road the sheer power of the Plus-8 makes this difficult terrain seem tame, except that the very long bonnet (approximately 6 ft. 10 in. from driver's eyes to the front of the bonnet, which itself is 4 ft. 2 in. long) masks the road on up gradients; there is the sensation, also associated with long-snouted pre-war cars, of sitting well back and having to steer the bonnet round bends.

The screen now has triple wiper blades but it no longer folds flat. Visibility is good, in as much as the n/s side lamp and part of the o/s headlamp cowl and vintage-type wing can be seen from the rather low driving seat by the average driver. Naturally, with its hood up things are less pleasant—but who wants to motor in a closed Plus-8, anyway? Especially as the hood's "lift-the-dot" fasteners required very strong fingers, or assistance from a coin or even a screwdriver, to budge them.

The brakes, which have a Girling vacuum servo, are powerful and seem free from fade. Oil pressure is normally approximately 50 lb./sq. in.

Coming to details, the new seats are very good—comfortable and offering good support. The squabs do not fold, which makes loading and unloading luggage into the carpeted well behind them difficult, hood up—but who wants the hood up, on a Plus-8? If it *is* put up, perhaps as a sop to some woman, snags arise. Apart from decreased visibility, which the area of transparency doesn't quite solve, although I have no serious complaints, but I have met hoods with better windows, the doors tended to jamb shut. As they have no external handles, and the side screens and hood cannot be ripped off, the occupants are trapped in the car. Although the doors can be locked, the sliding panels in the Perspex sidescreens have no grips externally, so how does one gain easy re-access, if they are locked? This could be serious in a racing accident, for an unconscious driver would be trapped in the car, with the hood up—and the Plus-8 is said to be faster closed than open, so might well be raced with hood erect. But who wants . . . etc.? Long legs can hurt knees on the back edge of the scuttle when entering the Morgan.

There is an open cubby hole on the n/s of the facia. The instruments, by Smiths, consist of a 140 m.p.h. speedometer, with trip-with-tenths and total mileage recorders, a matching multi-purpose dial (ammeter, fuel gauge, oil gauge and thermometer) and a smaller-dial tachometer before the driver. This means that the speedometer, as it sweeps towards 100 m.p.h., beg pardon, 70 m.p.h., is not easily read by the driver. The speedometer carries the name "Morgan". The dials are fairly casually calibrated. The ammeter shows 50–50+, the fuel gauge, which has a steady needle, E, ½, F, the oil-gauge 0, 50, 100 and the thermometer H, N, C. Between the two main dials are the press-button switches, which are not illuminated by the instrument lighting and are "fumbly" by day and by night. They are also insensitive for operating two-speed services, such as the wipers, heater-fan, and the lamps. They are nasty, American-inspired substitutes for flick-switches, in fact. On the Plus-8 they are in two rows, with those warning lights not located elsewhere, between them. The top row, l. to r., serve washers (inoperative on the test car), wipers, the Lucas sealed-beam fog and spotlamps, and heater fan. The lower row, l. to r., serve lamps, a hazard warning and parking lamps. The last-named cuts the ignition, to prevent driving off only half-lit. There is a handbrake-on warning light. A r.h.-stalk control, "borrowed" from a Ford Cortina, works turn-indicators, dips the headlamps, and sounds a subdued horn; it is very close to the facia in the full-beam position. The Lucas sealed-beam headlamps give excellent illumination, on full and dipped beam, better in narrow lanes than on main roads, however. Tucked up under the facia, for the driver's right hand, is a manual mixture enrichener and a right-angle socket for an ignition-key which can also lock the steering column.

The light doors have useful rigid pockets and quite a lot of luggage can be accommodated behind the seats, in an upholstered well.

CONTINUED ON PAGE 155

SOME ASPECTS OF THE MORGAN PLUS-8.—L. to r., the new instrument panel with push-button safety switches, the Rover V8 engine (note the slight dent necessary to squeeze in the air cleaner), and the tail with its exposed cast-alloy spare wheel.

NEW FOR '69 VEE-8 MORGAN

Powerful Rover engine in traditional Morgan

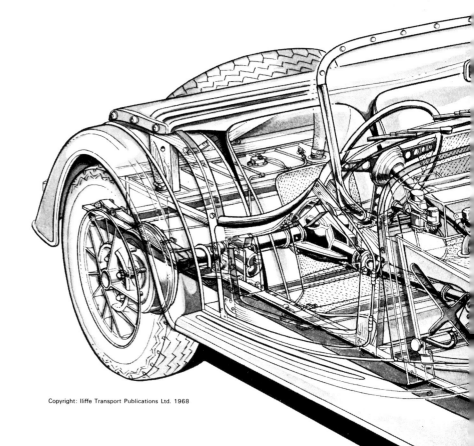

It has not been necessary to alter the body shape at all in order to get the Rover vee-8 engine under the bonnet. The traditional sliding pillar front suspension is retained and the gearbox is still attached via a short torque tube extension. The body is based on a wooden framework

The Morgan has a separate steel chassis which has not changed significantly for over 20 years. The body is detachable and construction methods are truly vintage

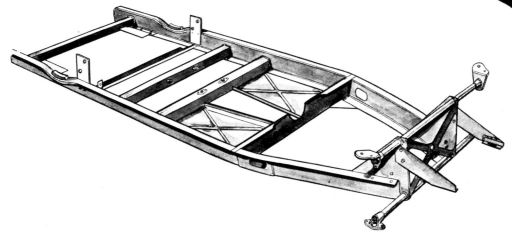

Autoc

Every Morgan four-wheeler built has had a four-cylinder engine, so the adoption of a new lightweight vee-8 unit (Rover's Buick-bought 3.5-litre) is new indeed. Traditional Morgan engineering still unchanged, new car capable of 124 mph with "vintage" body style. A replacement for the entire Plus 4 range and deliveries begin at once.

THERE can be no doubt that Morgan is an anachronism in the motor industry of the '60s; Peter Morgan admits it, the customers know it, yet the order books are always full for this most "vintage" of modern cars. Any change or development takes years to mature, so the announcement of a new and much more powerful engine is an important event indeed for the tiny Malvern company. The reasons are simple enough. Last year, Triumph changed their TR4A to a TR5, dropping the venerable old "four-banger" 2.2-litre engine in the process, and signalling the eventual end to TR4A engine supplies to Morgan. Enough were built to keep going for another season, but the Rover-Buick vee-8 engined car now takes over; though traditionally built in age-old Morgan fashion, there are many engineering changes to match the car to its much lustier power unit, and our road testers (see following pages) thought it was just as safe and roadworthy as any previous Morgan. Only the open two-seater version is available yet, though there is a possibility of a detachable hardtop in due course.

Compared with the Plus 4, the new Plus 8 has a 2in. longer wheelbase, much wider wheels and tyres (which automatically mean a wider track and slightly wider body), rather more rear suspension movement, a limited-slip differential, yet the same Moss four-speed gearbox. The facia design is new, and adjustable seats are new to Morgan.

Though the bulkier vee-8 engine would *just* have shoehorned into the existing chassis frame, it was so simple to extend the Z-section side members that another 2in., all forward of the passengers' toeboard, was included. Apart from adding judicious gussets and deepening the rear axle rebound clearance, the only major change has been to add steel floor boards between the scuttle and seat cross-member tubes to add chassis rigidity.

Front suspension uses traditional Morgan sliding pillars unchanged, as the light-alloy 3.5-litre vee-8 engine is slightly lighter than the 2.2-litre four-cylinder TR4A unit. Rear suspension changes are confined to re-aligning the long half-elliptic leaf springs (now sloping downwards to their forward ends, which—incidentally—help to induce slight understeer if ever the springs can be persuaded to distort) There is a little more rear wheel movement than hitherto, but the suspension is still extremely

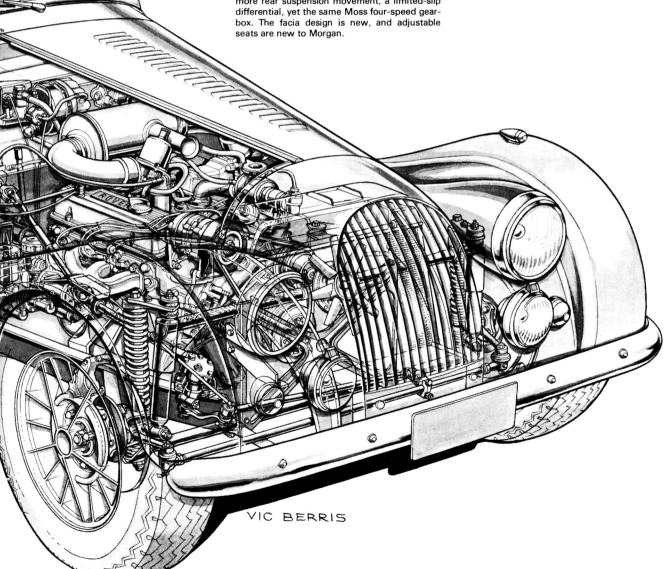

VIC BERRIS

VEE-8 MORGAN

stiff. Fat, cast-alloy road wheels, 15in. diameter with a generous 5.5in. rim, are standardized (there is no wire wheel option any longer) along with 185—15in. Dunlop SP Sport tyres, with Aquajets.

Girling front disc brakes have bigger 16P calipers (the Plus 4 has 14Ps) and a vacuum servo, while the 9 x 1.75in. rear drums are unchanged. Front pad area is only marginally up, and the 11in. discs are the same size as before, but the 16P calipers have much more fade resistance.

Traditional Morgan steering geometry, plus the Cam Gear steering box is retained, but a new steering column has been needed to circumnavigate the wider vee-8 engine. There is a universally-jointed shaft linking the lower column with an AC-Delco collapsible steering column.

The 3,529 cc Rover vee-8 engine is used with only minor changes—principally the substitution of Wood-Jeffreys thermostatically operated electric cooling fan, and a slight flattening of the air cleaner to squeeze it under the Morgan bonnet. Rover have yet to make a manual transmission version of either the 3.5-litre or the 3500, so a special flywheel, clutch, and starter arrangement has had to be designed. This is linked, in true Morgan style, by a short input shaft (and cast alloy tube) to the centrally mounted, remote Moss Gear four-speed gearbox. The box is also the same as on the Plus 4, and has no synchromesh on first gear. The handbrake is mounted well forward on the alloy tube, and the stubby gearlever sprouts straight above the selectors.

The rear axle is a Salibury 7HA unit, as used in the Plus 4, with a 3.58-to-1 ratio (the highest ratio available) and a limited-slip differential. Morgan would like to use an even higher ratio—something like a 3.4, especially for export—but Salisbury are not yet able to satisfy this need.

Though the Plus 8 body style may look exactly as before, in fact it is wider throughout, and there is very little interchangeability with the Plus 4. Forward of the toeboard the extra 2in. of wheelbase means that bonnet and wing panels are all new. In the cockpit, the facia is now completely covered in Ambla leathercloth, and re-styled. The AC collapsible steering column incorporates a steering lock, and for the first time on a Morgan the turn key starter is hidden under the facia board.

Somewhat of a revolution for Morgan is the provision of separate, adjustable seats, which have their own nicely shaped squabs in place of the bench back once known. Since there is only a two-seater sports body to consider, the space behind the seats (though fairly well filled with fuel tank) is useful for stowing soft luggage, and the folded hood lives there too. Under the floorboards in this area is the 12-volt battery, not shielded from the rear wheel mud and water. The hood assembly is as simple as ever; three hoops at varying angles fix into the hood itself, which attaches to the screen by press studs. Perspex sidewindows in the doors have sliding panels, or can be removed altogether.

Traditional features carried on include the chassis lubrication (engine oil by pipelines, pumped by a foot pedal at least once a day), tool box under the bonnet in the scuttle, and recirculating heater down by the passenger's feet.

The new car is already in production, with deliveries in rhd form beginning at once in this country. A lhd version will follow during the winter, but no Plus 8s will be sold in the USA for the time being—the big problem being supply of suitably modified vee-8 engines to satisfy air-pollution laws.

The Ford Cortina engined 4/4 1600 carries on unchanged for 1969, in both 74 bhp and 88 bhp tune, in open two-seater and four-seater form; the-seater coupé version has been discontinued.   □

Cast magnesium wheels are standard, as are the twin auxiliary lamps. Sidescreen detach, but the hood (inset) includes blind quarters when erected

Bonnet catches are strictly functional, and there is a long hinge down the centre. Accessibility is good (better than on the Rover)

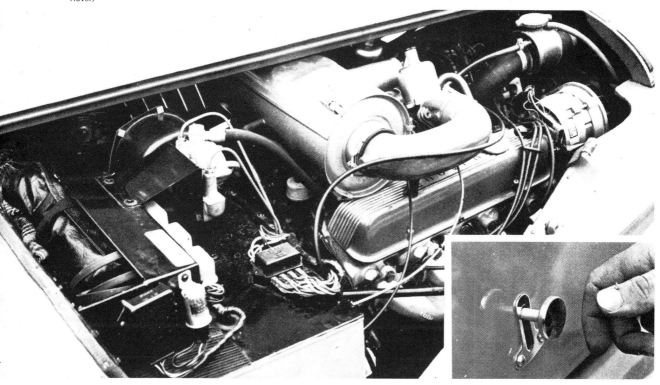

Cockpit layout follows closely on what is essential to satisfy the US safety regulations with padding and rocker switches. The spare wheel (inset) is totally exposed on top of the short tail

MORGAN PLUS 8

BY EOIN S. YOUNG

THE MORGAN PLUS 8 must be the newest old car in the world. Current boss Peter Morgan's grandfather thought up a keen way of putting independent front suspension by sliding pillars on his new car in 1910, and they've stayed pretty much the same ever since.

Now the car has been uprated to become the fastest Moggy of them all, with the 184-bhp ex-Buick Rover aluminum V-8 installed. That long, louvered bonnet has had to be lengthened two inches and widened two inches to cram everything in. So has the chassis. The new power makes the Morgan a 130-mph motorcar and a Salisbury limited slip differential has been installed to make sure that all the extra power gets to the road. Power is ample and there's plenty more to be extracted with development. The exhaust set-up almost looks like an after-thought. The Rover manifolds have a pipe bolted on either side, joined into one pipe at the fire-wall, and then runs down the left side of the Z-section chassis. There must be ten extra horsepower hiding away in that scramble of plumbing. New front hubs are fitted, as well as stronger stub axles, and an anti-sway bar is fitted across the front.

The price of the new model has sky-rocketed up to £1475 (abt $3500)—the previous TR-engined Plus 4 was £915 ($2200)—but although Peter Morgan obviously doesn't like the size of the tag, you get the impression that it will keep the clientele in the right bracket. Walking around the factory with the lanky tweed-suited head of the family business, you pass through a joinery shop where all the body frames are made. Fair takes you back, it does. You get the personal pride-in-their-work feeling about the people who make Morgans. If you bought one you wouldn't just be a customer—you'd almost be a friend of the family. They don't *want* cus-

tomers who are liable to make a fuss if their car is late or the ride is even more Spartan than they expected. It seems to be an honor just to have your name on the waiting list that was four months long on the Plus 8 before announcement! (You wait up to eight months for the 1600 Cortina-engined 4-4 model.)

The Plus 8 Morgan has become civilized. Not by current standards, but by Morgan standards. Sliding plexiglass side screens, a cramping button-down top, and no luggage room to speak of, are all part of the fun, but the new V-8 rejoices in a pair of black leather-trimmed Restall rally seats that are—wait for it—adjustable! No more bench-backs and blow-up cushions. It's the first Moggy where you can stretch your arms behind the wheel and switch from Nuvolari to Dr. Farina on the sliding adjustment.

Peter Morgan would be further along the road to passing American safety regulations if someone in the federal office stateside would answer his mail! They've put a Plus 4 through the crash test. The new Plus 8 has an AC-Delco collapsible steering column and the dash has a row of rocker switches. The usual big Smiths instruments tell driver and passenger everything they want to know and a little rev counter lives to the right of the new leather-padded wheel. Black leather trim is the in-thing at Malvern this year. The transmission tunnel is black-trimmed as are the cutaway door sills. You still have the reach-in door locks TF-style.

At the wheel you can't help but get a kick out of the long, louvered bonnet. The low screen will have three wipers like an E-type.

The slow Moss ex-Jaguar 4-speed gearbox still dwells along the driveshaft aft of the clutch. It's still a shift-one-two-shift box that adds to the vintage feel.

Progress sets in at Malvern Link

It will get from 0-50 in 5.2 sec, up to 70 in 8.6, and it does a standing quarter mile in 14.9 sec. The flexibility of top gear is quite something. Morgan talks about a possible 5-speed box but I don't reckon he needs it.

The Plus 8 has new cast aluminum 15 x 5½ wheels designed by Morgan when other manufacturers lagged on delivery. Turning circle is a hard-hauled 38 ft. Handling is typically Morgan, being neutral up to the point where you can choose whether to have under- or oversteer.

A 13½-gallon fuel tank slabbed on the back with a mounting for the spare wheel inset traditionally has a fuel filler on either side of the wheel to aid fast refueling in racing pitstops. The V-8 does between 22 and 25 miles to the Imperial gallon giving a range of around 300 miles.

Scuttle-shake was once a Morgan specialty but it has almost been eradicated on the Plus 8. Spot welded floor pans plus strategically placed gussets helps torsional rigidity immensely. Comfort seems to have been improved in direct proportion to the price hike!

Girling 11-in. servo discs are fitted in front with 9-in. drums on the rear. Rear suspension is by the usual archaic half-elliptics, although the front fixing points have been raised and the rears lowered which effectively increases spring movement by about an inch.

Morgan built a prototype with the Rover V-8 in mind 18 months ago when it was still a secret at Rover. Instead of the English engine they fitted a Buick V-8 into a Plus 4 chassis and did 40,000 miles of testing to sort out the shortcomings. When Rover was given a demonstration of what the new car could be like using their V-8, permission was given and Morgan now receives 10 engines per week.

The V-8 answered Peter Morgan's prayers since Triumph had phased out the 4-cyl TR engine he had been using in the Plus 4s for the past 18 years. He didn't fancy extending the chassis to take the long fuel-injected 2.5-liter 6-cyl Triumph engine. The compact Rover aluminum V-8 was the ideal answer. It weighed about the same as the TR, so there was no weight distribution problems.

The U.S. exhaust emission ticket is keeping Rover's 3500 out of America, and it will also bar the door to the new Plus 8 Morgan. But they are working at it. Our test car was a lurid sort of McLaren racing Orange and they intend to continue with their range of pop colors introduced extremely successfully at last year's Earls Court show at the suggestion of Peter Morgan's young son.

The Plus 8 is $3500 worth of rapid instant vintagery, ruddy cheeks and tangled hair. So who needs an Excalibur?

Thoroughly Modern Morgan

Simmer down, all you Stateside vintage-car lovers, this is not for you—at least not yet—but we thought you'd like to see it all the same. It's the Morgan Plus 8, destined for production at the rate of about two per day from a tiny factory in rural England, where they've been turning out cars of similar shape for 30 years. The Plus 8 puts Morgan squarely into the over-two-miles-a-minute category with the aid of Rover's ex-BOP 3528-cc V-8, an engine which meets Federal emission standards when coupled to an automatic transmission, but not with a manual box as fitted to the "Moggy." Although the cockpit has been partly "Fedded" and a car has been impact-tested satisfactorily, there are still many obstacles to be overcome before the U.S. market can be reopened for Britain's (and perhaps the world's) most "trad" sports car. Just to let you know what you're missing, performance is close to E-Jag standards, with a standing quarter-mile in about 15 seconds and 60 mph in well under 7 seconds. But, unlike the XK-E, it's as drafty as hell, the ride is firm enough to slip a disc, and controllability and creature comforts bang up to the very best 1938 standards. Some people have passionate love affairs with them... the masochists!

The smooth young gentleman in the equally smooth Jaguar XK-E sounded just a little charitable: "I say," quoth he as we exchanged greetings at the lights, "that's a rather splendid old motor car . . . And I'll bet she's still capable of a pretty brisk turn of speed, even now."

Then the green signal showed. And that, apart from glimpsing his stunned face in the mirror, was the last we saw of the poor bastard.

Now, Morgan's quaint little workshop — you can't, in all honesty, call such a sedate, Olde Worlde establishment a factory — has been building sporty motor cars for over 50 years. But the new Plus 8 makes all its illustrious ancestors look little more exciting than the 3½-hp Benz which, by wrecking itself on a steep hill back in 1899, first made H. F. S. Morgan think about building a car of his own.

It may look like the sort of thing pater drove before the Hitler war, but this spine-jarring anachronism has a maximum speed of 126 honest-to-God miles per hour and can streak from zero to 60 in just 6.6 dramatic seconds. Say a full second quicker than the XK-E roadster, 1/10th slower than Aston's fastback DB6, and only the mathematically pedantic are going to argue. Aerodynamically, the Plus 8 is probably little better than Worcester cathedral, a few miles down the road from Malvern, and this starts extracting its inevitable toll as speeds increase. Even so, the standing-start quarter-mile is covered in 15 seconds, with the needle hitting the 100 mark only 3.2 seconds later.

Peter Morgan, son of the firm's founder, started giving serious thought to the question of replacing the Plus 4 when it became known, in the summer of 1966, that Triumph planned to drop the 2.2-liter four-cylinder engine, which his car shared with the TR-4A. After scouting around and rejecting a number of possibles, including British Ford's V-6 and V-4, he opted for the V-8 3.5-liter then being developed by Rover to put some real guts into their saloons.

Based on a Buick design and used by Jack Brabham to provide the bones of the engine which won him the Formula 1 World Championship in 1966, this unit had all the obvious advantages. It was powerful, developing 160 (net) bhp at a leisurely 5,200 rpm. It was compact, and, thanks to being built of aluminum, remarkably light. In fact, the Plus 8's weight, including oil, water, and petrol, is only marginally heavier than 1800 pounds than the old Plus 4's. Its weight distribution, 48% front and 52% rear, is virtually the same as the Plus 4.

Unfortunately, Rover is still looking for a suitable manual gearbox, and Morgan has had to rely on the four-speed Moss unit used on the Plus 4. This is the new car's poorest feature — no synchromesh on first, and fast changes between second, third, and top produce ugly sounds if anything more than a modest dollop of power is being used. Peter Morgan makes no secret of the fact that he is keeping his eyes peeled for a suitable replacement, perhaps a five-speeder with a really high top to give 130-mph cruising.

What about suspension changes? Best prepare yourself for a shock, dear friend, because the Morgan has gone all soft . . . so soft it is now just a little difficult to tell whether that cigarette butt which just disturbed the wheels was plain or filter-tipped. All things, as Einstein told the world, are relative; Morgan's soft is the rest of the industry's granite.

The clock ticks slowly at Malvern, and it is going to take more than a piddling little 54% power increase to make them abandon the sliding pillars and coils up front, patented by H.F.S. not so very long after Queen Victoria turned up her toes. And acceleration figures, not to mention the difficulty of spinning the wheels, reveal that precious little urge is being wasted by the live back axle. Oh yes, a limited slip diff' must help.

The Plus 8 is actually a little longer and wider than its predecessor, a matter of no more than a couple of inches, and the Z-section chassis follows familiar, if judiciously strengthened, lines. How long must it be since a manufacturer last achieved added rigidity by replacing wooden floorboards with steel? As for the body, this still uses steel panels over an ash frame; Morgan must employ a higher proportion of carpenters than any other auto construction firm in the world.

Stopping this neo-vintage creation has been achieved by fitting servo-assisted, 11-inch-diameter Girling discs up front and 9-inch drums at the back, giving a total swept area of 325 sq. ins. Fade is very slight, thanks in part to the excellent heat-dissipation properties of the wheels, handsome affairs in cast magnesium with 5.5-inch rims to put plenty of rubber on the road. Tires are Dunlop's latest SP Sport radials, which provide a superb amount of grip, and are particularly good in the wet.

A greatly improved cockpit layout, along with a decent pair of bucket seats, indicate that a mention of ergonomics has filtered through to Malvern at last. A welcome newcomer is the anti-theft steering lock which should foil those tempted by the sight of such an invitingly open roadster. The driving position is as ever, closer to Nuvolari than Graham Hill, although a leather-rimmed steering wheel is a smart and practical gesture towards modern ity. There is none of this fancy fingertip-control business; man, you really steer the Plus 8, using steely wrists and hairy forearms. The gearing is superbly high, needing just 2.4 turns to get from lock to lock, but wider wheels and tires mean a turning circle all of 40 feet in diameter. You jockey for curbside spaces with the 600 Mercs, not the dinky little Healeys. But what the hell, it means the car can be placed on the road with hairsplitting precision, with just a twitch of the wheel needed to correct the chosen line.

It all feels very strange after the soft springing and relatively soggy steering of any modern motor, and the sight of that long, rakish hood, slashed by no fewer than 76 louvers, hardly helps make the driver feel at home — so initial impressions can be downright alarming. On

anything much rougher than a real billiard table surface, you fear for the fillings in your teeth and suddenly realize what those old clipper helmsmen must have gone through fighting the heaving decks while navigating around Cape Horn.

But this is all part of the running-in process. After a few miles, you begin to realize that hitting a rut or hump at the apex of a bend is not going to send the outfit bouncing off into the undergrowth like a frightened kangaroo. The wheels may deflect a little, sure, but it soon becomes second nature to automatically allow for this. The right foot starts exploring the bulkhead and, once the doubts have been banished, the Plus 8's vivid performance can be enjoyed to the full.

That 3,529-cc engine stuffed into such a light car

makes every mile seem like 880 yards, and opens up yawning chasms in the traffic rather than mere gaps. Plenty of power low down, and 210 lbs./ft. of torque at 3000 rpm let you start in top cog when feeling really indolent — not such a bad idea, the gearbox being what it is. In fact, third is good for up to nearly 110 mph, and provides tremendous reserves of effort when required. Even second, which can be held to 73, is more than useful for sorting out the slow movers. First? Say 40 mph.

Fuel consumption falls into the 15-19 miles-per-U.S.-gallon bracket, and roughly a pint of oil is used every 500 miles. Rover got a rather better figure on oil consumption; could it be, we asked innocently, because it doesn't have a little button on the floor to be pressed every morning, squirting en-

gine lubricant into the front suspension . . . ?

You really cannot compare this car with anything produced since the MG TC. Its shape and suspension characteristics are as out of place as a muzzle-loading musket would be in a space capsule. It lacks any number of refinements which the average motorist has come to regard as being as essential as gas, oil, and water. But this refusal to move with the times has been Morgan's strength rather than its weakness for nearly 20 years, keeping them in business while so many others have gone to the wall or lost their identity following mergers. However, one is left with the feeling that, immense fun though it may be, the Plus 8 could have been made slightly "softer," and therefore slightly better, without losing any of its characteristic panache. ⊕

THE ROVER

SCW exclusively tests the only Morgan plus eight to find its way Down Under.

VERY few motor car companies in England haven't been swallowed by British-Leyland. Most are specialist builders and one is Morgan. It will be a tragedy if they ever stop producing the famous square-riggers from the Malvern Link factory. Especially when they're quite as dynamic as the Plus Eight.

Morgan isn't as old fashioned as immediate impressions of the Plus Eight would suggest. In the next five years we could see a mid-engined V8 sporty as a stock production car. In the meantime, the Rover-ised Morgan is plentifully endowed with sufficient one-up-manship to put it not just in the next block, but the next block over the hill.

The Plus Eight is a paradox and an anachronism which enlivens the nasty Hyde traits in any performance bitten driver. Sidling up to the lights, adjusting your flat top and scarf, while milady puts a brush through her long blonde hair is sufficient intrigue for the GTO owner sitting alongside. But blasting-off in a swirl of tyre smoke and black marks at a rate adequate to capture the ton in 20 is a good reason for said Mr GTO to lodge an order for next year's model.

SPORTS CAR WORLD was privileged to test the only Plus Eight in Australia—and it's likely to be the only one for some time going on backlog orders. Correspondent Eoin Young drove one for SCW back in late 1968 when they were first released. He called it the CanAm Morgan because it sounded like a racer and laid rubber like one too. And it does. With scarcely run-in miles up

we kept the lid on 5000 for the owner's peace of mind and the car's future. But the standard Rover 3.5 V8 has so much sheer torque, the Dunlop Aquajets, despite sound support from an LSD, find it hard to move off without leaving half their tread behind.

The Morgan-Rover V8 mating has been successful for the extremely good balance achieved and lack of afterthought fittings, which inevitably come with hybrids. The lightweight V8 (it weighs only 3 lb more than the Rover TC four) is linked to the gearbox by a fully enclosed housing, so the gearbox is virtually between the driver and passenger with the gearshift coming directly from the selector forks. With this configuration distribution is 49/51 which *is* well balanced for a front-engined sports car.

The Plus Eight's cockpit treatment sums up the car perfectly. Everything functional and the latest gear is laid out in classic vintage style — right down to the hazard warning light operated by a safety rocker switch.

You take that character and apply it to performance and you have this dynamic acceleration in a car that would well fit in a war movie, when the hero sweeps up to his girlfriend's place on leave day. The V8 is stock—which didn't explain to us why it sounded like a 7-litre Cobra, Shelby-tuned. Nevertheless it does and on depressing the right pedal it gives silken smooth power right up to 6000 rpm. Up top 5500-6000 the twin SU HS6s are light-on with the mixture and the torque curve becomes asthmatic.

We used only 5000 rpm and ran 16.0 for the quarter—overseas tests go for 15.0 with 6000. What nobody told us until SCW r-t procedure picked it up, was the tacho is quite sympathetic to the engine to the tune of 750 rpm at 5000 rpm. In fact, our respectful 5000 was only 4250 which

ISED MOG

SPORTS CAR WORLD · ROAD TEST

Although the cockpit complies with safety regulations in the use of rocker switches etc, its design is still vintage, with the speedometer placed in such a position as to scare the daylights out of an unsuspecting female passenger.

The Plus Eight is immediately identifiable by its bonnet louvres, shallower front mudguard curve, two extra quartz iodine lights and dapper mags.

proves what alloy V8 ponies can do at a canter. Through the traps at 6000 on the tach (just one sneak run) showed a corrected time of 112.5 against 125 claimed. If the tacho were right, 131 would be the theoretical terminal but, wind push accounted for, it's more like 125 genuine and also as we said the V8 runs out of breath high-up, which probably makes that last 250 rpm fairly useless.

The virtue of no tweaking is rotary smoothness and Leyland bus tractability down low. Around town acceleration comes in short bursts followed by longer change pauses for sorting gears and integrating clutch movement. Just two and four makes it easier on the kidneys. If you've made good with five grand ($A) initially, fuel consumption is academic—hard driven during the test run tankful, 25 mpg. Not bad? Should be up 'round 30 for touring. With the Three Thousand Five's weight it goes to 15-20 mpg so fuel efficiency rating is on line for maximum. The book says its alloy head asks 101 octane which we used in the test Plus Eight. Octane 98 in the TT5 brought no protest though.

In Mog tradition, there is a little squirter to inject oil into the sliding pillar front suspension struts before you move off for the morning constitutional. Rear, bonk control is by leaf springs and lever arm shocks. Our test car had special box section reinforcements in the rear frame to tighten torsional twist for the Antipodes. The result is running gear which handles the V8 as though it had been the norm since three-wheeler days.

The Morgan Plus Eight isn't as old fashioned as first glances suggest. While still keeping its 40-year-old tradition, the Rover-ised-Morgan has enough one-up-manship to keep it in a class of its own for many years to come.

With LSD and torque rods, rear end control is excellent, though you will end up with a double handful of Mog out of the traffic lights in the wet despite the Aquajet set, if even half throttle comes on. The ride is quite soft and shockers feel well-used Morris Minor variety, as the Mog bounces happily over washboard. It feels happier on hotmix tarmac.

Obviously the shocks do work, because roll stiffness is high and roadholding confident, even with negative camber front wheels.

The man, brave enough to tell us whether a Mog under- or oversteers under natural road conditions (no sneaky track work here—we mean on-the-limit handling not bar room power sliding bravery) is either insane or on his way to heaven by fast Morgan V8. Generally there is so much torque to spare there's always a bit left to bring the Mog back on line. Alternately, how far/fast you wish to spin depends on your control of the throttle butterflies. The Aquajets hang-on exceptionally well but power-slide oversteer is predominant. Some understeer is detectable more especially on wet roads, but it's mostly understeer bounce from apex bumps.

In all honesty, the Plus Eight is not what we'd call a safe ton-up tourer, except on German autobahns — and they haven't started importing those Down Under yet. The cam and peg steering gear is jarringly direct and any suspicion of movement is relayed to the road with quick reflex action of correction or over-correction for quite small deflections and undulations. For mid-speed range the steering is fine and in the best tradition of true sports cars. Standing still, the big fat radials make it impossible to turn without imposing incredible strain on the box.

CONTINUED ON PAGE 37

MAKE	Morgan
PRICE	$4920
ROAD TEST MILEAGE	400 miles
OPTIONS	Nil

PERFORMANCE

TOP SPEED:

Fastest run (see text)	112.5 mph
Average	112.5 mph
Speedometer indication	118 mph
Rpm at max speed	5280 rpm

SPEEDS IN GEARS (mph):

		Equivalent rpm
First	41 mph	5750 rpm
Second	70 mph	5750 rpm
Third	101 mph	5750 rpm
Fourth	121.5 mph	5750 rpm

ACCELERATION THROUGH THE GEARS:

0-30 mph	2.3 sec	0-70 mph	11.2 sec
0-40 mph	4.9 sec	0-80 mph	13.2 sec
0-50 mph	6.5 sec	0-90 mph	16.3 sec
0-60 mph	7.7 sec	0-100 mph	22.0 sec

ACCELERATION IN GEARS:

	3rd gear	4th gear
30-50 mph	4.2 sec	5.1 sec
40-60 mph	4.1 sec	4.7 sec
50-70 mph	4.0 sec	4.7 sec

STANDING QUARTER MILE:

Fastest run (see text)	16.0 sec
Average of all runs (see text)	16.0 sec

FUEL CONSUMPTION:

Overall for test	25 mpg
Normal cruising	25-30 mpg

SPEEDOMETER ERROR (mph):

Indicated	30	40	50	60	70	80
Actual	30.7	40.2	50.0	60.0	69.5	78.2

CALCULATED DATA:

Mph per 1000 rpm in top gear	21.3 mph
Piston speed at max bhp	2426 ft/min
Power to weight ratio	216 bhp/ton

SPECIFICATIONS

ENGINE:

Cylinders	V8
Bore and stroke	89 mm (3.5 in.) by 71 mm (2.8 in.)
Cubic capacity	3530 (215 cu in.)
Compression ratio	10.5 to 1
Valves	OHV
Carburettor/s	2 SU H56
Power	184 bhp at 5200 rpm
Torque	226 lb/ft at 3000 rpm

TRANSMISSION:

Type	4 sp. 2-3-4 syncro
Clutch	sdp 9.5 in. dia
Gear lever location	central floor

Direct ratios:

1st	2.97	3rd	1.20
2nd	1.74	4th	1.00
Final drive (lsd)			3.58 to 1

CHASSIS AND RUNNING GEAR:

Construction	separate Z-section chassis steel body on ash frame
Suspension front	vertical sliding pillars, coil springs
Suspension rear	live axle, leaf springs
Shock absorbers	telescopic front, lever arm rear
Steering type	cam and peg
Turns lock to lock	2.4
Turning circle	38 ft
Brakes: type	disc front/drum rear, servo assisted tandem circuits
Dimensions	11 in. dia disc, 9 in. dia drum

DIMENSIONS:

Wheelbase	98¼ in.
Track front	47¼ in.
Track rear	50½ in.
Length	12 ft 9 in.
Width	4 ft 9¾ in.
Height	4 ft 1 in. (to roof)
Fuel tank capacity	13.5 gal
Touring range	325 miles
Tyres: size	185 by 14
Make on test car	Dunlop SP Aquajet
Ground clearance	9¾ in.
Weight (kerb)	17 cwt

Road Test

THE MORGAN PLUS 8

by Joseph Lowrey

CAR AT A GLANCE: Rover-built, Buick-designed V-8 power . . . Last of the classic sports cars . . . Tremendous high-gear torque . . . Traditional rigid suspension . . . One helluva lot of fun to drive!

If anyone tells you that Morgan never change their cars, show him the pictures on these pages. My 1927 three-wheeled Morgan, bought for $50.00 during World War II, had much the same kind of sliding-pillar independent front springing as today's V-8 Morgan. Also it had a torque tube separating the transmission from the clutch, as has its successor. There resemblances end.

Morgan have the Volkswagen idea, though, of not making changes for their own sake. When H.F.S. Morgan started building featherweight cyclecars (as they were then called) in 1910, he set out to offer people the fastest car at its price. His son Peter Morgan owns and runs the plant at Malvern now, the family objective is unchanged, and certainly in Britain today's Morgan Plus 8 is the fastest car at its price. To keep

Massive 15-inch wheels and tires curtail Plus 8's U-turn capabilities but the rear ones will lay a patch for as long as you have the cour

Export Morgans to come will undoubtedly fit sturdier bumpers. According to tester Lowrey, hood louvers function as a windshield defroster.

Triple windshield wipers and sturdy side shields plus a detachable rag top are sole concessions to bad weather. An effective heater there is not.

ahead of rivals on performance per $, the Morgan family changes whatever needs to be changed and perpetuates whatever seems better (or better value for the money) than any known alternative.

Back in 1937 when a four-wheeled sports car was first added to the Morgan range of three-wheelers, their car with a Coventry Climax engine was cheaper than the contemporary MG Midget for about equal performance. They had planned a simple chassis with Z-section side rails, its lower flanges facing inwards to carry the floor of a low, wood-framed body. The sliding-pillar front suspension was patterned after

their three-wheeler design of 1910, and half-elliptic rear springs were tucked inside the frame where it passed under the rear axle. They put a torque tube between the clutch and the 4-speed transmission, thus getting extra footroom alongside the pedals, shortening the open propeller shaft and avoiding any need for a remote-control gearshift.

Except that a 3.5-litre Rover (nee Buick) engine has replaced the 1.1-litre Coventry Climax, every word of that 1937 description is true today. But oh, how the details and the total effect have changed! That first Morgan four-wheel sports car would do 80 downhill whereas today's car hits 80 from a standstill in

12 seconds and can hold it up a 20% grade. It can reach 125 mph on level road.

Today's Morgan is no pastiche of a pre-1940 car then; its a pre-1940 design which has been modernized. Unique in character, it's 100% genuine, not a modern chassis spoiled by mock-antique coachwork.

As a tester I'm not impartial about Morgans: I ran two aged tricycles during wartime gas rationing, later owned a 2-litre Plus 4 for several years in the 1950s and still mistrust my own sales resistance. Cars of character have very good and very bad points. I still like the liveliness of ultra-simple Morgans and

SPECIFICATIONS FROM MANUFACTURER MORGAN "PLUS 8"

Engine in Test Car
Rover-built version of Buick aluminum V-8
Bore and stroke: 3.50 inches x 2.80 inches
Displacement: 215 cubic inches (3528 cc)
Advertised horsepower: 184 at 5200 rpm
Compression ratio: 10.5:1
Carburetion: Two S.U. constant depression carburetors
Transmission
9.5-inch diameter single dry-plate clutch
4-speed gearbox (synchromesh on 2-3-4) mounted on torque tube approx. 18 inches behind engine, with ratios 1.00, 1.205, 1.745 and 2.97; reverse 2.97
Salisbury rear axle with hypoid bevel, ratio 3.58:1 and limited-slip differential
Suspension
Front: Independent coil springs on vertical slides/steering swivels. Telescopic hydraulic shock absorbers
Rear: Half-elliptic leaf springs below axle, and lever-arm hydraulic shock absorbers
Steering: Cam and peg gear, 2.4 turns from lock-to-lock. Turning radius 21 feet, between walls
Wheels: Cast aluminum alloy, 5-lug with Dunlop 185-15 high-speed radial tires on 5½J rims
Brakes: Girling hydraulic, disc front and drum rear, with vacuum servo
Fuel capacity: 16.25 gallons
Oil capacity: 6 quarts
Lubrication interval: 3000 miles (also press one-shot pedal to lubricate front suspension every 200 miles or daily)
Body and frame: Chassis with Z-section side rails. Wood body frame carrying steel panels.
Trunk capacity: 4.5 cubic feet approx.
Wheelbase: 98.25 inches
Track: 47.75 inches front, 50.5 inches rear
Overall: Length 153 inches; width 57.75 inches; height 49 inches empty with top up, 37.25 inches to top of windshield
Curb weight: approx. 1925 pounds, 49% over front wheels

This version of the Plus 8 snapped at the London Show features optional Lucas road lights. Modest streamlining does not spoil traditional lines.

Tachometer would seem badly located but otherwise, dash is fully instrumented and functional. Extra padding and different wheel would be needed on U.S. models.

With customary honesty, Morgan does not hide fact that it is powered by a Rover-built V-8. Breather tube in valve cover proves plans for export.

am still forgiving of their faults. Sure, the ride on badly surfaced roads is lousy, but how many roads are badly surfaced today? Yes, various things broke or came loose on my Morgans, but only minor items that you could get fixed when it suited you. It was never anything major which left you at the roadside hitching a ride. Yes, top fabric which folds separately from its frame looks crude but it is durable and incredibly quick to erect. Yes, I do dig the instant acceleration and truly roll-free cornering, even if I am half-a-century old.

Did I say instant acceleration? Drop in the clutch in first gear and you leave two black stripes along the road behind you, stripes which go on until eventually you dare not ignore the tachometer any longer! The red sector started back at 5000 rpm but Morgan just happened to be able to get tachometers with that marking cheaply. Rover suggest a 6000 rpm limit and Morgan haven't found 7000 rpm destructive. Two upshift

around 40-45 and 70-75 and then the quarter mile mark passes at 89 mph in third after 15 seconds elapsed time.

Crunched upshifts? That Moss transmission is strong but it was designed a long time ago. It has synchromesh of a sort on three ratios but none at all on its nasty, grinding first ratio. Hell, you can run pretty smoothly at 10 mph in top gear, accelerating from 20 to 100 in it in only 24 seconds, so mostly you can ignore the transmission. Just treat the gas pedal a bit gently below 30 mph as the camshaft was designed to go with a torque converter rather than with a clutch.

It's amazing how a cart-sprung rigid axle without any tramp bars (but with a locked differential) handles so much power in a light car. Just a few changes of spring strengths and mounting points made the 2-litre car's layout OK for 3.5 litres. The springs are too hard by far for comfort on dirt roads, but have longer travel than on any previous Morgan and are adequate for modern roads.

Cornering is something to which modern road test phrases such as roll and understeer don't apply. It seems to involve geometric arcs undistorted by tire or spring flexing. Unhappily the steering mechanism does flex, and working against self-centering castor action, this feels a bit like understeer. If you want some oversteer, squirt some of the ample power through the rear wheels. You'll find it's the only way to make a U-turn within a 40-foot road since huge tires somewhat curtail steering in the normal fashion. Usually your courage rather than available tire grip limits

MORGAN

CONTINUED FROM PAGE 36

cornering speed, and the power-applied disc-and-drum Girling brakes cope easily with any last-minute cowardice.

This is just a two seater, a shade wider and much better upholstered than previous Morgans, but still your elbow will overflow onto the padded top of a cutaway door. A nice cubic space behind the seats takes modest luggage, a detail over which Morgans have almost been more practical than rival MG models. It's an impressive outlook from the driving seat along about five feet of hood, louvered from end to end so that the carburetors above the V-8 keep cool and the windshield gets de-iced.

It didn't rain whilst I had this Morgan, but the body is so like my old model that I'd wager a very little water gets in around lift-out sidescreens and through floor joints on really wet days. There's a heater of sorts to defrost your toes, but they figure you to wear clothes when driving a Morgan in winter.

Gas mileage? If you use the car, rather than just astounding big car owners with its acceleration, you can expect around 20 to the gallon or 300 to the tankful. One-shot lubrication of the front suspension slides from the engine's pressure system will put oil drips on the garage floor, but you won't find the quantity used measurable.

Some folk say that the Morgan Plus 8 is foolish but one helluva lot of fun. If you meet anyone who says this, ask him how much his own car cost, how its acceleration and top speed compare with the Morgan, and how much special equipment is needed to service or repair it. I'd not like to sit in a Morgan while two tons of Detroit iron were driven into its side, but I'd not like the experience in many other open cars either. Me, I'd say that if two seats and a moderate luggage trunk suffice for you, and if you seldom go off surfaced roads, getting Morganized can be a pretty shrewd way of having fun. ●

THE ROVERISED MOG

CONTINUED FROM PAGE 33

In terms of leverage to length of bonnet, the steering wheel (a tidy leather bound job) seems too small — a reverse to our normal criticism of wheels these days. But once you've mastered the idea this car really isn't a floating-on-marshmallow cocoa tin and every movement of any control is going to bring instant and precise reaction, you find the wheel is 100 percent suited.

Likewise the gearshift which is a rod protruding straight from the Jaguar-type Moss box is so precise you can just about feel which tooth you've meshed. The box is outstanding for its lack of syncromesh though the specs do say it exists on two, three and four. A ball and spring system, it requires suitable pauses and a sprinkling of double-de-clutching for graunchless changes. It's very exacting and would soon sort-out those bar room heroes again. But gearchanging is more placing the lever, than pushing it in the general direction of the next gear. And it's considerably hard on your wrist too. If your reflex sympathy is out, the selectors will bite, and hard. We can't remember a gearbox quite as exacting since the days of Austin 6/16 ownership (yes, the 1928 crash-box model, but it did have a ball not gate change).

Of course when you're really on the ball with the change and go for fast snick-free changes, ad lib driving a Mog V8 is suddenly what real motoring is all about.

With such taut suspension, the brakes gain that feeling of working without sensation, very similar to the prototype Bolwell we tested some years back. Stand on the brake pedal and any reaction is minimal. However you are stopping, and quickly. Lack of nosedive and a full harness belt leaning on you, only gently reduces the psychology of high G-forces. During all our testing the stealthy brakes were uninhibited by fade, water or dust. The 11 in. Girling discs and 9 in. drums are pumped by a dual circuit servo assisted hydraulic system. And you need the last feature, for a heavy foot is required even with the assistance. The handbrake is a genuine fly-off affair placed for'ard of the gearshift and quite "un-get-at-able" with a belt done up. There's also a large red warning light to tell whether it's flown-off or not.

Cockpit layout in general is ergonomically sound though vintage architecture does misplace some instruments for driver visibility — milady doesn't really need to be told that's a 107.6 mph slipstream pulling at her scarf. Switches are all the flat safety rocker type, and take in washers, wipers (two speed and three blades), spot lights, heater fan, lights, hazard warning flasher and an ignition isolation switch. A Cortina-type column stalk takes care of high and low beam, headlight flasher and horn.

Underneath the dash, against the firewall, is a "smog-recirculator" type heater which does keep your feet warm, top up or down. The steering wheel is a neat affair with bound rim and matt black alloy spokes, and to tame the safety experts, sits on the end of a collapsible column. Behind the rim is an afterthought Smiths tacho. It's a trifle hard to read and is symmetrically opposed to a commodious glovebox.

The Plus Eight is immediately identifiable for its bonnet louvres, a slightly shallower front mudguard curve, two extra quartz iodine peepers and those dapper mag alloy wheels — which we might add are an abortionate idea for easy cleaning. The big 13.5 gallon tank has two fillers which helps when it comes to available space on each side of the pumps and also eases the strain of burping. But it doesn't leave much space for luggage (4.4 cu ft) which fits in behind the seats, as there's no external rear opening. Two batteries beneath this deck make level checking slightly worse than a Mini.

Hood erection is yet another demanding exercise. In quite antiquated fashion hood stays are dropped into position before the fabric can be levered up into place. On a dark night as a Sydney cloudburst lets go, erecting the hood needs great fortitude and a stout bottle in the glove compartment. Mind you, once in place and the sliding perspex curtains screwed down, the interior is quite water tight. In continual heavy rain we had but a few drops instil iced shock to varying parts of the anatomy. The big secret is to ensure the side curtain rubber flap seal is running between the double overlap flaps of the hood. It's preferable to have the concierge do this from outside before you leave the lighted entrance patio. Entirely superior to fighting with rain-soaked flaps by yourself.

An inbuilt necessity with the Plus Eight (or any Morgan) is a chamois to keep both the exterior and interior clean of dust and water that plagues any open car, but more so with the Mog.

As the trim is all hand-stitched in a factory that must be the last front of cottage industry, the finish is superb. The centre section breathes well while there is excellent location for trying the SPs. The orange chrome paintwork was also most lustrous and only at the bottom of one guard and at one spot near the bonnet hinge was there any imperfection.

A fairly delicate chassis apart, the Mog V8 is probably more at home in Australia than the UK. To start with if *it* doesn't make the scene at Palmy for half the year round, *nothing* will; and for those winter months stepping it out at the sprints will re-write the ET book. Yes we did say sprints, chaps. Drags? In a Morgan? #

MORGAN PLUS 8

An anachronism,
but it's what motoring is all about, chaps

LET'S START OFF by admitting that a Morgan—any Morgan, including this new Plus 8—is a car you can't be indifferent to. In these days when cars seem to have less and less to distinguish them from each other, that in itself is a virtue. Morgans stir your juices.

Taking the progressive point of view, you could fill a small book with the reasons why a Morgan is a ridiculous and unnecessary anachronism. It rides hard, steers hard, isn't put together very well, it leaks in the rain, has a token heater, a cranky gearbox, etc., etc. You have to be a student of automotive history these days to even be aware of such things as sliding-pillar front suspension, wood body framework, side curtains and the Moss nearly-crash gearbox, but Morgans have them all. A Morgan's styling is about as up-to-date as "Stardust" compared to "Star Shine" and it has enough mechanical idiosyncrasies to make a grown engineer cry. But a

Morgan is nostalgia on wheels—genuine nostalgia, not plastic nostalgia—and if nostalgia is a legitimate state of mind, a Morgan is a legitimate car. Not being psychologists, we leave that decision to the reader.

Getting down to the nuts and bolts, the Plus 8 replaces the Triumph-powered Plus 4 in Morgan's lineup while the Cortina-powered 4/4 in standard 2-seater and competition 2- and 4-seater form remain. Built on Morgan's traditional steel ladder frame, it has the traditional ash body framework with steel panels laid over it. The wheelbase is stretched 2 in. from the Plus 4, as is the overall length; front and rear track are up by an inch apiece and the Plus 8 is 1½ in. wider. Apart from that it is altogether the same car as the Plus 4 and its styling goes right back to the original Morgan 4/4 of 1937 except for today's rounded-off radiator shell and a startling set of J. H. Robinson alloy wheels. The front suspension, whose sliding pillars keep the wheels parallel to the body sides and also form the steering axis, requires daily lubrication from the engine oil supply via a pedal the driver depresses, and the rear suspension is by trusty multi-leaf springs and a live axle carrying a Salisbury limited-slip differential that is stronger than that of the Plus 4.

The big news, as anyone keen on Morgans already knows, is the Plus 8's engine. This is the highly favored 3.5-liter aluminum V-8 formerly of Buick-Olds-Pontiac and now made by Rover in modified form. It gives 184 bhp and 226 lb-ft torque compared to the Plus 4's 105 bhp and 128 lb-ft (from the Triumph TR-4 engine). The V-8 weighs no more though some of the attendant changes have increased total weight by about 25 lb. A new clutch was needed to take the V-8's steam but the old Moss gearbox, which many will remember as the Jaguar gearbox until 1965, has plenty of torque capacity. It remains unchanged and is mounted as before in a midship position with a short driveshaft connecting it with the clutch. Some frame strengthening has been done and the fuel tank is nearly six gallons bigger.

Morgan still hasn't returned to the American market but hopes to do so in 1970, at which time the fully "detoxed" Rover engine will be used and the cars will conform to all the Federal safety standards. The Plus 8 tested had safety rocker switches in its redesigned instrument panel and uses the AC Delco collapsing steering column section. The test car was the property of Scott McMillan, a young writer at American Broadcasting's Hollywood studios who had brought it into the U.S. via the Canadian border. He had little trouble getting it through U.S. Customs, but we have inquired of the official position of the customs department on bringing in "non-conforming cars" and hope to report on it soon.

The BOP-R V-8 has a nice, throaty exhaust note—just enough to let everyone know that this isn't any Triumph-powered Morgan—and is its usual mechanically smooth self except for what seems to be less complete isolation from the body than you'd get in, say, the Rover 3500. Morgan hasn't opted for overly long-legged gearing, with the result that the Plus 8 feels really strong in any of its four gears. It lays a healthy streak of rubber getting off the line—nothing insane, mind you—and minding the 5200-rpm rev limit as well as taking the time necessary to shift without graunching we got the highly respectable quarter-mile time of 16.6 sec and a 0-60 mph time of 8.5 sec. A British magazine, using 6000 rpm and probably not nearly so concerned with preserving the gearbox as we were with this private example, recorded

15.0-sec quarters and a 0-60 time of 6.7 sec. Top speed is limited by the 5200-rpm redline to 105 mph. The V-8 fits neatly under the Morgan's vintage hood except for an amusing bash (undoubtedly done by a rubber mallet) in the Rover air cleaner to clear the center hood support and should be reasonably accessible for service although the front spark plugs are awkward to get at.

There's a great deal of pleasure to be derived from the V-8's strength, but the vintage gearbox very nearly spoils it. It's noisy and extremely hard shifting—we recall the stiffness as a characteristic of this box that gradually wears off as the miles accumulate—but its lack of a synchromesh first gear, together with synchros on the upper gears that range from hopeless (2nd gear) to marginal (3rd and 4th), make it a challenge to drive a Morgan well. As mentioned earlier, the published acceleration times could have been improved greatly if we hadn't taken over a second to complete the 1-2 shift and nearly a second each for the other two. Another annoyance is the limited-slip differential, which chatters wildly if torque is applied in a sharp, low-speed turn. We first thought the left rear wheel was about to fall off.

The excellent Dunlop tires, generously large for the Morgan's light weight, give it high cornering power—if the surface is glassy smooth. The strange front suspension geometry gives a prevailing understeer which can easily be overcome by applying plenty of power—this way you get a classic 4-wheel drift, more or less—but the undulations present in

MORGAN PLUS 8
AT A GLANCE

Price as tested. . . . .$2800 fob England
Engine. . . . . .ohv V-8, 3528 cc, 184 bhp
Curb weight, lb. 2005
Top speed, mph. 105
Acceleration, 0-¼ mi, sec. 16.6
Average fuel consumption, mpg. 16.0
Summary: the past lives on . . . sparkling performance of V-8 engine countered by poor ride, clumsy handling and terrible gearbox . . . brakes powerful & fade-free but tend to pull.

GORDON CHITTENDEN PHOTOS

MORGAN PLUS 8

the smooth pavement of Orange County Raceway were enough to get the front end "nibbling" as, apparently, the front tires gained and lost traction in a manner similar to that of a Volkswagen. This is not surprising because VWs share camber characteristics with Morgans.

The steering is quick—and extremely stiff. And it gets stiffer when the brakes are applied. Perhaps this might be a safety factor in an extreme situation but in everyday driving one does occasionally apply the brakes gently while steering and it's disconcerting to have the wheels feel as if they're unsteerable.

Like all the other controls, the Plus 8's brake pedal is a heavy affair, taking 55 lb of effort for a half-g stop even though there is a vacuum booster. In our simulated emergency stop from 80 mph they haul the car down nicely, with little tendency for wheel lockup on dry pavement, to a full stop in just over 300 ft. But in the fade test, in which they did not fade at all, they insisted on pulling to the left in varying degrees, a characteristic which is tough to correct because of the aforementioned stiffening of the steering under braking. We could have rated them "very good" but for this.

When it comes to a description of the Plus 8's ride, one word will do it: stiff. Even on a relatively smooth freeway the Plus 8's nose bobs up and down with the gentle humps of concrete strips, and when it comes to traversing really rough surfaces one does well to simply slow down to minimize the jarring, rattling and suspension bottoming. If there was ever a car for smooth roads, this is it.

The revised cockpit of the Plus 8 is basically well-planned, given the vintage car concept to start with, and has more room than some modern cars of similar size. The instrument panel is simple and attractive in the classic mode with modern rocker switches and simple but contemporary dials—surprisingly, there are no numbers on a temperature gauge that ran in the "hot" range all the time we were doing performance tests. The tachometer is a small dial on the left and is visible enough but the speedometer is off to the right and becomes very difficult to see if one drives with the righthand part of the tonneau cover snapped up. An arms-out driving position is out of the question but the seats themselves, new Restall items, are truly individual seats unlike Morgan bench

seats of old and give good lateral location for the back that is augmented by seat belts for the lower body. They certainly don't look modern-orthopedic, but they seem to work pretty well.

Looking out over the lengthy hood, which is covered by two long rows of (real) louvers, one is moved to a genuine love of the older and better things of motoring. The V-8 engine, or a 4-cyl for that matter, may not be a long engine but front wheels that are right out at the front and engine placed back toward the firewall results in far better weight distribution. Looking to the rear, we find a rearview mirror that's too small—and with the makeshift top in place rearward vision really gets bad, but then one does not drive a Morgan with the top up any more than absolutely necessary. A few cubic feet of luggage space is available in the well behind the seats if the top is up or if you've left the top and side curtains at home. There are three windshield wipers and an old-fashioned recirculating heater with a 2-speed blower.

Okay. So the Morgan Plus 8 doesn't measure up to any of the modern standards about shifting, handling, ride, noise, weather protection—you name it, it just doesn't *do* the things we expect a sports car to do these days. But we couldn't get any staff consensus at all on whether or not it is a worthy automobile in AD 1970. The Associate Editor said "Makes a man out of you—but then who wields broadswords these days?" The Engineering Editor said, "What fun is a sports car that doesn't do any of the sports car things well?" The Editor said, "This is what motoring is all about, chaps. Not driving, not touring, but motoring, damn it. It's romance—young love, moonlit motoring on winding blacktop roads and coffee stops in unlikely places. A car for F. Scott Fitzgerald heroes and heroines, yet surely as appealing to the pot generation as the hip-flask set." When we pulled into a drive-in market and parked alongside a young couple of the former category who volunteered, all smiles, that the Plus 8 (in its stunning chrome-yellow and black paint, to be sure) was a super groovy thing, we were convinced that the Editor had his point. If you thrive on *reasonable* automobiles, cars that do a required job well, forget the Morgan. But if you're old enough to be nostalgic about 1930-style sports cars, or young enough to simply groove on something kooky, the Plus 8 may be your thing. And even when you add in the $500-odd it will take to import it for yourself, it's not very expensive. We'd like to tell you to try one, but to our knowledge this is the only one in the country.

ROAD TEST
MORGAN PLUS 8

SCALE: 10" DIVISIONS

PRICE

Basic list.................$2770
(fob Malvern Link, England)
As tested.................$2800

ENGINE

Type....................ohv V-8
Bore x stroke, mm....88.9 x 71.1
  Equivalent in.......3.50 x 2.80
Displacement, cc/cu in...3528/215
Compression ratio.........10.5:1
Bhp @ rpm.........184 @ 5200
  Equivalent mph...........105
Torque @ rpm, lb-ft......226 @ 3000
  Equivalent mph...........59
Carburetion.........two SU H56
Type fuel required......premium

DRIVE TRAIN

Clutch diameter, in...........9.5
Gear ratios: 4th (1.00).....3.58:1
  3rd (1.21)..............4.33:1
  2nd (1.74)..............6.22:1
  1st (2.97)..............10.65:1
Synchromesh........on 2, 3 & 4
Final drive ratio..........3.58:1

CHASSIS & BODY

Body/frame: steel ladder chassis
  with separate steel body on ash
  framework
Brake type: 11.0-in. discs front,
  9.0 x 1.75-in. drums rear, vacuum
  assisted
  Swept area, sq in.........223
Wheels.......cast alloy 15 x 5½J
Tires........Dunlop SP 185VR-15
Steering type........cam & peg
  Turns, lock-to-lock........2.25
  Turning circle, ft.........37.0
Front suspension: vertical sliding
  pillars, coil springs, tube shocks
Rear suspension: live axle on leaf
  springs, lever shocks

ACCOMMODATION

Seating capacity, persons.......2
Seat width..............2 x 16.5
Head room..................38.5
Seat back adjustment, deg......0
Driver comfort rating (scale of 100):
  Driver 69 in. tall...........70
  Driver 72 in. tall...........65
  Driver 75 in. tall...........55

INSTRUMENTATION

Instruments: 140-mph speedo,
  6000-rpm tach, 99,999 odo,
  999.9 trip odo, oil press, water
  temp, ammeter, fuel level
Warning lights: generator, hazard
  flasher, high beam, directionals,
  handbrake

MAINTENANCE

Engine oil capacity, qt.........5.3
Daily: lube front suspension by
  depressing pedal
Every 5000 mi: change engine oil &
  filter, adjust carbs, lube chassis,
  various op'l checks
Every 10,000 mi: chg air filter elements, oil carb dampers, chg
  plugs, adj or chg points, lube
  distributor
Every 20,000 mi: clean eng flame
  traps, chg fuel filter
Tire pressures,
Warranty period, mo...........6

EQUIPMENT

Seat belts, as fitted to test car
  ($30) and tool bag

GENERAL

Curb weight, lb............2005
Test weight................2430
Weight distribution (with
  driver), front/rear, %.....46/54
Wheelbase, in..............98.0
Track, front/rear.......49.0/51.0
Overall length.............152.0
  Width....................58.0
  Height...................49.0
Ground clearance, in........6.5
Overhang, front/rear....19.9/34.1
Usable trunk space, cu ft.....4.4
Fuel tank capacity, gal......16.1

CALCULATED DATA

Lb/hp (test wt).............13.2
Mph/1000 rpm (4th gear).....19.7
Engine revs/mi (60 mph).....3050
Engine speed @ 70 mph.....3530
Piston travel, ft/mi........1480
Cu ft/ton mi...............156
R&T wear index............45
R&T steering index.........0.83
Brake swept area sq in/ton....184

ROAD TEST RESULTS

ACCELERATION

Time to distance, sec:
  0–100 ft................3.3
  0–250 ft................5.8
  0–500 ft................8.9
  0–750 ft...............11.5
  0–1000 ft..............13.7
  0–1320 ft (¼ mi).........16.6
Speed at end of ¼ mi, mph...82.5
Time to speed, sec:
  0–30 mph................3.1
  0–40 mph................5.5
  0–50 mph................6.7
  0–60 mph................8.5
  0–70 mph...............11.9
  0–80 mph...............15.4
  0–100 mph..............28.4
Passing exposure time, sec:
  To pass car going 50 mph....5.4

FUEL CONSUMPTION

Normal driving, mpg.......16.0
Crusing range, mi..........257

SPEEDS IN GEARS

4th gear (5200 rpm), mph.....105
3rd (5200)................85
2nd (5200)................60
1st (5200)................34

BRAKES

Panic stop from 80 mph:
  Stopping distance, ft.......307
  Max. deceleration, % g.......84
  Control.............very good
Fade test: percent of increase in
  pedal effort required to maintain
  50%-g deceleration rate in six
  stops from 60 mph..........nil
Parking: hold 30% grade......no
Overall brake rating........good

SPEEDOMETER ERROR

30 mph indicated......actual 29.0
40 mph.................38.8
60 mph.................58.3
80 mph.................77.8
100 mph................97.6

ACCELERATION & COASTING

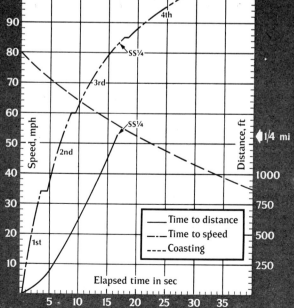

Time to distance
Time to speed
Coasting

Speed, mph — Distance, ft

Elapsed time in sec

Morgan
First of the Real Sports Cars

A
selection of
Morgan
publicity

Plus 8 2-seater. Powered by a superb aluminium V8 engine of 3528 c.c., this is our latest model. 0—70 m.p.h. in 7.5 seconds, with brakes to match. Wider, longer and more comfortable than ever, with a very full specification.

£1,647   5 10 tax paid.

4/4 1600 2-seater. This car is available in standard form with a lively 1600 c.c. crossflow engine giving good acceleration. This is enhanced by a mild stage of tune in the competition version which is capable of speeds well in excess of 100 m.p.h.

£1,085 18   1 tax paid.
competition model £1,125   1   5 tax paid.

4/4 1600 4-seater. Just about the only open 4-seater sports car available today—and there really is sufficient room for 4 people. The specification is otherwise similar to the 4/4 competition model which allows sufficient power for the larger body.

£1,164   4   9 tax paid.

Morgan   **MORGAN MOTOR COMPANY**
Malvern Link, Worcestershire. Tel.: Malvern 3104/5

Come back to open-air motoring in powerful style.
Owning a Morgan Plus 8 says that you know
how much fun life can be.

Morgan + 8 exciting

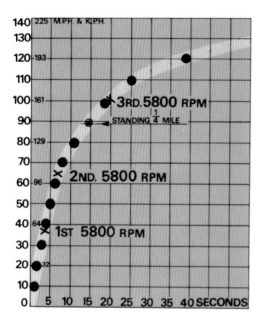

PLUS 8
GENERAL SPECIFICATION

Cubic Capacity	—3,528 c.c., (215 cu. ins.)
Number of Cylinders	—8
Bore and Stroke	—89 x 71 mm, 3.5 x 2.8 in.
Carburettor	—Twin SU HIF6
Compression Ratio	—9.35:1
Firing Order	—1,8,4,3,6,5,7,2
B.H.P.	—155 DIN PS at 5,250 r.p.m.
Oil Capacity	—5.7 litres (9.5 pints)
Torque	—198 lb.ft., 27.5 mkg at 2,500 r.p.m.
Fuel Tank Capacity	—13½ gallons (61 litres)
Fuel Consumption	—24 m.p.g. (11.77 litres/100km)
Valve Gear	—O.H.V. pushrod, hydraulic tappets
Ignition Timing	—Top Dead Centre
Dryweight of Complete Car	—1,826 lbs., 828 kg

All Morgans are capable of high cruising speeds. The 4/4, we think, performs rather well at quite a reasonable price. With the hood down it's surprising how seldom it rains!

Morgan 4'4 fantastic

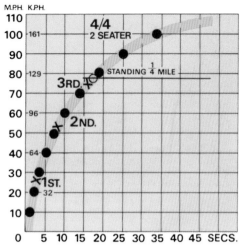

4/4 GENERAL SPECIFICATION

Cubic Capacity	— 1.599 c.c. (97.6 cu. ins.)
Bore and Stroke	— 3.188″ x 3.060″ (81 mm x 77.6 mm)
Compression Ratio	— 9:1
B.H.P.	— 84 DIN/SAE at 5.500 r.p.m.
Torque	— 92 lb.ft., 12.7 mkg. at 3.500 r.p.m.
Type of Carburettor	— Weber Twin Choke 32/36 downdraught
Number of Cylinders	— 4
Firing Order	— 1.2.4.3
Oil Capacity	— 7.5 pints (4.25 litres), 7 pints (4.1 litres), refill
Petrol Capacity	— 8½ gallons (39 litres)

1913 Morgan Grand Prix Models

1926 Morgan Family Model

1930 Jap engined Aero Morgan

4/4 AND 4/4 4-SEATER SPECIFICATION

- *Chassis Frame*—Deep Z-shape section with five boxed or tubular cross members. Easily detachable front end.
- *Gearbox*—Four speed and reverse. Synchromesh on all forward gears. *Overall Ratios*—Top 4.1; 3rd 5.7; 2nd 8.3; 1st 12.2; reverse 13.6 to 1.
- *Transmission and Rear Axle*—Propshaft with needle roller bearing universal joints transmits power to the tubular Salisbury rear axle fitted with Hypoid gears—ratio 4.1 to 1.
- *Wheels and Tyres*—Pressed steel rims fixed with four studs and covered by chromium-plated disc. Centre lock wire wheels are an optional extra. Radial tyres—165 x 15".
- *Brakes*—Girling hydraulic dual brake system on four wheels 11" dia. discs on front wheels. 9" x 1¾" drum brakes on rear. Cable operated hand brake.
- *Steering Gear*—Cam gear. Collapsible column. Steering lock ignition switch. Leather-covered spring alloy wheel, giving 2¼ turns lock to lock. Turning circle 32' (9.7 m).
- *Suspension*—Front wheels—vertically mounted coil springs on sliding axle pin. Double acting tubular shock absorbers. Semi-elliptical rear springs, fitted at both ends with Silentbloc bushes, and controlled by Armstrong hydraulic dampers.
- *Electrics*—Lucas 12 volt equipment; indicators, hazard warning, instrument panel lighting, two-speed wipers and fresh air heater.
- *Instruments*—Steel instrument panel includes speedo with trip mileage, rev. counter; oil, fuel, battery gauges and water temp. gauge.
- *Bodywork*—Sheet steel panels on ash wood frame. Black vynide upholstery (alternative colours or leather available at extra cost). Detachable tops can be stowed in luggage compartment or behind rear seats in four seater. Laminated windscreen.
- *Colours*—Deep Brunswick Green, Signal Red, Turquoise Blue, Nut Brown or Royal Ivory. Other colours available at extra cost.
- *Dimensions (approx.)*—Wheelbase 8' (244 cm). Track, front 3' 11" (119 cm), rear 4' 1" (124 cm). Length 12' (366 cm). Width 4' 8" (142 cm). Ground clearance 7" (18 cm). Height, 4/4 two seater 4' 3" (129 cm). Weight, 4/4 two seater 1,624 lbs (735 kg). 4/4 four seater— 1,680 lbs (760 kg).

PLUS 8 SPECIFICATION

- *Chassis Frame*—Deep Z-shape section with five boxed or tubular cross members. Easily detachable front end.
- *Gearbox*—Five speed and reverse Rover gearbox. Synchromesh on all forward gears. *Overall Ratios*—Top 2.76:1; 4th 3.31:1; 3rd 4.62:1; 2nd 6.90:1; 1st 10.99:1.
- *Transmission and Rear Axle*—Propshaft with needle roller bearing universal joints transmits power to tubular Salisbury slip axle with Hypoid gears—ratio 3.31 to 1.
- *Wheels and Tyres*—Cast aluminium, wide-based rims fixed with five studs. Radial tyres 195 x 14". Overseas option 185 x 15".
- *Brakes*—Girling hydraulic dual brake system 11" dia. discs on front. 9" x 1¾" drum brakes on rear. Fly-off, cable operated hand brake.
- *Steering Gear*—Cam gear. Collapsible column. Steering lock ignition switch. Leather-covered spring alloy wheel, giving 2¼ turns lock to lock. Turning circle 38' (11.5 m).
- *Suspension*—Front wheels independently sprung by vertical coil springs and telescopic hydraulic shock absorbers. Semi-elliptic rear springs with lever type hydraulic dampers.
- *Electrics*—Lucas 12 volt equipment; indicators, hazard warning, instrument panel lighting, two-speed wipers and washer. Twin spotlights and fresh air heater.
- *Instrument Panel*—Steel instrument panel includes speedo with trip mileage, rev. counter; oil, fuel, battery gauges and water temp. gauge.
- *Bodywork*—Sheet panels on ash wood frame. Black ambla upholstery (alternative colours or leather available at extra cost). Bucket seats with fore and aft adjustment. Detachable hood can be stowed in the 36" x 20" x 12" (92 x 51 x 30.5 cm) high luggage compartment. Laminated windscreen.
- *Colours*—Deep Brunswick Green, Signal Red, Turquoise Blue, Nut Brown or Royal Ivory. Other colours available at extra cost.
- *Dimensions (approx.)*—Wheelbase 8' 2" (249 cm). Track, front 4' 4" (132 cm); rear 4' 5" (135 cm). Overall length 12' 3" (373 cm). Width 5' 2" (158 cm). Ground clearance 7" (18 cm). Height 4' 4" (132 cm). Weight 1,826 lbs (828 kg).

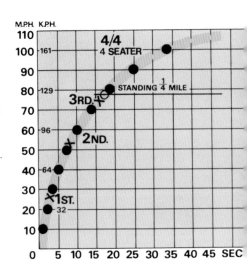

1937 Morgan "F" Super

1947 Morgan 4/4 Tower

1967 Morgan Plus 4 2-seater

Morgan 4/4 four seat fun

So like the 4/4, you'd hardly know the difference. But your wife and kids really have a proper seat each. Always keep a Morgan in the family.

The Driving experience

S itting behind the wheel of a Morgan is an unparalleled experience. Instead of an expanse of plastic so typical of most mass produced cars, in a Morgan the senses are delighted by the contrasting textures of hardwoods, aluminium and leather.

The cockpit inspires a sense of adventure - to seek out remote country roads and leave the mediocre behind. The long view over the bonnet and wings is unobstructed by heavy pillars. The sense of security offered by the low driving position is reinforced by the knowledge that both chassis and ash frame have passed rigorous testing.* This is a thoroughbred among cars - a unique fusion of traditional skills and modern technology.

Drive off and the car feels perfectly balanced. The controls are light, direct and responsive. Acceleration is exhilarating and computerised emission controls ensure that this is not at the expense of the environment.

From any point of view, the Morgan shouts no compromise.

Full safety and impact tests were successfully carried out on Morgan cars in 1996 by The Motor Industry Research Association (MIRA).

Morgan's unique Ash wood frame

Charles and Peter Morgan

Photo: courtesy of Autocar

---

plus 4 Technical Specifications

Engine:
No. Of Cylinders:	4 In-line
Cubic Capacity:	1994 cm³
Bore & Stroke:	84.45 x 89 mm
Compression Ratio:	10.0 : 1
Maximum Power:	99kw @ 6000 rpm (134 bhp ps)
Maximum Torque:	184nm @ 2500 rpm (136 lb/ft)
Valve Gear:	D.O.H.C. Belt Driven, Hydraulic Tappets 4 Valves Per Cylinder
Fuel Supply:	Electronic Fuel Injection
Ignition:	Digital Electronic
Petrol Capacity:	2-Str. 50 Litres/11 Imp. Gallons, 4-Str. 40 Litres/9 Imp. Gallons
Exhaust System:	Cast Manifold to Stainless Steel down pipe and Single Catalyst
Evaporative Cntrl:	Sealed System with Pressure Relief Valve to a Charcoal Canister.

Transmission:
Gearbox:	Five Forward Gears and Reverse
Ratios:	5th: 0.79, 4th: 1, 3rd: 1.397, 2nd: 2.087, 1st: 3.32, Rev. 3.43.
Clutch:	Single Dry Plate 241mm
Axle:	Tubular Live Axle with Hypoid Gears
Ratio:	3.73 : 1

Steering:
Type:	Steering Box with Worm and Roller 2.25 Turns lock to lock.
Column:	Separate universal shaft with Vibration Damper to collapsible safety Top Unit with Steering Lock Ignition Switch.
Wheel:	381mm/15" or 356/14" Diameter
Turning Circle:	10m/32'

Suspension:
Front:	Independent Sliding Pillar with Coil Springs and Gas Telescopic Shock Absorbers
Rear:	Semi-elliptic Leaf Springs with gas telescopic Shock Absorbers

Brakes:
Front:	AP Lockheed 4 Pot Callipers, 11" Dia. Disc Brakes.
Rear:	AP Lockheed 9 x 1.75" Drum Brakes
Hand brake:	Sporting Fly-Off Type.
Operation:	Hydraulic, Dual Circuit with Vacuum Servo Assistance.

Wheels and Tyres:
Wheels:	Centre Locking Wire Wheels with Rudge Hubs, 6" Wide Rims
Tyres:	195/60VR15

Chassis:
Type:	Separate Deep Z Shaped Section with 5 Tubular or Box Section Cross Members.

Body work:
Type:	2 Seater and 4 Seater, Handmade Steel or Aluminium Panels on Cuprinol treated Ash Wood Coach built Body Frame.
Upholstery:	standard: Black Ambla, optional: Connolly Leather in numerous colours.
Hood & Tonneau:	standard: Black Everflex, optional: Coloured Everflex and Mohair hooding
Seats:	standard: Bucket Seats, optional: Reclining or Sports Seats.

Electrical and Instruments:
Electrics:	12v electrical system, Indicators, Three Two Speed Wipers, Hazard Warning Lights, Fresh Air Heater and Demister, H4 Headlights, Reversing Lights.
Instruments:	Speedometer, Tachometer and Warning Lights in front of driver. Separate Panel With Oil Pressure, Water Temperature, Volts and Fuel Gauges.

Colours:
standard:	Connaught Green, Corsa Red, Indigo Blue, Black or Royal Ivory
optional:	Any Single or Two Tone combination from The ICI Autocolour Range

Dimensions:
Overall: Length:	3960mm/13', Width: 1630mm/5'4", Height: 2-str 1290mm/4'4", (approx.) 4str. 1350mm/4'5"
Wheelbase:	2490mm/ 8'2", Track Front 1280mm/4'2" Rear 1420mm/4' 8"
Dry Weight:	2-Str. 920kg , 4-Str. 1000kg.

All optional specifications at extra cost.
All weights and dimensions are average figures for standard vehicles.

All specifications are subject to change without warning but are correct at the time of going to press.

the Morgan plus 4
and the Four Seater

The ample rear seats of the four seater

1800 4/4 Technical Specifications

Engine:

No. of Cylinders:	4 In-line
Cubic Capacity:	1798 cm³
Bore & Stroke:	80.6 x 88 mm
Compression Ratio:	10.0 : 1
Maximum Power:	84kw @ 5750 rpm (114 bhp ps)
Maximum Torque:	160nm @ 4500 rpm (118 lb/ft)
Valve Gear:	D.O.H.C. Belt Driven, Hydraulic Tappets 4 valves per cylinder
Fuel Supply:	Electronic Fuel Injection
Ignition:	Digital Electronic
Petrol Capacity:	50 Litres/11 Imp. Gallons
Exhaust System:	Cast Manifold to Stainless Steel Down Pipe and Single Catalyst.
Evaporative Cntrl:	Sealed System with Pressure Relief Valve to a Charcoal Canister.

Transmission:

Gearbox:	Five Forward Gears And Reverse
Ratios:	5th: 0.82, 4th: 1, 3rd: 1.34, 2nd: 2.08, 1st: 3.89, Rev. 3.51
Clutch:	Single Dry Plate 216mm
Axle:	Tubular Live Axle with Hypoid Gears
Ratio:	4.1 : 1

Steering:

Type:	Steering box with worm and roller 2.25 turns lock to lock.
Column:	Separate Universal Shaft with vibration damper to collapsible safety TopUnit with Steering Lock Ignition Switch.
Wheel:	381mm/15″ or 356/14″ diameter
Turning Circle:	10m/32′

Suspension:

Front:	Independent Sliding Pillar with coil springs and Gas Telescopic Shock Absorbers
Rear:	Semi-elliptic Leaf Springs with Gas Telescopic Shock Absorbers

Brakes:

Front:	AP Lockheed 4 Pot Callipers, 11″ Dia. Disc Brakes.
Rear:	AP Lockheed 9 x 1.75″ Drum Brakes
Hand brake:	Sporting Fly-Off type.
Operation:	Hydraulic, Dual Circuit with Vacuum Servo Assistance.

Wheels and Tyres:

Wheels:	Centre locking wire wheels with Rudge Hubs *standard* 5″ x 15″ or *optional* 6″x 15″ Wide Rims
Tyres:	*standard* 165 TR 15 *optional:*195/60VR15

Chassis:

Type:	Separate Deep Z Shaped Section with 5 Tubular or Box Section Cross Members.

Body work:

Type:	2 Seater, Handmade Steel or Aluminium Panels on Cuprinol treated Ash Wood Coach built Body Frame.
Upholstery:	*standard:* Black Ambla *optional:* Connolly Leather in numerous colours.
Hood & Tonneau:	*standard:* Black Everflex *optional:* Coloured Everflex and Mohair hooding
Seats:	*standard:* Bucket Seats *optional:* Reclining or Sports Seats.

Electrical and Instruments:

Electrics:	12v electrical system, Indicators, three Two Speed wipers, Hazard Warning Lights, Fresh Air Heater and Demister, H4 Headlights, Reversing Lights.
Instruments:	Speedometer, Tachometer and Warning Lights in front of driver. Separate Panel with Oil Pressure, Water Temperature, Volts and Fuel Gauges.

Colours:

standard:	Connaught Green, Corsa Red, Indigo Blue, Black or Royal Ivory
optional	Any single or Two Tone combination from The ICI Autocolour Range

Dimensions:

Overall:	Length: 3890mm/12′9″ Width: 1500mm/4′9″, Height: 1290mm/4′4″ (approx.)
Wheelbase:	2440mm/ 8′, Track : Front 1220mm/4′ Rear 1240mm/4′ 1″ (6″Wire Wheels: Track, front: 1280mm/4′2″ rear: 1310mm/4′3″)
Dry Weight:	868kg.

All optional specifications at extra cost.
All weights and dimensions are average figures for standard vehicles.
All specifications are subject to change without warning but are correct at the time of going to press.

the Morgan 4/4 1800

---

plus 8 Technical Specifications

Engine:

No. of Cylinders:	V8
Cubic Capacity:	3946 cm³
Bore & Stroke:	94 x 71.12 mm
Compression Ratio:	9.35 : 1
Maximum Power:	140kw @ 4750 rpm (190 bhp ps)
Maximum Torque:	312nm @ 2600 rpm (235 lb/ft)
Valve Gear:	Single central camshaft, Hydraulic tappets, overhead valve.
Fuel Supply:	Electronic Fuel Injection
Ignition:	Electronic
Petrol Capacity:	56 Litres/12 Imp. Gallons,
Exhaust System:	Cast Manifolds to Stainless Steel Down Pipes and Twin Catalysts.
Evaporative Cntrl:	Sealed System with pressure relief valve to a Charcoal Canister.

Transmission:

Gearbox:	Five forward gears and reverse
Ratios:	5th: 0.79, 4th: 1, 3rd: 1.397, 2nd: 2.087, 1st: 3.32, Rev. 3.43.
Clutch:	Single Dry Plate 241mm
Axle:	Tubular Live Axle with Hypoid Gears and limited slip
Ratio:	3.45 : 1

Steering:

Type:	Steering Rack, 3 turns lock to lock.
Column:	Separate Universal Shaft with Vibration Damper to collapsible safety Top Unit with Steering Lock Ignition Switch.
Wheel:	381mm/15″ or 356/14″ Diameter
Turning Circle:	10m/32′

Suspension:

Front:	Independent Sliding Pillar with Coil Springs and Gas Telescopic Shock Absorbers
Rear:	Semi-elliptic Leaf Springs With Gas Telescopic Shock Absorbers

Brakes:

Front:	AP Lockheed 4 Pot Callipers, 11″ Dia. Disc Brakes.
Rear:	AP Lockheed 9 x 1.75″ Drum Brakes
Hand brake:	Sporting Fly-Off Type.
Operation:	Hydraulic, Dual Circuit with Vacuum Servo Assistance.

Wheels and Tyres:

Wheels:	*Standard:* Aluminium Alloy 6.5″x 15 *Optional:* 7″ x 16 Centre Locking Wire or Alloy Wheels.
Tyres:	*Standard:* 205/60VR15, *Optional:* 205/55VR16 on Wire Wheels.

Chassis:

Type:	Separate Deep Z Shaped Section with 5 Tubular or Box Section Cross Members.

Body work:

Type:	2 Seater, Handmade Steel or Aluminium panels on Cuprinol treated Ash Wood Coach built Body Frame.
Upholstery:	*standard* Black Ambla, *optional:* Connolly Leather in numerous colours.
Hood & Tonneau:	*standard* Black Everflex, *optional:* coloured Everflex and Mohair hooding.
Seats:	*standard:* Bucket Seats *optional:* Reclining or Sports Seats.

Electrical and Instruments:

Electrics:	12v electrical system, Indicators, Three Two Speed Wipers, Hazard Warning Lights, Fresh Air Heater and Demister, H4 Headlights, Reversing Lights.
Instruments:	Speedometer, Tachometer and warning lights in front of driver. Separate panel with Oil Pressure, Water Temperature, Volts and Fuel Gauges.

Colours:

standard:	Connaught Green, Corsa Red, Indigo Blue, Black or Royal Ivory
optional	any single or Two Tone combination from the ICI Autocolour Range

Dimensions:

Overall:	Length: 3960mm/13′, Width: 1600mm/5′3″, Height: 1290mm/4′4″, (approx.) (Wire Wheel: Width: 1700mm/5′7″)
Wheelbase:	2490mm/ 8′2″,
Track:	Front 1345mm/4′4″ Rear 1375mm/4′ 6″ (Wire Wheel: Track, Front: 1350mm/4′5″, Rear: 1450mm/4′9″)
Dry Weight:	940kg with standard alloy wheels.

All optional specifications at extra cost.
All weights and dimensions are average figures for standard vehicles.

All specifications are subject to change without warning but are correct at the time of going to press.

the Morgan 8 plus

MOTORING PLUS

Plus 8 plus goodies equals 140 mph

Morgan owners will be familiar with the name of Adam Bridgland, the Bridgland in Kerr-Bridgland Ltd (stockists of Morgan and most other go-faster bits) and enthusiast extraordinaire for the unique product of Malvern Link.

We were lucky enough to borrow Adam's own road/sprint Plus 8 which he pedals with great verve in club events (witness his win in the Plough Trophy meeting at Snetterton in appalling conditions). This car has been carefully and sensibly modified to allow it the occasional success while remaining totally usable and enjoyable for the road. That's why we tested it.

Outwardly only the decals and racing roundals betray 4 KYD's competition background, together with the inevitable Aley roll-over bar. In the cockpit everything seems familiar at first sight. But look again—that's a Moto-Lita wheel you're clutching and the speedo reads up to 160 mph. Adam says it's a joke, but there are funnier things around.

As he has modified the car for his own use he makes no apologises for the total cost of the mods, which is a little frightening. In consequence, our figures may look rather disappointing, but we were impressed with the car and could undoubtedly have made it go quicker if the owner had not insisted upon 'granny style' starts in the interest of preserving his Salisbury LSD.

A dab on the throttle and starting was instantaneous with the Holley 4-barrel carb. The hot Rover unit would then settle to a typical V8 burble at about 900 rpm. There seemed to be little loss in low-speed torque, but the engine objected to full throttle below about 1200 rpm in top. After that it would pull strongly with the real punch coming at about 3800 rpm and staying all the way to 7000 rpm. You didn't think the Rover would rev to 7000? Well, it will with a Sig Erson camshaft kit. This comprises performance camshafts, high revving hydraulic tappets and special double valve springs. Better breathing also comes from the Offenhauser inlet manifold and the exhaust is by courtesy of Janspeed.

Adam has also got at the spark. Mallory transistorised ignition replaces the original coil system and pushes the spark via silicone rubber covered stainless steel HT lead to the special Champion plugs. This just about covers the engine mods apart for the Bendix blue-top fuel pump which pushed the juice through at an alarming rate of 14 mpg—ie a tankful every 190 miles.

The standing starts were rather nerve racking—its very different to get the maximum possible acceleration while deliberately preventing wheel spin, especially when you've got rather a lot of horses prancing about under the bonnet. However we managed 0-60 mph in 6.6secs. and 100 mph in 17.7secs.—even with the ponderous Moss gearbox—not bad. You begin to appreciate the extra power of the Bridgland Moggie even more at 6200 rpm in top—about 132 mph—when the car is still accelerating hard. We estimate a top speed of over 140 mph, though it would take some time to reach it.

Just as impressive as the performance was the car's handling, especially in the wet. We were surprised, therefore, to learn that the

only mod to the suspension was the fitting of Koni rear dampers. Such was the resultant ride and handling that it took a really undulating or bumpy road to betray the car's vintage background. It is not unusual for Konis to transform a soggy saloon but one would not necessarily see them as the answer to a stiffly sprung sports car. The tribute for the wet weather grip must, however, go largely to the Avon radials which Adam not only uses for road work but also competes on. The conditions could hardly have been worse when we picked the car up from Harpenden and we commenced by treating the right pedal with great respect. Later, we discovered that the tail was very reluctant to break. Eventually when it did it was in a gentle, controllable way that was nothing but fun and certainly no cause for alarm. In the dry —at least on smooth roads—it was superb.

One thing that came to light during our short tenure of 4KYD was the remarkable ignorance of the public with regard to Morgans in general. A number of people had no idea what make of car it was and countless others expressed surprise at the V8 under the bonnet and wanted to know how 'we' had managed to fit it in. Having driven the standard model and this particularly pleasant conversion we suspect that there are many sports car owners who don't know what they are missing. After all, now that the Tiger and TVR Tuscan (V8) are defunct, what other British sports car has a V8 under the bonnet—one that most people could afford anyway. And how many other sports cars are there around in the prime of life after 43,000 road/competition miles? **Gordon Bruce**

		Standard +8	Bridgland +8							Standard +8	Bridgland +8
Maximum speed											
		mph	mph								
Lap	... ...	125.0	140+								
			(estimated)								
Acceleration					**In third**						
mph		sec	sec		mph					sec	sec
0-30		2.5	2.5		10-30	... ...				4.7	—
0-40 ...		3.5	3.5		20-40	... ...				4.3	4.7
0-50 ...		5.1	5.2		30-50	... ...				3.9	4.5
0-60 ...		6.7	6.6		40-60	... ...				3.9	4.4
0-70 ...		8.7	8.4		50-70	... ...				4.2	4.7
0-80 ...		12.1	10.8		60-80	... ...				4.5	4.7
0-90 ...		15.4	14.2								
0-100 ...		19.0	17.7		**Fuel consumption**						
Standing ¼ mile		15.0	14.7		Steady mph					mpg	mpg
					30	... ...				29.0	23.6
In top					40	... ...				31.0	24.2
mph		sec	sec		50	... ...				30.0	20.4
20-40 ...		4.9	—		60	... ...				29.0	18.9
30-50 ...		4.8	5.6		70	... ...				27.0	17.6
40-60 ...		4.7	5.8		80	... ...				23.5	16.7
50-70 ...		5.1	6.5		90	... ...				19.5	15.2
60-80 ...		6.1	6.8		100	... ...				15.0	14.4
70-90 ...		6.4	7.0		Overall	... ...				20.3	14.0
80-100 ...		8.1	8.4		Touring	... ...				22.2	—

Th handling is the Morgan's most important feature with high cornering power and precise control.

Strong and simple, traditional Morgan

Morgan motoring is one of those illogical things which cannot be satisfactorily explained. There are people who would never consider owning any other make of car, yet they cannot tell you why. We all know that sports cars are now mid-engined and have soft independent suspension, but whenever I parked the Morgan it collected a much greater crowd than even the Bora or the Dino. To the public, a real sports car still has wire wheels and a long, louvred bonnet, for the vintage tradition will never die.

Though I am an apostle of ultra-modern design, I am also secretly a Morgan addict and look forward to my road tests of these cars. I had intended to try the latest version of the Plus 8, but it was suggested that the 4/4 might be a more realistic vehicle for present conditions. As it happened, I was offered a beautiful yellow one, with centre-locking wire wheels, by the London Morgan distributors, Morris Stapleton Motors Ltd. Who could resist such a car? Certainly not Bolster!

Of course the Morgan still has the famous front suspension, which was first used on the firm's three-wheelers some 60 years ago. The stub axles slide up and down vertical pillars against coil springs and also turn around them for steering purposes. The separate steel chassis is of Z-section and passes beneath the rear axle, to which it is attached by very stiff semi-elliptic springs. The engine and gearbox are by Mr Ford, from the 1600 Cortina GT, and the body is hand built, with steel panels on an ash frame.

Though the headlamps are no longer on stalks and the radiator cowl is curved to re-duce wind resistance, the mudguards still have a vintage sweep and the long bonnet is hinged down the middle. The bonnet takes up so much of the chassis that the luggage space is pretty small and the spare wheel is attached outside — I would fit a padlock to it! There's a full width bumper at the front, but only rubber over-riders at the rear unless you pay extra.

Speaking of extras, my car had wire wheels, which add enormously to the looks, even if light-alloy ones are more functional. It did not have the separate bucket seats, but having achieved a long run on the standard object I would willingly pay for greater comfort. The hood is very cosy indeed and does not flap at speed. It can be put up quite quickly with practice, but two are better than one for this job.

The Morgan is an instant starter, even when coated with ice. There is a simple heater under the scuttle, which keeps the toes warm even with the hood down. Curiously enough, there is no tap for turning the heater off — at least I couldn't find one, though switching off the fan was fairly effective.

On the road, the car feels very lively indeed and has excellent acceleration. The simple pushrod 1600 cc engine has ample power to hurl the light two-seater along, and most people will average well over 30 mpg. The 4/4 reaches 90 mph very quickly, after

which the shape begins to encounter wind resistance. Though the car will not reach 100 mph when open, it will slightly exceed that speed with hood up and windows close.

Nevertheless, real Morgan motoring is done with the hood down. There's nothing like travelling through the fresh air, if one is sensibly dressed, and I thoroughly enjoyed it, even with frost on the grass. The car is then remarkably quiet, except for the exhaust and, really Peter, the police don't encourage such a healthy note! With the hood in position, the 4/4 is as cosy as any saloon, but the interior sound level is then rather high and the delightful ease of open motoring is lost. There is surprisingly little wind noise, but all mechanical sounds are magnified.

The ride is very hard indeed. On reasonable roads or under typical urban conditions, this is not particularly noticeable, but on country lanes the short travel of the suspension cannot be ignored. People who want this kind of car are prepared to accept such a ride and

Real Morgan motoring is done with the hood down.

softer springing would not appeal to them at all. It's all part of the character of the Morgan and the real addicts would not have it otherwise.

The handling is the car's most important feature. Initially, the characteristic is just about neutral but the tail can at once be hung out by lifting off in a corner. The cornering power is high and there is little deviation over bumps. Unlike many hard-sprung cars, the 4/4 runs straight and true at high speeds, being deflected neither by changes of camber nor gusts of wind. The steering is light and direct, giving a fine sense of control.

Naturally, the gearbox is most important in such a car and the Morgan has an ideal set of ratios, selected by a well-placed lever. The brake pedal demands fairly firm pressure but the retardation is swift and sure. A fly-off handbrake, once regarded as essential on any sports car, is a pleasant survival. Above all, the view down that long, louvred bonnet is superb, with proper mudguards to indicate the exact width, instead of the usual amorphous mass of pressed steel that one sees through the distortions of the modern curved screen.

The Morgan is a strong, simple sports car, with everything get-atable, and plenty of space for the amateur mechanic to work. It's still hand-made by traditional craftsmen who are proud of the job they are turning out. Though there is a considerable waiting list, the factory will not be extended, for men of this calibre are few and far between.

Perhaps I am wasting my time, writing this article. There may well be enough Morganatics already to snap up the products of that little factory in an unspoilt corner of England's green and pleasant land. Nevertheless, if there is still a man who hates air conditioning, power steering, and automatic transmission, it might be worthwhile for him to get in the queue for miracles have been known to happen.

SPECIFICATION AND PERFORMANCE DATA

Car tested : Morgan 4/4 open sports two-seater, price £1,569.43 including tax and VAT.

Engine : Four cylinders, 81 x 77.6 mm (1599 cc) ; compression ratio 9.2 to 1 ; 88 bhp (net) at 6000 rpm ; pushrod-operated overhead valves ; Weber twin-choke downdraught carburetter.

Transmission : Single dry plate clutch ; four-speed all-synchromesh gearbox with central remote control, ratios 1.0, 1.397, 2.01, and 3.1 to 1 ; hypoid rear axle, ratio 4.1 to 1.

Chassis : Separate steel frame with Z-section side members and coachbuilt body ; independent front suspension with sliding stub-axles, coil springs, and telescopic dampers ; cam gear steering ; live rear axle on semi-elliptic springs with lever-type dampers ; disc front and drum rear brakes with fly-off handbrake ; Centre-locking wire wheels (£68.52 extra) fitted 165-15 tyres.

Equipment : Speedometer, rev-counter, ammeter, oil pressure, water temperature, and fuel gauges ; heater ; windscreen wipers and washers ; flashing direction indicators.

Dimensions : Wheelbase, 8 ft ; track (front) 3 ft 11 in. (rear) 4 ft 1 in ; overall length, 12 ft ; overall width, 4 ft 8 in ; weight 1,624 lb.

Performance : Maximum speed 102 mph. Speed in gears : third, 75 mph ; second, 55 mph ; first, 34 mph. Standing quarter-mile : 17.2 s. Acceleration : 0-30 mph, 3.0 s ; 0-50 mph, 7.1 s ; 0-60 mph, 9.8 s ; 0-80 mph, 18.2 s ; 0-90 mph, 25.0 s.

Fuel consumption : 28 to 35 mpg.

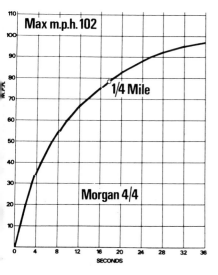

Above : interior showing cramped cockpit. Below : outside mounted spare wheel.

Ford Kent-series 1600 engine from the Cortina GT sits accessibly.

With rorty 1-6 litre power, the 4/4 is...
THE VERY BEST
MOG

A loud, rasping exhaust, an engine that revs and a light, fluent gearbox make the Morgan 4/4 an even better car than the Plus Eight. You really haven't lived until you've driven a Mog, top down in the rain . . .

BY NOW THEY'LL have painted the sign out. But until a month ago, the service station half a dozen kilometres outside Gisborne, Victoria, wore the faded name Smith's Motors, just as it had done for two decades.

It was a Neptune station for those 20 years, but now the pumps are being changed to Shell.

Now the repaint job is completed, the new name

Museum Motors is up there in bold letters and the showroom contains a stack of classic and PVT cars belonging to an enthusiast called Vic Kaye. The place has a higher purpose than selling petrol to Fred Tourist. It's the headquarters for Australia's last surviving traditional British sports car concessionaire, Morgan Distributors. It's the place to which you must travel to buy a Mog.

When you stand on the cement apron, look at the grass growing round the bottom of the petrol pumps, listen to the breeze moving under the eaves of the wood and iron showroom — it's barely credible this is a place where you can discuss trade-ins and options, finance and warranties, service problems and spare parts discounts.

It's hard to imagine Morgan in the motor merchandising game. The game that depends on images and premises and the color of a dealer's window sticker. The game that can turn one dealer into a millionaire in two years and send another one,

Long-nosed four-seater Mog isn't exactly beautiful with the top up. There's an obvious solution, of course, don't use it.

half a mile away, through the hoop in half that time because his place doesn't catch the eye of the locals as they wend their way home from the pub at 10.

Having an exclusive car dealership like this out in the bush at Gisborne is like Ron Hodgson or Kevin Dennis setting up a "move-30-a-day" used car joint at Woomera. Right?

Of course it bloody isn't. Morgans are different. Morgans are cars you travel hundreds of miles to see and to sample and you don't mind doing it, either. That's if you're serious.

We became pretty serious the day Vic Kaye rang us up to say he'd just landed a new four-seat, four-cylinder Mog and how would we like to drive it when it was run in? We were so serious that by the end of the day we had arranged a date and a time to drive the car. And we could already see ourselves fanging

around the countryside, hair blown to hell by the unruly slipstream and cracking a smile as we powered up the wooded country roads, round Mt Macedon, just like the ones in the Old Country.

The rain began half an hour before we arrived in Gisborne and we sat in the workshop listening to it drum on the tin roof for an hour talking to Patricia Kaye and Vic's mechanic, Ray Bishop until it dawned on us that however many sunny days we'd had before, on this particular one it was going to rain non-stop.

To be truthful it was only our timidity about the effect of the chilly winds and rains on our bodies which prevented us from getting into the four-seater and driving it off into the rain haze. Sure as hell it wouldn't do the car any harm. After all, isn't it a Morgan which they say should have wipers both sides of the screen because the purist never, never, runs with the hood up just because the weather's bad? The hood is there only for emergencies such as if the Mog driver — naturally a traditionalist — should come upon the Royal Daimler broken down on a rainy day and be obliged to offer to drive the Queen back to the Palace in as close as he can muster to regal comfort. For normal use? Never!

The four-seater we tested is Vic Kaye's own car. This one joins his Triumph engined "flat radiator" Morgan and half a dozen other cars, from a Dennis fire engine to an RME Riley, in being a car he'll never part with.

It's a French blue car, and if you can forgive the color's unpatriotic name, it's very attractive. It has the optional wire wheels and leather upholstery. Price is close to six grand and when you consider that you're getting a piece of English traditional sports car motoring whose future is ever so shaky (in Australia) and which is far more exclusive than a Lambo and just as well bred, it's a steal. There's no question that

Ford four is gutsy and crisp sounding. It breathes through a twin-choke downdraught Weber. It's a more sporty engine than the Plus Eight's 3½ litre Rover mill.

Vic could ask nine grand and sell just as many cars. Or have just as long a waiting list, to be more accurate.

If you read our It's Terapy story in SCW March, you'll realise Vic doesn't sell Morgans here to get rich. If more proof is needed, let us tell you that he'll soon be ordering what cars he thinks he'll be able to sell in the year 1977, not knowing whether the supply will be cut off in three months, or whether some desk jockey masquerading as "the authorities" will suddenly one day decide to register no more Morgans. Who but an enthusiast fighting to preserve the marque's foothold in Australia, would choose such a shaky investment avenue?

While we were in Melbourne, Vic told us confidently that his local member, former Seeker Athol Guy, has been encouragingly receptive to his attempts to point out the injustices of the Australian Design Rules for low-volume sports cars, and was doing what he could to ease the problem.

We could have sat around that workshop all day, because the rain continued to rattle on the roof, and there was always the hope that it might go away. But when photographer Ian Smith arrived wet through from another outdoor assignment earlier that morning, we knew the time had come.

So we walked out the back where the Morgan nestled among Vic's boxes full of Morris Cowley engine blocks, wooden spoked wire wheels and gearbox bits — all filed in the scheme of things under "future projects" and got in.

If you're fairly tall, you'll find that the four seater's driving seat is a little high for you and that your knees tend to foul the steering wheel a little, but apart from that entry is pretty easy. In front of you is the padded-rim steering wheel, not exactly small, but not bloody huge, like the early four-wheel Mogs had.

The wheel is at well-bent arm's length and is very close to and set at the same angle as the dash panel. It's an identical dash to the one in the Plus Eight with Smiths tacho right in front of you, large round composite gauge containing oil pressure, fuel level, charging rate and water temperature information visible through the wheel, then speedo away to the left because it's the least important dial, separated from the composite dial by a battery of seven rocker switches arranged in two rows.

The front passenger has a cavernous glovebox in front of him — and also the best view of the speedo. Rear passengers sit high and regal in surprisingly roomy style, with their knees just about level with

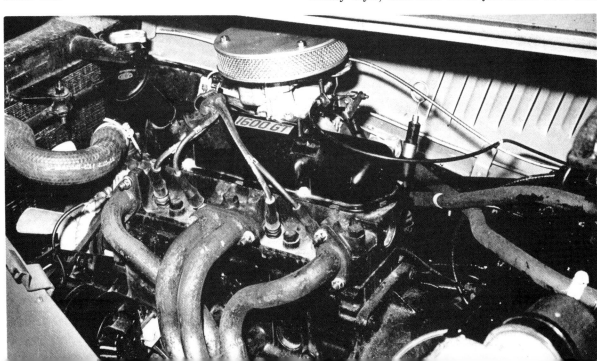

Dashboard is similar to that of four-wheel Morgans made 20 years ago, but tacho mounted in front of driver, smaller padded-rim steering wheel and matt-black dash are concessions to modernity.

the shoulders of those in front.

The four seater uses the old Cortina GT's 1600 cm³ crossflow engine and the smooth and light Ford four-speed gearbox. Output is 73 kW (93 bhp) at 6000 rpm and maximum torque of 135 Nm (100 lb/ft) comes at 3600 rpm. It's a lively enough engine, but it certainly isn't peaky or highly stressed. Healthy is the best description.

You turn the keystart and the Mog blasts into life because it has a pretty loud exhaust note at the best of times and you've got the hood down and you're inside an iron shed. With coat pulled around shoulders and windscreen wipers on you ease out of the shed into the rain, watching the droplets move progressively up the nose until they're bouncing off the windscreen frame, into your eyes and onto your shoulders.

The only chance you have of staying less than drenched is to get moving damn quickly, so that's what you do (as you've already warmed the engine in the shed). Take it up to five grand in first and just listen to the exhaust bellow. It's wonderful and so is the effortless snap-change to second. That lever can't be more than 12 centimetres long and it only moves half of that distance between gear slots, yet the action is light. It's so good that you don't notice for a time that the small black gearlever knob is still dry and that the cockpit isn't shipping water any more because your forward motion of 50 km/h or so is keeping it out.

Snick it into third at five thousand again and the mobile blizzard is starting to feel like a sports car. There's wind to buffet the hair and chill the cheekbones, and there's a constant patter of messages transmitted from the road through the flexible chassis to the seat of your pants. Steering is direct and dead accurate. Only a flick of movement is needed to twitch the long nose instantly to a new direction. It's

Morgan seating (showing evidence of a wet road test) has enough room for four adults. Rear passengers sit much higher than those in front. Upholstery is optional leather.

almost good enough to transmit your pulsebeat to the bitumen.

The power is an interesting thing. If you've driven only a Plus Eight before, the torquey, jack-rabbit-acceleration-from-low-revs feeling is noticeable by its absence. Even though the four can be catapulted up to high speeds quickly with use of the gears, the four feels gutless by comparison with the eight. It's only to be expected of course, it does have less than two-thirds of the eight's power.

But the curious thing is that the Morgan four is better for the lack of torque. It seems far more natural that this raw, English square-rigger should have a rackety four which transmits some vibration to the driver and which sounds crisp when used hard rather than a lazy engine which anyone can drive hard simply by flattening it.

THE VERY BEST MOG

CONTINUED FROM PAGE 61

It reminds us of the motoring philosophy of an Alfa owner friend of ours who is decidedly anti-V8. He says a well-used four-cylinder car can often provide similar point-to-point performance to a V8, provided the driver keeps it in the right rev range. But the four driver must be in the right gear at the right time for instant action, whereas the V8 man can have power anytime, so long as he's no more than two gears out.

That's how we feel about the Mog four, now that we've experienced it. It must be driven with verve and a good deal of finesse to cover the ground quickly, whereas the V8 can do everything on torque.

The four's gearchange is superb. Apart from the short movements we mentioned, there's such feel in the shift that any sympathetic driver can time his gearchanges to match the fall of the engine revs and change gears very smoothly. First runs to 45 km/h (28 mph), second to a commendable 85 (53), third is slightly short at 120 (75) and the top speed is a true 172 km/h (106 mph). The car has the mechanical ability to cruise for days at 135-145 km/h (85-90 mph) but at the speed you're buffeted around a good deal and it's a pretty uncomfortable bat. For comfortable long distance work, 120 (75) is top odds, and you'd be far more relaxed if you ran somewhere around 110.

It annoys us that some sporty sedan drivers still feel they've achieved something by burning off an open car on the highway.

To us sports cars are fun cars. They're built with a nice kind of 'rawness' which lets you get close to the road and the mechanical functions of the car so you can savor every moment of driving. Sedans are insulation cars. They iron out bumps, noise, wind and in many cases road feel. They're built so Larry Normal can be respectably smooth, even though he drives like Desperate Ivan, king of the one-armed desert racers.

In a sports car you buy fine, sensitive road behavior. And this Morgan had it in abundance. Let us start by saying that understeer in the 4/4, in any form, is out. The car is utterly neutral and faithful to your instructions until you're cornering quickly enough to have your passenger showing the whites of his eyes.

At the limit, the car moves into the merest touch of oversteer, and would go off backwards if you were fool enough to ignore abundant warnings. In the Mog four, oversteer comes in two brands — "power" and "twitch"

You can enter a bend on a wide line close to the limit and apply full power just before the apex, exiting in a rhythmic, shallow-angle slide. If you stay this side of sanity that's all you'll get unless the roads are wet. In that case you can hang the tail much more, but it's just as safe and controllable as in the dry, provided you're acceptably quick and sensitive in getting the opposite lock on (and off).

The second brand of oversteer is provoked by throwing the Mog into bends with a flick of the wheel; because of the steering's high gearing it doesn't need much. This can be used to good effect on tight bends to get the car round with a minimum amount of wheel winding.

On high speed curves — say good for above 130 km/h (80 mph) the Mog just goes where it's pointed. We tried cornering harder and harder through one corner — in fact to the limit of our courage and the best we could get was a sideways chirp at the rear and a movement of perhaps a few centimetres. On a hard drive through corners which you're only taking one go at you'll very rarely see a decisive handling characteristic.

The ride quality of the car was simply astonishing. It took to the uneven bitumen we put it over with ease and the faster we pressed it, the better it became. WHEELS editor Peter Robinson, who has covered more Morgan miles than the rest of our staff put together, had no hesitation in saying it was the best Mog he's driven.

The Plus Eight we tested early this year was enough of a revelation. After years of reading how a Morgan's ride was "rock hard" or "bouncy" or whatever, we found that it was firm, beautifully controlled and certainly fine for top-down touring. After driving the four farther and faster, we feel very strongly that the Mog has been maligned for years.

We don't mind saying that after an intoxicating afternoon's drive, we were ready to fight the next man who prattled about the impractical nature of the Morgan's ride. The offer still stands . . .

It was a motoring experience to be numbered among our very best and one which left us doing sums on the back of our chequebook to see if we could afford the price of a four cylinder Morgan.

This is a car which you would drive with all the finesse you could muster on Sunday mornings — strictly for enjoyment. It's a car in which you would do perhaps three thousand kilometres a year, one which you'd keep for ever and which, in 20 years you'd be proud to run in the vintage section of a club hillclimb.

It's a "forever" car, one you hate to give back, or even get out of. Anyone who watched a certain tall, spare roadtester with rain beads bouncing off his glasses as he blasted round and round our photography roads and refused to be flagged down could see that . . .

Test car from: Morgan Distributors PO Box 140, Gisborne, Vic.   *

TRADITION WITH POWER

MORGAN PLUS 8
MGB GT V8

*Text by
Reuben Archer.
Photos Douglas Newby,
Ken Goddard.*

Two British high performance cars powered by the same British built V8 engine—the Morgan Plus 8 and the MGB GT V8 are the subjects for this month's twin test. Tracing the background of the British Leyland offering is not really too difficult. One need only go back nine years or so to the MGB GT of 1965, based on the original 1962 B Roadster, which proved to be a selling formula. Its makers quoted it to be a car both solid and reliable, better value for money could not be found (the fact that second-hand models kept their price endorsed this point) and in this respect the V8 doesn't really differ from previous MGB models.

The family tree of the Morgan tells a slightly different story: basic design commenced way back in 1936 and progressed through the years incorporating little in the way of styling changes until the flat radiator was changed to a more stylish curved grille and the lines, although still basically rakish and simple, gave way to a more streamlined, smooth look in the shape of the 4/4. Not everyone's cup of tea, but a car most definitely in the traditional sports car image—old-fashioned to some, out of date compared to other car shapes of today, but that is the whole point and beauty of the Morgan concept. One might call the 'Moggie' old-fashioned indeed against the MGB silhouette but now I think of it, even the MGB could well be considered out of date by today's standards—although perhaps, like the Morgan, in a traditional way; both designs are relics of nostalgic eras and could end up as collectors' pieces.

That the Morgan Plus 8 is still a sports car through and through there is no doubt but the MG has now become something of a compromise. The manufacturers have retained a sporting performance, matching this with saloon appeal in order to capture a wider section of the motoring public. As for the Morgan, Malvern have tried to do nothing more than produce the old style of car, as the brochure states: 'A classic sports car with all the advantages of modern safety engineering'. As far as the last factor is concerned, there are cynics who disagree with Morgan's claims; these people, supposedly in the know, will tell you that the Morgan was unsafe even before Malvern installed the V8 between its chassis members, and as for the MGB GT V8: 'Thought the factory would have learned a lesson with the MGC but no, they stick a 3.5 V8 in the B!' In many respects one can immediately dismiss these opinions: in years gone by, the Morgan used several engines including the TR4 unit and later the 1600 cross flow Ford GT unit, while the Leyland car always used the B-series 4 cylinder in-line (except for the short-lived attempt to utilise the six cylinder engine). Those under the impression that the V8 unit would compromise the handling of either of these cars can rest assured, because this light alloy Rover unit weighs almost the same as those previously used; weight distribution is not a problem. However, what must have proved a problem to those concerned with the conversion was how to fit the width of the V unit into a shape designed to take only a 4 cylinder in-line engine. With nearly all cars that have been converted to accept V units, it is the exhaust manifolds that suffer and it is difficult to find a compatible gearbox. In standard form both models utilize twin SU carburettors, although Ken Costello's original MGB V8 used a single 45 DCOE twin-choke, side-draught carburettor mounted at the rear of the engine on a long-necked manifold. The Leyland car uses a similar set-up but with twin SU HIF6 carbs; in order to get the V unit to fit, the bulkhead of the MG's engine compartment has been altered to clear the manifolding.

There are apparent differences in engine specification between the two units: for instance, the MGB GT V8 specification indicates the bore and stroke of the V8 are 88.88 mm/71.12 mm, as opposed to Morgan specification of 89 mm/71 mm; MG rate their V8 with a compression ratio of 8.25 to 1, while Morgan specify 10.5 to

1. Maximum power produced from the MGB GT is 137 bhp (DIN) at 5000 rpm, but the Morgan is reckoned to produce 152 bhp at 5800 rpm. Considering we are talking about the same 3528 cc (215 ci) unit why do the specification figures differ so much? The answer to this must of course be the addition of the anti-smog equipment now fitted to the MG, which Morgan manage to do without.

One thing is certain, both vehicles now utilize the Rover gearbox (replacing the original Moss box used on the Morgan). It has four speeds (plus reverse), synchromesh on all four gears and uses a 9½" diaphragm clutch. Gear ratios differ considerably (the MG runs on 14" diameter wheels while the Morgan was 15"); the MGB has overdrive on top gear, activated by the right hand steering column lever, which knocks off a good 1,000 rpm from engine speed when utilised. Although the Rover V8 unit could be said to provide all the power necessary for sports performance, pleasing the driver with flexibility of torque and unfussiness, this is indeed more than can be said for the gearbox; for sports car handling and ultra-quick changes the MG box proves sluggish, notchy and unwilling to respond to the driver's wishes. Really hard acceleration with both cars produces acrid burning smells from the vicinity of the clutch. With both cars power is fed through a solid rear axle, though the Plus 8 uses a Salisbury limited-slip diff. Suspension on both cars is somewhat similar, both having independent front suspension and a live rear axle hung on leaf springs. The MGB uses coil springs, wishbones, lever-arm dampers working with the top wishbone and an anti-roll bar at the front, and at the rear it has a solid axle, half-elliptic leaf springs and lever arm dampers. The Morgan's independent front suspension consists of the same vertical sliding pillars it has always used, with coil springs and telescopic hydraulic shock absorbers, the rear set-up being similar to the MGB. The springs on both cars have been uprated to compensate for the extra power, although damper settings on the MGB remain the same. Overall length of the MGB is 12' 2¾" and it is 5' in height. The Morgan is 8¾" shorter in length and 8" lower and weighs 1876 lbs to the MGB GT's 2427 lbs. This provides another reason why it is not surprising that performance differs considerably—the 0-60 mph figure for the MGB V8 turned out to be 8.5 seconds which was slow compared to 8.4 seconds for the Morgan; up to the 80 mark we managed 15.3 seconds for the MGB and a shade under 11 for the Morgan.

Weight was obviously an important factor affecting these two cars, mainly stemming from the very different body/chassis construction. Whereas Morgan still construct their cars of sheet steel panels on an ash wood frame, the MGB uses the conventional, modern, mass-production

Top to bottom: Neat and simple Morgan cockpit layout; hinged bonnet gives access to Rover V8 unit; lack of luggage space; spare wheel and above where luggage has to go.

Top to bottom: MGB GT V8 cockpit, similar to B; Rover unit well shoehorned between bulkheads; spare wheel and tool kit housing; the hatch back, for luggage storage.

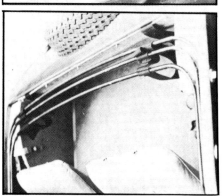

method of a steel monocoque structure. With the added material for the roof and heavier doors, bonnet and wings, the MG was bound to prove heavier.

Driving the two cars reveals further pointers to why the Morgan takes the edge as far as performance is concerned. When starting from cold, some use of the choke is necessary on both cars but because of its anti-smog apparatus, the MGB takes a good deal longer to warm up;

consequently choke is needed for a longer period. Further affirmation of the detrimental effect that the anti-pollution equipment has on performance is that below 2000 rpm the MG engine is sluggish and does not give the usual torquey feel that one expects from a V8 unit. However when correct running temperature is reached and the engine is revving nearer to its peak, the car becomes more of a performer and one soon develops a feeling of sympathy for drivers of the more conventional 4 cylinder model. Handling of the MG can prove at times a little disconcerting when one drives with a view to reaching full potential from the power available. Set the car up for a corner at reasonable speed under power and it will understeer considerably and then, on correction, oversteer; making the best of this situation is difficult because of the heavy rolling motion of the car due to its rather sloppy suspension. If one is to be really critical about handling then perhaps the Morgan will provide better results, although it too has its drawbacks. On good road surfaces a Morgan can be a pleasure to drive; it is easily set up using both steering and throttle to take a tight bend—real exciting stuff, but hit a loose patch or uneven surface and the Morgan will completely lose traction, the rear sometimes hopping a considerable distance off line. The rigidity of the car has a great deal to do with this problem, although one can plainly feel the flex and whip due to the traditional chassis body set up.

If one expects handling perfection with a car that leaves plenty of room for mistakes by its driver at any speed, neither car will fit the bill. Both need to be driven and kept on a tight rein. At high speed both can become rather unmanageable, especially in wet conditions—the Morgan more so, mainly because of its lack of weight. Steering on the MG is through a rack and pinion (the same set up as is used throughout the MGB range) but Morgan as always fit the cam and peg set up. Either way, at low speeds steering with these cars is heavy—quite tiring when parking, due to the amount of rubber making contact with the road, as both vehicles use 5½J road wheels and 185 section radials. Steering becomes progressively lighter as higher speeds are reached but the MG tends to stay on the heavy side and a long journey on winding roads soon tells on one's wrists. The clutch on the MG is also

rather tiring, being on the heavy side.

Considering the performance capabilities of both cars, adequate braking facilities have been provided and physical effort on the part of the driver is minimal. The Morgan is up to date in this respect, with servo-assisted 11" discs at the front and 9" x 1¾" drums at the rear (with cable-operated handbrake). The M.G. has a similar arrangement: 10" diameter discs at the front and similar-sized drums at the rear, also with a servo. Both cars' brakes proved efficient at all speeds, with no noticeable fade under quite strenuous use, although on the M.G. tested, a slight pull to the left could be felt—no doubt this tendency was peculiar to that particular example of the model.

Driving positions in both vehicles are similar; not what you'd call the straight arm style, more reminiscent of the close to the wheel 'arms and elbows' style which is, in a way, quite in keeping with the Morgan tradition—certainly not uncomfortable with either car. Both have adequately padded bucket seats, with a similar rake to the wheel.

Whereas the MGB dash incorporates tacho and speedo in a seperate nacelle behind the wheel (with oil pressure to the left and fuel gauge to the right), the Morgan has the rev counter flat on the dash above the column and the speedo, ammeter, oil pressure and rocker switches for minor controls are mounted in one steel panel, centre of the dashboard. Instruments are quite visible on both cars. Prize for the worst heater controls must go to British Leyland, who by now should have done something about the impossible heater knobs, inherited from the early 'B' and still fitted to the MGB V8: it is impossible to adjust them satisfactorily. Handbrake for the MG is close to the driver's elbow and with the Morgan you have to reach for it under the dash. Stubby gear shift on both cars is comfortably positioned.

On the subject of interior space and

passenger seating, one can dismiss the Morgan immediately as being a pure 2 seater, with some luggage space behind the seats. For my part, the BGT hatch-back has always been rather pointless; one cannot load the available space with much luggage because rear view would be impaired and the back bench seat, even with the front seats fully forward, constitutes room for only a very small child to sit in comfort. Quite apart from the unfortunate passenger who might have to travel in the rear of the car, the driver and his adjacent passenger travel in relative comfort and in view of the forward driving position, leg room in both cars is reasonably good.

Perhaps if a potential buyer were to try both cars one after the other, he might find it difficult to make the final choice. Steering away from the Morgan because of its hereditary ruggedness, he would perhaps go for the full-bodied MG but having sampled the prospects of sports car performance on a sunny day with only two windows to wind down, that must seem a little oppressive inside. Hood down, side-screens off, arms resting on the quaint cut-away doors, the Morgan could present an exciting proposition, but on a wet day with water dripping between hood and side-screens, a few drops to the back of the neck whilst buttoning up the flaps could swing the balance in favour of the other car. No matter which the choice, both cars can be docile enough for the shopping trip yet exciting enough for really fast open-road work. The facts—two cars, both with V8 power, the Morgan out in front with performance, the MG with its saloon bodywork proving the more civilised of the two. The Morgan also comes out best for price (about £2,000 opposed to £2000 plus for the MG). One thing is certain, the deciding factor will be the driver's character and with cars like these, that counts for a great deal.

TECHNICAL SPECIFICATIONS

ENGINE	MGB GT V8	MORGAN V8
Cylinders	90° V8	90° V8
Bore/Stroke	88.88 x 71.12mm	89 x 71mm
Capacity	3,528cc	3,528cc
Valve operation	Pushrod OHV	Pushrod OHV
Comp. Ratio	8.25-1	10.5-1
Carburation	Twin SU HIF6	Twin SU HS6
Max Power	137bhp @ 5,000rpm	152bhp @ 5,800rpm
Max Torque	193 lb ft @ 2,900rpm	226 lb ft @ 3000rpm

TRANSMISSION

	MGB GT V8	MORGAN V8
Clutch	9½in dia.	9½in dia.
Gearbox	4 speed all synchro with O.D. on top, plus reverse	4 speed all synchro, plus reverse
Back axle	Hypoid 3.07:1	Hypoid 3.31:1, Salisbury limited-slip.

SUSPENSION

	MGB GT V8	MORGAN V8
Front	Independent by coil springs and wishbones, lever type dampers	Independent by vertical coil springs and telescopic dampers.

	MGB GT V8 (Cont.)	MORGAN V8 (Cont.)
Rear	Solid rear axle, leaf springs plus anti roll bar, lever type dampers.	Solid rear axle, leaf springs, lever type dampers.

BRAKES

	MGB GT V8	MORGAN V8
Front	10.7 in discs	11 in discs
Rear	10 in drums	9 in drums
Servo	yes	yes

STEERING

	MGB GT V8	MORGAN V8
Type	Rack and pinion	Cam and gear

WHEELS AND TYRES

	MGB GT V8	MORGAN V8
Type	Aluminium centres with chrome steel rims	Cast aluminium
Size	5" x 14"	5½" x 15"
Tyre size	175 x 14	185 x 15

DIMENSIONS

	MGB GT V8	MORGAN V8
Length	12ft 10¾in	12ft 2in
Width	5ft	4ft 11in
Height	4ft 2in	4ft 4in
Weight	2,427lbs	1,876lbs
Price (inc. Special Car Tax & V.A.T.)	£2,408	£2,163

It may not be Formula One but......

the Morgan 4/4 is a real racing car nonetheless,
as Terry Grimwood found out.

WHAT sort of image does this description conjure up?

A sports car, eked out to a craving public at a rate of about eight per week; traditionally styled bodywork, hand built and hung on a wooden frame; sliding pillar front suspension hailing from the year 1909; ragtop weather equipment without the option; an owner-allegiance to the breed which only just stops short of pacts writ in life blood.

To me that whiffs of an amusing little anachronism of a car, dripping at the seams with character and driven by gauntletwearing, Biggles-helmeted, spotted-scarved Chaps with large mou'staches and eightydecibel laughs. Plus rather awful handling requiring much arm flailing and bicep rippling to propel the steed round corners at speeds which could be attained with a third of the effort in a 1965 Ford Anglia.

That, to me, was Morgan. Then I took up Production Sports Car racing and lo and

behold, there were these aristocratic thoroughbreds rushing about in true racing car fashion and, what's more, disdainfully leaving whole hosts of Lotus, Jags, TR's & MG's rustling around in the weeds. On top of which, in the final reckoning it was a Morgan which walked away with the overall championship after scoring an unbeaten record of class wins.

What an eye-opener. Sure, I'd seen a few Morgans thundering around in Modsports events but you can do so much with a fullrace conversion that I didn't really consider it had much bearing on the inherent value of the standard car; that sort of thinking is positively chilling in it's ramifications — I mean, it could lead you into buying a Skoda just because of John Turner's Super Saloon version. And if that isn't a cautionary thought, I don't know what is.

So, with Chris Alford winning the BRSCC Championship in his Morgan 4/4, I just had

to find out more. And finding out more meant a track test of the vehicle in question. Naturally.

But first, fair reader, a bit of a potted biog on Leighton Buzzard-domiciled Christopher. He is a 29-year-old sales manager for John Britten's Morgan emporium at Arkeley Road, Barnet, a reasonably sensible place to work if you happen to race a Morgan. Or does he race a Morgan because he works for John Britten?

Whatever the case, he had his first ever motor race on Boxing Day 1965, using a Jim Russell Lotus 20 Formula - almost - Three single seater, his reward for successfully completing the racing school course. He must have learned quite a lot, because he made pole for the race and finished second despite spinning off into the local flora. But what inspired him to go to the race school in the first place? I mean, you don't suddenly stop in the middle of what

urged along by an ex-Carlsson rally engine "which just happened to be laying around the workshop."

Not very quick, until halfway through the season when Cornish SAAB agent (that is, an agent from Cornwall who sells SAAB's, not a vendor of Cornish SAAB's) Mike Bennett loaned them an ex-Andrew Mylius works racing engine which all of a sudden made the little beastie rather competitive. A good few seconds and thirds were scored, until the car was subjected to "what happens to all good SAAB's." In other words, Chris rolled it into oblivion.

That was in 1967. In '68 young Alford did little, apart from campaigning a friend's road-going SAAB — for which Chris had paid for an engine tune and racing tyres — in the Snetterton 500 Ks race, finishing second in class by virtue of reliability.

Then in 1969 he started in F Ford using a very old, very tired, very converted 1963 ex-Formula 2 Lola Type-55. Whatever that is. Used to belong to Geddes Yeates, anyhow. He also used a Cooper S in some long distance Continental events, scoring a third in class at the Nurburgring.

The Lola was a real nail, however, and his best results were a seventh at Brands in a Leston Championship round and a sixth at Mallory right behind Bob Evans.

For 1970 Chris moved on to another sad Formula Ford, this time a Centaur "which was the biggest heap of crap in the World. Still, I always managed to be first FF home in Libre events."

He then got married, entered one of his periodic phases of retirement, before going through a series of FF drives in a Lenham, a Royale, and the ex-John Morrison Merlyn, with varying degrees of success.

And so to the Morgan. John Britten was himself campaigning a Plus 8 in Prodsports, and suggested that Chris should perform with a 4/4 in the middle class; he also suggested that he would rather like Alford's scruffy Merlyn off his premises, thank you very much. So John provided a new 4/4, and at the beginning of 1975 Chris found that he had suddenly become an active Prodsports contender.

But let me explain about Morgans. The 4/4 is a Ford 1600GT-powered Morgan, originally designated the 4/4 Competition when the car was also available in non-GT 1600 form. The Plus 8, as campaigned by John, is Rover V8-powered, and the Plus 4 (no longer produced) is similar to the 4/4 but powered by TR.

At the beginning of the year, the 4/4 looked no more than a fairly good prospect. It seemed likely that it could win the (b) Class — TR5's, TR6's, MGB's — at most circuits, but would probably lose out on the faster venues like Silverstone or Mallory. As it happened, the 4/4's domination of the class was about as total as you can get. Fifteen starts, fifteen class wins, twelve fastest laps, six records, eleven class pole positions. Chris ended the season as overall BRSCC Prodsports Champion by a healthy margin and Northern Prodsports Class (b) Champion without really trying.

All that success would suggest that a great deal of development has gone into the 4/4. On the contrary, modifications, especially to the chassis, are very limited even by Group 1 standards.

The bodywork is basically in steel, but with aluminium doors and bonnet. You see, The Morgan Company offers cars in either steel or aluminium according to choice, and

Above and clockwise: Morgan — a suitable car for winning. The BRSCC Championship — winning 4/4 of Chris Alford; the cockpit area, with Britax harness and Corbeau seat. The heading pic shows TG sliding through the Esses, while overleaf he chats with Chris Alford in the pits.

you happen to be doing and cry: "I think I'll be a racing driver!" like you'd say "I fancy beans on toast for tea," or "I think I'll wear the grey tie to work today."

So, delving back to prime sources we find ourselves standing spectating at the Nurburgring with Alford Senior, who is stationed with the RAF in Germany. Follow that up with 1000 - lires - worth of hired Go-Kart while on holiday in Italy, and we've discovered a seed in the process of germination (not to mention a rather cavalier attitude towards English grammar).

At the time of the Jim Russell course Chris was working for SAAB in Slough, earning a princely £7.00 per week — which is why he could only afford to do two of the Club races.

Nevertheless, he has only good things to say about the school course, rating it an excellent grounding for the would-be race driver ("I owe all my present success to the Jim Russell School," says Mr C.A. of Leighton Buzzard).

Although he could afford no more single-seater races, Chris managed to keep the competition flame well fanned by doing speed events with his road-going MGTC — which, incidentally, he cunningly sold just before prices took on an upward swoop. Inspires a lot of self-chastisement, that sort of thing.

Then Chris moved into 850 Special Saloon racing. With a Mini? No. With an Imp? Nope. It was with a SAAB.

"With a what?" I hear you murmur in hushed disbelief. Ah, but this wasn't just any old SAAB — this SAAB, sahib, cost all of £67 10s 0d. No expense spared, I can tell you. In fact it was so pricey that Chris had to halve the cost with fellow SAAB-employee Chris Partington.

The car was made from two written-off 850 two-strokes welded together, and

if they run out of steel during production they will often substitute alloy as a matter of course.

The suspension has been left completely standard, apart from the addition of second-hand adjustable Spax dampers at the front. The rather curious sliding pillar front suspension has the upright sliding vertically on a steel shaft with small coil springs above and below. Funnily enough, it all works rather well. The rear is far more conventional, with a live axle and semi-elliptic leaf springs.

One really important plus-factor is the brakes: nine inch drums at the back and eleven inch discs at the front. Chris runs standard friction material all round, after having used DS11 pads for a while but finding they glazed too easily. No problems have been experienced since going back to the ordinary stuff.

Chris initially ran the car with wire wheels, on which it arrived from the factory, but found they were not allowed, being wider than the more common steels (Prodsports regs specify the narrowest available standard rim). Rubberwear throughout the season has been the popular Avon Wide Safety cross-ply tyre, these being 6.5 x 15in diameter on 4in x 15in rims.

Strange though it might seem, Chris actually found himself quicker at certain circuits using the narrower rims, beating his own wire-wheel set record at Rufforth.

Perhaps the most impressive part of the car is the engine, a Ford 1600 GT modified to Group 1 specification by ace Formula Ford engine builder Dave Minister of Dartford, and giving 102bhp at 6000rpm.

"And it's legal," cries Chris, jubilantly.

The living area of the 4/4 is protected by a twin-hoop John Aley roll bar — a bit of a job to fit into a Morgan, with all those wooden bits in the way.

A bench seat is fitted as standard to the 4/4, so it's lucky that the regs permit a change of seating — in this case to a black vinyl Corbeau GT4, into which the driver is secured by a rather old model of Britax full harness. Other cockpit appointments include a Motolita steering wheel and a regulation-size fire extinguisher.

With the spare wheel removed the rear of the Morgan is left open, enabling passers by to admire the beautifully made Grand Prix Metalcraft foam filled ally tank, which holds about four gallons of best five-star.

There was little argument over where the test drive should be held; the final BRSCC Championship round was to be held at Snetterton in two weeks time, and both Chris and I agreed that a bit of practise at that circuit wouldn't do us any harm. We were lucky to have a really fine day for the drive, bright and sharp though rather windy at times — still, what we'd lose on one straight we'd gain on the other.

In keeping with usual track test procedure, Chris took the car out for a few exploratory laps to get things warmed up and generally sound out the track — rather he finds the oil patches than me!

Nothing seemed to be amiss with car or circuit, so Chris nodded me in the direction of the Corbeau seat. Felt pretty good, actually. It makes a change to drive an open car; Chris is a real Morgan man, and wouldn't dream of racing with the top up.

The first thing I noticed once safely buckled in was that the short gearstick was hidden away down front, somewhere under the dash panel. This is perfectly okay with

the standard bench seat, which gives an upright and forward driving position, but the bucket-like Corbeau places the driver further back in the cockpit, and makes gearchanging a finger-tip operation.

The engine fired up easily enough — as it should in virtually standard tune — and I eased my way down the pit road and out onto the circuit. Now with worm and nut steering, weirdo suspension, and a general feeling of being in something Nuvolari would have enjoyed wrestling with, I thought I was going to be in for a tough time with the 4/4.

Not so. The surprise was pleasant. In fact it would be no overstatement to say that the Morgan was one of those rare cars which provide pure, uncomplicated enjoyment.

Far from being heavy and vague, the steering, even with the smaller than standard wheel, was precise and, well, not light, but certainly requiring no special effort on the driver's part.

But the most impressive thing about the car was the way in which all functions — engine, roadholding, handling, brakes and steering — worked together with great compatibility to create a cohesive whole.

Each factor complemented the others, and made the car a real joy to drive.

The engine revved cleanly up to 7000, but really there was not a lot of point going much over six. In fact on one lap I exited from Sear onto the main straight and changed from third to top at five-five. The result was that I was pulling exactly the same revs at the end of the straight as I had when changing at six-two.

Roadholding was adequate but not high, but the handling was really superlative. On long fast bends the car would understeer mildly, eventually falling into a lazy kind of oversteer. On tighter corners the brakes, handling and tractibility of the engine could be used to maximum advantage.

The big eleven inch discs enabled me to go really deep into a bend before braking, then by lingering on the stop pedal while turning in, the tail could be put out of line until, once the car had found the apex, the power could be brought in to settle the car down and hold it in a graceful slide through the remainder of the bend, until it assumed a straight-on posture onto the straight. This required no special skills on my part — the car was so forgiving it went ahead and did it all for me. There was no snappy, rear-end breakaway requiring the driver to frantically bring the tail back into line or risk a spin. Forgiving was the name of the game.

These characteristics were really good in the new Esses complex, where the track leaves the long back straight and goes into a ninety left followed almost immediately by a sharp right. In the Morgan this sequence was best executed in third gear throughout; I found that the most effective way was to brake really late off the straight, lingering on the brakes and banging down to third right at the point of turning in to the left hander. This set the tail out nicely for the first bit, then as soon as the car was in a straight line I would climb hard on the brakes and let the tail swing in the opposite direction, positioning the car perfectly for the right-hander. Delicious.

At no time did I ever feel the 4/4 was getting away from me, there being so much feel through the suspension and steering that I always knew what the car was about to do. And the gearchange turned out to be no problem either — in fact I hardly noticed its awkward looking position when actually driving.

Now all I need is somewhere to buy those gauntlets and that Biggles helmet. ∎

THE MORGAN WASN'T BUILT IN A DAY

By David Allison

THE philosophy behind the building of a Morgan says that 99·99 per cent of the world's car makers must be wrong. "The Book of Common Prayer" is only slightly more resistant to change than "the first and last of the real sports cars".

In an age of mass production and automation, the world's oldest privately owned motor company still only makes eight cars a week, only two of which stay in England.

So how is a Morgan built today? In almost exactly the same way that it was built sixty years ago. For instance, Morgan front suspension is the same today, essentially, as when H. F. S. Morgan, the firm's founder, adapted it from a nineteenth-century Decauville design for his first three-wheeler in 1909.

The body, with its narrow, tapering hood, separate wings, cutaway louvres and angled tail, is built according to principles that flourished in the vintage era. Ash framing, carpentered by Morgan, is clothed in individually formed sheet metal panels. These are separately attached to and detachable from the timber skeletons -- a big time and money saver in the event of crash damage.

Peter Morgan dismisses the common belief that wood as a body material is prone to ills. There is, as far as he knows, only one species of beetle that attacks it and you can't find it nearer than China.

The trimming, upholstering and painting processes are all handled by Morgan at Malvern. The foreman trimmer, A. B. Gulliver, has been on the payroll since 1915 and C. Cummings, his sheet-metal colleague, clocked in ten years later.

As an extreme example of Morgan handwork, the body panels are cut out with tinsnips. Peter Morgan says they really *must* install power cutters sometime. Incidentally, where else but Morgan could you be given an option between steel or aluminium as a body material?

Day 7

With a little puffing and blowing, porters push what is already beginning to look like a car into the sixth of the seven bays. This is where the wooden subframe of the body is made and assembled, sometimes made with ash from the local Malvern Hills. The ash arrives at the mill kiln so that it can be used at once. The three men who work here know the machines here so intimately that using forty-year-old equipment doesn't worry them at all.

Day 1

The first step in the birth of a new Morgan is taken in the third of seven bays of the sheet metal shop; a factory porter brings a chassis from the stores and lays it on wooden trestles about half way down the bay.

While the chassis is being prepared, other workmen in the same bay are putting tyres on wheels and fitting certain parts such as the modified water pump and belt assembly to the engines.

Then such parts as the brake and clutch pedals are fitted, using a good do-it-yourself-style electric drill to bore out the holes. Later, from something that looks like the bellows of a giant piano-accordion, they take the metal bulkhead that covers the driver's and passenger's legs and feet.

Day 19

Eight men work in the body shop. They begin by gluing a damp course on to the upper surface of the chassis so that the wood is not bolted directly on to the metal. They then finish the parts that have been made in the mill and assemble them into complete subframes before bolting them onto the chassis. The wooden door frames are also made and hung in this shop, each one being individually constructed to fit perfectly. The thick board that protects the underside of the petrol tank is installed with the petrol tank above it and finally the floorboards are fitted. The car is then ready to leave the body shop.

The Morgan wasn't built in a day

all his painstaking effort is a perfect fit for every car; something tha no mass-produced car can hope to achieve.

Most Morgan bonnets are made with louvres. The machine use for the operation is a fly-press, entirely powered by human muscl The same machine has been used since soon after the First Worl War. Each louvre is individually pressed on pencil marks accurate drawn on the bare sheet metal. It is a slow process and one tha causes arm-ache, but this does not worry the louvre makers at Ma vern." (Extracts from Grogory Houston — Bowden's book *Morga first and last of the real sport cars.)*

Day 23

Probably the most intricate work in the body shop is the construction of rear wheel arches. To make these, thin ash boards are carefully selected and coated with a special hardening acid. Then beetle cement is applied so that they can be laminated and placed in special wooden clamps, ready to go into the drying cupboard. The clamps are simply made out of carefully shaped pieces of wood held together with stout bolts. After the laminated ash has spent about nine hours in the drying cupboard it will not lose its shape.

Day 33

When the body shop has fulfilled its duties, the factory porters are again called upon to take the car across the yard to the sheet metal shop. The work here is done in three separate stages. On arrival, the car is handed over to one particular man who makes its rear panels, its quarter panels and its door panels, and then fits them to the ash subframe. He cuts them out of sheets of metal and shapes them individually until they fit the car he is working on. The panels are numbered so that if at a later stage the work is thought to be substandard, it can easily be traced back to the man responsible. This, however, is a very rare occurrence.

The Morgan body is, in fact, chiefly held together with tin tacks and wood screws; this system pays good dividends if a crash or corrosion causes a panel to be replaced at some future date. It takes nearly two days to make the panels for a Morgan.

Day 35

When the job is complete, the car is pushed along the shop to the next man, whose job is to fit the wings and the front cowl. These are made with the same care and attention as the other parts of the body and are fitted to the car in just the same way. These are the only double curvature panels. "Finally the car is handed over to the bonnet-maker — the man with the trickiest job of all. The result of

Day 47

"With wings and doors securely mounted, the porters take the c through to the spray shop. Here the car is sprayed with primer a handed over to one of the Morgan 'putty' experts. These men ha the skill of sculptors and they need it, for they have the extreme tricky task of filling in all the little imperfections in the wings a especially in the welding that holds together the different section

"Once the putty is applied, it is smoothed down. The man w does the job is convinced that any kind of sanding machine wou have a disastrous effect at this stage, so he does all the rubbi down by hand, using different grades of silicone paper."

When these sculptors have finished, the whole car is given tw or three coats of grey paint called "primer surface". When this h ried overnight, they are carefully rubbed down by hand with a fine-grain silicone paper; then the undercoat is applied. There are at least two coats of this, but as some colours cover better than others, up to six coats are applied so that the sprayers can feel fully satisfied.

Day 90

After its second visit to the electrical shop, the newly born car is very nearly complete. Now it goes to the finishing shop where the final touches are applied: these include fitting the bumpers, the sidescreens and the Morgan badges. The car is then transferred to the test shop, where it is handed over to one of the most envied men in the Morgan world – the chief tester. At present the job is held by Charlie Curtis, now well into his seventies and wonderfully well qualified for the job. He began as a mechanic in the test department of Morgans shortly after the end of the First World War, and swiftly rose to the post of chief tester. Thus Charlie has, with very few exceptions, driven every Morgan that has been made since 1927. His regular run is about ten miles, carefully selected to include some twisty sections of Worcestershire country roads, some hills and some comfortable straight stretches. When he returns, his mechanic colleagues carry out any adjustments which have shown themselves to be necessary, and off he goes again. If the second test run proves satisfactory, the car is considered ready for despatch. It is then driven to the despatch bay where it awaits collection from either its owner or transporter.

In all, the building of the Morgan has taken some ninety days. It's not surprising there's a two-year waiting list for the car.

What is the Morgan's *raison d'être*? Two quotes are appropriate.

"The only possible reason for buying such a car", wrote *Motor* in a test report, "is the sheer fun of driving it fast on suitable roads . . ."

Dr Johnson once said, "The ultimate end of all employments is to produce amusement".

Morgans are sheer fun to drive and produce more amusement than a roomful of Playboy bunnies. ●

Day 61

The gleaming machine is taken through to the electrical shop where lights are fitted and wired up.

Then in the trim shop, the wires are covered with the upholstery and the wheel arches and door panels are fitted.

The intricate leatherwork which covers the gearbox and transmission tunnel is cut to shape and the seats are made here too.

The trim shop has a staff of nine, including three jolly ladies who work away on the slightly antiquated sewing machines.

All the upholstery, including tonneau and hood, is individually made for the car to which it is fitted. Nothing is pre-cut or ready-made, so that everything fits perfectly.

Day 73

Perhaps the smallest department is where the windscreens are fitted. After the windscreen has been put in place, the car is taken to the electrical bay where the wiring is completed and all the spaghetti is neatly tucked out of sight. It does occasionally happen that, when the electrical system of a new Morgan is first tested with a battery, a fine shower of sparks flies out. On these occasions the cause is usually a tin-tack driven through the harness by an over-enthusiatic trimmer.

Morgans lined up in the despatch bay awaiting collection. David Allison has acquired a four-seater Morgan and went to see how it was put together.

2-seater

1600 ENGINE (Ford CVH)

Cubic Capacity	—	1597 cm³ (97.42 cu.ins.)
Number of Cylinders	—	4
Bore and Stroke	—	79.96mm x 79.52mm
Compression Ratio	—	9.5:1
Maximum Torque	—	98 ft/lb @ 4000 rpm (135 nm)
B.H.P.	—	96 DIN @ 6000 rpm
Firing Order	—	1,3,4,2
Valve Gear	—	Single central O.H.C. Hydraulic Tappets
Oil Capacity	—	6.2 pints (3.50 litres)
Carburettor	—	Single Weber 3234 DFT twin choke
Petrol Capacity	—	12½ gallons (56 litres). (2 Seater)

Morgan
4/4 1600

For further details contact your local dealer (listed overleaf).

4-seater

Moggie line-up from left to right: John Atkins' tuned Plus 8; Chris Alford's prodsport 4/4 (with driver); and John Britten's racing Plus 8. Standing behind are Chris's mechanic, John Britten and a rather bemused Rex Greenslade

GUTEN MORGAN

Self-confessed sports car fanatic Rex Greenslade explains his love for rag-tops in general, and Morgans in particular. Here he tests two racers and a remarkable road car.

WHAT IS A sports car? If it means to you one of those effete in and glassfibre affairs generally available today, then stop here. If, however, you long for a *real* sports car, something out of the rut of computerised designs that you've been driving for the past few years, then read on. This is for you.

To qualify for the title, a sports car should, in my opinion, satisfy all the following criteria. It should offer ample accommodation for two people (plus, perhaps their luggage) and no more; creature comforts should take a distant second place to the all-important characteristics of handling, roadholding and performance; it should sound nice; it should, above all else, be open-topped. How people can refer to some machines as sports cars when the only concession to open-air motoring is the provision of wind-down windows and a pair of fresh air vents is beyond me.

If you've got this far then we're probably on almost the same wavelength. Any sports car you'd buy would almost certainly be uncomfortable, impractical to use as daily transport, a misery when it rains—but bloody good fun when the sun's shining. It won't quite put hairs on your chest, but it'll certainly put some colour in your cheeks, and a broad smile in the process.

For a real sports car you can't beat a Morgan. The Morgan Motor Co of Malvern Link in Worcestershire has been making cars since 1936 (before that they made those beautiful three wheelers) and the concept has changed little since. The current body design dates back to 1955, for instance, and Morgan's unique sliding pillar front suspension was first patented as long ago as 1912. Over the years they've got quicker and more modern under the skin; gone are the Moss gearbox and nasty protruding switches, for instance. But Morgans are still traditional sports cars in every sense of the word— from the tips of their flat windscreen to the extremities of their separate wings.

Just how good the 4/4 still is was shown last year by Chris Alford who, using a Ford Escort-engined Moggie, annihilated the opposition in the BRSCC's Prodsport Championship. From 15 starts he had 15 wins with 12 fastest laps and six lap records. Not surprisingly he ended up overall champion—a title all the more creditable when you realise that his class included competitors in MGBs and TR6s.

Prodsport races are controlled by regulations similar to those of production saloons. You're very limited as far as modifications are concerned and the cars have to run on ordinary road tyres; neglecting the open exhaust, showroom condition wouldn't be an inaccurate description. You need a blueprinted engine to be competitive, of course, and a set of adjustable competition dampers helps a lot. Chris chose Minister to tweak the Mexico engine (not, incidentally, to Formula Ford state of tune; Prodsports regs don't allow combustion chamber "fettling"), but the only alteration made to the suspension was the addition of a pair of second-hand Spax dampers at the front, and those only halfway through the season.

In Prodsports (unlike production saloons) you are allowed to use "demised" bits from earlier cars together with more recent parts—a 1975 TR6 can, for instance, use the original, much more powerful, engine. In the 4/4's case, it's permissible to adopt the 4.5:1 final drive ratio that hasn't been used since 1969; current 4/4s have a 4.2:1 cwp. Morgan also occasionally use alloy panels on their cars, so that the 4/4's doors, and bonnet of this material are also allowed. But all that (plus mandatory safety modifications) represents minimal alterations for a championship winner; it shows how good the 4/4 is in the first place. Although Chris says that he did virtually no sorting at all, I'd rate the 4/4 as the best balanced production car of any type that I've driven on a racing circuit—in this case Brands Hatch on a damp

muggy winter's morning. Hardly a day for records, you might think (and in any case, I make a point of not trying too hard on track tests), yet the 4/4 proved to be very quick indeed.

Unlike on many production cars the brake balance front/rear was near ideal, allowing deep braking into the apex of the corner. As the tail slid gently out of line, a quick application of opposite lock and a simultaneous prod on the throttle were sufficient to send the car rocketing out of the corner in a stable, and most satisfying, manner. Despite the slippery conditions, Graham Hill Bend (née Bottom Bend) could be taken flat in top, and given a certain amount of bravery, I reckon that a similar manoeuvre could have been used at Paddock; I just dabbed the brakes once lightly.

I was impressed by the car's traction out of the corner (no limited slip differential remember), by the normal slick Ford gearbox (though you need ape-length arms to reach first or third) and especially by the extremely torquey and smooth Minister engine; on Chris's instructions I was using about 7000 rpm on the rev counter, though I have little doubt that the instrument was more than a mite optimistic.

After 10 flying laps I was circulating in 64.0 sec (Chris' lap record is 63.6 sec), which is great testimony to the ease with which the car can be driven.

John Britten's Plus 8 was a completely different kettle of fish. Unlike the nimble, easily learnt, 4/4, the Plus 8 drives like it looks and sounds; big, mean and brutish. John has relatively little spare time these days as boss of John Britten Garages and sundry camera concerns (Chris Alford is one of his co-directors) but he managed to squeeze in 11 starts and get two outright wins, five 2nds and two 3rds, against some pretty stout opposition including V12 E-types and Chris Meek's Lotus Europa.

Like the 4/4, John's Plus 8 is a bit of a cocktail mixture being an early narrow track model converted to wide track but retaining the original high compression engine and low (3.58 instead of 3.3:1) final drive ratio. Racing Services prepared the engine which utilises the allowed Mallory twin contact breaker distributor, and suspension modifications are confined to Koni front and Armstrong rear adjustable dampers. For my test, John had replaced the normal Michelin XWX tyres he uses on the circuits with Pirelli CN36; early in the season John found that these tyres weren't easy to drive on, but the Michelins weren't available.

This was a great pity, for in the greasy conditions, the Plus 8 proved to be a great handful. Rush into a corner a mite too quickly and it understeers . . . and understeers . . . and under-

steers. A little bit more throttle accentuates this attitude until, when your arms have twisted themselves into a knot and you're least expecting it, the limited slip locks up with a jerk, the car surges forward with a great belt up the back and you're piling on the opposite lock like there's no tomorrow. And with the amount of lock you've already applied in the other direction to counteract the understeer it's no mean feat to get that opposite lock on cleanly and accurately.

I soon learned that the best method was to negotiate most of each corner on a trailing throttle and only squirt when the corner opened up. Hardly the most sophisticated technique (but it's the one which John also uses) though the car can still be hustled round at very respectable rates.

My best time was about 61.5 sec. With more neutral handling that would allow the power to be

Top: the 4/4 swooping through Graham Hill Bend. Above: understeer from the Plus 8 at McLaren (née Clearways)

poured on much earlier in each corner (and what power there is!) I reckon that you could knock a couple of seconds off that time immediately—and it would be keeping up with Mr Meek's Europa quite comfortably.

Understeer was no problem with John Atkins' Plus 8, one of the most beautiful Morgans I've ever seen, mainly because it's had more lavish attention in the past couple of years than most cars have in their lifetime. John is managing director of Jamesign (London) Ltd who make those super smooth Perspex number plates you see on most flash cars these days; he also deals in cherished numbers, which explains the Morgan's registration. But John's the first to give most of the credit for the work done to his friend John Eason; as a token of his gratitude, JA gave JE the number plate JEA 5ON for Christmas (think about it).

And what work has been done. The Plus 8 was bought by JA in 1972 as a virtual write-off after being crashed in Sweden. The two Johns had to rebuild it from the chassis up (for instance, fitting new brake and complete wiring systems), at the same time modifying it to their tastes. Early on they decided to fit an Alfa Romeo 2600 five-speed gearbox as it offered a superior gearchange and more ratios, though this transplant involved an immense amount of work. Eventually they found that the following combination worked well enough: a Rover bellhousing (with modified chassis); a one-off mating plate twixt this and gearbox; a Rover clutch pressure plate with Alfa centre disc; a one-off prop shaft made by Hardy Spicer; and a special remote shift designed and made by John Eason.

Williams and Pritchard widened the steel wings while the engine was highly modified with bits from a number of sources: Janspeed exhaust manifolds; Ian Richardson camshaft, valve springs, Holley four barrel carb and inlet manifold; Les Ryder gasflowed cylinder heads; and a special anti-surge sump that holds an extra four pints of Castrol GTX. The rest of the mods included Konis for the rear suspension, Corbeau seats, Wolfrace wheels, enormous SP Sport tyres, Cibie lights (what else?) while JA and JE did all the respraying, retrimming, decambering the front suspension and redesigning of the dashboard themselves. And I've still probably left something out.

How does it drive? Superbly, in a word. Even our most cynical and critical tester conceded that he'd had a bloody good thrash in it while others were ecstatic. Sure, like any Morgan, it gets thrown around on bumps and hurrying the Plus 8 along a winding road at speed can be very tiring; but the feeling of exhilaration during the drive and satisfaction at its finish are

Get the wind in your hair—or chicken out and wear a bobble hat. Beautifully flared arches, wide Wolfrace wheels and no bumpers give the Atkins Plus 8 its aggressive stance

Rearranged facia, stubby gearlever for the Alfa box and Moto-Lita steering wheel in the cockpit, and a highly modified engine under the bonnet

only too rare nowadays.

For a start, John's Plus 8 hangs on much better than any I've tried before, and in almost any given situation the amount of available power exceeds grip by such a large amount that the car can, to use that hackneyed phrase, be steered with the throttle. You soon learn to let the Morgan find its own way over humps and bumps taken at speed, though passengers find this meandering a little disconcerting; rarely, however, does a bump require a specific steering correction.

When it's warm, the Alfa gearbox gives a slick precise change, and perhaps even more importantly endows the car with a fifth gear ratio that makes 90 mph cruising quite relaxed (especially if the hood's down and the sidescreens are in place). The engine sounds woofly at low revs, but builds up to deep throated crackle above about 4500 rpm—a note somewhat reminiscent of a racing Cobra at its best. The two Johns are still sorting the carburation (that it's not right can be seen by black coating on the exhausts) and once completed it should be a real flyer—even in adverse conditions, it's already capable of reaching 100 mph in less than 18 sec.

Above all, I can't remember a car that evoked so much admiration from on-lookers. Leave the Morgan parked for a few minutes and it'll be surrounded with people marvelling at its smooth sleek lines and at the high standard of finish. Ferraris and Lamborghinis attract a different sort of gazer, the sort that idolise pop stars and yearn for the unattainable. The Morgan admirer is almost always older and a Person Who Knows About Cars. The chances are that he owned one or something like it in his youth, and that probably sums up the Morgan; it makes you feel young again. Grab that chance while you can.

Inside the "New" Morgan Plus 8

A different kind of replicar, because it's a replica of itself.

BY CHARLES FOX

• Fink and Miller's Bicentennial Morgan Plus 8 is a screamer: a fat, wide, low, tight screamer. It resembles the basic Morgan, but it drives more like a potent Chain Gang Frazer-Nash or San Remo Maserati. Old Moggies were meant to be caned through corners with much whip and spur and motioning of the elbows. They flexed and creaked like H.M.S. *Victory* in a hurricane. Not this one.

This one zooms. And bounds across whole lanes with a single bounce of its solid rear axle. Propane power means instant response and 155 DIN horsepower, undiluted with whips, chains, catalysts and pumps. Pushing only 1876 pounds, it means 100 mph in third gear and 20 seconds, and a quarter-mile in 15 seconds at 90 mph.

The engine is the 3.5-liter Buick/Rover V-8, coupled to a Rover four-speed, breathing through a pair of two-inch SU carburetors. Fink and Miller devised a way to feed the propane mixture into the SUs: The propane, kept under pressure in liquid form with a lock-off valve that remains closed unless the ignition is on, is brought forward from an 18-gallon tank to a heat exchanger that vaporizes it. It is then drawn into the cylinders by each piston on the intake stroke. Propane gives approximately five percent less mileage than gasoline (16 to 18 mpg) but is about 10 cents per gallon cheaper.

It produces no carbon, so spark plug life is longer. And there is no liquid fuel running down cylinder walls into the oil, so engine wear is reduced.

If you don't care for propane, a gas-powered Plus 8 will be available in 1977, after either the TR7 or Rover 3500 appears in the U.S. fitted with the Rover V-8. Fink and Miller will then put this de-toxed engine into the Morgan. As waiting time on Morgan orders is currently four to five months, you could presumably order a gasoline version immediately. Anti-smog equipment will cut power in the gasoline V-8 down to about 135 hp, which is why Fink is pushing propane.

He will be importing a propane version of the Morgan 4/4 (four cylinders, four wheels) with 1600cc Ford Cortina. With propane, this engine will develop about 84 DIN hp at 5400 rpm and 92 foot-pounds of torque. But Fink is proposing to turbocharge, which with a modest boost, will increase the horsepower to a 140, and give a good 30 mpg.

Both cars will have all-aluminum skins on ash frames set on a ladder chassis with five tubular cross members. The 4/4 comes with pressed steel-rim, four-stud wheels and 165x15 radials. The Plus 8 has cast-aluminum five-stud wheels and 185x15 radials. The Plus 8 has two inches more wheelbase (98 inches) and weighs an extra 250 pounds. Front track is 51 inches (compared to the 4/4's 45 inches) and is three inches wider. Both cars have independent front suspension and semi-elliptic springs at the back.

Price of the 4/4 is pegged at $10,500; the Plus 8 costs $14,500. It's a sign of the times. In England, a Plus 8 retails for $8000 and, on the flourishing black market, fetches $10,000; 4/4s go as high as $9000 under the table.

Once the cars arrive in San Francisco, Fink and Miller must strip them to install the roll cages, door guards, lights and bumpers. They must then be reassembled and painted. Cost per unit for this work is $3500.

Fink and Miller do a good job: a row of toggle switches on the leather-covered dash, real seats (gone are the air dough-

It was not conceived to
catch the eye; it was and is a
truly functional machine.

nuts on plywood), a thick padded wheel, an enormous speed-ometer and a small tach, full-weather equipment and enough luggage room for a short afternoon at the beach. The advantage of the optional roll cage at the rear and 1.5-inch tube that crosses behind the dash to take the side-impact guards in the doors is immensely improved torsional rigidity.

It makes the Plus 8 a different animal. But it's a curious car to drive, particularly if you are six foot or more. The seat adjusts, but barely, enforcing a driving style more after Froilan Gonzalez than Niki Lauda. That's to say that the wheel is a bare nine inches from your chest. Mercifully however, it is not so much the wheel, but the throttle that must be used to steer the Plus 8. To this end, the controls fall very readily to hand and feet. The shift may not be that precise, but then there is such a glut of torque (226 foot-pounds) that one seldom

needs to resort to the gearbox. And the disc/drum brakes are completely adequate.

The Plus 8 is a harsh device until you remember how to drive a solid rear axle. You must keep the back wheels in only light contact with the pavement. When the understeer strikes, you simply use more throttle. At that, the Morgan Plus 8 is transformed from strenuous to glorious.

The Morgan is a sufficiently antiquated design to have evolved into a replicar—a replica of itself. But something about its originality makes it different. It is not conceived to catch the eye, but as a functional machine. The motive makes a deal of difference. Replicars are made to commemorate the passage of the Golden Age. The Morgan is a true if tenuous thread to those days, a bare-chested-in-all-weather delight. There is definitely a place for the Morgan in this world. ●

MORGAN: The Second Coming

by Tony Swan

It's a definite maybe.

To most citizens of this realm, particularly those in certain sections of the Midwest and South, references to the Second Coming concern the possible reappearance of a certain long-absent gentleman from Nazareth (*not* Mario Andretti). But to the American devotees of a certain Neanderthal British sportscar, the Second Coming can mean only one thing: the return of the Morgan.

Although both of these events look like longshots, if you're a betting person put your money on the second possibility. Absent from the U.S. market since 1972 (except for the trickle of propane conversions put out by Isis Imports, in San Francisco), Morgan is now gearing up to return, probably sometime in 1978.

One of the keys to the return of the Morgan is the slick new Rover 3500, launched last summer in England. British Leyland plans to make the new car available in the U.S. sometime in 1978, along with its four-wheel-drive entries, the reliable old Land Rover and the newer Range Rover. Since the Morgan Plus 8 uses the same 3.5-liter V-8 engine as the Rover, a U.S. emissions-legal Rover means Morgan won't have to worry about certification programs. (Rumors persist of an Australian-developed 4.4-liter version of the Rover V-8 for use in the U.S. edition of the new car, and if this occurs, Morgan will likely continue with the 3.5-liter and run his own abbreviated—4,000-mile—certifications under the dispensations available to low volume manufacturers.)

The piggyback certification program also applies to the Morgan 4/4, thanks to the advent of the Ford Fiesta, due to arrive in the U.S. this fall. The Fiesta's U.S. engine, which will probably be a 1600cc version of the European Fiesta engines, should offer performance characteristics similar to the British Ford engine currently propelling the Morgan 4/4 in Europe.

The rather reluctant architect of the Morgan's Second Coming is Peter Morgan, son of the company's founder. A spare, scholarly-looking man in his middle years, Morgan exhibits many of the earmarks of the English country gentleman: a gently condescending air with American visitors, a resolute suspicion of anything smacking of hurry or change, and a slightly distracted but nevertheless unshakable self-assurance. At a national level, the syndrome is called "There'll always be an England." It's precisely the

spirit that carried the Morgan Motor Company, Ltd., through the "one bad year" that followed pulling out of the American market.

Morgan reflected on the lessons of that year for us:

"It was a bit difficult at first, of course," he said. "We'd gotten to the point where as much as 87 percent of our production was going to the North American market. So I said, 'well, we can't have just one market,' and we set about developing others.

"Now Germany is our biggest market, and we've got a bit of a problem generally with back orders."

By "bit of a problem" Morgan is talking about intervals of two to three and one half years between order and delivery, a wait requiring the patience of a . . . well, of a real Morgan fanatic.

"Ideally," says Morgan, "I'd like it to be about nine to 18 months."

If you feel this doesn't augur well for the actual implementation of the Second Coming, you're right. Time hasn't really leaned very heavily on the little factory fronting Pickersleigh Road in Malvern Link, a wide place in Highway A-449 about 20 miles south of Worcester. Morgan founder H. F. S. Morgan began a piecemeal move of his operations from across town to their current location back in 1914, completing the move in 1931. With that 17-year effort as a company precedent, haste would be more than conspicuous here; it would be simply gauche.

A walk through the plant is like popping through a time warp. This has to be the only car factory in the world with a carpentry shop (for the famous wood spaceframing) integral to the proceedings, and one of the very few where sheet metal is handshaped on the spot (with the exception of the fenders). The clangor in the sheet metal shop is incredible, like Santa's workshop amplified to match the general decibel level of Armageddon, and hand soldering is an everyday skill, as germane to this operation as automated spot arc welders to the assembly lines of Detroit.

The mood of the Morgan work force, all properly trades-unionized of course, seems to match the unhurried, anachronistic manufacturing techniques and the Edwardian look of the place. As one worker put it, "I've been in the motor trade all me life, and this is the easiest place I've seen yet."

It all adds up to an annual production figure that wouldn't even be a proper morning warmup for an American plant.

"It varies out a bit," says Morgan, "but it's generally between 410 and 440 cars per

A Musclecar for Traditionalists

□ There is this slur that certain fainthearts love to aim at the Morgan sportscar. Anyone who loves Morgans, they say, has never owned one.

I savor the full pettiness of this idea as the green Worcestershire countryside leaps toward me at speeds well beyond what the tongue cluckers of our own National Highway Traffic Safety Administration regard as safe. The wind snatches at the top of my head, poking well up above the windscreen, the country road seems to be doing its best to either elude me or dwindle to the general equivalent of a paved game trail, and there is a delicious feeling of grisly disaster barely averted at almost every turn.

The British call it motoring, and you have to be "keen" to do it. The car is the Morgan Plus 8, and it took only a very short turn at the wheel—which is all the petrol they allotted me—to understand a distinction that Peter Morgan had made only a few minutes earlier.

"In the U.S. with sportscars it's mostly a matter of open air touring," he'd said. "A lot of people don't really care about performance.

"But I don't really feel you have a right to call a car a sportscar unless it can perform in competition."

Morgan understands performance and competition, having spent many hours at the wheel of race-prepared Morgans both before and after World War II, in three-wheelers as well as four. His son Charles races them now, and the cars are still highly competitive in British club racing.

My brief communion with the Plus 8—the first time I'd ever had my hands on one—didn't allow any time for instrumented testing. But it did produce some vivid and lasting impressions.

The first, and strongest, was of pure *muscle*. This car isn't a 400-horsepower Corvette—in British road trim the 3.5-liter Rover V-8 delivers about 190 horsepower. But it is hardly a car that wins by finesse. Its power-to-weight ratio is favorable enough to deliver consistent sub-15-second quarter-miles at 90-plus, and getting to 100 miles per hour is a matter of 23 seconds. Top speed is in the 130 mile per hour vicinity.

There's something elemental and stirring about going rapidly in a car like this, and it's not simply the difference between an open car and a closed one, such as the new Rover I drove down from London. The Rover is far from slow—it cruises easily at 110—but it lacks the visceral elan of this automotive throwback. Concessions to modernity are at a minimum in the Morgan, and in hurling it down those country lanes (after 64 years of it, the locals have become thoroughly accustomed to the sight of madmen flying Morgans past their pastures) it was easy to believe in the time warp again: Suddenly it was 1937.

However, the bushy-haired caveman appeal of this car is also the quality that earns it criticism, and it's easy to imagine discomfort being a significant part of any long trip. It's undeniably crude. The seating position is almost bolt upright, and the steering wheel is close to the driver's chest in the classic old-timey elbows-out driving style. It's a big wheel, too; regardless of seat adjustment it brushed my thighs, hampering wheel movement. There's no foot room. The only place to rest the left foot is on the clutch pedal, although this malady presumably goes away in left-hand-drive editions. The 4-speed gearbox in my Plus 8 was marvelously British in its resistance to any change, down or up, but future Plus 8s will be available with the new Rover (and TR7) 5-speed, which is very smooth and easy to manage.

The handling qualities, surprisingly, are more up to date than the amenities. The car isn't exactly mid-engined, but the Rover engine—a lightweight unit to begin with, thanks to extensive use of aluminum—is set well back from the front wheels. The result is less understeer than I'd expected. It's not exactly a forgiving car, but it can be thrown about considerably, even during the getting-acquainted stage. The brakes—Girling discs—took a bit of getting used to. There didn't seem to be much of a problem with lockup, but the car seemed very busy, particularly under hard braking. To be fair, this car was so new the paint was almost sticky.

For all his disdain for the Morgan's detractors, Peter Morgan has resigned himself to giving his brutes a bit of taming before sending them off to U.S. consumers.

"I do feel we'll have to make the car a bit softer than it is now," he says, somewhat sadly. "It'll be more of an open tourer than a sportscar as it is here."

Morgan makes it clear, however, that his concept of "softer" does not in any way equate with the general emasculation of other British sportscars sold in the U.S. Which ought to suit everyone just fine.

—T.S.

year. And as you can see, it's not the sort of operation where you can simply double production overnight, even when demand is good."

Nevertheless, Morgan and his staff have been at work getting their cars ready for the scrutineers of the U.S. Environmental Protection Agency and the Department of Transportation. Beefing the Morgan up to meet safety standards has been easier than you might expect, because the car is basically quite solid.

"Mainly what we've had to do is add a brace beam in the door and cross member bracing under the dashboard," says Morgan. "A Mr. Jervis Webb, from Detroit, has come up with a reasonably good bumper arrangement (Isis' Bill Finks installs a similar system of his own on his conversions) for the five mile per hour standard."

What about the wood framing (not to be confused with the chassis, which is steel)?

"I don't feel we have to make any excuses for it at all," says Morgan. "We use ash, not quite as hard as teak, but immensely strong. It's forgiving, and even has certain recuperative powers, which one certainly can't say for metal. And of course it allows the owner to work on it himself.

"When we tested our three-point seatbelt anchoring system (the DOT standard requires the anchor to resist a 5,000-pound tug), the Rover people were on hand, probably waiting to pick up the firewood. But we came through first rate, no problem at all."

And as far as that beloved straight-from-the-genesis-year appearance is concerned, don't worry. A swoopy new Morgan in the new tradition of wedges and angles is about as likely as blue snow in Santa Monica.

"The new styling trends have helped us, really," says Morgan. "There was a period from about 1955 through 1965 when our styling made it terribly difficult to sell our cars in the home market and in Europe. During that time our American buyers really sustained the car's styling for us."

Morgan is the first to admit, though, that styling isn't quite the word for the way the car gets its looks.

"Nobody styles it," he smiles: "It simply evolves.

"But esthetically, I think it looks right. The reason you don't see a sweeping fender line like that anymore is because it's simply not economical to produce. We intend to keep it.

"And of course I'm *very* keen on building an open car as long as I can. I feel they're just as safe as closed cars, provided there's a rollover bar. And since we've got to have a rollover bar let's for God's sake make it *look* like a rollover bar, rather than some sort of Targa top. That wouldn't go with the looks of the car at all.

"About the only change we're planning at the moment is going to 14-inch wheels and a slightly wider stance."

Morgan carefully avoids being pinned down on his timetable for the Second Coming, rambling off into logistical complaints when pressed.

"Of course, you've got to have guaranteed supplies to make a big increase in production. All too often we're hand-to-mouth on that score even now. Tires, for heaven's sake! It's almost impossible to get tires, because there's hardly anyone going 130 anymore. And on the other hand, you must be able to order in big enough quantities to even interest a supplier."

For all his vagueness on dates, Morgan has definite ideas about a couple of matters concerning his place in the U.S. market: The prices of his cars and the remoteness of the possibility of producing them in kit form, *a la* the old Lotus Super Seven.

"I've never wanted to make a kit car," he notes, "because I believe you only make them twice: once when you're going into the motor business and once when you're going out.

"As for prices, I'd say that the 4/4 would sell for about $7,500 and the Plus 8 for roughly $10,000. I rather think the 4/4 will be the better seller, as much because of the U.S. speed laws as the difference in price."

With the British pound flopping around like a wounded tuna, putting a fine point on the price will be another wait-and-see matter—particularly when you consider the prices of the Isis cars (admittedly more expensive to put on the road): The Isis-treated 4/4 sells for $10,500, the Plus 8 for $14,500 and the new lightweight Plus 8 for $15,250. If you really want to fly, Isis is doing up a turbo Plus 8 that will cost roughly $17,000.

But while you're waiting for the Second Coming—and the news of how much it's going to cost you per unit—rest assured that the product will remain in trusty (read Morgan) hands. Yet another member of the clan, Peter Morgan's son Charles, 26, is hovering at the periphery, ready to carry on the family tradition.

"At the moment he's a TV cameraman," says Morgan. "Hasn't anything to do with the firm at all, although he runs a Plus 8 in competition. But then I didn't join the firm until I was 27.

"Charles is quite keen on motorcars generally. In fact, he's the only Morgan chap who's turned one of the cars over. He was all right, fortunately. And he's quite a good stylist; he's done quite a number of sketches on the 1930s look brought up to date."

Styling, of course, seems to be one thing the Morgan motor car doesn't particularly need, but it is reassuring, somehow, to know that there'll be another Morgan at Morgan, protecting this motoring institution. So while there may not always be an England, it seems likely that there will always be a Morgan. ■

MIGHTY MOGGIE

Traditionalists wait years to buy them, admirers move mountains to ride in them. In Plus 8 form the pride of Malvern Link is perhaps the last remaining example of the true hairy-chested sports car. With bobble hats aloft we tried the latest of the breed, the five-speed Plus 8

ORGANS ARE not only old-[fa]shioned in their design and [ap]pearance but in most aspects of [th]eir behaviour too. It is this anach[ro]nistic character that gives the car [its] charm, and the unique Malvern [fir]ms company its continuing suc[ce]ss. When you've got a product [th]at's unique and well made it's no [su]rprise to find customers queuing [for] the gates.

The basic essentials of traditional [M]organ motoring are still there, [in]cluding the antiquated sliding pil[la]r front suspension. But under the [bo]nnet of the Plus 8/77 there's a [r]over 3½ litre V8 engine which, in [it]s latest form, produces 158 bhp; [w]ith the help of the new Leyland [fi]ve-speed gearbox it endows the [Pl]us 8 with a performance that's [b]etter than most modern "sports" [an]d quite a few flash Italian jobs.

Today's Plus 8 differs from the [on]e that we tested back in 1968 in [h]aving a more sophisticated heater [(t]he temperature is now adjustable [fr]om inside the car, and there's pro[vi]sion for ram flow and demisting [ve]nts to the windscreen); a new facia [w]ith restyled, resited instruments [an]d fingertip stalks; and a body [wi]dened by two inches ("people [w]anted us to accentuate the separate [w]ings; only a few years ago they [w]anted us to hide them," says man[ag]ing director Peter Morgan). [H]ardly stunning changes, but sig[ni]ficant by Morgan standards.

The Lightweight version intro[du]ced a year ago has been dropped. [Cu]stomers can still order their Mor[ga]n with aluminium body panels [an]d save around 60 lb; but it will [co]st an extra £150. At £5,417 the [Pl]us 8 is not cheap, but then nothing [th]at's hand made today is.

The Morgan didn't quite stand [al]one in 1968, but it certainly does [no]w. What other new car offers the [sa]me exhilaration, the same *joie de [vi]vre?* If you've been nurtured on [co]mputer-designed, monocoque-[bo]died modern sportsters then your [fir]st trip down the road in a Moggie [is] likely to be an eye-opener. The [st]eering is heavy, the suspension [ro]ck solid and the body creaks and [gr]oans.

But then these were always [ac]cepted ingredients of the "tradi[tio]nal" sports car and many a wind-[in]-the-hair enthusiast wouldn't be [wi]thout them. Compensating for its [he]aviness, the steering is direct and [h]as plenty of feel. And although the [su]spension throws the car off line on [bu]mps, the fat 195/70 VR 14 tyres [in]variably restore adhesion before [yo]u need apply steering correction. [It] makes for an exciting motoring, of [co]urse, but that's the Morgan's [gr]eat appeal.

On smooth surfaces the handling [is] superb. The steering is so high [ge]ared that you point into a corner [ra]ther than steer round it. In the dry [th]ere's no understeer; the handling [is] pretty neutral unless you use too [m]uch throttle when it's oversteer all [th]e way. Even then the Morgan has [an] endearing ability to sort itself out [wi]thout any opposite lock correction [fr]om the driver. In the wet there's [m]ore than enough power to break [tr]action at the back round most cor[ne]rs, so a lot more delicacy is then [re]quired; but the Plus 8 is not the [so]rt of skittish beast that its fat

PERFORMANCE

MAXIMUM SPEEDS

Speed in gears (at 6000 rpm):	mph	kph
1st	40	64
2nd	63	101
3rd	94	151

ACCELERATION FROM REST

mph	sec	kph	sec
0-30	2.5	0-40	1.9
0-40	3.9	0-60	3.6
0-50	5.2	0-80	5.2
0-60	7.2	0-100	7.8
0-70	9.6	0-120	10.7
0-80	11.9	0-140	14.5
0-90	15.7	0-160	21.7
0-100	22.2		
Stand'g ¼	15.5		
Stand'g km	28.9		

ACCELERATION IN TOP

mph	sec	kph	sec
20-40	7.8	40-60	4.6
30-50	7.3	60-80	4.6
40-60	7.3	80-100	4.6
50-70	7.8	100-120	5.2
60-80	8.7	120-140	6.5
70-90	10.3	140-160	9.3
80-100	15.1		

ACCELERATION IN 4TH

mph	sec	kph	sec
20-40	5.6	40-60	3.3
30-50	5.3	60-80	3.3
40-60	5.6	80-100	3.4
50-70	5.6	100-120	3.8
60-80	6.2	120-140	4.8
70-90	7.5	140-160	6.2
80-100	9.4		

tyres, a weight of only 17 cwt and nearly 160 bhp might suggest.

Unfortunately a stretched alternator belt (the fan is electrically driven) and very high winds prevented us from obtaining what we expected to be some pretty staggering acceleration figures. On almost every occasion we roared away from

Left: the new facia with main dials in front of the driver and the minor gauges in the centre. Note the Leyland-style fingertip stalks

Below: what Morgan motoring is all about: a winding road, the wind in your hair and a smile on your face

a full-blooded wheelspin standing start, the belt got thrown from its pulleys because there was no more adjustment to take up the slack. Even with this handicap, a 20 mph headwind in one direction and only 1400 miles on the clock, the Morgan returned 7.2 sec to 60 mph, 15.7 sec to 90 mph and 22.2 sec (the effect of

the wind) to 100 mph. We had no opportunity to verify the maximum speed accurately but then during brief bursts we saw over 120 mph with the car still accelerating, so Morgan's claim of about 120 mph can't be far from the truth.

One of the big attractions of a light, large-engined sports car is that you don't have to rev hard to sustain extremely brisk progress. To accelerate from 30 to 50 mph in fourth takes only 5.3 sec, for instance; from 60 to 80 mph only a fraction longer at 6.2 sec.

Mated to the Rover engine was Leyland's 5-speed gearbox and clutch. With a high 3.31:1 limited slip differential this gives lower gear maxima of 40, 63 and 94 mph at 6000 rpm (as peak power is at 5250 rpm there's little point in hanging on any further). In the upper three changes the lever moves freely and easily, but into first and second it baulked, especially when cold, just as it did in the five-speed TR7. So our original enthusiasm for this 'box — so good in the first Rover 3500 we tried — is on the wane.

In other respects the Morgan is much as before. We like the new instruments and the fingertip stalks, and being able to regulate the heater's temperature from inside the car is an obvious advantage. Travelling with the hood down and heater full on to toast your feet was most exhilarating in March.

What better way to spend a Sunday afternoon than thrashing along a country road, with the wind in your hair, the crackle of the exhaust in your ears and a smile on your face?

VUY 195R

SUPERCAR!
Morgan Plus 8

......for Mad dogs and Englishmen

● Today's supercars generally look like something begotten by a space capsule, and we can only be thankful that features like the wheels, steering and light fixtures remain recognizeably automobile-like. Yet looks cannot be the sole criterion to the definition of a supercar. Above all else, supercars are so called for their speed and sheer gut-hitting power. The Lambo Countach is one, and the Ferrari Boxer. So, too, at the lower fringe, are the Alfetta GTV and the Porsche 924.

Sleek, speedy and oh-so-desirable. These are the supercars. But what can one say when confronted with something like the Morgan Plus 8? This happened to us recently in Penang, and we immediately thought of a bonnetted grandma. Well, looks can be deceptive, as we soon found out, for in terms of speed and raw power, few cars can come close to the Morgan. It'll put some of those sleek sportsters to shame, and this it can do without straining its carb. So back we went to our design board to cook up a

new definition for a supercar.

The Morgan Plus 8 looks like something out of the English country lanes of the thirties, and one can easily conjure up visions of it being driven by author Leslie Charteris or the Duke of Windsor. Its name also conjures up visions of King Arthur (Morgan Le Fey?). This element of medievalism and the carefree air of the thirties make the Morgan quaint in the modern context.

The shape is definitely that of the classic roadster. What is even more

emarkable, Morgan cars are not replicas, in the way that Panthers and
Felbers are. Instead, they are what one
may call anachronisms, and the irony of
it is that they thrive by being anachronistic. So year in and year out, the Morgan
stylists evidently take a holiday, because
the shape remains just as it was when
the company started making four-
wheelers back in 1936. And in all that
time the company has come out with only
two models worthy of mention, the 4/4,
based on the Vauxhall powerplant, and
the Plus 8, which is presently available
only with the Rover 3.5-litre engine.

Being a roadster in the classic tradition, the Morgan Plus 8 weighs less than
an equivalently engined saloon. It tips
the scales at a quite hefty 1876 lb, about
the same as Lancer sedan. But here the
similarity ends. Close to one-third of the
weight is taken up by the engine alone,
and the Plus 8 has a power-to-weight
ratio of 13.2 lb/hp, better than that of
the Lamborghini Urraco or the Maserati
Merak!

Underneath the topless profile of the
roadster lurks the 3,528cc engine of the
Rover 3.5 saloon. This V-8 powerplant is
slotted into the Morgan's maw virtually
unchanged. In this standard form the
unit delivers 143hp (DIN) at 5000rpm,
and 202 lb. ft. of torque at 2700 rpm.
This enormous amount of power and
torque propels the Plus 8 to a maximum
speed of 137mph. Top speed isn't everything, however, and in typical British
understatement, the manufacturers
claim a 0-50mph time of 5.1 seconds and
the standing quarter mile in 14.8!
Hmmmm. They must have had fun in the
thirties.

Our bright red test car was stock
standard, and very recently brought in
from Britain. Understandably, the owner
wasn't about to let us give it full rein. A
once-over included a long look at the
suspension system, which, even if
executed perfectly, would still be
labelled primitive. The Plus 8 uses a
system that is as anachronistic as its
styling. The front wheels are independently suspended, each with its coil
spring and telescopic damper. Linkage is
by vertical sliding pillars. At the rear is
found a rigid axle, with the usual semi-
elliptic leafsprings. Here, too, heavy
duty telescopic dampers take care of the
shocks.

With this kind of arrangement, one
would not expect the firmness of all-

round coils. The ride is soft, almost soggy, and on poor roads we experienced a lot of shaking and swaying. These, however, were not any worse than that experienced in a similarly sprung Japanese lightweight. In the same strain, roadholding could be termed adequate. Make no mistake; this car can go like a bomb, and with its antiquated suspension, the driver needs to be a really experienced driver to handle the Morgan properly. Poor surfaces can throw the car about in such a way that if there is a corner to be negotiated as well, one can easily get out of the chosen line. On these roads, too, the Morgan will show up some rattles from the panels and sidescreens.

The steering has a cam-and-peg arrangement, something most people have given up seeing, except in go-karts. In the Morgan, this gave a positive feel, the kind of directness that is in keeping with the character of the car. We would have preferred something more familiar, like the rack-and-pinion, but quite frankly this latter arrangement would be only for allaying our fear of·the unknown, for the steering worked flawlessly, with no discernable flat spots.

Slotting oneself into the Morgan poses no problem. Open the small door, sit, then swing in the legs. Getting out entails the opposite. However, the open top invites jumping in the way roadster drivers should, but doing this revealed one flaw: the door is not firm enough to withstand this kind of punishment.

Once behind the wheel, the driver is confronted with a dash vaguely reminiscent of the dogbone type found in the old Jags. This is one area where Morgan has given way to the demands of the times. Instruments are by Smith. The entire layout is so simple when compared to present-day saloons and sports cars. The speedo is located in line with the transmission tunnel, out of the driver's line of sight. Dead ahead of the driver is a similarly-sized dial, housing the temperature, fuel, charge and oil pressure gauges. At the extreme right, within the driver's line of sight, is the tacho, redlined after 5500 rpm. There are no stalks protruding from the steering column. The various functions are taken care of by rocker switches clustered between the speedo and the combination dials.

We found the gearshift a little tight, and, more serious, endowed with poor synchromesh. The first is unsynchronized, and we experienced a few crunches before we got the hang of it. Added to this, the clutch was heavy, and getting the Morgan moving smoothly would take the newcomer some time. One thing is certain, though. This car is not for ladies.

The wind-in-the-hair intention of this kind of car is really supported by the performance. With the owner in the driver seat, we clocked a top of 102mph before we ran out of road. The 60mph mark passed after a mere 7.1 seconds, and the ton mark in just another 12.5 second. The Morgan didn't give the sensation heart-in-the-stomach unpleasantness the Ferrari Boxer did, but the speed achieved is commensurate with a blue blooded sports car.

We left the Morgan with mixed feelings. This is one desirable piece machinery, but it costs about close thirty thousand to bring in. We may peasants in this respect, but that helluvalot of money if you're not fully love with something like the Morgan True, it's unique, but it's also a reflection of eccentricity. While its performance can be termed nothing less than superb, you'd have to be a little crazy doing the ton in an open seater. What next, goggles and beret?

● Test car courtesy of Lawerence Lo

BRIEF SPECIFICATIONS

Morgan Plus 8

ENGINE:
Rover V-8 3.5-litre; 3.528cc; 143 bhp (DIN) @ 5000rpm, 202 lb. ft. (DIN) @ 2700rpm; compression ratio: 9,25:1; material: light alloy block and head; coolant: water; carburettion: 2 SU type HIF 6.

TRANSMISSION:
Driving wheels: rear; clutch: single dry plate, hydraulic; gearbox: 4 speeds, 3.625, 2.133, 1.391, 1.000, rev 3.430; limited slip differential.

CHASSIS:
Ladder frame, z-section long members, tubular & box type cross members; suspension: front-independent, vertical sliding pillars, coil springs, telescopic dampers; rear-rigid axle, leaf springs, telescopic dampers.

STEERING:
Cam and peg; turns lock-to-lock: 2.5

DIMENSIONS:
Length: 146''; width: 59''; wheelbase 98''; track: 50''; ground clearance: 5'' Dry weight: 1876 lb.; fuel capacity: 13.5 gallons; turning circle: 38 ft.

PERFORMANCE:
Max. speeds: (1) 38mph, (2) 64mph, (3) 98 mph, (4) 137 mph. Standing ¼-mile 14.8 seconds; 0-50mph: 5.1 seconds.

MORGAN: WHERE TIME DOESN'T MATTER

The man himself: Peter Morgan in the grounds of the tiny Malvern Link works.

At Morgan, workmen use 50-year-old tools to hand-build their enigmatic cars and they deliver parts around the factory in wheelbarrows. It has never changed and the purists believe it never will. Peter Robinson stepped back in time to visit the factory where the past is the future.

WASN'T until I'd said goodbye and walked away from the funny old, reddish-brown factory that I realised it had been an anti-climax. The anticipated euphoria, even the bright eyes and goose bumps, were missing. Had I come half way round the world to have a dream turn into a matter-of-fact reality? No, it wasn't simply disappointment for I'd been totally delighted by what I saw, enthused by the quiet dedication of the men in the factory and charmed by the man whose father had created the whole crazy business 69

years earlier. Yet, as I unloaded my camera and packed my things in the little Alfasud for the journey back to London I knew something was missing.

In the back of my mind, perhaps the front of my soul, there was an inexplicable feeling that all had not been told; that rather than soak up the mystique through rosy eyes I had done a normal day's work and although all the questions had been answered I had still not gained an insight into the magic of it all.

On the other side of Pickersleigh Road,

Malvern Link, Worcestershire, England, from the Morgan Motor Company Limited there is a row of semi-detached wooden cottages. They are houses of workers. At 4.30 that afternoon two rather large, Coronation Street women in their 60s rested their heavy elbows against the picket fence. They stood not three metres apart as they gazed languidly in the direction of the small flow of traffic along Pickersleigh Road but they said not a word. Time, it seemed, was of no importance.

Would they, I wondered, know what the factory opposite represented? The first woman barely moved her lips and briskly referred me to the second without a glance in her direction. The second at least spoke in more than a monotone but didn't alter her expression at all.

"It's of no interest to me, I've never been in." There was a silence I filled with another question and then waited for the reply.

"Why don't you ask him, he worked there." She pointed to a man — was it her husband? — who walked down the path beside the house. He looked close to 70, his face showed no interest.

I started again, with the same questions. The response was slow.

"Yes, I know ... they build sports cars, they always have."

He leaned forward as if to whisper a confidence. "I worked for Morgans for eight years, then I retired. They were good, it's an old family business."

Now there was no need for questions.

"It was a very contented work force. I talk to the lads and they say it still is. Everybody is satisfied. You do a job and they leave you alone, there's no niggling."

He looked at me for the first time, as if to confirm that I was genuinely interested.

"Everything just goes happily on and I think it always will. The Guvnor wants to

Below: What's old is new at the Malvern Links works. Here an old and a young worker ready a car for delivery.

carry on the Morgan tradition. We all know he will. He doesn't want to get any bigger, expansion just brings an expansion of problems."

He looked at the Naples number plate on the Alfa.

"You know, they're always coming down here. You can see them saying the same words when they find the factory. And they always get out and take photographs and walk around. They come from all over the world."

With a self-assured, gentle understatement he went on, "We kind of feel proud".

I'd found my magic.

*   *   *

Malvern Link nestles tight up against the Malvern Hills in western England. It is a typical, small English village with the greenest of green commons contrasting subtly with the greenish-purple of the hills.

About 500 metres down Pickersleigh Road from the main street you will find the house of Morgan between Civic Engineering Contracts and Chance Brothers Limited. Moss grows between the slate tiles on the roof of a modest, low building that fronts the road. Three-quarters of the way along there is a small

Right: The Morgan pub isn't far from the factory and is yet another sign of the esteem in which the timeless cars are held.

Below: The enthusiast's dream: brightly-painted Morgans near completion.

entrance with twin swinging doors and an enquiries sign on the glass. "MM" is set into the brick at the top but a newer, larger sign that simply says "Morgan" shows you that you are at the right address. Lower down on the left-hand door that doesn't look as if it's been used for years there's another black sign that says "Morgan Motor Company Limited". There's nothing else except a tiny Messerschmitt Owners Club badge on one of the small panes of glass. The tenuous link is that they both once built three wheeler cars.

The door was locked so I tried the side entrance which leads into the factory. Morgans in various stages of construction littered the bitumen slope. A door on the left leads into the offices and spare parts store. A sticker on one of the windows says "I love God, country and Morgans (but not necessarily in that order)".

A young man walked past carrying an ice cream. I told him who I was and that I had an appointment with Peter Morgan.

"He's not back from lunch 'til two," he said. "I should take a wander around the factory." He had heard it all before.

Next to the offices is the delivery bay. Inside were 18 new Morgans — red, silver, green, white, brown and blue — awaiting their owners. Peter Morgan's Ferrari 365 GTC4 — his second Ferrari — stood out from the open cars like a Modigliani hanging alone in a room of Gainsboroughs.

It was the Monday after the annual Morgan Owners' club meeting which had attracted 300 Morgans and the works was full of visitors from Europe and America. The workers seemed oblivious to the intruders wandering through their factory. Just occasionally, they'd take the mickey out of any particularly rabid enthusiasts who asked a stupid question or got in the way.

At a little after two, three Morgans drove into the yard with Peter Morgan at the wheel of the leading Plus 8. I was to learn later he had been to lunch with the President of the American Club.

Peter Henry Geoffrey Morgan was born in Malvern Link on November 3, 1919, in a house next to the original Morgan factory that is now occupied by the local Ford dealers, Bowman and Acock. He is tall, and thin like the grey hairs above the friendly smile. His handshake is limp and there is just the right mixture of cultured aristocracy in his voice. There is no suggestion of arrogance. He is a charming man.

The office of the Morgan Managing Director is cluttered rather than untidy. Pictures of Morgans old and new hang on the walls, bound volumes of old car magazines and press clippings (called "press opinions" on the cover jacket) from the Olympia Motor Show of 1912 fill the bookcase. There is also a workshop manual for the Ferrari. There are two desks, the one against the wall is covered with letters and magazines, the one in the centre of the room has a leather top. Two bar radiators provide heating when it is needed. It is more a study than an office. There is no effective ventilation, so Peter Morgan's chain smoking soon fills the room.

We talk about Morgans, of course, and specifically the future. "I would like the Morgan name to continue and any Morgan male to be connected with it," he says. He hesitates, and then adds with a soft smile, "If he has anything to offer".

Charles Morgan is 26, a successful television newsman and occasional artist — he designed one of the Morgan brochures a couple of years ago. Based in London, he races the cars his father builds. Charles is also headstrong and an individualist according to his father and too young to take over the running of motoring's anachronism. And yet Peter Morgan knows that when the call from the somniferous little factory comes, Charles will return and life will go on much as before with a new, third generation "guvnor".

It seems there will always be a Morgan to give the constant stream of visitors the answers they want to hear as they watch their dreams screwed and bolted together on wooden trestles by carpenters and upholsters who are proud of their work.

Peter knows his history, it flows from the man easily. He has clearly said it all before, many times. Morgan, he points out, survived the intense competition of the '50s from MG and Triumph and the sales slump of the early '60s when the American market, which had been taking almost 90 percent of all Morgan production, dried up and left Peter with 17 cancelled cars on the water destined for America and another 60 finished cars in stock at Malvern Link. Not a lot of cars by most people's standards but nearly nine weeks' production for Morgan. It took nine months to get rid of the cars and production was reduced to just five cars a week. Peter Morgan swore he would never again allow one market to establish such dominance; today he exports to Europe, Australia, Japan and Africa and has just returned to the

Above: The "production line" at Malvern Link. Instead of mechanical monsters there are wooden trestles and tradesmen. The wheelbarrow, at left, is used to deliver parts around the factory.

Left: Part of the workbench area, where the bodies are built up from fine-quality Belgian ash — the same timber used to make top-name tennis racquets.

American market, on a limited basis, for the first time since the early '70s.

The resurgence for Morgan began in about 1965 when the French movie star set discovered the car and Brigitte Bardot, Catherine Deneuve and Jean-Paul Belmondo all owned Morgans (Peter claims Brigitte's Morgan lasted longer than Gunther Sachs). The British took longer to realise the rustic antique provided an instant vintage car when other sports cars were becoming softer and rounded, with wind-up windows and even half-way comfortable rides.

The once old-fashioned appearance of the Morgan became an attribute and interest in the cars increased, order books filled and demand has yet to taper off. There is no question that the proliferation of replicars has harmed sales of the Morgan — quite the opposite. If you are going to buy a car that pretends to look like something straight out of the past, why not have the real thing? The three-year waiting list for English buyers proves

that Morgan's quite deliberate policy of restricting production has paid off.

So Peter keeps his staff down to 110 or 115 and has no intention of growing beyond, perhaps, building up to 10 cars a week.

"If we built 30 cars a week we'd have to make concessions, they're pretty specialist cars," he says. "Most people who buy the cars know what they are in for."

His comment is a less than subtle reference to the ride, the one great compromise involved in Morgan ownership. The very limited suspension travel of the sliding pillar front suspension, used since 1910 on the Morgan three-wheelers and carried over onto the 1936 four-wheelers until today makes for a ride that is stiff beyond the experience of most drivers. Morgan recognises that "You need decent roads" to own one of his cars but counters that by adding "at least you don't have to modify the suspension for racing".

It seems the primitive ride is as much a part of the Morgan character as the classic this-is-the-way-a-sports-car-should-look styling and a more modern suspension system has no priority at all at Malvern Link. The heavy steering with its built-in slack at the straight ahead is something else. Peter admits he is experimenting with a rack and pinion system.

The present Morgan range of Plus 8 two-seaters — one four-seater has been built, (Morgan claims that four-up, the extra weight in the back upsets the car's balance), and one automatic — and Four/Four two- and four-seaters will go on indefinitely with minor improvements to "this and that" but no changes that are likely to alter the car's appearance. Even the small modifications will be, in a sense, forced on the cars because of government pressure in the areas of safety and engine emissions.

"We put the car in a wind tunnel and found a curved windscreen would improve it but it wouldn't improve the aesthetics," Peter Morgan says. "And it would be more expensive to replace."

Morgan's problems today are not so much worrying about what kind of cars it should be designing for the '80s but rather in ensuring a reliable flow from

Left: A young carpenter carries on the tradition of building Morgan bodies while behind, completed chassis wait to be fitted.

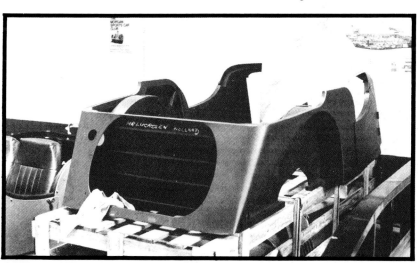

Above: The individual touch: the owner-to-be's name is chalked onto a partly-completed body. And of course, it's preceded by "Mr".

Not a car to drive on a bumpy road. The clearly-visible sliding pillar front suspension on these rolling chassis outside the factory is probably the biggest compromise a blinded-by-love Morgan fan has to make.

suppliers. The factory does not want to become dependent upon one engine supplier, a distinct possibility a couple of years ago when Power Torque — which supplies Morgan and all other specialist car builders with Ford engines — suggested the 1.6-litre ohv Ford engine was likely to be phased out. Leyland, it seemed, would be the only alternative.

Supply of the Rover 3.5-litre V8 was so difficult in the early days of the Plus 8 that Peter Morgan sometimes wondered why he didn't switch to the Ford V6 as he originally intended when Triumph dropped the four-cylinder TR engine in 1967.

Morgan still uses wood for the sub-frame — chiefly from Belgian ash — and glue, and hand saws, and wooden clamps, and hammers. Everything is done carefully although the finish at the end of it all betrays the primitive manner of construction. There is a trim shop with sewing machines, nothing is pre-cut or ready-made and the equipment looks as old as some of the workers.

Charlie Curtis, the chief tester, retired a couple of years ago after starting at Morgans as a mechanic just after the end of World War One. He drove nearly every Morgan built from 1927 onwards. Today, Taffy Burston runs the machine shop. He has been with the firm since 1920. By contrast there's young Gilmour — he wouldn't tell me his first name — who has worked at Malvern Link for a few years. "I envy them (the older men), they have all the knowledge," he said. "I just like what I'm doing, I want to learn as much as the foreman."

He means it . . . the work ethic is alive and well in Malvern Link.

Now Ford has decided to continue building the engine used in the Four/Four until at least 1985, so an engine change isn't likely until then.

In the two hours I'd been talking to Peter Morgan, the phone had rung twice, not because he had a bunch of secretaries protecting him but because that is the way things are at Malvern Link.

The Morgan factory moved to its present site after WW1 and the cars are still built the way they were 40 years ago. The cars are built by hand, and in a sequence that can change from car to car. There are seven factory porters who spend their days pushing wheelbarrows containing parts around the bays, dropping the bits in the appropriate spots or pushing the chassis from section to section.

*   *   *

On the way out of Malvern Link that placid afternoon I drove past Whitebread's The Morgan pub and reflected that only in England could such an enterprise survive.

For Morgan, the future is the past and there is no reason to suppose that it can't go on building cars in exactly the same way it has for 40 years. □

Left: A hand-beaten Mog body is hand-delivered to the next stage of its factory life.

Below: Morgan owners have their own brand of masochism. This German owner dropped into the factory before setting off to tow a caravan around Europe.

Morgan Plus 8

Classic old-style thoroughbred sports car from Malvern.
Rover 3½-litre V8 provides tremendous performance and flexibility.
Rover five-speed gearbox an improvement.
Excellent smooth road grip; violent ride spoils bumpy road cornering.
A car which deserves improvement it still awaits.

*It takes a bump to upset
the Morgan into the beginnings
of a slide (which followed this shot).
Bumps upset the Morgan a great deal
vertically but not too much laterally — catching
any rear end breakaway is relatively easy*

RE ARE
mber
nall
s today
ucing sports   cars of more
ss pre-war style. There is only
which can, without being un-
, be described as a pre-war firm
turning out pre-war cars. As far as
company is concerned, we are
ng about the first war; it was
ed in 1910 where its successor
stands in Malvern Link. The cars
creatures of the pre-second war
d essentially, although there
been lots of changes. Morgans
survivals, not pastiches like the
her J72 or Lima. There is a
g commercial reason for their
val — an order book currently
years long.

tocar was the first magazine to
Test the original Morgan Plus
the week of its annoucement (12
ember 1968). The Plus 8 is the

most
outrageous
survival of the Morgan
brood, since of course it uses the
Rover 3½-litre V8 engine to drive
an old-fashioned ladder chassis
based on a pair of torsionally whippy
cross-braced Z-section members,
with most of the body framing carried
out in ash, laminated or plain. Thanks
partly to the blessedly low weight of
the light-alloy engine, the car scales
only 19 cwt in the standard steel-
panelled version tested here. The
main reason for re-testing the car —
an excuse really, for we needed no
persuasion — is to see what effect if
any there is of the adoption some
time ago of the Rover five-speed
overdrive gearbox — the original
continued to use the famous old
Moss Gears four-speed, a distinctly
character-full unit which worked well
once you had been reminded that the
lack of any synchromesh on first and
not much on the upper three required

proper double de-clutching. More
importantly, we wanted to establish
whether this lovable veteran still deserves to be so loved.

What has changed?

Since the original Plus 8, that is;
the biggest difference is of course the
fitting of the Rover box. That has
done away at last with the short cast
torque tube separating the Moss box
from the back of the engine, and
brought the engine itself a little
further back. The Moss-box car used a
3.58 Salisbury 7HA final drive with
185VR15in. 80-profile tyres, setting
the overall gearing at a slightly short-
legged 22 mph per 1,000 rpm (the
124 mph top speed meant that the
engine was revving 450 rpm past its
power peak). The Rover transmission
has a 1-to-1 fourth gear and a 0.834
top. Tyre rolling radius has been
reduced with the adoption of 185/
70VR14in. tyres, but the final drive is
higher, at 3.31-to-1. Top gear mph

per 1,000 therefore comes out considerably higher than before, at 26.2,
while in fourth it approximates to the
old figure, at 21.84.
It is bigger than in 1968. Track is
larger, by 3in. in front and 2in. behind, so that overall width has increased by 5in. Wheelbase remains
at 98in. Partly because of the extra
size and partly because of a succession of small changes, the test car, a
standard steel-bodied one (all Morgans have aluminium alloy rear side
and back panels), is surprisingly
heavier, at 19 cwt; this is 1.3 cwt
more — an increase of 7½ per cent.
Has this affected performance?
The answer seems to be "not
much." Indeed, remembering that
when testing the 1968 car we were
blessed with near-ideal conditions —
0 to 5 mph wind — where this time it
was 10-22 mph's worth, there seems
to be little in it. Looking baldly at the
standing start figures (1968 ones in
brackets), 30 mph is reached in

2.2sec (2.3), 50 in 4.6 (5.2), 60 in 6.5 (6.7), 80 in 11.4 (11.8), the quarter-mile in an identical 15.1, 100 in 20.2 (18.4) and 110 in 31.0 (25.7). The wind is seen taking its toll from the quarter-mile onwards; the new car did 90 mph there where the old one was 2mph faster, with proportionate increases beyond. Interestingly, the old car shows up as consistently faster when you compare its top gear acceleration with the new car's near-similarly geared fourth — 10-30mph in 6.4 (5.8 old model), 50-70 in 5.2 (4.5) and 90-110 in 12.6 (10.9). We also managed to persuade the earlier example up to 120mph within the MIRA twin horizontals, which was not on this time.

Peter Morgan tells us that he would have preferred to have used the earlier 3.58 axle — now unavailable — with the new box, which would have lowered top gear to 24.2 mph per 1,000 rpm. When one examines the maximum speeds in fifth and fourth, one can see his point. The highest mean speed belongs, just, to fifth, at 123 mph, when the engine is making only 4,700 rpm, 550 rpm below peak power (5,250 rpm). In fourth, 121 mph corresponds to 5,550 rpm, which is 350 rpm over. Geared as it is, the two top ratios straddle the ideal. Changing gear at 5,250, the Rover box provides 34, 55, 82 and 115 mph which means progressively decreasing rev drops — nicely spaced ratios for general use, though a little wide for production sports-car racing. For the record, the Moss four-speed gave one 39, 66 and 95 in the intermediates at the same engine speed, and was necessarily wider-ratio'd, so that the heavier Rover transmission is a genuine improvement. It also brings with it a superb gearchange quality — light, precise, short of excess movement and always a delight to use, in contrast to the very stiff Moss one. Our only criticism is of the lack of enough spring protection against selecting reverse — certainly on first acquaintance, one tends occasionally to touch teeth when going into first. There is also totally reliable synchromesh on all forward gears.

Enough of figures for the moment; one must attempt to describe the tremendously satisfying performance of the car. The standing starts were sheer wanton pleasure — drop the clutch in at 3,000 rpm, and the limited slip differential encourages both big rear wheels to scream with spin most of the way to that excellent 2.2sec 30 mph time. Bang the lever through into 2nd and there is another yelp as the car leaps forward yet again. Both testers concerned remember faster times in more sophisticated cars, equally but no more exciting than in the Plus 8. It is a Vintage-looking roadgoing dragster. The Rover's effortless 198 lb.ft. of torque — at only 2,500 rpm — and its 155 bhp mean magnificent flexibility and super top gear acceleration, with instant pick-up at all times. In town you burble off the line in first, and plop it into top at 30. As before, just for the hell of it, we timed a standing quarter-mile done, with the help of clutch slip up to 7 mph (300 rpm), solely in the now higher top gear; it took 23.6 sec, passing the post at 70 mph.

You are certainly conscious of the engine's exhaust note from the two pipes, deep-voiced behind. It is easier than in many sporting cars to pass through inhabited places quietly in the Morgan, thanks to that flexibility. You can make yourself very audible, if you must, by opening the beautifully progressive, traditional roller-pedalled throttle — but there is no need for such crass behaviour where it might cause offence. There is also the clear clicking of the electric fuel pump behind your head; you hear that at town speeds too. At anything from 50 mph onwards with the hood up, wind noise grows to well-high appalling levels — it is a screaming hiss above 110 which is almost intolerable.

Economy

This is broadly speaking unchanged. The steady speed figures suggest that the new car is slightly less economical, but the overall consumption of 20.5 mpg is a little better than before (18.3). Exploit that flexibility and the car's lightness, combined with frugal acceleration, and some remarkable figures are possible — up to 27 mpg. But you have got to be a less than typical Morgan owner to drive like that all the time. Full-blooded use of the performance can reduce the figure to around 17 mpg. Oil consumption proved disappointing at 600 miles per pint (it was 500 last time, on a younger engine — 4,000 miles), due to the drain imposed by the daily bleeding of engine oil to lubricate the front suspension — you press a button above the pedals.

Handling and ride

Although we put these two subjects under the same heading in *Autocar* Road Tests, they can usually be treated virtually separately. It is not so with the Morgan. The handling is inextricably bound up with the ride.

The steering uses a Cam Gears worm and nut box, and is high geared, needing only 2.4 turns lock to lock for a 39ft 11in. mean turning circle. It seems paradoxical that a sports-car whose purpose is better agility, should have a restricted lock, but it has long been so in this case. Fortunately, the design of the car forces the driver to sit relatively close to the wheel, which helps him provide the muscle needed to steer at low speeds — and indeed at very high ones when cornering; steering effort

The heart of the matter — the Rover V8, nowadays mated to its own excellent five-speed gearbox. Access gets better if you undo the bonnet and remove it completely

Maximum Speeds

Gear		mph	kph	rpm
Top	(mean)	123	198	4,700
	(best)	124	200	4,750
4th	(mean)	121	195	5,550
	(best)	122	196	5,600
3rd		94	151	6,000
2nd		63	101	6,000
1st		40	64	6,000

Acceleration

True mph	Time (sec)	Speedo mph
30	2.2	30
40	3.5	40
50	4.6	49
60	6.5	59
70	9.0	72
80	11.4	82
90	15.4	92
100	20.2	102
110	31.0	112
120	—	

Standing ¼-mile: **15.1 sec**, 90 mph
kilometre: **28.4 sec**, 108 mph

mph	Top	4th	3rd	2nd
10-30	8.8	6.4	4.4	2.5
20-40	7.7	5.6	3.6	2.1
30-50	6.8	4.9	3.3	2.5
40-60	6.7	4.9	3.6	2.9
50-70	7.2	5.2	4.0	—
60-80	7.9	5.7	4.6	—
70-90	9.2	6.9	6.2	—
80-100	11.8	8.6	—	—
90-110	20.3	12.6	—	—

Consumption

Fuel
Overall mpg: **20.5**
(13.8 litres / 100km)
Calculated (DIN) mpg: 21.7
(13.0 litres / 100km)

Constant speed:

mph	mpg
30	33.1
40	31.8
50	29.9
60	26.7
70	23.9
80	20.7
90	18.3
100	16.3

Autocar formula
Hard driving, difficult conditions
18.3 mpg
Average driving, average conditions
22.3 mpg
Gentle driving, easy conditions
26.4 mpg

Grade of fuel: Premium, 4-star
(97 RM)
Mileage recorder: 1.6 per cent
over-reading

Oil
Consumption (SAE 20/50)
600 miles/pint

Brakes

Fade (from 90 mph in neutral)
Pedal load for 0.5g stops in lb

	start/end		start/end
1	40-45	6	50-60-65
2	40-45	7	55-60-65
3	40-50-45	8	60-60-70
4	45-60-45	9	60-65-70
5	50-55-60	10	60-65-70

Response from 30 mph in neutral

Load	g	Dist.
20 lb	0.15	201 ft
40 lb	0.35	86 ft
60 lb	0.60	50 ft
80 lb	0.90	33 ft
100 lb	1.03	29.2 ft
Handbrake	0.16	188 ft
Max. gradient 1 in 6		

Clutch Pedal 38 lb and 5 in.

Test Conditions

Wind: 10-20 mph
Temperature: 15 deg C (60 deg F)
Barometer: 29.7 in. Hg
Humidity: 55 per cent
Surface: Dry asphalt and concrete
Test distance: 978 miles
Figures taken at 11,000 miles by our
own staff at the Motor Industry
Research Association proving ground at
Nuneaton.

*All Autocar test results are subject to
world copyright and may not be
reproduced in whole or part without the
Editor's written permission*

Regular Service

	Interval		
Change	**6,000**	**12,000**	**25,000**
Engine oil	Yes	Yes	Yes
Oil filter	Yes	Yes	Yes
Gearbox oil	Check	Check	Check
Spark plugs	Check	Yes	Yes
Air cleaner	—	Yes	Yes
Total cost	**£35.76**	**£74.03**	**£75.23**

(Assuming labour at £6.50/hour)

Parts Cost

(including VAT)

Brake pads (2 wheels) — front	£11.65
Brake shoes (2 wheels) — rear	£17.54
Exhaust system	£103.12
Tyre—each (typical advertised)	£67.19
Windscreen	£36.18
Headlamp unit	£15.39
Front wing	£104.49
Rear bumper	£61.56

Warranty Period
12 months / 12,000 miles

Weight

Kerb, 19.0 cwt/2,128 lb/965 kg
(Distribution F/R, 47.4/52.6)
As tested, 22.6 cwt/2,528 lb/1,146
kg

Boot capacity: 4.8 cu. ft.

Turning circles:
Between kerbs:
L, 39ft 5in.; R, 40ft 5in.
Between walls:
L, 40ft 4in.; R, 41ft 4in.
Turns, lock to lock: 2.4

Test Scorecard

*(Average of scoring by
Autocar Road Test team)*

Ratings:
6 Excellent
5 Good
4 Above average
3 Below average
2 Poor
1 Bad

PERFORMANCE	5.89
STEERING AND HANDLING	3.77
BRAKES	4.62
COMFORT IN FRONT	
DRIVERS AIDS	3.82
(instruments, lights, wipers, visibility, etc)	
CONTROLS	4.10
NOISE	3.91
STOWAGE	3.75
ROUTINE SERVICE	4.17
(under-bonnet access: dipstick, etc)	
EASE OF DRIVING	3.66

OVERALL LENGTH 12' 3"
OVERALL WIDTH 5' 2"
OVERALL HEIGHT 4' 4"
GROUND CLEARANCE 7"
WHEELBASE 8' 2"
FRONT TRACK 4' 4"
REAR TRACK 4' 5"

Comparisons

	Price (£)	max mph	0-60 (sec)	overall mpg	capacity (c.c.)	power bhp	wheelbase (in.)	length (in.)	width (in.)	kerb weight (lb)	fuel (gal)	tyre size
Morgan Plus 8	**5,961**	123	6.5	20.5	3,532	155	98	147	62	2,128	13½	185/70VR14
Alfa Romeo 2000 SV	5,999	116	8.8	24.8	1,962	133	88.6	162.2	64.1	2,245	11.2	165HR14
Caterham Super Seven	3,948	114	6.2	28.3	1,588	126	89	133	61	1,621	8.0	165HR13
Lotus Esprit	10,171	124	8.4	23.3	1,973	160	96	165	73	2,274	13.0	205/60HR14
MGB	3,490	105	12.1	26.1	1,798	84	91	158	61.8	2,289	12.0	165SR-14
Panther Lima	5,564	115	6.7	21.8	2,279	160	97	142	63.4	1,949	10.0	185/70-13
Panther J72 3.8	—	114	6.4	14.3	3,781	190	109	160	65.5	2,504	28.0	E70VR-15

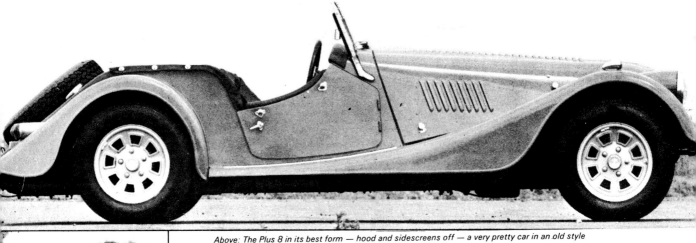

Above: The Plus 8 in its best form — hood and sidescreens off — a very pretty car in an old style

Left: Rear view through the hood is good, but there are bad blind spots to the side just behind the driver. Neat turned-up valar... carrying number plate is the type fitted for trials use; normal one turns down

Below: Sidescreens remove some of the side-draught when top is off, but obstruct vision with their frames

Inset right: Tonneau cover tidies up the back when the hood's down. Seats are comfortable, though one could do with more sideways support for the hard cornering of which the car is capable

is great enough when rounding a bend at the very high rates of which the car is capable for one to wish that the steering wheel spokes were made smoother near the rim.

There is plenty of feel, rapid self-centring, some (but not too much) kick-back, and quick response. There is also some perceptible play about the straight ahead, roughly 1in. at the rim. The weight of the steering makes fast corners excessively hard work, which is a pity because the car's smooth road limit is very high. It rolls very little. It is now slightly more rear-biased in weight distribution — 47.4/52.6 against 48.1/51.9 front/rear thanks to the new engine position — yet there is some marked understeer due partly one suspects to the limited-slip differential. It is very hard to make it break away behind even using all that 137 bhp/ton laden power-to-weight ratio — on smooth roads. Hit a bump, even quite a small bump, and the rear axle hops out readily, sometimes setting the back sliding if there's enough power on, at other times simply making the car wriggle sharply.

Obviously, the Morgan hop-steers, considerably and often, when so many roads even in Britain have bumps. On a few occasions, we also encountered some chassis-steer — true bump-steer — when a road irregularity made the car weave sur-

prisingly. It is a handful down a country road — not dangerous by any means, because in spite of its way-wardnesses, it is essentially very stable and will always put itself right — but you have to work hard. And of course the problem is mainly the ride, which is simply very bumpy. At the front the famous Morgan sliding pillar independent suspension allows 2¼in. bump, 1⅞in. rebound. Behind the movement range of the short half-elliptics is 3¾in./1in. The result is an understandably violent ride which is something else in 1978. You can argue that over many road in this country, the Morgan gets away with it adequately, which is quite true. After a while one takes pleasure in the stirring way the Plus 8 sweeps over open roads — the striding long-leggedness of the gearing and the always confident power allied to the short sharp pitches of the ride together translate into a wonderful bounding motion. But hit a heavier bump at speed, and there is a crash from behind as the axle hits some-thing, you bounce up in the seat — if the hood is up, your head sometimes hits a hood stick — and the car bucks itself briefly askew, wriggling straight again. There are bumps on some motorways which will do this sort of thing to the Plus 8 at high speed.

It must be understood that the Morgan is inherently stable. It has no

dangers in its suspension geometry which can build up into something out of hand after bump-induced in-stability. You can say that it is fun, which it is. Peter Morgan explains that he has not the slightest preten-tions to competing in the mass sports-car market. Whenever the ride is criticised he points out with a grin that "You get a pretty bad ride if you go hunting".

In our view, the Morgan is not a horse but an intrinsically charming sports car, and it need not ride so appallingly. As it is, driving a Plus 8 fast on the open road is unnecessarily hard work. Better suspension and steering would not automatically spoil the car's character.

Brakes

The disc/drum servo-assisted layout works well, indeed better than before in our experience, since over 1g is easily achieved at 100lb pedal effort where previously an annoying stick-slip tyre vibration at the front prevented the car bettering 0.92g at 85lb. The Michelin XWX tubed radials grip superbly in wet or dry, and the balance seemed just right. Our fade test revealed an interesting manifestation of the flexible chassis. By the eighth ½g stop from 90 mph, the pedal effort had stabilised reassuringly at 70lb maximum, 55 per cent higher than at the end of the first stop — the brakes had faded, but not unacceptably, recovering quickly

as they should. But during t... seventh stop, the front wheels beg... to tramp. During subsequent stop... the tramp would build up so mu... that one could see the front win... waggling in sympathy, showing th... the chassis was vibrating in twi... presumably due to some cycli... variable in the grip of caliper on d... when hot.

The handbrake is applied by... delightful fly-off lever. For the bene... of any reader unfamiliar with ol... sports cars, a fly-off handbrake is... effect a conventional handbrake w... the spring holding the release pawl... the ratchet working gently in t... opposite direction. To set the brak... you pull it back and press the t... down (which engages the pawl); ... release it, you simply pull the lev... back briefly and let go — hence f... off. The fly-off action on the test c... worked well, but retardation was ve... poor, at only 0.16g, and the bra... would not hold the car on any slo... steeper than 1-in-6. Restarts on 1-... 3 were performed with contemp... ous ease two-up.

Driving position and comfort

You sit, as mentioned earlier, clo... to the wheel by contempora... standards. There is just enough re... ward movement of the seat — a... justable in this respect which was n... always so on Morgans — to enable

96

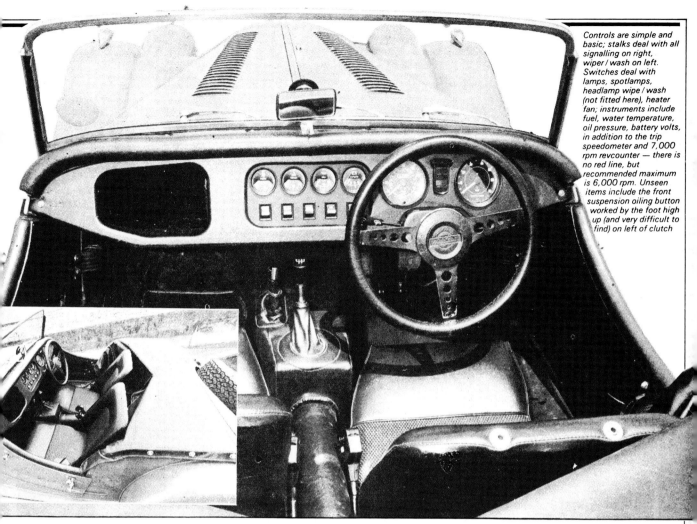

ix-foot driver to make himself comfortable, but it is a pity that there is owhere to put one's left foot except hreaded between the floor-hinged edals. Pedals themselves work leasingly, and heel-and-toe — heel nd side-of-foot in fact — changes are o problem. After one has caught a nee on it, one would be grateful for he elimination of the sharp rearmost orner of the scuttle; it catches you as ou get out. With the hood up, getng in and especially out is not easy, ecause of the tiny door. At maxihum speed, which for aerodynamic easons is achieved only with the ood up (running with it down costs 6 1ph) and indeed even at 70 mph, it is ood idea to clip the lift-the-dot faseners fixing the hood side valances o each sidescreen. It helps prevent ach sidescreen bowing out too much — but you must then remember to ndo the fasteners before opening he door.

.iving with the Plus 8

The view out over the bonnet is npressive, the lines of louvres apering towards the front, mphasizing the perspective. With ood up, there are serious blind spots ist behind one's shoulder, but the ear view is excellent. The mirror ibrates, so that one cannot always lentify everything behind. (A better rmer one is now being fitted, plus a cuttle-side mirror). The sidescreens

are almost more of an obstruction to view than a help, since for some drivers the eye level is roughly the same as the top sidescreen frame member. The car of course comes into its own with the hood down; removing and folding the hood is not difficult, though stowing the sidescreens is awkward. The sidescreens themselves cut down a lot of buffeting, but the car is nevertheless at its best without them.

There is a crude water valve heater, with two-speed fan. It delivers heat usefully, but with little temperature control and very slow response. One wonders how necessary it is, since a lot of heat steals through the bulkhead, making the car uncomfortably hot in warm weather in traffic driving, even with the hood down.

There are now three windscreen-wiper arms, toy-looking things in their proportions, which clear the flat screen well, leaving little unswept. The Leyland stalk controls put all signalling command on to the right-hand one, and two-speed wiper-wash on the left. Our only criticism here is for the horn to go back on to the steering wheel boss, where it surely belongs on this of all cars, and where it would in any case be easier to get at quickly. Headlamps give a useful light, assisted if necessary by the twin spot lamps.

Underbonnet space is crowded by the handsome vee-8, and for some

work one would be glad of the ease with which the traditional side-opening bonnet can be removed. Access isn't as bad as it is first seems.

Oddment space is limited to the open cubby in front of the passenger, and anything you can safely stow under your thighs in front of the seat. Even with the hood down, it surprises one what can be put in behind the seats — a reasonably minimum for two people's weekend luggage. One can lock the doors, but clearly you must rely on the steering lock to put off the thief happy to unclip the hood. It isn't the sort of car you'll put a radio in.

Conclusions

We can of course see why the Plus 8 has such a devoted following. Engine and transmission-wise it is more superb than ever, providing magnificent performance up to 100 mph; the fact that its built-in headwinds slow it appreciably thereafter doesn't matter much. Most of us would not want the shape changed; it isn't a modern car to look at and that is certainly part of its tremendous charm. And you *can* live with that ride. But it seems a waste not to match the power unit with chassis and suspension that allows it to realise much more of its potential. Sports car driving should not be unnecessarily difficult — and the Plus 8 although still tremendous fun, is needlessly hard work. □

MANUFACTURER:
Morgan Motor Co. Ltd.,
Pickersleigh Road
Malvern Link, Worcestershire

PRICES	
Basic	£5,095.00
Special Car Tax	£424.58
VAT	£441.57
Total (in GB)	**£5,961.15**
Seat Belts	Standard
Licence	£50
Delivery charge (London)	£20
Number plates	£10
Total on the Road	**£6,041.15**
(exc. insurance)	
Insurance	Group 7

EXTRAS (inc. VAT)	
*Michelin XWX tyres	£87.75
Aluminium body & wings	£117.00
Bonnet strap	£11.11
Non standard paint	£29.25
Leather upholstery	£117.00
Reclining seats	£70.20
Luggage carrier	£40.94
Spare wheel cover	£8.78
Headrests	£18.13
Carseal underseal	£18.48
Total Protection rustproofing	£55.58
Locking petrol cap	£2.34
*Door handles	£14.63
Towing bracket	£20.48
Badge bar	£8.78
*Fitted to test car	
TOTAL AS TESTED ON THE ROAD	**£6,143.53**

Full Bore
Morgan Plus 8

Michael Bowler tries a 10-year-old road test car that still wins races

– the truly versatile sports car

TESTING a modern Production Sports Car Championship winner may not, at first sight, seem to be the right sort of material for a magazine which respects the original; but, to start with, these cars run to very strict rules on standard parts so they can reasonably come within our scope; and secondly, the actual car that won the 1978 championship is doubly historic in that it, or at least some of it, was the original Morgan Plus 8 road test car, which I well remember driving and writing about for *Motor* in 1968. Then as now it bore the registration number MMC 11. In between it has been used by the Morgan Motor Company for more testing, development, the odd MCC Trial in the hands of Peter Morgan before passing to Peter's son, Charles, who has driven it so successfully in 1978 as well as in some outings in 1977.

A standard Plus 8 is no sluggard and is capable of reaching 60mph from rest in 6·7sec, 100mph in 19·0sec and a maximum speed around 125mph. This is achieved on a nominal output of 155bhp which reduces to some 115bhp at the rear wheels on a rolling road. Within the limits of the regulations which effectively allow "blueprinting" — hand-finishing of parts to exact manufacturer's dimensions — you can change the cam shape but not its lift, while carburettors have to stay the same size. Using the later cylinder head from the Rover SD with its manifolding, the power increase achieved is another 35bhp to 150bhp at the wheels. Because the car retains the old-style lighter chassis — albeit a new chassis following an accident — and because the ratios are better, this car still has the Moss-type gearbox rather than the current Rover 5-speeder and keeps the 3·58 axle ratio rather than the later long-legged 3·3:1.

Weight reduction is allowed with aluminium panels if these are a factory option which they are for the Morgan. Damping is free to your own choice but otherwise the suspension is standard. Wheels and tyres have to be those available from the manufacturer so it uses the 6-inch alloy 14-inch wheels with Michelin XWX tyres worn to a nicety — in older days of narrower wheels they would look like lightly patterned slicks.

I drove the car first in its ProdSports form with the full-width screen and a hood — hood-down adds a second to lap times. The Club Silverstone track was a bit greasy but the tyres hung on extremely well; you couldn't feel a lot through the steering at

that stage. You just realised that you were understeering in mid-corner and applied power; the resultant fairly sudden change to oversteer required some practice to catch cleanly, but it was quite possible and there was no lurch as it returned to an even keel — no noticeable roll. In these conditions of slightly slower lappery, third gear could be held all the way past the pits to Copse; fourth would be taken before the Maggots curve which I wasn't taking flat at that stage; third was then suitable for the tight Becketts which emphasised the good tractability of the V-8 pulling strongly and rapidly from 3000 to 6000rpm — hydraulic lifters have to be retained. As the track dried out the steering began to provide more feel with the higher grip and you could flick it into the corner knowing exactly what was happening at the front end, but with a surface still slightly damp it wasn't easy to catch the power oversteer cleanly.

I wasn't aware of any particular hood noise at speeds over 100mph although one obviously notices it in a standard road car on the road; the biggest noise apart from the muffled roar of twin V-8 pipes was from the transmission on the overrun after a hard season. Early lappery came down to 1m 13½sec which reduced to 1m 9s with the cornering line dry, but the rest still damp; Charles Morgan's Michelin time was 1m 7s.

We then had a lunch break during which time the Plus 8 was converted to Mod Sports form which, in fact, is a no-holds-barred formula, but for the Morgan it meant removing screen and hood and substituting an aero screen and changing the road tyres to Dunlop low-profile slicks, still on the 6-inch rims.

The effect of this was quite dramatic and particularly so bearing in mind that the suspension is standard Morgan apart from firmer damping; the ride is still firm and bouncy, even on smooth Silverstone and the car steps bodily sideways on the mid-Maggots bump at something like 100mph. The first flying lap, on a dry circuit now, was 1m 7·7s which came down to 1m 4·2s in about five laps, but it wasn't just the straight stopwatch differences that were impressive, the whole car felt quite different. The steering was now transmitting good feel of initial understeer and you could put the power down a lot earlier with a much more gradual transition to oversteer, it was much more controllable. In fact, I waited till my slowing down lap —

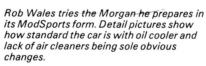

Rob Wales tries the Morgan he prepares in its ModSports form. Detail pictures show how standard the car is with oil cooler and lack of air cleaners being sole obvious changes.

just in case I spun – before really throwing it into Becketts with a boot-full of throttle, and it just went round in the most satisfying controlled opposite lock power slide that I have achieved for some time. I had been braking deeper and deeper into the turn-in without upsetting the car and doubtless might have gone faster, but I had learnt enough to know that the Plus 8 is a very safe and sure-footed track car as well as an entertaining road car. I had also learnt something about the effect of putting on slicks instead of good road tyres – for me it was something like $4\frac{1}{2}$ seconds difference (lower frontal area might have helped a bit) but even the regular driver shows nearly $3\frac{1}{2}$ seconds; and that was just using 195/600 × 14 Dunlop slicks against 195/70 × 14 Michelin XWX on the same width wheels.

The car has been maintained throughout the season by London Morgan specialists, Libra Motive Services (6–10 Rosemont Road, Hampstead, London NW3 6NE). Rob Wales started Libra six years ago having

earlier run a garage and got to know Peter Morgan. Libra had prepared Charles Morgan's 4/4 for racing three years ago and he asked Libra to do the same for MMC 11; while 1977 had been a reasonable season in terms of results the car had also doubled as a road car. For 1978 it became a track car and the results have been impressive with 10 wins, 4 seconds and a third with overall victory in the Production Sports Championship.

In its ProdSports form it feels just like a quick Plus 8; it is nice that someone is still producing a car that can so easily be converted into a competitive racer, but perhaps it couldn't go back to trialling with that 4-inch ground clearance. Retaining the style, despite the many improvements that have gone on over the years, hasn't affected the versatility that one used to expect from a real sports car in the 'thirties and rarely received in the 'fifties; with a Morgan you still can get that versatility in the 'seventies. ●

MORGAN
+8
TURBO

*For those who appreciate
their nostalgia straight-up*

PHOTOS BY DOROTHY CLENDENIN

THE YEAR 1936 was a momentous one in Great Britain: She had three sovereigns that year, with King George V dying in January, Edward VIII abdicating to marry the woman he loved, and his brother becoming George VI before year's end. In the midst of all this, one of her motorcar manufacturers, Morgan Motor Company Ltd, Malvern Link, Worcestershire, introduced its 4/4 model (that is, four each of cylinders and wheels) characteristically understating the point that 4-wheeled motoring might not be just something of a fad. To cover its bets, though, Morgan

kept its 3-wheelers in production almost to the end of George VI's reign, 1950 to be exact. Beg pardon, ma'am; that's the Moggie Trike, not George VI.

And if you're wondering why, in this twenty-eighth year of Elizabeth II's reign, we're making such a big deal of things that happened so long ago, you've not reached the proper frame of mind for appreciating the subject of this road test, the Morgan +8 Turbo. In our "10 Best Cars for a Changed World," R&T, June 1978, the Morgan garnered the coveted Henry N. Manney III Intransigence Can Be a Virtue Award. "After all," we noted, "if the basic design was good enough in the Thirties, it's surely adequate today." And prior to that, our last Moggie road test was back in December 1969, so you can see that the long view is important. Why this thoroughly delightful car evaded our road test scrutiny for the entire decade of the Seventies is partly that very little new happened to the Morgan, partly simple economics and partly a good dose of Gummint. For a long time, Morgan has had waiting lists that would be the envy of any other automaker. And Pete Estes, Henry Ford and Lee Iacocca know what we're hinting at—you get to a point where there are just so many cars you care to make, and that's it. Complicate matters with piles of paper required to show the car is safe and sanitized, and you eventually come to think the U.S. market is more trouble than it's really worth. As did Morgan in the early Seventies.

Enter Bill Fink and his Isis Imports, Ltd, Inc. and U.S. Morgan aficionados had cause for rejoicing. Bill set out single-handedly to import and legalize the marque, and his offerings today, both 4- and 8-cylinder models, are absolutely charming blends of old and new. And when we say old, we're not simply talking about last year's chrome trim being carryover.

Let's start at the front end by noting that Morgan's sliding-pillar independent suspension hasn't changed radically since the good H.F.S. Morgan set pen to drawing board in 1910. (Curiously enough, that's the year George V ascended the throne. See how much history we're learning?) In any case, the Morgan front suspension has steel tubes supporting two vertical pillars on which slide the hub/stub axle assemblies suspended by coil springs; disc brakes, hydraulic tube shocks and an optional decambering by Bill bring things more or less up to date. The rear suspension is a bit more modern, but then you've got to recall that the Morgan had only one wheel back there for the first 26 years. A live axle with Salisbury limited slip is suspended on semi-elliptic leaf springs and damped by lever-action shocks, those marvelous box-like contraptions whose sealing characteristics were always hinted at by the presence of little refill plugs.

These components attach to what is actually half the real suspending medium, a steel ladder frame of perhaps less than

are attached, another structure behind the cockpit on which the door latch posts reside, and Bill carves out a bit of ash door-frame to mount aluminum beams. Little of this shows, of course, but you can still see a painted edge of ash here and there, as is quite proper, after all.

Bill handles the fed's dodgem bumper regs cleverly, with hydraulic pistons taken from the Volkswagen Rabbit and attached to steel tubes backing up the stock Morgan bumpers. These and the relocated taillights look considerably less out of place than several factory botch-ups that come to mind.

Under the bonnet comes the real news since our last road test of a Morgan: The Isis/Jaguar Rover Triumph/nee Buick V-8 is now propane-fueled and turbocharged. The first is a standard feature of Bill's 25-per-year output; the turbo installation is a $2500 option for those desiring added kick to their nostalgia. The switch to liquid petroleum gas (propane or butane) makes particularly good sense for a couple of reasons. First, it allows a complete lack of emission controls and the attendant problems with certification, durability testing and the like, what with LPG running as clean as Joan Claybrook escaping a Detroit steam bath. As an added benefit, propane's 105 octane means the 9.4:1 compression ratio is perfectly compatible with the Rajay turbo's 6-psi boost. There's no need for water injection or other detonation protection, and Bill says he can tighten the screw to even more boost if you're really intent on excitement.

The conversion to LPG uses a 19.3-gal. tank located approximately where Morgan fits its ordinary fuel tank. However, Bill notes that regulations dictate a 20-percent air volume, so the tank's effective capacity is more like 15.4 gal. Also, with LPG refueling capacity being temperature-dependent, a visit to the filling pump (actually, it's a valve) may result in less than 15.4 gal. filling an empty tank. This activity is accompanied by considerable ceremony, starting with unlatching the rear-deck-mounted inlet and bleed valves, screwing in the filler nozzle, opening it and the bleed, then waiting until a piquant mist of propane from the

state-of-the-art rigidity. The tires are the other half of the suspension; think of the springs as merely something to grease occasionally. An ash framework is assembled atop the ladder chassis, and this in turn is cloaked in steel panels (or, as is the case with our test car, several of optional aluminum alloy). Neat, effective and, as we noted as recently as 1969, if it was good enough for the Thirties, why not today? Well, in fact, the feds have stomped in since then, and Bill responds with some added structure to fit the required door anti-intrusion beams. There's a hoop of rollbar stock behind the dash to which the door hinges

latter signals a fill. And it costs quite a bit less than a visit to the gasoline pump: By shopping around, we found propane at 77¢/gal. Now there's nostalgia, admittedly of the short-term variety.

By the way, our experience indicates that all propane or butane suppliers aren't necessarily able to refuel a car; this, because of motor-fuel licensing requirements. And there was one lad, probably fresh from viewing a Great War dirigible movie, who refused to refuel our test Moggie because thunderstorms were forecast.

The propane travels from the tank to a firewall-mounted ⟫→

vaporizer that's heated by engine coolant. There's also a vacuum-operated fuel lock/filter that keeps everything shut down when the engine isn't running. A single-barrel Impco propane carburetor replaces the V-8's two SUs fitted at Malvern Link and the propane system carries an automatic enrichment device for cold starts. Bill fiddles with the Lucas Opus electronic ignition to optimize the engine's propane compatibility: seems that propane wants more initial ignition advance than gasoline, but not quite as much overall. He says a turbo V-8 put out 200 bhp at the rear wheels during dyno development, so we'd estimate 225 bhp (SAE net) as peak horsepower at 5000 rpm with the Rajay wastegate set for 6-psi maximum boost. Some added guesswork gives the estimate of 240 lb-ft of torque at 3000, but neither of these figures suggests the beautiful driveability and responsiveness of this engine.

In fact, the total experience of driving the Morgan evokes memories that have improved with age. You clamber into the cockpit by folding your right knee under the scuttle, tucking that foot down to where the pedals lurk, sliding in and maneuvering your left leg to follow. Do all this in the correct order, and you find yourself facing a handsome wood-rimmed Nardi wheel. In fact, you do more than face it—you're up near this lovely example of Italian craftsmanship. But not to worry, because once you experience Morgan steering, you'll realize that laid-back straight-arm driving is for sissies. This is steering that exercises shoulder muscles, not just biceps.

The ignition switch is hidden beneath the dash, and the first few times it takes a couple tries to get the key in it. Evidently a Morgan concession to anti-theft considerations, and apparently the only one because with no outside door handles the locking latches inside seem awfully silly. All this can get reasonably complicated with the top and side curtains in place: Whether the car is locked or not, you slide a plastic panel of the side curtain open, reach in, fumble around a bit and unlatch the door. Speaking of top and side curtains, we can note that the Moggie's are exemplary of what English weather protection used to be. And honestly, it's not all that difficult to assemble or disassemble, roughly midway between the superb ease of a Fiat Spider's, say, and the Erector-Set fiddling of a Jeep CJ's. Having the top up is a mixed blessing, however. It does give some space behind the seats for storage, but anyone except for the shortest driver gets only crooked-head side glances at whatever might be happening to the

right or left. And the bowing-out, flapping and general lack of seal had our Engineering Editor calling his 90-mph sound level measurement of 98 dBA "the positive hinges of hell." No matter, chaps; the best course is to leave the top and side curtains at home in the garage anyway.

Top up or down, the Morgan's cockpit is a nice snug one. Directly ahead of the driver is full instrumentation, including a speedometer calibrated to 170 mph, a Smiths unit evidently left over from the D-Type Jaguar or some such. You like to think Peter Morgan got a deal on the last batch of them. The steering

column stalks are straight out of JRT right-hand-drive models, with the directionals/high beam/flasher/horn on the right and wiper/washers on the left. The handbrake along the driveshaft tunnel is of the genuine fly-off variety: Its button locks it on; a quick pull rearward and release unlock it. And also down on the tunnel is a device resembling a foot-actuated dimmer switch. This is Morgan's One-Shot Auto-Lube control, the depression of which causes a squirt of engine lube to pass onto the sliding-pillar front suspension. It's the only thing that's automatic about a Morgan's lubrication, what with a total of 10 sites around the car profiting from grease every 3000 miles.

But enough of these details. A twist of the key, and the V-8 throbs to life. Snick the stubby lever into 1st, ease out the clutch, and you're burbling away, looking down that long louvered bonnet at one of the classic views in motoring. Stomp the throttle (one of those little roller types many of us learned to heel-and-toe with), and gobs of torque at the bottom end turn into raspy turbo power as the revs build past 3000. Redundant though they may be with all this power, the gear ratios are nicely spaced and it's a gearbox you enjoy shifting for the sheer pleasure of it all. And if you get downright serious, you can go from 0 to 60 mph in 6.8 seconds and turn the standing quarter mile in 15.1 sec at 93.5 mph.

As for ride and handling, you've got to remember that terms like oversteer, understeer and suspension compliance were coined long after key elements of the Morgan were already in place. Essentially, it's a car that likes to wash out its front end first, although there's enough power available to provoke the rear end too. From a relatively rearward seating position, you sense the road at all four corners and watch that lovely bonnet bob up and down, back and forth. All the while, you come to appreciate the close-to-the-wheel seating because the Moggie's cam-and-peg steering gear is extremely stiff and notchy, just about impossible to turn at rest and affected with that characteristic remembered by MG TC drivers of combining lots of center freeplay with very abrupt response once the slack is used up.

At its lofty top speed, and this car will redline 4th fairly easily, things get busy indeed. Driven more sedately, though, the Morgan provides excellent input to the driver and it responds decently despite its heavy controls. It enjoyed a tight line through our slalom, for instance, with absolutely no lean and little squirts of power between pylons as it posted a commendably quick 61.1 mph. It bobbed its bonnet around our skidpad with a lateral acceleration of 0.791g. Not bad for Thirties suspension, eh? Yet both of these are smooth-surface evaluations in which the Morgan's ample tire patches, predictable understeer and quick steering fill the bill. No staff member felt it would be anything but a handful down a less than smooth twisty road at speed, and sure enough it was, exhibiting behavior that one staff member termed "St Malvern's Dance."

The brakes reinforce this feeling of vintage motoring. Even though they're modern enough disc/drum combinations, they're free of vacuum assist and required a super-high 60-lb pedal pressure for our 0.5g stops. However, they pull the car down evenly with excellent control, and distances from 60 and 80 mph were quite short at 157 and 269 ft, respectively. On heavy braking, the front end chatters up and down as the sliding-pillar structure deflects in reaction to the most definitely post-vintage width of the Michelin XWX 195VR-15s. Bill Fink notes that he's experimented with added bracing of the front end that mitigates this hopping routine.

But you can bet he's not going to change any of the essential features, because Bill is a believer. And after spending some time with this latest Morgan, we definitely understand its attraction. Modern machinery is easier to drive, but what's often traded away is the enjoyment of challenge and accomplishment. To drive a Morgan properly, you get to forget your daily concerns; you have to concentrate on the car and its operation. For awhile there, with the louvered bonnet leading the way, the transmission tunnel warming your right leg and the cold wind tousling your hair, you and the Morgan are very good friends indeed.

SCALE: 10 in. (254 mm) DIVISIONS

PRICE

List price, FOB San Francisco $23,500
Price as tested $27,625
Price as tested includes standard equipment (propane conversion), turbo sys ($2500), aluminum alloy body ($550), adj seats ($350), brown top, tonneau cover & side curtains ($350), Nardi steering wheel ($185), badge bar & badges ($115), decambered front suspension ($75)

IMPORTER

Isis Imports, Ltd, Inc, PO Box 2290, U.S. Custom House, San Francisco, Calif. 94126

GENERAL

Curb weight, lb/kg	2285	1037
Test weight	2475	1124
Weight dist (with driver), f/r, %		44/56
Wheelbase, in./mm	99.0	2515
Track, front/rear	52.0/53.0	1321/1346
Length	157.0	3988
Width	62.0	1575
Height	52.0	1321
Ground clearance	6.0	152
Overhang, f/r	23.5/34.5	597/876
Trunk space, cu ft/liters	4.4	125
Fuel capacity, U.S. gal./liters	15.4	58

INSTRUMENTATION

Instruments: 170-mph speedo, 7000-rpm tach, 99,999 odo, 999.9 trip odo, oil press., coolant temp, turbo boost, voltmeter, fuel level
Warning lights: oil press., brake sys, hazard, seatbelts, high beam, directionals

ENGINE

Type		ohv V-8
Bore x stroke, in./mm	3.50 x 2.80	88.9 x 71.1
Displacement, cu in./cc	215	3528
Compression ratio		9.4:1
Bhp @ rpm, SAE net/kW	est 225/168 @ 5000	
Equivalent mph / km/h		128/207
Torque @ rpm, lb-ft/Nm	est 240/325 @ 3000	
Equivalent mph / km/h		77/124
Carburetion		Impco propane (1V)
Fuel requirement		propane/butane, 105-oct
Exhaust-emission control equipment: none		

DRIVETRAIN

Transmission	5-sp manual
Gear ratios: 5th (0.83)	2.76:1
4th (1.00)	3.31:1
3rd (1.40)	4.62:1
2nd (2.08)	6.90:1
1st (3.32)	10.99:1
Final drive ratio	3.31:1

ACCOMMODATION

Seating capacity, persons		2
Head room, in./mm	37.5	953
Seat width	2 x 19.5	2 x 495
Seat back adjustment, deg		40

CHASSIS & BODY

Layout		front engine/rear drive
Body/frame		separate, aluminum & steel on ash/steel
Brake system	11.0-in. (279-mm) discs front, 9.0-in. x 1.8-in. (229 x 46-mm) drums rear	
Swept area, sq in./sq cm	226	1458
Wheels		cast alloy, 14 x 6
Tires		Michelin XWX, 195VR-14
Steering type		cam & peg
Overall ratio		na
Turns, lock-to-lock		2.2
Turning circle, ft/m	38.0	11.6

Front suspension: vertical sliding pillars, coil springs, tube shocks
Rear suspension: live axle on leaf springs, lever-action shocks

MAINTENANCE

Service intervals, mi:	
Oil/filter change	5000/5000
Chassis lube	3000
Tuneup	20,000
Warranty, mo/mi	12/12,000

CALCULATED DATA

Lb/bhp (test weight)	11.0
Mph/1000 rpm (5th gear)	25.5
Engine revs/mi (60 mph)	2350
Piston travel, ft/mi	1095
R&T steering index	0.84
Brake swept area, sq in./ton	183

ROAD TEST RESULTS

ACCELERATION

Time to distance, sec:
0-100 ft	3.3
0-500 ft	8.3
0-1320 ft (¼ mi)	15.1
Speed at end of ¼ mi, mph	93.5

Time to speed, sec:
0-30 mph	2.7
0-60 mph	6.8
0-100 mph	18.0

SPEEDS IN GEARS

5th gear (5000 rpm)	128
4th (5500)	117
3rd (5500)	81
2nd (5500)	56
1st (5500)	35

FUEL ECONOMY

Normal driving, mpg	16.0
Cruising range, mi (1-gal. res)	230

HANDLING

Lateral accel, 100-ft radius, g	0.791
Speed thru 700-ft slalom, mph	61.1

BRAKES

Minimum stopping distances, ft:
From 60 mph	157
From 80 mph	269
Control in panic stop	very good
Pedal effort for 0.5g stop, lb	60

Fade: percent increase in pedal effort to maintain 0.5g deceleration in 6 stops from 60 mph ... 8
Parking: hold 30% grade?	yes
Overall brake rating	very good

INTERIOR NOISE

Idle in neutral, dBA	65
Maximum, 1st gear	90
Constant 30 mph	82
50 mph	86
70 mph	93
90 mph	98

SPEEDOMETER ERROR

30 mph indicated is actually	27.5
60 mph	54.6
80 mph	73.1

ACCELERATION

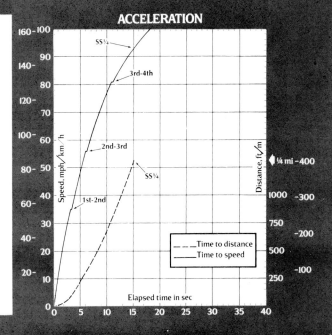

103

Pieces of eight

We look at Morgan's unique blend of tradition and performance that keeps them ever popular

It's a strange irony that while much of British industry is suffering from the effects of ageing plant and out of date methods, one company is perenially successful in that most fragile of businesses – small scale car manufacturing – simply through building an obsolescent model in an ageing factory with very old fashioned methods.

Morgan is the company, of course; to step into their red brick Malvern factory is to step back 50 years, back to a time when wood was as important a material in car manufacture as steel and cars were all hand built by skilled craftsmen. Nostalgia for these times has created a boom in modern day replicas of classic sports cars, but the difference is that Morgan don't build replicas – they still make the real thing.

Car buffs know the difference and that is why Morgan sit in a unique niche with waiting lists for their cars longer than Rolls Royce and customers just as prestigious, while some replica builders have learned the hard way that they can't muscle in overnight.

There's more to Morgan's enduring success than just building the right cars, though. They have been shrewd enough to keep the supply/demand equation always balanced well in favour of demand; content to leave waiting lists at an almost absurd length of four, five and more *years* rather than greedily mop up these customers with extra production beyond the nine or ten cars a week that has been their routine now for several years.

It might seem commercial nonsense to treat potential customers like this but by ensuring that demand always greatly exceeds supply Morgan have effectively isolated themselves from the vagaries of the economy. Even now, at the height of a depression and with exports to the USA priced high by the exchange rates, production hasn't faltered. All they have noticed is that some would-be buyers have withdrawn when they have reached the top of the waiting list – only to be replaced with eagerness by those below.

The hundred strong workforce that build the cars use methods that were the norm before the last war for all but the few mass manufacturers of popular saloons. But these days Morgan must train their own employees for the skills they require have become lost arts in the rest of the motor industry; few companies now need the services of skilled carpenters to fashion body frames or metal workers who can hand form body panels from steel or aluminium (though Morgan's craftsmen do get poached away occasionally by surprisingly exotic rivals).

There's still precious little automation to be seen at Malvern; the cars are moved by hand through a series of inter connecting buildings on a seemingly haphazard route that is actually a legacy of the time when the present factory was simply an extension of one across the road.

Assembly begins on the chassis (which are fabricated outside the company) to which are attached the mechanical running gear. No car starts the assembly process without having a firm buyer agreed – a tag on each car identifies it and notes any specific customer requirements.

Most of the mechanical components come from outside the company – and problems with suppliers are a continuing major headache. The two basic models are the Ford engined 4/4 and the Rover V8 powered Plus 8. The Plus 8 has a larger, beefier chassis frame and the Rover five speed gearbox but otherwise the two share a generally similar mechanical specification – both having Morgan's unique sliding pillar front suspension and semi-elliptic sprung live rear axles, or cart springs as the unkind say.

As the rolling chassis are being built up, so body frames are being formed from ash timber in the adjoining workshop. The ash, incidentally, comes from Europe and the shop's machines occasionally jam on buried pieces of shrapnel the legacy of two world wars. Th frames are clothed with panels steel and aluminium, rolled ar finished by hand, then the cor pleted bodies are mated up wi the rolling chassis before movir on to the paintshop. Here, too, th spraying and finishing is done b hand. Final stage of the assembl process takes place across the ya in the trim shop.

But traditional as the cars ar their methods of building may b Morgan still have to cope with th burgeoning bureaucracy that su rounds car manufacturing today and that is their biggest headach With exports going all over th world they have to cope with a international welter of regulation and red tape just as complex that faced by the industry giant The real problems are in copir with the Type Approval and oth regulations whilst not compromi

All Morgans are still made largely by hand in the traditional manner. Abo left: many components come from outside suppliers which can cause problems. Left: the start of the production process as bare chassis are built up with the mechanical components. Left bottom: in the metalwork shop body panels are formed by hand and fitted as the car takes shape

ing the traditional design of cars. It's a battle that Morgan ha been winning so far – but steadily getting tougher.

After visiting the factory we to a Plus 8 out for an all too brief dr through the nearby beautiful He fordshire countryside. If to look the flowing wings, the long bonn and the flat screen is to be tra ported back to the thirties, then drive the car is a rather harsl reminder of how things ha changed. It's a brute of a machin

Pictured on its native Malvern hills, the 3.5 litre Rover V8 powered Morgan Plus 8 combines classic looks with breathtaking performance (below) and a top speed of 125 mph. But vintage-style handling and roadholding can make it a brute to drive on all but the smoothest surfaces. Cornering power on wide alloy wheels and tyres (bottom) is impressive, though, on a good road. Order one now but don't expect delivery before 1986

that needs to be mastered in a way few of today's more sophisticated modern designs demand.

There's the sheer power to begin with. The 152bhp 3.5 litre V8 is sitting in a body weighing just 16 hundredweight – that's half a ton less than its usual Rover home – so it really can shift the Plus 8; 6.8 seconds to 60 mph and 125 mph top speed are figures reaching towards the supercar class. More impressive still is the seemingly boundless pull of the big engine in the light car; once on the move there's scarcely any need to change gear such are the reserves of power, while the rumbling V8 note is music to the ear.

But in the Plus 8 this wealth of power is allied to a chassis that it is not unkind to describe as crude. The suspension reacts to poor road surfaces by hopping and skip-

ping about, while the worm and roller steering is heavy enough to make cornering a really physical effort. The Plus 8 has to be fought round a bumpy bend with pure muscle power. Roadholding can be remarkable on the right surface, thanks to the roll-free cornering and wide tyres, but with that excess of power to weight the tail can be unstuck and the car slid gloriously around tight bends on the throttle.

It's not a formula for everyday motoring – except for the diehards – in Britain's all too often cold or wet climate. The spine jarring ride, noise and heaviness would make it just too wearing. But tucked in the garage beside a dull modern tinbox, waiting for the sun to shine and ready for a glorious, hooddown cross-country blast – that's a very different story.

MORGAN PLUS 8

A legendary car with a cult following, Morgan's formidable Plus 8 lives on, and how!

WE LAST tested a Morgan Plus 8 14 years ago. A carefully crafted anachronism, assertively old fashioned in everything but performance, we concluded that it was simply unique. And very quick.

Since then, men have walked on the moon, the micro-chip has revolutionised computer technology and the energy crisis has changed the face of motoring. But the Plus 8, like the Rock of Ages, doesn't change. With the advent of cars like the Panther Lima and Brooklands (née J 72), it's no longer unique, but with demand necessitating a delivery time that runs to years rather than months for each of the three Plus 8s that emerge from Peter Morgan's Malvern premises every week, the Panthers pose little threat to the big Rover V8-powered Moggie.

The inevitable detail modifications which accompany the production of any car have been modest but significant in the Morgan. In the days when Rover's 3.5-litre Buick-derived V8 came from the factory with automatic transmission only, Morgan mated it to a dreadful four-speed Moss manual gearbox (like that fitted to early Jaguars). Today, the Rover's engine and five-speed gearbox are supplied as a package to Morgan who only alter the postion of the clutch and fit "bannana" type exhaust manifolds before installing it. The Girling system brakes (discs at the front, drums at the rear) have also been improved. But perhaps the most

The seats are thinly padded but well shaped and supportive

important concession to today's technology is the recent adoption of fat 205/60 VR Pirelli P6 tyres on wider (6in instead of 5.5in) 15in alloy wheels. Inside, the facia — basic but not rudimentary — has been tidied up and the hood operation refined.

But essentially the Morgan Plus 8 is the same as ever. There's the graceful yet aggressive steel and aluminium body which is supported by Z-section side members and boxed cross members and rests on an ash frame; the Vintage sliding pillar front and leaf-spring rear suspension; and the antiquated cam and peg steering. New car specifications don't come more nostalgic than that.

Assuming you could walk into a showroom tomorrow and buy a Plus 8 (which you can't), it would cost £10,496. Whether this represents good value for money clearly cannot be judged objectively beyond the obvious fact that you get plenty of performance-per-£. A lot depends on your appreciation of such nebulous qualities as character and style and individuality. But that's not to suggest that the Morgan has the monopoly on charisma in the fast car ranks. The area of the market in which it competes is blessed with a rich variety of desirable machinery. Cars like the mid-engined Lotus Esprit S3 (£13,979), the semi-convertible Reliant Scimitar GTC (£12,490), the open-top version of TVR's Tasmin (£12,744), and Porsche's rapid 924 Turbo (£13,998), while lower priced exotica can be had in the shape of the mid-engined Lancia Monte Carlo Spyder (£9240).

These days, Rover's superb 3530cc all-alloy V8 has a compression ratio of 9.35:1 (in 1968, it was 10.5:1) and develops 155 bhp (DIN) at 5250 rpm with a walloping 198 lb ft of torque at 2500 rpm. We need only to add that the Plus 8 tips the scales at a comparatively modest 17.8 cwt to complete the picture of a high performance car, despite the far from aerodyne form its blunt shape must present to the air. Top speeds are often rather academic with fast open top cars like the Morgan since it can become physically painful to travel at more than 90 mph with the hood down, while the level of wind noise tends to prohibit going much faster with the hood up. Suffice it to say that the Plus 8 is good for more than 120 mph in short blasts, though even at this speed the long-legged (27.4 mph/1000 rpm) gearing ensures

The facia is businesslike, but the fly-off handbrake is a bit of a stretch on the far side of the transmission tunnel

that revs are kept down to a leisurely 4380. So high speed cruising involves no mechanical strain, at least.

What's more remarkable, though, is that the long gearing imposes not the slightest penalty on flexibility, which speaks volumes for the big V8's torque spread. In fact, its punch from low revs is right in the supercar class. Even in fifth, it covers the 30-50, 40-60 and 50-70 mph increments in just 5.3, 5.5 and 5.6 sec. Drop down to fourth (still 21.7 mph/1000 rpm) and the same increments are disposed of in a mind-blowing 4.1, 4.4 and 4.7 seconds. What this means is that, should you wish, you need never change out of fourth (apart from getting rolling) and still have enough performance to see off most quick cars, however slick their drivers' gearchanges. Just to put this into perspective, in fourth the Morgan accelerates from 30-90 mph in 15.2 sec. *Through* the gears a quick two litre

like the Lancia Monte Carlo takes 19.4 seconds. Even the earnest Capri 2.8 Injection driver (14.9 sec) wouldn't be able to get away from the lazy Morgan driver.

Neither would the Lotus Esprit driver away from the traffic lights. Aided by the fat footprint of the P6 tyres and a limited slip differential, the Plus 8 catapults off the line to reach 30 mph in just 2.2 sec and 60 mph in 6.7 sec. The Lotus pips it to 60 mph (6.5 sec) and pulls away thereafter as aerodynamics begin to play their part. But the Esprit is well over £3000 more expensive than the Moggie and unless you buy a Sunbeam Lotus (£7948, 0-60 mph in 6.8 sec) or the component-form Caterham 7 Twin Cam (£5916, 0-60 mph in 6.0 sec) there simply isn't anything else for less money with similar performance.

Figures aside, the Plus 8's usable performance is immense. In the lightweight Morgan, Rover's V8 is a giant of

an engine, a reservoir of smooth power that can be unleashed from 500 to 5000 rev in any gear to devastating effect. Overtaking is effortless and ultra safe. Above 5000 revs the engine becomes a little harsh and throbby, but you're less aware of this with the hood down. Then all you hear is the unmistakable exhaust burble of a fine, small-block V8, which all our testers found addictive.

Accepting that the Morgan's performance was exploited to the full, its overall consumption of 20.8 mpg is a reasonable result and not significantly worse than the consumptions returned by its mostly slower rivals; the class average is around 22 mpg. Our usually reliable Transflow meter was out of order during our MIRA session, so it was not possible to measure the Morgan's consumption at steady speeds. However, it would not be unreasonable to expect 25 mpg in reward for restraint and, on that basis, the car should travel around 340 miles on every 13.6 gallon tankful of four star.

Rover's five-speed gearbox can be excellent and the one fitted to the Plus 8 was among the best we've tried. Not blessed with the lightest of actions, the stubby lever can nevertheless be snicked through the well defined gate with confidence and speed. The clutch is rather heavy but exceptionally smooth and progressive. With so much torque to hand, the spacing of the ratios is rather academic but, at 6000 rpm, the first three gears run to 39, 62 and 93 mph.

The Plus 8's sliding pillar and coil spring front suspension dates back to 1911 and the first Morgan three-wheelers. To put modern generation tyres at the business end of such an antiquated and unsophisticated system might seem a bad idea. But according to Peter Morgan, the suspension is ideally suited to the low-profile P6s since, even when subjected to high cornering loads, it keeps the wheels perpendicular to the road, which is as it should be if the square-shouldered Pirelli's are going to grip to maximum effect.

This would certainly seem to be the case on smooth sweeping bends. Here the Morgan can generate quite extraordinary cornering forces and feel superbly stable. On more typical roads, however, the Plus 8 remains something of a brute, though not an unlikable one. It isn't car whose steering wheel you casually control betwixt forefinger and thumb. When you want to get a move on in the Morgan you must take a firm grip of the steering wheel with both hands and *drive* it.

One problem is the car's initial understeer, which gives the effect of reluctance to turn into a bend, es-pecially if the approach is bumpy. Once committed to a line, however, the understeer can be effectively neutral-ised by feeding in the power while, on tighter bends, the same ploy can be used to kick the tail out — though if the bend is a particularly bumpy one it doesn't need much prompting. Around town, the steering is undeniably heavy with only mild self-centring, though it does tend to free-up with speed. There is about an inch of free play in the steering too, which doesn't engender a feeling of precision about the straight ahead though fortunately the car tracks reasonably straight and true at speed.

Over big bumps and humps the ride is diabolical and the Morgan can actu-ally take off, but the small bump ride is contrastingly quite good, which may be a side benefit of the P6's low inflation pressures. The brakes perform well, with a good combination of progres-sion and power.

The Plus 8 is a strict two-seater with no boot but enough space behind the seats to squeeze a couple of squashy overnight bags. Legroom is restricted only inasmuch as the footwells are rather narrow and constricting though the pedals themselves are well spaced and ideal for heel and toe gearchanges. The driving position places the steering wheel close to the chest, which is no bad thing in view of the leverage it affords on the heavy steering, while the thinly padded seats are more com-fortable than they look.

The plain and simply furnished in-terior can seem a little claustrophobic with the hood up and seeing out at acute junctions can be a problem. Tak-ing the hood off, however, is a straight-forward exercise and, if the weather is right, open-topped is the only way for the Morgan to be. If the side screens stay in place so will your hair-do up to about 50 mph, but even at 70 mph the buffeting remains gentle. Other-wise, they can be removed by un-screwing a knurled wheel and stowed, with the hood, under the tonneau be-hind the seats. The heater needs to be powerful and is, while the instrumenta-tion is both comprehensive and reason-ably clear, only a couple of the minor dials being obscured when the tonneau cover is fitted over the passenger side. This, like the hood, is well made and reflects the generally high standards of finish evident throughout the car.

Old fashioned it may be, but the Morgan Plus 8 must rank as one of the world's great cars. Elegant yet elec-trifying, it marries such disparate ele-ments like no other car. Peter Morgan has been careful to preserve that and we think he's right. When the world is full of standardised shoe boxes, it's cars like the Plus 8 we'll miss most.

Centre-hinged bonnet allows good access

PERFORMANCE

WEATHER CONDITIONS

Wind	0-10 mph
Temperature	57°F/14°C
Barometer	30.5 in Hg/1032 mb
Surface	Dry tarmacadam

MAXIMUM SPEEDS

	mph	kph
Estimate	125 (see text)	200
Terminal speeds:		
at ¼ mile	85	137
at kilometre	107	172
Speeds in gears (at 6,000 rpm):		
1st	39	63
2nd	62	100
3rd	93	150

ACCELERATION FROM REST

mph	sec	kph	sec
0-30	2.2	0-40	1.8
0-40	3.4	0-60	3.0
0-50	4.7	0-80	4.7
0-60	6.7	0-100	7.2
0-70	9.0	0-120	10.3
0-80	12.2	0-140	15.6
0-90	17.0	0-160	21.6
0-100	21.8		
Stand'g ¼	15.0	Stand'g km	28.5

ACCELERATION IN TOP

mph	sec	kph	sec
20-40	5.4	40-60	3.2
30-50	5.3	60-80	3.5
40-60	5.5	80-100	3.5
50-70	5.6	100-120	3.9
60-80	6.7	120-140	4.7
70-90	7.6	140-160	6.9
80-100	9.8		

ACCELERATION IN 4th

mph	sec	kph	sec
20-40	4.2	40-60	2.6
30-50	4.1	60-80	2.7
40-60	4.4	80-100	2.7
50-70	4.7	100-120	3.3
60-80	5.5	120-140	4.1
70-90	6.5	140-160	5.6
80-100	8.0		

FUEL CONSUMPTION

Overall	20.8 mpg
	13.6 litres/100 km
Govt tests	NA
Fuel grade	97 octane
	4 star rating
Tank capacity	13.6 galls
	62 litres
Max range*	340 miles
	547 km
Test distance	534 miles
	859 km

based on an estimated 25 mpg touring consumption

NOISE

	dBA	Motor rating*
30 mph	74	21
50 mph	81	34
70 mph	93	79
Maximum†	88	56

*A rating where 1=30 dBA, and 100=96 dBA, and where double the number means double the loudness
†Peak noise level under full-throttle accel eration in 2nd.

SPEEDOMETER (mph)

Speedo	30	40	50	60	70	80	90	100
True mph	28	38	48	58	68	78	88	98

Distance recorder: 4.7 per cent fast

WEIGHT

	cwt	kg
Unladen weight*	17.8	904
Weight as tested	21.5	1092

*with fuel for approx 50 miles

Performance tests carried out by Motor staff at the Motor Industry Research Association proving ground, Lindley.

Test Data: World Copyright reserved. No reproduction in whole or part without written permission.

GENERAL SPECIFICATION

ENGINE

Cylinders	V8
Capacity	3528cc (215.1 cu in)
Bore/stroke	88.9/71.1mm
	(3.50/2.80in)
Cooling	Water
Block	Aluminium alloy
Head	Aluminium alloy
Valves	Pushrod ohv
Cam drive	Chain
Compression	9.35:1
Carburetter	Twin SU HIF 6
Bearings	5 main
Max power	155 bhp (DIN) at 5250 rpm
Max torque	198 lb ft (DIN) at 2500 rpm

TRANSMISSION

Type	5-speed manual
Clutch dia	9.5in
Actuation	Hydraulic
Internal ratios and mph/1000 rpm	
Top	0.792:1/27.4
4th	1.000:1/21.7
3rd	1.396:1/15.5
2nd	2.087:1/10.4
1st	3.321:1/6.5
Rev	3.428:1
Final drive	3.31:1

BODY/CHASSIS

Construction	Separate chassis; part steel, part alloy body on ash frame

SUSPENSION

Front	Independent by vertical sliding pillars; coil springs telescopic dampers
Rear	Live axle with semi-elliptic leaf springs; lever arm dampers

STEERING

Type	Cam and peg
Assistance	None

BRAKES

Front	Discs, 11.0 in dia
Rear	Drums, 9.0 in dia
Park	On rear
Servo	Yes
Circuit	Split front/rear
Rear valve	No
Adjustment	Manual

WHEELS/TYRES

Type	Alloy, 6½ x 15 in
Tyres	Pirelli P6, 205/60 VR 15
Pressures	20/20 psi F/R (normal)
	22/22 psi F/R (full load/high speed)

ELECTRICAL

Battery	12V, 50 Ah
Earth	Negative
Generator	Alternator, 65 amp
Fuses	3
Headlights	
type	Cibie Halogen
dip	100 W total
main	120 W total

Make: Morgan
Model: Plus 8
Maker: Morgan Motor Co Ltd, Pickersleigh Rd, Malvern Link, Worcs WR14 2LL
Tel: 06845-3104
Price: £8425.00 plus £702.08 Car Tax plus £1369.06 VAT equals £10,496.14

TheRivals

Other possible rivals include the Datsun 280ZX Targa (£10,871), Ferrari 308 GTSi (£22,699), Fiat X1/9 (£6,345), Mercedes 280SL (£16,930), and Panther Brooklands 4.2 (£22,950)

MORGAN PLUS 8 £10,496

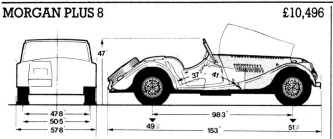

Power, bhp/rpm	155/5250
Torque, lb ft/rpm	198/2500
Tyres	205/60 VR 15
Weight, cwt	17.8
Max speed, mph	125e
0-60 mph, sec	6.7
30-50 mph in 4th, sec	4.1
Overall mpg	20.8
Touring mpg	—
Fuel grade, stars	4
Boot capacity, cu ft	N/A
Test date	May 15, 1982

Perhaps the last remaining example of the true sports car. Combination of vintage chassis and low-profile Pirelli P6 tyres gives tremendous grip on smooth bends (though bumps can make life interesting). Rover V8 has huge low and mid-range punch and 5-speed gearbox is a joy. Classic looks, fine finish. Nothing like it in the right conditions.

LANCIA MONTE CARLO SPYDER £9,240

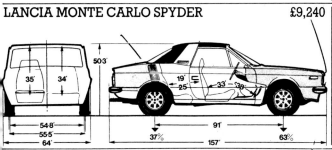

Power, bhp/rpm	120/6000
Torque, lb ft/rpm	126/3400
Tyres	185/65 HR 14
Weight, cwt	19.7
Max speed, mph	115.8
0-60 mph, sec	9.0
30-50 mph in 4th, sec	6.9
Overall mpg	23.3
Touring mpg	28.0
Fuel grade, stars	4
Boot capacity, cu ft	6.3
Test date	May 30, 1981

A car of uneven ability, Lancia's revised Montecarlo no longer misbehaves in the wet, has excellent roadholding and good handling and brakes, a comfortable ride, and good performance with reasonable economy. Comfortable for medium size drivers but badly cramped for tall ones, instruments badly placed, and heating and ventilation poor. Worst fault is excessive engine noise which some testers considered unacceptable; others enjoyed the car despite its failings.

LOTUS ESPRIT S3 £13,979

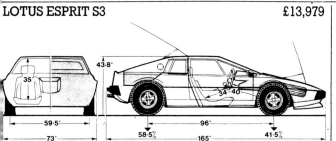

Power, bhp/rpm	160/6500
Torque, lb ft/rpm	160/5000
Tyres	195/60 VR 15; 235/60 VR 15
Weight, cwt	21.0
Max speed, mph	135e
0-60 mph, sec	6.5
30-50 mph in 4th, sec	6.9
Overall mpg	23.1
Touring mpg	24.5
Fuel grade, stars	4
Boot capacity, cu ft	6.6
Test date	August 22, 1981

A very much improved car in its latest S3 form, with outstanding handling and roadholding and a comfortable ride. Excellent performance backed up by impressive economy, safe brakes and a reasonably good gearchange. Greatly reduced noise levels make it much more pleasant to drive, but very poor visibility (worsened by stray reflections in instruments and glass division) is an inherent fault. Fair accommodation for two people with soft luggage.

PORSCHE 924 TURBO £13,998

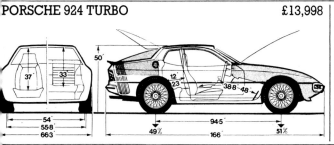

Power, bhp/rpm	170/5500
Torque, lb ft/rpm	181/3500
Tyres	185/70 VR 15
Weight, cwt	23.7
Max speed, mph	140†
0.60 mph, sec	7.0
30-50 mph in 4th, sec	8.8
Overall mpg	21.0
Touring mpg	—
Fuel grade, stars	4
Boot capacity, cu ft	4.8
Test Date	January 26, 1980
†Estimated	

Turbocharged version of Porsche's 2-litre, four-cylinder, front-engined but rear wheel drive 924. Performance when the turbocharger is on boost is in the supercar class, but is poor at low speeds and revs — claimed to be better on latest models, as is fuel consumption, which was excellent even in 1980 form. Too much road noise, poor ventilation, low-speed handling and gearchange are minor flaws in an otherwise superb machine.

RELIANT SCIMITAR GTC £12,490

Power, bhp/rpm	135/5200
Torque, lb ft/rpm	152/3000
Tyres	185 HR 14
Weight, cwt	26.3
Max speed, mph	114.1
0-60 mph, sec	9.7
30-50 mph in 4th, sec	8.5
Overall mpg	23.7
Touring mpg	27.4
Fuel grade, stars	4
Boot capacity, cu ft	6.6
Test date	June 14, 1980

Using the same formula of four seats and a soft top, the Scimitar GTC plugs the market gap left by the Triumph Stag. Like the GTE on which it's based, the GTC, now powered by the 2.8-litre Ford V6, combines flexible performance with impressive economy in an attractive, if expensive, package. Precise handling and excellent hood are plus points a hard ride, dated interior and poor gearchange earn black marks.

TVR TASMIN CONVERTIBLE £12,744

Power, bhp/rpm	160/5700
Torque, lb ft/rpm	162/4300
Tyres	205/60 VR 14
Weight, cwt	21.5
Max speed, mph	128e
0-60 mph, sec	7.8
30-50 mph in 4th, sec	8.9
Overall mpg	22.4
Touring mpg	—
Fuel grade, stars	4
Boot capacity, cu ft	3.5
Test date	April 18, 1981

Plugging the gap between ordinary and exotic sports cars, and one of the few traditional convertibles left, the Tasmin has strong performance (albeit not in the same league as the Morgan), powerful brakes, satisfying transmission and comfortable interior for two. Plush finish, good ventilation and respectable ride reflect TVR's increasing maturity. Good fuel consumption but too much wind noise; steering kick-back we criticised in our test is now claimed to have been eliminated.

FACTORY VISIT
Morgan Motor Company

THERE is something pleasantly reassuring about a visit to the Morgan Motor Company's factory in Malvern Link. "Just write what you wrote last time!" grinned the jovial Geoff Margetts, the company's accountant, as we began our stroll round the old, but surprisingly light and airy plant. And he wasn't intending to be sarcastic or flippant in any way. The Morgan company hasn't changed its attitude and philosophy for years now: not because it's consciously *resisting* change, but simply because it knows what it can do best and has accumulated a loyal *coterie* of enthusiasts who acquire these vintage-styled sports cars with an impressive regularity. It is 101 years since H. F. S. Morgan was born at Stoke Lacy Rectory, Hereford. This ambitious man served an apprenticeship as a pupil of the famous Great Western Railway chief engineer William Dean in the years around the turn of the century before abandoning a career as a budding locomotive engineer and turning his hand to mastering the intricacies of the "new fangled" internal combustion engine. By 1911 H. F. S. Morgan had made his first three-wheeler, powered by a 7 h.p.

Peugeot engine, and thus laid the first foundations for a company which survives in his family's ownership to this day, now presided over by his son, Peter.

Peter Morgan sustains a bubbling, infectious enthusiasm for matters motoring and, in particular, matters Morgan! He has controlled the company since his father's death in 1959 and the way in which his office door seems ever open to his 115-plus employees is indicative of the man's character. While he's quite obviously the boss, he remembers the Morgan company's hard times with clarity and in no sense is a chief executive ruling in isolation. Mrs. Peter Morgan, it should be said, helps out in the accounts department and with son Charles campaigning the company's products round Britain's club circuits (when he's not working as a London-based film cameraman), there is clearly still a strong element of family continuity in the operation of the company.

In a world where we're used to hearing about small specialist car companies getting into financial deep water, how has Morgan survived? Peter Morgan's philosophy is firmly rooted in personal family experience. "My father learned one commercial lesson very early on," he smiled broadly. "Back in 1923, I think it was, father built no fewer than 2,000 three-wheelers. Then along came the Austin Seven and once that took off in a big way, suddenly our demand dropped

dramatically. It was that experience that prompted him to always remind me 'never forget that demand should always run slightly ahead of supply'. And I've tried never to forget that advice."

Quizzing Peter Morgan a little further on the enormously long waiting list quoted for Morgan products, he's also very realistic. He admits quite frankly that, on paper, there are orders running forward for the next five or six years. "But I feel that the list would shorten quite dramatically if we were suddenly to tell all those people who've ordered a Morgan 'you can pick your car up next week — and can you arrange the money', then I think that the waiting list would shrink somewhat!" When a car is ordered, the factory does not ask for a deposit, only asking for a nominal £500 when work on the specific car begins — which means it is between three and four months away from completion.

The current Morgan range comprises the Rover-engined Plus-8 offering 155 b.h.p. from its GM-derived power unit, and the 4/4 which is available with the Ford CVH 1,597 c.c. four-cylinder engine (as marketed in the XR3) or the

1,584 c.c. twin overhead camshaft Fiat motor. Peter Morgan reflects that a total of 4,000 Plus-8s have been made since the car's introduction in 1968 and a lot of minor changes have been incorporated in the design since that time. When the car was first launched, Morgan had to adopt a Moss gearbox because the Rover saloon in which the engine was first publicly launched was only fitted with automatic transmission. From 1972 a four-speed gearbox was offered on the Plus-8 and now, of course, it boasts the excellent five-speed change from the contemporary Rover 3500 V8 saloon. Supply of outside components can always be a bit of a headache: Peter Morgan cites the change from Rubery Owen to Rockwell Thompson for chassis frames and an element of concern over the 4/4's engine supply once it was appreciated that the push-rod "Kent" four-cylinder Ford unit would no longer conform to emission requirements for the USA.

"We tried Ford's single overhead cam engine but it was too tall for the 4/4 chassis layout," he continues, "so we then had a look at the Fiat twin-cam only for one of Ford's senior management men to come onto our stand at the Motor Show intent on ordering a 4/4. He looked aghast when he saw it had got a Fiat engine and said 'we can't have that'. . ." That chance meeting turned Peter Morgan's attention to the CVH engine which has thus been available in the 4/4 since April 1981. "It's a British engine, built in Bridgend in South Wales," says Peter Morgan with some pleasure, "but I reckon we're still taking 20 per cent. of our 4/4 orders to be fitted with the Fiat engine". But Morgan will continue to offer both engines as alternatives for their 4/4 customers, the company obviously unwilling to put all its eggs in one particular basket.

This vulnerability of small firms to the whims of outside suppliers has been a factor with which Morgan has become occasionally acquainted. Back in the early 1950s there was some tension between Morgan and Standard's Sir John Black (who'd been a draughtsman with the Malvern company when he was younger, incidentally!) when it was found that the Standard Vanguard engined Morgan proved to be quicker than the

Triumph TR2! At one point the supply of Vanguard engines was reduced to a trickle, but when Triumph realised that Morgan was never going to encroach on the volume sports car market the problems eased. It was the same in the late 1960s when Morgan sought permission to use the GM-derived V8 in the new Plus-8. At the same time, Triumph were anxiously trying to get permission to fit this V8 into the TR4A but, while permission was eventually given by GM to allow Morgan to have this engine, there was never such sympathetic reaction for the bigger manufacturer! Peter Morgan admits with a wry smile that permission to use the V8 was granted "as long as you don't make too many. . . ." With only three Plus-8s emerging complete from the Malvern factory in 1982, there was never much problem about that.

Over the years Morgan has built up an impressive export market and today 47 per cent. of their output go to deals in Australia, Austria, Belgium, Canada, Denmark, France, Germany, Holland, Italy, Ireland, Japan, Luxembourg, Spain, South Africa, Sweden, Switzerland and, of course, the USA. In the early 1960s Morgan had developed to a point where almost 80 per cent. of their production was exported to the United States, so when there was a recession at that time in North America, the Malvern factory was hard hit. For eleven months, Morgan's West Coast US dealer didn't take a single car. It was on occasions such as this that Peter Morgan's adherence to his father's principles of not overstepping himself paid off. The company was able to ride out the problem, even though things were a bit marginal for a time. This attitude has also enabled Morgan to fend off the occasional takeover bid: Peter Morgan may be mild-mannered, but it's obvious that he cherishes the company's independence above all else.

A walk round the production shops reveals that

CONTINUED ON PAGE 125

METHODS of Morgan construction have hardly changed for a generation. On the opposite page (top), the wooden body frames are seen receiving their steel panels. The two pictures at the bottom of page 1048 show the basic chassis frames receiving their running gear and the body frames themselves being fashioned from Belgian ash. Driving power behind the company is Peter Morgan (centre) whose personal Plus-8 is seen in the two shots below on this page. Above, Morgans of varying specifications and colours can be seen crowded into the trim shop just prior to completion.

MORGAN 4/4

It's twenty years since Motor last tested a four-cylinder Morgan. Now powered by Ford's Escort XR3 engine, the 4/4 has good economy to its credit, but can it match the charisma of its V8-engined big brother?

WE NEVER tested a Morgan 4/4 powered by Ford's crossflow Kent engine. Now we've missed our chance. More than two years ago, Peter Morgan knew that the ubiquitous pushrod unit must soon succumb to tougher European emission regulations, and was already searching for a replacement. Ford offered their 1.6-litre single overhead camshaft engine (as used in the Cortina and Capri) but Morgan thought Fiat's 1.6-litre twin-cam looked more promising, an added attraction being the five-speed gearbox that went with it. Development went ahead and a Fiat-engined test car was built.

Ford's interest in the future of the

4/4, however, was far from dead. At the 1980 Motor Show in Birmingham, a high-ranking Ford official came on to the Morgan stand looking concerned. He asked if it was true that future 4/4s would be Fiat-powered. His probing was more than professional since he had one on order and, being a Ford man, he would have to cancel it if the Morgan was going to arrive with a Fiat engine under its long, louvred bonnet.

The incident prompted Ford to revise their stance and Peter Morgan was told that the new Escort CVH engine — the high-tune 1.6-litre XR3 version — would be made available. But there were snags. This engine had been designed for mounting transversely and

driving the front wheels. Ford, however, were only too willing to help and eventually solved the problem by replacing the standard XR3 sump with the more tapered variety from a Cortina so that when the Morgan-designed flywheel was fitted, the engine would mate with a Capri bell-housing and a Cortina gearbox for installation "north to south" in the 4/4. In addition, new engine mountings and a new exhaust system had to be devised along with a special recessed bulkhead to accommodate the rearward projecting distributor.

So now Morgan customers have the choice of either Fiat or Ford power for their 4/4 and it's the XR3-engined ver-

sion we test here. As well as being a modern, efficient sohc design, the 1597cc CVH engine is also a good deal more powerful than the old Kent unit (96 against 84 bhp), and even a little torquier (98 against 92 lb ft). As for the rest of the specification, it remains as antiquated as the engine is new, with worm and nut steering, sliding pillar type suspension at the front (leaf springs at the back) and a Z-section steel chassis supporting an ash wood frame to which the steel and aluminium body panels are fixed. Braking is by 11 in discs at the front and 9 in drums at the rear, but there is no servo or pressure limiting valve. The styling hasn't changed in 25 years and evokes a period even earlier. It's graceful and superbly balanced.

The retail price of Morgans is rather academic. Demand for these cars so far outstrips supply that anyone contemplating purchase now must either pay over the odds for a car straight away or wait years for delivery and watch the price climb with inflation. Nor can the usual criteria be used to judge value for money. The 4/4 makes a virtue out of being old-fashioned; its ride and handling on bumpy roads would simply appal anyone used to even the most stiffly sprung of today's sporting saloons, yet some would argue that for a quasi-Vintage car such things are only right, even desirable. We're inclined to say that a Morgan with modern steering and suspension would be even more desirable.

At £7,245, the 4/4's only direct rival is the Panther Lima (£6,455) which, indeed, embodies the "old-style-with-modern-mechanicals" philosophy to reasonably good effect, though its styling lacks the look of authenticity and is even less practical than the Morgan's. In complete contrast, Fiat's X1/9 (£6,345) and, from the same stable, Lancia's capable but ill-starred Montecarlo Spyder (£9,240) offer a degree of open-air motoring — both have removable roof sections — and two-seater accommodation, but with standards of grip and responsiveness only a mid-engined chassis configuration can provide. Both the Italian cars are quicker than the Morgan, too, the near 120 mph Lancia by a big margin. VW's fwd and fuel-injected Golf GLi Cabriolet (£7,812) is another nimble mover with crisp handling, and combines these virtues with a completely retractable hood and full four-seater accommodation. For those who don't mind being closed in, Porsche's efficient and fine handling 924 (£9,494) is yet another alternative.

Weighing just over 15 cwt and propelled by the XR3 engine's 96 bhp (DIN) 6,000 rpm and 98 lb ft of torque at 4,000 rpm, the 4/4 is no slouch itself though the fact that the 2.5 cwt heavier XR3 is both faster and more accelerative is a measure of just how aerodynamically inefficient the 4/4's shape is. Round MIRA's banked circuit with the hood up, the Morgan achieved a top speed of 103.0 mph (XR3, 111.2 mph) and the 0-60 mph time was 10.0 sec dead (XR3, 8.7 sec). This puts the 4/4 neck-and-neck with the X1/9 for spirited ability — but adrift of the Porsche, Lancia and VW. On top speed, not surprisingly, it trails the field.

Accelerating in top gear, the Mo-

gan's 30-50 and 50-70 mph times of 9.3 and 11.9 sec show it to have a wide torque spread and respectable mid-range punch, though this must be helped in no small measure by its unfashionably low gearing in top (17.9 mph/1000 rpm). This combination means that it is seldom necessary to change down for most overtaking manoeuvres, which is no bad thing; Ford's 1.6-litre CVH engine revs well but rather harshly above about 5,500 rpm, though it never gets intolerably noisy and in normal driving it's really quite refined, its muted exhaust note seeming oddly out of character with the car's vintage appearance.

Not that changing gear is a chore. The four-speed Cortina gearbox has a typically slick, positive action complemented by a progressive medium-weight clutch. The low overall gearing isn't mirrored by the intermediate ratios, however, as the first three gears allow maxima of 33, 61 and 88 mph at 6,700 rpm.

Nor has it, or the poor aerodynamics, had an adverse effect on economy. Over a test period of over 900 miles, the Morgan returned a commendable overall fuel consumption of 29.3 mpg which is almost 1 mpg better than the (four-speed) XR3 managed in our hands, albeit a reflection of one's

continued over

...ove: cosy accommodation for two, with luggage space behind. The seats are ...mfortable, though the wheel is close to the drivers chest. Switchgear, below, is ...ndily placed and the handbrake is of the 'fly-off' variety

Instrumentation is comprehensive, traditionally attractive in appearance, and clear apart from some tendency to reflections

tendency to settle for lower cruising speeds than in more modern machinery. Unfortunately, there's not much room for further improvement with gentle driving, as our computed touring consumption of 30.1 mpg illustrates. At this rate, the 8.5-gallon tank would need refilling with 4 star every 250 miles or so.

With its primeval front suspension, virtually extinct worm and nut steering and crude leaf-sprung rear axle, it would be unrealistic to expect much in the way of handling finesse from the Morgan. Yet on smooth roads few would find its chassis behaviour wanting. The major drawback is the heaviness of its steering on lock at any speed. Even sitting close to the steering wheel in traditional style, it requires real physical effort to wrench the 4/4 round a tight bend. Criticising Morgans for their heavy steering, of course, is nothing new, and it is encouraging to note that about the straight ahead position, the steering is reasonably light and precise with less "free play" than we encountered on the Plus 8.

Like that car, however, the 4/4 grips smooth roads well, cornering quickly and securely with virtually no body roll and only moderate understeer. Without the V8's tremendous torque, there's little the driver can do to modify the cornering balance on the throttle in the dry, though he will experience no difficulty provoking oversteer in the wet or, indeed, controlling it. On poorer surfaces, things are less predictable, the 4/4 getting jarred and even thrown bodily off line by mid-corner bumps. Over sharp undulations, the ride is so bad it's often necessary to take a firm grip of the steering wheel to at least ensure some physical contact with the car; the absorption of small bumps is,

contrastingly, quite good. And the brakes, although requiring a firm push, are powerful and progressive.

Legroom in the 4/4 is restricted only in as much as the footwells are too narrow and constricting at the business end; the pedals are well-spaced for heel and toe gearchanges, though few of our testers cared much for the roller-bearing type accelerator pedal. The Vintage-style driving position places the steering wheel close to the chest (no bad thing in view of the leverage required to turn it), while the seats, although small and thinly padded, provide good all-round support and proved comfortable on long trips. There is no boot but just enough room behind the seats to squeeze a couple of squashy overnight bags.

The plain interior is smartly finished but can seem rather claustrophobic, as well as being difficult to see out of with the hood up. With it unfastened and stowed behind the seats, however, the Morgan is in its element, and if the sun shines so much the better. The heater wasn't as powerful as it needs to be for chilly weather, but the instrumentation is both comprehensive and reasonably clear, only a couple of the minor dials being hidden with the tonneau cover fitted over the passenger side. This, like the hood, is well made from hard wearing material and reflects the high standards of finish and construction evident throughout this handbuilt car.

The Morgan 4/4 doesn't thrill like its big brother, the Plus 8, that we tested earlier in the year. That car had charisma, the 4/4 merely has charm. It also has faults, some of which are hard to live with. We'd still like to see Morgans with modern suspension and steering. In the meantime, with the XR3 unit, the 4/4 at least has a modern engine.

PERFORMANCE

WEATHER CONDITIONS
Wind	10-20 mph
Temperature	52°F/11°C
Barometer	29.5 in Hg/999 mbar
Surface	Dry tarmacadam

MAXIMUM SPEEDS
	mph	kph
Banked circuit	103.0	165.7
Best ¼ mile	109.7	176.5
Terminal Speeds:		
at ¼ mile	78	125
at kilometre	94	151
at mile	99	159
Speeds in gears (at 6,700 rpm):		
1st	33	53
2nd	61	98
3rd	88	141

ACCELERATION FROM REST
mph	sec	kph	sec
0-30	3.1	0-40	2.4
0-40	4.9	0-60	4.4
0-50	7.0	0-80	6.9
0-60	10.0	0-100	10.7
0-70	13.4	0-120	15.5
0-80	18.0	0-140	24.6
0-90	27.4		
Stand'g ¼	17.3	Stand'g km	32.6

ACCELERATION IN TOP
mph	sec	kph	sec
20-40	8.8	40-60	5.4
30-50	9.3	60-80	5.8
40-60	9.9	80-100	6.8
50-70	11.9	100-120	9.0
60-80	15.1		

FUEL CONSUMPTION
Touring*	30.1 mpg
	9.4 litres/100 km
Overall	29.3 mpg
	9.6 litres/100 km
Fuel grade	97 octane
	4 star rating

Fore-aft installed XR3 engine has electronic ignition and self-adjusting tappets for enhanced reliability and ease of maintenance

Tank capacity	8.5 galls	
	39.0 litres	
Max range	256 miles	
	412 km	
Test distance	937 miles	
	1,508 km	

*An estimated fuel consumption computed from the theoretical consumption at a steady speed midway between 30 mph and the car's maximum, less a 5 per cent allowance for acceleration.

SPEEDOMETER (mph)
Speedo	30	40	50	60	70	8
True mph	33	43	53	63	73	8

Distance recorder: 8.0 per cent slow

WEIGHT
	cwt	kg
Unladen weight*	15.2	772
Weight as tested	18.9	960

*with fuel for approx 50 miles

Performance tests carried out by Motor staff at the Motor Industry Research Association proving ground, Lindley.

Test Data: World Copyright reserved. No reproduction in whole or part without written permission.

GENERAL SPECIFICATION

ENGINE
Cylinders	4 in-line
Capacity	1,597cc (97.42 cu in)
Bore/stroke	80.0/79.5mm
	(3.15/3.13in)
Cooling	Water
Block	Cast iron
Head	Aluminium alloy
Valves	Sohc
Cam drive	Belt
Compression	9.0:1
Carburettor	Weber 32/34 DFT
Bearings	5 main
Max power	96 bhp (DIN) at 6,000 rpm
Max torque	98 lb ft (DIN) at 4,000 rpm

TRANSMISSION
Type	4-speed, manual
Clutch dia	8.5in
Actuation	Cable

Internal ratios and mph/1,000 rpm
Top	1.000:1	17.9
3rd	1.37:1	13.1
2nd	1.97:1	9.1
1st	3.65:1	4.9
Rev	3.66:1	
Final drive	4.1:1	

BODY/CHASSIS
Construction	Ash wood frame with steel panels; separate "Z" section steel chassis
Protection	Paint (rust-proofing optional)

SUSPENSION
Front	Ind. by vertical sliding pillars; coil springs; telescopic dampers
Rear	Live axle with semi-elliptic leaf springs; lever arm dampers

STEERING
Type	Worm and nut
Assistance	No

BRAKES
Front	11.0 in dia discs
Rear	9.0 in dia drums
Park	On rear
Servo	No
Circuit	Split front/rear
Rear valve	No
Adjustment	Manual

WHEELS/TYRES
Type	Pressed steel 15×5½ J
Tyres	165 HR 15
Pressures	20/20 psi F/R (normal) 24/24 psi F/R (full load/high speed)

ELECTRICAL
Battery	12V 40Ah
Earth	Negative
Generator	Alternator, 35A
Fuses	4
Headlights	
type	Halogen
dip	110 W total
main	120 W total

Make: Morgan
Model: 4/4
Maker: Morgan Motor Company Ltd, Pickersleigh Road, Malvern Link, Worcestershire WR14 2LL. Tel: 068 45 3104 or 3105
Price: £5,815.00 plus £484.58 Car Tax and £944.94 VAT equals £7,244.52 total.

114

TheRivals

Other rivals include the Panther Lima (£6,455) and the Mazda RX-7 (£9,199)

MORGAN 4/4 £7,245

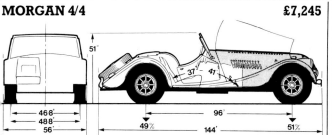

Power, bhp/rpm	96/6,000
Torque, lb ft/rpm	98/4,000
Tyres	165 HR 15
Weight, cwt	15.2
Max speed, mph	103.0
0-60 mph, sec	10.0
30-50 mph in 4th, sec	9.3
Overall mpg	29.3
Touring mpg	30.1
Fuel grade, stars	4
Boot capacity, cu ft	—
Test Date	September 25, 1982

An old car with a new engine, the Morgan 4/4 offers most of the charms of Vintage-style motoring with few of the day-to-day hassles. XR3 engine delivers punchy, untemperamental performance with good economy, but becomes rather harsh when pressed. Ancient suspension design means a rock-hard ride and somewhat erratic progress over bumps, though smooth road cornering is secure. Wonderful looks, fine finish, rare and exclusive.

FIAT X1/9 £6,345

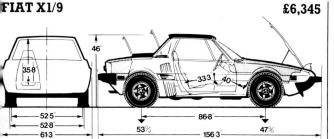

Power, bhp/rpm	85/6,000
Torque, lb ft/rpm	86.8/3,200
Tyres	165/70 SR 13
Weight, cwt	18.0
Max speed, mph	107.7
0-60 mph, sec	9.9
30-50 mph in 4th, sec	7.4
Overall mpg	29.0
Touring mpg	34.0
Fuel grade, stars	4
Boot capacity, cu ft	5.3
Test Date	January 27, 1979

The X1/9 has peppy performance with its very noisy, but revvy 1500 engine. Economy very good for the performance, aided by slick five-speed gearbox. Handling and brakes still superb, with a good ride. Cosy interior features neat instruments, and glove locker, but seats are not particularly comfortable. An excellent small sports car with detachable roof; great fun, and yet practical with it.

FORD ESCORT XR3 £5,750

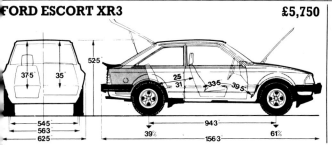

Power, bhp/rpm	96/6,000
Torque, lb ft/rpm	98/4,000
Tyres	185/60 HR 14
Weight, cwt	17.7
Max speed, mph	111.2
0-60 mph, sec	8.7
30-50 mph in 4th, sec	8.5
Overall mpg	28.4
Touring mpg	34.2
Fuel grade, stars	4
Boot capacity, cu ft	10.3
Test Date (Group Test)	April 10, 1982

Now supplied with a five-speed overdrive gearbox as standard, Ford's XR3 Escort combines very good performance with excellent fuel consumption. Styling, packaging, finish, gearchange, heating and ventilation are other good points. Excellent brakes, and smooth road handling and grip impressive, but ride comfort is still its worst feature while the steering is surprisingly lacking in feel. Good driving position, and now quite competitively priced since recent price cuts.

LANCIA MONTECARLO SPYDER £9,240

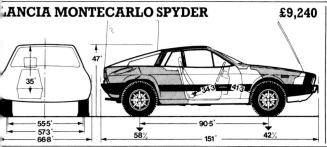

Power, bhp/rpm	120/6,000
Torque, lb ft/rpm	126/3,400
Tyres	185/65 HR 14
Weight, cwt	19.7
Max speed, mph	115.8
0-60 mph, sec	9.0
30-50 mph in 4th, sec	6.9
Overall mpg	23.3
Touring mpg	28.0
Fuel grade, stars	4
Boot capacity, cu ft	6.3
Test Date	May 30, 1981

A sad flop the second time round (and soon to be dropped), Lancia's revised Montecarlo no longer misbehaves in the wet, has excellent roadholding and good handling and brakes, a comfortable ride, and good performance with reasonable economy. Comfortable for medium size drivers but badly cramped for tall ones, instruments badly placed, and heating and ventilation poor. Worst fault is excessive engine noise.

PORSCHE 924 £9,494

Power, bhp/rpm	125/5,800
Torque, lb ft/rpm	121.5/3,500
Tyres	185/70 HR 14
Weight, cwt	20.2
Max speed, mph	121.3
0-60 mph, sec	9.3
30-50 mph in 4th, sec	7.3
Overall mpg	25.2
Touring mpg	—
Fuel grade, stars	4
Boot capacity, cu ft	4.8
Test Date (Group test)	November 24, 1979

Front-engined, rear-wheel drive "baby" of the Porsche range has good performance for a 2-litre (though 2.5 litre 944 is much faster) both cars offering excellent economy in relation to their performance. Excellent steering, brakes, transmission and handling, but ride is firm, and noise suppression — notably of road roar — and ventilation could be better. As in all Porsches, quality of finish and build is excellent.

VW GOLF GLI CABRIOLET £7,812

Power, bhp/rpm	110/6,100
Torque, lb ft/rpm	103/5,000
Tyres	175/70 HR 13
Weight, cwt	16.5
Max speed, mph	111.6
0-60 mph, sec	8.2
30-50 mph in 4th, sec	6.4
Overall mpg	27.4
Touring mpg	—
Fuel grade, stars	4
Boot capacity, cu ft	8.6
Test Date (Group Test GTi)	April 10, 1982

VW's smart new drophead version of the highly-successful Golf GTi. Unlike most rivals, it has the advantage of being a full four-seater. Although heavier than the saloon, performance from fuel-injected engine is lively matched by excellent handling and ride. Gearchange is slick and brakes progressive. Main disadvantage is the poor rearward visibility due to lack of rear quarterlights when hood is raised. When hood folded it does not lie flat. Refined and well-equipped.

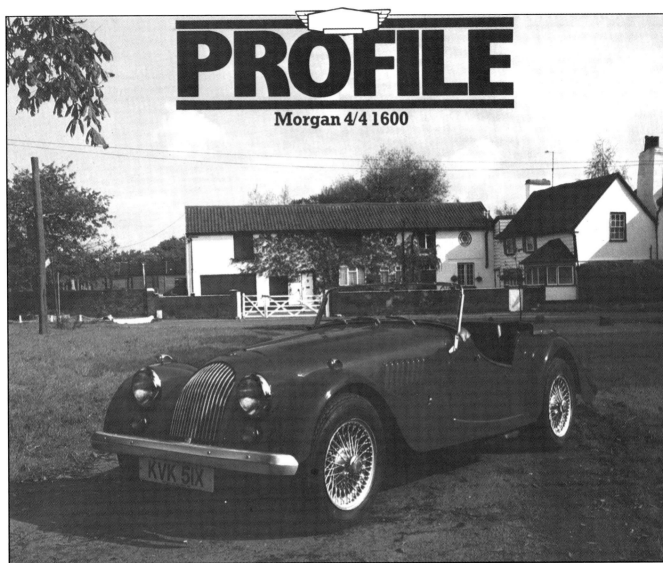

This 4/4 may be X-registered but to all intents and purposes it's pure 1935 in character. It's also cheaper to buy and more economical to run than its larger Plus Eight brother

Malvern tonic

If your finances can't quite stretch to running a Plus Eight Morgan, then the Ford-powered 1600 4/4 must surely be the next best thing. Peter Nunn discovers the secrets of motoring the Morgan way

There can be no other car in the world quite like a Morgan. On one side it has the reputation for being the last 'proper' sports car in the truest sense of the term, and yet viewed dispassionately it's an archaic bone-shaker, an expensive anachronism that would amaze any self-respecting modern car maker. Paradoxically, it is these latter shortcomings that, to some extent, reinforce the marque's enduring popularity and cult appeal.

Visually, it's all there. Combine the long, louvred bonnet, flowing wings, cut-down doors, sidescreens, tail-mounted spare, bonnet strap and aeroscreens (these last two items are, admittedly, optional extras) with a respectable turn of speed, notoriously hard ride and 'vintage' driving position, and you're beginning to get some idea of what the car's all about. Then there's the company's ancestry, which stretches back as far as 1910, competition heritage and sporting image to consider. The character and technical outline of the first four-wheeled Morgan (the prototype was created in 1935, with production cars following the next year) broadly matches that of the cars being built in penny numbers at the Malvern

factory in 1982. This means that, in this nostalgia-conscious age of hideous glass-fibre Replicas, the Pickersleigh Road machines, while hardly innovative, certainly have time, not to mention tradition, on their side.

Timeless formula

The four-wheel Morgan story is a fairly simple one in that the basic formula hasn't changed at all within the last 40-odd years. There was one famous break with tradition between 1963/1966 when the factory introduced a closed coupé model to the range ('the car that terrified 10,000 Morgan owners' as it was once described), but this theme was dropped discretely after only 26 cars had been built. Today, these coupés are prized collectors' items. Rightly or wrongly, Morgan has never made any significant attempt to modernise its 'classic' sports car nor update its laborious method of construction although with the recent demise of MG and Triumph's TR series (with, of course, Austin Healey and other revered names) in mind the factory's reluctance to change is, perhaps, understandable.

The story behind the many four-wheel Morga manufactured since 1936, though, does becom complicated when the talk turns to Plus Fours, P Eights, 4/4s (there are six separate types of this c alone), flat rads, curved rads, drophead coupés, fo seaters and so on. Any Morgan enthusiast worth salt should have the details of these engraven on heart but if you're a Morgan novice, how best to p your way through the maze, bearing in mind m Morgans look pretty much the same? Answer: tak quick look at the model table which appears on pa 53, and then read on.

When the idea of the 'Profile' was first mooted, subject matter seemed simple. A piece on fo cylinder Morgans made since the War. Much been written in magazines and books concerning hairy Plus Eight, the Rover V8-powered Mog introduced in 1968, but little on the cheaper models. Despite its age-old under-skin configurat (engine apart), the Plus Eight really is a latter-d Super Car; traditional Morgan looks, rubb scorching performance and exhilarating open-motoring, are just some of the Plus Eight's endear

rong suits. But sadly, Plus Eights cost a lot of
money to buy and run – for sure, OPEC is no great
[al]ly of this big-hearted road burner. A sensible
compromise, then, is to run one of the smaller-
engined cars offered by the factory. But which one to
[ch]oose?

As a general rule, Morgans tend to be bought by
[tw]o types of customer. The archetypal dyed-in-the-
[wo]ol enthusiast, who will insist on driving with the
[ho]od down in all weathers as a matter of principle –
[an]d the less committed individual who finds the
[po]werful image the marque creates a strong
[at]traction. A Morgan, don't forget, is the genuine
[ar]ticle, often imitated, never quite equalled. It's
[in]stant thirties nostalgia available new in the
[se]venties and eighties. The traditional enthusiast's
[ca]r will be regularly exercised in competition; it may
[be] a Plus Eight or perhaps a TR-engined Plus Four.
[In] any event it will *go*. A 4/4 1600, the subject of this
[p]rofile, may not match the performance of these
[M]organ favourites but it's definitely no slouch. It
[po]ssesses qualities which appeal to both the
[ha]rdened enthusiast and Sunday driver.

4 1600 a practical choice

From a practical point of view, the 4/4 1600
[p]roduced between 1968-1982 after the Plus Four
[wa]s dropped) must emerge as an appealing
[ca]ndidate. A Plus Four Super Sports is, for many
[M]organ drivers, the ultimate but many of those (in
[co]mpany with a large percentage of sixties Morgans)
[we]re destined for the United States. In fact Plus
[Fo]urs in general seldom seem to change hands
[no]wadays and when they do, the sums of money
[in]volved tend to be somewhat frightening. A
[se]venties 4/4 1600, on the other hand, is a far more
[re]alistic proposition. In the first instance, it was
[pr]oduced in far greater numbers than any other
[M]organ, and that includes the Plus Eight; there
[sh]ould, therefore, be plenty around still in good
[co]ndition (having had less time to rot!). Secondly,
[th]e power train used was taken straight from the
[Fo]rd Cortina so spares and servicing are no problem,
[ev]en for the home d-i-y mechanic. Thirdly, it's
[ec]onomical; 30/35mpg or even more is easily within
[re]ach whereas the thirsty Plus Eight will struggle to
[be]tter 20mpg. And lastly, it's cheap to insure –
[gr]oup 5 in place of the Plus Eight's more worrying
[gr]oup 7.

A 4/4 has one further advantage, still. It's a
[M]organ. This may sound like an obvious remark but
[th]e fact that the car was hand-built over some 90 days
[at] the factory where all Morgans have been built is
[sig]nificant. The lengthy gestation period has
[tra]ditionally (that word again . . .) meant the waiting
[lis]t for a new one is measured in years as opposed to
[mo]nths and this, in turn, has led to an abnormally-
[hig]h resale price structure as demand is always so
[hig]h. Thus 4/4s – or any Morgans come to that –
[do]n't depreciate nearly as fast as their rivals although
[wh]ether the cars are holding their own or falling
[sli]ghtly with inflation, in real money terms, is open to
[deb]ate. Whatever the true picture a 4/4 1600 must
[be], in reality, one of the world's *cheapest* sports cars;
[it h]olds its value seemingly against all odds (almost
[ind]ecently one might say) and is comparatively
[ine]xpensive to run and insure. Possibly your biggest
[he]adache will be finding one that suits your needs or
[ma]ybe raising the necessary cash . . .

[S]o far we haven't mentioned where the 4/4 1600
[fit]s in the overall Morgan picture. The first 4/4 model
[of] 1936 was also the first four-wheel Morgan to go
[in]to production, but with the introduction of the
[ear]ly Plus Four in 1950 the 4/4 disappeared
[tem]porarily, only to be re-introduced five years later
[at] the Earls Court Show as a down-market
[com]plementary model to the new 2-litre car. The
[pro]duction 4/4 of the late thirties used a four-cylinder
[Co]ventry-Climax engine of 1122cc capacity mated to
[a M]eadows gearbox, although following hostilities a
[12]7cc Standard unit and Moss 'box were
[sub]stituted. From late '55 when the 4/4 reappeared
[on] the scene, Morgan adopted, in succession, a
[num]ber of Ford engine/transmission units to power
[the] 4/4, culminating in the 1599cc Ford 'Kent'
[oversh]rod engine in January 1968. Morgan still make a

From this angle, a 4/4 looks near perfect, the archetypal thirties sports car. Its proportions and detailing are hard to fault

The traditional Morgan winged badge, in 4/4 form

The trusty Ford Cortina GT engine powers the 4/4

John Bolster smokes away in his 1974 road test 4/4. His Autosport *report described the car as 'strong and simple.'*

4/4, of course, using either Ford CVH (from the
Escort XR3) or Fiat Mirafiori twin cam units and
recent tests indicate that the replacement engines still
provide this 46-year-old design with plenty of zest.

The outline of the 4/4 1600, however, follows the
time-honoured Morgan pattern of manufacture. A
separate, steel chassis (underslung at the rear) with
characteristic Z-shaped side sections supports an ash
frame and attractive steel body. Aluminium panels
are used on some cars as an option although the
radiator cowl – Morgan changed from a flat radiator
to the current streamlined design, much to the

disgust of contemporary enthusiasts, during 1954 –
and front scuttle are always made from steel. The
suspension (which generates perhaps more Morgan
jokes than any other) consists of a primitive coil
spring, sliding pillar and telescopic damper
arrangement at the front with simple semi-elliptic
springs and lever arm dampers at the rear.
Wishbones and anti-roll bar? How dare you sir!
Contrary to some other Morgan jokes, the 4/4 does
actually go round corners by means of a Cam Gear
worm and nut arrangement. But again, it's hardly the
last word in refinement. Brakes are by discs at the

front with drums at the back; dual circuits came in during October 1971 although you won't find a servo in standard trim. A Salisbury live axle appears at the rear.

The early 4/4s adopted a similar transmission layout to the Plus Four in that engine and gearbox were separated by a stout tube. Not all 4/4s benefited from this arrangement, however, which prompted Morgan to specify a remote control slide-and-pull set-up to the gearchange mechanism. This enabled 'changes to be made in a more civilised fashion without the need to lean right forward to reach the lever. As far as the 4/4 1600 is concerned the engine and four-speed gearbox are as one, with the gear lever positioned sufficiently far back to prevent the need for a transmission tube or push/pull adaptation. The Ford engine should need no introduction. At the end of the sixties, though, Morgan were using both the 'ordinary' and GT versions of the newly-introduced Ford cross-flow engine in the 4/4 1600 and 4/4 1600 Competition models respectively. History records that the 'ordinary' engine gave way to the GT unit during November '70 because enthusiasts who chose the Competition model (after all, who wants an 'ordinary' Morgan?) were experiencing trouble with their insurance companies – it was the 'Competition' name that was worrying brokers. So Morgan decided to drop the less popular model of the two and the 'Competition' part as well. Result: the 4/4 1600 with the GT engine soldiered on until the arrival of the new Ford and Fiat engines at the start of this year.

Cramped driving position

4/4 1600s were produced in two basic styles – as a straightforward two-seater sports model or as a four-seater with a pair of extra seats overhanging the rear axle. From an aesthetic point of view, the four-seater is not the happiest of compromises. Entry via the back of the front seats (which slide forward) has to be experienced to be believed and once you're there, headroom is, shall we say, limited with the hood up. Luggage space is simply non-existent. Still, for the family man with two small children a 4/4 four-seater does makes sense.

Out on the road, a 4/4 holds few surprises. It goes like it looks. Even before you move off, the cramped driving position (necessitating bent elbows for the steering wheel is, in true 'vintage' fashion, very close to your chest) becomes apparent. Then there's the long reach forward under the dash for the gear lever and fly-off handbrake. The view down the long bonnet is mightily impressive but, alas, the woolly steering, and terrible lock, soon begin to irritate. Drive a representative model and you'll find the Kent engine pulls well from virtually any point in the rev range; it really is an excellent unit with few vices. It could do with a few decibels of V8 burble, however! Gearchanges are generally clean, commendable and precise.

And so to the ride. On properly macadamed roads, it's not nearly as bad as popular opinion would have you believe. True, the feel is decidedly firm – thus causing the front wings to bob rhythmically up an down as the car goes along but surely this is part of the car's overall character? It's only when driving over less-than-smooth surfaces that the seat belts are needed to prevent you from being bounced straight out of the car. Once the steering technique has been mastered – and pushing the seats back doesn't help a great deal here – the 4/4 can be hurled about with some degree of confidence for its handling and roadholding are fun to exploit.

On the race track, the Morgan four-wheeler has a fine competition record as befits such a sports orientated machine. Arguably the highlight of the marque's race career occurred back in 1962 when Chris Lawrence and Richard Shepherd-Barron took their famous Plus Four, TOK 258, to an excellent class win at Le Mans, finishing 13th overall. On the 4/4 front Chris Alford re-wrote some headlines during 1975 by winning all 15 rounds of the BRSCC Prodsports Championship in his remarkably standard 4/4, RA 444. Morgans are still ultra-competitive, though, witness the startling times put up by Charles Morgan's Plus Eight, the annual Moggie race at BDC Silverstone in August and the

Chris Alford walked away with the 1975 Prodsport championship, winning all 15 rounds in his 4/4 two-seater

controversial result of this year's Snetterton 24 Hour Race . . .

How to sum up the pluses and minuses of a Morgan 4/4? One of the most widely-held notions is that the car could easily be improved technically without altering its character one iota. The traditionalists would undoubtedly complain long and hard and resist any changes, but really by now you would have thought the steering and suspension could be altered *slightly* to bring them into the eighties? A Morgan with slightly more forgiving steering would be a joy to behold . . . Without doubt, a 4/4 two-seater running on optional wire wheels, with the hood and sidescreens removed is a superb means of fun transport for a summer's day. It doesn't look as butch or as menacing as a Plus Eight but in our estimation, it really looks the part. Alternatively drive it on a cold winter's night with the hood up and it's a real claustrophobic misery. But isn't that what traditional sports cars, *real* sports cars, are all about?

Production history

The four-wheel Morgan story starts with a prototype car in 1935, production beginning the following year and continuing, of course, to this day. Up until 1954, the characteristic flat radiator was fitted but to the utter dismay, shock and horror of Morgan traditionalists, this gave way to the current curved-style grille during that year.

Two basic 4/4 models have been offered over t[...] years – an open, two-seater tourer and a four-sea[...] with the same essential configuration. In [...] excellent book on the subject, *The Four-Wheel[...] Morgan*, Ken Hill records that one 4/4 drophe[...] coupé (with full-width doors) was constructed [...] Morgan to Series 2 specification but this is thought [...] be a unique car. The 4/4 1600, introduced in Janua[...] 1968, succeeded four different 4/4 models, each o[...] slightly more powerful than the last. It was initia[...] offered in two forms – as a two-seat tourer w[...] 'standard' 1600cc Cortina engine fitted, or as [...] Competition version powered by the slightly mo[...] potent Cortina GT motor. The Competition boast[...] a twin choke carburettor, a wilder camshaft profile, uprated compression ratio and pushed out 96b[...] as opposed to 74bhp. Unfortunately this 4[...] derivative (which echoed similar Competiti[...] versions of the Series II and V) did not go down [...] well with insurance companies – the 'Competitio[...] tag was the problem – so with the introduction of t[...] new breed of Ford OHC engines, Morgan decided [...] drop the engine altogether. From November 19[...] then, both types of 4/4 (two-seater and four-seat[...] were fitted with the GT engine that, incidental[...] also found a home under the bonnet of the 1970-19[...] Escort Mexico and early versions of the Capri 1600.

4/4 specification changes are few and far betwe[...] but can be summarised as follows. The facia w[...] brought in line with that of the Plus Eight in Octo[...]

What it's all about: many have tried to copy the famous Morgan lines over the years but few, if any, have succeeded

Model	Engine cc	Years produced	Production total
4/4 Series II	1172cc (Ford)	Oct 1955 - Oct 1960	387
4/4 Series III	997cc (Ford)	Sep 1960 - Oct 1961	59
4/4 Series IV	1340cc (Ford)	Oct 1961 - Feb 1965	206
4/4 Series V	1498cc (Ford)	Jan 1963 - Jan 1968	639
4/4 1600	1599cc (Ford)	Jan 1968 - Mar 1982	3513
Plus 4	2088cc (Standard)	Oct 1950 - May 1958	893
Plus 4	1991cc (Triumph)	Oct 1953 - May 1962*	2237
Plus 4	2138cc (Triumph)	Jun 1962 - Sep 1969	1523
Plus 4 Super Sports	1991cc, 2138cc	Mar 1961 - Jan 1968	101
Plus 4 Competition	(Triumph)	Oct 1965 - Nov 1966	
Plus 4 Plus	2138cc (Triumph)	Oct 1963 - Dec 1966	26

* The 1991cc engine continued as an option after this date. From Jan '82, the 4/4 became available with Ford CVH or Fiat twin cam power units.

...ouldn't all Morgan dashboards look like this one?

Federalised interior of a late-model 4/4 two-seater

'69 in that the rev counter was moved to the right of ...e steering wheel and rocker switches appeared on a ...ntral oval panel. A collapsible steering column was ...ted in November 1970, the month in which the ...andard' crossflow engine was dropped. A ...echanically-operated clutch was also specified. By ...e next Motor Show the braking had dual circuits, ...e facia more padding and the tail lights extended ...ckwards instead of being flush-fitting. May '73 ...w an improved fresh air heater introduced to the ...nge, with new windscreen demisting vents ...llowing in November '74. An aluminium-body ...tion was offered from early '77 and another facia ...date arrived in the middle of that year.

Ford CVH and Fiat twin cam 4/4s became ...ailable from January 1982 which meant that, ...icially, the pushrod Ford 1600 was superseded in ...ecember 1981. In reality, however, the final car left ...e Malvern works in March 1982. A total of 3513 4/4 ...00 Morgans were produced by the factory between ...69 and 1982.

Rivals when new

The Morgan 4/4 1600 doesn't really have a rival as far as tradition, looks and cult appeal are concerned. Perhaps the car which comes closest is Colin Chapman's stark Lotus Seven, manufacture of which was taken over by Caterham Cars in 1973. On the performance and handling fronts, the Lotus wins hands down but the Morgan makes up for these deficiencies by being slightly (?) more practical and economical. A Morgan, *any* Morgan, will also be worth much more than a Seven which has a similar, though less fanatical, following in comparison to the Morgan.

As far as prices are concerned (always a touchy subject when buying a Morgan), the two cars were evenly matched when new; at the close of '81 a Caterham Seven and 4/4 1600 two-seater were within a few hundred pounds of each other but there the similarity ends. The Lotus, exciting four-wheel motorbike though it may be, doesn't even begin to compete with the 4/4's five/eight-year waiting list, *Sunday Times* buyer's premiums and all that the two entail. This may or may not be a good thing, depending on your viewpoint.

The origins of the 4/4 lie as far back as the thirties. Panther tried unsuccessfully to emulate the magic Morgan formula with the ghastly Lima but the project didn't quite come off. Run-of-the-mill sports rag tops (TR5, TR6 and TR7 together with the MGB) ran the 4/4 quite close on a number of counts and provided dramatic wind-in-the-hair motoring for the masses – but could they match Morgan's charisma? We think not. Civilised, up-market open-air competition, meanwhile, was provided by Alfa Romeo's 1750 and 2000 Spiders and, to some degree, by the Lotus Elan Sprint and Jensen Healey. The TVR Taimar convertible (although a full 3-litre) might be yet another choice.

Clubs, specialists and books

Last year, the Morgan Sports Car Club – the extrovert organisation that caters for all four-wheel Morgans, celebrated its thirtieth birthday. Of all the one-make clubs in existence today, the MSCC must surely be one of the most light-hearted and informal. For evidence of this last statement, just run down the list of local club branches (there are 27 of them in the UK and three overseas). We particularly like, for example, the official nicknames of the Barrow-in-Furness, Brighton, Bristol, London, Reading and South Coast centres; in order, they read FurMog, SmogMog, GrogMog and SogMog!

The heart of the club's activities revolves around the monthly magazine *Miscellany* which is always crammed full of centre news, race reports and tempting advertisements for Morgan maniacs. The

The 4/4's heritage follows that of the Plus Four, shown here in two guises, and beyond. On the left, a rare drophead coupé; on the right, a four-seater. 4/4s look very similar . . .

SPECIFICATION	4/4 Series II	Plus 4	4/4 1600
Engine	In-line 'four' (Ford 100E)	In-line 'four' (Triumph TR2, 3)	In-line 'four' (Ford Cortina GT)
Construction	Cast iron block and head	Cast iron block and head	Cast iron block and head
Main bearings	Three	Four	Four
Capacity	1172cc	1991cc	1599cc
Bore × stroke	63.5mm×92.5mm	83mm×92mm	81mm×77.7mm
Valves	Sidevalve	OHV (pushrod-operated)	OHV (pushrod-operated)
Compression	7:1	8.5:1	9:1
Power	36bhp at 4500rpm	90bhp at 4800rpm	88bhp at 5400rpm
Torque	52lb.ft at 2500rpm	117lb.ft at 3000rpm	96lb.ft at 3600rpm
Transmission	Three-speed manual	Four-speed manual	Four-speed manual
Top gear	17.0mph per 1000rpm	21.0mph per 1000rpm	17.9mph per 1000rpm
Final drive	Hypoid, 4.4:1 ratio	Hypoid, 3.73:1 ratio	Hypoid, 4.1:1 ratio
Brakes	Drums, drums	Drums, drums*	Discs, drums
Suspension F.	Ind. by coils, sliding pillars, telescopic dampers	Ind. by coils, sliding pillars, telescopic dampers	Ind. by coils, sliding pillars, telescopic dampers
Suspension R.	Live axle, semi-elliptics, lever arm dampers	Live axle, semi-elliptics, lever arm dampers	Live axle, semi-elliptics, lever arm dampers
Steering	Cam gear	Cam gear	Cam gear
Body	Steel body and chassis	Steel body and chassis	Steel body and chassis
Tyres	5.00 - 16	5.25 - 16	6.5 - 15
DIMENSIONS			
Length	12ft	12ft	12ft
Width	4ft 8in	4ft 8in	4ft 8in
Height	4ft 1in	4ft 4½in	4ft 3in
Kerb weight	13cwt	16½cwt	14.5cwt
PERFORMANCE			
Max speed	72mph	98mph	102mph
0-60mph	26sec	11.6sec	9.8sec
Standing ¼ mile	23sec	18.6sec	17.2sec
Fuel con.	30/32mpg	27/30mpg	28/32mpg

Note: specifications refer to the two-seater sports model in each case. *Front disc brakes as standard from September 1960

club, as a whole, has an excellent competition record as club members have an embarrassing habit of cleaning up in important races and sprints. The social side of clublife, though, is not forgotten as a glance through *Miscellany* or a trip to one of the many club 'noggins' will testify.

Full details of the club and its wide-ranging activities can be obtained from Chas Smith, Top Lodge, Crown East, Worcester.

When the talk turns to Morgan specialists, the prospective 4/4 owner has a bewildering number of outlets to choose from. The following firms, however, have been recommended by members of the MSCC. Libra Motive, 6/10 Rosemont Road, Hampstead, London NW3 6NE; F.H. Douglass, 1A South Ealing Road, Ealing, London W5 4QT; The Light Car and Cyclecar Restoration Co., Unit 226, Artic Trading Estate, Droitwich Road, Hartlebury, Worcestershire; Allon White & Son (Cranfield) Ltd, The Garage, High Street, Cranfield, Bedford; Mike Duncan, 92 Windmill Hill, Halesowen, West Midlands.

Rutherford Engineering, Stanley Old Colliery, Station Road, Stanley, Derbyshire; Colin Musgrove, Newburn, Hob Lane, Balsall Common, Near Coventry CV7 7GX; Harpers, 2 King Edward Road, Shenley, Herts; General Insurance Agency, 56 High Street, Huntingdon; SGT Station Garage, Station Road, Taplow, Bucks; Black Phey Ltd, Raleigh Cottage, Takeley, Bishops Stortford, Herts; Burlen Services, Greencroft Garage, The Greencroft, Salisbury, Wilts; Phoenix Motor, The Green, Woodbury, Exeter; I&J Macdonald Ltd, Maiden Law Garage, Lanchester, Co. Durham and Melvyn Rutter, 3 The Green, Wanstead, London E11 2NT.

John Britten Garages of Arkley, Barnet, Herts and Richard Bourne Ltd of 63 Sangley Road, London SE6 2DX are two further useful Morgan addresses.

Heading the list of Morgan books currently available must be *Moggie* by Colin Musgrove. It's an extremely useful guide to the joys and sorrows of Morgan ownership and well worth its £8.95 cover price. Finding a copy to buy, though, might be slightly tricky nowadays but if you have difficulties, write to Colin Musgrove at the above address. Musgrove has also penned the *1980/1981 Morgan Yearbook* (the only one so far). Ken Hill's two books on four-wheel Morgans are both a must for any self-respecting owner but only the second volume, *The Four Wheel Morgan Volume 2* is relevant to our story.

Morgan The First and Last of the Real Sports Cars by Geoffrey Bowden is a delightful history of the company's exploits. It's well illustrated and especially strong on the early years but, alas, only goes up to 1972.

Other recommended titles include a trio of Brooklands Books *Morgan Cars 1936-1960*, *1960-1970*, and *1969-1979*, and *Morgans in the Colonies* by John Sheally. *Postwar MG & Morgan* (in the Survivors series) by John Blakemore and Henry Rasmussen is essentially a coffee table book. Finally, the Morgan Sports Car Club produced their own booklet two years ago to celebrate the company's 70th birthday. Entitled *1910-1980 70 Years of Morgan Motoring*, it's full of interesting stories and illustrations.

Paint bubbles around wing joints could be ominous

Not much left of this ash frame sill board!

Buyers spot check

A few general points first. Try to buy the latest, cleanest 4/4 you can afford unless you're planning a full restoration on a car you want to keep forever. Most Morgans tend to need some form of rebuild after three or four years so one way to stave off a large restoration bill is to track down an original, low-mileage car that hasn't deteriorated too far. From an economical point of view, the coaxing back to life of a 'basket case' 4/4 1600 is not yet a viable proposition although Morgans have always had that happy knack of being infinitely rebuildable. Furthermore they are seldom, if ever, written off by insurance companies (too valuable) or stolen by vandals, as they're too conspicuous.

The traditional Morgan method of construction leads to several problems, notably in the paint department. The body flexes a great deal in the normal course of duty and this induces cracking in vulnerable areas, particularly around the rear wheel arches, headlamp and sidelight surrounds and along the bonnet centre strip. The front wing joints also suffer in this way. The problem is exacerbated to a certain extent by the factory's habit of spraying the

complete car with all wings and panels in place – yo may find, for example, that as you unbolt a fro wing, the inner section won't have been ful painted.

Watch out for signs of bubbling and possib corrosion around the doors, bonnet, wings (front a rear) and the rear ¾ panel between the door ar wheel arch on either side. This last panel has bee made from aluminium from '78 onwards but was common rust trap on earlier cars. Note that c aluminium-bodied cars, the front cowl and scutt are always steel.

A simple way to check the rigidity of the ash bo frame is to give the body a firm shake! A small degr of movement is permissable but be extremely wary any apparent slackness in the structure as a whole. the frame does seem unwieldly, we'd advise leavir the car alone if the asking price is high since a fu professional repair job will not be cheap. A saggi frame on a soon-to-be rebuilt car, on the other han is awkward but not too disastrous.

Tell-tale danger areas include the sill boards (the are partially exposed to the elements from new!) ar the B post uprights. Unfortunately the sill frames a normally covered with trim and water-absorbe foam both of which make it difficult to check t wood properly. The only way is to look undernea and/or gently pull back the trim – not a pleasant ta when the vendor is looking over your shoulder. , *extremis*, the door shut faces can also rot away.

If you have removed the interior trim it's a go idea to check (as best as you can) the inner chass members below the doors for rust damage. Chas cracks occasionally originate around the engi mountings and the rear spring hangers on, we' told, '69/'70 cars although it would seem prudent check the chassis carefully on any Morgan. T bulkhead assembly and exhaust mountings al merit close examination.

Front suspension king pin bushes wear out in time at all – between 9000 and 20,000 miles says o source, or if things go badly wrong within 300 according to another expert! The engine one-sh lube system is partly to blame here, apparently. recognised way to lengthen the life of the bushes is replace the supply pipe with a grease nipple – sensible idea that maybe the factory should adop Watch out, incidentally, for cracks around the ou joints of the lower king pin mountings – we have se examples that have broken away completely.

The Ford engine and gearbox should not prese any problems, being simple, robust and trouble-fr Ridiculous though it may seem, a measure of freep in the steering (as much as 1in) is perfectly wit limits . . . Inside, check that the seats and trim are good condition as refurbishment of either is specialist art. Ergo it won't be cheap.

Prices

List prices for the first 4/4 1600s in early 1969 rang from £877 for the basic two-seater to £909 for faster Competition. The four-seater was priced £948. At the close of manufacture in late '82 the prices has risen to £6603 for the two-seater or £7 for the cumbersome four-seater. The Competiti had long been dropped.

So much for history. The above figures we gleaned from contemporary motoring magazines they tell you precious little about the 4/ performance on the new/used markets. Demand, course, has far exceeded supply. Until quite recen a brand new car with only delivery mileage could sold by an unscrupulous individual the same day fe handsome £1500 premium over list price. T situation is doubtless much the same today with Ford and Fiat-powered 4/4s – so how does the ol 4/4 shape up on the current used market?

According to Chris Alford of John Britten Garag (a noted Morgan agent), even a worn-out/abus wreck of a car can be worth an indecent amount money. The absolute bottom line, in his opini starts at £3000 but don't expect too much at t figure except a car ready for an imminent rebui Sound examples without too much adrift ran between £4000/£6000 with late, low-mileage cars A1 condition topping the £8000 mark.

European Morgan enthusiasts gather together at Dover, on their way to Mog '82 – the MSCC's summer rally in Worcestershire

failure to anticipate market ...ds and move with the times has ... to the obliteration of many a ...ous motoring name, but ironically ...of Britain's specialist car builders ... a seemingly inbuilt resistance to ...nge are thriving and are able to ...erate enviably long waiting lists.

...he two companies – Morgan and ...erham – simply keep on building ...cars more or less the way they've ...ays been, and that seems to ...ain the best way. Over the last ...ade or so a new breed of kit cars ...'replicars' has sprung up – ill-...portioned and ungainly looking ...tions in the main – and this has ...ed only to highlight the ...endous style of these two origin-...which easily outclass the tacky ...ducts of the classic car renaiss-...e of recent years.

...s not possible to mention the ...erham Seven or the Morgan with-...going into their respective back-...nds, and though the finished ...ucts appeal to a rather different ...of fresh air fanatic, they are put ...ther on similar principles, the two

...rey, are not the company responsible for starting off the Seven in 1957, but that they are the company who saved it from a tragic end when towards the end of the '60s Lotus found that the little road-going racer could no longer fit in with their social-climbing image.

Caterham Cars, who had been the distributors for the Lotus Seven, took

THE FIVE-YEAR WAITING LIST JUST MIGHT GIVE YOU THE CHANCE TO SAVE UP FOR A 1990 MORGAN IF YOU ARE ON A DECENT INCOME

over production in 1973 lock stock and barrel, buying up jigs, mouldings, and any spares which they could lay their hands on. The company continues to sell cars from the same premises, friendly-looking workshops which are adorned with the inevitable paraphenalia from the '60s when the Lotus Seven became a real cult car thanks to that fascinating but strange TV serial, The Prisoner.

It seems almost incredible that

sists of four basic models; 1.6-litre Ford or Fiat-powered cars, or two versions using the Rover V8 3.5-litre unit, with or without fuel injection. Chassis sizes for the two different engine are slightly different, but whatever model is specified, production methods are exactly the same, starting with the steel frame, which is bought in from outside.

All models have Morgan's unusual system of sliding pillar front suspension, and at the rear good old fashioned cart springs are used. Steering is worm and roller on all models except the Vitesse-engined car which has rack and pinion, though rack and pinion is optional on all models made by Morgan.

On to the rolling chassis, complete with engine, are grafted ash panels, and then the assembly is clothed in those familiar curvacious body panels, in a choice of aluminium or steel, of course. At all stages of production, each car has a little ticket attached showing each customer's specification, so in fact few, if any, Morgans will turn out the same. Customers are encouraged to visit the factory so they may get a full understanding of all the options available.

Final stage is the trim shop, where the cars are upholstered – be it in black vinyl or white leather, and then the finishing touches are put on. Indeed it's an awe-inspiring scene; bearing in mind the Morgan's rarity on the roads, the sight of 20 gleaming new examples is almost too much for the eye to take in!

But traditionally designed and built or not, Morgan do have to make some concessions to automotive developments and Department of Transport bureaucracy. In order that Morgans may be continually refined and improved, the firm runs several 'hacks' (one of which is Peter Morgan's 'company' car) on which all the development work is carried out.

When we visited the factory we drove the prototype Rover Vitesse-engined car, and the 'M' registered V8 model we tried in 1981 was still to be seen in the workshop, having doubtlessly been the testbed for many new components since then.

The price? Well let's say that the five-year waiting list just might give you the chance to save up if you're on a decent income. The 4/4 1600 two-seater starts at £8569 (Ford powered) and the Plus 8 carburettor model is £11,651, while the injected Vitesse powered car is £13,000-plus, but who knows what it will be in 1990.

Down at Caterham the build process may seem a little less steeped in historical methods than it does in the Malvern Hills, but proprietor Graham Nearn has no less commitment towards the car, having been involved with it for as long as it has been in production.

As with the Morgan, the chassis – more like a race car frame – is

brought in from outside, and then fitted with any of three different engines; Ford 1.6-litre units of 84 bhp (GT), 110 bhp (Sprint), and the legendary 130 bhp Twin Cam. A pair of massive-looking twin-choked Weber carburettors with small chrome covered air filters gulp in the mixture.

Caterham's cockpit is a cramped, no-frills affair that gives little creature comfort. Morgan's (below) is a more comfy alternative that can be trimmed in any kind of leather

Suspension seems almost a concession on the Seven. Short little coil springs are mounted on wishbones at the front, and on trailing arms at the rear. Steering is rack and pinion with only two and a half turns lock-to-lock.

The cars are built with the same absence of automation as with the Morgans, but of course there is one step not included in the building process, and that is the attention to luxury or equipment. Once the bare driver necessities are installed in the Caterham that's it; creature comforts are not included because the Seven is a car designed to be enjoyed, rather than out to cut a dash, though of course with its unique style it cannot help but do that as well.

It's simply a road-going racer, so there's no need for doors, a boot, or any kind of noise insulation, though

Wild ones

Remnants of an era long gone by, the Caterham Seven and Morgan V8 can both still cut a dash in today's world of refinement

...panies between them sharing ...years of hand building.

...e Morgan Motor Company Ltd, ...alvern Link, Worcs, operate from ...rt of the English countryside as ...utiful as the cars which emerge ...the old brick-built factory, the ...e of the company since before ...rst world war. Its present chair-...and managing director is Peter ...gan, before him the firm was in ...hands of Henry Morgan, who ...ded the company in 1909.

...must surely be general know-...e that Caterham Car Sales and ...chworks Ltd, of Caterham, Sur-

even although people are waiting five years to take delivery of their Morgans, the company refuse to step up production which runs at less than 10 cars a week. This may result in a long queue of frustrated future owners, but from Morgan's point of view it makes sense. Keeping supply way, way below demand, Morgan are able to ensure the mystique of the marque is in no danger of dying, and perhaps more importantly, it means there is no need to even consider changing from the traditional, labour-intensive production methods.

The current Morgan line-up con-

Sleek and flowing lines of the Morgan (above) reveal the car's early origins, while the Seven looks exactly as it should: a Lotus-inspired road-going racer with no compromises

the exposed exhaust system running along the nearside of the body does have the luxury of a heat deflector to stop passengers burning legs as they struggle to get out. Bodywork is aluminium, and wings and nose cone are fibre glass.

But although the Seven is a car synonymous with spartan trim and performance, it is possible to have one custom built, and while we watched Caterham's men at work we saw a twin cam version destined for South America which was, of all things, having leather trim fitted instead of the very basic plastic.

Unfortunately while Caterhams have not changed much over the years the price certainly has. The basic 84 bhp model costs £6440, and the Twin Cam is £8093, though you can buy a rolling chassis less engine for just over £5000. Seats don't adjust; so if you're a human beanpole you have to buy the long cockpit version for £185 extra.

Driving either the Caterham or Morgan is a rare treat for a journalist; to drive them back to back on a sunny day and on twisty roads makes a really withwhile day out.

This meant driving the Caterham from its Surrey home to the Malvern Hills, and covering the distance predominantly on motorways and dual carriageways: the diminutive sportster passed the first stage of the test. Low geared and incredibly draughty it may be, but the Caterham feels well put together and there are none of the shakes, rattles and vibrations you might expect in this type of firmly-

sprung, race-bred car at high speed.

But if the Seven acquits itself adequately on a motorway, then it excels once B-roads are reached. Take off the hood – which, almost ridiculously, is not high enough for anyone more than average height – and the Seven becomes open-topped motoring at its most uncompromising.

If the side screens are dispensed with too, then sitting in the Caterham really is akin to being in a go-kart. The ground is just inches away, and a

THE SEVEN IS A CAR DESIGNED TO BE ENJOYED RATHER THAN TO CUT A DASH, THOUGH IT DOES THAT AS WELL

small flat token effort of a windscreen keeps the flies out of the driver's eyes, but little more. There's none of the civilised windows-up draught-free ride you find in the Escort or Golf Cabriolets; it's old-fashioned wind in the hair all the way along.

Quick isn't the word for the Caterham's performance, shattering is more suitable. With a featherweight chassis it just rockets away, the engine revving unburstably – there is no red line on the rev counter – until it seems sensible to change up. Something of a rarity nowadays are the twin double-choked carburettors with little air filters which hiss aggressively when the throttle is blipped, and the almost straight-through exhaust that gurgles and pops deliciously when throttling back at over 4000 rpm.

Acceleration is aided by the excellent traction and also by the speed with which the gears can be selected. A stubby little lever moves only a couple of inches in total and gears (ratioed uncompromisingly low for maximum acceleration) engage with the utmost precision.

Handling too is terrific. Grip is absolute at both back and front, and it takes courage and confidence to get the rear wheels sliding out under power. Ride comfort is surprisingly good considering; it's firm but not as harsh as might be expected.

On a sunny day and on quiet winding roads the Caterham is sheer delight, but could you live with the car every day, summer or winter? Well that's where the rub is as far as the Caterham is concerned, for the car is just totally impractical.

For a start there is probably only enough luggage space to accommodate a couple of volumes of this magazine stacked on top of each other. And two normally-sized adults will rub shoulders whether there're on good terms or not.

Getting in and out really is difficult, and anyone not up to gymnastic fitness standard will feel a right charlie trying to make a dignified entry or exit, particularly as the car seems to attract so much attention anyway. For getting in, the trick is to gently lower oneself down, aided by one hand on the transmission tunnel, one on the side panel. If the hood is in place, then it's more difficult.

On the road the Malvern-built machine is a distinctly different kettle of fish. The V8 with its 205 bhp (Morgan's provisional claim) has a mighty kick to it, and the tendency is to keep the huge motor working at around 2000-3000 rpm. Dropping the clutch at high revs will produce very rapid acceleration, but it seems the wrong sort of treatment for this sort of classic car.

Handling on the Morgan is good, and rather better than the previous

Morgan's Vitesse engine gives over 200bhp, while Seven's sprint unit (below) gives 110

model we tried, due to the late version's rack and pinion steering. Ride is hard, of course; on the bumpy roads around the Malvern Link factory we felt every single little rut.

But there can be few cars with such a breaktaking view out of the driver's seat. The long, handsome bonnet becomes more pointed towards its leading edge, and is nicely flanked by the upper halves of the protruding headlamps. Inside, the Morgan has a touch of class too. The facia is classic; a flat panel with dials and switches lined up in an ordinary fashion, style being more important than ergonomics. The prototype we drove had the plain plastic trim – the thing to have is, of course, your own particular choice of leather.

ONE THING THEY SHARE: THEY ARE ALL ABOUT FUN, AND IN THIS ERA OF 'EUROBOXES' THAT IS VERY REFRESHING

Despite its size there's actually little more stowage space in the Morgan than the Caterham, just a very small area behind the two seats which is really there for the hood when it's down. But that needn't be a problem – an exterior luggage carrying rack is optional.

When the hood is down the Morgan is about as open as any open car could be, but keeping the side screens in place is advisable to retain some degree of warmth. With them, the wind howls in around the low-cut doors and it can get a bit tiresome on a long run. And in keeping with the vintage image, heaters have only just become standard on most of the Morgan line-up.

But over the Caterham at least it has doors, though getting in and out still isn't the easiest of tasks. One must first of all plant one's body in the seat, and then carefully insert legs under the steering wheel. But even although the Morgan is hard refined car, it crosses the great divide of motoring civility that the Caterham fails to negotiate.

It's difficult and perhaps unfair to compare these two cars, as despite having a lot in common, they are machines to suit different motoring temperaments; the Seven is the fun little point-to-point racer, and the Morgan is for the wealthy fresh air devotee who needs just about the ultimate in style. But one thing they do share, they are all about fun and in this era of 'Euroboxes' that is refreshing.

Another thing is clear – these cars will be enjoyed all the more if their owner has a double garage which can also contain a more practical and mundane car, to be pressed into service for the all-too many occasions, when the compromises necessary for the Morgan or Caterham become just too much.

Morgan Plus-8

ROAD TEST

Elsewhere in this issue you will find a bevy of convertibles. Though they represent a broad variety of manufacturers and range in price from $11,000 to $66,000, they have a number of common features: air conditioning, AM/FM stereo, and roll-up windows. Wimpy stuff that wouldn't even have been considered by the true sporting driver of two or three decades ago.

by Michael Brockman

PHOTOGRAPHY BY BOB D'OLIVO
AND PAUL MARTINEZ

State of the art of open-air motoring back then—and in all the decades that went before—sneered at all that foo-foo stuff. What you needed was a long, louvered bonnet, with a leather strap to hold it down, running boards, and a tolerance for weather. Make that a positive *enthusiasm*

for weather.

But can this be, in 1984? Yessir, Mr. Orwell, there is hope for the pure of heart. Thanks to a few hearty souls, namely Peter Morgan, for carrying on his family's work in England, and Bill Fink, for his undaunted persistence in making the Morgan legal in America, we were able to have a Morgan Plus-8 on our 1984 convertible run.

The Morgan is one of the very few real traditional sports cars available in the

world today, and is truly a holdout from another age. The chassis literally starts life on a pair of saw horses. Ash wood sub-framing is used beneath the coachwork and a total-loss oiling system for the front suspension is standard equipment. Speaking of front suspensions, this one was first designed in 1909. The sliding pillar suspension, as it is called, is patented and is actually a sliding kingpin setup with vertical coil springs above and below the spindle in conjunction with telescopic hydraulic shocks. The lubricant for the sliding pillars is taken from the engine and applied via a pushbutton on the firewall known as the "One Shot": one shot every morning on long trips or one shot every 200 miles or so under everyday driving conditions.

The rigid rear axle is overslung on semi-elliptic rear springs with lever-type hydraulic dampers. Modern technology had appeared on the Plus-8 we drove in the form of telescopic rear shocks and, believe it or not, rack-and-pinion steering. The brakes too had moved into the present with 11-in. discs in front and 9-in. drums in the rear, held up by Pirelli P205/60VR15 P6s on 6.5-in. cast aluminum wheels. With this fat footprint and a great deal of pedal effort, the 2270-lb Morgan stopped in an impressive 130 ft from 60 mph. Interestingly, the combination of fat tires and telescopic

shocks kept the tail in on the skidpad, holding us to 0.75 g.

All these pieces are put to good use on the Plus-8, which gets its power from a healthy Rover 3.5-liter aluminum V-8 (nee Buick) connected to a 5-speed Rover gearbox. The combination is delightful and makes for great seat-of-the-pants-style driving. Admittedly, the suspension works best on smooth surfaces, and the steering and braking require some manual labor; but overall the Morgan Plus-8 is a real kick in the knickers to drive.

Another interesting and unusual aspect of the current Morgans in the U.S. is that they run on propane. Once again, credit must be given to Bill Fink of Isis Imports Ltd. in San Francisco, America's largest (and only) importer of the oldest (75 years) ultra-low-volume (400 to 500 cars per

year) manufacturer in the world. You see, Mr. Fink has a long-standing love affair with the Morgan and has fought long and hard to make the marque available in the U.S. When it looked like Moggies were going to be kept out permanently because of emissions, Mr. Fink cleverly decided to use propane, which happened to be neat, clean, and relatively cheap. Not to mention kind to internal combustion engines.

When asked about the pros and cons of using propane, the only con seemed to be availability to ordinary consumers, and this poses little problem with some thought and planning. The pros, according to Mr. Fink, are many: longer engine and plug life, quicker throttle response (dry fuel doesn't have to be vaporized), to mention just a few. Propane has about 10% less BTUs for a given quantity than gasoline, but with a little manifold work (by Offenhauser) Fink reckons his Morgans put out about the same power (160 SAE net) as their English brothers.

We decided to test the merits of propane-based muscle, and the results were impressive. Times at the dragstrip were fairly quick, registering a 15.12-sec quarter mile at 90.2 mph.

Making the engines legal is not Mr. Fink's only concern. Upon arrival in the States, the cars are partly disassembled and bracing is added in the doors and the rear compartment (the doors, quarter panels, and rear deck are aluminum). Five-mph bumpers—a clever combination of VW Rabbit bumper shocks and stock Morgan bumpers—and an assortment of lights, reflectors, and other gadgets are installed to make Uncle Sam happy. This is a time-consuming process requiring some 100 man hours in the Isis garage, romantically housed in Pier 33 on the San Francisco waterfront.

Now that we know what makes this holdout from another time tick, what about driving it? On the convertible run

The top can be put up in three or four minutes, depending on how hard it's raining

...ie thing was sure: No matter if someone ...ved it or hated it, everyone had some-...ing to say about it. What makes the Plus-...unique today is what got so many of us ...volved with cars in the first place—you ...ave to drive it; a cruise control on this car ...ould be the equivalent of neon signs in ...e Sistine Chapel. There are no tricks or ...mmicks, it's just a no-frills approach to ...odtime motoring. This approach is not ...thout merit; the cars have looked and ...en built the same for years, and the fac-...ry can't produce enough cars to meet de-...and.

It should be mentioned that weather ...ar (a top and side curtains) is included in ...e package, and it works with relative ...se. There are no buttons to push and it's ...t a one-hand job like those you see in the ...s, but the top can be put up and the side ...rtains installed in three or four minutes, ...pending on how hard it's raining. When ...side, with all the gear up, you either have ...be very short or bend your neck a lot to ...e out the sides. Oh, there's a heater, too.

The cars are available in the U.S., even ...ough there is some six-year backlog in ...gland, at the rate of 30 cars a year. This

number also includes the more classical-looking 4-cylinder version, with either a 1600 Ford CVH or a 1600 twin-cam Fiat engine, both using propane.

So if you like to drive, like the nostalgic thought of zipping down the lane with that long, louvered hood stretching out in front,

and you don't mind getting your hair blown and being bounced around a bit, if you don't mind everybody staring and every other body asking, "What is it?" and "What year is it?" and you have an extra $26,000, call Bill Fink in San Francisco (415/433-1344). You'll have a ball. **M**

☑ SPECIFICATIONS

Morgan Plus 8

GENERAL
Vehicle type ....Front-engine, rear-drive, 2-seat, 2-door roadster
Base price................................$26,000
Price as tested $26,663

ENGINE
Type & displacement ....V-8, liquid cooled, cast aluminum block and heads, OHV, 3528 cc (215 cu in.)
Induction system ....Impco propane (IV)
Max. power (SAE net)............160 hp @ 5250 rpm
Max. torque (SAE net) ....198 lb-ft @ 2500 rpm
Recommended fuel................Propane/Butane 105 octane

DRIVETRAIN
Transmission..........................5-sp. man.
Final drive ratio 2.75:1

CHASSIS
Front suspension ....Independent, sliding pillar, coil springs, telescopic shocks

Rear suspension ....Live axle, semi-elliptic leaf springs, telescopic shocks
Brakes, f/r ....11.0-in. discs/9.0-in. drum
Steering type ....Rack and pinion
Turns, lock to lock 2.2
Wheels......................................15 x 6.5-in. cast aluminum
Tires..205/60VR15

DIMENSIONS
Curb weight............................1031 kg (2270 lb)
Wheelbase ....2515 mm (99.0 in.)
Overall length ....3988 mm (157.0 in.)
Overall width ....1575 mm (62.0 in.)
Overall height ....1321 mm (52.0 in.)
Power to weight ratio............14.1 lb/hp
Fuel capacity...........................58.0 L (15.4 gal)

PERFORMANCE DATA
0-60 ....6.49 sec
Standing quarter mile ....15.12 sec/90.2 mph
Braking 60-0 ....130 ft
Skidpad ....0.75 g
Fuel economy (test average) ....19.0 mpg

---

MORGAN — continued from page 111

little has changed about the way in which these hand-crafted cars are made since the Second World War. One of the long sheds contains a row of bare chassis frames, rested gently on wooden trestles, which are carefully built up into rolling chassis, there never being more than between ten or a dozen under construction at once. With Rover V8, Ford CVH or Fiat twin cam engines installed, the chassis are then moved round into another section of the factory in which the ash-framed body is completed and fitted to them. The scuttles and cowls of all cars are finished in hand-beaten sheet steel, but the remainder of the body panels can be supplied in alloy as an optional extra. Belgian ash is used largely for the chassis frames themselves (it has even been known to find traces of World War II shrapnel in some of this wood!) while marine ply, which has been soaked in a vat of creosote, is employed for the Morgan floor panels. Eventually the completed cars are mounted on slave wheels for the spraying process before being fitted with either Pirelli P6s (Plus 8) or Michelin XAS (4/4) on pressed steel or wire wheel rims. When Dunlop ran down their facilities for making wire wheels in 1979/80, Morgan concluded an arrangement for continued supply of these components from the London-based Motor Wheel Services who took over a lot of the Dunlop equipment. Interestingly, in order that the Rover V8 can circumnavigate the strict US emission control regulations, all Plus 8s destined for that market are adapted to run on propane. Only petrol engined cars are obliged to conform to these stringent regulations and, as anybody who has driven a Rover V8 thus stultified will testify, the engine hardly performs at all thus modified. Morgan's ambitious US dealer, Bill Fink in San Francisco, is also working on the idea of a propane powered, turbocharged Plus 8 for those who require even more power in the land where absurdly restrictive 55 m.p.h. limits hold sway!

The final act in the construction of this bespoke motor car is its visit to the trim shop where a

handful of ladies cut and stitch the upholstery — be it vinyl or expensive Connolly hide. At the time of our visit the trim shop was crowded with a kaleidoscope of Plus 8s, 4/4 two-seaters and 4/4 four-seaters in a wide variety of specification and a wide variety of colours.

No visit to Morgan would be complete without a whirl up the road in one of their products. On this occasion Peter Morgan found us two cars to play with: his own personal Plus 8 and a development 4/4 fitted with the new Ford CVH engine. I have to confess that in twelve years of motoring journalism, this was my first flirtation with a Morgan. As far as the Plus-8 is concerned, this is quite a brute of a machine, rather like a scaled-down AC Cobra. With a modest overall weight of 1,826 lbs. and 155 b.h.p. to play with, this is no machine for the meek and it doesn't forgive sloppy driving in any way. We were fortunate enough to be able to try the latest Plus-8 in ideal "Morgan weather": a beautiful summer day under a burning sun and with never a thought about whether or not we should have to erect the hood. With 198 lb./ft. of torque at 2,500 r.p.m., there is no problem about flexibility either. That at least gives you the opportunity to come to grips with the hunched-up driving position — you steer with effort from your shoulders rather than your arms — and the relatively heavy steering which, some might find unacceptable when manoeuvring at low speed. This is one aspect of the Plus-8 about which Peter Morgan is certainly concerned and developments to improve this quirk are currently in hand.

On anything less than smooth surfaces the Plus-8's ride is lively to say the least although its P6s allied to the independent coil spring front suspension mean that its directional stability is pretty good. Smooth dry tarmac is the ideal environment for the Plus-8 and in these conditions it's truly great fun, the evocative view down that impressive bonnet and the deep burble of that splendid V8 engine reminding one of what sporting motoring must have been like in the days when the World was young and interminable

urban traffic jams still lay, happily, well in the future. Although it's a little dificult for someone with as large a frame as the writer to squeeze in behind a Morgan steering wheel, I was pleasantly surprised as to how comfortable it was.

The Plus-8 is currently priced at £10,496 .14p inclusive of car tax and VAT and, after we'd returned it to Peter Morgan's care, we had the opportunity of trying out the model at the opposite end of the range, the CVH-engined 4/4 which stands potential customers in at £7,244.52p. I found the smaller engined two-seater a delight, real fun to hurl about the country lanes in conditions where one thought twice about hurling the bigger engined car through tight corners. The sliding pillar front suspension that has been a Morgan hallmark for so many years is retained on the 4/4 and although the ride seemed significantly choppier than in the V8 machine, limits of adhesion were predictably lower and it was much easier to "play bears" without fear of dire consequences. The purpose of the 4/4 is to provide the enthusiastic motorist with an extrovert sports car for the same price as a decent family saloon: in that respect the CVH-engined Morgan fits the bill quite admirably.

If you're seeking the standards of ride offered by a Lotus or the mechanical refinement provided by sports saloons such as Volkswagen's Golf GTi, then you won't look at a Morgan. But if you keep your sense of perspective and want a dyed-in-the-wool sports car and like the idea of blowing the cobwebs away not simply on sunny days, then a visit to this modest Malvern factory may result in your coming away converted to the Morgan habit. If you judge the products by contemporary standards you will almost certainly emerge disappointed, but really, that's not fair on the Morgan Motor Company. They have no pretensions and simply get on with offering a concept that has pleased successive generations of loyal enthusiasts. Change for change's sake has no place in the Morgan world. And, as I said at the start of this article, that is a trait which many people will find attractively reassuring. — A.H.

AT THE bottom of the sloping yard not far from the trim shop is a handful of rolling chassis, their unpainted aluminium bodies shining in the July sun. Opposite a row of men in blue overalls put their backs against the factory wall and settle down for a tea break. Up the hill is the wonderfully ancient petrol pump with its circular face marked in gallons almost totally obscured by years of grime on the glass and a few paces away Peter Morgan talks enthusiastically about his latest car.

It is not only the "Ultimate Driving Machine" — to borrow a BMW slogan — to come from the red-bricked Malvern Link factory but also as big a step in engineering terms for Morgan as perhaps any since the fourth wheel was added.

The car bears the famous MMC 11 number plate — always referred to as MMC two, not eleven — but only a small air scoop in the right side of the louvred bonnet gives any clue that this particular Morgan is a prototype for a new line of Moggies.

A kerb weight of just over 17 cwt and 155 bhp from the Rover V8 engine means the current Plus 8 is no sluggard but the new machine is in a higher class altogether as the fuel-injected V8 from the Rover Vitesse provides a mind-boggling 190 bhp. If you thought the Porsche 944 was a fast car forget it! MMC 11 has a power-to-weight ratio almost 50 per cent better than the four pot Porsche.

But if the Morgan faithful are amazed that the hammer and screw driver engineering that has been the marque's hallmark for 75 years should now have to share space with electronics — for the fuel injection — then a glance at the front suspension will fill them with disbelief.

The sliding pillar set-up, designed in 1913, has been stripped of its crude cam and peg steering box to be replaced by a steering rack. Hard to believe really but, yes, a Morgan with rack and pinion steering. They will be putting stays on the doors next or even fitting heaters that really work; just

don't expect a radio in this £13,000 Mog.

It seems inconceivable that 190 bhp can be happily transmitted through a live axle held in place by nothing more than a pair of cart springs, yet it is. But there is one surprise as the old lever arm dampers have been replaced by some gas-filled telescopic ones though they are still "under development".

As we moved off in MMC 11 I realised that Peter Morgan had been right. Asked how much better the turning circle is with the steering rack he had replied, "Well this one turns round in the yard." In Malvern quoting turning circle in feet and inches is of secondary importance.

After we had turned round by the paint shop in one sweep it was clear that gone are the days when a parking manoeuvre would be accompanied by graunching noise from under the wings as the tyres rubbed against the chassis on full lock.

And the driver struggled manfully with the large steering wheel and something as rapi

MACHO MOGGIE

Morgan slips a 190 bhp Rover Vitesse engine in its Plus-8 two seater, gaining a dragster-style power-to-weight ratio and a new model to top its range at October's NEC Motor Show.
Daniel Ward has been driving the prototype

Photography by Maurice Rowe

as a three-point turn was experienced only rarely.

The precision of the fuel injection is responsible for a more even but still very satisfying burble from the exhaust pipes.

Jump from a Peugeot 205 GTI into the Morgan and it would be difficult to claim the Plus 8 has the worst ride. The soft-walled Pirelli P6s do a good job of softening the blow to the front end while the new dampers relieved our backs of the expected jarring and only once did a transverse slot in the road catch the car out, causing the axle to crash loudly less than a foot from our spines. Compared with my old Plus 8, the ride was indeed supple but still distinctively Moggie-like.

With the beautiful Malvern hills moving away to our right as we began to get up some speed it was not the fierce power under the bonnet that demanded first attention but the steering. Unlike the engine it is totally different.

Drive a Plus 8 fast through the country-

side and it is the fight with the steering wheel that opens the pores of your armpits. The marked bump steer is there to catch the inexperienced, manifesting itself at the first bump and causing the pilot to wrestle with the wheel until the last one has been safely passed. The other former joy was derived from the steering box.

In the cam and peg box, the shaft upon which the cam was mounted simply butted up against a flat plate and adjusting out the free play just increased the resistance. This made the steering even heavier but worse, the box wore out more quickly. So at high speed the Morgan driver would have to accept up to two inches of free play at the steering wheel rim.

Fast cornering on a bumpy road would therefore become a moment of frenzied elbow waving as the driver tried to prevent being outwitted by the bump steer and slack in the steering.

The rack and pinion on MMC 11 couldn't be more different. As the long steering arms come from the centre of the rack — previously there was a single track rod — bump steer has all but been eliminated. Difficult to say that it is gone completely because on a really bumpy lane taken at speed the still very firm suspension is bouncing the driver around a great deal but at least there is a feeling of predictability about the bucking motion.

With the free play gone the steering now

Far left: In its natural habitat, a Morgan in Elgar country with the Malvern hills behind
Top: There is no way of identifying this as the fastest production Morgan
Above: Super grip, on smooth roads at least and no body roll — the ultimate roller skate
Below: The view no Morgan enthusiast would swop as there is no substitute

has a satisfying fluidity to it that makes wringing the fantastic performance out of the Plus 8 a more pleasurable experience. Naturally that will not stop purists, and Morgan has its fair share of those, from arguing that the steering has lost its character and there is a loss of feel at high speed. Also the increase in turns lock to lock from 2¼ to 3¼ is a retrograde step despite the advantage in reducing the 38 ft turning circle.

But this car is really about sheer gutsy performance and in the world of open top cars it has few if any rivals. At 4,500 rpm the ordinary Plus 8 is still pulling hard but it has already delivered its superb mid-range punch and particularly in the higher gears the Morgan's house brick style aerodynamics are beginning to take the edge off its acceleration. Fuel injection changes all that.

There is now incredibly smooth power from 800 rpm to 5,280 rpm, where the engine is producing at least 190 bhp, and beyond. Having the soft top down only adds the excitement of the memorable acceleration as you floor the antiquated roller throttle pedal and hang on to the large steering wheel. Stay in third gear as the rev counter needle flicks round the gauge and the mechanical frenzy under the long bonnet steps up a notch and you will have moved into the pain barrier as the wind and engine roar assault your ears.

This would get to 100 mph in a time only supercars could hope to match.

The massive quota of horsepower means MMC 11 will spin its wheels to order off the line. For cornering this has its advantages as the pleasant initial understeer is never allowed to build up as the throttle always commands the power needed to determine the car's attitude perfectly as it exits from the bend.

In this burst of exciting driving the car's shortcomings do not come readily to mind even when your pulse has returned to a semblance of normal. Yet the immense power does make the gearing in second and third in particular feel too low despite appearing fine on paper. They are simply used up too quickly. And the brakes are heavy even before any retardation is achieved. They don't haul the car to a stop rather just slow it adequately.

That said, the Morgan story has been running for 75 years and it has an admirable new hero.

PLUS INJECTION

We arrived back at Malvern Link, cold, senses battered by the gale blowing into the cockpit, irreparably dishevelled, but grinning from ear to ear. The ride in the Morgan is not as denture rattling as you might expect and the results of the 190bhp engine, easily offset by the huge 11 inch discs on the front and nine inch drums behind that reveal another Morgan foible — involuntary cadence braking. It might not appeal as daily transport, but as a car to make your adrenalin pump, it is no wonder the customers keep on queuing

The mighty Morgan Plus Eight has received an added boost not from a turbocharger as seems to be the fashion these days, but by the addition of the fuel injection Rover Vitesse 3.5 litre V8. **Art Markus** sampled the car on home territory

Even standing still, Morgan's +8 looks a brute. The family resemblance is obvious, but the +8 is a full 6″ wider, and sits on a 2″ longer wheelbase than its lesser brethren; the tyres are far wider at 205/60 x 15. The look is menacing, like a sleek cat stalking its prey, muscles coiled and tensed, ready to spring.

We approached our drive in the prototype Vitesse-engined fuel-injected (there is no official designation yet) +8 with some trepidation. This engine, when fitted to the Rover, develops an intimidating 190bhp. In the lightweight Morgan, the addition of tubular exhaust manifolds (the engine could not be persuaded to fit with the standard cast exhaust manifolds) should produce a modest gain in output. A new camshaft design is expected soon from Austin Rover, and should boost output still further to a massive 220bhp. At a dry weight of 1826lbs, the +8 should then boast a racing-car-like power-to-weight ratio of 269bhp per ton! We had to make do with a mere 233bhp per ton.

The Morgan Motor Company's location in picturesque Malvern Link gave us easy access to some excellent territory to sample the delights of traditional motoring in the Morgan style. Their "test facilities" around the Malvern Hills, and the Black Mountains of South Wales proved to be ideal. Its simply not done to drive any Morgan with the hood up, so despite indifferent weather, we set off with the hood safely stowed.

After the initial fiddling with seat adjustments, mirrors and so on, we found the +8 extremely habitable. On the outside corner of each seat-back, we found a clip through which the shoulder strap of the seat-belt passes, and which did an excellent job of holding the strap in position when the seat was unoccupied, and holds it at exactly the right position and angle when in use — an excellent idea, well executed. The seats, upholstered in black ambla, don't look anything special, but we found them to be quite satisfactory during a day's spirited motoring. The cockpit is obviously very compact, and dictates a rather upright seating position, but this has some practical advantages when it comes to wrestling with the largish leather-bound three-spoke steering on the twisty bits, when you really need to put your back into it.

The dashboard and controls are a model of clear, logical layout and simplicity, with large white-on-black speedometer and tachometer either side of the wheel, divided by a vertical row of warning lights. In the middle of the dash is a slightly recessed panel, containing a row of five tumble switches, and gauges for fuel tank contents, water temperature, oil pressure, and amperes, left to right. A small, open cubbyhole on the left completes the picture, while each door panel contains a shallow map pocket. Storage space is at something of a premium in the +8. Stalk controls take care of lights, indicators, and wipers. Turning on the wipers causes a surprise — three blades pop up from their resting places, and proceed to oscillate busily. Three short blades are required to ensure adequate coverage of the unusually wide, shallow screen.

A somewhat elusive reverse gear, and an unfriendly handbrake (of the fly-off variety) both of which we believe to be a typical, made low-speed manouevring rather tiresome. All was forgiven, though, and forgotten, once we were on the move, and headed for the open road, with the prospect of some exhilerating motoring ahead adding to our sense of keen anticipation. Our initial impression was that every word ever was written about the Morgan's ride was true. But after a mile or two, traversing the outskirts of Malvern Link at moderate speeds, in which circumstances it can be assumed that the car is at its worst, is not harsh — a subtle but important distinction. Road shocks seem somehow to be transmitted through the whole structure, so that one senses the chassis and body flexing independently, the whole car seeming to come alive. This impression is reinforced by the knowledge that a second-hand Morgan will usually betray hard usage and indifferent maintenance by crazing and cracks in the paint and bodywork. However, the result is a ride that is not quite as denture-rattling as one has perhaps come to expect.

Onto the open road, then, and our first chance to step on it. We had already been impressed by the injected engine's smoothness and flexibility, and its willingness to potter along in High Road traffic with a minimum of revs and just a whiff of throttle. Now it was time to see what would happen when we opened the taps. The results are simply astonishing.

Above: The dashboard and controls are a model of clear, logical layout and simplicity
Below: A new camshaft expected from Austin Rover should boost power from 190bhp to 220bhp

The mighty Morgan simply leaps forward, virtually regardless of road speed, engine speed or gear ratio when the long-travel accelerator pedal is pressed down. The pedal is stiff in operation, and requires a determined prod; occasionally when surging forward, we were surprised to discover that the throttle was not fully open, and that even greater acceleration was available. Launches from a standing start are similarly exciting. Weight distribution, two-up, is purportedly near-equal (slightly biased to the rear, if anything) and with both wheels spinning furiously, courtesy of the standard-fitment limited slip differential, getaways are blindingly fast.

A car with this amount of poke seems almost obscene on the open road, but by jove, it's exciting!

So far we have discovered racing car ride quality and performance. What about roadholding and handling? First, the steering. Morgans have frequently been criticized for their heavy and imprecise steering, and it was hoped that the new rack-and-pinion steering would counter most of the criticisms. Although it is still no finger-tip job, we could find little to criticize, with little kick-back or freeplay at the wheel rim (both former weaknesses), and reasonable precision. The wide Pirelli P6's seem to offer plenty of grip, but in fact, a rational analysis of the +8's handling is extra ordinarily difficult. One is always aware of that, should the tyres let go, the car could rapidly develop a will of its own, for there is absolutely no subtlety or refinement about its progress. Slow in — fast out seems to be the recipe, which is great, for it gives one frequent opportunities to enjoy the electrifying performance, and the glorious sound of that mighty V8 powerplant, to the full. Bumpy corners will send the front wheels pattering wide, at which time the general flexibility of the car also becomes apparent, when everything becomes a little vague. We aren't convinced that the new steering arrangement may not be slightly detrimental in these circumstances, as a degree of bump-steer seems to be quite unavoidable when with rack-and-pinion steering, even with the extra-long steering tie-rods employed, is combined with Morgan's unique sliding pillar front suspension. No doubt Morgans customers will soon let the manufacturers know if this is the case.

Nevertheless, one would need to be foolish indeed to find oneself in serious difficulties with the +8, despite the massive performance available, and the unrefined nature of the roadholding. Provided one heeds the golden rule, slow (relatively) in — fast (very fast) out, one can have great fun, rushing from corner to corner, Morgan bucking and roaring beneath one. The brakes are very reassuring, as they should be with 11″ discs up front, and 9″ drums behind, operated by dual hydraulic circuits, in such a lightweight car. Hard usage of the brakes revealed another interesting Morgan foible — involuntary cadence braking! After the initial hard application of the brakes, when the nose dips, it then bobs up again, and a porpoising motion is set up, with a chirp, chirp, chirp from the tyres as speed comes down. Very disconcerting at first, but the phenomenon gave us no concern when we had learnt to expect it.

After our drive, photographer Peter Robain and I arrived back at Malvern Link, cold, senses battered by the gale blowing into the cockpit, irreparably dishevelled, but grinning from ear to ear. The Morgan has that effect on people. We could readily appreciate the appeal of the marque, not as daily transport, perhaps, but as a fun car/adrenalin pump, the +8 has no peers, especially when value for money is considered. No wonder that the people at Pickersleigh Road enjoy building 'em, and the customers keep queueing up.

RoadTest

In its 75th year of production the Malvern firm has built the ultimate Morgan, a Plus 8 with the 190 bhp fuel injected engine from the Rover Vitesse. Its fantastic acceleration puts the Plus 8 firmly among the fastest Porsches!

MORGAN PLUS 8
INJECTION

When it comes to wanting more performance, Morgan owners are no different from those who queue up to buy Porsches. The Morgan Plus 8 may be an exceedingly rapid sportscar with its Rover V8 engine punching the light weight Malvern car to 60 mph from standstill in rather less than seven seconds but when the Austin Rover engineers boosted the power of the aluminium V8 to 190 bhp it was inevitable that the ultimate Morgan would soon emerge.

Yet the company was beaten in the race to produce a convertible with the fuel injected Rover V8 by Blackpool-based TVR which launched the exciting 135 mph 350i Tasmin last year. The car's enthusiastic reception has produced a string of customers. For

Morgan, limited resources for developing a new model and restricted supplies of the new engine — used to power the Rover Vitesse — meant more time was needed. To launch the ultimate high performance Plus 8 in the year of the company's 75th anniversary was an obvious attraction.

In 'Vitesse' form the 3,528 cc all aluminium alloy V8 engine has its twin SU carburetters replaced by Lucas L system fuel injection which is British designed but for the Bosch injectors. The improved fuel system combined with a rise in compression ratio from 9.35:1 to 9.75:1 encourages another 35 bhp from the V8. This lifts maximum power from 155 (DIN) at 5,250 rpm to 192 bhp at 5,280 rpm and maximum torque rises from 198 lb ft at 2,500 rpm to 220 lb ft at 4,000 rpm. In the Plus 8 the engine is linked to Morgan's own design of tubular exhaust manifolds accounting for the 2 bhp gain in power compared with the Rover. The engine drives through the familiar five-speed Rover gearbox to a live rear axle with a limited slip differential. Leaf springs are the only location for the axle even on the injection model; the dampers remain the lever arm design. Front suspension is also

unchanged with its sliding pillar design first seen 75 years ago. But the most surprising news for Morgan enthusiasts is that the beloved steering box has been replaced by rack and pinion steering. Built to Morgan's design by Jack Knight it has a central take-off point for the two long steering arms, this being intended to eliminate the car's notorious bump steer. The new steering set-up is standard on the fuel-injected Plus 8s (there is no official name for the 190 bhp monster) and optional on the carburetted model. Wheels and tyres are unchanged with 205/60 VR 15 Pirelli P6s on all corners.

Since we last tested a Plus 8 in 1982 the brake servo has disappeared and in its place a straightforward unassisted dual system with the same size solid discs at the front and drums at the rear.

The Plus 8 Injection's combination of incredible acceleration and open top motoring is rivalled by few cars and arguably anybody prepared to wait up to five years for delivery has decided he or she simply must have the only ash framed sports car still in production — nothing else will do. A list price of £12,999 (that is before extras like reclining seats and door handles) puts it between the less

expensive Reliant Scimitar GTC (£11,990) and the excellent Lotus Esprit S3 (£15,985). Representing good value for money and perhaps the closest character to that of the Morgan is the Panther Kallista 2.8 Injection (£9,245) — normally aspirated version costs a modest £7,990. Costing over £3,000 more than the Morgan is the TVR 350i (£16,400) which shares the same engine while uncrowned king of the soft top slingshot market is the 911 Porsche. The 911SC Cabriolet costs £25,556, almost the price of two Morgan Plus 8 Injections. Other possible rivals would have to be hard tops and are likely to include the Lotus Excel (£14,990), Lotus Esprit Turbo (£19,980) and the Porsche 944 (£16,073).

When considering the Morgan's performance, top speed and acceleration have to be treated as two very different things. The Plus 8 Injection can manage only a relatively feeble 122.2 mph flat out in fourth gear with the engine running at 5,600 rpm. Underlining the Morgan's poor aerodynamics, the TVR with the same engine manages a 135 mph top speed while the slightly more powerful Porsche (204 bhp) achieves an impressive 147 mph

maximum speed. The carburetted Kallista 2.8 we tested — arguable the car most similar in body to the Morgan — reached a maximum speed of 110.9 mph.

In terms of sheer acceleration the ordinary Plus 8 is super quick reaching 60 mph from standstill in 6.7 sec and pushing on to 100 mph in 21.8 sec. With its extra power the injection version turns in a 0 to 60 time of 6.1 sec which though very rapid is a disappointment compared with the reports emanating from Malvern of "mid fives" 0 to 60 mph time. Also the 911 manages the dash in 5.8 sec despite weighing (23.2 cwt) over 5 cwt more than the Morgan and the TVR (22.8 cwt) managing 6.0 sec admittedly with slightly lower gearing.

With the speedo checked for accuracy — surprising good and under reading if anything — we realised the ratios of the lower gears were rather longer than suggested by the 37, 60, 89 mph maxima claimed for 1st 2nd and 3rd by the Morgan. Unfortunately our enquiries revealed that our test car — Peter Morgan's personal Plus 8 and the only prototype Injection model — had suffered a gearbox failure just before collection and Rover had supplied a close ratio

Above: and Left: The archetypal British sportscar, superb looks with lovely flowing wings and a row of louvres on the bonnet to stare at as you drive. Below: Simple and snug interior, freezing in winter, boiling in summer

gearbox in double quick time as a replacement. Fourth remains a direct gear but first gear in this special 'box is incredibly high and good for 53 mph, 77 mph in second and an amazing 96 mph in third. Fifth is much less of an overdrive gear as its ratio is changed from 0.79 to 0.833.

Bearing this in mind it is easy to see that the Plus 8 Injection would easily break the 6 second mark for the 0 to 60 mph dash with lower gear ratios. To its credit it beats the TVR to 100 mph (15.7 sec compared with 16.5 sec) although a little behind the Porsche (14.2 sec). In top gear the injection model with 'that' gearbox is slower than the carburetted Morgan. This is the penalty of the engine modifications raising the speed at which peak torque is developed to 4,000 rpm. That said it is not until the 70 to 90 mph increment that the 911 can come within reach of the Morgan, the same goes for the TVR. In fourth gear the Morgan has the legs on the 911 and 350i but only above the 60 to 80 mph increment does it out gun its own stable mate.

On the road the 'Vitesse' engine feels markedly smoother than the carburetted one, starting more easily from cold or when hot and idling evenly. Unhappily the super long lower gears marred the tremendous acceleration as it is above about 4,000 rpm that the big difference is noticed. Instead of the punch beginning to diminish, the Plus 8 Injection is really starting to fly as the rev counter flicks up to 5,000 rpm and past. The car gets to 100 mph in just 15.7 sec but press on to 110 mph and it feels as if it has run into a wall as the terrific wind buffeting kills its acceleration.

In this class of high performance car 20 mpg economy is average and in this respect the Morgan fares well, returning 20.2 mpg. Although this is marginaly worse than for the carburetted version (20.8 mpg) it should prove the most frugal in normal use. Considering the TVR has the same engine and a more slippery body its consumption of 18.4 mpg is poor compared with the Morgan.

The Rover gearbox is a super affair, matching a meaty heaviness which is in character with the car, with an impressive slickness to make gear changing both rapid and pleasurable. But it is not perfect as the short lever often requires both hands to be raised for selection of reverse. The clutch is also heavy.

The change in the feel and action of the steering is perhaps more noticeable on a brief run in the car than the extra power. No longer do your biceps need to be flexed as the Plus 8 is parked, it really is quite light now. At speed the steering is a great deal more precise as the inch or two of free play at the wheel rim has disappeared. On the debit side it lacks feel — as the steering box set-up did — and at speed this is lighter than desirable and due to little castor angle does not get any heavier on lock.

With the rack and pinion steering it is no longer necessary to have such a large steering wheel. The number of turns lock to lock has been increased from 2¼ to 3¼ which is perhaps a retrograde step for a sportscar but at least the appalling 38 ft turning circle

has been reduced. Though on the test car we measured 34 ft on left lock and 38 ft on right lock!

The big step forward for Plus 8 handling and roadholding came when the old fashioned 70 series tyres were replaced by Pirelli P6s. And to be expected the Injected Morgan handles like the slower sister car with the exception of bump steer which is now hardly noticeable. Yet driven fast on anything less than smooth roads the Morgan is still a considerable handful but there has been a distinct improvement. The handling balance is essentially moderate understeer which is easily turned to neutral or oversteer depending on how much power is unleashed. The wide tyres give the car plenty of dry road grip and the marked rear weight bias ensures traction is good.

The Morgan is one car where handling and ride cannot easily be separated. The bump steer might be all but eliminated but it requires a confident driver to tackle a bumpy road at Porsche-speeds because the car will be thrown around at will with the poor pilot requiring all his concentration and making continuous steering inputs. Over bumps it soon becomes evident that the uncompromisingly firm front suspension is not complemented by the compliant rear which results in the car pitching badly front to back.

There are no ventilated discs and with good reason as the Morgan's brakes run cool, if anything, due to the openness of the wings and the car's light weight. And with no servo this means light pedal pressure achieves little retardation, presenting a rather dead feel to the driver. Warm the brakes up and press hard and the brakes prove progressive with excellent bite.

With the hood down occupants are in for buffeting if the Morgan's performance is to be used. The rival TVR is much better in this respect. With no sound deadening to speak of the Plus 8 is inevitably noisy with the hood up yet it is the wind noise that proves the most wearing on motorways.

Inside the Morgan nothing has changed since we last tested the car. Unless the optional leather seats are specified they come in black PVC. With no space for hip hugging Recaros, the standard sears are a compromise but sadly offer little lateral support. Legroom is quite good but most of our testers experienced the large steering wheel rubbing their knees.

The instruments include fuel, water temperature, volt and oil pressure guages but the rev counter lacks a red line.

To consider whether the Plus 8 Injection is good value or a better car than its rivals is simply to miss the point. If you want a Morgan nothing else will come close and if your wallet will stretch to £13,000 then this, the ultimate high performance Morgan is the perfect choice. The modest cost premium over the carburetted Plus 8 will surely make the full blooded injected model the natural choice for anybody who has waited five years for a Plus 8, and the magic call from Malvern.

MOTOR ROAD TEST No 40/84

MORGAN PLUS 8 INJECTION

PERFORMANCE

WEATHER CONDITIONS

Wind	10-11 mph
Temperature	81 deg F/27 deg C
Barometer	29.73 in Hg
	1006.7 mbar
Surface	Dry tarmacadam

MAXIMUM SPEEDS

	mph	kph
Banked Circuit (4th gear)	122.2	196.7
Best ¼ mile	125.0	201.3
Terminal speeds: at ¼ mile		
at kilometre		

Speed in gears (at 5,750 rpm):

1st	53	85
2nd	77	124
3rd	96	154

ACCELERATION FROM REST

mph	sec	kph	sec
0-30	2.5	0-40	2.1
0-40	3.6	0-60	3.3
0-50	4.7	0-80	4.7
0-60	6.1	0-100	6.6
0-70	7.8	0-120	8.6
0-80	9.9	0-140	11.8
0-90	12.6	0-160	15.8
0-100	15.7	0-180	22.8
0-110	20.9		
0-120	28.3		
Stand'g ¼	14.7	Stand'g km	27.1

ACCELERATION IN TOP

mph	sec	kph	sec
20-40	7.5	40-60	4.6
30-50	7.2	60-80	4.4
40-60	6.8	80-100	4.5
50-70	6.8	100-120	4.8
60-80	7.1	120-140	5.7
70-90	9.3	140-160	6.6
80-100	12.0		
90-110	15.5		

ACCELERATION IN 4TH

mph	sec	kph	sec
20-40	5.2	40-60	3.1
30-50	4.8	60-80	3.1
40-60	4.5	80-100	2.6
50-70	4.8	100-120	3.5
60-80	5.3	120-140	4.0

70-90	6.1	140-160	4.7
80-100	6.6	160-180	5.6
90-110	8.6		
100-120	11.8		

FUEL CONSUMPTION

Overall	20.2 mpg
	14.0 litres/100km
Govt tests	waived
	mpg (urban)
	mpg (56 mph)
	mpg (75 mph)
Fuel grade	97 octane
	4 star rating
Tank capacity	13.6 galls
	62 litres
Max range	340 miles (estimated)
	547 km
Test distance	1,000 miles
	1,690 km

NOISE

	dBA	Motor rating*
30 mph	76	24
50 mph	85	44
70 mph	91	69
Maximum†	97	100+

*A rating where 1 = 30 dBA and 100 = 96 dBA, and where double the number means double the loudness
†Peak noise level under full-throttle acceleration in 2nd

SPEEDOMETER (mph)

True mph	30	40	50	60	70	80	90	100
Speedo	29	39	49	60	70	80	90	99

Distance recorder: 2.6 per cent slow

WEIGHT

	cwt	kg
Unladen weight*	17.5	887
Weight as tested	20.8	1,056

*with fuel for approx 50 miles

Performance tests carried out by *Motor's* staff at the Motor Industry Research Association proving ground, Lindley.

Test Data: World Copyright reserved. No reproduction in whole or part without written permission.

GENERAL SPECIFICATION

ENGINE

Cylinders	V8
Capacity	3,532 cc
Bore/stroke	88.9 × 71.12 mm
Cooling	Water
Block	Aluminium alloy
Head	Aluminium alloy
Valves	Pushrod, hydraulic tappets
Cam drive	Chain
Compression	9.75:1
Fuel system	Lucas L system
Ignition	Breakerless
Bearings	5 main
Max power	192 bhp (DIN) 142 KW at 5,280 rpm
Max torque	220 lb ft (DIN) 298 Nm at 4,000 rpm

TRANSMISSION

Type	5-speed manual
Clutch dia	9.5 in
Actuation	Hydraulic

Internal ratios and mph/1,000 rpm

Top	0.833/26.0
4th	1.000/21.7
3rd	1.300/16.7
2nd	1.611/13.4
1st	2.330/9.3
Rev	3.428:1
Final drive	3.31:1

BODY/CHASSIS

Rust warranty	12 months or according to treatment
Aerodynamic drag coefficient (Cd)	N/A

SUSPENSION

Front	Independent by vertical sliding pillar, coil spring telescopic dampers
Rear	Live axle suspended on semi-elliptic leaf springs; lever arm dampers

STEERING

Type	Rack and pinion
Assistance	None

BRAKES

Front	Solid discs, 11 in dia
Rear	Drums, 9.75 in dia
Park	Rear
Servo	None
Circuit	Front/rear split
Rear valve	None
Adjustment	Manual

WHEELS/TYRES

Type	Aluminium alloy, 6.5 × 15 in
Tyres	205/60 VR 15
Pressures	18-20 psi F/R (normal) Up to 36 psi F/R (full load/high speed)

ELECTRICAL

Battery	12V, 57 Ah
Earth	Negative
Generator	Alternator, 65 Amp
Fuses	4
Headlights	
type	Halogen
dip	110 W total
main	120 W total

Make: Morgan **Model:** Plus 8 with fuel injected engine.
Maker: Morgan Motor Co. Ltd. Pickersleigh Road, Malvern Link, Worcs, WR14 2LL Tel: 06845 3104.
Price: £10,434.00 plus £869.50 Car Tax plus £1,695.53 VAT equals £12,999.03.

TheRivals

Other possible rivals include: Porsche 944 Lux (£16,073), Panther Kallista 2.8 Injection (£9,245), Lotus Excel (£14,990) and Lotus Esprit Turbo (£19,980).

MORGAN PLUS 8 INJECTION   £12,999

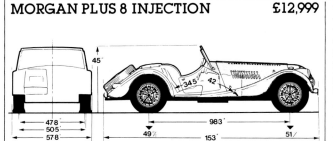

Power, bhp/rpm	19/5,280
Torque, lb ft/rpm	220/4,000
Tyres	205/60 VR 15
Weight, cwt	17.85
Max speed, mph	122.2
0-60 mph, sec	6.1
30-50 mph in 4th, sec	4.8
Overall mpg	20.2
Touring mpg	—
Fuel grade, stars	4
Boot capacity, cu ft	N/A
Test Date	September 1, 1984

Fuel-injection mods from the Rover Vitesse have given the Plus 8 an extra 35 bhp making it even faster accelerating. Non-standard gearbox in test car means acceleration times could be improved upon. Rack and pinion steering provides lighter loads at parking speeds and elimination of bump steer but is too light at speed and lacks feel. Non servo brakes good but require firm push. Classic looks of the Morgan remain one of its biggest attractions.

LOTUS ESPRIT S3   £15,985

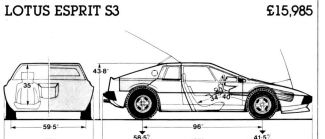

Power, bhp/rpm	160/6,500
Torque, lb ft/rpm	160/5,000
Tyres	205/70 VR 14/205/60 VR 14
Weight, cwt	21.0
Max speed, mph	135e
0-60 mph, sec	6.5
30-50 mph in 4th, sec	6.9
Overall mpg	23.1
Touring mpg	24.5
Fuel grade, stars	4
Boot capacity, cu ft	6.6
Test Date	August 22, 1981

A very much improved car in current Series 3 form, with outstanding handling and roadholding and a comfortable ride. Excellent performance backed up by impressive economy, safe brakes and a reasonably good gearchange. Greatly reduced noise levels make it much more pleasant to drive, but very poor visibility (worsened by stray reflections on instrument panel and glass division) is an inherent fault. Fair accommodation for two people with soft luggage.

PANTHER KALLISTA 2.8   £7,990

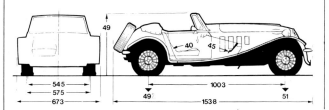

Power, bhp/rpm	135/5,200
Torque, lb ft/rpm	162/3,000
Tyres	185/70 HR 13
Weight, cwt	18.6
Max speed, mph	110.9
0-60 mph, sec	7.9
30-50 mph in 4th, sec	6.6
Overall mpg	22.8
Touring mpg	26.0
Fuel grade, stars	4
Boot capacity, cu ft	3.3
Test Date	February 19, 1983

At under £8,000, Panther's Kallista offers head-turning looks, straight-line perforamnce, and fine smooth-surface handling. Add in the delights of hand-built craftsmanship, easy-to-service Ford mechanicals, and the package looks strong. Weaknesses include handling on bumpy roads, a high level of interior noise and an draughty interior. If fun is a pre-requisite of your driving — rather than day-to-day practicality — then it could be a winner.

PORSCHE 911SC CABRIOLET   £25,556

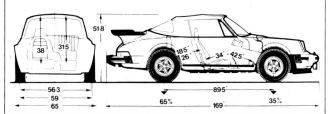

Power, bhp/rpm	204/5,900
Torque, lb ft/rpm	195/4,300
Tyres	185/70 VR 15/215/60 VR 15
Weight, cwt	23.2
Max speed, mph	147.3
0-60 mph, sec	5.8
30-50 mph in 4th, sec	6.0
Overall mpg	20.1
Touring mpg	—
Fuel grade, stars	4
Boot capacity, cu ft	9.8
Test Date	June 4, 1983

First soft-top Porsche for nearly two decades, the 911 SC Cabriolet ranks as one of the most impressive open cars ever made. Superb 3-litre flat six delivers storming acceleration and 147 mph top speed yet returns more than 20 mpg. Tremendous handling becomes tricky in the wet and ride is very firm around town, but as a practical day-to-day supercar, the Porsche has no peers. Hood is beautifully made (in keeping with the excellent build), and easy to use.

TVR TASMIN 350i   £16,400

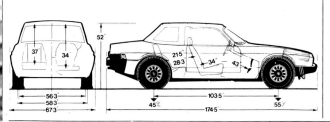

Power, bhp/rpm	190/5,280
Torque, lb ft/rpm	220/4,000
Tyres	205/60 VR 15
Weight, cwt	22.8
Max speed, mph	134.8
0-60 mph, sec	6.0
30-50 mph in 4th, sec	6.0
Overall mpg	18.4
Touring mpg	—
Fuel grade, stars	4
Boot capacity, cu ft	3.5
Test Date	August 27, 1983

With terrific performance, excellent handling and brakes, a satisfying gearchange and comfortable driving position, TVR's new muscle car has all the fundamentals of an ideal driver's car. Good ventilation and plush trim are unexpected bonuses, ride comfort and fuel consumption reasonable in this sporting context. Exhaust noise is excessive and hood-up wind noise disappointing, though the lack of buffeting with the hood down is most impressive.

RELIANT SCIMITAR GTC   £11,990

Power, bhp/rpm	135/5,200
Torque, lb ft/rpm	152/3,000
Tyres	185/HR 14
Weight, cwt	26.3
Max speed, mph	114.1
0-60 mph, sec	9.7
30-50 mph in 4th, sec	8.5
Overall mpg	23.7
Touring mpg	27.4
Fuel grade, stars	4
Boot capacity, cu ft	6.6
Test Date	June 14, 1980

Using the same formula of four seats and a soft top, the Scimitar GTC plugs the market gap left by the Triumph Stag. Like the GTE on which it's based, the GTC, now powered by the 2.8-litre Ford V6, combines flexible performance with impressive economy in an attractive, if expensive package. Precise handling and excellent hood are plus points, a hard ride, dated interior and poor gearchange earn black marks.

MORGAN

a suitable place for treatment

For over 70 years, Morgan has been building hand-made sports cars using traditional skills and crafts. It is still a family business, but now has a world-wide following for its individualistic, and much-loved, products.

Current owner Peter Morgan

Body frames are made of ash — it's light, strong and repairable

The feminine touch is given to the neatly-pleated upholstery

Panel beating is still carried out in the traditional way

Engines of various shapes and sizes will fit under the bonnet

Final assembly, with the new cars almost ready for the road

I T WAS BACK in the early 1900s that HFS Morgan bought a 7hp twin Peugeot engine, intending to build a motorcycle. Although he was a keen cyclist, his dislike of motorised two-wheel transport prompted him to build the Peugeot engine into a light, three-wheeled tubular chassis which he had already designed — a decision which was to change the destinies of all concerned: the first of the now world-famous Morgan three-wheelers had been born. This very first model was completed in 1909 and was called the Morgan Runabout — a single-seater with tiller steering.

Morgans clearly attract the slogan writers. A sticker on one Morgan we saw read: 'Have you hugged your cat today?' For the uninitiated let's explain that Morgans are often lovingly referred to as Moggies. Another sticker read: 'I love God, country and Morgans — but not necessarily in that order'.

HFS took it to London in 1910 and secured only five or six orders, but there was plenty of interest and, at the Olympia motor show, it was suggested it would sell well if it could carry two people. He went back the following year with a two-seater and the orders poured in. Still poor HFS couldn't find anyone interested in buying the project so, with a £3000 loan from his grandfather, he set about building the cars himself.

The present owner, Peter Morgan, joined the company in 1947, becoming first a draughtsman and later managing director. HFS died in 1959, just four months before the company's 50th anniversary celebrations.

Peter has a son and two daughters, but his son Charles has become a star cameraman with ITN. While Peter hopes his son will take over one day he adds: 'I am not terribly interested in the paternal angle. The car has been built for many years and many people are interested in seeing it go on.'

Today, Peter employs more than 100 people and drives to work in a Ferrari. 'You don't become a millionaire overnig but you want to be profitable has been difficult in recent years because the Morgan does appeal to the young, bu nowadays they don't have th money they did'.

But young people do buy them, somehow, and there a always secondhand ones. Other owners have invested many hours in restoring wrecks, for a Morgan is neve thrown away. Adds Peter: 'Recently we supplied one to the King of Spain, who had a cover made for it so it could live on his yacht.

'Today you may have to w up to six years or as little as months for a Morgan, but in the early 1960s we had diffic times. The car's style wouldr allow it to sell in Britain or Europe but, luckily, the US

A stuffed owl looks balefu down on the final-assemb shop — and it isn't there f decorative reasons. Birds (t feathered sort) used to flutter and leave droppings on the ne cars — particularly, for som reason, the blue ones. Morga hasn't had that problem for 2 years, thanks to the owl . . .

took 87% of our production. That was why, in 1963 I developed another body, the Plus 4 Plus, but people didn't like it. Then surprise, surprise interest came back and by 19 demand was strong again. Th interest has held up ever sinc

Those much disliked Morgans must now be very collectable indeed. Only 28 o the Plus 4 Plus were made, a they were scattered about world-wide.

Says Peter: 'We didn't mak any money, but it did at least show that Morgans can chan if necessary.' □

WHAT IS THE connection between French sex symbol Brigitte Bardot and the King of Spain? The answer is that they both own Morgan cars — those unique sports machines that are still hand-made in a Worcestershire factory set in some of Britain's most spectacular scenery, the Malvern Hills.

Here, in Elgar's inspiring countryside, the hills are alive to a new sound — the roar of a 3.5-litre fuel-injection Morgan Plus 8. That's £13,000-worth of vintage-style soft-top sports car propelled by a vicious 190bhp of Rover Vitesse engine. It sounded like music to the ears of Supertest driver BOB OXFORD, who went north to investigate . . .

SUPERMOGGIE!

Photography: John Rigby

How it goes

The company will be 75 years old this year, and these days it is in the hands of Peter Morgan, son of the founder known to all as H F S Morgan. Plans are well in hand for celebrations, and thousands of Morgans from all over the world will be visiting Malvern to join the festivities.

'I am willing to change anything on the car except the general shape and style,' says Peter Morgan. 'That is somewhat individual, to say the least, and I wish to retain it. With the general contraction in the motor industry, all cars are going down the same road — they all look like Fords. I like the look of the Morgan'.

About eight cars are built each week — about half are 4 Plus 4s, half the powerful Plus 8s. The Plus 8 is built only as a two-seater, and this new car with the fuel-injected Rover Vitesse engine was the car that we had come to drive.

The Morgan starts life as a rolling steel chassis, to which is mounted an ash (yes, that's right) body-frame, which is eventually panelled. Certain panels which are likely to rust are now aluminium instead of steel, but for an extra £242 buyers can have an all-aluminium body. The ash-frame is light and strong, giving little trouble in Europe — although the same cannot be said for cars that go to the heat of Saudi Arabia!

The new car has just over 190bhp and, according to

normally carburettored version.'

What else could a Morgan enthusiast consider? Says Peter: 'I think we always have competition to a point, but we have no direct competition. The last serious rivals were MGs, and I was sorry to see them go. I didn't want to see the demise of the open car. Happily, people are making open versions again, the Golf and the Escort for instance, and this helps us. But while a lot of people like the looks of the Morgan — it looks more sporty

indeed going out with two-litre twin-cam Fiat engines installed, which would be nice here, too.

With the fuel-injected Vitesse engine the Plus 8 will now be fast enough for the German autobahns, and a lot of interest is already coming from there. Indeed, there is a Morgan club in virtually any country you can name, and the first injected Plus 8 was due to leave with its diplomat owner to go to Warsaw. Five more Morgan owners from Britain are driving there, too — just for the sheer fun of it.

So far the new fuel-injected version of the Plus 8 has no name. People have suggested that it should be called a Super Sports, but Peter Morgan objects to that. 'I call a car a Super Sports only when it has really achieved something. I last introduced the name when Chris Lawrence won the two-litre class at Le Mans in 1962. We can't do that again, but there are events angled towards sports cars like ours. There's a 24-hour event at Snetterton which Morgans won three years out of four. We have had some good names in our time. The original three-wheeler was the Runabout, and then we had the Aero. If we had an aerodynamic car we might resuscitate that one.'

The new car may well reach 130mph — though as DRIVE discovered, such a maximum speed is slightly academic: the open car does get noisy when you venture beyond 75-80mph. As Peter Morgan puts it: 'We can't take on Mercedes for quietness at high speeds.'

Make no mistake about it — the injected Plus 8 Morgan is a very exciting car to drive. It's one of those rare hairy-chested

If the Morgan waiting list did not exist, the feeling is that only 25% of the interested parties could pay for their car immediately. Many buyers place their names on the list in the hope that, by the time the car is ready, they will be the managing director of their company. That said, one buyer actually took out a second mortgage on his house to indulge his dream.

Is there a vast profit to be made from buying a Morgan and selling it the next day? Not any more. Snag is that the car market is very 'down' and those premium prices to jump the queue have disappeared. You might get a little over the odds for a 4/4, but certainly not for a Plus 8. They retail at list price and can be slightly less — although two years ago they fetched £2000-3000 more than list price. The speculators have moved out of Morgans and the factory was glad to see them go. Buy now and sell in Morgans can hold their value well, however. three years' time, and you should get back what you paid.

Peter: 'It's great — quicker and more powerful at higher revs. Acceleration feels about the same — you should get 0-60mph in around 5.3sec and a top speed of 130mph. I have the greatest respect for the Rover engine because it's so flexible — superb for passing someone quickly and then dropping back to your speed. This car will cost about £13,000 — about £1500 more than a

than many a modern sports car — one way and another there's quite a lot against it.

'Our market is small. It can be a first car, but I'd put it this way: if a husband is keen on competition to a small degree he might have a Plus 8 and his wife might have a hatchback. Alternatively, the husband could have a Rover or Jaguar and he'd buy the wife a Morgan for shopping.'

New versions in the pipeline could include a two-litre version to fill the obvious gap. We were surprised to see that some export models were

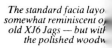

sports cars that are disappearing faster than the British Empire.

How comfortable

First thoughts are that the car's cockpit is somewhat cramped, with nowhere to stow luggage and the driver sitting rather too close to the large, leather-covered steering wheel. The pedal arrangement is such that there's nowhere to brace your left foot properly.

Newcomers frequently turn on the windscreen wipers — there are three of them, by the way — when intending to indicate. These days a Morgan must be the only car made outside Japan with indicators on the righthand stalk. It seems, too, that ECE

regulations insist that the rear-view mirror must be glued on to the centre of the screen — effectively cutting one's view of the nearside front wing.

One quickly realises that the car's light weight and big engine are a recipe for very exciting motoring. Tyres are 205/60 VR 15 Pirelli P6s, designed to complement the special machinery, and the car's low centre of gravity ensures that cornering speeds can be high. That said, on the wet roads we experienced during much of our test driving, the power needed to be applied with care. The Morgan could quickly teach a newcomer the meaning of oversteer...

Instrumentation is easy to read — although on our car the steering wheel's rim obsured the voltmeter, and when the tonneau cover was zipped across the passenger side, other gauges disappeared, too. The tacho is not red-lined so presumably, if your ears can stand it, you can go all the way to 7000rpm. The speedometer proved to be very accurate indeed and was graduated up to 170mph.

Minor switch gear consists of a row of rocker-switches reminiscent of the early E-type Jaguars. They could be confusing in the dark, and oblige you to take your eyes off the road to locate them. We were disappointed to find the

*...years young — and
...anges are something
...at Morgan owners
...n't want to see.
...evertheless, over the
...ars evolution has
...eant the introduction
...more powerful
...gines and wider
...heels and tyres to cope
...ith the increased
...rformance*

SUPERMOGGIE!

mph	time (sec) 5th	time (sec)
20-40	6.6	5.2
30-50	6.9	4.8
40-60	6.9	4.8
50-70	7.7	5.2
60-80	8.0	5.4
70-90	8.7	6.2

0-60mph through the gears
6.1 sec.
Overall fuel consumption
25mpg

wipers had no intermittent setting — merely two speeds and a flick-wipe facility.

The steering deserves a special mention, for this is the only Morgan available with rack-and-pinion steering as standard — normally a £311 extra. It is light and informative — but already some drivers are saying it is a little too light. Maybe a smaller steering wheel would solve the problem if it is regarded as such.

Being a prototype, our test car was fitted with two different types of seat — one reclining, one fixed — so that both types could be tested at once. With Morgans being rather like bespoke suits, buyers can have any type of seating they like. While ours were covered in plastic, most buyers specify leather for an extra £373, and very nice it would look, too.

While on the subject of extras, the Morgan company must be the only one to charge an extra £25 for door handles — 'You do want door handles, don't you, sir?' It's not as silly as it sounds, really, because Peter Morgan believes the car is more secure without them, and they are not strictly necessary.

Who says they don't build 'em like they used to? They do in Malvern

There wasn't time to complete a full track test, but nonetheless we put a watch on the Morgan. Would it really live up to the factory's claims?

Well, we couldn't check-out the top speed, but we did get some good in-gear acceleration times that testify to the V8's good spread of torque …

VERDICT

The Morgan's ride is firm — downright bone-jarring on bad roads, but otherwise, it's tolerable. Combined with the noise, though, it made us dubious about wanting to live with one.

On our car, the heater blew hot air when switched off, and remained impossible to 'fine-tune'.

But forget the niggles. This Morgan offers 190 bhp, a lightweight body and thrill-a-minute motoring. Let's hope it is still around in another 75 years.

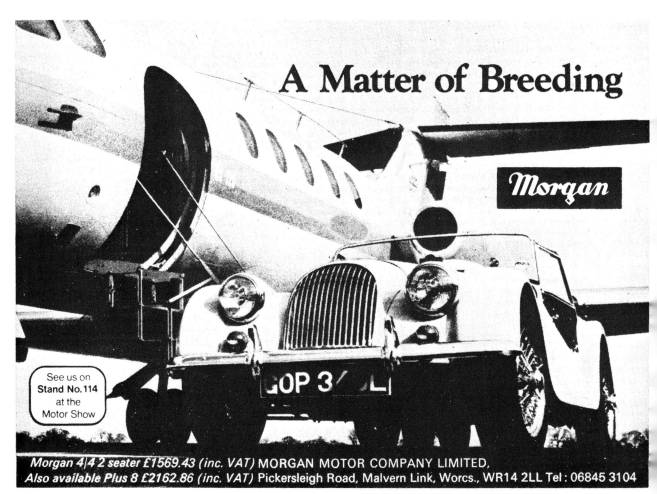

A PAIR OF MORGANS

Honoring Morgan's 75th Anniversary, we drive Toly Arutunoff's 17-year-old National Champion Morgan 4/4 and its street car companion

BY PETER EGAN

THIS BEING MORGAN'S 75th Anniversary, we decided to spare no effort in celebrating this banner year in the company's history. Dennis Simanaitis, Engineering Editor and resident Morgan buff, was dispatched (or possibly dispatched himself) to the home factory at Malvern, England. Naturally, Steve Kimball and I boarded a plane for Tulsa, Oklahoma.

Tulsa, you say. Why, of all non-English places, Tulsa?

Because that's the home of a gentleman Morgan racer with the unusual name of Anatoly Arutunoff (pronounced Are-uh-TUNE-awv). Those who follow SCCA road racing will remember that Arutunoff won the National Runoffs in 1981, driving his H Production Morgan 4/4 brilliantly in the pouring rain, the square-edged roadster outskating an angry swarm of Bugeye Sprites by eight seconds.

It was a popular win, because he'd won the Runoffs in 1973 in the same car, only to be disqualified for slightly oversized valves. Arutunoff, who had been assured by the engine builder

that the engine was dead legal, was as surprised as anyone.

When Arutunoff won in 1981, the car cruised through its teardown inspection without a hitch and Anatoly was awarded the President's Cup for his fine drive; an award he received while wearing a T-shirt silkscreened as a tuxedo.

About a year ago, Arutunoff sent us an invitation to come to Tulsa to sample his National Championship Morgan, adding that he had a very nice street Morgan of the same vintage for comparison purposes. That, together with the fact that Arutunoff is the owner of Hallett Motor Racing Circuit northeast of Tulsa, made the offer irresistible. Not many people, after all, have two Morgans and their own test track.

Arriving at Arutunoff's race shop (housed in the rear of the import car dealership he owns), we met his team mechanic (carpenter?) Tim O'Toole, who showed us around the place. This sizable garage contains, besides the two Morgans, such other objects of Arutunoff's affection as a 1954 Cooper/Ford, a 1969

McKee 4-wheel-drive Can-Am car and a half-dozen other un-usual cars, of mostly Italian extraction.

The two Morgans are both Series V 4/4 models, bought right off the Morgan assembly line in 1967 (for $1760 each!) while Arutunoff was visiting England. The British Racing Green street car, originally purchased as a parts car for the racer, is powered by its original 1498-cc Ford 116E 4-cylinder pushrod engine, while the British Racing Flesh (Peach, actually—a Ford truck color) competition car has been backdated to the Series IV 1340-cc Ford 109E engine for H Production.

Modifications to the racing car include Koni shocks, gussets at the front to support the sliding pillar suspension, fiberglass fenders, fuel cell inside the spare tire bay, alloy bonnet, Good-year slicks on 15 x 6-in. Minilite racing wheels with 1-in. spacers to widen the track, and an extensive roll cage to steady the Mor-gan's flexible wood and stamped steel ladder frame and body structure. "In stock form," mechanic O'Toole told us, "the chassis is pretty gooey and likes to walk around a lot. We had an Orkin man check the wood in the chassis and he declared it termite free. We have a termite certificate in the office."

The race engine has oversize Hepolite Powermax flat-top pis-tons, a Crane cam and a ported cylinder head. The compression ratio is 10.5:1 and the redline is 7500 rpm. Arutunoff says the last time they checked, it produced 87 bhp at the rear wheels.

The car has 11.0-in. discs at the front and 9.0-in. drums at the rear, which provide firm, easily modulated stopping. From the driver's seat, the Morgan feels like a wider MG TC with real brakes, better steering, more horsepower and a higher-pitched, less raspy exhaust note.

Arutunoff passed us on the highway, and by the time we reached Hallett he was unlocking the gate to the track. Hallett Motor Racing Circuit is a 1.8-mile track built on the highest point of land for miles around in the rolling Oklahoma countryside. Its four straights and 10 turns go up- and downhill, a mixture of blind and off-camber corners with a couple of sweepers and a 3/10-mile main straight.

Arutunoff gave me a track tour for several laps in the RX-7, then switched places so I could practice and learn the lines. Finally getting comfortable with the circuit, I took the green street Morgan out first.

After touring in an RX-7, a dead stock Morgan 4/4 on a race track seems very much a think-ahead car in braking, shifting, turning in, etc; stable but not as cat-quick as a modern sports car. There is also a feeling of fragility, a tendency to go easy on the car out of respect for the age of its design, if not for the age of the car itself. The Morgan corners flatter, with less roll than the RX-7 and feels as though there is no rubber in the suspension, but merely flex in the chassis. The relative stiffness and harsher ride initially give you less feel for the road surface.

After a time, however, the Morgan builds confidence. It doesn't break or go off the track and the only evident handling quirk is a predictable amount of understeer, most noticeable in tight corners. Once you get into the rhythm of driving the Morgan it can be pushed fairly hard, and the notion that it has to be coddled or treated like an antique vanishes. The faster you drive, the more compliant and sure-footed it feels in corners (a sensation aided, no doubt by the Avon 165SR-15 radials). The car is amazingly forgiving at all speeds, and when the tail is flung out it stays flung but never threatens to come around or change attitude. Compared with the Mazda, it feels more a race car in the traditional sense, a slightly stiffer, less compromised machine, all its body motions horizontal rather than vertical. Put simply, the Morgan is, by any standard, a fine handling car.

Slow down for a cool-off lap and the other side of the Morgan personality comes back into focus. Sitting low in the driver's seat and holding on to that big 3-spoke steering wheel, you look down the long louvered hood and feel a little like a youngster on his first driving lesson around the family estate (Carlyle, take my son out and teach him to drive), circa 1937. As a machine, it's like some kind of motorized pram for daring children, a wood-and-leather contraption dusted off and brought down from the attic. At low speed the race car goes away and the Morgan becomes purely romantic; a low, handsome roadster, completely, unquestionably English.

Arutunoff warmed up the race car while I dug out my helmet and official race car driver's outfit. I slid into the driver's seat and tightened the belts.

Driver's seat may be something of a misnomer. What the car actually has is a rectangle of plywood to sit on and a curved piece of aluminum to support the back and ribs. The driver sits, essentially, on the floor. The gearbox, a Lotus Elan 5-speed with 1st and reverse locked out, has the optional Morgan remote shifter that brings the gear lever to the driver rather than the other way around. After the mellow hum of the 1499-cc street engine, the 1340-cc race engine was quite a change, with its cammy idle and staccato exhaust note. I slipped (clashed) the gear lever into 1st and motored out onto the track.

The first thing I noticed was the smoked plastic windscreen, the top of which cut directly across my vision. Craning my neck I could see over the top, while slumping I looked—sort of—through it. Road bumps produced an over/under/over/under effect reminiscent of a nickel flip show. I took Corner 1 a little faster than expected because the DS-11 competition brake pads had not yet warmed up and found that my weight against the

The green street car, having been refurbished a few years ago the Morgan factory, is in very nice condition. Not concours, but comfortably broken in and well cared for; a car that gets driven as well as admired. It has black leather factory-option bucket seats, wire wheels and a completely stock appearance except for a minuscule K mart tachometer at the top of the instrument panel.

O'Toole loaded the race car onto a 1969 Chevy transporter for the 45-mile trip to Hallett, while Arutunoff folded down the windscreen on the street Morgan. "You can follow the transporter with the green car," he told us, "and I'll be along in a few minutes with my RX-7." He produced a proper rakish driving cap from behind a toolbox and gave it to me for the trip.

Steve Kimball and I settled into the low Morgan buckets and I started the engine, which immediately settled down to that wonderful light sewing machine clatter peculiar to British pushrod engines. Inhaling the slightly musty smell of wood and leather, I eased the push/pull gear lever forward and accelerated through open garage doors and onto the highway.

On the road, the Morgan has a stiff but fairly comfortable ride, handling dips and rises better than it does the sudden shock of potholes and road seams, which bring out the stern side of the suspension. The shifter, poking out in a straight horizontal shaft from beneath the instrument panel, works smoothly and easily.

aluminum transmission tunnel caused it to lean against the prop shaft with appropriate scuffing noises.

After a few warm-up laps I had still been unable to bring the pads up to clasping temperature. This was a real problem because the race car has a locked differential that causes it to go straight in a corner unless power is applied, and it's difficult to apply power while sailing into a corner 20 mph faster than expected. After a sharp spin in the downhill kink, I decided it would be fun to go easy in the tighter corners and concentrate on the faster bends, where less braking was needed.

In those the Morgan is stable and neutral, with a harsh ride (plywood seat amplified) but no discernible body roll. It's the quintessential coal cart production racer with four fat tires and a highly tuned engine, all held together by a sturdy roll structure. The steering is quick but feels short on caster, with a tendency to take a set and dolly toward the apex after the wheel is turned in. That and a slight amount of play in the steering box give the front end a twitchiness that takes some adaptation. With practice, however, you almost get used to it. Almost.

After about 5 more laps I felt I had done enough penance to atone for all my sins and came in to turn the car over to its rightful master, for whom I had a new respect. Arutunoff had won the Runoffs in this car—in the rain—an act of finesse and fine judgment performed in a very spartan car with (I imagined) fairly limited steering feedback under slick road conditions. I concluded that the Morgan racer was like a good German shepherd or Doberman guard dog; a 1-man car whose purpose in life was not necessarily to make strangers comfortable.

When I turned the car over to Arutunoff, I mentioned my vision problems with the windscreen. He nodded. "I hate it," he said. "I've had the same problem ever since we put that thing on, and I haven't gotten around to fixing it."

He drove for a few laps, spun in the downhill kink and returned to the pits. "This car simply has no brakes," he said. We checked the brake fluid (okay) and concluded that, as the pedal was firm, the problem must be glazed or oil-soaked pads from the car's last race.

It was sundown by then and we loaded the race car onto the transporter to follow Arutunoff's RX-7 back toward Tulsa. Kimball and I drove the street Morgan, cruising along under a dusty red summer moon. This time we put the windscreen up, to ward off winged creatures of the night. Crossing the rollercoaster terrain of northern Oklahoma, it was warm on the hilltops and refreshingly cool in the bottomlands. Almost too refreshing.

We looked for a heater switch or valve of some kind, checking on and beneath the dash in the dim light of the instruments, but couldn't find any. It was quite possible the car had no heater. We shrugged and decided to ignore the chill, concentrating instead on the road and the pleasant drone of the engine. "Not a car for frill-seekers," I mumbled, remembering a phrase from a Morgan ad I'd read long ago. ⓂⓋ

MR ANATOLY ARUTUNOFF

THE NAME IS Armenian by way of St Petersburg; Anatoly's father and mother escaped from Russia just about the time Lenin had designs on that ancient city's name. "An especially zealous band of revolutionaries was coming through the neighborhood shooting every man without calluses on his hands, and my father, an engineer, didn't have any," says Anatoly.

It was Russia's loss. The family came to America, where the young engineer designed the first successful immersible pump for use in oil wells, an invention that coincided neatly with the great Oklahoma oil boom. The Arutunoffs moved to Bartlesville, Oklahoma, a town just north of Tulsa and formed the REDA (loosely translated, Russian Electric Dynamo Arutunoff) Pump Co Inc, selling enough pumps to buy a large house across the street from the Phillips family of Phillips 66 fame. It was into this house that Anatoly was born in 1936, and where he lives still.

An early interest in things mechanical got Anatoly into the sports car movement of the Fifties. In 1957 he bought a Porsche Carrera Speedster and began road racing at airport and fairgrounds tracks. His first race was at Garnett, Kansas in 1959. "Jim Hall was there with a Maserati. My total race preparation consisted of taking off my air cleaners and bolting on a pair of velocity stacks. The fuel truck had lots of gas left over after the race, so they just filled everybody's tow car for free."

After that he raced a 1962 Studebaker Hawk GT in SCCA events as well as at the 1964 Sebring sedan race, where he beat Jim Clark "because a wheel fell off Clark's Lotus Cortina." Other favorites were a 1962 Lancia Flaminia, raced by Arutunoff at the Nürburgring, the Targa Florio and Spa endurance races in 1963; a 1964 Appia Zagato and a 1960 Alfa 2000. Other than the Morgan, his most successful racing car was a 1961 Lotus Seven America, a car that was eventually destroyed in a towing accident, but resurrected by Allan Girdler.

"In 1966 I looked at the rules to see what could win, and got interested in a Morgan for H-Production. They had 15 x 6 wheels vs the Sprite's 13 x 5 in. wheels, so I figured we could outcorner them." Which he did, of course, many times, finally winning the rain-soaked SCCA Runoffs in 1981. "If I could concentrate just 15 minutes a day the way I concentrated in that race," he reflects, "I could be Emperor of the World."

Arutunoff now has a growing interest in vintage racing, running his Cooper-Ford whenever possible between Showroom Stock races in his Honda Prelude. "Vintage racing," he says, "is now 95 percent of what SCCA racing used to be; five serious guys out in front, and everyone else having a lot of fun."—*Peter Egan*

PROFILE

Morgan Plus 8

Cutaway shows construction — separate chassis, wooden body frame and near vintage mechanical layout

MALVERN MUSCLE

**One of the last true 'blood-and-
guts' sports cars is Morgan's Plus
8. Mike Walsh is your guide to its
fascinating story and what to look
for when buying one**

here is one intriguing question about the Plus 8. Why did Peter Morgan wait until the late sixties to put his vintage 'hot rod' into production?

The chemistry of a strong sports car chassis blessed with excellent roadholding and graceful, classic style mated to a lusty V8 powerhouse has continually proved a success, particularly with supercars from the fifties such as the Allard J2X, and the AC Cobra, Sunbeam Tiger and TVR Tuscan from the sixties. America, before the days of restrictive emission control and tight safety legislation, craved for a traditional English sports car with the performance to out-pace and out-corner Detroit muscle or Italian exotica. MG had long proved that England was closer to American hearts than Italy. The cross-breeding of Shelby's Cobra clearly proved the market potential, and even during the thirties the Ford V8 roadsters were the budget pocket rockets with snappy acceleration and jazzy styling that could embarrass many highly priced sports cars.

The Plus 8's ancestry harks back to a golden age when H.F.S. Morgan fitted a flat-head 22hp V8 to a chassis. This one-off is fondly remembered by Peter Morgan, the company's present Managing Director. He used this demon Moggie more than anyone else, and covered some 9000 miles in it. With its early 'flat rad' sitting further forward on a lengthened frame to accommodate the V8, its body always in grey primer, and driven on trade plates, it was a superb pre-war Q-car.

"It ran out of speed at about 95mph," says Peter Morgan, "and its cable operated drum brakes suffered from ghastly fade. No-one knew how to cure it in those days." He remembers vividly a cross-country chase with Forrest Lycett in his famous Bentley 8-litre special after the celebrated Donington Grand Prix of 1937: "The Morgan managed to keep ahead on the twisting country lanes, but a long straight near Beaconsfield saw the Bentley draw alongside, Lycett smugly glancing down at the Morgan and then changing up to top to power ahead. A fabulous machine."

Sadly, car taxation changed and the V8 was replaced by a Standard 8 engine with an Arnott blower. "From the sublime to the ridiculous," Peter recalls. His biggest regret was never fitting a 30hp V8.

Rational softies

It was not until 1968, when the Morgan's trusty TR engine had become obsolete, that Peter Morgan was forced to look for a suitable replacement and that V8 power was seriously considered again. The Ford V4 and V6 had been investigated, but somehow just didn't impress. Peter had the foresight to see that the Morgan needed performance to match the new exclusive breed of supercars and to take Morgan into the seventies. The concept of popular open sports car had slowly been replaced by the 'hot-shot' saloon package and the 'GT' revolution, very much enforced because of the scare that America was going to ban open cars! The new breed of sporting enthusiasts were rational softies who fussed over their hair styles, whose girlfriends hated cold draughts and uncomfortable seats. The Morgan had to become more exclusive, and needed stunning performance to give the image real credibility.

Peter Wilks at Rover proposed the idea of a sports car utilising the aluminium Buick V8. Peter Morgan was keen to keep the company independent, yet was desperate to get the new engine. As it turned out he had great difficulty in getting engines, although drawings and detailed information of Rover's modifications to the GM block were only too forthcoming. Rover could see the image boost for their range from the Morgan sports car.

At about this time, the cheery, experienced Maurice Owen, acknowledged by many as the father of the Plus 8, entered the story. Maurice had recently fitted a Buick V8 to George Keelock's Cooper hillclimb car, and knew the whereabouts of more Buick engines, one of which was used in a McLaren. He also saw the potential of a stunning road car with considerable horsepower, and realised that the Morgan chassis was an ideal choice. He visited an excited Peter Morgan, and subsequently found full employment in the Malverns to supervise and develop the new project.

The transplant of the Buick engine (Rover versions were still not available) went very smoothly. In the small workshop in the corner of the factory where he still works, Maurice beavered away on the secret project. The chassis was extended forwards to accommodate the new engine, and the location of the rear springs was changed to stop axle tramp with the extra power. The original prototype (chassis no R7000) had twin bulges in the bonnet to make room for the carburettor, and the brakes and steering were beefed up. The car was registered OUY 200E, and this first Plus 8 was entered for the MCC Edinburgh trial in 1967 "to see if anything fell off or needed strengthening."

These events had a long tradition for Morgan development, and created an ideal testing ground, although the more cynical critics have claimed that trialling and motor racing are extreme conditions, and that Morgans forgot they were designing a car for the road! The only problem on the trial was fuel starvation

143

Latest Vitesse-engined Plus 8 is little different from its predecessors — there's rack-and-pinion steering, more power, and the wheels are now back to the early style

on very rough ground but this was cured by a conversion to later SUs with integral float systems. The Buick engine in fact was lighter than the TR unit, and was virtually indestructible in conventional motoring.

The Plus 8 could have debuted at Earls Court in 1967, but still no affirmative decision from GM had been made. But Peter had an influential friend at GM who happened to own a Morgan, and the car was regularly parked in a prominent position at the Detroit headquarters — the right people were impressed. It soon become clear that the American company had no objection to Morgan using the V8, but when Triumph took over Rover, Donald Stokes had rather different views, and saw the Morgan as a market threat to the TRs.

Buick commitment

Peter Morgan then visited Triumph's Harry Webster and was shown the Stag V8 and the slant-four Saab engines, but made it clear that he was already committed to the Buick as the prototype had been completed. Still no firm decision was forthcoming. Eventually Stokes and George Turnbull agreed to visit Morgan, and to their amazement were actually able to test the car. They were impressed, and agreed to allow the use of the engine "as long as they didn't make too many and made sure it's a Morgan in the traditional mould." There was no need for them to fear the car on either count.

The delay was in fact very useful, as it allowed time for refinements to the prototype. The chassis was widened by 2½ins to drop the engine and thus remove the 'suggestive' bonnet bulges that so worried Peter Morgan. The wire wheels were replaced with the distinctive finned alloy designs which have since returned to the latest production Plus 8s with a wider rim size.

Two more prototypes were built, R7001 carrying the personalised company registration MMC11 and R7002 carrying AB16, now on Peter's own Ferrari 400i. The total cost of development, incredibly, had not exceeded £15,000.

The Plus 8 was launched to the public on stand 127

at Earls Court with two cars and a bare chassis just in case anyone didn't notice the transplant. The car, not very far removed from that original design, remains in production today 17 years later, and you still have to wait five or six years for a new one.

How then has this antiquated design lasted so long, and how does it still have a healthy future provided that supply of Rover V8 engines is forthcoming?

No one can ignore those classic lines that evoke such a strong image of carefree open air motoring, much like that other true original, the Lotus Seven. It's a pure exposed driving thrill — driving any other sports

car is like paddling in Wellington boots. Once behi the wheel, you revel in the stirring way the Plus 8 tak sweeping roads in its stride, inherently stable w that wonderful throaty V8 sound that goes with fier acceleration, and of course that majestic view dov the bonnet. Give the chassis a smooth road and its gr is tenacious, the Plus 8 handling beautifully produce an experience that few other sports cars c match and one which you will never forget. That's biased view of Morgan fever for which there is no cu

It's easy to be critical of this 'vintage' animal. T standard of the finish often leaves much to be desire

Woodwork class — Morgan bodies being handcrafted

A handful of cars awaiting their turn in the paint shop

The hand-built construction is inherently fragile, and needs constant love and attention. Five or six years of hard driving will definitely require a body rebuild. The trim is often carelessly fixed, the vision with the roof up is poor, the footwells are like ovens, and there's an annoying lack of clutch foot space. Value for money is certainly not the strong point of a Morgan Plus 8. And all this is apparent before you drive the beast. The driver sits close to the wheel, and 'Mr Universe' physique is needed to steer at low speeds. As well as being heavy (with a terrible 40ft turning circle), the steering is too vague, and almost an inch of play is present when driving straight ahead.

It is very hard to break the tail away even with 137bhp. If anything, marked understeer is the dominant characteristic, due possibly to the limited slip differential. When you hit a bump, even a small bump, the rear hops out readily, making the car a real handful, or challenge depending on your viewpoint. It is not dangerous, and the chassis is essentially very stable. A very bumpy road induces sharp pitches, bouncing you out of your seat, creating the complete vintage motoring experience.

Hard work

Road test comments usually echo those of Mel Nichols in *Car*: 'It seems a waste not to match power unit with chassis and a suspension that allows it to realise much more of its potential . . . sports car driving should not be unnecessarily difficult, and the Plus 8 is needlessly hard work.'

Peter Morgan explained to me that for a company without a test track motor racing is crucial for development, and claimed that much of the assessment of the Morgan was by its performance in production races. But he seems to forget that race tracks have very few bumps.

Why has it taken so long to produce a rack and pinion steering system for the Plus 8? Maurice Owen has had one fitted to his car for many years, yet it has taken 12 years to persuade the boss. The new system is excellent, and was engineered by Jack Knight at great expense. Unlike several conversions available, it is a genuine rack with a centre take-off rather than from a drag link. The new system virtually eliminates bump steer, but at great expense. It is only available on the

entifying points for the Plus 8 are the wider wings and alloy wheels — but only on post-1973 cars, with a lower rear axle ratio

at Morgan motoring is all about — top down, a sunny day, and a wide open road. The styling of the car is literally timeless, part of its incredible and long-lasting appeal

Vitesse, and to convert an old Plus 8 would be very costly. Now the system is almost redundant with the availability of a Gemma recirculatory ball type steering box from France, which is now in production on the standard Plus 8.

A small company like Morgan relies very heavily on the co-operation of major manufacturers. But the bigger the company, the more remote it becomes. To find components suitable for developing the existing chassis is a major problem, and Morgan certainly don't have the facility or resources to introduce new designs. Re-design or modification has generally only taken place when existing components are no longer produced, or when new specification components have become available.

It is too easy to be rational about the Morgan Plus 8. And if you are, you will never buy one in the first place. The Morgan is a breed apart, and many have said its owners are too. If your lifestyle desires such stimulation, you pay the price at the cost of refinement and comfort. Yet nearly every exhilarating physical experience has painful side effects, so why should the Morgan Plus 8 be any different?

Production history

Although the Plus 8's character has not changed essentially throughout its production life, there have been quite significant changes to its detail specification. From the model's introduction until 1971, separately mounted Moss four-speed gearboxes were fitted to 484 Plus 8s; after that date Rover were able to offer an all-synchromesh manual transmission, fitted in unit with the engine. Although ratios were not as close and sporting as the previous 'traditional' Moss 'box, the new change was much more refined. The chassis cross-members had to be modified to accommodate the new specification, and the first such car — R7475 — produced in April '72 also had improved cooling thanks to a larger radiator.

Later that year the front and rear tracks were increased to 4ft 3ins and 4ft 4ins. This, with the wider profile tyres and a new 3.3:1 rear axle, meant that the wing profile had to alter subtly to match the track, and much like the AC Cobra 427, the later cars lost the purity of line of the original. EEC exhaust emission control also meant a lower, 9.25:1, compression ratio compared to the 10.5:1 of the early models.

In 1975 the 'Sports lightweight' was offered to the committed enthusiast — there were alloy panels and 14ins wheels, but only 19 owners were tempted. In total 702 Rover four-speed 'box cars were built.

More major changes were made in 1977 with fitment of the more powerful 155bhp engine, an altogether more lively unit, even though peak torque was lower. More important was the availability of Rover's new five-speed gearbox with its 'overdrive top'. This, along with the Plus 8's new 14ins wheel design and 195/70 section tyres, meant overall gearing was higher than ever before, while the car's performance image was rather over-stated — more 'hot rod' than 'vintage' car. In addition to the stretched width of 5ft 2ins, the Plus 8 was given a new padded facia and a revised instrument layout. Customers were now allowed the option of aluminium panels. Although the first five-speed car was chassis R8151, production really began with R8200.

In 1977, revised full width alloy bumpers were adopted, while in 1978 the braking system lost servo assistance and gained new calipers. 1982 saw the SU carbs replaced with Strombergs with their cursed automatic choke (due to new emission controls). Later that year the classic wheel design of the original Plus 8 returned with rim modification and P6 tyres, which greatly improved the car's style. 1984 saw the introduction of the ultimate Plus 8 development, not only with the fuel injected 190bhp Vitesse engine but, at last, rack and pinion steering. The system is optional on standard Plus 8s which are now fitted with an excellent recirculating ball steering box from Gemma of France.

Buyer's spot check

The construction of the Morgan Plus 8 may be very simple — to many it's downright primitive — but this does not mean that the car is any less prone to the wear-and-tear of everyday motoring. The design is

Maurice Owen in the workshop where the Plus 8 was born

Early cars (this is the first test Plus 8) have narrow wings

Rover V8 engine breathed through SU carbs until 1982

essentially pre-war (who would want to change it?) and consequently has little protection against corrosion, unlike modern sporting cars.

It pays the Morgan owner to maintain his car regularly, even be over-cautious, particularly with regard to the wooden frame. These simple chores are an everyday fact of Morgan motoring which are usually carried out with pride, but many cars, particularly Plus 8s, get into unsympathetic hands and the cars suffer from lack of maintenance. To the unsuspecting buyer poor condition can casually be blamed on the car's design, so it is always worth contacting a Morgan specialist or a friendly experienced owner to check the car over before buying.

The body is the most crucial part of any Morgan, and the frame itself is constructed of unprotected wood. It is especially exposed to the elements on the underside of the chassis, while there are also internal moisture traps. The structure must be kept dry, so if the car is not used regularly a garage is essential.

First check points are the bead edges under the doors — look here for any sign of corrosion, particularly on earlier cars which could have been over-painted recently. A pen-knife is a useful tool, and you can check condition of the exposed wooden sill boards and the rocker frame by poking the knife along the inside of the running board. Any sinking feeling should cause suspicion. The chassis leg behind the rear wheel arch carries a lower frame member which is exposed to spray from the wheels and will soon rot if not wiped clean regularly. Also steam from both exhaust pipes does not help sill life.

Most higher frame members will generally be very sound, although joint fracture occurs after high mileages, and continuous wet weather driving causes the upholstery to trap moisture and eventually rot the frame if not properly dried out. Also check the fit of

the doors. If they don't align properly it could simp[ly] be worn hinges, but when gently rocked any body fl[ex] or worn joints will clearly indicate the frame structural condition. The bodies on earlier cars c[an] quickly be checked by lifting the rear frame to look f[or] movement.

It is worth emphasising that even a relatively lo[w] mileage Plus 8 could need body attention and it [is] generally reckoned — even by the factory — that mo[st] bodies will need work after five or six years if t[he] cars are driven as they are meant to be. Any woodwo[rk] is a specialised task and should only be carried out [by] craftsmen with Morgan experience, but they a[re] generally as sought after as the car itself, so do[n't] expect the job to be done overnight.

The bodyshell itself is less of a problem, but it [is] worth checking the potential rust points. Look ag[ain] at the skin under the door, around the bottom edges [of] the scuttle, the headlamp pod mounts on the fr[ont] wing as they corrode around the joints where the wi[ng] joins the main body. Aluminium panels tend to l[ast] longer than steel ones, but are more susceptible [to] catalytic reaction, and to stress fracture. Glass-fib[re] wings may not help the value of the car, but they l[ast] longer than steel panels. Earlier wings are now v[ery] hard to come by.

The Rover engine is generally the least of [the] problems when buying a Plus 8. The V8, due to [the] car's lightness, is very under-stressed, and provid[ing] it is well serviced should last up to 100,000 mil[es]. Engine oil, particularly with the unit's hydrau[lic] tappets, should always be clean, and (as with all al[loy] blocks) the correct inhibitor should be used to ens[ure] water passages are kept clean. The early engines [were] prone to overheating due to a radiator of insuffic[ient] capacity and water pump cavitation, but fittin[g a] larger pulley and radiator from later cars can eas[ily] cure the problem. Holley carburettors tend to cre[ate] flat spots and are more difficult to tune than SUs.

Clutch replacement is an engine-out task costin[g in] the region of £200, so it is worth checking carefully [for] signs of wear. The gearboxes are generally indestru[ct]ible, although the lower ratios on the pre-'72 M[oss] 'box are prone to wear. The internals for the Moss u[nit] are no problem as Morgan still have most of the pa[rts] on the shelf, but a damaged casing will be alm[ost] impossible to replace. The Moss was a no[toriously] primitive design when new, with virtually straight [cut] gears, and very border line selection. If you [are] unfamiliar with its character ask an expert to check[.] To consider a conversion to the later Leyland gear[box] would mean extensive modification to the chassi[s as] the cross-members are completely different on la[ter] cars. Replacement Rover 'boxes are no problem [—] even good scrapyards could yield one.

The back axle is another crucial area. They are v[ery] expensive to replace, with exchange units cost[ing] around £500, and internals as expensive as [the] complete item. A good check is to drive around a t[ight] roundabout, and listen for graunching and crack[ing] which could indicate that the limited slip differe[ntial] is worn. It is worth looking at service records as [it is] crucial that lsd oil has been used. The grease nip[ples] on the rear hubs are worth investigating — exces[s] under the axle by the spring anchorage will mean [the] nipple has been over greased, which will mean new[er] seals will be needed. The Armstrong shock absorb[ers] are simple to replace.

If you are suspicious about the car's past, check [for] damage by moving the seat forward, removing [the] metal covers and looking at the bolt spacing on the[se] spring shackles to ensure they are even on both si[des]. It is worth examining the chassis members in fro[nt of] the bulkhead for any hint of creasing or rip[ple.] Bonnet fit is a good indicator of previous acci[dent] damage.

The front suspension is a more common prob[lem] area, but signs of wear are quickly evident once o[n the] road. At about 50mph a horrifying wheel wo[bble] which literally shakes the whole car will manifest it[self] — this immediately indicates that kingpins [or] bushes should be attended to, a task which c[osts] around £100. It is also worthwhile ensuring that [the] pedal operated one-shot lubrication system, w[hich] uses engine oil, is working or has been used. M[any] owners have now disconnected the system and f[ill]

ease nipples. Be very suspicious of a dry and
glected front end.
Also look at the damper blades which run from
hind the hub to the chassis sides, where they should
immed up to prevent spring wind-up. They should
ove in and out but not forwards or backwards, and if
ey are badly corroded it will mean the task of manual
rication has been ignored. It is worth checking also
unnatural tyre wear — if it occurs on the inside, it
uld possibly mean a bent chassis, while wear on the
tside provides a good indication of worn kingpins
d bushes.
Very heavy steering could mean that greasing the
ck rod ends has been neglected, any wear in the
umn UJs could mean short shaft replacement,
ile a worn top bush will produce column
ovement. Don't be too worried about play in the
ering, because even when new the worm and peg
tem had almost an inch of slop. A worthwhile and
pular conversion is to the new recirculating ball
ering box, now standard on all Morgans except the
esse.
The split circuit brakes are excellent and generally
uble free on the Plus 8, but post-'78 cars do not have
uum servo. Many cars have been converted with a
ling twin servo kit, but pedal pressure should
ays be sure and firm.
Generally Morgan owners care passionately for
ir cars, and that kind of attention is essential to
intain a Plus 8's condition. It is recommended you
y your Morgan from this type of enthusiast. It has
been said that rebuilt cars are a far better buy than
ginal cars providing the restoration has been
ertly carried out. That is out of no disrespect for
lvern production, but a loving owner generally
es more care in assembly and protecting and
roving the weaker areas of construction, thus
ating a stronger car.

ubs, specialists & books

e Morgan Sports Car Club has achieved the perfect
ance between a friendly club atmosphere and very
cient organisation, with a fine cross-section of
nts from relay teams and club races, sprints and
climbs to informal regional social activities.
There are some 27 club branches with names like
gmog, Jock Mog, Grog Mog and for the Brighton
tre Sex Mog, no less. The club produces an
ellent monthly magazine called *Miscellany*, packed
of gossip, technical tips and classified ads as well as
ails of the club's extensive spares register. It can be
ly said that club membership is essential to life
h a Morgan and full details can be obtained from
-president Chas Smith, Top Lodge, Crown East,
rcester.
s well as being the only factory recognised service
nt, Libra Motive offer a range of worthwhile
difications to Plus 8s. A recommended conversion
eir new steering box which improves and lightens
standard system (and is in fact being fitted to the
Morgans). The conversion replaces their rack
pinion modification and costs half the price, about
0. Other refinements are a front anti-tramp bar, a
ative camber conversion which not only improves
road-holding but also saves valuable rubber. To
rove the ride they recommend Konis instead of
rather primitive lever arm dampers. The
version costs in the region of £200, improves both
ride and handling, and gives longer service than
original design. Libra Motive are based at 8-10
emount Road, Hampstead, London NW3 (tel:
435 8159) and as well as offering expert Morgan
ice will willingly sell you a new Vitesse Plus 8.
Morris Stapleton not only offer the regular car sales,
es, and servicing facilities but also the tempting
r of hiring a Plus 8 for a weekend, with unlimited
eage, for £150 plus VAT, if you are uncertain about
manent ownership or you can't wait six or seven
s for your order. Should you be tempted for this
kend of agony and ecstasy they can be found at
ce Mews, London SW7 (tel: 01-589 6345). Mike
ican is an absolute authority on Plus 8s, and will
e all your Mog problems at Packer-Duncan,
erloo Garage, Hagley Road, Oldswinford, Stour-
ge, W. Midlands (tel: 03843 5186). They also
e a large selection of secondhand cars.

MMC 11, owned by the works, is raced by Charles Morgan

Friendly gatherings are part of the fun of Morgan ownership

Bliss is pointing the prow of a Plus 8 along a country lane!

Other specialists in Malvern magic are Colin
Musgrove and Associates, Newburn, Hob Lane,
Balsall Common, Nr Coventry (tel: 0676 33836);
Autopride, Whitehouse Farm, Wedmore, Somerset
(tel: 0279 725725); Lifes Motors Ltd, West Street,
Southport, Lancashire (tel: 0704 31375); Harpers,
The Bothy, Essex Lane, Hunton Bridge, Kings
Langley, Herts (tel: 40 67796); and the oldest Morgan
specialist, Douglass at 1a South Ealing Road, Ealing,
London W5 (tel: 01-567 0570). Allon White & Son
Ltd, The Garage, High Street, Cranfield, Beds also do
first class Morgan work.

Melvyn Rutter Limited offer a wide range of
services to Morgan fanatics, and are particularly
recommended for spares including a range of their
own pattern parts. They can be found at The Morgan
Garage, Little Hallingbury, Nr Bishops Stortford,
Herts (tel: 0279 725725). Vic Champness is highly
regarded for his woodwork on Morgans, and is based
at Black Phey Ltd, Raleigh Cottage, Takeley, Bishops
Stortford (tel: 0279 870698) should your Mog require
a new frame. John Smith is highly respected not only
for his tuning preparation, but also for invaluable
work on back axles and Moss gearboxes. He is at
Inworth, nr Colchester, Essex (tel: 0376 70438).

Rutherford Engineering not only offer a spares
facility, but produce their own glass-fibre front wings
which cost half the price of standard steel replacement
wings, and have been reinforced in the right places.
They also manufacture rear wings, cowls and a
distinctive hard top, a worthwhile extra for winter
motoring. They are based at Cottage-in-the-woods,
Whinlatter Pass, Keswick, Cumbria (tel: 0596 82
409). John Worrall Exclusives at 12 Burnt Oak Drive,
Parkfield Road, Stourbridge, West Midlands (tel:
03843 75189) offer an extensive range of body
fasteners and accessories.

John Britten Cars offer one of the largest
secondhand selections of Morgans including the Plus
8 that graces our cover and colour pages. They can be
found just off the A1 at Barnet Road, Arkley, Barnet,

Herts (tel: 01-449 1144) and Chris Alford will
willingly offer advice to enthusiasts. Don't forget that
the factory offers technical advice and an excellent
spares service.

There is only one book specifically about the Plus 8,
published by Osprey as part of their excellent
Autohistory series. Author Graham Robson presents a
comprehensive guide to the model, including buying
tips and design improvement as well as production
history. At £7.95 the book is good value, but unlike
the other titles in this series it lacks a genuine personal
involvement with the subject.

Two Brooklands Books, *Morgan Cars 1960-1970*
and particularly *Morgan 1969-1979*, offer a fascinating
selection of road tests including those on the Plus 8,
and are excellent value at £5.50. Other titles of more
general interest to the four-wheel Morgan fanatic are
the second volume of Ken Hill's history, *The Cowled
Radiator Models*, which is rather dated and far too
obsessed with competition, at £7.95; *Moggie: The
Purchase, Maintenance, and Enjoyment of the Morgan
Sports* provides an excellent practical guide to Morgan
addiction at £8.95; and *The Morgan: 75 years on the
road* presents a fascinating selection of Morgan
advertisements throughout the marque's history. It is
£10.95.

Rivals when new

Value for money should never be the criterion for
buying a Morgan. Its very special charisma is matched
by few. Today only the Caterham Seven comes close to
its exhilarating driving experience and classic style,
although it is essentially less practical, if that is
possible, than the Plus 8. The Panther J72 is closer to
Brook Stevens Excalibur ideals, looking more at home
in Liberace's garage than one time Morgan owner
Mick Jagger's. The Panther Kallista is the nearest
modern competitor, and although more refined and
perhaps better value, it still looks decidedly phoney.
The Plus 8 is essentially a 'vintage' car with reluctant
acknowledgements to eighties motoring, while the
Kallista is a modern car trying desperately to look
vintage. This essentially retrograde design policy is
the Panther's major failing.

1973	0-60	Max speed	Price	Fuel
Morgan Plus 8	6.7s	125mph	£1966	20mpg
Panther J72	6.4s	114mph	£5285	15mpg
TVR 3000M	7.7s	121mph	£2464	24mpg
Triumph TR6	8.5s	117mph	£1605	20mpg
Lotus Elan Sprint	6.7s	121mph	£2436	22mpg
Porsche 911S	6.2s	145mph	£6235	13mpg
1985				
Morgan Vitesse	6.1s	122mph	£13996	20mpg
Panther	7.9s	110mph	£9625	26mpg
Caterham T-C	6.0s	115mph	£8216	24mpg
Porsche 911 cab	5.4s	160mph	£26461	23mpg

Prices

The most important factor in the value of a Plus 8 is its
condition, much more so than specification or year.
Providing Plus 8s are properly maintained they rarely
depreciate, and if an owner spends £1500 on a body
rebuild it is quite realistic that the Morgan will
appreciate by as much. There are very few cars that
present that sort of financial guarantee.

Early cars (pre-'72) with the Moss gearbox are
priced around £5000 in sound, original condition
while a reconditioned example could cost over £6000.

A sound four-speed Rover gearbox specification car
(pre-'76) will begin at £6500, while five-speed models
(post-'76) can cost anything over £7000 depending
ultimately on condition.

A Plus 8 that has very personalised modification
with expert performance tuning and chassis development, plus a custom built body to high standard,
could fetch over £10,000.

Some discerning Morgan enthusiasts feel that the
original, pre-'72, Plus 8s with their pure styling,
10.5:1 compression engine, Moss 'box and 3.58 rear
axle ratio will become *the* collectable Mog, helped
partly by their rarity.

With the waiting list as strong as ever for a new
Vitesse there is little sign of any definite depreciation
in the Plus 8 market.

Morgan's Plus Four revived

YOU START to live dangerously once you put motorised wheels past the sign that warns of a penalty of £50 for driving on a path made for one-horsepower only. But there is precious little room to turn round – and we wanted to get to the top.

The Malvern hills loom large over the bustling old-fashioned town. We were driving the prototype of Morgan's latest model, the new Plus Four, and reckoned a spot of trials-driving would be highly appropriate. Swallow the guilt for putting a car on a bridle-path and you find yourself gunning second gear hard, climbing steeply, and working up the slimmer's treatment on a few hairpins.

We paused at St. Anne's Well – a small building shaped like a stone MG badge, totally hexagonal. The sign said coffee, and with a gale-force wind that penetrated the most efficient of rally-jackets we abandoned the Morgan and the photographers for the beckoning glow behind the windows.

It turned out to be nothing resembling a cafe at all... it was a kite factory! It seems that Malvern is famous the world over not just for the very traditional sportscar – but also for Malvern kites.

As I thawed out against a Calor gas heater, the owner explained: "There is a great joy to be had when flying a kite! There is a serenity about it that moves the inner spirit..." Fly a kite?

The Editor becomes the first to drive Morgan's new two-litre twin-cam Plus Four

I heartily agreed, and said I was off to do just that. And returned to the blustery gale. I sensed a pair of eyes watching my return trek back up the path to the Morgan – for I had left empty handed. Chapter 15 of David Copperfield has Charles Dickens waxing very lyrical on the benefits of kite flying. "It lifts themind out of confusion." Driving an open Morgan on the Malvern hills is exactly the same.

When you swing open that cutaway door, and clunk the heavy door catch of the type that really should have been banished to the autojumbles when the MG TF last went out of production, you soon find yourself marvelling at the way the 'Men of Malvern' continue to succeed in tracking down the constant supply of parts that keeps Morgan going.

Those little lights that sit on the top of the front wings... who else uses those?

122 bhp is good enough to get a 0-60 mph under 8 secs, weight is no more than a Morris Minor...

Photos: Clickstop Sports Photography

How does Morgan make a hand-built performance car without it costing more than a mass-produced Rover with the same engine?

The Morgan is an anachronistic as the kite factory in the old coffee shop. Recessions come and go. (Or now come and stay!) Inflation has its ups and downs. But the waiting list for Morgans still runs into years.

There are still a couple of cars to be built in 1985 that were ordered way back in 1979, (when a pound note was worth 2½ dollars!) but Peter Morgan, the son of the founder who guides the whole place with his feet planted very firmly on the ground, now reckons that the waiting list is virtually "down to about three years."

He has just launched a new model that should give the marque a shot in the arm. It's a revival of the Plus Four name that was once given to two-litre Triumph TR powered Morgans. Lighter and better handling than the Triumph, it was a terrific car in the early Sixties – particularly in its tuned, all alloy form known as Supersports.

Peter Morgan has for some time been aware of how the costs of the mind-blowing supercar performance of the lusty V8 has been creeping upwards, widening the gap of the smaller 4/4. He looked for a 'middle model' to revive the Plus Four name.

The Ford-powered 4/4 had ran into engine supply difficulties and he found

Backroom Boffin: Maurice Owen,
Morgan's one-man Development
Department, who made room for
Fiat's injected two-litre.

that the twin-cam Fiat engine could be obtained at exceptional value, with a five-speed box. It's an engine that has an excellent reputation — you can cane them all day long and they keep their tune. Only the reputation of Fiat bodywork tarnished the whole Fiat image. But an Italian engine in a very British sportscar? That made quite a few sit up and think... it also helped Peter Morgan to deal his cards with masterly fashion in his long-standing links with the Ford Motor Co, who reluctantly agreed to supply a re-engineered version of the f.w.d. Escort engine. That Morgan initiative was followed up by Panther and a few other specialist car builders.

So the 'real' Fiat twin-cam in two-litre form was a natural direction to look. Britain doesn't have a sportscar engine of this size, and saloon-car engines such as the 'O'-series from BL's Princesses and Marinas is simply nowhere near as good — or as cost efficient.

The alloy-headed twin-cam shoves out 122bhp in the Morgan, with fuel injection. The engineering of this engine is what gives it its sportscar qualities. The engine is from the Argenta, and Fiat proved so helpful they gave a fuel-injection version to Morgan right-away, the same-spec Argenta mill is not due for public announcement until April. It is a classic engine that has won all manner of international rallies, and is capable of delivering a lot more power with Abarth mods — 250 bhp could be reached by a racer without resorting to turbos.

The idea of a two-litre Fiat powered Morgan has occupied the minds of Morgan for quite some time. When we returned from our escapade on the Monte Carlo Raly in Peter Morgan's V8, one backroom boffin told us: "The Boss is very impressed by the potential of a new engine... no names no packdrill, but its just won a rally you've been on!" The winner was Walter Rohl in a works Fiat two-litre twin-cam.

In the early part of 1981, work began. The factory soon had two cars running, in carburettor form. The extra mid-range punch was welcomed by the factory and the conversion worked well, but it was realised that a shot more power would not go amiss... Fiat mentioned fuel-injection, reckoning it was also a smoother engine in this spec. Other ideas were also tried. This engine is very closely related to the two-litre Lancia unit, and when the Volumex supercharged Lancia was announced, Maurice Owen, Malvern's Development Engineer, measured up the Lancia engine with its 'blower'.

How he managed to squeeze under

that narrow bonnet a V8 with all its fuel-injection gubbins, and the computer to work it, is simply a marvel. *(See the first published report on that car in our Morgan Scoop of October 1983.)*

The Lancia engine and its supercharger *just* squeezed in. Says Maurice: "That project *was* certainly a go-er".

But costs come into it. So too does the main strategy of providing a middle-range car, that will fit in neatly in performance terms between a 1600 4/4 and the rip-snorting V8.

The new Plus Four should be priced for a shade less than ten-grand. It is quick, and is also probably the best-made Morgan ever put on the road.

It has a vastly improved ride. Careful attention to build-quality has a lot to do with it. The rear springs are down from a six-leaf to a five-leaf version, and the curvature of the springing has been re-engineered. A fraction more movement has been found front and rear.

The difference is very marked indeed. We commented on this development when we drove the prototype of the 190 bhp Vitesse-powered Plus Eight. All Morgans now have revised suspension that run a lot softer, with more forgiveness on the bumps.

The main alteration that makes the new Plus Four visibly different from its small brother is in the wheels, which are centre-laced six-inch Cobra wires, carrying 15-inch Avons in low 60-profile rubber.

You would think that a low-profile tyre would only serve to feed extra harshness into an already hard ride. It didn't go that way when the V8 moved to P6s. The sliding-pillar suspension at the front keeps the contact-patch angled squarely against the ground as it rises and falls, unlike a wishbone suspension system, which tends to move the wheel through an arc. It was this 'McPherson-strut'-like characteristic which provided the Morgan's 1911-Veteran front suspension to adopt readily to modern, high-tech rubber. But a traditional high-profile tyre has extra depth of air to help cushion the ride. Morgan men don't deny this... but say try the low-profiles, "and you'll soon find out what works best in practice."

This led to one main problem. Malvern wanted wire wheels. Spokes are flexing the whole time and can not be made air-tight where they go through the rim. That means tubes — in the traditional manner. You can't put tubes in low-profile tyres.

"NO, NO, NO!" screamed Pirelli technical people when we told them we were going to spend our own money buying a set of P6 tyres to test... on a Healey 3000 for the RAC Golden Fifty Raly. Bunk, we replied, and duly finished sixth overall, and first in class.

Then we stripped the tyres and tubes from the 6J TR6 wire wheels, a combination that had worked so well. We then saw the dangers of it all... the tubes all bore the characteristics scuff marks of having been badly pinched. It

could have been dangerous had we gone much further.

Morgan were told the same thing — fit wire wheels and you can't have our tyres. They got that from Michelin, Pirelli, Goodyear — everybody. Only Avon bothered to promise to look into it... they came back with the answer. Special tubes do exist, and they are now imported specially from Sweden for low-profile tyres.

So the new Plus Four sits on Avon 195-60 profile Turbospeeds... they are super predictable in the wet, in true Avon tradition. They certainly suit the new Morgan very well indeed.

The steering is also different on the new Plus Four. Cam Gears ended their supply, a frequent sort of experience for Malvern. They get round most of these problems, though — this time going to France for a similar steering-box, lighter and better-made, from Gemma.

The super-rack-and-pinion set-up specially developed by Jack Knight of Woking is reserved only for the Plus Eight. Again, Malvern say it is a way of keeping the price in order.

At the back is the same Salisbury 7HA axle of the 4/4 with its 4.1 ratio, with no limited slip diff (that's only in the Plus Eight) but a limited slip diff is a possible future development. So too is telescopic shockabsorbers, the new car retains the old lever-arms.

On the road it felt exceptionally well balanced, the two-litre engine is virtually the same weight as the 1600 4/4 engine. It turns in much easier than the V8, and the narrower track of the 4/4 chassis blesses the car with a much better steering lock than its big brother. You get a snap in the neck on quick take-off. Without resorting to clutch-slipping tyre-shreiking take-offs, we just got under the eight-second barrier in a standstill to 60 time.

Top whack is good for a fraction over 115 mph, in the kind of weather we had to put up with... on a calm day possibly 120 mph — almost matching its horse-power.

Stomping it hard up the slippery tracks was a revelation. First and second are low, making it a 5,800-revs thrash in second before going for third. And the sheer grip is nothing short of astonishing... you shake your head in disbelief when you are told it has no limited slip diff in that axle. It rode the ruts and bumps far better than any Morgan we have driven before and that is real progress.

It's simply ideal for taking to the hills... as a sort of glorious form of adult's kite-flying. **P.Y**

THE NAMING of new models from the 76-year-old Malvern concern is neither haphazard nor a deeply researched affair. Morgan knows what is right and what its ever-loyal customers expect. So the fuel-injected Plus 8 launched last year did not get the Supersports title some expected it might; that name remains in waiting.

But when Morgan decided to ditch the 1.6-litre carburetted twin-cam Fiat engine — retaining the 1.6-litre Ford CVH engine for the 4/4 — in favour of the 122 bhp 2-litre injection unit from the Italian company, the name Plus 4 was doubtless the obvious choice. It had done 18 years' service on the first Plus 4 between 1950 and 1968, starting the trend at Morgan of putting powerful engines into the Z-section ladder chassis and ash-framed cars to produce excellent performance. The old Plus 4 was slightly more than 2 litres, using the 2088 cc Standard Vanguard 68 bhp engine. Its notable torque combined with the compactness of the 4/4 chassis to produce an admirable sports car with a character of its own.

The concept of the new Plus 4 is remarkably similar to its predecessor. It uses the smaller 4/4 chassis, but with Plus 8 wings cut down to cover the generously proportioned 195/60 tyres on 6×15 in wire wheels. The result is a car with the shorter wheelbase of the 4/4 — 96 in (2.44 m) and 2.3 in (5.8 cm) less than the Plus 8 — and a rear track of 49 in (1.2 m) which is a useful 3 in (7.5 cm) narrower than the V8-engined model.

The Fiat twin-cam is by no means a new engine, but when considering alternatives such as the Saab 2-litre and small BMW sixes, Morgan decided that the Italian engine was the best bet. Its long life and continual development is assured — important for a small concern like Morgan — because the twin-cam will be turned transverse and see duty in Fiat's forthcoming Type Four large hatchback. The engine produces a respectable 122 bhp at 5300 rpm and healthy 127 lb ft torque at 3500 rpm. The fuel and ignition system is a mixture, employing Bosch LE-Jetronic fuel injection but Marelli Digiplex fully programmed ignition.

You would be forgiven for assuming that the traditional Morgan suspension — coil sprung sliding pillar front suspension, steered via a worm and nut steering box, with a leaf-sprung live axle at the rear — had remained unchanged, but this is not entirely true. The familiar 2 in of free play at the steering wheel has disappeared, along with the worm and nut steering box, as Cam Gears no longer makes it. In its place is a rather more modern reciprocating ball box from the

French Gemmer company.

Criticism of Morgan's rock-hard suspension appears to be eliciting a response at last from the engineers at Malvern; the front suspension has now been softened by shortening the coil springs. Rather more work went into the changes at the rear which, after experiments with numerous designs of leaf-springs, has resulted in a change from a six- to a five-leaf design. Although the spring rate is the same, a marked reduction in friction should result in an improved ride. Armstrong lever arm dampers are still used at the rear but there is work on a compact telescopic damper set-up.

Compared with the 4/4, the Plus 4 has an increased fuel tank capacity: from 8.5 to 12.5 gallons.

A price of £10,901 for the Plus 4 (£11,711 for the four-seater) places the newcomer between the Ford-engined 4/4 1600 two-seater (£9300) and the carburetted Plus 8 at £12,498. Morgan's production will be split between two Plus 4s a week, four 4/4s and three Plus 8s. As ever, the waiting period for a new Morgan is measured in years, not months.

If you want to have a Morgan in the garage, arguably nothing else will do. Closest rival must be the Panther Kallista (£10,875) powered by the carburetted Ford 2.8-litre V6 to produce 135 bhp. For searing performance the Caterham 1700 Supersprint looks cheap at £7624 and has the merit of excellent build quality. Similarly priced is the plastic-bodied Reliant Scimitar SS1 (£7795) while the thoroughly modern Toyota MR2 (£9499), though cheaper than the Morgan, is really in a different world from the ash-framed car by virtue of its mid-engined layout and fixed roof.

Top speed may be academic

MORGAN PLUS 4

A year after the mighty Plus 8 injection appeared, Morgan has launched the Plus 4 powered by the Fiat 2-litre fuel injection engine. It could be the best yet from Malvern

for a Morgan, as it involves passing the aural pain barrier. Nevertheless the Plus 4 managed a creditable 111.3 mph, putting it on a par with the similarly un-aerodynamic Panther (110.9). The MR2 is naturally streets ahead with a 121.8 mph maximum.

A 0 to 60 mph time of 9.0 sec is respectable enough and a full second faster than the 4/4, keeping the Plus 4 in touch with the MR2 (8.8 sec) but the lightweight Caterham turns in a scintillating 5.5 sec time.

The torquey character of the Fiat twin-cam comes through on the in-gear acceleration times. It actually beats the lithe Toyota in the 30 to 50 mph increment in fourth gear (6.8 sec) and is barely outpaced by the Caterham and Panther. By compari-

son, the four-speed 4/4 record-ed a tardy 11.9 sec for the increment.

The Plus 4 takes 11.4 sec to accelerate from 50 to 70 mph in its 20.55 mph per 1000 rpm top gear, an identical time to the shorter geared MR2, though inevitably outpaced by the four-speed Caterham (7.0 sec).

Subjective assessments of the Plus 4's performance can be deceptive, because the engine doesn't feel particularly sporting and its marked mechanical harshness above 5000 rpm deters the frequent use of the full range. Power is on tap all the way to 6000 rpm (no red line) and the engine always pulls strongly, it is just that the best technique is to make full use of the engine's excellent torque, keeping the engine revs between 3000 and

Left: Muscular rather than refined, Fiat's Bosch injected 2 litre engine produces 122 bhp

ingly neutral. The sure handling is matched to unservoed brakes which need a firm shove but lack enough feel to prevent premature locking up on some surfaces.

Like any Morgan, the Plus 4 should be driven with the hood down, because the wind roar at speed with the hood erected is horrible and tiring. The engine is not notably noisy unless extended. The interior is unchanged from the 4/4, which means the driver has a speedo and rev-counter directly in front on the flat facia, complemented by a row of four auxiliary gauges. The open glove box and small ledge behind the seats are the only concessions to practicality. Legroom is adequate but there is nowhere for the driver's left foot other than the clutch pedal, and tall drivers will find the wheel set too low for comfort.

Arguably the Plus 4 is the nicest looking Morgan; it is more purposeful than a 4/4, less roller-skate-like than the bulkier Plus 8. The wide wire wheels are apt, and will delight enthusiasts.

The new Malvern car emerges at the heart of the Morgan philosophy, offering more punchy performance than the evergreen 4/4 while trading the sheer power of the Plus 8 for agile, sharp handling and fine balance. A very pleasant surprise.

500 rpm when it is acceptably smooth. It may not have the gut-wrenching acceleration of the Plus 8, but is nevertheless a rapid cross-country performer.

The SEAT-built gearbox (Fiat design) has a stubby lever and short precise action. It is never light to use, nor notably rapid, and the narrowness of the gate can cause errors until the driver becomes used to it. The ratios though are well spaced, producing maxima of 27 mph, 48 mph, 72 mph and 98 mph at 5750 rpm. The clutch is heavy, but progressive.

The improvement to the steering cannot be overstated, being superior to even the rack and pinion set-up of the injected Plus 8 which suffers from lack of feel and overly light weighting. By comparison the Plus 4 is endowed with relatively heavy steering but is now consistent in feel, with none of the free play and high friction of the old box.

The combination of the chassis improvements and the new steering takes the Plus 4 into a higher class of road manners than previous Malvern models. The ride remains very firm, but the chassis copes with bumpy country lanes taken at speed with much more ability, no longer requiring the extremes of concentration and reflex action to handle the bucking body. Apportioning the credit is not easy, but the supple-walled Avon 60-series tyres certainly make a valuable contribution.

The weight distribution of the Plus 4 is almost perfectly split, while the wide tyres ensure that the inherent balance is enhanced by excellent grip. For cornering ability the Morgan is as enjoyable as it is surprisingly good. Hustled fast into corners there is a hint of understeer, yet make full use of the grip by applying more power and the stance is satisfy-

MOTOR ROAD TEST **MORGAN PLUS 4**

PERFORMANCE

WEATHER CONDITIONS
Wind	7 mph
Temperature	60.8 deg F/ 16 deg C
Barometer	29.8 in Hg 1009 mbar
Surface	Dry tarmacadam

MAXIMUM SPEEDS
	mph	kph
Banked Circuit (5th gear)	111.3	179.1

Terminal speeds:
at ¼ mile	79
at kilometre	98.2

Speeds in gears (at 5750 rpm):
1st	27
2nd	48
3rd	72
4th	98

ACCELERATION FROM REST
mph	sec	kpg	sec
0-30	3.1	0-40	2.3
0-40	4.5	0-60	4.1
0-50	6.5	0-80	6.4
0-60	9.0	0-100	9.7
0-70	12.2	0-120	4.3
0-80	17.1	0-140	21.7
0-90	24.0		
Stand'g ¼	16.9		
Stand'g km	33.5		

ACCELERATION IN TOP
mph	sec		sec
20-40	9.1	40-60	5.6
30-50	8.9	60-80	5.6
40-60	10.2	80-100	6.7
50-70	11.4	100-120	8.3
60-80	13.7	120-140	12.3
70-90	20.3		

ACCELERATION IN 4TH
mph	sec	kph	sec
20-40	6.9	40-60	4.1
30-50	6.8	60-80	4.5
40-60	7.3	80-100	4.8
50-70	8.2	100-120	5.7
60-80	9.4	120-140	7.6
70-90	12.2		

FUEL CONSUMPTION
Overall	25.7 mpg
	11.0 litres/100km
Fuel grade	97 octane
	4 star rating
Tank capacity	56 litres
	12.5 gallons
Max range*	353 miles
	569 km
Test distance	792 miles
	1275 km

*Estimated. No Govt fuel consumption figures available

STEERING
Turning circle	11.2 m	36.9 ft
Lock to lock	2.75 turns	

NOISE
	dBA
30 mph	77
50 mph	83
70 mph	94
Maximum†	97

†Peak noise level under full-throttle acceleration in 2nd

SPEEDOMETER (mph)
True mph	30	40	50	60	70	80	90	100
Speedo	29	40	50	61	72	82	93	104

Distance recorder: 1.0 per cent fast

WEIGHT
	Kg	cwt
Unladen weight*	848	16.7
Weight as tested	1036	20.4

*No fuel

Performance tests carried out by *Motor*'s staff at the Motor Industry Research Association proving ground, Lindley, and Millbrook proving ground, near Ampthill.

Test Data: World Copyright reserved. No reproduction in whole or in part without written permission.

GENERAL SPECIFICATION

ENGINE
Cylinders	Four in-line
Capacity	1995 cc
Bore/stroke	84.0/90.00 mm
Max power	122 bhp (91 kW) at 5300 rpm (DIN)
Max torque	127 lb ft (172 Nm) at 3500 rpm (DIN)
Block	Cast iron
Head	Aluminium alloy
Cooling	Water
Valve gear	Twin overhead camshafts, belt driven, two valves per cylinder
Compression	9.0:1
Fuel system	Bosch LE Jetronic fuel injection
Ignition	Digiplex fully programmed
Bearings	5 main

TRANSMISSION
Drive	Rear wheels
Type	Five-speed manual

Internal ratios and mph/1000 rpm
Top	0.83/20.55
4th	1.0/17.06
3rd	1.36/12.54
2nd	2.05/8.32
1st	3.6/4.74
Rev	3.24
Final drive	4.1:1

AERODYNAMICS
Coef. Cd	N.A.

SUSPENSION
Front	Sliding pillar mounted on a crossframe, telescopic dampers
Rear	Semi elliptical leaf springs, lever arm dampers

STEERING
Type	Recirculating ball
Assistance	None

BRAKES
Front	Discs, 27.9 cm dia
Rear	Drums, 22.9 cm dia
Servo	No
Circuit	Split front/rear
Rear valve	No

WHEELS/TYRES
Type	Wire 6 x 15 in
Tyres	195/60R15
Pressures	F/R
(all conditions)	24 psi 1.7 bar

ELECTRICAL
Battery	12V, 40 Ah
Alternator	35 Amp
Fuses	8
Headlights type	Halogen
dip	110 W total
main	120 W total

GUARANTEE
Duration	12 months, unlimited mileage
Rust warranty	None

MAINTENANCE
Major service	10,000 miles
Intermediate service	5000 miles

COMPARISONS

Make/model	Price £	Eng. cap. cc	Power bhp/ rpm	Torque lb ft/ rpm	Max speed mph	0-60 mph sec	30-50 mph sec	mph/ 1000 rpm	Over. mpg	Tour. mpg	Weight kg	Boot cap. m³	Drag coef. Cd.
Morgan Plus 4	10901	1995	122/5300	127/3500	111.3	9.0	6.8	20.55	25.7	—	848	—	—
Caterham 1700 Supersprint	7624	1691	135/6000	122/4500	115e	5.5	6.6	19.06	29.5	—	520	—	*
Panther Kallista 2.8	10875	2792	135/5200	162/3000	110.9	7.9	6.6	26.6	22.8	26.0	941	0.09	—
Reliant Scimitar SS1	7791	1596	97/6000	98/4000	105.3	10.5	9.1	20.5	26.5	34.1	837	0.14	0.40
Toyota MR2	9499	1587	122/6000	105/5000	121.8	8.0	7.7	18.6	28.2	38.4	1020	0.13	0.34

e = estimate.

Make: Morgan **Model:** Plus 4 **Country of Origin:** Britain
Maker: Morgan Motor Co Ltd, Malvern Link, Worcestershire, England Tel: Malvern 310415
Total Price: £10,901.04
Options: Luggage carrier (£67.50), rust proofing (£82.50), aluminium body and wings (£240), door handles (£25)
Extras fitted to test car: Leather interior (£360), aluminium body and wings (£240)

Creature comforts are still limited, and the ride remains rather rudimentary, but this is the essence of the car.

More magic from Malvern

Imitation, they say, is the sincerest form of flattery, and no company has been more flattered than Morgan — in my opinion, it was the continued success of the little company from Malvern which gave rise to the current fad for replicars. But where others have attempted to amalgamate modern mechanicals from large companies with 'traditional' styling, Morgans are the result of steady, continuous development of a basic theme, which makes them, in my eyes, much more complete cars. There's nothing like the real thing, and therefore nothing like a Morgan.

However, the almost wholesale turn-around from front-engined, rear-wheel drive cars to transversely mounted front engines and front-wheel drive created some problems for Morgan: there was a point where it looked as if their traditional source of engine/transmission units, Ford, wouldn't be able to supply. Morgan cast around and found a very nice combination, though, at Fiat. (Ford, happily still supply units for the 4/4 however).

The specification looked very good to Morgan. With a capacity of 1995cc, it featured belt-driven twin overhead camshafts and Bosch LE Jectronic injection with Digiplex ignition, enough to give 122bhp (DIN) at 5300rpm, and 127lb ft (DIN) torque at 3500rpm. Allied to this was a five-speed gearbox with a direct fourth and an overdrive fifth. With a vehicle weight of 16cwt, this was enough to give the Morgan what should be on paper a very respectable performance — enough in fact, for Morgan to revive the Plus 4 appelation, last seen back in the sixties on the Triumph-engined version, a lusty beast if ever there was one.

The Plus 4 is based essentially on the 4/4 rather than the Plus 8, the main difference being greater width due to wider mudguards covering fatter 195/60R15) tyres — 175/15s on steel wheels are standard on the smaller-engined car.

We therefore see a very traditional specification. There is a Z-shaped separate chassis with five boxed or tubular cross members. Front suspension is of the sliding pillar type as ever, while the

rear axle is live and suspended on leaf springs. This is all covered by the ash-framed, steel-panelled body of exceedingly traditional shape — upright (well, curved but upright) radiator, long bonnet, small cockpit with cutaway dors, flared mudguards and spare wheel open for all to see on the tail. (For those with a

small family, there is a four seater version as well.) Steering has come in for attention, and is now of the reciprocation ball type made by the French company Gemmer, but old-fashioned lever arm dampers are used at the rear. Brakes are discs at the front, drums at the rear, and there is no servo.

The Fiat engine has, indeed, given the Plus 4 some grunt, to use modern parlance. Neither *Autocar* nor *What Car?* have tested one yet, so we cannot as usual quote their figures, but, using a deserted stretch of unopened motorway, we noted a steady and held maximum of 115mph which, corrected, comes to about 112mph. In absolute terms, of course, this is no great shakes — almost anything with a GTi label on it can match, and many can beat, this figure, but the question of top speed with a Morgan is really rather academic. With its non-

aerodynamic shape — its drag fa would probably give any aerodynam the colly-wobbles — you wouldn't ex it to be sensationally rapid at the top and it isn't. But then, if you want with a higher top speed there's alway Plus 8 . . .

Again, a hand-held watch and the peedo (corrected) were used for a rc ind ready acceleration runs, and averaged about 9.5s to 60mph fro standstill. This again isn't particu fast, and puts it on a par with machines as the Fiat Uno Turbo, Escort XR3 and others of that ilk. difference is that the tin-tops rec many revs and a lot of cog-swappir achieve a decent on-the-road perf ance: with the very torquey and Fiat engine you find you have more enough urge at almost any speed a almost any gear. In this respect, in of its high-tech specification, the engine is much more like the so power plant you expect in a Morgar

Mellow engine note

In fact, one of the best things abou Plus 4 is the engine/gearbox comb tion. Previous experience with it ha been too happy, as we've found it i past to be harsh and strained and cla at the top end of its rev range, but ir application it sounds and behaves right: the sharp crisp bark of the ext in Fiats has been mellowed to a plea smooth, clean burble at low speeds a not too rorty at the top.

The gearchange is especially del ful, with very small throws and a na gate so it behaves like a flick-swit action.

The clutch, on the other hand, felt heavy and had a curious, Pors like, over-centre feel: when you re it, it comes back and kicks the unde of your foot. You become acclimatis it quite quickly, but it's never pleasant.

The steering, too, came in for criticism. It feels rather heavy and st so the initial impression of the handl one of obdurate and stodgy unders as if all the car wants to do is pl straight on. In fact, this isn't the because once you overcome the h ness of the steering you find tha chassis is nicely balanced. It pays to it in a slow-in, fast-out way, for the tail squats slightly, the fat Avons d and the car simply scuttles arounc corners without any dramatic effects, though to get it to oversteer requires braking in a corner or upse

The Plus 4 fits into the Morgan range between the Plus 8 and the 4/4, with rather more in common with the latter.

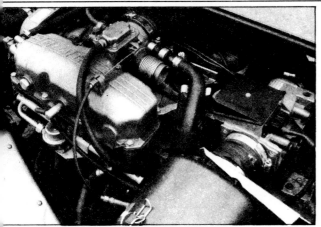

Plus 4's motive power comes from Fiat's 2.0-litre 122bhp twin cam engine.

ail before it. Levels of roadholding in er wet or dry are excellent, proving the Morgan really is a sports car with at implies.

ople don't buy Morgans for creature forts necessarily, but in fact it scores e highly here. It's a bit of a tight fit e, but the seats are comfortable and driving position excellent, though ewhere to put you left foot other than r under the brake pedal wouldn't go s. None of the controls are unreach-, but the handbrake lever is over the enger's side, while the gear lever is er the dashboard somewhere.

sually, the dashboard is a bit of a ppointment, but Morgan cannot be ed for that. The car has to meet ral safety criteria and, when you're ed to bits from someone else's parts this doesn't leave you much room in eauty stakes. For the same reasons, n't care for the position of the nal rear view mirror—it is sited just e it cuts out much of your vision (for of my height anyway) on left hand ers.

litional ride

e ride of the Morgan is *very* itional. Everything seems to flap, e or rattle, and not necessarily in , but this is acutally one of the facets e car that appeals to Morgan owners ms, judging by those I've spoken to. act the actual ride, once you've issed the noise and body movement

rgan is still an art-form.

that accompanies it, isn't too bad from a comfort viewpoint. Bumps still, howev-er, can have each end of the car hopping around to the detriment of roadholding, especialy when compared to much more modern machinery, but don't get the impression that you drive the car from one take-off point to the next—in fact its ability to cope with bumpy roads has been improved over the years and is now just about acceptable. After an hour's or so driving, though, you know you've been well shaken, if not stirred . . .

Of course the only way to drive a Morgan is with the top down, which I did, so I cannot comment on the hood's ability to keep out rain or draughts, but, with side-screens in place, there is enough wind in the hair buffeting to keep any traditionalist happy yet also keep more sybaritic types such as myself warm and cosy.

Yes, the Morgan *is* old fashioned. Yes, smaller engined, more aerodynamic saloons will see it off the traffic lights, and even around the corners. Yes, it is cramped, with zero luggage space. Yes, it is noisy. Yes, the ride is harsh. Yes, it shakes, rattles and rolls over the lumpy bits of the road. But that, precisely, is its appeal. If you cannot understand all that, you never will, no matter how much I write. A Morgan is a Morgan is a Morgan. Nothing will ever usurp it, or replace it, or copy it effectively. No matter how hard the rule-makers try, it must never be allowed to disappear. ∎

MORGAN PLUS 4
£10,901

Specification

Cylinders/capacity	4 in line, 1995cc
Bore/Stroke	84.0 x 90.0mm
Valve gear	Twin OHC
Fuel system	Bosch LE Jetronic fuel injection
Power/rpm	122bhp (DIN) at 5300rpm
Torque/rpm	127 lb ft (DIN) at 3500rpm
Gear ratios	3.6, 2.05, 1.36, 1.0, 0.83:1
Final drive	4.1:1
Steering	Recirculating ball
Brakes	Discs/drums
Wheels	6x15 in wires
Tyres	195/60 R15
Suspension (F)	Sliding pillar, coil springs
Suspension (R)	Live axle, leaf springs

Dimensions

Length	153ins
Wheelbase	96ins
Track (F/R)	47/49ins
Width	57ins
Weight	15.9cwt

Performance

Maximum	112mph
0-60mph	9.5s
Fuel consumption	
(urban/56mph/75mph)	N/A
Test consumption	24.3mpg

THE MORGAN PLUS-8 SPORTS TWO-SEATER

Engine : Eight cylinders in 90° vee. 89×71 mm. (3,530 c.c.). Push-rod-operated overhead valves. 10.5 to 1 c.r. 161 (net) b.h.p. at 5,200 r.p.m.

Gear ratios : 1st, 10.63 to 1; 2nd, 6.24 to 1; 3rd, 4.4 to 1; top, 3.58 to 1.

Tyres : 185×15VR Dunlop SP Sport, on bolt-on cast-alloy wheels.

Weight : 17 cwt. 3 qr., unladen, but ready for the road, with approximately 7 gallons of petrol.

Steering ratio : 2.4 turns lock-to-lock.

Fuel capacity : 13½ gallons (Range approximately 260 miles).

Wheelbase : 8 ft. 2¼ in.

Track : Front, 3 ft. 11¾ in.; rear, 4 ft. 2½ in.

Dimensions : 12 ft. 9 in. × 4 ft. 9¾ in. × 4 ft. 1 in. (high-hood up).

Price : £1,155 (£1,487 2s. 9d., inclusive of purchase-tax and compulsory safety belts).

Manufacturer : Morgan Motor Company Ltd., Pickersleigh Road, Malvern Link, Worcestershire, England.

CONTINUED ON PAGE 21

Reverting to the Plus-8 on the road, the engine gives a subdued vee-eight exhaust beat (although I was disappointed to find only a single tail-pipe) and is otherwise practically inaudible, although the lower gears howl. The heater wafts plenty of really warm air about, so that hood-down driving is no hardship. The Morgan looks low-hung but didn't bottom over rock-strewn surfaces. The centre-hinged bonnet opened easily on the o/s, but one of the two press-down catches on the n/s panel was very stiff. The present output of this intriguing Plus-8 is two a week, but the intention is to increase this to about five a week by 1969.

The fuel tank has twin quick-action fillers and holds 13½ gallons, giving a range of at least 250 miles in ordinary conditions. Indeed, on mostly main road driving, I recorded 23.6 m.p.g. The intention had been to do a further check, motoring fast over a familiar Welsh mountain road, but in this I was hampered, and had to abandon the idea, because ponies were being taken over it to the November pony sales at Tregaron. Driven hard, consumption would no doubt fall to around 20 m.p.g. The only fault which developed during a three-day test, apart from the difficulty at times of opening the doors (chassis flexion?) was failure of the o/s sidelamp, which responded to the time-honoured thumping on the first occasion but not thereafter. Driving this truly exhilarating car with the hood down, in distinctly cold and wet November weather, to gain the enjoyment and benefit of fresh air, I was disappointed to notice a trace of exhaust fumes in the cockpit. These are probably sucked forward by the aerodynamics of the tail, and no doubt, assuming this was not a fault of this particular car, a longer or different exhaust tail pipe will be experimented with to cure this annoying shortcoming. With the rigid sidescreens erect draughts are successfully excluded and open-air driving is otherwise a joy.

The Morgan Plus-8 is a true sports car, and a very quick one at that. It weighs around 21 cwt. laden, with some 160 b.h.p. to propel it. As I drove it, sighting along the louvred bonnet, air playing around my head, the smell of hot mud coming from the exhaust and that vee-eight wuffle from behind, nostalgia for the days of pre-war trials, of exploring good country in exciting cars, and memories of V8 and V12 Allards came crowding back. For that alone, I was grateful to this all-yellow Morgan. Regarded purely as a 1968 automobile, the Morgan may be something of a joke. But as a fun and fresh-air car perhaps the only thing comparable (even preferable) to a Plus-8 would be a 30/98. And a brand-new Morgan costs only £1,487, including p.t. and seat belts.—W. B.

MORGAN
PLUS 8

*A classic car, a coastal
road and thou*

BY DENNIS SIMANAITIS
PHOTOS BY JEFFREY R. ZWART

ONE OF THE more subtle advantages of taking a trip in a
Morgan Plus 8 is that folks along the way tend to find
you more charming, interesting, trustworthy and
intricate than the same people might find you in, say, your
Porsche, Pontiac or Peugeot. Maybe we're a country of
unadulterated Anglophiles after all. Maybe, as David Frost
has so aptly observed, we 20th-century Romans look to

"We've obtained steady-state cornering equivalent to a Lamborghini Countach's."

Great Britain as our Greece, our heritage in things classic and refined.

A Morgan, classic? Most definitely. Refined? Er . . . perhaps we could show you something in a Reynolds or Gainsborough?

The first of 4-wheel Morgans entered production in 1936, things haven't changed overly much since then, and thus driving a Plus 8 today is sharing an experience with motoring enthusiasts of a half-century ago. Never mind that this V-8 version was introduced as recently as 1968. And in traveling down California's celebrated coastal Route 1, we can report that our Plus 8 was headed only once, by a daring and possibly over-enthusiastically driven ponycar. This should come as no surprise to those in the know: The Plus 8 doesn't weigh a great deal, it has some 175 bhp to do its bidding, and its suspension is fully up to the task of transmitting this power. In particular, you needn't be concerned that important elements of the design are essentially unchanged over the company's 76-year history.

For example, let the front wheels' location be defined by having them slide on vertical pillars, and they'll always be vertical. So reasoned H.F.S. Morgan in 1909; nor is it a bad idea today. The concept works best with stiff springs, well snubbed damping and limited suspension travel, but not to worry because the Morgan has all three, to classic extreme. Its tires, however, are perfectly modern and they team up with the rest of these vintage components to give really impressive handling. How impressive? We've obtained steady-state cornering equivalent to a Lamborghini Countach's. And slalom performance a bit better than that of a Porsche 944.

Peter Morgan, son of H.F.S. and current managing director, is smart enough not to leap into vogue technocracy. For years, Morgans used a cam-and-peg system that rendered the steering well nigh impossible to turn at rest and not all that much lighter at speed. Nor did it err in the direction of excess precision. Now, the company has rack-and-pinion steering as an option (and it's fitted to all Plus 8s destined for our side of the Atlantic). Thus, steering a Morgan comes into the realm of activities discussed by athletic ladies rather than only broad-browed single-purpose diehards. A similar passage of history is evident at the rear of the cars: Telescopic shock absorbers, indeed of the state-of-the-art gas-over variety, reside back where traditional lever-arm dampers used to function. How times do change.

"That's the one with the wooden frame, right?" asked the pleasant man in the bookstore in Monterey. Well, yes. After a fashion. But actually the frame is a steel ladder with Z-section rungs. Then comes the wood, a framework of Belgian ash forming, more or less, a skeleton for the bodywork. Things like door openings are precisely fit, simply because no two are exactly alike. With this in mind, the company's brochure notes that the dimensions listed are only approximate. The hand-formed bodywork is of steel or aluminum, the customers' choice, and its handsome shape has a way of evoking appreciative comments from the strangest quarters.

"Hey, what a cute car." This, in downtown San Francisco from a striking young thing with a winning smile and purple hair. We felt simultaneously quite old and kind of darling. But we understood her enthusiasm for the long louvered hood, the raked rear deck complete with exposed spare, the multiplicity of compound curves defining radiator opening, headlamp and fender top. It is just as good inside looking out, we told her.

Later, as we were about to leave that lovely city, we were chatted up by the owner of an art gallery. He had owned a Morgan while living in England and found the lines heartbreakingly beautiful. We talked for awhile, and when our stocking cap didn't fall readily to hand upon departure,

our new-found friend instantly offered his brand-new tam-o'-shanter in celebration of seeing a Morgan in front of his gallery. It's that kind of car.

There's a 7-year waiting list for new Morgans in their home market. It's said British enthusiasts buy one and order the next one simultaneously. Our situation here in the U.S. isn't quite this complicated, though a certain air of exclusivity still prevails. Bill Fink evidently came to appreciate Morgans during his university days at Oxford. He liked rowing as well and Oxford's Isis Boat Club gave its name to Isis Imports, Ltd (PO Box 2290, U.S. Custom House, San Francisco, Calif. 94126; 415 433-1344). This operation resides in San Francisco's Embarcadero, at Pier 33, close to some of the best restaurants known to man. Bill brings in some two dozen cars a year, performs the necessary DOT-izing with subtly worked door beams and bumpers,

LAST OF THE REAL SPORTS CARS

THE MORGAN MOTOR Co, Ltd, Malvern Link, Worcs, claims the distinction of being the oldest privately held motorcar manufacturer in the world. Not only has Morgan been in the business of producing cars since 1909, it has been continuously, dedicatedly, some would say doggedly so.

And they've all been sports cars.

The first of them was H.F.S. Morgan's Runabout, a spindly 3-wheeler advertised as "Not an EXPERIMENT, but a well-tried Machine." A British tax dodge encouraged its 3-wheel nature, wherein such cars were considered motorcycles and taxed at the lesser rate. And trike owners had

a real edge on motorcyclists, not to say the taxman, what with even the earliest Moggies offering better weather protection than any cyclesidecar combo.

Both 2- and diminutive 4-seaters were available, with either air- or water-cooled engines hanging off the front and driving the single rear wheel. By the Twenties, a factory brochure identified the Super Sports model as "probably the nearest approach to the ideal sports car." And indeed if three wheels were enough for you, perhaps it was.

The demand for a 4-wheel Morgan was initially met in 1936 with introduction of the 4/4, so named to account for the number of its cylinders and wheels. Subtle refinements followed, the war intervened, and availability of a more powerful 4-cylinder engine brought forth the Plus 4 in 1950. This was the last year, by the way, in which trikes could still be had. To put 3-wheel Moggie popularity in perspective, ponder that

roughly half of Morgan's total production had been in trikes.

Morgan variously could/could not obtain small 4-cylinder powerplants, coinciding with which it produced/didn't produce the 4/4 model. And in 1954, purists wrung their hands when Morgan's classic flat radiator shell gave way to a sloping design made necessary by supplier changes.

But the real shock came in 1963, when the factory introduced the Plus 4 Plus, an aerodynamically styled coupe—with fiberglass bodywork, for goodness' sake. Only 26 were ever produced.

Another company's engine lines again ruled Morgan's fortunes when the Triumph 4-cylinder ceased production, but the Triumph/Rover/nee Buick V-8 became available. Exit the Plus 4; enter the Plus 8.

In the beginning, they were all sports cars. And now, more than three-quarters of a century later, the Morgan Motor Co continues to thrive.—*Dennis Simanaitis*

and converts the cars to propane fuel in a deft exemption of EPA emission regulations. All this brings the total to around $25,000 for a Plus 8; figure around $2000–$3000 less for either of two 4-cylinder variants. And turbocharged versions are available for those intent on extreme excitement.

As we all know, it isn't easy being special, and it isn't easy to find propane either. A handy booklet identifies who and where, more or less, but it comes nowhere near identifying the ritual that accompanies refueling. You do get to meet some more interesting people, though.

We were refueling in Salinas and this time the Morgan's admirer was a pilot with worn leather jacket and properly jaunty scarf. "I love my airplane, my motorcycle and my wife," he told us, "but not necessarily in that order . . . and I could see that car in there somewhere too."

It's easy to understand why folks enamored by flying and cycling would like Morgans. For one thing, their touring is similarly complicated by deciding what to bring and where to stow it. There's hardly any room behind the Plus 8's seats for luggage, but then again if your touring is in the winter you'll probably want to wear everything you brought along anyway. The side curtains help to deflect the wind, but only to around nose level. Don't worry about your feet, though, even in the dead of winter: The heater does a marvelous job of keeping feet and shins toasty. Maybe even too marvelous in its single-minded sort of way.

It rained during part of our trip and we wanted to protect the leather, so it was good to know the top could be erected in relatively few steps. These are steps, however, that profit from a dry run, literally and figuratively. There's a certain coziness in the resulting construction, though outward vision does suffer a bit and it's so much nicer with the thing properly stowed where it belongs.

"This is a new Morgan, isn't it?" asked the hotel parking attendant. Yes to the Plus 8 query. Yes, propane. Yes, Isis. Some hotel parking attendants are very knowledgeable indeed. And most considerate. "Why don't you park it over there. It'll be safe and I'll keep an eye on it for you."

U.S. SPECIFICATIONS

GENERAL

Curb weight, lb/kg	2250	1022
Wheelbase, in./mm (approx)	98.0	2489
Track, front/rear	52.0/53.0	1321/1346
Length	157.0	3988
Width	62.0	1575
Height	52.0	1321
Fuel capacity, U.S. gal./liters	15.4	58

ENGINE

Type		ohv V-8
Bore x stroke, in./mm	3.50 x 2.80	88.9 x 71.1
Displacement, cu in./cc	215	3528
Compression ratio		9.4:1
Bhp @ rpm, SAE net/kW		est 175/130 @ 5000
Torque @ rpm, lb-ft/Nm		est 210/285 @ 3000
Carburetion		Impco propane (1V)

DRIVETRAIN

Transmission	5-sp manual
Gear ratios: 5th (0.83)	2.76:1
4th (1.00)	3.31:1
3rd (1.40)	4.62:1
2nd (2.08)	6.90:1
1st (3.32)	10.99:1
Final drive ratio	3.31:1

CHASSIS & BODY

Layout	front engine/rear drive
Brake system	11.0-in. (279-mm) discs front, 9.0 x 1.8-in. (229 x 46-mm) drums rear
Wheels	cast alloy, 15 x 6½
Tires	Pirelli Cinturato P6, 205/60VR-15
Steering type	rack & pinion
Turns, lock-to-lock	2.2
Suspension, front/rear: vertical sliding pillars, coil springs, tube shocks/live axle on leaf springs, tube shocks	

-Injected with Enthusiasm

Three thousand five hundred and twenty eight cubic centimetres of Rover V8 engine give the driver of our fuel-injected Plus 8 an enthusiastic approach to the sportier aspects of motoring. This 5-speed, front disc-braked, P6-shod masterpiece is hand-built in small numbers for those enthusiasts who number excitement amongst their requirements. It is recommended that those who aspire to a unique experience such as this car provides, and who are capable of controlling a quick vehicle, should inject a deposit at their nearest Morgan dealer, without delay. Morgan Sports Cars are currently available from £9,300 to £13,995.*

Allon White & Son
(Cranfield) Ltd.,
The Garage, High Street, Cranfield,
Beds. MK43 0BT. (0234) 750205

Otley Motors Ltd.,
Cross Green, Otley,
West Yorkshire. LS21 1HE
(0943) 465222

John Britten Garages Ltd.,
Barnet Road, Arkley, Barnet,
Herts. 01-449 1144

I. & J. Macdonald Ltd.,
Maiden Law Garage, Lanchester,
Co. Durham. (0207) 520916

Malvern Sports Car Company,
2A Howesell Road, Malvern,
Worcs. WR14 1TH
(06845) 63767

Burlen Services,
Greencroft Garage,
The Greencroft, Salisbury,
Wilts. SP1 1JD
(0722) 21777/8

John Dangerfield Garages,
115 Staple Hill Road, Fishponds,
Bristol. BS16 5AD (0272) 566525

F. H. Douglass,
1A South Ealing Road, Ealing,
London. W5 4QT 01-567 0570

Packer Duncan,
Waterloo Garage,
153 Hagley Road, Stourbridge,
West Midlands.
(0384) 395186

Robin Kay (Motors),
Marine Road,
Eastbourne, Sussex.
(0323) 26462

Lifes Motors Ltd.,
32-36 West Street, Southport,
Lancs. PR8 1QN.
(0704) 31375

Parker Bros. (Stepps) Ltd.,
63 Cumbernauld Road, Stepps,
Glasgow. G33 6LS.
041-779 2271

Phoenix Motors,
The Green, Woodbury, Exeter,
Devon, EX5 1LT. (0395) 32255

Cliffsea Car Sales,
Bridge Garage, Ness Road,
Shoeburyness, Essex. SS3 9PG.
(03708) 5323

Mike Spence (Reading) Ltd.,
School Green, Shinfield, Reading,
Berks. (0734) 883312

Sports Motors (Manchester) Ltd.,
214/216 Ashley Road,
Hale, Altrincham, Cheshire.
061-928 8143

Morris Stapleton Motors,
6 Kendrick Place, Reece Mews,
London, SW7.
01-589 6894

Station Garage, Station Road,
Taplow, Nr. Maidenhead,
Berks, SL6 0NT.
(06286) 5353

SERVICE AGENT
Libra Motive Services Ltd.,
8/10 Rosemont Road,
Hampstead, London. NW3 6NE.
01-435 8159

*Includes Car Tax, VAT.
Special equipment/colours extra.

'The Real Sports Car'
Morgan

Morgan Motor Co. Ltd., Malvern Link, Worcestershire, England. Telephone: Malvern 3104/5

I'M MOGGIE – FLY ME

The Vitesse-engined Morgan Plus 8 offers supercar performance at under £15,000 — plus a six-year wa Howard Walker jumped the queue and took one for whoosh along the Welsh borders *Photographs by Maurice Rowe*

The all-too-few residents of Hole in the Wall would surely have heard us coming. The deep, glorious bellow from the Morgan's exhaust as we scorched along the twisting, winding A449 in deepest Herefordshire could have raised the dead.

Yet there was no time for Hole in the Wall*ians* to respond. Hard on the brakes to haul the racing green Plus 8 down to a more circumspect pace as we passed through the sleepy hamlet, then down two gears and back on the throttle to once more release the Morgan's great flood of power.

The effect is like flicking a switch. There's no gradual build-up, no valve-bounce revving; the injected Rover V8 unleashes its 192 horses as if some invisible rider has prodded his invisible spurs into the hind-quarters of all 192 of them at the same time.

It seems to matter little which gear you've selected; just squeeze the throttle and hang on to the steering wheel as the power presses your body hard against the seat back. It's the same sensation as sitting in a jet on take-off; that deep, gutsy cacophony of rumble and roar mixed with this tremendous force on your body. Hi, I'm Moggie, fly me.

We left Ross-on-Wye behind and went in search of hard driving roads on the Welsh borders. Down along the busy A40 towards Monmouth, we used the Morgan's sensational overtaking performance to whip past the lines of heavy lorries thundering their way south to Newport and Cardiff. There was no fuss, no trauma, just haul the stubby lever connected to the Rover five-speed box down to third, wait for the gap, and whoosh you were past.

And there's no need to bury the rev counter needle into the red to get the best sprinting ability. Extend the revs past the 4500 mark and the engine takes on a rather hammery note, as if those big hydraulic valves are beginning to rattle against their seats. No, change just after 4000 rpm comes up and the flow of power continues unabated with the same urgency as before.

We had come to Morgan country to reassess the mighty Plus 8 in its 1986 guise. Not that revolutionary changes have been made to the classic two-seater. Not that many changes have been made at all. There's a new single pipe exhaust system in preparation for a catalytic converter being fitted for markets like Germany and Switzerland, plus there's some new trim.

When we last tested a Vitesse-engined Plus 8 the car had been fitted with the wrong gearbox ratios, with hopelessly tall first,

cond and third cogs. With the ...ht ratios in place, the standstill ...60 mph sprinting time drops ...m 6.1 sec to an impressive 5.9 ...c. That's Porsche 911 ...rformance.

From bustling Monmouth we ...aded north following the River ...onnow along the winding ...347. It was testing stuff, ...essing on hard, guiding the ...organ through fast, sweeping ...nds and along arrow-straight ...en roads. The car was in its ...ment; top down, being worked ...rd with smooth asphalt ...neath its sticky Pirelli P6 boots. ...n the dry, the way the car grips

the road is terrific. Just past Newcastle, the road takes an unexpected dive to the right – I'm sure it's there just to test that the driver's brain cells are working well. A sharp intake of breath, a tug on the wheel and the Morgan swept round as if held on line by some invisible rail. Impressive stuff.

Less impressive is the steering, which was recently changed from quaint cam and peg to more modern rack and pinion. While it's now much lighter at parking speeds, there's little in the way of feel at speed and the small degree of castor angle

RFORMANCE

KIMUM SPEEDS

...kimum speed, mph	122.2
...t ¼ mile, mph	127.4

CELERATION FROM REST

	sec
	2.2
	3.5
	4.5
	5.9
	7.9
	9.9
	12.7
...0	16.6
...0	22.1

CELERATION IN TOP

	sec
...0	7.9
...0	7.3
...0	7.9
...0	7.9
...0	8.8
...0	9.7
...00	12.2

CELERATION IN FOURTH

	sec
...0	5.3
...0	5.1
...0	5.2
...0	5.3
...0	5.5
...0	6.1
...00	7.2
...10	9.6

L CONSUMPTION

...rall mpg	25.8

Above: Interior is beautifully trimmed in beige leather. Driving position is dominated by over-large steering wheel

means that the wheel has to be almost wound back from lock. But at least it's got rid of the couple of inches of free play in the system that was always tolerated as part of the Morgan's character.

Smooth roads don't last for long in Wales, and soon the bumps and the ruts returned as we turned off left on to the white roads in search of the Black Mountains, their snow-capped peaks looming in the far distance.

There's one particular track – calling it a road would be flattery in the extreme – that runs across the mountains from picturesque Pandy, past the mediaeval priory at Llanthony, through Hay Bluff at 2200 feet and down to Hay on Wye. The only trouble with most Welsh minor roads is that breathtaking views across the valleys are almost non-existent because of the great high hedgerows they plant at each side of the road. Don't want the

sheep gettin' run over, boy-yo, do we?

The Morgan coped with the mountainous climb admirably which is more than could be said for the occupants, who were developing acute hypothermia by the second. It's not that the temperature of the air from the heater wasn't hot enough, the problem lay with quantity and the lack of it. Even with the noisy fan on full blast, I swear that icicles were forming on the end of photographer Rowe's nose. Not a pretty sight.

Over the bumpy lanes, the latest Plus 8 seemed to cope far better at retaining its composure than did the last Mog we sampled. While no suspension modifications have been made, Peter Morgan did explain that spring suppliers were now tempering the rear leaves to a more consistent standard than before. The new car certainly pitched far less and was thrown off line less often than with the previous car.

But don't misunderstand me, this is no boulevard cruiser; when you hit the ruts and potholes it sets your eyeballs shaking, making the view ahead look like a colour photograph on the front page of the Daily Shah.

Back on smoothish surfaces, we left Hay in our mirrors and headed off towards Hereford along the old Roman Road, more commonly known as the A438. It's straight and flat and allowed the Moggie to stretch its paws.

The Rover gearbox is a super affair; it's got the meaty weightiness that's in keeping with the traditional image of the car, yet it has an impressive slickness that makes changes quick and pleasurable. It's certainly not without its shortcomings and occasionally needs a couple of attempts to persuade it to go into first, while finding reverse can occasionally be a two-handed affair. And the clutch is certainly not for the lily-legged.

That's true for the brakes, too. There's no servo assistance, so hauling the car down from speed often requires all the energy a driver can summon. And even then braking is a rather slow affair. That said, the brakes do improve when they've been warmed up.

The same could have been said for the Morgan's occupants. We'd braved the elements for long enough and as we were both fresh out of bobble hats and thermies, the hood had to go

back on. You would be doing well to get the fitting time down to five minutes and if you didn't have sufficient strength to stretch the hood to meet the windscreen fasteners, you might as well give up.

Once fitted, the hood fits tightly and snugly and even at the car's top speed of 122.2 mph, it didn't threaten to part company with the body. Sliding sidescreens are still a feature of Morgan motoring and however well you make them, you're still never going to get a good fit at speed. The only answer is to wrap up warm against the bombardment of draughts.

Yet that said, the Morgan's cockpit has a wonderfully cosy feel to it and the cream leather trim that was fitted looked terrific. Most drivers would be comfortable behind the Morgan's wheel, though most would also say the wheel itself was miles too big. I would agree. Legroom is good with plenty of seat travel to suit the tallest of drivers, though it's irritating to have nowhere to rest your left foot apart from on the clutch pedal itself.

Getting in and out can be a bit of a problem, partly because the door is so small and partly because of that oversized steering wheel. With the hood in place, visibility leaves a lot to be desired with more blind spots than actual sight spots. Yet no self-respecting Morgan owner drives his car with the hood raised.

The thrill of blasting along the Welsh country lanes was tainted, I suppose, by the long haul back along the M4 motorway to suburban Surrey. Motorway monotony is not what the Plus 8 is about. Noise levels, largely from gales around the sidescreens mixed with road noise and a whiney back axle, certainly dulls the excitement of Morgan motoring.

But for £14,834, the Plus 8 Injection offers a lot of motor car with truly stunning supercar performance. I can't say hand on heart that I could live with a Morgan day in, day out, sharing a commuter haul every morning, but as a car to keep in the garage and bring out on sunny days to get the adrenalin pumping through your veins, there's little else to touch it. That's if you have any adrenalin that's worth pumping after you've just waited six years to take delivery of your new pride and joy.

PRICE £15,436, **TOP SPEED** 122mph, **0-60mph** 5.6secs

FOR Price, handling **AGAINST** Ride, refinement

THE PLUS FACTOR

The chassis design may date back to the dawn of motoring history, the ride may well be all you could expect from cart springs and sliding pillar suspension, but the combination of the fuel-injected V8 and open motoring works wonders

Have you got £15,500 burning a hole in your pocket? Want to invest in the future with a little piece of the past? A Morgan Plus 8 could well be the answer.

If you are one of the people who think Morgan owners are a bunch of bobble-hatted loonies who potter about in their cars at weekends do not turn to the feature on the C2 BMW

Morgan has managed to combine lines redolent of the '30s with modern wheels and low-profile tyres attractively

Alpina or the Corvette swanning up the west coast of the States. Carry on reading about a car with *real* supercar performance and enough character to satiate even the largest ego: a Morgan Plus 8.

Morgan began producing cars back in 1910 from a small factory in Malvern Link in Worcestershire and nothing much has really changed. The present day factory is still small with a long-serving and loyal staff who build cars to order on the same site as 77 years ago. What has changed is the length of the waiting

list. It can be as long as five years.

There have been many changes over the years to the mechanicals and drive train but the Morgans of today still look the part: a pre-World War II car, the real thing. There are quite a few other small manufacturers who have jumped on the bandwagon in recent years but none has managed to ascend to the Morgan pinnacle.

We last tested a Plus 8 in 1978 but we did not need an excuse to reacquaint ourselves; if we had, the fact that the Plus 8 is now powered by the fuel-injected 3528cc Rover V8 engine would have been reason enough.

The all-aluminium V8 engine is a development of an American GM unit and in 'Vitesse' specification incorporates reprofiled inlet ports for improved gasflow plus a higher compression ratio — raised from 9.25 to 9.75:1.

The twin SU carburettored version of the V8 which used to be slotted into the Plus 8 developed a maximum power of 155bhp at 5250rpm with peak torque of 198lb ft occurring at 2500rpm. The uprated 'Vitesse' engine fitted to the test car, however, raises the maximum power to 190bhp at 5280rpm and the peak torque to 220lb ft at a much higher 4000rpm — a substantial increase over the previous output and one which raises the Plus 8 into the rarified atmosphere of the ▶

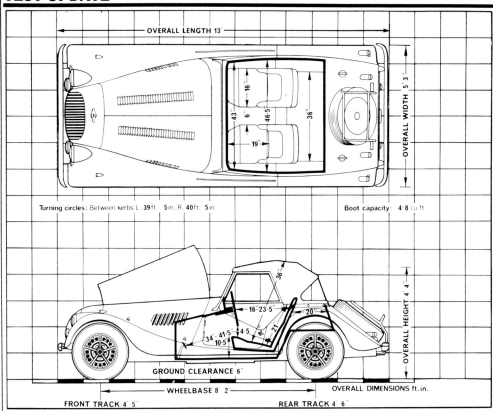

Turning circles: Between kerbs L 39ft. 5in., R 40ft. 5in.   Boot capacity: 4·8 cu.ft.

GROUND CLEARANCE 6"

WHEELBASE 8' 2"   OVERALL DIMENSIONS ft.in.

FRONT TRACK 4' 5"   REAR TRACK 4' 6"

MODEL

MORGAN PLUS 8
PRODUCED AND SOLD IN THE UK BY:
Morgan Motor Co Ltd,
Malvern Link,
Worcestershire

SPECIFICATION

ENGINE
Longways, front, rear-wheel drive.
Head/block al.alloy/al. alloy. 8
cylinders in 90 deg V, wet liners, 5
main bearings. Water cooled, electric
fan.
Bore 88.9mm (3.5in), **stroke** 71.1mm
(2.8in), **capacity** 3528cc (215 cu in).
Valve gear ohv, 2 valves per
cylinder, chain belt camshaft drive.
Compression ratio 9.75 to 1.
Breakerless ignition, Lucas 'L' Jetronic
fuel injection.
Max power 190bhp (PS-DIN)
(142kW ISO) at 5280rpm. **Max torque**
220lb ft at 4000rpm.

TRANSMISSION
5-speed manual, Borg and Beck
clutch, 9.45in dia

Gear	Ratio	mph/1000rpm
Top	0.79	27.59
4th	1.00	21.76
3rd	1.39	15.65
2nd	2.09	10.41
1st	3.32	6.55

Final drive: hypoid bevel, ratio 3.31.

SUSPENSION
Front, independent, sliding pillar and
leaf, coil springs, telescopic dampers.
Rear, live axle, leaf springs, lever
arm dampers.

STEERING
Rack and pinion. Steering wheel
diameter 14.5in (14.0in on test car), 3.4
turns lock to lock.

BRAKES
Dual circuits, split front/rear. **Front**
11.0in (279mm) dia discs. **Rear** 9.0in

(228mm) dia drums. Vacuum servo.
Handbrake, centre lever acting on rear
drums.

WHEELS
Al alloy, 6.5in rims. Tyres (Avon
turbospeed on test car), size 205/
60VR15, pressures F22 R22 psi
(normal driving).

EQUIPMENT
Battery 12V, 58Ah. Alternator 65A.
Headlamps 110/120W. Reversing lamp
standard. 21 electric fuses. 2-speed
plus flick wipe screen wipers. Electric
screen washer. Water valve interior
heater. PVC seats. Carpet floor
covering. Scissor jack; 6 jacking points
on chassis. Laminated windscreen.

PERFORMANCE

MAXIMUM SPEEDS

Gear	mph	km/h	rpm
OD Top (Mean)	120	193	4350
(Best)	126	203	4570
4th	122	197	5600
3rd	94	151	6000
2nd	63	102	6000
1st	39	63	6000

ACCELERATION FROM REST

True mph	Time (sec)	Speedo mph
30	2.0	35
40	2.9	48
50	4.3	59
60	5.6	70
70	7.9	81
80	9.7	91
90	12.3	102
100	16.4	113
110	21.3	123
120	29.6	134

Standing ¼-mile: 14.4sec, 95mph
Standing km: 26.7sec, 117mph

IN EACH GEAR

mph	Top	4th	3rd	2nd
10-30	8.6	5.9	4.0	2.3
20-40	7.2	4.9	3.4	2.2
30-50	6.8	4.6	3.2	2.3
40-60	7.3	4.8	3.3	2.5
50-70	7.6	5.1	3.4	—
60-80	8.1	5.2	3.6	—
70-90	9.4	5.6	4.7	—
80-100	11.7	6.4	—	—
90-100	15.7	8.5	—	—

CONSUMPTION
FUEL
Overall mpg: 20.9 (13.5 litres/100km)
4.6mpl

Autocar formula:	Hard 18.8mpg
Driving	Average 23.0mpg
and conditions	Gentle 27.2mpg

Grade of fuel: Premium, 4-star (98 RM)
Fuel tank: 14 Imp galls (64 litres)
Mileage recorder: 6 per cent long
Oil: (SAE 10W/40) negligible

BRAKING
Fade (from 95mph in neutral)
Pedal load for 0.5g stops in lb

	start/end			start/end
1	70-55		6	90-180
2	65-80		7	90-180
3	70-100		8	90-170
4	80-115		9	90-160
5	80-170		10	90-140

Response (from 30mph in neutral)

Load	g	Distance
20lb	0.10	301ft
30lb	0.21	143ft
40lb	0.37	81ft
50lb	0.51	59ft
60lb	0.64	47ft
70lb	0.72	42ft
90lb	0.96	31ft
Handbrake	0.47	ft

Max gradient: 1 in 3
CLUTCH Pedal 55lb; Travel 5in

WEIGHT
Kerb 18.1cwt/2022lb/915kg
(Distribution F/R, 48.1/51.9)
Test 21.3cwt/2382lb/1078kg
Max braked towing weight 1232lb/
559kg

COSTS

Prices

Basic	£12,390.00
Special Car Tax	£1032.50
VAT	£2013.38
Total (in GB)	**£15,435.88**
Licence	£100.00
Delivery charge (London)	N/A
Number plates	£20.00
Total on the Road	**£15,555.88**
(excluding insurance)	
Insurance group	7
Total as tested on the road	**£15,555.88**

SERVICE & PARTS

		Interval	
Change	5000	10,000	20,000
Engine oil	Yes	Yes	Yes
Oil filter	Yes	Yes	Yes
Gearbox oil	Yes	Yes	Yes
Spark plugs	No	Yes	Yes
Air cleaner	No	Yes	Yes
Total cost	£136.77	£171.14	£171.14

(Assuming labour at £20.00 an
hour inc VAT)

PARTS COST (inc VAT)

Brake pads (2 wheels) front	£20.29
Brake shoes (2 wheels) rear	£23.66
Exhaust complete	£175.69
Tyre—each (typical)	£220.80
Windscreen	£74.75
Headlamp unit	£9.75
Front wing	£346.15
Rear bumper	£95.17

WARRANTY
12 months/12,000 miles

EQUIPMENT

Ammeter/Voltmeter	●
Automatic	N/A
Cruise control	N/A
Economy gauge	N/A
Electronic ignition	●
Five speed	●
Limited slip differential	●
Power steering	N/A
Rev counter	●
Self-levelling suspension	N/A
Trip computer	N/A
Headrests front/rear	N/A
Heated seats	N/A
Height adjustment	●
Lumbar adjustment	N/A
Seat back recline	N/A
Seat cushion tilt	N/A
Seat tilt	N/A
Split rear seats	N/A
Door mirror remote control RH/LH	N/A
Electric windows	N/A
Heated rear window	N/A
Interior adjustable headlamps	N/A
Tinted glass	N/A
Headlamp wash/wipe	N/A
Central locking	N/A
Child proof locks	N/A
Clock	●
Fog lamps	●
Internal boot release	N/A
Locking fuel cap	£7.16
Luggage cover	N/A
Metallic paint	£265.05
Radio	†
Radio cassette	†
Aerial	£7.16
Speakers	£50.14

● Standard N/A Not applicable
† Part of option

TEST CONDITIONS

Wind:	9-17mph
Temperature:	0deg C (32deg F)
Barometer:	30.0in Hg (1017mbar)
Humidity:	86per cent
Surface:	dry asphalt and concrete
Test distance:	682miles

Figures taken at 10,811 miles by our own
staff at the General Motors proving
ground at Millbrook.
All *Autocar* test results are subject to
world copyright and may not be reproduced in whole or in part without the
Editor's written permission.

est mean speed *the Plus 8 achieved was 122mph. However, it is standing-start acceleration that is the car's true forté*

over V8 engine *develops 190bhp at 5280rpm*

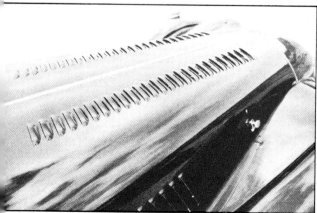

e long, sleek *bonnet hides the startling 178bhp/ton secret*

◀ supercar in terms of out-and-out performance. A power-to-weight ratio of 178bhp/ton as tested is a mouthwatering figure to conjure with and one which will stifle the mutterings of any car enthusiast.

Aerodynamics, or to be more precise a lack of them, play a large part in determining the Plus 8's maximum speed. The effects can be felt as 100mph is reached and at 120mph there is a definite feeling that the Morgan is beginning to struggle. A wind gusting up to 17mph around the high-speed bowl at Millbrook meant that conditions were not exactly ideal for a maximum speed run but on the day the Plus 8 managed to record a mean maximum in fifth gear of 120mph (4350rpm) with a wind-assisted best of 126mph (4570rpm). Fourth gear produced a mean maximum of 122mph (5600rpm).

As there was no red line indicated on the rev counter we took 6000rpm to be a sensible limit and this produced maximum speeds of 94, 63 and 39mph in third, second and first gears respectively.

Maximum speed, however, is fairly academic for the Plus 8 as it is not the *raison d'etre* of the car. Where the Morgan really shows its mettle is in the in-gear and standing start acceleration times.

The incremental times in each gear demonstrate admirably the flexibility of the Rover V8 engine and 3.4secs to go from 50-70mph in third gear is not

to be sniffed at as the comparison table shows.

Despite the age of the design the Plus 8 manages to gain an enormous amount of traction off the line, helped in no small way by a limited slip differential and the low-profile 205/60R 15ins tyres. The main problem off the line is wheelspin but with a bit of practice this can be brought under control and used to launch the car most effectively. It is not often that we test a two-wheel-drive car which reaches 30mph in 2secs from a standing start.

The benchmark 60mph comes up in an impressive 5.6secs in second gear with the quarter-mile post reached in 14.4secs — eat your heart out GTI drivers.

During its 682 miles with us the Morgan Plus 8 returned an overall fuel consumption figure of 20.9mpg, an improvement of 0.4mpg over the carburettored Plus 8 we last tested. The intermediate consumption figures range from 19.0mpg during the strenuous test session to 22.0mpg for prolonged motorway driving.

Unlike most other cars we test where the fuel consumption an average motorist could expect to return is better than the figure we manage, a Morgan owner is likely to record similar figures. The Plus 8 has to be taken by the scruff of the neck and *driven*; it is in its element being hustled around sweeping country lanes at speed and this is the way an owner is likely to drive it. As a ▶

Instrumentation *is utilitarian, as it should be in a car like this*

Driver *is forced to sit very close to the steering wheel*

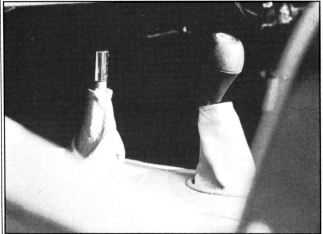

Handbrake *is sited forward of the gear lever on the tunnel*

Spare wheel *is conveniently mounted on boot lid*

◀ consequence economy will suffer.

The Plus 8 is fitted with a 14-gallon fuel tank — and it is literally a tank strapped to the back of the car — which gives it a very respectable range of nearly 300 miles.

The Morgan of the '80s retains the infamous sliding pillar independent front suspension and the resultant ride quality was described as "something else" in the last test of the Plus 8. It may have been something else nine years ago but it has to be described as diabolical in 1987.

The decrepit state of the majority of British roads — motorways included — does not help, but hit a bump, even a small one, at speed and there is bump steer as the front goes over it and then a resounding crash from the rear axle. The driver is thrown sharply upwards and if the hood is up there is a tendency for the top of your head to make contact with one of the hood sticks. This can be disconcerting the first time it happens

on the motorway as the driver feels momentarily out of control.

Look down the long bonnet line of the Plus 8 from the driving seat on the motorway and the motion of the front end bears a strong resemblance to the nose of a bloodhound hot on the trail — constantly moving from side to side. Because of the bouncing tendency it is a handful when driven hard down a country road but not dangerous by any means because in spite of its waywardness the Plus 8 is essentially a very stable car and will always put itself right. But the driver has to work hard.

In a lot of ways, however, it is this side of the Morgan's character which probably appeals to owners in this pampered age of power steering and boat-like ride. Back to basics and feeling every — and that means every — bump in the road.

Steering on Morgans used to be via a Cam Gears worm and nut box with only 2.4 turns lock-to-lock. Thank-

fully things have changed. Rack and pinion steering is now standard on the Plus 8 and with 3.4 turns lock-to-lock it is far more manageable, if still on the heavy side. The driving position is classic British sports car; straight legs and bent arms, with the driver sitting close to the steering wheel. There is a very good reason for this.

Driven hard into a tight corner the Plus 8 understeers initially, and understeers heavily. Being so close to the steering wheel gives the driver sufficient leverage to control the car, but be warned: if nothing else, Morgan driving builds up the chest and shoulder muscles. It is not a car for the faint of heart.

Speaking of the faint of heart, back off the throttle on entering a corner and the understeer disappears to be replaced by oversteer. The back end swings out of line and can then be caught on the throttle to power the Plus 8 round a corner in a most satisfying way.

Despite the antiquated chassis and suspension design the Morgan Plus 8 is a joy to drive as far as handling is concerned, and no matter what people say it is ultimately safe.

Refinement and convenience are two categories which form an important part of our full road test. In the case of a Morgan they are two sections which should not even be considered. Neither are inherent in the thinking behind the concept of the car.

There is enough room behind the seats for two soft overnight bags and the hood — it should always be carried in case of a prolonged downpour — and the engine and wind noise are at such a high level that fitting a radio/cassette player is a waste of time.

Instrumentation is utilitarian, as it should be in a car like the Plus 8. Comprehensive dials show the driver how the engine is coping but very little else.

The Morgan Plus 8 is in a class of its own. There is nothing quite like it: real old-fashioned wind in the hair motoring with performance that puts most modern 'fast' cars in the shade.

So do you have £100 burning a hole in your pocket? That is all you need to place a deposit on a piece of modern history. But there is a catch. The waiting list at the moment is in the region of four to five years.

It is by no means a car everyone will like. It is for those people who really enjoy the pleasures of seat-of-the-pants motoring and who are bored with the mass-produced boxes so often seen on the roads these days. True, the modern car is a sophisticated and ultimately competent piece of machinery and despite the fact that there really is no excuse for the atrocious ride of a Morgan Plus 8, it wins hands down in terms of character, performance and sheer driving pleasure. A car which really separates the men from the boys. ■

HOW THE MORGAN COMPARES

Morgan Plus Eight	0-60 5.6secs	50-70 3.4secs	Price £15,436
Audi Sport quattro	4.8	3.0	£47,621
BMW M635 CSi	6.1	3.8	£40,950
Chevrolet Corvette	6.0	3.4	N/A
De Tomaso Pantera GT5-S	5.4	2.7	£47,621
Ferrari Mondial	6.8	3.7	£41,250
Ford Sierra RS Cosworth	6.2	3.7	N/A
Lamborghini Jalpa 3500	6.2	3.8	£43,656
Lotus Esprit Turbo	6.1	3.1	£24,980 (HC)
TVR 350i Series 2	6.6	3.8	£17,865

140bhp Rover M16 2-litre engine should take the new Plus Four to 60mph in well under 7secs

Morgan Plus 16

Sparkling 16-valver bridges the gap between the Plus Four and fiery Eight

MORGAN'S BABY PLUS FOUR has been re-launched with 16-valve 140bhp power. As with the big Plus Eight, the source is once again Rover — the new engine is the twin-cam M16 from the 820 series.

With multi-point injection, the new engine should give the wooden framed/aluminium bodied 1900lb Plus Four a power to weight ratio of 160bhp per ton. Morgan is not claiming any performance figures but is waiting instead for an *Autocar* test. However, director Charles Morgan admits that the company would be disappointed if the car couldn't make the 0-60 sprint in under 7secs. "Around 6.5 would be nice," he says.

The decision to switch from Ford to Rover propulsion was taken to give the Plus Four a separate, mid-range identity between the Four Four and the Plus Eight. "We liked the Rover engine for a number of reasons," Morgan explains. "It's not only good, but also has tremendous development potential — Rover has very much kept its qualities under its hat. It's a low key unit, too, which is appreciated here. But above all we wanted it because it's British.

"We looked abroad — for instance I went to Fiat to have a look there. Without doubt, there are some very

good engines on the Continent, but we all thought this one would give us the best deal, keeping in mind those future developments which are top secret right now."

Morgan had little work to do on either the engine or the chassis to mate the two. A new back plate is fabricated at Morgan to match the engine to Morgan's own Rover 77mm gearbox from the Plus Eight since Rover does not have an end-on M16 gearbox.

The clutch was modified, along with the linkage, to cope with Morgan pedals that rise out of the chassis — unlike the 820 series cars which use a more traditional pedalbox. The engine has been mounted further back in the chassis than the Ford it replaces to improve weight distribution which, complete with driver, is said to be a near perfect 50/50 split.

There have been other minor modifications to the chassis to improve the new Plus Four's ride and handling. Both front and back springs have been changed, the rear leafs to include the latest hot oil tempering technology for greater flexibility. In addition, the axles have been beefed up to handle the new engine's greater torque — around 130lb ft in the Rover.

The exhaust system has been designed and built for Morgan by

Tube Investments, long time suppliers of the Malvern Works company. The new system, boasts no less than three silencer boxes.

Morgan at least quotes a fuel consumption figure — 35mpg for the M16 engined Plus Four. Given the 12.5 gals rear mounted tank, that should mean a range of around 430 miles.

The 15ins wire wheels, on Rudge hubs manufactured by Morgan, are shod with 195/60 low profile tubed Avon tyres.

The new Plus Four will be built at an initial rate of two a week, and the order book runs to three or four years. Customers for the old model will be offered the £13,500 new car.

There is also a choice of steel or aluminium coachwork, with narrow or wide running boards.

Chassis components can be specified in galvanised steel or coated in plastic. Inside there are the options of leather or fireproofed vinyl, a burr walnut or ash facia, and a mohair hood and tonneau.

The performance of the new car narrows the gap between the 20-year-old Plus Eight and the rest of the range — but there are no plans to increase the size of the V8 to 3.9 litres.

■ **Michael Harvey**

This was the vision through the little windscreen: the long green bonnet weaving over the bumps; the lights on the wings jumping with each gearshift; the brightwork shining in the morning cold. This was the view down the nose of a Morgan Plus Eight taking us up the Great North Road. We knew the next 200 miles were going to be hell, but we knew it would be worth it. Two hours jolting over the joins and through the roundabouts of the A1. Two hours overwrapped against the cold on our backs while our feet slowly cooked below. Two hours with just our thoughts for company, with conversation negated by the noise. Two hours of sensual battering for two days in the most charming parts of these isles, with the most beautiful, charming car they produce.

We were on our way to the North Riding or Yorkshire. They call it Cleveland now, but it was the North Riding when I grew up there. I wanted a Morgan to go back there because they're the perfect match. The Morgan, the dales, and the moors seem to evoke the character of this country. For me they are Englishness.

And the nose that lead us safely along the length of the A1, stopping just once for fuel, soon brought us, in the rain, to the long swoops that carry the A15 onto the biggest single span in the world — the Humber Bridge, the very gateway to the North Riding. It was drizzling, but against the greyness, the pale stone towers took on a magical quality. So simple, so elegant in their design and construction it's difficult to see them as man-made. It seems as if it's been there forever, not just six years.

The Morgan rumbled across. The whine from the gearbox, the creak of the suspension, the rush from the tyres, and that great blood-stirring blast from the V8 seemed to echo through the bridge. We slowed, the engine muttering its disapproval with a cackle. The reflections of the thousands of cables holding the countless steel sections in place danced over the bonnet louvres, distorting in the simmering heat now gently drifting out.

We parked below the northern tower and eased our stiff way out. It's not an uncomfortable car as such: your legs are bent just enough to relax, you sit reclining just enough to take the weight off your bottom, the wheel seems to sit in your lap and your elbows rest on the tunnel and door top either side. But after 200 miles, even on the smoother surface of a main trunk road, the combination of bumps, draughts, that rocking motion and the noise wear you down. Still, this car was designed long before anyone thought of the first motorway.

We consoled ourselves with the thought of the roads that lay ahead over the Wolds to Scarborough and beyond. Roads where the backdrops lack the desolation of the moors, or the solitude of the dales, but are nonetheless as open, wide and clear as any further north.

The change of mood was reflected in the weather. From where we stood on the Humber Bridge we could see the clouds starting to break, the sheets of rain being prised apart by a great bolt of sunlight that followed the line across the bridge then behind us, lighting our route into the Wolds.

As we took off towards Scarborough the sun was shining but the roads were damp, so the hood we'd taken off at the Humber Bridge soon went back on again. It wasn't so much to keep the cold out — the sidescreens and first rate heater see to that — more to guard against the filthy spray from the roads. Besides, we'd been travelling since crack of dawn, had a lot further to go yet, and deserved the odd comforts.

We raced into the North Riding, the Plus Eight revelling in the thrill of the long straight roads climbing the Wolds, then dropping away on the other side. The Morgan invariably crested these rises with a crash as the back of the car lifted.

COUNTY OF NORTH YORKSHIRE

TESTER'S CHOICE

DRIVER *MICHAEL HARVEY*
CAR *MORGAN PLUS EIGHT*
DESTINATION *NORTH YORKS.*
OBJECT *600 MILES WITH A LION IN WINTER*

A TASTE OF MORGAN MAGIC

Michael Harvey takes the bone-shaking but potent Plus Eight into the dales and moors of his beloved Yorkshire and comes squarely under the nostalgic spell of a car that is quintessentially English. Photographs by Jim Forrest

The Plus Eight *dives across the Wolds into the North Riding (above). The Morgan's suspension failings were never more evident — the car crashing over each rise. On the smooth roads across Arkengarthdale (left) we could use the Morgan's performance to the full. Only 2520lb at the kerb and with 197bhp at 5280rpm and 220lb ft torque at 4000rpm, the Plus Eight returns supercar performance. Engineering from the '50s and '80s, the Plus Eight by the Humber Bridge, world's longest single span*

The sun was shining brightly as we neared Scarborough. And I wished we'd left the hood off, for it was first-rate Morgan territory. As the bonnet would point towards the sky near the top of a hill, I'd feel myself longing for the descent to be clear. Then I could push that heavy lever into third and gun the car down the hill. They don't put red lines on the Smith's tachometers in Morgans, but they don't need to. You can hear everything as it happens, the chokes opening up, the thrashing cam gears, even a little squeak from the fan belt. No modern car is as physical to drive as a 190 bhp Morgan Plus Eight.

Scarborough is a special place to me. I wouldn't want to bore you with shared memories of childhood day trips, but if you go there don't be put off by the veneer of tacky penny arcades and fish and chip shops. Look a little harder for the Victorian and Edwardian magnificence of this former spa resort. It is very beautiful.

I took Jim Forrest to see the best views: the Grand Hotel, the Castle and the fishing harbour. Then we trundled off along Marine Drive that cuts into the base of the cliff around the North Bay, a cobbled drive strewn with the flotsam and jetsam from the last high tide. The Morgan made bumpy progress out of the town. We were starting to get weary and it was starting to get very, very cold.

Ten miles out of Scarborough we were on the edge of the moors, the A165 to Whitby: Dracula country. We stopped at Robin Hood's Bay to clear the traffic that had kept us at painfully slow speeds since Scarborough. Robin Hood's has changed so much. In the summer, the car park above the almost inaccessible village is now crammed with day trippers.

Out of season, on the fringes of this cold November evening, it was almost deserted. Not a soul watched our uncomfortable descent to the bay. As we parked at an uneasy angle on the slipway, a few faces appeared at the windows of the tall, narrow Bay Hotel. It's difficult to imagine anybody coming in and out after winter sets in, and the faces at the window seemed to resent us being there.

I breathed a sign of relief as we pulled out of, and away from, Robin Hood's Bay to head towards Whitby, the big lights picking our way through the moors. Morgan fits big, old-fashioned driving lights to Plus Eights and with the main lights they make driving after dusk a pleasure.

There's a lot to see in Whitby: the graveyard at St Hilda's where on a windy day you can feel the sea air blasting into your lungs; Yorkshireman James Cook looking out across the North Sea from the West Cliff; the Whalebone arch in memory of Captain WM Scoresby Senior, inventor of the crow's nest; and the River Esk estuary harbour, now a mixture of fishing boats and cruisers taking respite from the North Sea.

And then there's the Abbey. Its feeling of Godlessness wasn't helped by Irishman Bram Stoker, who chose Whitby as the place where Count Dracula landed on these shores. As we trundled up the hill towards the abbey the wind buffeted the Morgan, every tiny leak in the hood admitting a draught of icy air.

We'd wanted to spend our second day away from the moors amid the wild greenery of the Dales. Hemsley, just on the edges, seemed about right.

We were there just before the early evening traffic, allowing us to run the Morgan at ten tenths from time to time. That great fat band of Rover V8 power took the grind out of changing up and down as we heaved around bend after bend. Then, when we encountered a bus or slow car, it was down to third with the tachometer needle skipping around the clock and the back wheels twitching against the power as they fought to follow the front. The soft babble that had been there before was now a roar as that big heart thrust us towards Helmsley. We'd grown used to the battering the car seemed to take at anything over 60, and besides — like a middle-distance runner kicking out as he saw the line — the signposts were now counting down the miles.

We raced the last five miles, lifting off as we passed the sign into Helmsley. We were weary, cold, and stiff; our ears humming with the noise. And we were hungry and thirsty. After about 300 miles in the Plus Eight we deserved the comforts of the Black Swan, which faces the market square. We could see a fire roaring inside as we locked the Morgan up for the night. It was the perfect tonic for the last 300 miles.

Across the square a pub serves Theakston's Old Peculiar. We met there after dinner, and as we returned past the Morgan on the way to our beds we couldn't help but notice that the sky was clear as far as the eye could see. We agreed that a dawn run to Sutton Bank, 10 miles down the road, would be wonderful. With that, we slept like children.

The world seems to end at Sutton Bank, and as we headed gingerly along the icy roads that morning it did seem as though you could see for ever. The distance to the horizon is, apparently, 90 miles. We parked for a while, and the cold air shook every last drop of sleep from us. By the time we'd driven up and down the bank — with a lurid slide round the long hairpin reminding us of the temperature — it was time to return to the Black Swan for kippers.

By the time we'd eaten and set about taking the hood off the the day, the sun was shimmering, but steely-cold. It seemed another world from London, and we leapt into the Morgan vowing to leave the hood off all day.

It feels a very different car without the hood or side screens. Underneath the bulbous vinyl top you feel vulnerable and claustrophobic. You pick up all the creaks and groans from inside the car, as well as all those generated outside. With the hood down, you feel the cold air fresh against the top of your head, and a great sense of liberation.

It seems a much smaller, more controllable car like this and, wrapped against the cold, we headed off towards the Dales to enjoy the Eight to the full.

inspired by the beauty, in front, to the left, to the right, and behind us. This was why we'd come to the North Riding.

I dropped the Morgan back to third and eased the tiny roller-type throttle pedal down, feeling the roller twisting against my sole. Ahead the neat grey ribbon of road dropped and twisted, climbed and turned for mile after mile. The nose lifted to the icy blue sky each time the heavy clutch sank home again. The noise became louder and louder, we snuggled deep into the tiny leather seats to be closer to the warmth.

Nothing could have been more perfect. You could have been more comfortable in a German sports saloon, or travelled faster in an Italian, but you wouldn't have felt as if you really *belonged* up here.

With an eye to the rivers of ice either side, and the attentive audience of sheep, I raced on through the bends, only coming back down to earth as I struggled with the brakes, heavy and ineffective and abdicating their duty to the engine's own impressive stopping power. I kept an eye open, too, for bumps and potholes on the sides of the roads. Keep out away from these disruptions, and the Morgan is bliss to drive. Whether you hurl the tail out deliberately or push it out slowly with gentle pressure on the peculiarly effective throttle, it's superb. Push the other way on the heavy leather wheel and leave your right foot where it is, and the Morgan jumps back into line like a well-drilled soldier. Considering its age, the chassis does well. It's only the bumps that it doesn't like.

Feeling a great rush of reacquaintance and purged by the bracing fresh air we left Arkengarthdale to explore the tiny road that drives over the dale back to Swaledale. You will have seen this road if you watched Scotsman James Herriot's *A Creatures Great and Small* television show. This is the little road where the Austin Seven splashed through the tiny ford.

The road is lined with mile after mile of dry-stone wall which looks as if it's been there forever. Always the same height, always the same width, yet not single brick or drop of cement. Leaving Arkengarthdale behind us now, we headed across toward Swale. We couldn't see the new dale as we approached: the road's so steep the nose of the Morgan pointed to the sky, its green bonnet blue in the clear, icy light.

We sat on the solid wings of the Morgan, each with an arm resting on the hot bonnet and waited for the sun to go. Across from us were the fields of Swaledale, still white with the morning frost; they don't get much sun at this time of year. The sun turned orange in the sky but the dales remained colourless, uniform patches of the palest green. The light picked up the long chrome strip running down the middle of the Morgan's bonnet, curiously clean while the rest of the car was covered in grime.

In the past two days we'd grown used to Plus Eight motoring. After it, the most basic Lada would seem civilised — and our journey back to London was as uncomfortable as any in the previous 48 hours. That didn't matter.

Three hours later the road-stained car sat tick-ticking back in London, its ash frame creaking as the aluminium cooled all around it. We must have done more than 600 miles all told, and stepping back into a "normal" car made the point: the Morgan must have something very special to make all the suffering worthwhile.

It's two things really. One is the way it looks. It's tired cliché to talk of the way the car shouts its pedigree amid the uniform tin boxes, but you only have to watch the way people react to see how charming its appearance is. The second is its performance. In a Plus Eight you do so much more than floor the throttle and hang on. It takes care and sensitivity to make this car go fast. You feel it working all around you and little by little you learn to work with it. The bottom line is character. After this, you'll know how strong its appeal can be. ∎

From Helmsley, we couldn't miss the chance of visiting the striking ruins of Rievaulx Abbey, which nestles in a small valley a few miles down the road. The Morgan had already warned us twice that morning that it didn't generate a lot of grip through its Pirelli P600s, and with the ice glinting on the road we slipped into Rievaulx, the engine's enormous compression taking us down safely — if a little noisily — to the tranquil corner.

There's a world of difference between the solitude of the desolate moors, and the solitude of this abbey. We spent an hour walking the ruins, with the cold air broken only by an RAF Tornado working above, and the sound of the Rover V8 when we crept back up the hill.

We were off to the Dales now and that, alas, meant crossing the bleak industrial plane around Middlesborough with its dirty black halo of smog. Being back on the busy roads was an uncomfortable contrast with the peace of Rievaulx. Now the little

Morgan stood knee-high to the lumbering pantechnicons of the A1 and we soon resented the filthy air coming over the top of the screen, covering our clothes in grime.

Thirty miles later, we pulled off towards Catterick and Richmond. The running boards and arches displayed an impressive covering of caked-on salt. The screen was filthy inside and out, and the midday sun was blinding as we hobbled across the cobbles into the beautiful castled town of Richmond. As at Helmsley, it was market day and the Morgan was a bit of a handful around the tight crowded streets. We managed to find the right road out, passing by the light-stone castle standing guard above a long, meandering River Swale.

Still blinded by the sun we followed the River Swale out towards Grinton and Reeth, then left the main road behind and headed out on to Arkengarthdale, leaving the Swale to lead up into Swaledale. Five minutes out of Reeth we were shouting,

The Morgan in Helmsley (above and left). With the sun shining we kept the hood off all day. Despite a tendency to shrink when cold, it was a snip to take on and off. 'Lift the dot' fasteners across the 'screen and Dzus at the back are painful to cold fingertips though. Hand-beaten panelwork is supported on an ash frame, now Cuprinol-dipped to prevent woodworm

DUEL!

The new Rover-engined Morgan and Caterham's latest Super Seven fight it out in the Cotswolds. Mark Hughes discovers they fulfil different promises. Photographs by Stan Papior

Morgan uses Rover's 1994cc twin-cam 16-valve M16 engine delivering 138 silky bhp. Caterham achieves amazing 135bhp from Ford pushrod 1597cc engine

Superficially the Caterham Seven and Morgan Plus 4 have much in common. Throwbacks to a past era, both have quirky, appealing, unaerodynamic and distinctive shapes. Both are hand-built by small-scale manufacturers whose production levels today are higher than ever before, yet waiting lists — nine months for the Caterham, several years for the Morgan — show that demand is unabated. Both defy marketing logic to provide a very different driving experience as minimal two-seater sports cars offering few concessions to practicality.

The comparisons, however, cannot be taken too far. For all their similarity, these two revised versions of existing cars are at opposite ends of an anachronistic branch of motoring. Whereas the Caterham has been continually developed to remain at the sharp end of modern dynamics standards, the Morgan clings stubbornly to its traditional qualities. The Caterham can be measured against the best current performance machinery, but the Morgan is unashamedly vintage in character, its maker resisting any temptation to tamper with a proven formula.

Graham Nearn and his staff at Caterham recognise that the Seven's appeal centres on exhilarating performance and the class of chassis. Taking the best hot hatches as their yardstick, they are determined to keep the Seven's acceleration, handling and roadholding abilities ahead of all non-exotic opposition. This aim has seen a package of improvements for 1988 — the car, tested here in 1700 Super Sprint form, has not been so intensively re-engineered for years.

Braking and suspension are the main areas of change. Disc brakes appear at the rear of the Seven for the first time. These 9ins discs — the same size as those at the front — carry Sierra

Cosworth calipers and asbestos-free pads. There is a significant reduction in unsprung weight at the rear and the car continues without servo assistance.

After Lotus borrowed a Seven during its M100 development programme, the trade-off for Caterham was advice on a batch of front suspension changes. Caster, camber, toe-in, spring rate and bump steer alterations have given more bite to the front wheels. Interestingly, after years of progress towards eliminating bump steer, Lotus suggested that more should be introduced to improve stability on poor roads. Work continues on stiffer spring rates, but the test car had springs of double the normal stiffness.

The pedal box has been redesigned for the first time in 30 years to eliminate the old Seven problem of the driver's feet getting damp when it rains: water used to seep down through the bonnet louvres. Although the car's traditional stove-enamelled spaceframe withstands corrosion well, the entire chassis is now coated with epoxy powder. Sevens have also been known for marginal cooling, a problem partially corrected by fitting a larger radiator and a better cowl for the electric fan.

Otherwise the Seven recipe is much the same as Colin Chapman's original 1957 concept. The car looks eccentric with its skimpy aluminium bodywork, glass-fibre wings and bug-eyed headlamps. Its suspension is a sophisticated mix of double wishbone front and De Dion rear, with telescopic dampers and coil springs all round. At around 10cwt it is incredibly light and the 135bhp punched out by its Caterham-modified 1698cc Ford ohv 'Kent' engine gives a formidable power to weight ratio.

Morgan also has something new to offer in the car pitched here against the Seven. The Plus 4 is the most powerful four-cylinder car Morgan has ever made. For the last two years, Ford's 1597cc ohv engine has been used in all four-cylinder cars since the Fiat twin-cam unit

was phased out two years ago after a production run of 126 owing to servicing difficulties.

After examining many engine options Morgan chose Rover's 1994cc, twin-cam 16-valve M16 unit, complete with multi-point fuel injection. The engine itself is unaltered from the 138bhp form in which it is used in Rover's 820 range, but a new transmission backplate has been added so that the Plus 8's end-on gearbox, driving a Salisbury rear axle, can be used.

Apart from its new engine, the Plus 4 is substantially unaltered from traditional Morgan specification. The powder-coated steel chassis frame — galvanised steel is optional — retains two-deep longitudinal sections with five boxed or tubular crossmembers. On to this base is mounted an ash frame to support hand-beaten steel or aluminium bodywork. In the time-honoured way, the ash frame is entirely cut and screwed/glued together by hand, but a recent innovation is a 40-minute dip in Cuprinol. The whole structure is strong but not very torsionally rigid. Indeed, Morgan owners can sense the handling feel change slightly with the weather, since a prolonged dry spell causes the ash frame to stiffen.

This craftsmanship and the car's aggressively traditional appearance are the key to its enduring appeal. Back in the early '60s Morgan put a toe in the water of modernity by designing a sleek coupé, the Plus 4 Plus, but it flopped completely. Ever since, Peter Morgan has learned his lesson and steadfastly maintained Morgan's traditional values. If it doesn't look like a Morgan, the customers say, it's not a Morgan.

Morgans must look like the '30s sports car that they continue to be in essence under the surface. They have a few concessions to modern requirements, like indicators and windscreen washers, but otherwise they are full-blooded nostalgia machines, all the way from the chrome-plated brass radiator grille to the raked rear quarters. Many replicas attempt

Morgan is arm and elbow car. You have to grasp the wheel and will it through corners. Tyres provide enough grip to allow Morgan some poise but it's unsettled by slightest bumps

to imitate the charisma of a Morgan, but none carry it off as well as the real thing.

With traditional looks you also receive a fair dose of archaic specification. The suspension is truly primitive, with leaf springs and lever type hydraulic dampers controlling the live rear axle. Front suspension is a sliding pillar independent system which looked old-fashioned in the '30s. Brakes are discs at the front and drums at the rear. But the steering is rack and pinion.

The stark differences between Caterham and Morgan are brought home as soon as you sit in the Seven. You need to be agile to prise yourself into its tiny black cockpit, but once you have slipped your legs down into the narrow footwell everything feels comfortable, tight and cosy. The adjustable vinyl seats, hug your body perfectly if you are of average height and build and the optional Motolita leather-rimmed steering wheel sits nicely in the hands. The hollow in the newly-designed sidescreens give an amazing amount of elbow room compared with Sevens of old. If you ignore the equally minimal passenger space on the other side of the high transmission tunnel, this feels exactly like a little single seater racing car.

The facia is merely a flat panel of vinyl-covered metal, with dials and switches neatly arranged across its full width. A 7000rpm rev counter with no red line marked, and 110mph speedometer are just visible through the steering wheel if you lower your head and keep your hands out of the way. In front of the passenger seat are small gauges for fuel, water ▶

Tremendous chassis makes cornering the Caterham very rewarding. You never feel it's going to let go. Corners require just a subtle flick of the wrists and bootful of power

Seven remains close to Colin Chapman's original concept: it has skimpy aluminium bodywork, glass-fibre wings. Very light, it has formidable power to weight ratio

◀ temperature and oil pressure. A toggle switch sprouting from the facia by your left hand looks a primitive means of operating the indicators but works well, and similar switches take care of the horn and headlamp flashing — there are no conventional column stalks. The rest of the switches are rockers and include one to operate the optional heated windscreen: the familiar Seven winter problem of seeing through misted glass has been eliminated.

The Morgan's interior is far more plush, although less convenient. Since the cars are hand-made, almost any combination of trim colours and materials can be requested — 33 are available in leather. The test car had red leather with blue piping and a coloured facia instead of optional burr ash or walnut. It feels nice to sit in, far more spacious and upright than the Seven, and not so uncompromisingly designed for driving efficiency. The seats, although very comfortable, provide woefully little side support on the backrests, while the column stalks for indicators, horn and wipers are uncomfortably close to the dash. The three-spoke steering wheel feels twice as large as the Seven's, but the size is right for the steering weight. The view through the windscreen, swept by three stubby wipers, is just as evocative as the Seven's, and you sit equally low in both cars.

Large dials for speed (calibrated in white on black to 140mph) and revs (to 7000rpm, with no red line) sit directly in front of you. In spite of the steering wheel's size, their top sectors are obscured. A large rectangular panel in the centre contains rocker switches and gauges for fuel, water temperature, oil pressure and volts. The gearlever is tucked away under the facia and to its left is a fly-off handbrake.

If the interiors don't convince you of the Caterham's chalk to the Morgan's cheese, the performance of the Seven certainly does — from the very first time you ease up the light clutch and open up the accelerator. The Super Sprint engine whips the car forward with a

E750 FMV

The car whips forward with a force unbelievable from a Cortina engine, no matter how modified

force unbelieveable from a Cortina engine, no matter how heavily modified and balanced. Response is instant and electrifying. The Seven catapults itself up the rev range in an instant through the first three gears, recording spectacular figures as it goes — 0-50mph takes just 5.3secs.

You are so low to the ground, so exposed to the elements, that this incredible acceleration feels subjectively even faster than the figures suggest. For all the world you could be sitting in the fastest object on four wheels as you open up down a quiet lane. The wind knocks your head about, the twin Weber 40DCOEs snort eagerly and the exhaust crackles like machine-gun fire as speed builds. The raw edge of exhilaration of most performance cars becomes blunted with familiarity, but the Seven's slingshot progress remains just as vivid to the senses a thousand times later. In a perfect driving environment, such as we found in the Cotswolds on a sunny spring day, you never tire of this car.

The engine is very flexible, but from 3000rpm to the 7000rpm limit it really lights up, quickly asking for another split-second pull of the short, delightfully snappy gearchange. It does not move quite so forcefully through fourth and fifth gears as the wind starts to create an invisible wall, but at 90mph the car feels quite fast enough. With sidescreens removed, the windscreen's protection is minimal: you have to squint to keep grit out of your eyes and the wind flares your nostrils. But then one of the greatest joys of the Seven is that you can experience its gutsy performance at useable speeds.

Measured against the Caterham, the Morgan's performance feels civilised and almost gentile, although this too is a quick car. A severe misfire above 4500rpm prevented us from taking figures, but Charles Morgan reckons that the Plus 4 should just nudge into the 6secs bracket for 0-60mph.

Undoubtedly the V8-engined Plus 8 would

be a far closer match for the Caterham's acceleration.

The Rover M16 engine is a lusty performer, although it needs to be revved hard beyond 4500rpm to deliver its best. Acceleration is reasonable up to this point where maximum torque of 130lb ft is developed, but there is a subtle increase of urge beyond it. At lower engine speeds the Morgan emits none of the tingling sounds of the Caterham, the gentle whine of 16 valves dominating this engine's character. But higher up the scale a transmission harshness — we assume it is a result of the Plus 8 gearbox, since none is present on the Rover saloon — begins to intrude and spoil the smooth installation. Towards its 6500rpm limit it sounds distinctly breathless, even though this is where its strongest performance is delivered.

The Morgan's gearchange works pleasantly and firmly, but does not have the Caterham's trigger-like quality. In fourth and fifth, the car feels far more long-legged and high-speed progress is more refined, although with these cars we are talking comparatively. You could travel further in greater comfort in the Morgan since it cruises more readily and protects you just a little more thoroughly from the elements when the hood is down. But its acceleration is nowhere near as thrilling as the Caterham, or indeed the Plus 8.

Cornering quickly in the Caterham is just as rewarding as stamping on its throttle thanks to its fine chassis. The test car was fitted with optional 185/60R14 tyres on 6J alloy rims and adhesion is tremendous: you never feel that the car is about to let go. With such a quick steering ratio and tiny wheel, darting into corners requires just a subtle flick of the wrists and then a bootful of power to balance the car through. This is classic rear-wheel drive poise and only the most single-minded provocation upsets rear end grip. The car is light to control, utterly faithful to sensitive commands and immensely fast on a twisty road.

The Plus 4 is also quick. It can get from 0.60mph in less than 8 secs

Although you sit close to the rear axle line, the Caterham's ride quality is a surprise. You feel every ripple, of course, but the springing and damping efficiently round the bumps to eliminate any jarring. You feel deliciously in contact with the road at all times, which inspires great confidence in the Seven's tremendous cornering power.

On smooth roads the Morgan also has capable handling, but it is entirely different in character. This is an arm and elbow car, with much slower and heavier steering giving little self-centring effect. You have to grasp the wheel and will the car through corners, using the power far more deliberately to counter initial understeer. Grip from the 195/60R15 tyres is good enough to allow the Morgan to take corners with fair poise and speed, but the slightest bumps are very unsettling.

This is where the Morgan's primitive design sets it into a past era most persuasively. The steering kicks and the live axle rear end crashes up and down when the road surface breaks up, destroying all the handling pleasure which the car can provide on a smooth road. This is never dangerous because the back wheels sort themselves out happily enough when they meet the road again, but this bouncy, twitchy progress, accompanied by old-fashioned chassis flex, makes the Morgan an effort to drive on imperfect roads. A good A-road is its favourite environment, whereas the Caterham loves nothing better than the most sinuous, bumpy B-road. Right-handers are much easier to manage in the Morgan because the mirror's position, bang in the middle of the windscreen, completely obscures your view through left-handers. Both cars have good brakes, although the Caterham'a all-round discs win on bite and efficiency, while the Morgan on the other hand asks for more pedal pressure to operate its front discs and rear drums.

The cars, both fun machines, are contrasting and totally impractical ways to enjoy performance of rare character. You revel in the

battering of the wind, the rush of the tarmac inches from your backside and the feeling of wearing the cars, rather than sitting in them. But each is different. There is the thoroughness of the Caterham's engineering for uncompromised ability. But the Morgan has a simpler appeal which wallows in pure nostalgia. The Seven is a driver's car, but the Morgan suits a gentler traveller. Both have strong merits, vivid personalities and offer an evocative driving experience, but the Caterham is much the better car . . . and cheaper by £3000. ∎

HOW THEY COMPARE

DRIVETRAIN	CATERHAM	MORGAN
Cylinders	4	4
Capacity	1690cc	1994
Bore/stroke (mm)	83.3/77.6	84.5/89.0
Head/block	cast iron/cast iron	al alloy/cast iron
Valve gear	2 per cyl	4 per cyl
Valve operation	push rod	DOHC
Compression ratio	9.7:1	10.0:1
Induction	2 Weber 40	Lucas multi-
Power/rpm	DCOE	point
Torque/rpm	twin choke carbs	fuel injection
Gearbox	135bhp/6000	138bhp/6000
Drive	122lb ft/4500	131lb ft/4500
Final drive ratio	5-speed	5-speed
Mph/1000rpm top	De Dion rear	live axle rear
Tyres	3.92:1	3.73:1
	20.3	24.4
	185/60 HR 14	195/60 R15

DIMENSIONS		
Length (ins)	133.0	156.0
Width (ins)	62.0	63.0
Height (ins)	44.0	52.0
Wheelbase (ins)	88.5	98.0
Track f/r (ins)	50/52.5	53/54
Kerb weight (lb)	130g	2042
Distribution f/r (%)	49/51	57/43

PRICES		
Total in GB	£10,691	£13,500

FUEL CONSUMPTION		
Overall mpg	19.3	—
Fuel tank (gals)	8.0	12.5

TOP SPEED		
Mean	114	109

ACCELERATION (secs)		
0-30 mph	1.9	2.7
0-40	3.0	4.3
0-50	4.1	5.6
0-60	5.3	7.7
0-70	7.6	10.5
0-80	9.7	13.6
0-90	12.5	18.0
0-100	17.0	26.1
Standing ¼mile	14.6/95mph	15.2/86
Standing km	27.6/111mph	29.0/104

In each gear — CATERHAM

mph	top	4th	3rd	2nd
10-30	—	—	6.1	3.9
20-40	10.5	8.2	5.3	3.2
30-50	9.9	6.4	4.6	2.8
40-60	8.6	5.7	4.3	2.9
50-70	8.8	6.2	4.3	—
60-80	11.4	6.0	6.0	—
70-90	15.1	7.2	7.2	—
80-100	22.6	10.8	10.8	—

In each gear — MORGAN

mph	top	4th	3rd	2nd
10-30	—	9.8	6.0	3.5
20-40	13.4	8.3	4.9	3.3
30-50	11.2	7.2	4.8	3.3
40-60	10.9	7.3	5.1	3.6
50-70	12.2	8.1	5.2	—
60-80	14.6	9.5	5.7	—
70-90	25.0	10.9	7.9	—
80-100	—	13.0	—	—

Morgan's interior is plush red leather with blue piping. More spacious than Seven but seats give little side support. Column stalks too close to dash. Wheel obscures tops of dials. Gear lever is under facia. Steering is slow and heavy, but handling is capable and grip good

Seven feels like a single seater. Seats adjust and fit well. Facia is just a flat panel with dials and switches across its width. There are no column stalks. Toggle switch operates the indicators. The 1988 1700 Super Sprint has very much improved suspension and handling

THE FOUR FOR FOUR

Ash frame is altered for four-seaters

Road behaviour is like two-seater's, but ride is worse on rough roads

Picture a Morgan and you always see a two-seater car in the style of the new Plus 4 featured here, but 20 per cent of Morgan's four-cylinder production comprises four-seater cars. They are mechanically identical to the two-seaters, needing only ash frame modifications to make room for two rear seats. A four-seater contains 116 wooden pieces compared with the 96 of the two-seater — total weight increases by around 60lb.

"Kids love riding in these cars," says Charles Morgan, who now works full-time at the Malvern Link factory founded by his grandfather. "I have a three-year-old and there is no way he could travel in a two-seater. The rear seats are quite high, so he can see everything on a journey. I think people tend to forget that we build four-seater cars. No magazine has featured one for 10 years, but they are particularly popular with British buyers. Most Morgan enthusiasts sooner or later find themselves with a young family."

The style of the rear seats is like an ample version of an old-fashioned 'dickey' seat as rear occupants sit rather higher, above the rear axle, than those in the front. Legroom is tight for adults but for children this would not be a problem.

Although there is no luggage space in the four-seater — the space behind the rear seats is just a slender slot large enough for the hood — a couple of suitcases can be carried on the seats, the only spare space. For transporting two people, this is a more practical car than the two-seater.

The hood is a bizarre construction which balloons high above the driver's head to allow decent headroom for rear occupants.

So much of the desirable optional mohair is interrupted by plastic panels to the sides and rear that visibility with the hood raised is excellent. The usual sidescreens attach to each door and a secondary pair of smaller sidescreens sit behind these. With the hood down and all four sidescreens in place there is far less buffeting inside the cockpit than you experience in the two-seater.

Lowering the four-seater hood is not the work of a moment. You have to unbolt the rear sidescreens then unclip the hood from the rear part of the body and the windscreen rail. The hood is a large piece of material which has to be laid on the ground to be folded up neatly and stowed before you hinge back the tubular supports and secure the mohair cover.

With practice, the entire operation takes around three minutes. Although it looks a 'Heath Robinson' arrangement, the hood was completely watertight during a spell of heavy rain.

The Plus 4 four-seater feels virtually identical to the two-seater on the road, with the only discernable difference being that the ride deteriorates even more over rough roads, presumably because all the extra weight is carried by the rear wheels. The test car, in fact, weighed less than our two-seater since its wings and bonnet were made of aluminium. Range is slightly reduced because a 10 gallon fuel tank has to be fitted in place of the usual 12 gallon item.

List price is expected to be around £14,500, but the test car was fitted with a number of extras. Full Connolly leather upholstery costs £630, a light ash burr dashboard is £125, a mohair four-seater hood is £704, metallic paint is £187, chromed wire wheels are £311, and an aluminium bonnet and wings are £343.

Rear seats give little leg room but children love them

New heart for an old soul

A fresh engine beats beneath Morgan's aged shell. But the character's the same/LJK Setright

IT MUST BE A VERY LONG TIME since anyone bought his Morgan through Harrods. The London store was one of the first dealers to represent Mr HFS (Harry) Morgan's new company after his successful showing at Olympia in 1911; but things have changed since then. Harrods, I should say, has changed a lot more than Morgans: the latest Plus Four has an astonishing amount in common with all its ancestral line. There is no such thing as a new Morgan.

The most that can be said about the latest one is that it has a different engine: beneath that centre-hinged and louvred bonnet stands the M16 engine from Austin Rover. But different engines have never made any difference to Morgans: since the earliest days of the three-wheelers, the factory has treated them as of no abiding significance – has treated them more callously than Don Juan at his most arrogant might have dismissed his conquests. Like 'Pa' Norton in his motorcycles, Harry Morgan started with a V-twin Peugeot that he happened to have handy; since then, the only consideration

preventing the list of engines starting with Anzani from ending with Zundapp is that Morgan always thought it preferable and politic to buy British.

That has never been a more important policy than it is today, when the sheer Britishness – dammit, Englishness, and never mind the proximity of Wales – of the cars is demonstrably one of their most endearing features. It does not leave the company a lot of scope, though: Ford does make engines in Britain, and Morgan has used them since the 1930s, but when Ford goes on strike it leaves only Austin Rover as an alternative supplier.

Rover has been delivering a steady trickle of V8s for 20years; another two or three a week from Austin will now make Morgan a much better customer, for the M16 incorporates costly elaborations such as no earlier Morgan has enjoyed.

Four-valve combustion chambers, for instance, served by hydraulic tappets, a multi-point electronic fuel injection system tolerant (with electronic ignition) of unleaded petrol, and a fluent exhaust system emitting no more emissions – toxic or noisy – than the most stringent European requirements will tolerate. This lean-burning 16-valve engine is derived from the 2.0litre O-series four, and it develops 140bhp at 6000rpm.

Plus Four ride is uncompromising and suspension archaic. View is uncluttered, a joy. Interior and footwell cramped

By the very latest standards, that is not a lot, even though it represents a bmep of 152lb per sq in. It does not have a lot to propel, though: if the open two-seater, despite its exceptionally smooth bottom, has a frightful drag coefficient, it does not present much frontal area. Weight is a more serious matter: because the M16 is heavy, the Plus Four scales 1900lb. Add 12.5gal of fuel and a two-man crew, and the whole lot rates 136bhp per ton.

It does not feel even that good. Explosive wheel-spinning starts are possible, in the absence of a limited-slip

differential, but the acceleratic is no better than decent. This no fault of the engine, which delivers quite respectable torque (about 130lb ft), but is entirely the fault of the gearing

It must have been tempting easy to choose the Rover 75m five-speed gearbox, the same serves the 3500 V8; but it does the Plus Four a disservice. It is hard work to operate, so shor the lever; it also has very wide spaced ratios. Add to that a 3.73:1 back axle and 195/60R tyres, and you have maxima o 36, 58, 87 121 and 153mph.

At least, that is what you fin if you believe the data given ir the homologation sheets. Elsewhere in them, figures for km(*sic*) per 1000rpm indicate that 6000rpm would give 38, 6 90, 125 and 158mph, which is even sillier. Dial readings in th car suggested something less extreme, but the speedometer was about eight percent fast a 90mph and there was no tellir how inaccurate the tachomet might have been. At any rate, not only will the Plus Four not reach maximum revs in fifth, it will not do it in fourth either. T most I could see, two up and hood down, was 105. Putting hood and sidescreens up wou have helped the car to go fas I do not doubt; but that is no way to drive a Morgan.

Here is the nub of the deba It does not matter a twopenny cuss how fast a Morgan will g how long it takes to get to 60mph, or whether there be ra in the air. Either you enjoy driving a low long-bonneted old-fashioned sporting open two-seater, or you do not. Either you like Morgans for w they are (what you *think* they are, perhaps?), or you suffer.

At least they have adjustab seats nowadays, but there is still very little room for the feet around those long-travel ped that Morgan still make uprigh with broad pads for hefty pressure on clutch and brake and a roller on the accelerato There is even less room betwe steering wheel and thigh: my gloved hand would jam, and there can be few as skinny as Setright. But oh, the joy of finding flat glass before you a nothing else to intercept the vi

And then to discover a genuine frabjous fly-off

ndbrake. You know, there are
this world things that really
atter intensely and are beyond
planation: the action of a
artini rifle, the docility of a
eviot tweed, the lucidity of
rpetua Italic, these and their
rallels are not to be
aluated but only to be
preciated. For all the
ousands of mean and
lculating pragmatists who are
ncerned to know what any
r does, there is an occasional
ocent aesthete who cares for
at a particular car is.
Only such as he could delight
the rather ramshackle
ding-pillar front suspension
ich has graced the front of
ery Morgan since 1910, or be
vocate for the flimsy Z-section
de-rails which have defined
 chassis of every Morgan
ur-wheeler since the first
ur-Four of '35. Anybody else
ght suspect the old Malvern
m of dim-witted archaism or
arge it with exploiting its
stomers' sentimental
manticism.

The thousands may – almost
tainly will – dismiss the
rgan as a stupid relic of the
t of Edwardian amateurism
e expected when a
rcester prebendiary sends
 public-school son to learn
gineering at Crystal Palace.
e Morganatic will cherish it as
ecious relic of the untrained
ity and intelligent simplicity
ch once made engineering
es clearer than they have
ce become.

One can still corner flat
hout anti-roll bars. Held
ly by its live rear axle,
mped to long underslung
-elliptic leaf springs, the Plus
ur does just that. The front
pension scarcely helps: it
s the front roll centre at
und level, but the car is so
w that its centre of gravity
not be far from its roll axis.
ng just ahead of the back
e, you lean against the
ering wheel and move the
g bonnet into approaching
ves, rather like pulling the
se of an aeroplane
und the horizon. As in the
oplane, any discursions of
nose betray some want of
ntrol. If the road surface is at
umpy, the underdamped
k end bounces and weaves,
ps sideways and then

**Latest power plant
is M16 four valves
per cylinder four
from Rover 800.
Has 140bhp.
Corners flat,
entertainingly**

resumes its efforts all over
again; but it takes only a little
more power to make the
reliable tail sit down and
persuade the car that it ought to
go where you want. Faster than
it feels because it is so flat, the
Morgan does go around
corners even when it
seems unlikely.

There have been Morgans
that were even lower, but only
one of them had four wheels, a
GN axle having been grafted
onto the back of a three-
wheeler. Sitting in my own
Moggie, a 1927 Aero tricycle
with a V-twin watercooled JAP
engine and a two-speed

transmission (36mph in bottom
chain, 67 in top chain), I could
touch the road with my knuckles.
One could palm the road from
the seat of a wide-tracked
Supersports trike, but mine
cornered flat enough: a steady
diet of three-wheeled drifts
breaking wheelspokes with
infuriating frequency. The wire
wheels of today's Plus Four are
much more robust on their
Rudge hubs: Avon has satisfied
itself that its tyres are safe with
inner tubes, and Morgan
machines the hubs itself.

The best Moggie handling has
in my experience accompanied
disc wheels, not wire-spoked
ones. I knew it could be done
when I watched a chap called
Sparrowe drifting blissfully
through the bends of Silverstone,
at an International meeting in
the very early 1950s, in a pre-war
Le Mans Morgan fitted with
Coventry Climax engine. A
decade later I did it myself
around Goodwood in the little
Ford-engined Four-Four, when
skinny bias-ply tyres were still
the norm and handling was all

the more delightful for roadholding being so slight. By 1968,
when the brutish Plus Eight
made my task around the same
circuit much more difficult,
radial-ply tyre grip had
increased enormously and
handling had gone for a Burton.

I dare say the factory has
done a lot of work since then, but
that was the last time I drove a
Moggie, and I never laid my
hands on the original Vanguard-
engined Plus Four that I thought
such a good idea, let alone the
TR2-powered version.

Other cars may accelerate
quicker, go faster, corner
harder, on paper or on a track;
on the road, they may – but they
do not. The three-dimensional
bends which abound in
Worcestershire, Herefordshire,
and adjacent counties, are a
challenge to any modern car;
they are an invitation to a
Morgan. I drove four new high-
performance saloons in the
same area the day before and
the day after, so the comparison
was particularly vivid. Perhaps if
you get your MacPherson
Marvel properly tweaked up, and
you concentrate entirely on
driving it, the thing will strut-
and-strumpet its rubbery way
through such corners faster
than this; but where the modern
hotfoot requires you to
subjugate the road, the cool-
headed Morgan approach is to
enjoy it. The immediacy of an
open car is inimitable, but there
is more to it than that. It is the
difference between immediacy
and directness: beyond being
open, the Morgan is also frank.
It is a simple apparatus,
designed by hand and eye,
manufactured by knife and fork,
as close to the basic notions of
motoring as a spade is to
digging. A powered rotary
cultivator may do more work, but
can its operator feel the soil?

The Morgan driver feels the
road. Too literally, if it be at all
bumpy, he will feel it in his
shaken stomach and blurred
eyeballs; but he feels more than
the road surface, he feels the
land flanking it, the air
blanketing it, the light bathing it,
the earth-force quickening it.
For all that, £13,000 – call it
£14,200 including such
reasonable extras as door
handles and Connolly leather –
may not be too high a price.

MORGAN: a suitable case for treatment. You all know the plot, of course: Vanessa Redgrave is the harassed wife, trying to tear herself away from David Warner, endlessly amusing as Morgan, the dotty academic who's becoming more and more like the primates that appear to be his sole obsession.

And in the end? Well I can't remember precisely what happens as it's a rarely-repeated film from the middle '60s when I was still driving Dinky toys and Morgan technology was only 40 years adrift of the times. But I seem to remember that by the time the credits came up all had turned out well for Mr and Mrs Morgan and our hero had finally been talked out of his ape-like state and persuaded to rejoin the 20th century.

There's naturally no danger whatsoever of something so unthinkable happening to the wooden wonder we all know and love – which is where the film and four-wheeled scripts part company. It's an interesting parallel all the same – a man so at

odds with his contemporaries that he takes refuge in an altogether more primitive form of existence, and a motor car that, while not exactly travelling back in time, has remained so rigidly rooted in an early era of design that any merits of the original vehicle have been long since forgotten and the ancientness of the machine has become a virtue in itself.

The idea occurred to me in one of those blinding flashes that sometimes come when you're struck smartly on the head – except that in my case the blow came from a rather different direction.

It should by all rights have been one of those perfect moments those long-held fantasy scenes that psychoanalysts are always supposed to ask you to describe. An idyllic country lane, perfect and peaceful with its undisturbed hedgerows and primrose verges. A mere splash of spring sunshine glinting on the long louvred dark green bonnet ahead and on the country cottages beyond. Peering over the slender screen with spring air filling the

THE WAY WE WERE

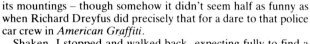

At just over £11,000, the Morgan 4/4 is
notable more for its rustic pleasures
than its pace or handling. Tony Lewin
found several plus points beneath the
archaic exterior

CLICKSTOP

its mountings – though somehow it didn't seem half as funny as when Richard Dreyfus did precisely that for a dare to that police car crew in *American Graffiti*.

Shaken, I stopped and walked back, expecting fully to find a sump, some shattered spring leaves or, at the very minimum, the remains of a differential on the road. But I couldn't even locate the bump that I had hit – unless it was that tiny, transverse road-mend that no other car would have even noticed at my 40mph amble. But that's what it must have been, I decided, making a mental note to steer clear of even the tiniest bump that threatened to hit both rear wheels at the same time.

And it wasn't long before I realised that dodging the bumps was in fact one of the main priorities when driving a Morgan, even at moderate speeds; the sustained jolting and jarring that still came through was, I figured, the acceptable minimum level of discomfort for the stiffly-sprung machine on its chosen back-road itinerary.

The adventure had in fact begun a few hours earlier in smart west London mews surroundings where couturiers and antique shop owners mix with double-barrelled car dealers (sorry, purveyors of *motor* cars), and where Bill Wykeham not only sells Audis, Seats and Morgans but rents out Morgans too, claiming to run the only organisation in the world to offer such a service. Here we were scheduled to pick up the rental 4/4 that was to be ours for a couple of days, but as there had been a last-minute rush on Wykeham's rental fleet we were given a near-new 4/4 demonstrator instead.

I wasn't complaining. Our very dark BRG car, complete with matching dark green non-chromed wire wheels, played the vintage part to perfection – far more convincingly than the shocking scarlets or polar whites, in my opinion. Photographer Simon Childs wasn't so happy. "It's bound to look black in the pictures," he mumbled, "worst colour of all to photograph. . ."

Of the Morgan's finish there could be no complaints, however. "They've got a proper paint process at last," explained Bill. "There are ovens and so on, and wings are now sprayed off the car."

What that means in practice is an end to the notorious paint-cracking that invariably spoilt Morgan wing/body joints. "And there aren't any brush-painted panels under the bonnet any longer," added Wykeham, though we certainly did find plenty of brushmarks on components such as the hood stays.

And after a brief run-through of some of the less conventional of the 4/4's controls (including a baffling explanation of the very rudimentary heating system, which had Bill pointing under the dashboard, and explaining that I'd only be in trouble if the weather got *really* hot), I wriggled awkwardly into the leather bucket seat, turned the key and fired up the lusty, er (and here it's a bit embarrassing) Ford Fiesta engine. It's an XR2 unit, actually, and therefore less inexcusable with very nearly 100bhp – which, after all, is far more than older Morgans ever dreamt of. The gearbox is five-speed (Sierra), too, though there's still a good old-fashioned Salisbury back axle.

Even as I eased out of the cobbled mews I could feel that axle deflecting the car from side to side, but I'd been expecting as

ungs and fluttering the hair of you and your chosen companion.

It wasn't quite so ideal for a variety of reasons – not least of which was an empty passenger's seat and a crumpled road map instead of the regulation young lady as companion. Nor was there much rural tranquility, I thought to myself, as car and conductor rattled and shook in obvious disharmony over that seemingly well-surfaced B-road stretch. And just as I was wondering whether this was what Morgan motoring was really about, there came the crash.

Not a crash in the conventional sense of an unplanned impact with another vehicle, an immovable tree or an ill-placed wall, but an impact with the road itself. The ground seemed to slam up into the Malvern machine's underside, threatening to catapult unbelt-ed individuals over the screen and give others a severe shaking. At first I didn't know what had happened; so loud did the bang seem that I initially thought the back axle had been ripped from

187

much. And knowing Morgans all too well of old, I had already drawn up a plan to make the most of my limited time with the car, making certain that I stuck to the smaller and quieter lanes rather than fighting it out in traffic or on motorways.

It's a car in which you automatically seek the solitude of the countryside, where you instinctively pack old maps showing B and C roads and tiny villages rather than newer editions covering the latest motorway intersections; it's a car to which modern highway hardware such as flyovers, roundabouts and even traffic lights are uncomfortably alien, where any evidence of the 20th century comes as an unwelcome intrusion on the olde worlde tranquillity of vintage motoring.

My plan, such as it was, was to head out west through as many parks as possible to pick up the A3 to Guildford, my only real stretch of major road. From Guildford minor roads would take me in a great circle eastwards just outside the orbit of the M25, skirting the foot of the North Downs, sometimes venturing up and over, sometimes enjoying the sunny southerly views from the ridge and at other times taking to the occasional easier A-road to recuperate. That way, I reckoned I'd be able to make it to Maidstone or thereabouts before dusk or, more likely, exhaustion suggested a southward turn to the Morgan's East Sussex overnight stop.

Threading my way through the rush of airport-bound traffic along the Cromwell Road that early April afternoon, the 4/4 was nothing but easy to drive. The high-geared steering was perhaps a shade heavy through that huge and close leather-rimmed wheel and the fly-off handbrake not only awkward to reach but singularly useless once applied. However, with a progressive throttle, smooth clutch and light gearchange this mildest of Morgans made a good impression. I found the seating position quite comfortable, too, though by the time I'd navigated through Richmond Park, deer and all, I had begun to feel confined for elbow space when negotiating tight bends, unless I engaged in a humiliating driving-test type wheel-shuffling routine.

Kingston's customary hold-ups gave me more chance to admire the Morgan's workmanship, from the leather dash-top scroll to the polished screen surround and the sheet-metal open glovebox with just a flash of white timber peeping though from behind (a reminder of the 4/4's ash-frame bulkhead and chassis), and the way it uses almost no plastic whatsoever. The break into the 70mph stream of the A3 underpass was something of a shock, though: there's not

really very much go to the Morgan's CVH engine and one feels doubly vulnerable as other traffic buffets its way rudely past and the shaky road surface does its best to deflect the car from its course.

A friendly wave from a mean-looking pair of motorcyclists one on a chopped Triumph and the other hog-bound, means that the Morgan had the approval of the alternative establishment, despite its gleaming coachwork and E registration. Interest of a less welcome kind kept arriving in the form of large vibration-distorted images in the tiny rear-view mirror. Morgans it seems, attract tailgaters like no other vehicle on the road, most apparently intent on reading the tread rating on the spare tyre or in the case of a giant Scania truck, using the advantage of height to peer down the *decolleté* of a possible female passenger.

But I soon became fed up with this three-lane tedium, tired of watching those instrument needles all tremble in unison with the engine, tired even of admiring those exquisite chromed teardrop sidelights shaking away on the front wings – sidelights which lack only that neat red tell-tale and the Lucas 'King of the Road' roundel for true vintage authenticity. Tired, too, of the sheer physical battering delivered at 70mph, not so much from the wind but from the rough-riding chassis and its ill-sorted steering.

I still cannot decide whether the steering is either too sensitive or too vague. Either way, its tendency is to allow the car to wander at speed. It's a system unique to Morgan and hasn't been used by anyone else for 2,000 years: described intriguingly as worm and peg or worm and finger, one can only boggle at how it actually operates, beyond suspecting that concealed somewhere in the 4/4 handbook there's a small print paragraph saying "inspect steering box daily; adjust every 500 miles; drain and refill every 1,000."

It was with some relief, therefore, that I cut loose from this madness and headed for the hills to seek the peace and freedom of Britain's forgotten back-roads – and to discover the appeal of the Morgan which, frankly, had thus far eluded me.

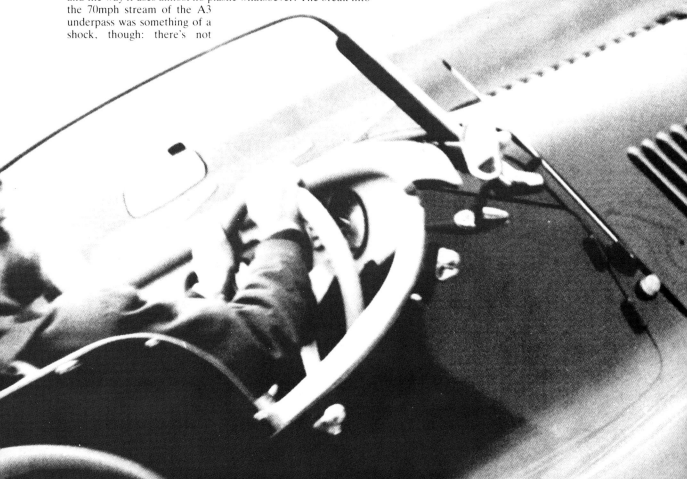

There were times when, chugging through sleepy villages or storming up steep hillside tracks, I thought I'd come close to appreciating the spirit of the vintage age, if not actually subscribing to it. There were times, too, when I seriously wondered what I was doing. Cruising down a normal B-road at a normal speed on a beautifully sunny day the Morgan must have made an enviable sight. Yet, at the wheel, the reality was rather different: the bouncing, jostling ride, chill wind, numbing vibration and hammering harshness of the chassis – it felt more like the astronauts' punishing test programme in *The Right Stuff* than an idyllic drive through the countryside.

Pampered by comfortable, convenient and smooth-riding modern machinery I might be, but I do at least expect a sports car, whatever its vintage, to stay in some semblance of a straight line when being driven sensibly. This the Morgan will do if the roads are smooth and flat: even in 4/4 form and with only modest power on tap it will handle well and corner quickly in response to a strong effort at the wheelrim. And though the Plus Eight, with almost twice the horsepower, is master in this respect, even the junior 4/4 offers the ever so slight possibility of deliberate power-on oversteer if you get the timing right. That, I reckon, is when Morgan driving begins to be real fun.

Change the road, however, and the whole equation changes. Introduce any un-

evenness whatsoever into the surface and the Morgan begins to have difficulties: on straights with any kind of camber or imperfection it's a full-time job to keep the car straight, the front wheels following every detail of the road like a puppy follows a scent. Combine an uneven surface with ups and downs or corners and the driver has an added struggle on his hands, the chassis bucking and bouncing from bump to bump, the steering kicking sometimes violently and the rear end jumping sharply out of line in the middle of a bend. It's just as well the steering wheel is big and tough: I found myself grimly clinging on to it as much for support in the leaping cockpit as for control over the front wheels.

And looking at the unique layout of the Morgan's suspension it is easy to see why it behaves in that way: at the front the sliding post system appears to rely on copious quantities of black grease to stop it from sticking, but travel is in any case severely restricted. And the live rear axle on hefty semi-elliptic leaf springs is again a recipe for limited travel and, in this case, seemingly poor axle location, too.

It's perhaps unfair to criticise a Morgan for these well-known faults, I mused, as I turned the long and louvred bonnet south towards home. After all, primitive engineering and the dynamic consequences that go with it are an essential part of the whole Morgan ethos, just as getting cold and wet are accepted drawbacks of dinghy sailing or paying the bill at the end is the unpalatable part of eating a decent meal out. So why not think positively and enjoy the good side?

And, indeed, I was already beginning to draw some comfort from the feel of the machine on the fast-improving roads. Free from serious bumps and jumps, I could now place the 4/4 as accurately into bends as its rather unresponsive steering would allow and, barring unseen surface changes or wet patches, I could also power it out again on a reasonably predictable line. Even the unservoed brakes suddenly seemed to have more bite.

Come dusk, it was time to stoke up the heater properly as the rural air was fast taking on a chill – this required a halt as I had been unable to locate the heater flap under the dash while driving along. It was then that I discovered two things: the radio (hidden so far under the dash that you almost have to operate it with your toes) and how not to get out of a Morgan. The radio's not vital, for it's rarely audible if you've got the hood down, which is how you should always drive anyway, but the getting out is very important indeed. Try it the wrong way and you'll wedge yourself painfully between the large steering wheel and the door frame, thus betraying yourself as a Morgan newcomer; do it correctly and you'll pass for a serious enthusiast of long standing. I leave you to guess to which school I belong.

Big round headlights now flooding the familiar (and suddenly unaccountably bumpier!) roads ahead, the Morgan returns to base and is safely zippered-up for the night – which looks like being a frosty one.

Hardly ideal Morgan conditions, you might imagine, and as I set off the next morning at seven for the photographic rendezvous, hood down and well wrapped up against the minus three degree frost, I did seriously think that I must have the odd 2BA bolt loose somewhere. The Morgan certainly had one: my three-year old son had cunningly slackened off the wing nut retaining the spare wheel, but I discovered the problem in time as the wheel began to thump alarmingly on the aluminium rear bodywork.

Against all the odds it turned out to be an exhilarating cross-country run, fast and free through the wide-open roads of West Sussex, the easier conditions and smoother surfaces clearly suiting the 4/4 very much better and the skipping tyres at last being given the chance to stay on the ground and grip. I was very nearly converted, too: swinging through successive series of well-spaced, well-sighted and well-surfaced bends, the Morgan at last got into its proper stride and I was beginning to feel as if it was actually travelling quite quickly.

I'd thought that at one stage the day before, too, as I heaved the heavy steering to keep the car on line through a sequence of dual carriageway bends, only to be overtaken by a Passat estate in the process. Summoning every last ounce of steering effort I at last caught up with the Passat; there was some gratification in discovering that it was a five-cylinder, but I promptly lost my flapping map overboard and with it my bearings and sense of chase.

For that's really what Morgan motoring boils down to: a heroic struggle not just with the elements, but with the car itself. More modern machinery may allow you to sit back and finely judge revs, braking, clipping points and steering angles, but a Morgan grants no such luxuries. And that's the key difference: with the Morgan you're fighting the car as well as the conditions, and it's bound to be an uphill struggle. After all, chassis engineering that may have been the latest thing in the '30s cannot hope but give second best today, even to something as excruciatingly ordinary as a Nissan Sunny.

And that's the 4/4's big dilemma. With almost any car you'd care to name outdoing it in terms of performance, handling, comfort and value for money, the £11,206 Morgan is left with only style, craftmanship and antiquity (in other words, what the car looks like, rather than what it does) as its real *raison d'être*. This in turn would brand Morgan owners as snobs, show-offs or antique dealers, which they plainly aren't, so perhaps it's best if we simply label them enthusiasts for the marque and leave it at that.

And would I volunteer for active service in this hardy brigade?

Yes, if only out of curiosity. Yes, if I had the space in my garage and the cash in the bank. Yes, if I had the essential extra of a normal car for routine running.

And yes if, and only if, that Morgan were a Plus Eight or the forthcoming 16-valve Plus Four. Only then would there be the proper kind of performance to make that brave battle against the elements truly worthwhile

ALL'S WELL IN WALES

A weekend of delightful wandering

BY THOS L. BRYANT
PHOTOS BY RICHARD M. BARON

E VERY NOW AND then in this business you walk through the front door of a factory and get caught up in the history of the automobile. Your head swims with the multiple images of cars and roads and drivers from the earliest days of motoring to the present. And just being there, in that place, gives you a sense of being a small part of the glory and romance of the automobile. ▪ Those were the thoughts I was having as Richard Baron and I stepped up to the front door at Morgan Motor Company Ltd on Pickersleigh Road in Malvern Link, England. In the car enthusiast's universe, not many manufacturers that started prior to World War I are still building automobiles. And I can't call to mind a sin- gle one that has re-

mained a family-owned-and-operated business. H.F.S. Morgan launched his car building effort in 1910 with money borrowed from his father, Prebendary Morgan, unveiling the original Morgan 3-wheeler. Two years later, the Morgan Motor Co was established, and it continues on to this day, now in the hands of the founder's son, Peter, and his son, Charles.

Richard and I had driven to Morgan in the latest Ford Scorpio 4x4, complete with air conditioning, sunroof, multi-faceted stereo radio/cassette player, and here we were, ready to pick up a Morgan Plus 8 for the weekend. The contrast was certain to be remarkable.

W E STEPPED through the door and into a lobby that is probably the size of your living room. Unadorned, plain to the point of sterile, yet exuding history. A small, glass-front counter offers the Morgan fan a variety of products for purchase: tie pins, scarves, wallets, key chains. Doors lead off on three sides of the room, and through one of them steps a young lady to greet us. We tell her we're there to see Mr Morgan and she

disappears through another door, returning in a moment and ushering us to his office.

Peter Morgan is an affable, unpretentious man in his late sixties. After a brief chat, he tells us he is giving us his personal Plus 8 to use for the weekend, and we all walk out to the parking lot so he can get his coat and papers out of the car. He then hands over the keys, wishes us Godspeed, and suggests we might like to have a look around the works. Unlike other automotive factories, where guided tours are formally conducted, at Morgan you get pointed in the right direction and then set off on your own, free to tarry as long as you like in each department. (For more on the factory, see the accompanying feature by John Lamm.)

As the factory closed, we set off in tandem with the Ford and Morgan, making our way northwest on secondary roads for the town of Ludlow and the famed Feathers inn, which would be our home for the next two nights.

The Feathers is one of those marvelously English inns you dream about, giving you a feeling of having stepped through the looking glass into an entirely different world. It was used as a private residence in 1603, the last year of the reign of Queen Elizabeth I,

daughter of Henry VIII and Ann Boleyn. According to the management, though, there are records that a house stood on the site prior to that, so this has been a place of abode for perhaps 400 years. The first record of the Feathers as an inn appears in a deed dated 1656. It has been in the family of current proprietor Osmond Edwards since 1947, and the family is dedicated to preserving the inn and a level of service all too rare these days.

The town of Ludlow has quite a fascinating history, too, having been the Seat of the Lord President of Wales from 1478 to 1694. And Wales was to be our destination for our first full day of Morgan touring. Ludlow is in Shropshire and it's a 15-mile jaunt due west on the A4113 to the border of Wales, where the road signs take on an entirely different language. Our first destination in Wales was Tref-y-Clawdd (you're on your own for pronunciation!) where we picked up the A488, skirting the Radnor Forest and heading for Llandrindod Wells on the A483.

At that point, we turned north on the A470, making our way along the Wye River

Valley to Rhaeadr, and a well-deserved lunch stop. Thus far, our route had taken us through gently rolling hills, over and along some mountain ranges with sweeping vistas of the countryside, and through any number of quaintly beautiful villages. And in the Morgan, it was easy to lose yourself in the romance of driving just for the fun of it, motoring along with a sense of how it was 40 or 50 years ago, prior to the era of motorways and fast-food eateries.

AFTER LUNCH, and despite the chilly, fresh spring weather, we had to lower the top and experience the rest of the day's journey in grand, open-air style. Fortunately, the previous day I had purchased a heavy, waxed gamesman's coat in Ludlow, which turned out to be the perfect thing for *al fresco* motoring. Our trail from Rhaeadr took us southwest on the B4518 through a hamlet named Elan and on to the edge of Caban-coch Reservoir. From there, we drove north again along a small road

without number that skirts the Pen-y-garreg and Craig-goch reservoirs.

This part of Wales is rather barren and sparsely populated, mostly inhabited by sheep herders, and the hillsides and valleys were alive with great flocks of sheep and newborn lambs. I reckon the Morgan Plus 8 is the ideal car for this sort of journey, with ample heat available to keep your feet and legs warm even with the top folded down. And, of course, the view out is unsurpassed. The 3.5-liter V-8 engine provides power for passing on the narrow, 2-lane roads, and yet docilely idles along at a snail's pace when the scenery and roads demand it. There's so much torque you can virtually leave the 5-speed gearbox in just about any gear—3rd, 4th, or 5th—and trundle along without shifting.

At the northern end of the Craig-goch Reservoir, we crossed the Elan River, motoring up a beautiful, rugged valley full of abandoned mines. We then encountered the B4574 road and turned west to Cwm Ystwyth and the town of Devil's Bridge, passing through a corner of the Ystwyth Forest. Then it was northward on the A4120 through Ysbyty Cynfyn to Ponterwyd where we intersected the primary road, the A44. The afternoon was marching steadily on toward evening as we wandered through such towns and villages as Llanidloes, Old Tylwch, Pantydwr and back again to Rhaeadr. From there, we retraced our route to Ludlow, with a stop for tea (and souvenir purchases) at a small establishment near Bleddfa. Then we crossed the Welsh border back into Shropshire.

Our Sunday drive was more of a transit stage, moving from The Feathers to our next stop, the Cottage in the Wood in the Malvern Hills, just west of Malvern. After checking in and enjoying a grand luncheon, we were off again in the Morgan, exploring the Malvern Hills and the Severn Valley to the east. It seemed only a short time had passed before the sun went down and it was time to return to our lodgings.

Our Morgan weekend had been filled with exploration of byways, hamlets and scenic wonders. And the best part of the entire two days was the Morgan itself. What had at first seemed a cramped and rough-riding car had become a cozy bit of history, perfectly suited for weekend wandering in the countryside of Wales and England.

Morgan+8

. . . and the sparks fly as we head down some of the country's best driving roads with Brita
fun with the top down surely do not exist but, as Andrew Frankel reports, the most impor

meets M3

heirloom and Germany's £37,000 ragtop technocrat. Two more diverse ways to have
ig is what binds this rather unusual couple together. Photography by Peter Burn

F ORGET APPEAR-ances, the vast price difference and the chalk and cheese chasm in technical detail: Britain's belt and braces Morgan +8 and Germany's computer literate BMW M3 convertible do the same job. And you know it the first time you drop their tops and aim them down a favourite road on a sunny morning. It's not just that either blasts to 60 in six wind-in-the-hair seconds or less, it's that both offer an unforgettable drive. But what conclusively different cars they are.

This is indeed a prizefight with a difference: the Morgan, hairy-chested and with the support of the crowd, facing a car trained by science and the racetrack to the peak of physical fitness. The battleground: the Lake District and the Yorkshire Moors . . . and the sort of roads for which both cars were born.

In the whole of motoring there are surely not two more opposed routes to what is ultimately the same result. The Morgan gets its punch from the old and ubiquitous pushrod Rover 3528cc V8. It produces 190bhp at 5300rpm and 220lb ft of torque at 4000rpm. When this kind of power is dropped into a car weighing little more than 2000lb, shattering performance is guaranteed.

With sliding pillar front suspension and a live rear axle located by leaf springs — ye gods, even lever arm dampers — the Morgan's suspension is pure pre-war. The car costs £17,703 and you will have to wait up to four years for delivery.

The BMW's 2302cc four-cylinder engine has twice as many valves per cylinder, operated by two overhead camshafts. The engine is unique to the M3 and was designed primarily as a racing unit. In roadgoing tune it develops 200bhp at 6750rpm and 177lb ft torque at 4750rpm.

Suspension sounds identical to that of any other 3-Series: MacPherson struts up front, semi-trailing arms at the back, coil springs and telescopic dampers all round. But BMW Motorsport has been to work here. With a combination of fine tuning and geometry revisions it has produced a chassis of rare quality.

BMW GB charges a ridiculous £37,250 for the M3 convertible. Only 40 left-hand-drive cars are being imported this year.

Straight-line performance in either car is sensational but the Morgan is the quicker. It can reach 60mph in just 5.6secs and up to 100mph in 16.4secs. The BMW manages 6.0secs and 16.6secs. Above 120mph the German's vastly superior aerodynamics mean the BMW can start to regain lost ground and

Morgan hustles through well-surfaced corners at cracking pace but handling falls apart on poor B roads. Hit a bump and whole car hops sideways. Driver needs to work but rewards are ample

pull away from the Morgan. In the gears, too, the Morgan is quicker. Between 50-70mph in fourth the car accelerates in 5.1secs, and in fifth 7.6secs; the BMW requires 6.4 and 9.5secs. It is only on top speed that the Morgan has to give best. Its 122mph cannot live with the BMW's 144mph.

Driving the cars on public roads shows this performance gap to be even wider than the figures suggest. For much of our two-day jaunt the Morgan was simply held up by the BMW, at least on straight roads. One event illustrates the point: overtaking a column of dawdling traffic, I dropped the BMW down from fourth to third and powered past on full throttle. The Morgan came too, but requiring neither a gearchange nor a foot on the floor.

It may seem hard to believe that Rover's ageing pushrod V8 could be a more effective engine than the multi-valve marvel produced by BMW Motorsport, but in these cars there is no contest. First there is the Morgan's torque. Even with very high gearing — 27.6mph/1000rpm in top — it will pull cleanly from walking pace in any gear. It will continue to deliver a flood of power to the 5500rpm limit we imposed, with no 'coming onto the cam' or fall off in power at high revs — it delivers its performance in one clean, solid shove. Then there is the noise. A classic V8 burble at low revs, rising to a deep-chested roar as it is extended. The effect is inspiring.

Taken in isolation, the BMW four is a great engine. It has a tremendously successful track record and in road trim it combines its power with a quality edge that the V8 lacks. But still there are racing traits: below 4000rpm, for instance, there is not much urge. Above this it unleashes its power and the rev-counter will charge to the limiter at 7400rpm with superb response. So you have to work at the BMW, with frequent gearchanges the key to keeping it on the boil. Fail to do this and the power disappears from under your feet.

There is not the engine music either. The engine sounds less distinguished than that of a Golf GTI up to 5000rpm and there's some roughness too — certainly it's not as smooth as any BMW six-cylinder unit. After 5000rpm it issues a mechanical howl to remind you of its racing aspirations, but still it does not seduce like the Morgan.

The BMW waits until the corners before it seduces you. The M3 has as good a claim as any to having the most competent *and* entertaining front-engined chassis in production. Remarkably, the convertible has lost none of the saloon's ability. Turn-in is sharp and the grip from the 225-section Michelin MXX tyres is of the very highest order.

The convertible will understeer or oversteer on demand, but its basic cornering stance is one of strong neutrality. Push on harder and it just feels better and better, neutral cornering ▶

M3 convertible has lost none of saloon's ability. Chassis is one of the best. Steering full of feel, turn-in sharp, and car will understeer or oversteer on demand. Grip is of the highest order

	BMW M3 Convertible	Morgan +8
DRIVETRAIN		
Cylinders	6, in line	8, 90 deg V
Capacity	2302cc	3528cc
Bore/Stroke mm	94/84	89/71
Valves per cyl	4	2
Valve operation	dohc	sohc
Compression ratio	10.5:1	9.8:1
Induction	Bosch ML-Motronic fuel injection	Lucas 'L' fuel injection
Power/rpm	200bhp/6750	190bhp/5300
Torque/rpm	177lb ft/4750	220lb ft/4000
Gearbox	5-speed manual	5-speed manual
Drive	Rear wheel drive	Rear wheel drive
Final drive ratio	3.25:1	3.31:1
Mph/1000rpm top	21.3	27.6
Tyres	Michelin MXX 225/45 ZR16	Uniroyal 205/60 VR15
DIMENSIONS		
Length (ins)	171	156
Width (ins)	66	63
Height (ins)	54	52
Wheelbase (ins)	101	98
Track f/r (ins)	56/56	53/54
Kerbweight (lb)	3105	2022
Distribution f/r	50/50	48/52
PRICES		
Total in GB	£37,250	£17,703
FUEL CONSUMPTION		
Overall mpg	22.2	20.9
Fuel tank (gals)	12.2	14
TOP SPEED		
Mean	144	122
Best	146	126

ACCELERATION (secs)		
0-30mph	2.1	2.0
0-40	2.9	2.9
0-50	4.7	4.3
0-60	6.0	5.6
0-70	8.0	7.9
0-80	10.7	9.7
0-90	12.0	12.3
0-100	16.6	16.4
0-110	22.5	21.3
0-120	28.3	29.6
Standing ¼ mile	15.8secs/90	14.4secs/95
Standing km	27.7secs/119	26.7secs/117

In each gear

mph	top	4th	3rd	2nd
BMW				
10-30	—	8.7	5.6	3.5
20-40	10.6	7.3	4.6	3.1
30-50	9.2	6.5	4.2	2.8
40-60	9.3	6.4	3.9	2.9
50-70	9.5	6.0	3.9	—
60-80	9.2	6.0	4.3	—
70-90	9.5	6.1	—	—
80-100	10.0	7.6	—	—
90-110	11.2	9.0	—	—
100-120	15.2	10.2	—	—
MORGAN				
10-30	8.6	5.9	4.0	2.3
20-40	7.2	4.9	3.4	2.2
30-50	6.8	4.6	3.2	2.3
40-60	7.3	4.8	3.3	2.5
50-70	7.6	5.1	3.4	—
60-80	8.1	5.2	3.6	—
70-90	9.4	5.6	4.7	—
80-100	11.7	6.4	—	—
90-110	15.7	8.5	—	—

Both cabins well finished and comfortable, Morgan's seats compensating in part for ride deficiencies. Refined interior of M3 is further improved by supportive and heated leather seats

balance eventually giving way to mi benign oversteer. The steering, so full of fe lets you keep the front wheels pointing in t desired direction, without drastic correctio and the car follows this line faithfully. It has hidden vices, no ghastly secrets.

Driving the same road in the Morg induces acute culture shock. Grip is not t problem if the road is smooth. With o 2000lb to persuade to change direction, t 205-section Uniroyals allow the +8 to hustled through well-surfaced corners at cracking pace. Put it on the pockmarked roads of the Lake District and the story is ve different. The car hops wholesale across t road as soon as look at a bump. The ride is tr appalling.

And the otherwise dead steering c generate the sort of kickback that wrenches t wheel from your hands. You drive this car fro the seat of your pants. Do this, and it is without its rewards. Fight the steering, kill heavy understeer with a bootful of throttle, ready to catch the inevitable tail slide and y will have one of the most invigorating rides t side of a rollercoaster. Despite the de steering, the Morgan can be placed accurate but it takes practice.

On the practical side, the BMW is stre ahead, and Morgan wouldn't have it any ot way. Hood up in the M3 you could be i saloon up to about 70mph. Engine noise prominent, and there is a distant rumble fr the fat Michelins, but wind roar, thou audible at motorway speeds, is very v suppressed.

The refinement is heightened by hea leather seats which are comfortable a supportive. With comforts like these worries of left-hand drive soon disappear.

Driving the Morgan roof-up on the mo way is not recommended. The tall gear keeps engine noise to a minimum but since wind drowns any attempt to hear anything, rather academic. The wind causes the hoo billow skywards — creating some m needed headroom — and assaulting you fr every hole in the ill-fitting side-screens.

The Morgan does do some practical j surprisingly well. The seats are comforta even if the ride is not. The two-stage he keeps you warm in freezing conditions. driving position is not terrible, even if it is s on leg room. However, none of this can m the car anything but fatiguing to drive in than ideal conditions.

The M3 convertible is the only BMW come with an electric hood. Raising lowering it is a simple matter of pulling levers and pressing a button. The mechan required to achieve a taut cover that is b water and air tight is not to be underestima The hood has to go through a complex rang manoeuvres, all of which are achieved v

absolute millimetre-perfect precision.

The Morgan has a typically belt and braces hood. A skeleton frame provides the basic shape. You have to hang the hood over it and clip it to the top of the windscreen and the back of the car, having already screwed on the sidescreens. The job could conceivably be done inside five minutes. Unfortunately our time with the car was spent in freezing conditions with a howling gale, when the job becomes nigh on impossible.

Both cars are beautifully built. Scuttle-shake, which can reduce a sound saloon into a rattling undesirable, is only apparent in the BMW on badly broken surfaces. Paintwork is deep and lustrous, and body panels fit tightly and evenly.

If anything, the Morgan is more impressive. The test car was Morgan's demonstrator and even after 40,000 miles of the suspension trying to shake the car to pieces it still felt and looked like new, save for the odd stone chip. Drive one and you will know that this is no mean achievement.

The BMW teaches lessons you never forget. It extends the boundaries which the comprised structure of a convertible has previously had to observe. It is fast and flattering, and as practical a drop top as anyone could wish.

Still, there is something not quite right about this car. It's partly in the price. A 325i convertible costs £17,000 less. A saloon M3 is nearly £14,000 cheaper. This cannot be justified by leather seats and an electric hood. The car seems to have been conceived as a money-making exercise.

The Morgan has no such problems. Apart from straight-line speed, it is no match for the BMW and nor, perhaps, would it want to be. What it offers is an unrivalled tactile experience. You can get out of the BMW, unruffled, after a hard blast down a fell road and marvel at the car's ability. Do the same in the Morgan and you get out with a real sense of achievement.

Then there is the way the car looks. Beside the Morgan the BMW, for all its flared arches and spoilers, looks anonymous. The Morgan looks classically beautiful. It has a hint of fragility that makes you want to look after it. For all the money it costs, the BMW is much less of an individual.

The Morgan has only one real problem. It is pointless driving it in anything other than ideal conditions. The car's comprehensive inability to transport its occupants for long distances in anything but severe discomfort is something that only the most die-hard nut will discount. But when the roads are dry and the sun shines, you cannot have too much of it. The Morgan ladles out fun like the BMW never could.

The essence of it is that in the BMW you enjoy the car, while in the Morgan you enjoy yourself. ∎

M3 is only BMW with electric hood. Raising or lowering it is simplicity itself. Morgan's hood posed problems for testers in howling gale but whole operation can take less than five minutes in ideal conditions

TWO-SEATER sports cars, most built along traditional lines, do not just survive in 1989. They prosper with vigour alongside the shriller hot hatchback clamour. From just under £10,000 to £31,000, Caterham, Westfield, Panther, Reliant, Morgan and TVR offer multiple model choices. Cars that shoot the breeze at the drop of a hood.

During 1989 the two-seater soft top sector will be further expanded by Mazda's 1.6-litre, rear-drive, 16v entry level competitor and a new, front-drive Lotus Elan. Yet it is unlikely that their clean and current style will appeal to the '30s-inspired Panther and Morgan buyers.

Whilst Caterham occupies the low price ground of traditional sports cars, their list costs reflect component form delivery. The traditional duo you see on our pages are fully-built, new cars. The Panther offers particular value at £10,975 (£12,089.76 in test trim), complete with Anglo-Korean alloy body.

Morgan prices start at £11,766 for their equivalent of the Panther's carburetted Ford XR2/3 motivation, but the posh leather-trimmed Mog we assessed was the spirited Plus Four with 16v Rover 820Si power. Priced from £14,183.81, another £1,100 or so brings a rear seat. *Fast Lane*'s metallic blue example was a two-seater, wearing a fair selection of the many options offered; a duplicate new car would be at least £15,678.81.

Both machines are built on the simple principles of pre-WW II tackle. Lightish (kerb weight 1,984lb) bodies cover separate steel chassis. A retention of front engines driving rear wheels via live axles is to be expected as part of the formula, but construction methods vary sharply.

Morgan have their unique combination of Z-section steel chassis and an ash frame to accommodate alloy or steel body panels. Galvanisation of the steel chassis is optionally available. Morgan state, "the ash hardwood body frame is soaked in a tank of Cuprinol before it is fitted to the chassis," which may not please health conscious purchasers.

Remember, it takes time to build each Morgan at Malvern on the individual order and assembly basis. The waiting list on all models measures "five to six" *years*, not months.

The Panther has the basic alloy body and its pressings made in Korea, but British finish and assembly. Panther's move to Harlow has allowed production of eight Kallistas a week, "most of them bound for export."

Panther, now minus the optimistic YC Kim, is directed by the unrelated BU Kim, but Kim-1 retains a 20percent shareholding. Got that? Fine, next subject.

Where is the Ford-Cosworth 204bhp Solo? We have been told by the company's PR representatives that 120 deposits have been placed on the shy Solo, 30 of them taken at the 1988 Birmingham Motor Show. The protracted production initiation is expected "for the second quarter of 1989, the first cars likely to be delivered to their owners during August of the same year." The first 100 Solos are expected to be rhd, and it will be at least 1990 before lhd output commences.

DATE WITH DESTINY

A December assignation with two uncompromising sports cars certainly sounds just punish-

Bright'n'Breezy

"**A December assignation with two uncompromising sports cars certainly sounds just punishment for turning the editorial passenger's locks a little greyer**"

ment for turning the editorial passenger's locks a little greyer in Mr Pork's Carrera-4 during its French launch.

I poured another litre of water into the test Panther 1.6L (*shurely shome repmobile badge mistake? – Ed*). Preparing to do battle with the pre-Christmas rush hour, there was no premonition of the fun factor in store.

Instead, there was a mounting dread of abandoning my Honda CRX and a fervent hope that the Hales-repaired water hose would remain intact under M25 pressure. All was well, but

throughout its stay with us the Panther's water temperature needle flirted in the 200-210° sector if the claimed maximum of 95mph was approached. Worrying, since there was no further detectable loss of water and the outside temperature were low. Decidedly chilly, in fact.

First impressions of the Panther are dominated by that enormous snout, which seemed to occupy 80percent of the Kallista's modest 12.76 length. Luckily the rack and pinion steering allows a good lock. Navigating out of Cheam' base camp car park did not produce th

The trad two-seater sports car lives, but do you take the harsh original or the softer and slower repro piece? Jeremy Walton referees. . .

Both cars hold the road well; Morgan in particular is difficult to provoke on a dry surface.

xpected thwacks of concrete bollard and shred-ed flank of dozing executive car. In fact there ere two immediate, and pleasant, surprises.

Number one was the sheer quality of the nish. "Panther Kallista Aluminium Body" pro-aims a proud plaque. The bright red example e tried exhibited a very high standard of fit and nish. Options such as the stainless steel running oards and chrome wire wheels helped here (and here were probably more we missed on that xtensive list), but nothing alters the initial npression of quality.

Items such as a walnut-veneered facia and oor cappings are standard along with carpets nd cloth covered seats; leather trim is offered

for just about every item. Amongst 18 choices were leather-clad sun visors at £57.05; hide-bound seats claim £614.72.

Priority has also been given to ease of driving and (by the standard of this uncompromising class) a comfortable low speed ride. Thus the Panther drifts onto urban trails with light steering and controls.

The five-speed gear changes are of acceptable Sierra-based grace, although first is buried beneath the dashboard. Stopping, via a mixed 9.75in front disc and 9in back drum braking system, is happily achieved at lowish speeds and kerb weight.

Below 45-50mph it all seems to make sense:

distinctive looks, easy driving and even the optional Blaupunkt radio could be heard. Instrumentation is from West Germany too, VDO supplying the 140mph speedometer and plain 7,000rpm tachometer. We blinked at six dials, the oil pressure gauge a £43.78 extra.

Below 3,500rpm the CVH engine sounds wheezy rather than charismatic. Classic carburation flat spot aside, the overhead camshaft Ford compliments a cabin full or minor Ford controls and an absence of rattles and thumps that is an object lesson to others in this category.

The trouble starts as soon as you hit what passes for open road in the South East. As the de-restriction signs of the M3 flicked past that elongated bonnet, the Kallista accelerated with the unremarkable flow of mass production hardware. The "FordVaux" pack surged smoothly away whilst the Panther's CVH fought to assert 93PS (used to be 96bhp in XR3 days) against optimistically tall gearing.

An indicated 3,000rpm and 70mph is bearable with the hood down. In fact, with pain-deadened practice you can sustain a lot more than that. Hood up it is a different story. The CVH flogging toward a quoted 5,750rpm power peak produces surges of harsh sound, but little in the way of perceptible performance.

At 4,000rpm the CVH becomes vocal, by 5,000rpm you would swear it is on redline 10,000. It takes a determined tormentor to push it beyond 5,800. By then it feels though Ford's foursome is clattering nails into echoing tin boxes that have been miraculously transplanted within your ear.

Panther, who now deal direct with Kallista custom from their Harlow base, claim 0-60mph

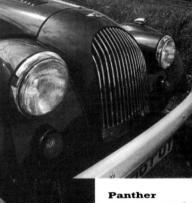

Panther captures style of Morgan, but is no performance rival in 1.6L trim.

in 12.5sec for the 1.6L. They do not speak of 100mph being approached.

If you want more than 95mph and above average acceleration (*circa* 7.7sec, 0-60mph) Panther offer much the same machine with 2.8/135bhp or 2.9i/150bhp Ford V6s. In both cases the company is honest enough to admit that you are unlikely to exceed 110-112mph. The shape that saps top speed also has an effect on fuel consumption, which is unlikely to exceed 25-27mpg in our experience.

The chassis and braking which feel so acceptable around town have their country lane foibles, but the basics are there. The double wishbone front suspension and the radius arms/Panhard rod location of the coil sprung rear axle are capable of generating enough private airfield cornering force to wish that the seats retained the driver a little longer.

The brakes always co-operated, but there was more slack in the pedal action than was needed for consistent reassurance. Extra retardation in response to higher pedal pressure might bring customer heartbeats back to normal.

When the Panther's tail switches – which is only under severe provocation, or with the aid of a slippery surface – the suspension and steering effect a tidy recovery. The Goodyear 175/70 NCT Eagle R13s are not so happy about holding the front in line on greasy surfaces. Fluent steering accuracy is not accompanied by sufficient slippery road feedback to be absolutely sure whether your supply of street credibility remains intact.

Despite the lack of straightline performance, most of our staff enjoyed themselves at the Panther's diminutive XR3i steering wheel. Now to the acid test, how would the Morgan original feel by comparison?

"Brutal" is the one word answer, but "brutally effective," is fairer, for this Moggie has another 45bhp in nominally the same kerb weight as the Kallista 1.6L. Plus the mid-range might of a bonus 33lb ft of torque.

Commanded by an odd, but efficient, accelerator ball pedal, Rover's 138bhp at 6,000rpm and 13lb ft of torque provide stunning acceleration.

We would not be a bit surprised to find this 1,994cc 16v was in company with the turbocharged Sierra RS Cosworth on the 0-60mph sprint (*circa* 6.0 to 6.5sec). In fact the slightly long stroke two-litre (84.5 × 89mm) from ARG seems to provide better mid-range gains than we remember from 110bhp Caterham Sevens, which is praise indeed.

The engine is by far the most advanced feature of Morgan motoring in 1989, the Lucas L multipoint injection and a 10:1 compression ratio electronically managed. They provide emissions-conscious lean burn characteristics and mighty all round performance. Just the kind of overtaking ability you need in Britain.

What hinders that accelerative ability, more than in any other car offered in 1989, is the road surface ahead. As I wrestled with a stranger's hopeless unfamiliarity in the darkened Morgan cockpit, a passing Peter Dron quipped, "hope

> **"Most of our staff enjoyed themselves at the Panther's diminutive XR3i steering wheel"**

your back gets better soon."

At that point I had only the fading memories of the CVH and Rover V8 Mogs. I did not think the ride could possibly be as bad as remembered. That much was true; it was worse!

The sliding pillar front coil spring layout still requires a dashboard-activated fix of lubricant every 400 miles. The back suspension has the semi-elliptic leaf spring principles that even Ford abandoned with Capri in 1986. And the Capri did not suffer the Armstrong lever arm hydraulic dampers . . .

Sensitively steered by Gemmer gear, the Morgan is a bumpy B-road handful. In fact, on anything less than the increasingly rare, unrippled A-class road, the Morgan is more like a frisky pony than a car.

Such manners are a pity, for the steering is superbly aware of surface and is geared faster than any road car we can recollect; just 2.25 turns lock-to-lock. Yes, it is heavy at rest, but the effect is almost like leaning on motorcycle handlebars for immediate response at speed. The 195/60 Avon Turbospeeds also deserve a contemporary chassis, showing high levels of grip whenever they were allowed to touch down.

The foward-mounted handbrake and stiffly obsolete Rover SD1 gearbox reluctantly freed the Mog from its Cheam car park berth. In amongst the Leyland switchgear and five Smiths dials there were some immediately obvious benefits over the Panther: the bonnet, beyond

Kallista cabin is well-built (below), and user-friendly, but lacks Moggie's leather-bound class (bottom).

triple and efficient wipers, was not quite so ludicrously prolonged, there was more storage space behind the seats (downright generous, hood up) and there was a neat foot rest recess. By contrast, Panther left a clutch foot hovering uneasily when redundant.

As on another wheeled legend, Porsche's 911, the Morgan's foot controls sprout from the floorboards and there is the accelerator ball oddity. None of these quirks cause any real difficulty. You can still heel and toe accelerator and brake, even via size sevens.

However, the brake action created by the centre pedal is memorable. Ryan Baptiste described it best as "wooden" and Simon Arron thought it simply "not there". The pedal to prompt generous 11in front discs and capacious rear drums has less slack than anything outside a competition car. Allowed practice and a reasonable surface, the system works best under heavy pressure.

The braking snag is that the chassis does not want to stay straight on any kind of camber or bump. The test Moggie always exhibited disconcerting desires to veer to the left.

As at Panther and Caterham, the body style steals any hope of more than an honest 115mph; the most we saw was 110mph at 5,800 in fourth. It lost speed if fifth was engaged during miles of reasonant research into this hood-up topic.

Neither the Morgan nor the Panther features severe hood operational problems, but the Morgan is definitely the more fiddly to lower, because of its stud fittings. Panther compensates by obstructing rearward vision most heartily when it is folded under a bulging tonneau. Once the hoods are down the Morgan is the draughtier, and you can make it more so by removing the side screens and sliding plastic panes. The Morgan also has a hood cover that does not fit as well as that of a Kallista.

Because this operator is as Neanderthal as the Morgan is felt to be by some of our staffers, there was also a persistent problem with the safety belt's retractor action. It was impeded by a folded hood and its cover.

The plus points, even on foggy winter days with a tight schedule to meet, are that open air motoring just seems to put a grin on your face whether you are 25 or 45. In the Morgan you get the bonus of losing the considerable transmission whines. Plus the nasal treats of that leathery trim, blended by Sussex bonfires and *Air du Ferodo, frappé.*

Despite the snags, both convertibles added enjoyment to routine and recreation motoring. Have no doubt that both cars are far better driving experiences with their hoods down, rather than raised.

VERDICT

IF THESE two cars had come to us in 1.6 Ford CVH form, there is no doubt that the cheaper and better-finished Panther would have got the nod. The coarse CVH brings out the worst in the Morgan, without performance compensation.

Given the under-rated Rover engine, the Morgan becomes a rapid performer that de-

"We cannot see why Malvern do not make the change to contemporary chassis techniques"

serves consideration against any rival. As a confirmed Caterham Seven addict the writer might well stray this Morgan's way, and it seems a sportier choice than a wuffling Morgan V8.

This cannot be a complete endorsement of the Morgan, however. We cannot see why Malvern do not make the change to contemporary chassis techniques under the traditional outline. The bucking ride over anything approaching the average, pock-marked, British B-road (terrain surely created to put the Morgan in its element?) handicaps both enjoyment and the considerable cross country speed that the marque would otherwise display.

Ford-powered Panther (above) runs out of steam at top end; Rover's 16 valves give Morgan decent performance throughout the range (below).

Driving Impressions in England:

A NEW MORGAN!?

Stop the presses! Or at least slow them down.

BY DENNIS SIMANAITIS
PHOTOS BY THE AUTHOR

CONTRARY TO POPULAR belief, changes *do* occur at Morgan Motor Co Ltd. Let's see, in 1936 a fourth road wheel transformed the Moggie trike into the 4/4. In 1953 a dwindling supply of classic headlamps encouraged the flat radiator to give way to the current sloping cowl. And in the exuberance of the mad and gay Sixties, the Plus-4-Plus even had all-enveloping bodywork. Saner heads prevailed, of course.

Moggie power has run the gamut as well, everything from the trike's Vee-twins to the Plus 8's Rover-nee-Buick V-8, sandwiched in between which were 4-cylinder engines of various lineage. Including (pause here for a little nervous jingoistic clearing of the throat) an I-Tie 4-banger. Briefly, the Plus 4 Mk II used Fiat's spirited twincam 2.0-liter, until the latter mill went front-wheel drive.

Enter British engineering, hem hem, in the guise of Austin Rover's M16. This 1994-cc 138-bhp 16-valver typically propels home-market 4-cylinder versions of what we call the Sterling. A few more fortunate ones, however, are diverted to Pickersleigh Rd, Malvern Link, Worcs, for the Plus 4 Mk III.

Not many, mind. Charles Morgan, son of Peter, grandson of H.F.S., told me that, one of these days, production would be upped to 10 cars per day. The scheduled build is to be three Ford-engine 4/4s, two Plus 4s and five Plus 8s. UK and German enthusiasts get most of these. Bill Fink's Isis Imports up in San Francisco gets maybe two dozen, Plus 8s and 4/4s only, at the moment.

With this extreme exclusivity in mind, I was delighted during a recent visit to England to scam Charles's own Plus 4 for several days. The weather cooperated, more or less, and I was reminded once more of what sweethearts Morgans are. The classic seating, low and well aft of centerline; the louvered bonnet and bobbing wings; the natural way these Anglicisms replace hood and fenders.

But what about the M16 drivetrain? First, you should know that I, for one, lamented the recent retirement of that shoulder-to-the-wheel steering duo, Cam and Peg.

So it is with mixed (or is it not fully stirred?) emotions that I report on a Morgan powerplant absolutely loving to rev. It feels smooth, modern and all that. But somehow it's a bit out of character with the rest of this wonderfully classic assemblage.

On the positive side, there's ample torque, quite enough to handle the Plus 4's particularly tall 5-speed gearing. (It turns just past 2500 rpm in top at 60, for example.) My hand-juggled stopwatch showed acceleration to this speed in around 9 seconds, adequate if not particularly awe-inspiring these days. However, a recorded fuel economy of around 29 miles per U.S. gal. struck me as pretty impressive. Just between you and me, I'd fit shorter gears, trading away some mpg for increased scat.

My driving impressions now span more than half a century of Moggies, from a 1937 F-Type 3-wheeler to this Plus 4. Plenty of changes, sure; yet there's a continuity of enthusiasm, an elemental consonance of things mechanical.

I'm delighted there's a new Morgan. And I'm especially relieved it's not too new. ⓜ

Reminiscences in
4/4 Time

What it really called for was silly hats and shooting sticks — the classic Quints-style coverage complete with tub-thumping and peasants in aspic — but with the period props tucked away in some dusty cupboard, and Romsey himself in temporary retirement (some say his writing future is all talk), it looked like I had no alternative but to play this Morgan assignment totally straight. Then again that was probably just as well, because if ever a car has suffered a surfeit of 'color' yarns it's the Morgan.

No, what was wanted here was some hard reporting, something a little bit more concrete than the usual near-sighted nostalgia and wind-in-the-hair, joys-of-motoring-in-spring stuff that Morgans generally inspire. Trouble was, that the more time we spent with the Morgan and Victor Kay, the managing director of

Reminiscences in 4/4 Time

Australian concessionaires, Calder Sports Cars, the more the story started to lean towards that sort of thing — the Morgan is simply that type of car. Still, as the Rolling Stones have been known to advise, even though you can't always get what you want, you just might find you get what you need.

That was the way it turned out anyway, but to begin with things weren't looking too bright and when I pulled up (late, and feeling very second-hand) outside the address I'd been given for the Morgan meeting I wasn't sure that things were going to come together at all. I knew it was the wrong time, but a large family home in Melbourne's most-burgled suburb, North Balwyn, hardly seemed like the right place, and the enormous 'Forthcoming Auction' sign hanging off the fence did little to reassure me.

It *was* the right place though — after all how many suburban houses have a silver and burgundy Morgan squatting at the bottom of the driveway, let alone one with a photographer busily plying his trade about it — so with a sigh of relief I girded my loins and strolled in to meet Victor Kay.

From his brown brogues, through the corduroy trousers, to his houndstooth jacket, and all the way up to the pork-pie hat he donned for the photo session, Victor Kay carries the aura of the antiquarian — he appears a man enchanted by the rare, delighted by the uncommon, and a man for whom the past holds more satisfaction than the present. It is an apposite air for a man who sells what many regard as an

automotive antique, but it is no affectation for within the house that has served as Morgan's sales and service centre for the past three years lie treasures such as a handcrafted concert-size harp and a chair with hardwood arms sculpted in the form of its maker's own limbs.

When Kay talks of his 20-year association with Morgan he flavors his speech with an appreciation of the British manufacturer's tradition and history but he is by no means blind to the product's place in the automotive scheme of things. He describes the Morgan factory and the craftsmanlike manner of the cars' construction as 'one of the anachronisms of the motoring world' but it is not an unkind description, and if the three-months it takes to build each vehicle restricts Australia to a maximum of 18 cars per annum he is not disturbed.

"Sales," he says, "are rampant. And the reason that the demand is there is that, as each year goes by, the Morgan is constantly bifurcating away from the mainstream of motor car construction. While other cars are becoming increasingly more of a technological nightmare the Morgan retains a lovely agricultural sort of appeal." Kay is a lover of country life, so when he says 'agricultural' his reference is to the pastoral romanticism that made Constable famous rather than the heavy-duty ironwork that did the same for Massey Ferguson (though

there are elements of both in a Morgan), and indeed he is the first to acknowledge the fact that Morgan sells on idealised nostalgia and romance.

"We sell to people that have the sense to look at the Morgan for what it really is," he says. "People that will seek out something rare and individual — people that appreciate the fact that every panel is hand-made; that the grille is solid brass and each piece hs been sweated together by hand. All those nice little things you won't find anywhere else. We've always said we don't sell a car, we sell a way of life ... a work of art on four wheels if you like..."

But what is this four-wheeled artwork really like, and how does the rare and individual hold out under the hard and pitiless gaze of a cynical motoring journalist? Well, I must admit that I was keen to find out because besides having long admired the Morgan's classic lines, and to some extent having succumbed to the period charm of its mechanical design, the closest I'd ever got to one of the beasts was trying to wade through the aforementioned 'wind-in-the-hair' magazine articles in a mainly futile attempt to penetrate beyond the car's obvious charisma.

Of course charisma is really what the Morgan is all about, but let's ignore that for the moment and focus on the mechanicals — in this case the running gear of the only unsold Morgan left in the country, a four-seater 4/4.

Okay, let's go for the nuts and bolts. The chassis is a simple Z-section steel ladder frame supporting a semi-eliptic sprung, lever-arm damped live axle (slung above the frame) at the rear and Morgan's own sliding pillar independent arrangement at the front. Semi-eliptics and live axles you are doubtless familiar with, even lever-arm shock absorbers, but the sliding pillar front end is definitely worth further explanation.

Dispensing with A-arms, struts and the like, the sliding pillar system uses a stub axle which moves up and down along a fixed tube (hence the pillar and the sliding) passing through its vertical axis — rotational movement is also permitted to

210

*...Not a car,
but a way
of life*

Reminiscences in 4/4 Time

allow for steering. Springs mounted either side of the stub axle (longer above than below) control movement of the stub axle, while damping is provided by tubular shock absorbers. Patented by Morgan way back in 1910 the 'sliding pillar' arrangement is quite an ingenious suspension system, which, besides offering low unsprung weight ensures that camber and castor values remain constant throughout the range of travel. On the negative side it is prone to binding under side loads, and requires lots of lubrication.

Right, that's the difficult bit over and done with ... from here on in its all pretty simple. Steering is by cam gears worm-and-nut, brakes are discs front, drums rear, wheels are 15-inch, 72-spoke wire jobs carrying 195/60 rubber, and the engine is an sohc 1597cc CVH Ford unit (from the transverse-engined small British Fords) backed by a five-speed gearbox. Producing 71.6kW at 6000rpm and 133Nm at 4000rpm this motor pushes along a car that weighs around (Imperial measures don't always translate that well) 800kg, and covers a patch of road 3657mm long and 1422mm wide. Good for a tad over 160km/h and zero to 100km/h times around the 10 second mark.

Then, of course, there's the body, or should I say the coachwork. You can see what it looks like from the photos so all that remains to say is that it is hand-beaten steel over a wooden subframe — Belgian ash to be precise. Or perhaps that's not all that remains to be said, because hand crafted doesn't always mean (in fact it seldom means) absolutely perfect and though each panel was gloriously sculpted and beautifully smooth, edges and joins don't always match up with the accuracy that computer-aided manufacture allows today.

Nor yet does it ensure that the trim comes out without blemish. Morgan uses Conolly hides, and though sumptuously in both appearance and scent, this particular car was let down by the rather lumpy looking padded trim along the top of the scuttle. For some the fact that the Morgan

has obviously been finished by fallible human beings rather than assembly line robots is what it's all about...

Still, whatever your views on craftsmanship, you have to admit that the Morgan is very solid. Victor Kay wasn't exactly enthusiastic about the prospects of a long-term road test, but we did manage to cover enough kilometres to form more than a few impressions about the Morgan, and one of the most telling facets of its personality was the lack of scuttle shake and panel flap that you usually encounter with 'vintage' style cars. One of the reasons is that, unlike older Morgans, and those sold in markets other than Australia, Kay specified an additional tubular brace running across the scuttle from frame rail to frame rail. Couple that with the rigidity endowed by the full chassis and the body's wooden frame and you have one strong (but light) motor car.

All of which brings us around to the

wind-in-the-hair bit and the 'What's it like to drive' question. Well the answer to that one, in a nutshell, is *strange*. This is a vintage car, and there's no way the modern instrumentation or the contemporary engine/transmission can hide that fact — not that they try to.

Just getting into the Morgan makes you realise that here is something decidedly different. With the low elbow cut-outs the doors seem almost redundant, but there's no gracious way in without opening them, least of all when the sidescreens (held on little knurled knobs threaded into castings on the door) are in place. It's not exactly Lotus 7 stuff, but there's a fair amount of threading your legs around the seats and down the footwell — more so on the way out.

Once ensconced on the plush leather seat (fore/aft and recline adjustable) you sit decidedly upright with elbows bent (the right resting naturally on the door cut-out) and the wide, leather-rimmed wheel close to the chest. There's not a great deal of clearance between the wheel and the scuttle either so shuffling the wheel through your hands is the required driving technique, and while you're adjusting to that there's the bottom-hinged pedal layout to contend with. It all comes together pretty quickly once you get the hang of it, although I must confess correct operation of the fly-off handbrake eluded me throughout our test drive.

With a modern powerplant the clutch and shift lever action are pleasantly light and performance isn't lacking but the real Morgan driving experience doesn't start

It's hand-built, traditional, bespoke and oh-so British.

til you hit 60km/h. With the engine
itting a subdued burble, the sun warming
ur shoulders and the wind playfully
'fling your hair (etc., etc.) it all seems
te good fun ... until the first bump
rranges the position of your kidneys.
s, that 'vintage' chassis offers almost
dieval ride quality and, adding insult to
ssible injury, as speeds increase the front
pension does its dolphin impression to
extent that the porpoising is clearly
ible from kerbside. By modern (even not
modern) standards it's more than
oying — the Morgan is a smooth-
d/low-speed carriage and that's that
ess you're prepared to strap on a kidney
.

goes around corners though ... by
key it does. Well, smooth corners,
way. With a driver on board the
rgan's weight distribution is almost 50/50
d this is reflected by a neutral cornering
e. Body roll is there, but the only reason
n confirm this is because the rear tyres
ld be heard rubbing on the bodywork —
erwise you'd swear the car cornered
d flat. Naturally since this car was the
'saleable' Morgan in the country we
ren't exactly tackling the edge of the
'elope, but with the tyres just starting to
eal you're pulling enough Gs (gs?) to put

your ribs hard up against the doors almost
to the point of pain. God help you if you hit
a bump though!

All that aside the 4/4 was not a hard car
to drive, it wasn't even hard to drive it
fairly quickly, but I'd imagine you'd have to
be a man of steel to drive one really fast. I
dare say those brave souls with Plus 8
Morgans just put the boot down on the
straights and button off for the corners, but
then again even the country lanes in
England are smoother than the average
Aussie highway.

But ... but, but you just can't help but

enjoy it. The incongruity of the thing is part
of the fun — it's almost a delight to be
battered into submission by the antiquated
chassis and a thrill to feel those front-
wheels pogo their way through the corners.
Some of the Morgan's appeal is its hand-
crafted exclusivity, part of it the fact that
you'd look right at home driving through
Darraby in an episode of All Creatures
Great And Small, and the rest of it is simply
the regular fun of open-air motoring.

What it all boils down to is that the
Morgan feels fabulous but is not the type of
car you'd want to drive every day — it's a
real Sunday car. $68-1/2K, the prices of this
particular car is a lot to pay for a weekend
driver though, a fact which caused Morley
(young whipper snapper that he is) to
comment that you'd probably be better off
buying a TD 2000 because you'd get more
use out of it. I must admit he has a very
valid point, but then as Victor Kay would
doubtless point out the Morgan is the real
thing. It is, but bear in mind the warts.

■CAR

213

PLUS 8 & 4/4

Ask the Morganists you know

PHOTOS BY LESLIE L. BIRD

HARRODS, THE FAMOUS Knightsbridge establishment, was only an up-and-coming department store in 1911. But its proprietors were quick to recognize a good thing: It was Harrods that became the first agency for Morgan motor cars. And, more than three-quarters of a century later, both firms continue to prosper, thank you, each epitomizing that which is traditional and best, not to say English.

In keeping with this heritage, let's do more than simply list the virtues of those Morgan sports cars currently available to us. Let's savor some other Moggies that are rather less available, either because of time or place.

In 1910, for instance, H.F.S. Morgan showed his first 3-wheeler at the First International Cycle and Motor Cycle Exhibition in London. The idea of three wheels was, and continued to be, a tax scam. Trikes qualified as motorcycles with an annual tax of only £4, much less than any ordinary motor car. Nor was the Morgan any ordinary trike, most being a particularly tacky means of transportation.

The marque soon proved itself in competition, with 1912 ads noting Morgan at the top of the pack in the highly contested Hour Record. "Only a few yards short of sixty miles in the hour," 59 miles 1120 yards, to be exact, and H.F.S. had reached 62 mph in his Runabout's fastest lap.

The Moggie's basic design flour-

■ Outstanding in the field, the only-sold-in-Europe Plus 4.

ished well into the Twenties. At the front of a twin-tubular frame perched a V-twin powerplant, its driveshaft connected to a 2-speed chain drive at the rear. The single rear wheel rode on a pair of quarter-ellipic springs, but it was the Moggie's front suspension that proved distinctive. Each front hub slid on a pillar, more or less vertical and incorporating a concentric coil spring. Such was the efficacy of this sliding pillar design that it remains a feature of Morgans to this day.

Not that there haven't been changes over the years. It's just that the concept of change is gauged somewhat differently when assessing Morgans. The Thirties, for example, were a period of positive unrest at Pickersleigh Road, Malvern Link, Worcestershire. In 1931 came a 3-speed gearbox. In 1933, a 4-cylinder Model F (identifying its Ford engine) augmented the line. And, in 1936, after having experimented on and off with the idea since the very beginning, Morgan introduced the 4/4, modestly signifying the number of wheels as well as cylinders. With wonderfully few changes and only a brief hiatus, the 4/4 designation continues to this day.

Also of historical note are 1950, when the first-generation Plus 4 added power; 1952, when the last 3-wheeler left the works; 1953, when the classic flat radiator gave way to our now-classic cowled nose; and 1963, when British Motor Show attendees were shocked by an aerodynamic, fiberglass-bodied Plus 4 Plus (only 26 were

PHOTO BY DENNIS SIMANAITIS

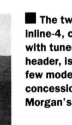

■ The twincam Rover inline-4, complete with tuned exhaust header, is one of the few modern concessions made on Morgan's Plus 4.

ever built). Bringing things up to date are 1968, when our current Rover V-8-powered Plus 8 arrived; and 1988, with U.K. introduction of the Rover-twincam Plus 4 Mk III.

No other automaker of such longevity could have its models summed up so concisely. And Moggie enthusiasts wouldn't have it any other way.

Consider, for example, the current Plus 4 shown in these pages. Alas, it's unavailable to U.S. buyers at this time. But we were fortunate in being able to drive and photograph the car in its home setting.

As with all Moggies, its sliding pillar front suspension dates from the very beginning. Its rear suspension of a live axle on semi-elliptic springs hasn't changed markedly since 1936, when that fourth wheel made its appearance back there. Its traditional lines are fabricated in a traditional manner as well. The coachwork is of steel panels attached to a framework of Belgian ash, all set atop a straightforward steel chassis. (Note, the Moggie *doesn't* "have a wooden frame," as some pundits would have you believe.)

At first, the Plus 4's 4-valve twin-cam powerplant may seem a bit out of place (or time). This Rover 1994-cc inline-4 loves to rev and does so smoothly indeed. But if you think its dohc looks strange under the Moggie's classic bonnet, imagine how modern the Matchless V-twin's ohv design must have appeared, at a time when most engines wheezed through side-valve layouts. Over the years Morgan has always bought engines from the best available sources.

And in the Plus 8, a Morgan that *is* available to U.S. enthusiasts, its 3528-cc Rover V-8 buys real excitement as well. This is the most recent Morgan we've put through our road test procedure, and its performance figures shown on the last page of this story are decidedly up-to-date. How's 0 to 60 mph in a mere 7.4 seconds? Or a skid-pad value of 0.80g? (We didn't slalom this particular car, but an earlier one weaved around our cones in 62.0 mph.) Glance through these pages at data panels of other so-called state-of-the-art machinery, and then reflect for a moment on old fashioned virtues of sliding pillars and Belgian ash.

The Plus 8 and its 1.6-liter Ford-engine 4/4 sibling enter the U.S. in absolutely tiny numbers, around 24 cars

each year, through Isis Imports Ltd (Box 2290, U.S. Custom House, San Francisco, Calif. 94126; 415 433-1433). Isis' Bill Fink, a Morganist of the highest order, has been U.S. agent for some years now. Bill converts the cars to EPA-pleasing propane, carries out the necessary bumper and other DOT jazz, and manages it all tastefully indeed. The minuscule volume has its price, however. The Plus 8 costs $37,500; a turbo option is $3000. A 4/4 is $28,000.

Bill says most buyers opt for the Plus 8. I'm partial to the 4-cylinder, though, for reasons of historical feel. And, just to show you the full spectrum of Morganists, there are those who profess that the only proper Moggie is a V-twin 3-wheeler.

Not long ago, I drove such a wonderful machine, thanks to the kindness and enthusiasm of Spence Young, a regular competitor in historic racing with his 1934 Matchless MX4 Super Sports. And what a thrill! You angle your legs over the side and down around an oversize cord-

wrapped steering wheel. Somewhere down there you feel a brake pedal on the right and clutch pedal on the left. The throttle is one of three levers on the steering wheel, mixture and spark control being the other two. A central gear change on the floor actuates the crash-box 3-speed. An adjacent hand-brake appears to be there mainly for show. It certainly has little enough retardation effect.

The sound is pure motorcycle as you learn to blip the throttle with your thumb, Morganist-style. Then, engaging 1st, you work to coordinate thumb and foot as you get under way. Clutch in/thumb down, shift up, clutch out/thumb up, and you're into 2nd with only a little grunch. Repeat the process and you're motoring along in top gear at 25 mph with the V-twin pounding out 1500 thumps/minute. A card on the dash shows Spence that he's traveling 68 mph at 4000, but you'll take his word for it. Actually, the hand throttle is less disconcerting than you expected. For one thing, the Super Sports' steering is very tall-geared, only ¾ turns lock to lock. The only time the throttle lever isn't recognizably on the right is when you try backing up at extreme lock. After a bit, you even attempt a double-clutch downshift into 2nd. Not bad—and hey, this is fun!

By this point, you know enough about Morgans to place yourself in one of two groups. Those in the first group will ask, "So why waste all this time telling about driving some old car?" Those in the second will not.

If you're in the second group: Welcome, fellow Morganist.

—*Dennis Simanaitis*

PRICE

List price, all POE $37,500	Price as tested $37,530
Price as tested includes: bonnet belt ($30)	

ENGINE

Type ..... ohv V-8
Displacement ..... 3528 cc
Bore x stroke ..... 89.0 x 71.0 mm
Compression ratio 9.8:1
Horsepower, (SAE): 190 bhp @ 5280 rpm
Torque ..... 220 lb-ft @ 4000 rpm
Maximum engine speed ..... 5500 rpm
Carburetion ..... Impco propane (1V)
Fuel ..... propane

GENERAL DATA

Curb weight ..... 2140 lb
Test weight ..... 2290 lb
Weight dist, f/r, % 45/55
Wheelbase ..... 98.0 in.
Track, f/r ..... 52.0 in./53.0 in.
Length ..... 157.0 in.
Width ..... 62.0 in.
Height ..... 52.0 in.
Trunk space ..... 5.0 cu ft

DRIVETRAIN

Transmission			5-sp manual
Gear	Ratio	Overall ratio	(Rpm) Mph
1st	3.32:1	10.99:1	37
2nd	2.08:1	6.88:1	58
3rd	1.39:1	4.60:1	85
4th	1.10:1	3.64:1	est (4700) 120
5th	0.83:1	2.75:1	est (4000) 125
Final drive ratio			3.31:1
Engine rpm @ 60 mph in 5th			2180

CHASSIS & BODY

Layout ..... front engine/rear drive
Body/frame ..... steel, ash frame/steel
Brakes, f/r 11.0-in.discs/
9 x 1.8-in. drums
Wheels ..... cast alloy, 15 x 6½
Tires ..... Pirelli P6, 205/60VR-15
Steering ..... rack & pinion,
Turns, lock to lock 3.3
Suspension, f/r: coil springs on sliding axle pin, tube shocks/semi-elliptical springs, tube shocks

ACCELERATION

Time to speed	Seconds
0–30 mph	2.5
0–40 mph	3.8
0–50 mph	5.3
0–60 mph	7.4
0–70 mph	9.8
0–80 mph	12.6
Time to distance	
0–100 ft	3.0
0–500 ft	8.2
0–1320 ft (¼ mi)	15.6 @ 88.1 mph

BRAKING

Minimum stopping distance	
From 60 mph	148 ft
From 80 mph	297 ft
Control	fair
Overall brake rating	fair

FUEL ECONOMY

Normal driving	19.5 mpg
EPA city/highway	na
Fuel capacity	17.5 gal.

HANDLING

Lateral accel (200-ft skidpad)	0.80g
Speed thru 700-ft slalom	na

na means information is not available.

WILD

Archetypal British sports cars with untypical amounts of power,

that's the Musgrove 4.5-litre Plus Eight and SPR Caterham Seven.

John Nutting is the one with wind in his hair, bugs in his teeth

Photography: Nathan Morgan

CARS

The history of high-performance cars is littered with the debris of shattered hopes based on the premise that power, and the more the better, provides the easiest route to success. You'd think the lessons would be carved in tablets of stone by now. 'Forget ye the craven pursuit of brute power', they might say, 'for ye shall suffer on the alter of wheelspin. And lo, thou shalt be blown off by the fleet of foot'.

A far more effective way of achieving electrifying performance is to tackle both weight and power. Better still, start with a car that's light to begin with. For some keen exponents of the pursuit, it's not enough to find a car that weighs less than three-quarters of a ton (and that is a rare thing in itself) but to aim for a car that is close to the weight of a couple of motorcycles. Now that's light.

When you approach that weight bracket, you start looking at power-to-weight ratios that make your hair stand on end. Three hundred brake horsepower per ton is the sort of ratio you'd find in a premium sports car – the type of thing you could buy off the shelf with a fat enough wallet. But we're talking about 350bhp per ton. At least. You

It is easy to provoke strong oversteer in the Caterham Seven and control the rear end with the throttle

know, the sort of potential enjoyed by competition drivers in the confines of a track. The sort of potential that allows those short bursts of acceleration up to the ton and back before anyone's had a chance to realise what's going on. But we are not necessarily talking about juvenile fun; this is all about primary safety too. A car that is more responsive to its driver, in all ways, is bound to be potentially safer, taking less time in overtaking and with all-round better handling.

Not everyone subscribes to that notion to the letter, of course. Eric Wigart, a 30-year-old Swede who made such a success of reporting on opportunities in the construction industry worldwide that he sold his research company to one of the majors, is such a person. His idea of 'a fun car for the weekends' takes the form of a red Morgan Plus Eight. At least, that's what it appears to be.

A Morgan Plus Eight is as light as they come, turning the scales at a feathery 1850lb. Even with its stock 3.5-litre V8 turning out a modest 190bhp, there's not much that will get in its way on a twisty road. Wigart's sights were set quite a bit higher

than that, though. What he ended up with, after Morgan specialist Colin Musgrove from Kenilworth had finished his handiwork on it, was the four-wheel equivalent of a rustic country squire with the brute power of Arnold Schwarzenegger.

ROVER POWER

Open the hood and the engine bay is bulging with £12,500 worth of 4.5-litre Rover V8, complete with a twin plenum chamber fuel injection system run by a hotwire programmable engine management system. It's a long-stroke unit, which Musgrove achieves by selecting crank forgings with more meat for machining to bring the capacity up to 4492cc. The end product is 305bhp at 5750rpm, gurgling through a racing-based exhaust system which sounds just on the verge of legality. More significantly, 75 per cent of the peak torque of over 300lb ft is available right down at 1300rpm!

From the outside, there's no indication that this is anything other than a stock Plus Eight. It's only when you fire it up, let out the clutch and squeeze

I squinted through the goggles down the Morgan's bonnet, and as the helmet strap rattled in the breeze, I could have been at the joystick of a Spitfire. . .

Pippa Jacobsen and John Lyon (top) believe the real strength of the Caterham's 165bhp Ford engine is its flexibility

the long-travel accelerator that you're left in no doubt that this car isn't standard. There's an enormous amount of power from just above tickover and pulling away from a standstill can be brutal unless you're gentle. Subtle it most definitely is not. But that's hardly surprising with a peak power-to-weight ratio of 369bhp per ton.

Our test drive started innocently enough as I cautiously got to know the responses from each of the controls. But each dab on the throttle brought another delirious surge of power, and I was lured on. Changing up with the stubby wood-tipped lever relaxed the revs, but the punch remained as we burbled along at 90mph, with me in the hot seat doing a Biggles impression with a leather helmet, and Wigart probably wondering if it had been wise to let me loose in his pride and joy.

If you like a bit of fantasy, the Morgan provides all the stimulation you need. I squinted through the goggles down the bonnet, and as the leather strap rattled in the breeze I could have been at the joystick of a Spitfire.

The euphoria was rudely shattered when we let

Outwardly, it is difficult to tell that Eric Wigart's standard-looking Morgan has an extra 115bhp under the hood

the Morgan loose for the acceleration tests at Millbrook. The first run resulted in wild wheelspin and left the cockpit reeking of burning rubber and clutch material. Yet it still reached 60mph in just over five and a half seconds. Balancing the massive torque against traction brought better rewards, with 60mph coming up in 5.1 seconds and 100mph in 12.2 seconds. The car is probably quicker than that except that the gearchange is slow and heavy, taking ages to come out of first and down into second across a stiff neutral.

For an indication of the engine's astonishing pulling power, look at the fourth gear acceleration figures: the crucial benchmark test of 50-70mph comes up in just 3.9 seconds. Compare this time with, say, the 4.9 seconds of the Sierra Cosworth, a respected mid-range surger. And 80-100mph is dispatched in 4.4 seconds, leaving the Ford flummoxed on 5.6 seconds.

One preconception of mine was that Morgans have a, well, uncompromising ride. Not this one. It's firm, but fair. Thumping over a couple of rail crossings brought no uncomfortable jolts. But

that's not to suggest the Plus Eight/450SE can be let loose with abandon. Floor it on a ripply country road and there's enough bump steer to have the car dancing about, and if you launch out of a corner in the lower gears without first setting up the navigation, the back end promptly swings out; that's the downside of using the standard rear rims. Had wider rims, fitted with BF Goodrich or Yokohama tyres rather than the stock 205/60 x 15 Avon Turbospeeds, been opted for, it is likely that the benefits of Musgrove's suspension changes would have been more positively demonstrated.

'ANTEDILUVIAN' SUSPENSION

When even a Morgan devotee like Musgrove describes the standard Morgan suspension as 'antediluvian', you can be sure that it compares poorly with modern practice. Therefore, he has adopted modern techniques to bring the Morgan as up-to-date as possible.

Up front, the sliding pillar and coil arrangement is uprated by adding brake reaction rods to stop

'I wanted a classic combined with a supercar. If that's the sort of car you want then there is only one to buy, and that's a Morgan. Any other car, such as an AC Cobra, is twice the price'

The Morgan's Rover V8 engine has been bored out to 4.5 litres, while magnolia Connolly hide adorns the interior

the upper frame tube from twisting under the increased braking loads generated by the 290mm ventilated discs with AP four-piston alloy calipers. Negative camber plates bring the camber specifications up to scratch. Finally, Musgrove recommends the fitting of Spax shock absorbers.

The real fun starts with the rear suspension. Ideally, the leaf springs would be junked, but to satisfy the requirements of the various classes of racing in which Musgrove competes, they have to be retained. The next best thing is the addition of a pair of trailing links on either side to augment the anti-tramp bar mounted on the centre line. Because axles on leaf springs move in a complex fashion rather than the normal arc provided by a simple trailing link, Musgrove enlisted the help of computer-aided design, so that the path of the axle provided by the linkage is correct at all but the very top of its movement. Further refinements include the use of vertically-mounted shocks and a Panhard rod for fuel-injected cars.

All these expensive modifications beg the question of why Wigart should go to the trouble

Morgan fans Colin Musgrove (left) and Eric Wigart

Lightweight shells with shattering performance: Eric Wigart's Morgan, front, and John Lyon's Caterham Seven

when real classic cars would cost little more than the £40,000 he's already spent.

'The reason I bought this Plus Eight is that I would have liked a classic car but didn't want all the hassle you get. I wanted a classic combined with a supercar. If that's the sort of car you want then there is only one to buy, and that's a Morgan. Any other car, like an AC Cobra, is twice the price.'

ROMANTIC VIEW

Wigart admits to being a bit of a romantic. And the Morgan's looks fit in with his view of motoring. 'It's very stylish. That's why I didn't want to alter anything on the outside. I couldn't bring myself to put on any boy racer wheels because it's the completely wrong type of car to do it with.' It's the sheer performance that he likes most about the Plus Eight/450SE. 'The torque is fine, but it's the outright performance when you accelerate with it that's best. It shoots by anything.'

If Eric Wigart's delight is indulging in an orgy of acceleration in what appears to be an 'old-fash-

ioned' car, then John Lyon's approach to high performance on the road is altogether more subtle. Lyon, 53, runs High Performance Cars in Isleworth, West London, which he founded in 1958 after working as a civilian police driving instructor. He built on that experience to offer high performance driving courses and, as you'd expect, over the years he's not only driven a wide variety of fast cars, but he has been able to see how most ordinary drivers cope with them.

So he doesn't need to prove anything in powerful vehicles. Instead, he drives for the sheer pleasure of it, using what has, for him, become a finely-honed driving tool – a Caterham Seven.

The measure of Lyon's enthusiasm for the Caterham is that for the past three years he has used the car on the road as well as for competing in the ten-round Caterham Seven race series. The fact that he drives the car to and from the circuits hasn't detuned his track skills either – in 1987 he won class C (near standard cars) with ten wins and seven lap records, in 1988 he won class B (slightly modified) with nine wins and six lap records, and

last year, as the competition got wise, he only just won the series with three outright wins.

'I treat motorsport as sport', he says, 'and I always feel that if you want to get to know your car very well then you should compete with it. And particularly now there should be a moral responsibility about driving at high speed anywhere on the road. The only place to drive at really high speed is off the road and on circuits'.

Lyon's Caterham Seven has been prepared and set up by SPR Engineering of Bishop's Stortford, which provides tuning services for several of the Caterham Seven series competitors. In its current form, his five-year-old class B car is powered by a 1700cc BDR pushrod Ford engine with forged steel crank and rods that allow safe revs up to 9000rpm. Output is now 165bhp at 7600rpm, breathing through 40 DCOE Webers, but according to SPR's Pippa Jacobsen, the real strength of the engine is its flexibility, with power usable from 5000rpm and level from 7600rpm to 8500rpm. What makes Lyon's Seven remarkable is that it's so usable on the road as well as the track, and much of that comes from the car's light weight of just 1172lb, which, if you're interested, works out to a power-to-weight ratio of 315bhp per ton.

USABLE PERFORMANCE

If you're disappointed that the Caterham falls short of the Morgan in this department, be sure that it makes up for it in many other ways. I found the performance much more usable, even though the Yokohama tyres had been set too hard for road use and it was still easy to lose traction at the back. But the car had been set up beautifully, and powering out of corners with the front end understeering like mad was real fun. Back off and it would take care of itself. Lyon's racing cockpit had been retained, complete with harness, and I must admit to missing the occasional cog in the straight-cut close-ratio 'box and giving the sintered bronze racing clutch more than its share of abuse.

But the engine was a gem, sounding crisp through the large-diameter pipe running down the left side of the alloy body. Caterham use a tubular space frame with simple independent front suspension and a fixed rear axle – in Lyon's older car this is a mundane BMC Marina unit but modern Caterhams have a better rear axle. The car's attraction is in good weight distribution, small overall

On the first attempt, our computer was suffering from a loose connection, and then the Caterham devoured most of the teeth off one side of the differential

dimensions and responsive steering. On country roads, there's probably nothing that can match the way it snaps through bends, with the engine howling in your ears and the guards over the front wheels bobbing up and down over bumps.

I might as well come out with it and admit we had a few problems when we figured the car. On the first attempt, our computer was suffering from a loose connection caused by vibration, and then the Caterham's rear axle complained and devoured most of the teeth off one side of the diff. A second session was more productive, with several acceleration runs producing a 0-60mph time of 4.8 seconds and 100mph coming up in 11.0 seconds.

Then we went on to the high-speed bowl to measure top speed. First, Lyon went for a lap and returned almost immediately saying the car's engine had 'gone off'. Engine builder Roger King, who was present, whipped out the plugs to find that one had melted and he deduced that the carburation was running slightly weak at the top end. 'It's unusual for a car to be run absolutely flat out constantly', he philosophised.

SPR had brought along another Caterham, belonging to director Robin Rex, just for the hell of it. This one had an extra 100cc of engine capacity but was otherwise in the same state of tune as Lyon's car. It had the latest chassis, including a de Dion rear end and a higher final drive ratio. Taking it out on to the banking produced a maximum speed of 126mph, with 7600 to 7800rpm showing on the tachometer in fourth gear. A fifth gear was fitted to this car, but it dropped the revs below a usable level. Incidentally, the car was perfectly stable at that speed, although the wind rush was deafening and the exhaust noise raucous.

Earlier, this car had recorded 5.0 seconds for the 0-60mph sprint, with 100mph coming up in 11.3 seconds. An indication of the Caterham's poor aerodynamics is that 0-90mph took 9.0 seconds but the next 10mph took a further 2.3 seconds.

Country roads off the beaten track are what Lyon has set up the car for.

'I enjoy driving a car which has the ride and handling to drive on the road. My car has a softer ride than a lot of Sevens – certainly a softer ride than a Morgan – and it handles very well indeed. The performance is extraordinary, but the Caterham isn't for driving at high speed. It's a question of having good overtaking ability. The ability to overtake in second and third gear in effortless style really makes a Seven. I think a Seven has the finest primary safety of any car there is.' ○

"Morgan has created a monster"

THE BBC series *Trouble Shooter* has been repeated recently. It was another chance to see Sir John Harvey-Jones' damning visit to Morgan Motor Company in Malvern. Charles Morgan thinks

the BBC did a job on his family's firm. "We were set up," he says of the whole programme, in which Sir John recommended the use of modern production equipment, increased prices and a less whimsical approach to the business of making motor cars.

Sir John's office says he is not commenting further on Morgan as he feels "it only leads to more hot water". This sentiment has not prevented a repeat of the series nor the publishing of *Trouble Shooter* the book.

In some ways, the Morgan Car Company represents all that is good about British car making. Our history in terms of automotive mass production has been lackadaisical at best, but companies like Bentley, Rolls Royce, Aston Martin, Jaguar and, to some extent, Morgan show the British forte at producing idiosyncratic, specialist cars. With the exception of the latter, all the aforementioned marques have become part of larger groups, which supply long-term investment, research facilities and security in return for

MORGAN PLUS 8 3.9

ANTIQUE ROADSHOW

association with a great name of motoring.

Faced with a massive order book, annual production pegged at just over 400 cars, 130 employees and little investment cash, the Morgan family agreed to appear as a target for the wit and wisdom of Sir John. The family didn't agree with what he had to say, and that's about the beginning and the end of it.

For what it's worth, we feel that the Morgan family showed a naïve faith in the idea of an industry guru. Rain forests tumble by the day to

Andrew English gets to grips with the latest version of a popular modern anachronism

support a burgeoning business book industry. Japanese management, European harmonisation, investment, working capital, autonomous work groups . . . no subject remains untouched. They might supply guidance, or pointers to a better course of action, but no book can or should change the whole direction of a company, even if it comes with the impressive title of *Trouble Shooter*.

By the same token, Sir John failed to grasp the

singular nature of the Morgan car. The first model appeared in 1909 and, apart from gaining another wheel in 1937, the concept has not changed much since. Using a bought-in drivetrain fitted to an in-house chassis, the Morgan is a lightweight, usually two-seater sports car with separate wings, exposed spare wheel and an optional leather flying helmet in the glove box.

It is the archetypal enthusiasts' car, produced by hand tools with love and care. That process is part of the purchase price of the Morgan, and to

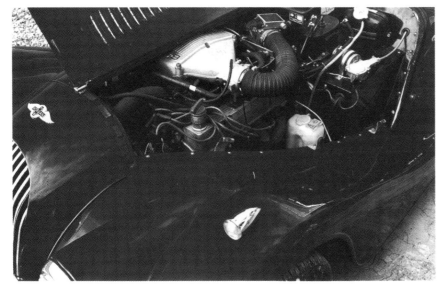

many owners it is as important as the car itself; its production is its credibility.

Charles Morgan says he is looking at new equipment for the works: computer-controlled machinery, laser cutting tools and computer-aided design. "This has nothing to do with the programme, I promise you," he says. "It's the sort of thing that happens in factories all the time."

It may be the wrong direction to take. Morgan currently has a waiting list of around eight years. The deposit to secure a place on this list is £100, and we can only think that this must encourage dealers and speculators to join the queue. Victor Gauntlett of Aston Martin makes his buyers pay a considerable proportion of the final cost of the car as a deposit; he claims it reduces the speculative element in his order books. If Morgan made the deposit £1,500, for instance, then at current interest rates, without compounding, it would gain nearly £10,000 towards the cost of building the car over the eight years.

DRIVELINE

IF THE investment cash is getting left behind, then the engines certainly are not. The latest specification Plus 8 models have been fitted with the 3.9-litre, twin-exhaust catalyst version of the Buick/Rover V8. The catalysts have soaked up some power, although the engine revolutions have been reduced as well. It delivers 188bhp at 4,750rpm, and torque is marginally up to 230lb ft at 2,600rpm. The gearbox is the Rover five-speed unit from the SD1.

Apart from the engine change, the Plus 8 remains the same. A cheque for £22,363.70 will buy you the basic car with a steel, two-seater body and fabric upholstery. A further £774.50 buys leather, £529.48 an aluminium body and wings. The style hasn't changed much from the flat-radiator pre-1954 cars, let alone the first 184bhp Plus 8 models that appeared at the Earls Court Motor Show in 1968.

The chassis frame is a steel ladder and the body is formed over an ash frame. Front suspension is an independent sliding pillar, and the live rear axle is still supported with semi-elliptic leaf springs. Rear damping is now done with telescopic units which mount onto a new hoop frame between the chassis rails.

FRONT SUSPENSION

IT IS the sliding-pillar front suspension that ensures the Morgan a place in every motor technicians' text book. The system has the advantages of light weight and simplicity, which is why it was adopted on a number of specials in the 1930s. It was also used on the 1922 Lancia Lambda with some success. The mountings for the suspension protrude from the side of the car and are fixed. The wheel's hub unit slides up and down on a coil-sprung pillar between the two mounts, with the vertically-mounted damper attached to the hub and one of the mounts. Morgan has fine-tuned the system over the years;

with sufficient lubrication, it gives few problems.

Inherently, however, the arrangement allows the front wheel camber angles to change when the body rolls. With modern low profile tyres, this can drastically reduce the available tread on the road. To prevent the body roll that causes this, Morgans have very hard front suspension. Charles Morgan says that a softer front suspension is on its way, so we can only assume that the body roll problem has been solved with anti-roll bars or somesuch.

PERFORMANCE

GETTING INTO the car can be a bit of a chore. The cutaway doors are very short, and the B-post catches on clothes, leaving the driver unable to escape. Apart from that, however, the Plus 8 is surprisingly roomy. There is plenty of space around the pedals for big feet, and the relationship between steering, pedals and seat, although far from perfect, is better than some moderns. There is a large parcel shelf behind the seats for soft bags, and even the glove box is copious.

This is just as well, for there is plenty to do in the Morgan, and one needs plenty of room to do it in. Starting the engine in the dark requires the splendid set of keys from various British Leyland eras to be poked and prodded into the slot until one turns. The exhaust note is disappointingly quiet at first and, like most V8s, there is a considerable delay between actuation of the tiny accelerator pedal and the rev counter rising up. The lazy nature of the engine is further confirmed on the road, where fourth gear seems adequate for most occasions.

It is difficult to find places where the engine can be used to the full. The handling always dictates caution before the revs do. Smooth open A-roads seem to bring out its best, and the waffly torque means the speedometer should be watched. Unfortunately, the speedometer is completely obscured by the steering wheel apart from the bit that reads '120mph'. As this is the top speed, life should be interesting for owners.

In-gear acceleration times are the key to the car's prowess. Overtaking is never a problem, and changing down the notchy 'box with its grabbing clutch should not be necessary. The fourth gear acceleration times are a match for most supercars, although aerodynamics start to slow the charge towards 90mph.

We only managed one timed acceleration run before the tired limited-slip differential ate some of its teeth. A 0-60mph time of 5.2sec in one run hardly begins to describe the violence of the experience. The diminutive leaf springs become Ess-shaped, the rear axle steers the car, the engine roars and the axle tramps, thumping the springs and wheels against their restraints. It was as though a dozen men had started to wallop the rear of the car with sledge hammers; no one would want to do this to any car they owned.

That said, we consider that a run in the opposite direction would have achieved a similar time, which means the Morgan could stomp on a few supercars in a traffic light Grand Prix. There are only a handful of cars that can undercut 0-60mph in 5.2sec, and they cost considerably more than £22,400; consider the Morgan a performance bargain.

HANDLING

I DROVE back from the office on one of my favourite roads, through National Trust forest. Narrow tarmac, blind crests, sharp bends and long, long, undulating straights comprise the most part. I can safely report that, in almost every area, the Plus 8 proved deficient, except in performance, braking and fun.

Any surface apart from smooth tarmac sets up a crashing from the body with which one soon becomes familiar. The steering bumps and jerks around in the hands, the wings wobble, the body rattles and my kidneys hurt. Most of the springing comes from the side walls of the 60percent profile Pirelli P600s. It is a hard life in a Morgan.

On the test track, the handling is surprisingly neutral. The imbalance between the soft rear/hard front suspension and heavy, front-mounted engine means that the car will always understeer like mad. As long as one anticipates this, however, the rear can be steered round on the throttle. It takes a deal of lifting off to provoke any sort of oversteer, and it is easy to see why Morgans make such successful racing cars. The brakes are brilliant, with little evidence of fade; firm, controlled stopping is always available.

VERDICT

IT IS too easy to criticise the Morgan for being old-fashioned and bumpy. If it wasn't, it wouldn't be a Morgan and we would be criticising the air conditioning or the vanity mirror. A lot of the unchanged bits are still very good. The hood mechanism, although fiddly, is very secure. The side screens keep the wind off effectively. Perhaps most of all, the car has a life and spirit that evades most mass produced cars; hammers and dollies moulded the curves, steam and craft bent the ash for the frame. It fulfils Cecil Kimber's demand of MGs; that they should look fast even when standing still.

Most of our criticisms are minor: we don't like VDO instruments, nor the amateurish wrapping round the exhaust pipes to keep the heat off the wings. Our biggest complaint is more fundamental, however. In some ways, Morgan has created a monster which is almost uncontrollable. The progression of the Buick/Rover V8 to 3.9 litres illustrates more than ever that the chassis simply is not up to the job of containing it. It is all very well to talk of torque rather than power, but there is too much of both. The rear axle calls out for some more location, and the front needs a properly engineered wishbone system. All these things were around in the 1920s, and could easily be accommodated within the Morgan bodyshell. The company has persevered with the sliding pillar suspension for long enough; as no one has beaten a path to their doors for the system, isn't it time Morgan beat a path to someone else?

Morgan Plus 8

PRICE £22,362.70p for basic car plus £774 for leather upholstery and £529 for aluminium body and wings

ENGINE

CYLINDERS	V8, front-mounted
CAPACITY, cc	3,946
BORE/STROKE, mm	94×71.12
CAMSHAFT	in-block with two overhead valves per cylinder, operated via push rods
COMP RATIO	9.35:1
FUEL SYSTEM	Lucas electronic fuel injection system with twin exhaust catalysts
FUEL	min 95 octane unleaded
MAX POWER,bhp/rpm	188/4,750
MAX TORQUE,lb ft/rpm	230/2,600

TRANSMISSION

TYPE	five-speed all synchromesh manual driving the rear wheels
INTERNAL RATIOS AND MPH/1,000rpm	
Fifth	0.79:1/27.5
Fourth	1.00:1/21.7
Third	1.39:1/15.6
Second	2.08:1/10.5
First	3.32:1/6.6
FINAL DRIVE	3.31:1

CHASSIS

SUSPENSION	
front	independent with sliding front pillars, coil springs and telescopic hydraulic dampers
rear	live axle supported with semi-elliptic rear springs and telescopic hydraulic dampers
STEERING	rack and pinion
BRAKES, front/rear	disc/drum
WHEELS	6.5/15inch aluminium alloy rims
TYRES	Pirelli P600 205/60/15 radials

DIMENSIONS (inches)

LENGTH	WIDTH	HEIGHT	WHEELBASE
156	63	48	98

TRACK, front/rear	FUEL TANK, gall	KERB WEIGHT, lb
53/54	13.5	2,068

PERFORMANCE

MAXIMUM SPEED, mph			120
ACCELERATION IN FOURTH, sec			
30-50	40-60	50-70	60-80
4.1	3.9	3.9	4.2
70-90	80-100		
4.7	5.7		
ACCELERATION IN FIFTH, sec			
30-50	40-60	50-70	60-80
5.7	5.7	5.7	5.9
70-90	80-100	90-110	
6.7	7.9	10.2	

FUEL CONSUMPTION

OVERALL TEST FIGURES, mpg 19.1
MAKERS: Morgan Motor Co, Pickersleigh Road, Malvern Link, Woorestershire WR14 2LL. Tel: 0684 573104

Rage On

THE MORGAN PLUS 8 ROADSTER, FOR MANY YEARS ONLY
AVAILABLE IN THIS COUNTRY WITH PROPANE POWER, IS NOW US-LEGAL
WITH A GASOLINE-BURNING V8 EQUIPPED WITH TWO BIG CATALYSTS.
KEVIN BLICK TOOK THE WHEEL OF A PLUS 8 FOR A DRIVE TO
THE WELSH COAST. **D. EXIDIUS DEWBERRY** WENT ALONG TO SHOOT
THE PHOTOS, AND ENJOY THE LOCAL CUISINE.

SIR JOHN HARVEY-JONES, retired chairman of the international chemicals giant ICI, wears gaudy ties and has hair longer than the corporate norm. He also expresses his opinions in a forthright but entertaining fashion. And he's not short of opinions.

All of which makes him a natural for the role of television personality. His recent British television series "Troubleshooter" proved far more popular than its obscure format might have suggested. In the programs, Sir John visited various firms and advised them on how to solve problems, some of which the companies weren't even aware they had. One of those firms was The Morgan Motor Company, founded 1909. The result was classic television. What the good Sir John found made him almost apoplectic with indignation and amazement.

Rage On

Machinery which he remembered as being old when he himself was a young apprentice. A haphazard assembly system that involved pushing partly finished cars backwards and forwards between sheds in a pattern of Masonic mystery. Rustic-looking workers who'd been employed there all their lives, yet couldn't recall any change of note in production methods.

And in charge of the whole operation a benign and smiling chairman, Peter Morgan -- son of the founder -- and his own son, Charles, a former television news cameraman and Morgan racer, now production director.

Sir John couldn't grasp why Morgan, with a five-year waiting list for its cars, didn't step-up production from a pitifully low nine to ten a week and push up prices (which start from under $25,000 in Britain) as well.

Peter and Charles listened quietly, then politely declined to take any of his advice. Sir John left the scene, shaking his head in disbelief.

SMALL IS BEAUTIFUL

The Morgan philosophy is one born of experience. The company has known the bad times as well as today's good ones. Schumacher's motto "small is beautiful" might have been coined to describe its survival. Hence today's restricted production and waiting lists that seem to stretch to infinity.

And the prices? With ingenuous frankness, Morgan says its cars are for real enthusiasts (letters and photographs around the factory walls testify to that) so it will not price them as rich men's toys. And if this means a few speculators can sell their new cars for a profit, then so be it.

As for the cars themselves, the Morgan ethos is simple: don't change unless you really have to. What was merely normal in the 1930s became unfashionable in the 1950s and is now at the height of nostalgia-led popularity. Plus ca change. But with savage irony, keeping the cars unaltered is actually harder than would be changing them. Component suppliers regularly stop making the vintage-style parts that Morgans rely on (why should they continue, when no company but Morgan with its tiny turnover needs them?). Engines come and go, too, with the ebb and flow of outside supplies.

But toughest of all are the demands of the bureaucrats. The mountains of paperwork that dictate myriad rules and regulations, which would never have been dreamed of when H.F.S. Morgan built his first three-wheeler. Safety was tough enough. Now Morgan is facing up to exhaust emissions as Europe follows the lead set by the US and goes catalyst in 1992.

GREEN MACHINE

Enter, with a nose discreetly thumbed in the direction of Sir John,

the twin catalyst-equipped Plus 8. For, as Morgan proudly points out, its new green machine is actually a pacesetter. Its version of the Rover (nee Buick) V8 has actually passed tougher emission tests than Rover's own. With three-way catalysts and a fuel evaporation system, the Morgan V8 meets emissions regulations that won't be in force in Europe until 1995.

What this also means is that, for the first time in years, Morgans in the US will be powered by gas -- as in gasoline -- rather than gas, as in propane. Morgans in the US have been propelled by propane for many years now.

All of which may be jolly good news to Morgan enthusiasts, but it's still scarcely a point they're likely to boast about. No one buys

beer beside the open fire in cozy, thatched roof pubs; and cricket on the village green. Images of fun and innocence encapsulated forever in those flowing fenders, the long, louvered hood, and the tiny, flat windshield. Driving a Morgan is always a trip down memory lane -- even if the crude suspension can jog some unpleasant memories, too -- but the Plus 8 is more than an exercise in nostalgia.

Arguably, the all-alloy V8 was the best thing that ever happened to the Morgan roadster. Instead of being a homely little runabout bought by retired gents wanting to revisit their youth, here is a rip-snorting monster. The 200 horsepower motor in a wood-frame chassis with minimal bodywork that all together weighs less than 2,000 pounds gives a power-to-weight ratio that would embarrass more than a few supercars. The Morgan V8 has the acceleration to match most Italian exotics.

Exciting stuff, especially when combined with a suspension that wouldn't have looked out of place on a horse-drawn carriage. And in a chassis with the torsional rigidity of a banana.

WELSH SEASHORE

But this is all part of the fun. And so -- if you're a real enthusiast -- is the weather. Perhaps it would be tiresome to drive a Morgan in California. No need for rain-soaked, wind-chilled fingers to tug at "Lift the Dot" fasteners. No need to wrestle in the rain with too-taut canvas, or to drive in a misted-up cabin while the rain drips through cracks and crevices. No fun at all without such suffering.

For some, perhaps, but not for me. Standing, soaked through, on a Welsh seashore and fighting to put up the reluctant top, I would gladly have forsaken the Morgan

for the sanctuary of a warm sedan.

At least things had started well. We collected the Plus 8 on a crisp, bright winter's morning, dropped the top immediately, and squashed our few belongings for the two-day trip into the tiny space behind the seats. Whichever way you turn from Malvern leads toward beautiful countryside. We went west, to the sparsely populated hills of mid-Wales and on to the coastal sands of Pendine, venue of epic and ultimately tragic land speed record attempts during the 1920s.

By any commonsense yardstick, the Plus 8 is an absurd machine. The cockpit is cramped and noisy. Two occupants sit shoulder to shoulder, yet can converse only when halted at traffic lights. The seats are flat and formless. The footwell is cramped, the clutch is heavy, the unboosted brakes much heavier still, and the long-travel accelerator pedal all but impossible to push to its far limit. The tiny gearstick shifts cogs with palm-bruising stiffness. The large,

organ because it has a catalyst. It ay be a necessary condition of organ motoring these days, but had better not try to spoil the rty.

And thankfully, it doesn't. The is 8 may be as green as the lvern Hills that are its home, t the driving experience is as d-blooded as its scarlet intwork. Malvern is quintes-

sentially English, famous for its water (consumed by The Queen, among others) and the high Hills whose spectacular views inspired Sir Edward William Elgar's majestic music. You couldn't ask for a more appropriate site for a maker of terrifically British cars, cars that conjure up images of Spitfire pilots with stiff upper lips and handlebar moustaches; pints of warm, brown

INSTEAD OF BEING A HOMELY
LITTLE RUNABOUT BOUGHT
BY RETIRED GENTS WANTING TO RE-
VISIT THEIR YOUTH, HERE IS A
RIP-SNORTING MONSTER"

· ·
ove Right: Morgan Pub in Malvern. Lower right: Hay-on-Wye bookstore.

Rage On

"LATER, SITTING IN THAT DANK AN
STEAMY INTERIOR, ON A WE
LEATHER SEAT, WITH SOGG
TROUSERS, SOAKED COAT, AN
FROZEN FINGERS, HOW I CURSE
THE MORGAN

. . . .

Left: Writer Blick peering into seaside shack of Welsh poet Dylan Thom
Lower Right: The Pendine Sar

Rage On

vertical steering wheel is cumbersome and heavy to handle.

Daft, yet delightful all the same. With the sun shining and the canvas and perspex sidescreens stopping the chill wind from doing anything worse than whipping around our necks, we rumbled energetically through the English

border country, the lusty V8's bellow reverberating off the hedgerows and low stone walls.

The fuel injected V8 simply oozes torque from every pore. There's 220 lbs. ft. of the stuff as well as 190 horsepower. The gear change might be stiff, but you can more or less forget it. Fourth is enough for most occasions and if you happen to be in fifth, that will probably do just as well. Likewise, the throttle may have huge travel, but you rarely need bother to tread it right down. A half-hearted squeeze will deliver all the thrust you need to swallow a country straight or leap past a dawdling,

worn-out farm truck.

The German magazine *Auto Motor und Sport* found the pre-cat Plus 8 to be quicker from 50 to 75 mph in fifth gear than anything it has tested. That's anything, Ferraris, Porsches, and Corvettes included. The trip needs just 7.9 breathtaking seconds.

In short, the Plus 8 goes -- and quickly. Anywhere and everywhere, the merest hint of a straight, a prod on the throttle, and you're hurtling at the horizon. Accelerating is what it does best. Cruising becomes irksomely noisy, and trying to run flat-out just batters the senses into submission.

HAY-ON-WYE

After 30 breathtaking miles that felt like 300, we came to the small town of Hay-on-Wye, which literally straddles the England-Wales border. In Hay every other shop sells books. It all started when Richard Booth opened what he claims is "the largest secondhand bookshop in the world." Now Hay and its books are firmly on the tourist trail.

Outside Hay, the Plus 8 posed for pictures on the awesomely beautiful Gospel Pass. Nearby, a handful of hippies parked their battered bus to search for hallucinogenic "magic mushrooms." Apparently Wales has had a record crop this year.

We left them to their trip and continued our own. The bleak hills of the Brecon Beacons were the next stop and though the sky was darker, the rain still held off.

There's a lot you can tolerate in the Morgan so long as the top stays down. The ride, for one thing. Cart-sprung at the rear and using Morgan's own sliding pillar front suspension (a system of dubious theoretical efficiency and even less practical merit), the Plus 8 rides like a bronco.

There was a time when the Plus 8 would hop and bounce like a jumping bean on a poor road surface, but Morgan has fiddled with spring and shock settings of late. The result is a ride that is different. Not a lot better, to be frank, just different. True, the car isn't so stiff, but it is much bouncier. So what. That's the nature of the car. Take it or leave it. You could never satisfactorily change things without ruining the car as a whole.

Handling is almost as agricultural. Stiff, low, and on fat 205/60VR-15 Pirelli P600 tires, the Plus 8 has a high level of grip. Far higher than that hopping, flexing, and jarring ride would have you believe. To handle the car, you need a certain amount of bravery, but you also need to know when to turn and run in order to avoid getting a nasty bite.

The steering is heavy, higher-geared, and disappointingly uncommunicative. Dial in lock and it gets heavier still. Essentially the car understeers -- which is sensible -- and only a great amount of

throttle will make the limited differential rear end slide ou shape on a tight bend. But the not much fluidity to cornering isn't easy to keep the car on a line down a twisty road. If press too hard, you'll find the l 8 getting increasingly unruly unwilling to obey your commar That said, give it a smoother face and sweeping bends rai than tight turns and not many will be nicer -- or quicker -- to dr

Black Mountain, a favorite ha of every British motoring write a road like that. It climbs sinuo out of mid-Wales, then desce into the industrial south. It wa minutes of sheer good fun.

MISERABLE TOP

Rain was falling now and at it was time to put up the to wrestling match that can tak experienced operator five min And in five minutes you can very wet. There are some th you would like to see changed Morgan and, stuck in a rainstc the top comes at the top of the We finished the day in the stean up cabin, toasted by the eng heat (the crude heater is eithe or off). Claustrophobic, gloc and noisy. It's not much fun most better to keep the top d and get wet, in fact.

The sun was out again the lowing morning as we drop down the steep hill into Penc Today, it's a scruffy little sea town with amusement arcades burger stands. It's a poor mem to the heroes who graced its sa all those years ago. A simple pla on the Beach Hotel (itself a fa relic of the past) pays tribute to epic duels that were fought ac the six-mile stretch of coast.

In 1924, Malcolm Camp driving a Sunbeam raised the w land speed record to 146.16

o years later he upped it to .87, only for Parry Thomas to ak it the same year with 169.30 then 171.02 mph in his special, s. In 1927, Campbell drove his oier to 174.88 mph. Finally, on rch 3, 1927 Parry Thomas was ed when the chain drive of Babs ke as he tried to recapture the ord. The car was buried where it shed and lay there for nearly 50 rs until it was dug up for resto-on as a monument to the driver. That was the end of Pendine ds as a record-breaking venue. eds were too high for even its jth. Today the military uses t of the coast as part of a firing re while at low tide the sands town serve as a playground vacationers.

Gazing into the lonely, deserted ance, with the watery morning glistening off the wave-rippled Is, it was hard to imagine the age of men prepared to race across those flats at previously un-known speeds in cars whose me-chanical sophistication would probably be surpassed even by our Plus 8.

As we photographed, a low gray cloud moved over the town and the rain began to fall, gently at first, then fiercely. Even when a bright blue, sunlit sky shone tantalizingly all around, that gray cloud refused to move and still the rain fell. Eventually there was no choice but to get wet, so we ran from under the shelter of the building where we had been hiding, unzipped the Morgan's tonneau, and wrestled once again with that top.

Later, sitting in that dank and steamy interior, on a wet leather seat, with soggy trousers, soaked coat, and frozen fingers, how I cursed the Morgan. But around the corner of the bay we were in sun-shine again, watching "pale rain over the dwindling harbour" as Dylan Thomas put it. He must have known well the vagaries of Welsh weather for he lived in Laugharne where we now were, just a few miles along from Pendine. He was buried in the local churchyard af-ter his death at the age of only 39.

Laugharne has looked after its local hero better than Pendine re-members its famous. The small hut where Thomas wrote *Under Milk Wood* and many of his poems has been restored to look just as it did when he worked there. The hut and the nearby Boat House where he lived look out over a gorgeous seascape of apparently timeless beauty -- the "mussel pooled and the heron priested shore" of the River Taf estuary and out on to the "sloeblack, slow, black, fishing boat bobbing sea."

Times do change, though. No fishing boats bob there now. In-stead, aircraft dive noiselessly over the distant ranges, their bombs ex-ploding like muffled thunder out to sea.

And for the equally timeless Morgan, times have changed, too, with catalysts and charcoal canis-ters and a whiff of sulphur in the desmogged exhaust. Yet, anachro-nistic as it may be, frustrating as it can be from time to time, defiant against every piece of management dogma as it certainly is, despite (or probably because of) all this, the Morgan lives on. The world's old-est surviving privately owned motor manufacturer is in venerable but far from decrepit old age. More from Dylan Thomas seems appro-priate:

"Do not go gentle into that good night,

Old age should burn and rave at close of day.

Rage, rage against the dying of the light."

Rage on, Morgan.

sci

TRUE BRITS

Look forward over that long, louvred bonnet past the bug-eyed headlamps and cycle wings and you couldn't mistake this for any other car. The looks are pure 1950s, right down to the chromed teardrop side lamps on top of the wings, and Morgan enthusiasts wouldn't have it any other way.

Glance around the cockpit and the detailing all harks back to a similar era — a flat, walnut dash with a collection of conventional black on white instruments, and beautifully-crafted Connolly hide on seats that are about as far away from the form-hugging security of a Recaro as it's possible to imagine. There are no frills either — simple sliding side windows, no stereo or ashtray and a heater that boasts just a choke-type control knob and a single rocker switch for the fan. It's narrow in here, a snug fit for two, though the driving position is first class and the leather-rimmed three spoke wheel perfectly placed.

But thanks to 190bhp and a kerb weight of just over 2000lb the performance is anything but 1950s. This is a Morgan Plus 8, powered by the latest 3.9-litre fuel injection version of the Range Rover's V8 engine and the quickest car Morgan has ever produced. Not only that, but this car shows the way forward for Morgan in these environmentally-conscious times — equipped with twin three-way catalysts, it complies with the most stringent emission regulations in the world.

Compared with the 3.5-litre Rover Vitesse-powered Plus 8 it replaces, the 3.9-litre version gets an increase in bore from 88.9mm to 94mm, changes to camshaft, intake and exhaust manifolding, and a substantially revised Lucas fuel injection system. The extra cubes have not been used to increase peak power — which at 190bhp remains the same — but to offset the penalty introduced by the catalyst and boost the torque spread at low rpm.

For the record, at 122mph the bigger engine delivers much the same top speed as the 3.5-litre Plus 8, although on the same gearing the engine is now spinning much closer to its peak power rpm — about 4500rprn. The car is actually limited to this top speed thanks to a top speed governor built into the electronics — this cuts the power for a couple of seconds at a time as the car edges past 122mph, and without it the Plus 8 would certainly go faster. In truth though, no one will buy a Plus 8 for its top speed potential — by no stretch of the imagination is a Morgan a relaxing high speed cruiser.

Again, with the same peak power you'd expect standing start acceleration figures to be similar, and in fact thanks to a wet track the Plus 8 was actually slightly slower off the mark — we recorded 0-60mph in 5.9 seconds, a standing quarter-mile time of 14.7 seconds and 0-100mph in 15.6 seconds. The extra traction afforded by dry tarmac would only have made a slight difference because getting a Morgan off the line quickly is a knife-edge balancing act between wheelspin and violent axle tramp.

Where the fatter torque curve does make itself felt though is in the gears, the 3.9-litre car being substantially faster than its predecessor through every increment, the benchmark time from 50-70 mph in top gear taking just 6.1 seconds — faster than an Esprit Turbo SE and only a tenth slower than the king of mid-range stomp, Audi's 20v quattro.

But this is not a car to enjoy on the test track — rather a unique driving experience to savour on the open road. Undo the 20 or so press stud fasteners, fold the hood back (an operation a good deal simpler than it looks) and remove the side screens. Sitting close to the ground and peering through the low, flat screen, you fire up the V8 with a twist of the key (one of four, different for each lock on the car) and listen to the frothy burble. It's not as loud or

A rush of blood

In the first of a new series looking at how British-made performance cars are facing up to the 1990s. Howard Lees drives the latest cat-equipped 3.9-litre Morgan Plus 8

G91 EWP

● *Paint and details such as wing-mounted sidelights (above) are beautifully finished*

deep chested as in the past, the catalysts have seen to that, but at a standstill or on the move you are never left in any doubt that there's a big V8 under the bonnet.

Depress the heavy clutch and snick the short travel, rifle bolt of a gearchange into first. Pull the stubby, fly-off handbrake next to it backwards to release the ratchet and you can ease off down the road. The Plus 8 carries well over half of its weight over the rear wheels, so there's plenty of traction available, but still it's all too easy to light up the rear tyres if the roads are damp or slippery. There's instant grunt available from very low revs in any gear, so though its almost impossible to resist using that short throw, lightning quick gearchange just to listen to the engine changing note, the Plus 8 will pull hard out of corners in any gear.

Winding through the Malvern hills away from the factory, the car was in its element. Braking deep into the corners with the heavy but reassuringly powerful un-servoed brakes, while heel and toe shifting down through the gate of the Rover five-speed gearbox, it was easy to be intoxicated by the sound and feel of motoring as it used to be. Turning in needs a big handful of lock, because the Plus 8 is a modest but determined understeerer and although the rack is geared at 3.5 turns lock to lock, the turning circle is the size of a small truck. The 205/50 ZR15 Pirelli P600s provide plenty of dry road grip and once in the corner, a tease of throttle tightens the line and holds the car in perfect balance. On the flip side, the steering forces build with increasing cornering speed to an alarming degree — this is a car to build your biceps, no question.

Though too much power will bring the tail out of line, this is by no means a mischievous car to drive fast. Thanks to the perfect camber control of the live rear axle it stays stable under a trailing throttle too, and in fact controlling the occasional tail slide would be child's play if it wasn't for the huge effort needed at the wheel.

Bumps and ridges send crashes and shudders though the body, and the rear suspension is all too eager to bottom out, but Morgans have always been like that and there are those who argue that it forms part of the appeal. In fact thanks to softer front springs this particular car was a good deal easier on the spine than previous examples.

When it rains you'll be glad to hear that erecting the hood is actually less fiddly than taking it down, and providing you remember to fold out the outer flap at the edge of the roof once you have closed the door, it doesn't leak — certainly the torrential rain that dogged our session at the test track was as severe a test of waterproofing as anyone could have devised. Despite the primitive controls, the heater fan does a good job of demisting the screen, although the first time you see the three tiny windscreen wipers flick across the screen I guarantee it will make you laugh.

Though it doesn't let the rain in and provides plenty of headroom, the hood is less successful when keeping the wind at bay. Wind noise is pronounced at 50mph, loud at 70mph and simply deafening at higher speeds. It doesn't take long to realise why Morgan doesn't fit a stereo — you simply wouldn't be able to hear it.

At £22,362 the Plus 8 is hardly over-priced given the degree of care and quality of materials that go into its manufacture, while at £13,797 the basic Ford-engined 4/4 looks like a bargain. There's no denying either that despite the age of the Morgan's basic shape, it still looks superb.

Enthusiasts on Morgan's five-year waiting list won't be deterred by such trivia as the uncompromising ride, ferocious wind noise and lack of creature comforts. What matters to them is the Plus 8's blistering performance, a driving position, gearchange and brakes that are pure sports car and a hood down motoring experience that's quite simply unique — drive one and you'll begin to understand.

● **Walnut facia (above) is a dash of elegance housing simple instruments in functional cockpit. Range Rover engine (below) meets latest emission standards with no drop in performance**

MORGAN PLUS 8

All tests with a crew of two and a full tank of fuel

THROUGH THE GEARS (seconds)

0-30mph	2.6	0-70mph	7.4
0-40mph	3.4	0-80mph	9.5
0-50mph	4.7	0-90mph	12.3
0-60mph	6.0	0-100mph	15.6

STANDING 1/4 MILE	14.7/98 (secs/mph)
AVERAGED TOP SPEED	122mph

ACCELERATION IN 3rd/4th/5th (seconds)

30-50mph	2.7/4.0/5.7	60-80mph	3.5/4.5/6.7
40-60mph	2.9/4.2/5.9	70-90mph	-/5.2/7.4
50-70mph	3.1/4.1/6.1	80-100mph	-/6.1/8.8

MAX SPEEDS IN GEARS AT 5500rpm

FIRST	33.4mph	FOURTH	110.9mph
SECOND	53.3mph	FIFTH	123mph at 4800rpm
THIRD	79.8mph		

OVERALL FUEL CONSUMPTION	20.3mpg/13.9 l/100km
TRACK CONDITION	Wet
TEMPERATURE	+6°C
WIND SPEED	2mph
ATMOSPHERIC PRESSURE	1009mb

SPECIFICATION

ENGINE TYPE		Longitudinal V8
DISPLACEMENT		3947cc
BORE	94.0mm **STROKE**	71.1mm
COMPRESSION RATIO		9.75:1
FUEL AND IGNITION		Lucas electronic fuel injection and mapped ignition
CYLINDER BLOCK		Aluminium alloy
CYLINDER HEAD		Aluminium alloy, ohv, two valves per cylinder
MAX POWER (DIN)		190bhp @ 4500rpm
MAX TORQUE (DIN)		235lb ft @ 2600rpm
GEARBOX		Five-speed manual
GEAR RATIOS		
1st	3.32 **4th**	1.00
2nd	2.08 **5th**	0.79
3rd	1.39 **Reverse**	3.42
FINAL DRIVE RATIO		3.31:1
SPEED PER 1000rpm IN TOP		25.5mph
FRONT SUSPENSION		Sliding pillars, coil springs, telescopic dampers
REAR SUSPENSION		Leaf spring, telescopic dampers
STEERING		Rack and pinion
BRAKES		Disc front, drums rear
WHEELS		6½in cast alloy
TYRES		Pirelli P600 205/50 ZR16
WHEELBASE		98in
TURNING CIRCLE		38ft
FUEL TANK CAPACITY		13.5 galls/61 litres
UNLADEN WEIGHT		2068lb
TEST WEIGHT		2403lb
BASIC PRICE (INC TAXES)		£23,859
PRICE AS TESTED		£23,859
OPTIONAL EXTRAS FITTED TO TEST CAR		Leather upholstery £775, locking petrol cap £6.23, aluminium body and wings £529, walnut veneer facia £186.88

TRUE BRITS

Morgan & Son

A year on from the BBC's Troubleshooter series, Morgan is riding out the recession. By Howard Lees

In the shadow of the Malvern Hills, a ramshackle shed houses both the past and future of Britain's oldest sports car producer. Racks of rough-sawn ash planks exposed to the elements will season there for at least a year before being cut to form the body frames of a Morgan.

And though the Morgan Motor Company has been owned by the family of the same name since its inception in 1909, each of these planks will have come from a tree 20 years older. It's the way things have always been done, and no-one here looks set to change something so central to the Morgan's hand-built appeal.

That's not to say that Morgan will never alter the design of its cars or the way they are built. Managing director Peter Morgan, son of founder HFS Morgan, is acutely conscious of the fine balance between tradition and evolution. 'I've never looked further ahead than five years, but changes will occur,' he says.

Whatever form those changes take, they won't be along the lines suggested by Sir John Harvey-Jones in the BBC TV's 'Troubleshooter' series. Morgan went to great lengths to distance

itself from the conclusions reached; whether the former chairman of ICI would stand by his pleas to double production and increase prices in the light of the current dire economic situation is debatable.

There's still resentment at the factory about the way Morgan was portrayed in that programme, but in the end it didn't do the company any harm — in the month after it was shown, sales director Derek Day took 400 orders.

Despite an increase in production from nine to ten cars a week, the people whose cars are going through the factory now put their £250 deposits down over six years ago. After that length of time the number of people still prepared to go ahead when they are advised production is about to start can fluctuate wildly, but once a further deposit of £500 has been banked it is very rare for people not to take delivery.

Morgan has always seen itself as producing affordable sports cars, and its prices are based very much on the costs of

building the car and the need for a reasonable return. Despite the hand-crafted nature of the cars, prices range from under £14,000 for the basic 1.6-litre 4/4 to just over £22,000 for the 3.9-litre V8-powered Plus 8.

The policy has stood the company in good stead through hard times — Peter Morgan's son Charles says the only obvious effect of the current recession is that the premium available to people who sell their delivery mileage cars has come down from around £7000 to perhaps £1000. Orders, he says, have not fallen off, and the cars are now going to people who really want them rather than speculators.

Every car produced at Malvern is built to order, and as soon as work is started on the bare steel ladder chassis a tag with the customer's name and the exact specification is attached.

There are very few parts of the car where a choice isn't offered — the chassis is usually black powder-coated, but galvanising is an option and the options list carries two different types of

TRUE
BRITS

produced every week and with the whole process taking ten weeks there are about 100 cars in production at any one time — this is no mass production line, but at least Morgan has gone metric.

Bare chassis frames are produced by an outside supplier then gain the familiar leaf-spring rear and sliding pillar front suspension, brakes, rear axles and wheels in the first of the series of single-storey brick buildings that have been Morgan's home since 1920.

Engines and gearboxes are installed next to avoid any body damage that might occur if they were lifted in later — a 1.6-litre 95bhp Ford CVH for the 4/4, 138bhp Rover 2-litre 16-valve M16 engine for the Plus 4 and 190bhp 3.9-litre Efi Land Rover V8 for the Plus 8, with either Ford or Rover five-speed manual gearboxes. On average, of those ten cars a week, four each are Plus 8 and 4/4 and the remaining pair the M16-engined Plus 4.

Over in the wood shop, those ash planks are sawn, planed and shaped to form the 76 different pieces of wood in a Morgan two-seater (110 in the four-seater models that make up 10 per cent of production). Most of the frame assembly is carried out next door, and the bare Morgan chassis starts to evolve into that familiar shape. An oven in the corner is used to cure the rear mudguard assembly, the three layers of cross-grained hardwood curved

additional rust-proofing. Though the nose section and front bulkhead are formed from mild steel sheet and the rear panel where the spare wheel sits is always aluminium alloy, the bonnet, wings and doors can be either steel or light alloy — the difference being 88lb and £530.

Morgan's production process might look a bit like organised chaos, but it actually works very smoothly.

There are separate shops where the various fabrication and assembly stages go on — chassis assembly, sheet metal shop, wood shop, body assembly, machine shop, paint shop, trim and final assembly and so on, and the company employs 130 people. Most stages takes about a week, there are ten cars

and glued together into a very strong, stiff assembly that doubles as the seat belt anchorage. The frame itself is glued and screwed together, then dipped in Cuprinol overnight before being mated to the chassis. Floor panels too are wood, but this time cut from sheets of deal.

Over in the sheet metal shop, the different panels — steel and light alloy — are cut, rolled and beaten to shape over formers. This is a noisy place — all the large panels are made by hand, and the hide mallet rather than the hydraulic press reigns supreme. With the body frames bolted to the car, the panels are

fixed to the frames with zinc-plated screws, allowing them to be replaced relatively easily if they are damaged.

Meanwhile a big machine shop with dozen of lathes, mills and drills makes a great many of the machined components — Morgan's policy is to make as much as it can afford to itself, rather than buy-in parts. Brakes, hubs, and stub axles are all machined here, though forgings and castings are not produced on site. These are old machines, and there's no sign of any computer or numerical controlled machine tools — the closest thing you'll find to automation are a few big capstan lathes. Batch quantities are small, and with many of the machines set-up to do a particular job, they are by no means all in use at once.

The company's brochure says 'the beauty of a Morgan is more than skin deep' but Morgan spends a great deal of time on that skin. Each car spends longer in the paintshop than anywhere else — there are three priming processes and between five and seven coats of two-pack acrylic paint are baked on. The results are glorious, without exception the cars having a smooth, lustrous finish that's way ahead of the mass-produced norm.

Next stop is the trim shop, where as well as gaining seats (mostly upholstered with optional Connolly hide), carpets, dashboard and windscreen, the cars are wired up and generally prepared for the road. Once finished, after setting the lights

● *Production is painstaking with not a robot in sight. Bare chassis (left) await suspension*

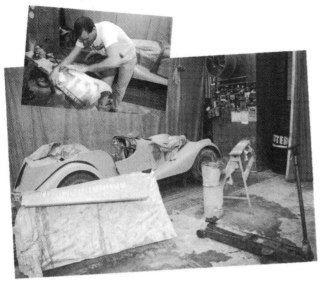

● Car spends more time in paint shop than anywhere else. Wood dashes (left) hanging about

the race track.

The track, or at least motor sport in general, has always been important to Morgan. The reception area at the factory is decorated with fading wooden boards listing trials and rally successes from the 1920s, and in the US the Morgan was the car to beat in production races for many years. In 1962 a TR3-engined Plus 4 won its class at the Le Mans 24 Hour race, and in 1978 Charles Morgan piloted a works Plus 8 to the Production Sports Car Championship in the UK.

Those BRSCC and BRDC championships have now gone, but Peter Morgan reckons the Plus 8 is still a car to be reckoned with: 'We can hold our own with almost anything on a track. We might lose out on the straights, but make it up under braking and round the corners.' Morgans are still raced, but not by the factory — engineering director Maurice Owen made an impassioned plea at the recent NEC Autosports congress for the minimum production quantities to be

lever arm dampers at the rear, and similar units are used at the front. But the sliding pillar front suspension and leaf-sprung live rear axle will not be changed in the near future — Charles Morgan says that development will concentrate on fine-tuning the existing layout, though he admits to considering a new or heavily modified chassis. Peter Morgan believes there is some mileage left in sliding pillar front suspension 'if only we could reduce the stiction', but reckons the suspension is just the job on

The frame

is glued and

screwed together,

then dipped

in Cuprinol

overnight before

being mated

to the chassis

waived so that Morgan could take part in production car racing again, but it fell on deaf ears.

Morgan knows that the appeal of a traditional, craftsman-built car that looks like it was designed in 1954 (it was) is what keeps the orders flooding in, though Peter Morgan says he is 'amazed that the style has been accepted — in the '60s we couldn't move the Plus 4'. The company isn't happy with the length of the waiting list, but it won't attack the problem by raising prices — that would alienate the enthusiasts the company sees as its real customers. Charles Morgan plans to make a few more cars, but without any significant change in the way the car is built: 'I want to increase production by 10 per cent a year, but there will be no new factory, no double shift working and no huge increase in overtime.'

As for the car itself, it has already changed a good deal under the skin, and there's clearly more to come. Peter Morgan has the last word: 'If we are smart, we won't alter the style, but if change is needed then we'll change it.'

and checking the emissions, each car is road tested for 20-30 miles before it is released to the customer.

Because it sells half of its production abroad — a tradition that began after the war to secure extra supplies of valuable steel — Morgan is only too aware of the current and impending legislation. The last couple of years have seen a tremendous amount of work on emissions control — the Plus 8 is now catalyst-equipped for everywhere except the UK, and the Plus 4 and 4/4 will follow soon. Apart from the durability test, which is going on now, the Plus 8 already complies with Californian emission standards — which are tougher than both US and impending EEC limits. Energy absorbing bumpers and side impact protection have also been developed, and air bags will be next.

Suspension is another area where Charles Morgan admits there is work to be done. Already, considerably softer front springs have taken much of the harshness out of the ride. New telescopic dampers from Gabriel in the US have replaced the old

● Handcut louvres in sides of aluminium bonnet give distinctive 1950s appeal

Morgan Plus 8

The V8 version of Morgan's timeless roadster demands respect but is a unique and rewarding driving experience

Price as tested *£25,229* **Top speed** *121mph* **0-60** *6.1secs* **MPG** *20.1*

For *Strong performance, old-fashioned looks, sheer entertainment*
Against *Hard ride, tricky handling, buffeting*

Driving the Plus 8 is a rewarding experience for those who can tolerate the boneshaking ride and buffeting. The car must be taken by the scruff of the neck and driven with enthusiasm. Hand-beaten aluminium and steel panels cover an ash frame and ladder chassis that is deliberately designed to flex

OWN AT MORGAN'S RED-BRICK factory tucked away from the glare and blare f city life beneath the Malvern hills, they on't like to rush into things headlong. Apart om a handful of detail changes over the years nd the change to a more sloping tail and miliar curved radiator grille in 1956, the urrent Plus 8 looks much as the 4/4 did when was made before the war. Sports cars caring the Morgan name have been crafted ithin those same walls for more than 70 ars, initially in three-wheeler form before rning to four wheels in 1936.

Even now, every Morgan retains leaf rear rings with an underslung chassis, ash-amed hand-beaten bodywork in aluminium d steel, and unique sliding pillar front spension that dates back to the very first organ of 1909.

But the Morgan's unique vintage character no contrived marketing ploy. It stems from e continuous manufacture over more

than five decades of a pre-war car by vintage methods in a vintage factory. It takes 10 to 12 weeks to build a Morgan, and just 10 ready-made antique cars roll out of the factory gates every week. It's no surprise, then, that there's a six-year waiting list for these instant classics.

Discuss future developments with Charles Morgan, production director and grandson of company founder H F S Morgan, and he'll tell you that Morgan customers wouldn't entertain any major changes. In spite of progress, or perhaps even because of it, the Morgan lives on intact, and is likely to do so for many years to come. It's that same vintage character that provides the appeal; drive a Morgan on a sunny day with the roof down and you've found the antidote to stressful modern living.

But there are other reasons for Plus 8 ownership. One of the more compelling ones has eight cylinders and crams full the space beneath that long, louvred bonnet. Rover V8-powered Morgans have thundered through

England's leafy lanes since 1969, but these days the all-alloy engine carries a Land Rover badge, electronic fuel injection and catalytic converters, while the capacity has been stretched from 3528 to 3947cc.

There's no substitute for cubic capacity, goes the saying, and few would argue. Even so, the latest 190bhp engine is no more powerful than its predecessor, as a result of those power-sapping catalytic converters, although it does lug with more gusto. Torque is up 7 per cent to 235lb ft at a much lower peak of 2600rpm. Real stump-wrenching stuff, this.

In this top-model form, the Morgan Plus 8 is listed at £22,849 — a little extra if you want door handles. Add the test car's optional aluminium wings and bonnet (as standard, both are in steel), together with leather trim, mohair hood and walnut dashboard and the cost climbs to £25,229.

At the other end of the scale, Morgan ownership starts at a bargain £14,098 for a ▶

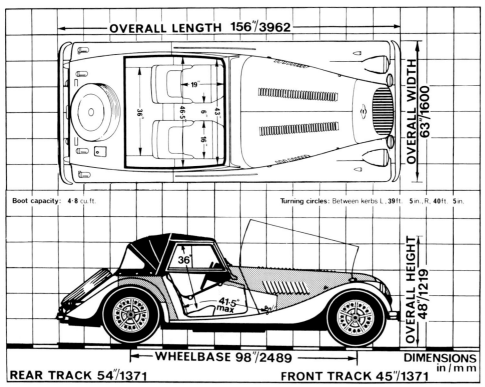

OVERALL LENGTH 156"/3962

19"

36"

46.5"

6"

43"

16"

OVERALL WIDTH 63"/1600

Boot capacity: 4·8 cu.ft.

Turning circles: Between kerbs L, 39ft. 5in., R, 40ft. 5in.

36"

41·5" max

OVERALL HEIGHT 48"/1219

WHEELBASE 98"/2489

DIMENSIONS in/mm

REAR TRACK 54"/1371

FRONT TRACK 45"/1371

SPECIFICATIONS

ENGINE
Longitudinal, front, rear-wheel drive
Capacity 3946cc, 8 cylinders in 90deg vee
Bore 94.0mm **Stroke** 71.1mm
Compression ratio 9.35:1
Head/block al alloy/al alloy
Valve gear ohv pushrod
Ignition and fuel Lucas electronic fuel injection and mapped ignition. Catalytic converter
Max power 190bhp (PS-DIN) (140kW) at 4750rpm
Max torque 235lb ft (312Nm) at 2600rpm
Specific output 48bhp/litre
Power to weight ratio 207bhp/ton

TRANSMISSION
Five-speed manual

Gear	Ratio	mph/1000rpm
Top	0.79	27.6
4th	1.00	21.8
3rd	1.39	15.6
2nd	2.09	10.4
1st	3.32	6.5

Final drive ratio 3.31. Limited slip differential

SUSPENSION
Front independent, sliding pillar, coil springs, telescopic dampers
Rear live axle, leaf springs, telescopic dampers

STEERING
Rack and pinion, 3.5 turns lock to lock

BRAKES
Front 11.0ins (279mm) discs
Rear 9.0ins (228mm) drums

WHEELS AND TYRES
Al alloy 6.5in rims, 205/60 VR15 Avon tyres

SOLD AND PRODUCED BY
Morgan Motor Co Ltd
Pickersleigh Road
Malvern Link
Worcestershire
Tel 0684 573104

COSTS

Total	£22,848.85

Options fitted to test car

Leather trim	£763.75
Exterior door handles	£57.28
Alloy body and wings	£540.99
Mohair hood	£827.40
Walnut veneer dashboard	£190.94
Total as tested	£25,229.21
Delivery, road tax, plates	£112.00
On the road price	£25,341.21

SERVICE
Major service 6000 miles (time 4-5hrs)

PARTS COST (inc VAT)

Oil filter	£11.73
Air filter	£8.94
Spark plugs (set)	£14.78
Brake pads (two wheels) front	£15.88
Brake pads (two wheels) rear	£25.54
Exhaust complete (inc VAT)	£350.85
Tyre — each (typical)	£119.06
Windscreen	£100.00
Headlamp unit	£24.12
Front wing	£438.53
Rear bumper	£111.76

WARRANTY
12 months/12,000 miles

EQUIPMENT

Anti-lock brakes	—
Alloy wheels	●
Auto gearbox	—
Power-assisted steering	—
Steering rake/reach adjustment	—
Seat tilt adjustment	—
Lumbar adjustment	—
Head restraints	£127
Internal mirror adjustment	—
Flick wipe	—
Programmed wash/wipe	—
Revcounter	●
Lockable glovebox	●
Radio/cassette player	DO
Electronic windows	—
Central locking	—
Catalytic converter	●
Metallic paint	£255

● Standard
— Not available
DO dealer option

PERFORMANCE

MAXIMUM SPEEDS

Gear	mph	km/h	rpm
Top (mean)	121	195	4385
(best)	122	197	4420
4th	121	195	5560
3rd	94	151	6000
2nd	63	102	6000
1st	39	63	6000

ACCELERATION FROM REST

True mph	Time (secs)	Speedo mph
30	2.4	32
40	3.7	42
50	4.7	52
60	6.1	62
70	8.5	72
80	10.6	82
90	13.7	92
100	18.4	101
110	23.6	111

Standing qtr mile 15.1secs, 93mph
Standing km 27.8secs, 111mph
30-70mph through gears 6.1secs

ACCELERATION IN EACH GEAR

mph	Top	4th	3rd	2nd
10-30	—	4.9	3.3	2.1
20-40	6.0	4.2	3.0	2.0
30-50	5.8	4.1	2.9	2.1
40-60	6.0	4.2	3.0	2.5
50-70	6.3	4.3	3.1	—
60-80	6.7	4.5	3.6	—
70-90	7.5	5.1	5.0	—
80-100	8.9	6.1	—	—
90-110	12.0	8.5	—	—

FUEL CONSUMPTION
Overall mpg 20.1 (14.1 litres/100km)
Best mpg 23.5 (12.0 litres/100km)
Worst mpg 15.5 (18.2 litres/100km)
Fuel grade Unleaded (95 or 98 RM)
Tank capacity 12 galls (55 litres)
Max range 282 miles

BRAKING
Fade (from 30mph in neutral)
Pedal load (lb) for 0.5g stops (mean)

1	60	6	95
2	60	7	95
3	65	8	90
4	85	9	90
5	90	10	90

Response (from 93mph in neutral)

Load	g	distance
20lb	0.05	600ft
40lb	0.35	86ft
60lb	0.65	46ft
80lb	0.90	33ft
100lb	1.1	27ft
Parking brake	0.25	120ft

WEIGHT
Kerb 2059lb/935kg
Distribution % F/R 49/51
Test 2429lb/1103kg

TEST CONDITIONS

Wind	5mph
Temperature	8deg C (47deg F)
Barometer	1017mbar
Surface	dry asphalt/concrete
Test distance	1221 miles

Figures taken at 18,569 miles by our own staff at the Lotus group proving ground, Millbrook.

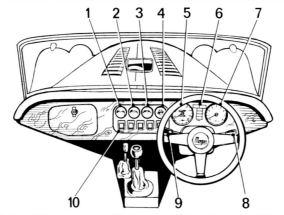

1 Fuel gauge 2 Temperature gauge 3 Oil pressure gauge 4 Voltmeter 5 Speedometer 6 Warning lights 7 Revcounter 8 Horn, main beam dip and flash stalk 9 Windscreen wash/wipe stalk 10 Lights, hazard warning and ancillary switches

◄ 4/4 two-seater with Ford 1.6-litre power. Between this and the Plus 8 comes the Plus 4, powered by Rover's two-litre 16-valve engine and priced from £17,407. Or, more realistically, it will cost £250 as a deposit and a six-year wait.

Fifty-five years ago, the 4/4 came with an 1122cc 34bhp Coventry Climax engine and sold for £194; a full £28 less than an MG TA Midget. These days, any price comparison would be nonsensical — the Morgan is unique — but it can be a fascinating eye-opener to compare the Plus 8's performance figures with those of its more modern counterparts. Not that you need any complex timing equipment to tell you that the Plus 8 is extraordinarily accelerative.

Plant your right boot hard down on the roller-type throttle pedal until it meets the floorboard — yes, it really is wood — and no matter what gear it happens to be in, the Morgan gathers itself up and launches itself at the horizon with an explosive surge of seemingly unstoppable torque.

Porsche 911 Turbo drivers eat your hearts out: for in-gear grunt at normal speeds (in other words, less than 80mph) you won't catch the Morgan. Examine the respective 30-70mph in-gear acceleration times in third, fourth and top gears for these opposite ends of the sports car spectrum and the message comes across loud and clear. The 911 Turbo does it in 7.5, 13.0 and 19.7secs respectively. For Morgan, read 6.0, 8.4 and 12.1secs. An unfair comparison, bearing in mind the 911 Turbo's far superior performance at higher speeds? Not really; they both have to ►

Squeezing behind the wheel isn't easy, but once in place the cockpit feels just right with an upright steering wheel and stubby gear lever close at hand. The 3.9-litre Rover V8 sounds good beneath the long louvred bonnet and provides stunning acceleration, particularly at lower speeds

contend with British roads, and we don't have unlimited speed *autobahnen* over here.

Although the figures show a big improvement in in-gear times compared with the 3.5-litre Plus 8 tested four years ago, the Morgan's top speed remains about the same at a modest 121mph. Acceleration from a standing start has dropped back a little, too. The old car sprinted to 60mph in 5.6secs and to 100mph in 16.4secs. Now, it can't quite break the six-second barrier to 60mph and is two seconds slower to 100mph: figures that the 911 Turbo driver would merely find vaguely amusing.

A fault in the fuel delivery certainly contributed to the disappointingly low top speed, and may also have affected the acceleration times, but by any standards the Plus 8 remains an absurdly quick machine to drive on the road. Most of the time, sufficiently rapid progress can be made without extending the engine beyond about 3000rpm. And that's just

as well; this engine isn't one that feels happy at higher revs and lets the driver know it through the thrummy coarseness that vibrates the whole structure of the car.

Despite the sanitising effect of the catalysts, there's never any doubt that a V8 lies beneath the bonnet — the waffly, slightly uneven exhaust beat sees to that. Yet in this application the muted bellow of the exhaust and the underbonnet intake roar never seem out of place or unacceptably loud.

Even when the car is driven hard, fuel consumption rarely drops below 20mpg. Our overall figure of 20.1mpg reflects a high proportion of hard charging. It takes enormous restraint to drive a Plus 8 any other way. The 14-gallon tank and pessimistic gauge mean fill-ups are far too frequent.

There are specific types of road to which the Morgan seems perfectly suited. Equally, there are others on which it seems hopelessly inadequate. Its intentionally flexible ladder

frame chassis and ash framework, together with short-travel suspension and an axle located by nothing more than a pair of leaf springs, might seem a perverse combination to an engineer in this age of stiff monocoque and precisely controlled all-independent suspension. In theory, the Morgan should handle as though it's hinged in the middle and should rattle like a bag of assorted nails, in spite of changes to soften spring rates and improve damping.

In truth, the Morgan feels tightly assembled even after a high mileage (the test car's odometer was way beyond 18,000 miles), but it only feels truly at home on well-surfaced winding A and B-roads — the sort that would have been the primary routes of the '50s before motorways took over. Here, the Plus 8's suspension isn't taxed beyond its limits and the considerable grip of the Avon Turbospeed tyres can be exploited.

With the hood up, a howling gale scream

Smooth, winding roads are what the Morgan likes best; it feels ill at ease on bumpy roads with its short-travel suspension and flexible chassis. Oversteer can be provoked at the touch of the accelerator – but it all feels quite natural in this car. Quick reactions are essential, but if you can get it right the rewards are great

inches away from your ears and makes fast progress an unpleasant experience, while the buffeting is brutal with the sidescreens tucked away in the only available luggage space behind the seats. Hood down and sidescreens up is the only way to drive a Morgan.

If it's cold, fumble around beneath the dashboard and sooner or later your hand will come into contact with the pull-switch for the heater. It pumps copious quantities of hot air into the footwells, although this can't be directed towards the hands to keep them as well toasted as the feet.

The driving position is just right for sporting motoring and there's room enough for lanky drivers. The wheel is just far enough away for comfort, although it's a little too upright. The gear lever is just a palm's span away. Seated thus, in the far-from-cosseting leather driver's seat, with the bonnet stretching away a furlong or two into the distance, the front wings bobbing gently up

and down over successive road undulations, and a responsive engine burbling away under the bonnet, you quickly begin to understand the appeal of the Plus 8. You can almost feel it straining at the leash.

But this isn't a car you'd want to pamper. Take it by the scruff of the neck and drive. Accelerate hard and the engine responds with a brutal thump to the small of your back. The unservoed brakes are very heavy but up to the job and superbly progressive.

Slice down a couple of cogs and you realise that the clutch needs a big push and the short-throw gear lever a firm, decisive hand. Swing it into a bend and the steering weights up challengingly as you fight against the understeer. Boot the tail out of line on the exit with a whiff of throttle — it seems quite natural with the Morgan — and again, you have to wrestle with the low-geared steering to keep it on the island. And all the time, you feel everything that's happening through the seat of the pants. This isn't a car for wimps. Total involvement is the message here, sheer exuberance the key to its charm.

But that's only one part of the Plus 8's character. Drive a Morgan for an hour or two on the motorway and you would willingly swap it for a clapped-out Capri at the next Road Chef. If it's raining, you might consider hitching a lift as a better alternative. Creature comforts are nil. It's surprisingly watertight with the hood up, but the deafening wind roar makes fitting a radio a pointless exercise, and although the comical triple wipers clear the screen reasonably well, the rest of the windows mist up so badly that every lane change

spells potential suicide. Every road joint is imprinted faithfully on your backside before it jolts your spine yet again.

The Morgan is equally ill at ease on bumpy back roads. This is where shortcomings in the suspension make themselves ever-present. Damping control is poor, particularly at the rear, suspension travel is inadequate and the rear axle hops and leaps across the road at the least provocation; occasionally it even bottoms out completely. Morgan's idea of a progressive bumpstop is when the propshaft comes into contact with the top of the propshaft tunnel.

Add a smattering of rain and the task of keeping it all on line is a precarious balancing act that taxes the quickest of reactions. A restrained throttle is essential, but again it's the Morgan's seat-of-the-pants feel that serves as an invaluable asset to help you to maintain control. Even so, a Peugeot 205 GTi would scuttle away from the Morgan without fear of being caught.

Yet for some, this intimate involvement of man and machine against all the odds is the very essence of why the Morgan remains such a dream machine. It offers a tactile experience entirely absent from the cocooned opulence of so many of today's executive cars. Drive a Morgan quickly and the driver gets a real sense of achievement. It sets the pulse racing.

The Morgan may be a relic of a bygone era — it could even be thought of as an irrelevance in the '90s — but so long as it continues to create the excitement and challenge epitomised by a tidily driven Plus 8, progress can wait as far as a certain red-brick factory in Malvern is concerned. ■

80 years is a long time and yet the chances are that at most weekends of the year you will find at least one example flying the flag somewhere in the country. It may be hillclimbing or trials testing but the chances are that it will be doing what it is best at, and that is track racing.

It has not always been like that of course. In the early years the 3-wheeler Morgans were famous for their trials successes; even as early as 1911 HFS Morgan winning a gold medal in one of his cars on the ACU Six Days' Trial, which was to be the first of a huge number accumulated by the marque over the next 25 years.

It was in the Twenties that the company partially diverted its attention to record-breaking with the likes of Ware, Hawkes, Fernihough, and Lones setting the pace while in 1925 Beart's 1100cc car covered the flying start kilometre at 103.37 mph becoming in the process the first 3-wheeler to be officially timed at over 100 mph. These activities rather compensated for the fact that 3-wheelers were forbidden to take part in car races at Brooklands from 1924-1928.

Even when the first 4-wheeler was produced in 1936, it continued the company's tradition in rallies and trials, George Goodall making the small open-car class of the RAC Rally his own with victories in 1937, 1938 and 1939. This was backed up in that last year before the outbreak of war by HFS Morgan who dominated the closed-car category in the drophead coupé introduced that year.

Track activities were of much less importance to the company despite a win first time out in the 1937 Ulster Trophy driven by R Campbell, a sucess which was backed up by McCracken's win in the Leinster race that year and Campbell's second place at Limerick in 1938. Examples were also raced at Le Mans that year, Miss Fawcett and White coming home in 13th place and White and Anthony 15th a year later.

Even in the Fifties, the Plus Four with the 2088cc Standard Vanguard engine, which superseded the 4/4, was used far more extensively in rallying than for anything else. Outright victory in the 1952 and 1953 London Rallies, the team award on the 1951 RAC Rally, class victories in the Lisbon and Evian-Mont Blanc that year, second place, the team award, the ladies' prize and two class victories in the 1953 MCC Rally, overall victory in the 1954 Scottish and a class win the next year, plus third place on the 1956 RAC Rally backed up by a class win, were just some of the successes achieved by the company's products.

It was not until the turn of that decade that Morgans began to be seen more often on the track, more due to the efforts of Morgan enthusiasts and specialists, in particular Chris Lawrence of Lawrencetune, than due to the company itself.

The results were never as impressive in international racing as they had been in rallying, but second place in its class in the 1961 Spa GP for GT cars, a class victory in

Colin Musgrove puts his Morgan Plus 8 through its paces on a very damp track.

A Breeding Improvement

the Guards Trophy at Brands Hatch, 13th place and first in class in the 1962 Le Mans event and eighth in the TT were nonetheless encouraging. It was at this time, though, that the Morgan was to find its true niche in life, and one in which it has flourished ever since - that of club racer.

There are a number of reasons for its popularity which range from general reliability, the relative ease of tweaking more power out of the engine, and simple mechanicals, to that nostalgic feeling of driving a car from the vintage era with bonnet stretching out ahead of you. It also has a reputation for handling well thanks to its flexible chassis which is stiff across the front and not much roll resistance at the rear which endows the car with a pleasant handling characteristic, especially in fast corners.

Morgans race in several championships ranging from HSCC events to the Morgan club's own championships sponsored this year by the Morgan factory. In the former series they are up against Porsches, Lotus and Caterham 7s, Marcoses etc and fool everyone, especially newcomers, with their competitiveness. It is in their own championship, however, that the gloves come off and those at the serious end of the grid look for that "unfair" advantage. One of those is Colin Musgrove, Morgan specialist, who prepares his own car for Peter Garland to drive.

Such was the competition last year and such was the complexity of the regulations that Garland missed out on the championship by 0.07 of a point. This year, though, the rules have been simplified so that everyone knows what he has to do to win.

Musgrove's car started life as a bog standard 4-speed Plus 8 in 1973, but was rebuilt by Colin Musgrove Racing and developed over the years for racing but at the same time, it was still road registered and legal. This year, though, has seen a major modification which has proved to be

very successful.

"We've taken off the Weber 48 carburettors, which we were running on last year, and replaced them with a Micos injection system to improve torque." The system has been mapped by John Eales of JE Motors, the company which prepared the map of the 4.4s for the works Range Rovers in the Paris-Dakar, Musgrove's car, in fact, using Patrick Tambay's spare Micos system. The cam has been changed from 248 to 256 which gives slightly improved power at higher revs.

"The advantages of fuel injection is that it has colossal tractability, plus the fact that all we wanted to do was make the quantum leap from being one of the best prepared carburettored engines to being the first running with fuel injection. We now have the start, but there is a lot more to come.

It is a complicated system which requires various back-up systems to understand it, so you need an IBM-compatible lap computer so you can actually check the system out. The Micos susyem is very good insofar as it has a jack plug into which a computer is plugged for all the basic readings that are required straightaway "so we can see immediately where there's a mistake in any one of the sensors. Rectifying it is another matter, but at least you can pinpoint where it is."

"The only problem we've had was a chance in a million when one considers that these things reached Dakar from Paris through sand and desert, but when fitted to our car, we had a broken main hall-effect sensor which is the main crankshaft speed sensor." The hall-effect system is the one which actually measures the crankshaft to almost one second of rotational degrees, which it does by forming a square time wave. Instead of having a point going past another point which becomes less accurate the faster it goes, this system actually measures it coming, going and passing, rather like the Doppler effect with a train, so that it is much more accurate.

"At Brands Hatch, at the beginning of the season, it was misfiring in practice, but in the race the thing completely went out. When we took it off the actual magnet, which is rather like a crystaline material, was completely broken and had disappeared."

"The main advantage of the system, apart from the increased torque and tractability, is that we are now at the base of the development of this system as opposed to the limit of the development of the old system. So there's a long way to go with it whereas there wasn't anywhere to go with the previous system."

Is this not an unfair advantage, especially if his is the only car with it? "No, I don't think so. The standard car was fuel injected. The original system we were going to employ was the Weber Alpha system which is available over the counter for £1500, cheaper, almost, than carburettors and manifolds. We bought that, but unfortunately we had some problems with Weber being unable to run at high revs as the spark was breaking down and the ECU was not really compatible for running a high-revving multi-cylinder engine. It's very good on a 4-cylinder engine running to 11,000 rpm but on the V8s, the spark is breaking down between 6200 and 6300 rpm. Weber suggested running two ECUs but that was a bit of a fatuous suggestion," scoffs Musgrove. The engine can now rev to 7200 rpm, the normal rev limit, with another six thousand revs left in the spark box before there is any sign of a spark breakdown.

The advantage of using an engine management system is that the car can run on unleaded fuel and the air/fuel ratio mixture can be programmed over a huge range. On the day Musgrove's car had been mapped to allow a 12 to 1 air/fuel ratio mixture all the way from top to bottom, from 600 to 7000 rpm.

Musgrove maintains that his customers always benefit from his racing activities. "People think it is a nice way to indulge myself in my life-time passion and even get paid for it. But that's not the case as it means that anything we try out on the racing cars are offered on the road-going cars. Development through motor racing, especially at the level we race at, can be passed on to the customer. The brakes, for example, are uprated. There is a good argument to say that the factory spec ones are not good enough for a car of this performance, and the front discs on the Morgan are virtually the same as on an Opel Manta. They are adequate but not brilliant. Our disc brake system is a direct bolt-on replacement for the drum brakes; we think Morgan ought to be using it anyway."

Everything about the car is functional: the dashboard, with a large red oil pressure warning light; the prominent oil temperature gauge; the rev counter, where the first 4000 revs hardly register; the defunct speedometer which has been relocated in front of the passenger's seat; and the lack of leg-room for a passenger due to the installation of the dry sump system.

Rear vision is interrupted by the roll-bar,

The beautifully arranged engine bay with the dry sump system.

while to the front, trumpets peep through the louvred bonnet. To keep the car as close to the deck as possible, the car has a large front skirt which is louvred so that the air can be extracted for greater downforce. In place of the spare wheel at the rear, plumbing for the 10-gallon fuel tank takes up all the available space and includes the external installation of a pump usually found inside most production petrol tanks. This is altogether a functional, but well constructed, machine.

With first gear a dog-leg away on this five-speed gearbox, it takes some getting used to the gearbox, but once mastered, the gears clunk home with a reassuring feel, giving the feeling that if there are any problems on the car, they are unlikely to involve the transmission.

This is a racing machine, so a fairly brutal use of the strong clutch, combined with 4000 rpm on the tachometer, is required to get any kind of getaway from stationary for racing purposes. Normal road driving, however, requires nothing more than a gentle 1200 rpm. It is prepared to amble down the road, obeying every speed limit, never pushing the driver to flout the law. It is, however, rather like the cat that ate the canary. It takes only a small prod of the throttle to realise that there is something very special about this car, that there is something not quite normal under the bonnet. It is an exhilarating experience opening up the throttle. The car leaps forward, the back tyres scrabbling for grip, but the BF Goodrich tyres hardly complain. Such is the power of the engine that even in

No room for a spare wheel on this Morgan because of all the extra plumbing required.

a straight line you can induce wheelspin without too much trouble, which can make life very interesting when pressing on along twisty and bumpy country lanes. The Musgrove brakes, however, offer some sort of compensation in their effectiveness, although even here one has to be careful in their application lest the tail begins to slip out of line.

As is to be expected, the ride is quite hard but a great improvement on the standard model, although the dampers on Musgrove's car can be adjusted for road or track use. The car can get caught out when steaming through a bumpy corner, some understeer snapping into sudden oversteer at the limit, but that is only likely to happen on the race track. The over-riding memory of the car, however, is that rorty, powerful V8, wailing through the gears up to the rev limiter, begging to be abused, daring you to take it nearer the limit, but one that demands respect.

After the disappointment of the opening race at Brands Hatch, the season started to improve. A second place at Donington, where they beat the lap record by some two seconds, and a win and fastest lap at Pembrey in the Morgan championship, another victory (by 57 seconds) and fastest lap in the Morgan Club's 40th anniversary race all stand testimony to the car's competitiveness and preparation. The greatest thrill for the team this year, however, was the poleman's award they won in July at Donington for winning pole by the greatest margin. What put the icing on the cake for Colin Musgrove was the fact that they were presented the trophy by the Managing Director of Securicor in front of 35,000 people and had beaten the British Touring Car teams to it. They then went on to win the race by 40 seconds.

This is undoubtedly one of the fastest Morgans still suitable for the road around at the moment. The fact that it is winning races wherever it appears and the fact that all the feedback from its racing activities are finding their way onto those cars which go through Musgrove's hands, are a couple of very good reasons why Musgrove should continue racing — and not be accused of letting others pay for his hobby!

WPK

MAGNIFICENT MORGAN

Tony Dron races a state-of-the-art Plus 8 and finds
upholding Morgan honour is hard work but rewarding

Above, it looks almost like any other Morgan but opening the throttle releases almost twice the horsepower of a standard Plus 8, with immense torque

Right, Morgan maestro Musgrove gives our Editor a few words of advice before the race: "Just remember we've won this event for the last two years." Gulp!

Below, Avon racing slicks were fitted for the Morris Stapleton Trophy race

Photography: Maurice Rowe

NO other car handles quite like a Morgan: technically, the cars from Malvern may seem to be quite primitive but you should never under-estimate a Morgan, as a long line of disappointed would-be rival manufacturers will testify! This inimitable traditional sports car has always possessed its own traits but when the going gets tough the opposition can be surprised to find that the old Morgan is still in there pitching hard, despite its latter-day Vintage looks and those constantly mentioned clichés of Malvern tradition, its 1910 pillar front suspension and its live rear axle. Maybe it's something to do with its Thirties trials background but a Plus 8 even goes well in snow as Charles Morgan, grandson of founder H F S Morgan, has repeatedly proved in winter Historic events in recent years. Tough but flexible, dogged but adaptable, the Morgan is rather like its human devotees in character.

Colin Musgrove's state-of-the-art racing Plus 8 is no different in character from any other Morgan – it is simply very, very quick, another piece of the jigsaw which has seen the constant development of the marque since Morgan turned to production four-wheelers way back in 1936. Weighing in at 900kg, with 360bhp on

MAGNIFICENT MORGAN

"... the two red Morgans in close formation ..."

tap, sees to that and the fact that it dates from 1974 is neither here nor there; in the factory, they are all too aware of the constant development that goes on but to the world at large the marque remains timeless. After all, what's a couple of decades in Morgan terms?

I had one go at racing this car at Snetterton earlier this year; in practice my 6ft 5in frame stuck out into the airflow so much that it was agony taking the full force of it on my neck and chest. Drastic modifications to the seat got me down inside it and, by dropping the clutch at 4,000rpm, a lucky guess, I got a great start from the front row of the grid. As I approached the first corner, in third gear and glancing in the mirror, it was clear that I already had a surprising lead; I just had time to think that I don't mind easy wins, then the throttle cable broke, so that was that. For that race the Musgrove Morgan was on road tyres, BF Goodrich R1s which I know well from several seasons of Porsche racing, and it felt very well sorted even if it was quite hard work to drive.

Colin was clearly irritated that his pride and joy had been let down by someone else's faulty work on the throttle cable; he puts a remarkable effort into keeping his Morgan racer on top and this was a very silly failure in an otherwise immaculately prepared car. So he invited me to drive it again, at Silverstone in August in the Morris Stapleton Trophy Race: "Mind you, it's the most prestigious Morgan race of the year and we have won it for the past two years," Well, who doesn't enjoy a sense of occasion? All right, but the sense of responsibility it carried began to weigh heavily!

There's a lot to learn in a very short space of time when you're going to race a car just once but at least this time I had driven the Morgan in a 15-minute practice session earlier in the year and I had the luxury of a test session the day before this race, the only trouble being that it was wet; good fun, but it didn't tell me much.

On race day, regular driver Peter Garland would drive the car in the Morgan Motor Company championship race, Class A of which he was then leading and has since won. Then it would be changed to slick racing tyres and I would drive it in the Morris Stapleton Trophy race, after which it would be left on slicks for Peter to drive again in the Allcomers Scratch race in this Bentley Drivers Club meeting.

Peter claimed pole position for his race; an hour later, in my official practice, I was alarmed to find that the very full grid contained cars of widely varying performance; the entire 20 minutes seemed to be spent steering round slower cars, which meant that I never had a full lap on the racing line, but it was the same for everybody and I was surprised to find that I had got pole by 1.6secs with a time of 1m 6secs, an average speed of 89.9mph.

This Morgan's performance calls for purple prose; it just thunders down the straights like a rocket, leaving racing AC Cobras in its wake as Peter Garland was to prove in the last race of the day. The engine in this car is basically the standard Morgan Rover V8 which is bored out to 3.9 litres but in this case is fully race-prepared, including Micos fuel injection with an incredible electronic management system which was mapped out by famous engine specialist John Eales.

You need a computer to understand and adjust the system which apparently measures the crankshaft

tion in some manner along the lines
the Doppler effect; it has things like
ll-effect sensors', whatever they
y be, and the engine map can be
presented by yards of paper, which
all demon stuff. Colin Musgrove has
t the hang of it but to someone like
e, who understands good old Lucas
tributors and Weber carburettors
ite well, it is utterly mystifying
hnically.
One effect of all this wizardry is to
oduce the most amazing near-flat

torque curve, making the engine pull
like a train from 3,000rpm right up to
7,600rpm, a fact which paradoxically
nearly caught me out in the race, but
we'll come to that!

All Morgans stop well and the
Musgrove car, with its big ventilated
discs, is extra good under braking. The
Getrag five-speed gearbox takes a bit
of getting used to at speed, probably
because the driver is being thrown
around inside this violent and exciting
machine, but the 'box feels

everlastingly tough. Heavy steering
adds to the driver's workload and I felt
that although the car and I might have
beaten the opposition to pole, the car
was going to wear out this driver long
before I did it any damage!

It puts up a really physical wrestling
match when you get it going properly,
but it is still pure Morgan at heart;
push too fast into a corner and it
understeers severely, losing any
chance of a decent lap time as it tries
to run straight ahead. Get the entry

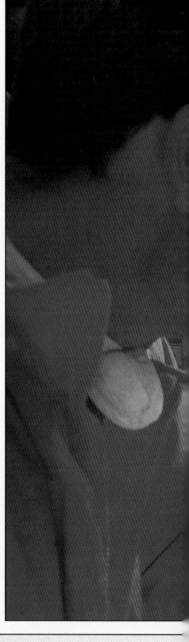

MAGNIFICENT MORGAN

speed right for the corners and you can feed in the power, releasing awesome forces that have the tail wriggling and hopping. You need to beat the heavy steering with considerable muscle-power, yet without losing your accuracy in the quick application of opposite lock. It's a demanding car, all right, but if you get all this right it does leave the corners very quickly.

Alongside me on the front row of the grid were none other than Peter Garland himself, driving his own Plus 8, and Matthew Wurr in another similar car, though neither of them had the sophisticated Micos injection. Behind us, there was the fine sight of a gridful of Malvern machinery of all ages and specifications.

At Snetterton I had got a fabulous start on the road tyres, using 4,000rpm. With more grip from these slicks I tried 4,500rpm when the Union Jack fell – yes, this was the Bentley Drivers Club and we had the nostalgic experience of a flag start rather than lights. My start was no more than reasonable this time and I got a bit too much wheelspin, so both Peter and Matthew just beat me away from the line; still, I had the inside line and all the way down the straight

" . . . a red car sitting close in my mirrors all the way . . . "

five and he was still right there on my bumper . . . it was turning into hard work.

Next time, out of the tight right at Luffield which leads onto the main straight, Matthew came up on the inside and simply out-accelerated me into the lead. We crossed the start/finish line, normally a gentle sweep but made into a real corner by these fearsome machines, with the two red Morgans in close formation. This was exciting wheel-to-wheel racing and I had to think quickly: fortunately I was still close enough to slip back into the lead under braking for the next corner, Copse.

Unwittingly, Matthew had revealed a vital secret: the Musgrove Morgan, with its immense torque, had felt fine through the Brooklands/Luffield complex of corners in third gear but, I asked myself, how come he had out-accelerated me? The answer was obvious: he had to be using second gear in the complex while I was in third. And that was it, there was a basic error in my programme: the

Above, keeping the accelerating projectile aimed the right way in corners needs strong, fast muscles

I was alongside Peter's rear wheel which enabled me to slip into the fourth gear right-hander at Copse ahead of the field.,Very soon, Peter dropped out of the picture; he had left his oil filler cap open and by the time he had stopped and worked out where the smoke was coming from the race was over.

On that first lap, it occurred to me that with nearly two seconds a lap advantage in practice over everyone else, this race should have been easy, but there was a red car sitting close in my mirrors all the way. Matthew Wurr must have found a demon set of slicks like those on the Musgrove car! I pressed on, getting down to 1m 5.6secs on lap five – half distance – but Matthew also did 1m 5.6secs on lap

SPECIFICATIONS

	Standard Plus 8	43 MOG
Capacity	3,942cc	3,942cc
Heads	Standard	Big valve, fully ported
Block	Standard	Cross bolted
Rods	Standard	Cosworth steel
Crank	Standard	TWR X-drilled electron aligned
Pistons	Standard	Omega forged
Lubrication	Wet sump	Dry sump
Induction	Lucas plenum injection	Weber throttle body injection
Electronics	Lucas hot wire	Micos engine management
Sparks	Standard coil	Lucas hall-effect
Clutch	Standard	Sintered metal 4-paddle
Gearbox	Rover std 5-speed	Getrag Race 5-speed (direct 5th)
Propshaft	Morgan	TWR Vitesse shortened
Axle	Salisbury 7HA	Salisbury 4HA (ex-Scimitar)
Suspension – Front	Sliding pillar	Sliding pillar, reaction rods
– Rear	Leaf spring & U-bolt	CMR trailing link with coil-overs, Panhard rod, anti-tramp
Brakes – Front	11in solid 2-pot	13in vented & X-drilled 4-pot AP racing
– Rear	Drums	11in vented 2-pot AP racing
Master Cylinder	Std integral	Twin with adjustable bias
Steering	Rack and pinion	Gemmer recirculating ball
Coachwork	Alloy/steel over ash frame	Alloy over ash frame
Wings	Alloy or steel	GRP
Chassis	Standard Morgan	Standard Morgan
Wheels	6.5in mag alloy all round	Front: 8in alloy Speed & Design
		Rear: 9.5in alloy Speed & Design
Camber	1/2° negative	1.5° negative
Power	200bhp @ 5,000rpm	360bhp @ 7,500rpm

Above, Colin Musgrove, in cap, discussing his car with the Editor after practice at Silverstone

"... a great day for all the Morgan enthusiasts ..."

same argument held true at Becketts and I managed to recover a comfortable lead of around two seconds.

There were no more quick laps as by this stage we were lapping backmarkers, but Colin Musgrove Racing got the honours once again in the Morris Stapleton Trophy race, much to my relief! Had Matthew simply sat behind me right through to the last corner of the race before making his move, he might have won, but luckily for me he gave the game away and I was able to pick up that all-important little tip which I had missed up to that point through my inexperience of the car.

As Peter had won the Tony Morgan-Tipp Memorial Race, a round of the Morgan Motor Company Challenge Race Series, it was a great day for Colin Musgrove Racing. It was in truth a great day for all the Morgan enthusiasts at Silverstone: they are an open-hearted, friendly gang of real people. Tony Morgan-Tipp, a Chartered Surveyor whose Plus 8 racer was track-tested in *Classic Cars* in 1988 (page 104, January issue), was very much a Morgan man – driving his racing Plus 8 to meetings on the road. He was tragically killed in a very unlucky road accident but his mother was at Silverstone to present the Morgan awards.

After that, only the Allcomers' Scratch Race remained and this has to be recorded as Matthew Wurr's well-deserved moment of glory; on pole

from Andy Shepherd's AC Cobra MkII, Matthew faced the threat of Peter Garland starting from the back of the grid (because of an administrative cock-up: Peter had been quickest in practice), so an exciting race was in store. The front row of the grid was completed by Big Sam, the 1974 Datsun 240Z originally raced by Win Percy: discovered and restored for owner Nick Howell by Tim Riley. I was invited to drive it in this race but that rebuild and race are for next month's issue of *Classic Cars*. Peter drove a storming race through the field but just lost out to a very on-form Matthew in this last event of the day, which had the Morgan fans right up on their toes.

FIRST DRIVE

Given a little rain now and again, an Arizona desert can be dense with cacti of all sorts. The big ones are saguaros.

PHOTOS BY DOROTHY CLENDENIN

Morgan Plus 8
Another technical coup for Malvern Link!

BY DENNIS SIMANAITIS

IT'S NOT EASY being the Morganite here at R&T. For years I had to put up with "cookout" jokes, what with Morgan U.S. agent Bill Fink sensibly converting his cars to propane to avoid all the EPA hassles of dirty old gasoline.

Now, after considerable development work, comes something quite different from Bill's Isis Imports (P.O. Box 2290, U.S. Customs House, San Francisco, Calif. 94126; [415] 433-1344); namely, a gasoline-fueled Plus 8. And what do I hear around here?

"Isn't it just like Morgan? Everyone else is plunging headlong into alternative fuels—and Morgan goes gasoline."

Not inappropriately, however: Like Belgian ash body structure and sliding-pillar front suspension, there's something quite traditional these days about gasoline as a motor fuel.

For the unenlightened (if, in fact, any of you have actually been able to duck my Morgan proselytizing), these products of Pickersleigh Road, Malvern

Link, Worcester, are wonderfully traditional English sports cars, built with few significant changes since 1936. That was the year when founder H.F.S. Morgan sensed that his 3-wheeler business, going strong since 1910, might profit from something new in the catalog with an additional wheel back there. Just to cover his bets, though, he kept the trike in production until 1952.

The Plus 8 is the most potent of current Moggies, with power provided by the Rover (nee Buick) 3.9-liter V-8.

And, as I've already implied, gone are the days of frantically searching out the local propane supplier before he went home to fire up his own backyard barbecue.

This time around, photographer, adventuress, pal and spouse Dorothy Clendenin and I traveled some 1000 miles through Arizona with nary a refueling fear. The reason for this drive was the Second Annual Copperstate 1000, an old-car tour held in benefit of the Phoenix Art Museum. (See "Moggin'

Our rolling car museum visits the copper-rich region of Bisbee. The Frazer Nash, immediately behind Moggie, beat us by a chain length.

Along the Mogollon Rim," November 1991, to read about the inaugural event.) True, our Isis Imports Plus 8 was a 1992 model, but Copperstate organizers graciously invoke a Great Grandfather Clause for any Morgan.

So what is the attraction of misting yourselves with spray bottles of water to promote evaporative cooling and postpone sunstroke as you take a classic open sports car across blazing desert in unseasonable 105-degree heat?

For one thing, a navigator who's passed out does you damned little good through the timed regularity section. And, for another, it wasn't *all* blazing desert. For instance, an entertaining run 12 miles up the twisties to Kitt Peak National Observatory gave us a view you wouldn't believe. The Plus 8 handled the climb with aplomb, never once probing the upper reaches of its temperature gauge. Indeed, cars as varied as Jerry and Barbara Riegel's stylish 1929 duPont Model G, Ed Henning's Devin SS and Arizona friend Ned Curtis' 1935 Frazer Nash Colmar made it as well. In fact, "Captain Archie," as Ned calls his car, maintained a brisk pace throughout.

Generally, I would say, the marvelous collection of cars on Copperstate II was less challenged by the extreme heat than were their nonetheless enthusiastic occupants. And I'd guess that, once re-freshed, whole passels of these perfectly normal people will be back next year for Copperstate III (whose information number, by the way, is [602] 952-0380).

Certainly the Morgan thrived on it all, its torquey V-8 burbling along with a decidedly modern note; its long, louvered bonnet bobbing this way and that, thus establishing a proper vintage aura.

On smooth roads, the Morgan's classic sliding pillars at the front and leaf-spring live axle at the rear give predictable, flat cornering. This, some say, because Morgan springs are so stiff that only the car's limber frame actually deflects. And, true, on bumpy roads there is a certain 4-point hydroplane feel.

Brakes are disc front/drum rear, without vacuum boost. Thus the brake pedal is a heavy one, but honest and straightforward in its modulation.

Steering seems a concession to modernity, an easy and accurate rack-and-pinion system having replaced that hair-shouldered duo, Cam and Peg. Truth is, the company that produced this earlier steering gear found it uneconomic to continue supplying Morgan's tiny numbers.

It was a similar occurrence in 1953 that caused the demise of flat-radiator Morgans. Malvern could still produce the radiator and cowl, but its supplier of classic headlamps couldn't comply.

Anyway, Morgan is doing just fine in 1992, thank you. Bill sells perhaps two dozen cars a year, mostly Plus 8s these days, though the Ford-engined 4/4 is still available, still propane-fueled. Prices reflect a lot of handwork on either side of the Atlantic, $50,000 for the Plus 8; $35,000 for the 4/4. And loads of character is part of Morgan standard equipment. It always has been.

For part of the run, Dottie swapped places with Copperstate chairman Brad Bayse. He sampled some vintage motoring; between photo ops, she savored the air conditioning of a Mercedes-Benz (one of the event's sponsors).

Morgan 4/4 1800
Gavin Conway reports

Don't get me wrong; I'm no tweed-brained Jolly Ho type that gets all stiff upper lippy at the sight of some copper-wired disaster posing as a sports car. I've been called a cynic on occasion and I won't deny looking somewhat askance at the reverence in which truly awful cars are held simply because they have wire wheels and running boards.

And I had supposed that a Morgan 4/4 1800, even with Ford's Zetec engine, would hardly be the tool to beat down my cynicism.

I'd gone 500 miles that day, top down, leather cap and goggles fitted for survival against a bitter Welsh wind. It was late, very late indeed, and I was a long way from home. A full moon looked over my shoulder, playing fantastic tricks with the light rippling across a silvery reservoir. The green and red glow of the dash lights reflected in my goggles and Glenn Miller played big band tunes in my head, crackling and popping like an old tube radio.

The Morgan's long, beautifully vented bonnet bobbled along at 85mph, chassis talking back like an air raid siren. Elbows flailing, sawing at the wheel with a little more enthusiasm than was really called for, another corner four-wheel

Once you get used to it, the 4/4 isn't just fun — it's wizard

drifted through the dark, another straight taken flat. I felt heroic, a real driver in a real car, against the weather and against kick-back steering and handling that demands respect. Hunched over the wheel, I imagined myself in newsreel film, wheels all oblong with speed, dust rooster-tailing, everything in grainy black and white.

"It has faults of omission and commission as seen through eyes accustomed to the entirely modern plan of car," said an *Autocar* road test of a Morgan Plus 4 that, staggeringly, was written nearly half a century ago. A 'modern' Morgan still shares much of the 'old' car's technical heritage.

A new Morgan is in effect a brand new antique. Not a replica, not some glass-fibre retrobody on new mechanicals and not some cynical recall — read MG RV8 — of a past and much-loved design.

It has the heritage and history of an old crock, but it will start on a cold morning and won't strand you in the middle of nowhere; try that in your Singer Nine, Mr Tweed.

Try as they might, though, there is one area where Morgan's anti-development engineers have failed to halt the insidious march of progress; Morgans have always borrowed their drivetrains from more modern kit, and the latest high-tech lump to find its way under Britain's prettiest bonnet is Ford's 16-valve 1.8-litre Zetec engine.

Once the XR3i engine has recovered from the shock of its antiquated surroundings, it settles down to produce 121bhp at 6000rpm and an axle-hopping 115lb ft of torque.

The Morgan is a relatively light car, weighing in at just 840kg (1850lb), so the Zetec engine has an easy job of it. To use the words of that same road test, "it gets up very quickly indeed". Spiffing, I'd say.

The 0-60mph sprint takes 7.8sec and the stout-hearted Morgan will hang on until 111mph. Leave the stick in third gear and the 4/4 will race from 50 to 70mph in 5.2sec. Not slow by anyone's measure.

You'll need to be a bit careful when really pressing the Morgan, though; in a perverse attempt to give the Zetec a little old-world retro feel, there is no rev limiter. It isn't that much of a problem, though; once the revcounter passes 6000rpm the noise and vibration soon tell you to ease off.

So the Morgan has plenty of performance, and the five-speed Ford gearbox is slick enough, although shorter throws (and a shorter gear lever) would be useful.

Handling? Well, now, that's another bag of snakes.

Drive the Morgan a few miles and you might well emerge appalled at the flexing chassis, the bounce-you-off-line suspension and the bus-sized steering wheel controlling steering that is just a little less than eager to centre. Just think, the Morgan is still suspended on a solid rear axle with leaf springs at the rear and sliding pillar front suspension; the body is still hung on an ash frame.

But this is the thing: the Morgan is by its own admission an antique and the way it goes down the road largely reflects that. If you can accept that, you've got a driving experience that is endearing and, with patience, an absolute blast.

It takes a while, but drive the

Ford's 16-valver from XR3i

Morgan a few more miles and you'll discover that those initially frightening responses are actually quite predictable, that the engine has just the right amount of power for getting the tail out, that initial understeer turns gently into oversteer and that the most glorious four-wheel drifts are easy and secure on the narrow 165 SR15 tyres.

Every time the Caterham Super 7's side pipe barked back at me, I knew the tiny roadster — a supercar compared to the Morgan — was about to explode into the distance. I also knew my colleague wasn't trying very hard, but we were both surprised at the Morgan's ability. And boy does that chassis communicate, yapping away like Ruby Wax, telling you things you'd rather not ▶

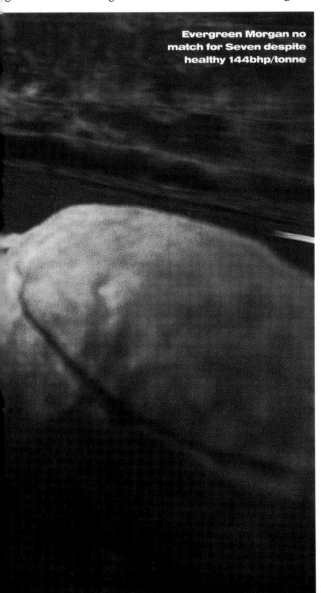

Evergreen Morgan no match for Seven despite healthy 144bhp/tonne

Factfile

Morgan 4/4 1800

How fast?

Acceleration from rest

Mph	sec
30	2.7
40	4.1
50	5.7
60	7.8
70	10.4
80	13.6
90	18.3
100	25.4

Max speed	111mph
30-70	7.7sec
1/4 mile	16.1sec
Standing kilometre	30.0sec

Acceleration in each gear (sec)

mph	top	4th	3rd	2nd
10-30	–	–	5.5	3.1
20-40	–	6.9	5.1	3.1
30-50	10.3	7.4	5.1	3.1
40-60	10.7	7.6	5.2	–
50-70	12.0	8.2	5.2	–
60-80	14.9	8.8	5.9	–
70-90	19.4	9.9	–	–
80-100	–	14.1	–	–

How much?

£16,256 **On sale in UK** now

Fuel consumption

Overall mpg on test	25.5
Best/worst on test	28.3/19.4
Touring	28.3
Range	311 miles

Weight (claimed)	840kg (1850lb)
Fuel tank	50 litres (11 gall)

Engine

Max power 121bhp/6000rpm
Max torque 115lb ft/4500rpm
Specific output 67bhp/litre
Power to weight 144bhp/tonne
Installation front, longitudinal, rwd
Capacity 1796cc, four cyl in line
Made of alloy head, iron block
Bore/stroke 80mm/88mm
Compression ratio 10.1:1
Valves 4 per cyl, dohc
Ignition and fuel electronic ignition
and Bosch indirect fuel injection

Gearbox

Type 5-speed manual
Ratios/mph per 1000rpm
1st 3.89/4.75 **2nd** 2.08/8.9
3rd 1.34/13.8 **4th** 1.0/18.5
5th 0.82/22.5 **Final drive ratio** 4.1:1

Suspension

Front independent with sliding
pillars and dampers
Rear solid axle, leaf springs,
gas dampers

Steering

Type rack and pinion
Lock to lock 2.7 turns

Brakes

Front 280mm discs
Rear 228mm drums
Anti-lock n/a

Wheels and tyres

Size 6x15in **Made of** steel
Tyres Uniroyale Rallye 165 SR15
Spare full size

Made and sold by

Morgan Motor Co, Pickersleigh Rd,
Malvern Link, Worcs WR14 2LL.
Tel: 0684 573104

◀ know about the road surface. And somewhere in all that cacaphony there are messages that will get you around that next corner in one piece.

Drive the Morgan really hard and it is almost possible to forget the ride quality, concentrating as you are on the non-stop chassis monologue. It is, to put it mildly, a very firm ride. Bloody unpleasant on bad surfaces, actually.

The environment inside the Morgan is convincingly retro, too. The huge, upright steering wheel is just over an inch from the dash with an equally upright driving position, and you'll find little lateral support in the seats.

The fit and finish of the thing is also superb, reflecting the fact that it is still largely hand built in a factory that would be Santa's workshop if it didn't happen to be producing Morgans. And that little fly-off handbrake is just plain cute.

Two up, the Morgan is a cosy affair, but there isn't much in the way of luggage space; a little shelf behind the seats and that's all.

Some of the younger bloods at Morgan have been overheard muttering about fully independent suspension and, believe it or not, aluminium honeycomb structures as a potential way forward for the Morgan. The old boys down on the shop floor, the ones who actually build the cars, shake their heads and smile as if to say: "No, sir, not in my lifetime." Anti-lock brakes? When hell freezes over. Maybe.

The cynics can whinge about the Morgan's antiquity all they like, but the fact is that Morgan has six years' worth of orders to satisfy; there are obviously an awful lot of folks willing to wait a long while for the privilege.

Half a century ago, *Autocar* staffer Montagu Tombs had his own idea about the Morgan appeal. "It isn't difficult to believe that owners of such cars will become very fond of them because of their fundamentally honest outlook and achievements." Amen, Montagu.

FIRST DRIVE

UNLIKE MG, TRIUMPH, Austin-Healey and Sunbeam, whose management simply rolled over and played dead in the face of changing American tastes and regulations during the Sixties and Seventies, Morgan maintained the commitment the other British manufacturers had lost.

Although the rest are just a memory in America, Morgan still lives and every one of the 30-odd cars that the company sends across the Atlantic each year gets fully street-legal.

That's the good news. The better news is that it's going to stay that way: Through the good works of Isis Imports' Bill Fink, Morgan's San Francisco-based agent, and lots of others, these wonderfully vintage cars will soon have driver and passenger airbags.

Morgan knew that the installation of airbags in its ash-framed cars was going to be a difficult task. Proving that the installation would work would be even more difficult, so the company called on Britain's Motor Industry Research Association (MIRA) to see if it could help.

The thing that the MIRA team leader, Dr. Viv Stephens, found most attractive about Morgan was its adaptability. Prototype parts were turned around by the Malvern craftsmen in less time than bigger manufacturers would need to complete the paperwork to set the work in motion.

Although MIRA was "incredibly realistic about costing," as Charles Morgan describes it, the organization used some of its most modern facilities for the exercise. First it ran computer simulations to check the physical limitations of the Morgan cockpit. Then more computer work found suitable bag installations and monitored their theoretical behavior and the way in which

Morgan 4/4 1800
The Moggie gets airbags
BY IAN NORRIS

they would interact with the sports-car's steel chassis and traditional ash-framed aluminum or steel body. Once the right package was found, physical tests were carried out on a Morgan buck.

The final system to be fitted to the Morgans will comprise full-size driver and passenger bags and a knee bolster on the passenger side. Fitting the passenger airbag into the Morgan's dash behind a hinged wooden cover means that none of the traditional appeal will be lost, while the new steering column with airbag will be welcomed by taller drivers, who find current Morgans a little constrained in the leg-room department. And I was very pleased to hear that plans are afoot to rearrange the body behind the seats to give an extra inch or two on the seat runners.

Taking advantage of the massive research-and-development money Ford spent on the Mondeo, Morgan now offers the 4/4 with the brand-new 1796-cc Ford Zetec engine, which produces 121 bhp at a free-revving 6000 rpm. Environmentally friendly, fuel efficient, and with spares available across the world, the Zetec (originally known during development and in these pages as the Zeta) is an ideal power unit for Morgan, which has always counted mechanical simplicity among its virtues.

It says much for the 4/4 that the pleasures of driving it overcame the initial impression—with the top up in bad weather, the view from behind the wheel for a 6-ft. 4-in. driver is somewhat akin to driving an ill-fitting ski mask. Switching on the triple windshield wipers does little to dispel the misgivings, although the mini-XKE setup does a fine job of clearing the screen. However, when you engage a gear and move off, the unique appeal of the car comes through.

Comparing a Morgan to any modern automobile is a waste of effort. The antiquated sliding pillar front and live rear suspension design may score poorly on today's noise, vibration and harshness tests, but sit low in the 4/4, feeling the wheels' interaction with the road so close beneath you, and you'll comprehend in an instant what "seat-of-the-pants" driving is all about.

As for potential Morgan owners in the U.S., don't worry. You can place an order for a 4/4 1800 now and know that when the car is delivered—which can take up to six years—it will have full airbags and be as legal as anything built at home.

THAT RIVIERA FEELING

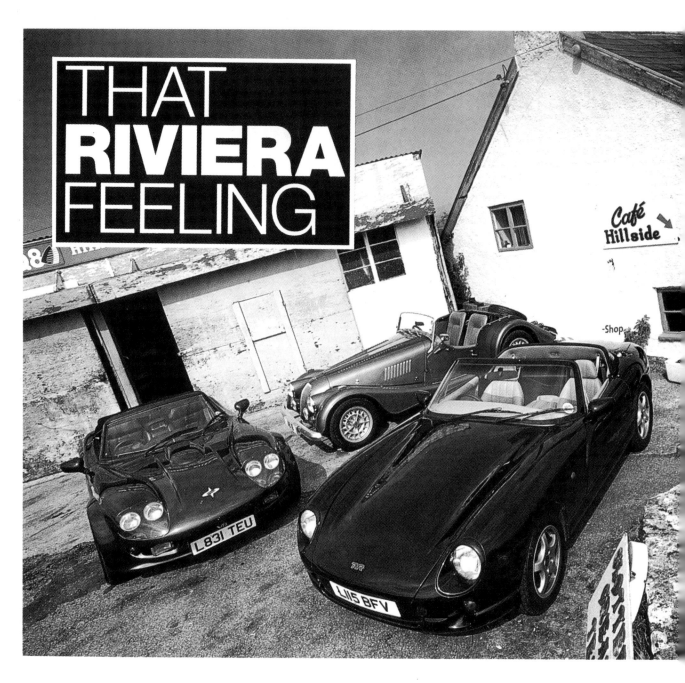

Café Hillside →

-Shop

If you look very closely to the right of the picture above, you can see the reason why Tom spent so much time complaining about how difficult it is to get in and out of these cars; he's photographed here tucking into his 37th fruit scone with a large dollop of clotted cream and strawberry jam. The interiors of our cars, (right, left to right) once we'd levered Tom into them, were very different. The Marcos is sporty but walnut-trimmed, the Morgan highly traditional, with a big, thin-rimmed wheel, and the TVR sort of '80s modern

The three of us are driving west in line astern, and there's no more dual carriageway for a few miles. The trouble is, progress is being hindered by a removals van belching diesel fumes directly into my sun-drenched, leather-clad cockpit. Clearly, something has to be done.

With nearly four litres of V8 muscle throbbing beneath the bonnet, overtaking in this light-weight two-seater shouldn't be a problem. But heading south-west, the A303 tightens and twists a little more after the wide open stretches of Salisbury plain, so finding a suitable place to pass invariably requires true commitment coupled with absolute readiness to act decisively when the way ahead is clear.

But this is all part of the fun. With the roof down, the engines and exhausts provide an almost salacious thrill. Hanging back from the van a little bit further than you would in an ordinary motor is advisable because, if you're not watchful, this car will catapult you straight into the back of the obstacle before you've managed to pull out into the oncoming lane.

Now I can see a small gap ahead. Sure, there's something coming a little way off, but this is my opportunity. I floor the throttle and tug the wheel delicately to the right, swiftly change up, tug the wheel back to the left and I'm past. The air is fresh again, the road is clear and I'm still accelerating hard.

This isn't work, it's cracking recreation. It's a Tuesday morning, Spring is in the air and we're driving down to Devon – more specifically, the 'English Riviera' – for a diet of incorrect food and drink. For a blast. The traffic is light, and the car? Well, it could easily have been any one of three but, for the record, I was in a Marcos Mantara Spyder at the time.

Big fun was also on tap in the other two, for, like the Mantara, the Morgan Plus Eight and TVR Chimaera use 3.9-litre Rover V8 power.

I'd started off this trip a few days earlier by driving the Morgan away from the factory in Malvern, down to the home of Marcos in Westbury, Wilts. From there, we would bundle the pair back down the M4 to rendezvous with the TVR in London. The weather wasn't up to much – grey cloud formed a giant blanket across the sky and the temperature was definitely on the cool side of comfortable.

I learnt quickly that the clutch pedal on this Plus 8 required delicate control for a smooth take-off, but other than that, my main concern was whether the weather would brighten up enough to get the hood down.

It didn't – but I took it down anyway, because driving a Morgan with the hood up is like making love with, er... swimming with wellies on. Although visibility is OK, you feel cocooned, and anyone prone to claustrophobia will feel as though they've been stuffed into a tiny canvas-and-leather-lined letterbox. But to hell with the weather, this is real motoring.

Apart from a few modern marvels like electronic ignition, fuel injection, a catalytic converter and disc brakes, Morgans are put together in the traditional way, using coachbuilding techniques that were common in the 1930s. This, as any driver who is old enough to remember will tell you, was The Golden Age, and no other car in current manufacture can replicate the thrill of this bygone era so convincingly.

With 188bhp and bottom-end torque by the barrel load, the Plus Eight demands and rewards full attention from its driver.

I've already mentioned the tricky clutch, but other major controls also warrant a brief description. The brakes – discs at the front, drums at the rear – aren't servo-assisted and at first they feel as though they may not be quite up to the job. Unless you're a size 14, your heel has to be off the floor to get good purchase on the pedal and at lower speeds, the feel is a bit wooden. The gearstick needs a firm hand, and a blend of strength and technique to get it into reverse first time (though the most recent cars have a revised gearbox with a lighter action).

The steering will be completely foreign to anyone familiar only with anodyne saloons. The wheel itself is close to your chest and, although there's no power assistance, it's not too heavy. But all the same, corners are better negotiated by having both hands firmly on the wheel, backed up by positive steering inputs going into, through and exiting a turn.

At normal speeds none of this is overly demanding on the driver. The suspension is firm, transmits bumps through to the chassis, and is manifested most noticeably in the long, louvred bonnet bouncing about in front of you. But after an hour or so at the wheel, the Morgan's idiosyncratic behaviour becomes not just tolerable, but darned good fun. The brakes prove to be strong and progressive, the steering comes alive in your hands and grip is good. The chassis rewards smooth considered driving.

By the time we had collected the Marcos and tanked up with fuel, there was little time left to delight in Wiltshire's A-roads. With even dodgier weather on the horizon, I piled on many layers of clothing and pointed the Morgan towards the M4 and London.

On a modern motorway the Plus 8 looks like

a fish out of water, but with its lusty 3.9-litre V8 burbling away at little more than tickover at 70mph, you don't feel particularly out of place. With no radio fitted, there's little to do but listen to the muted burble of the exhaust, occasionally check that the heater knob is still pulled out to its full-on position and sit there comfortably, thinking of England.

Coming into London, I was frustrated by the usual traffic jam running from Heston services to Hammersmith, but also entertained by the antics of a couple of Japanese businessmen, who caught sight of me crawling alongside them in the drizzle, gesticulating frantically with their noses pressed hard to the window as though they had just caught sight of Princess Di rollerblading topless.

The Marcos is a very different tool to the Morgan. Designed like some sort of Gerry Anderson-created high speed pursuit vehicle that's just rolled down a ramp from the belly of Thunderbird Two, the Mantara is low, sleek and seriously aggressive-looking. In fact, with Marcos' Stage One engine conversion bumping horsepower up to 230bhp, it's more than aggressive – it's perfectly pugnacious.

The Mantara was to provide my seat for our trip down to the 'Riviera', but you don't so much sit in it as lie back in it. The seats are an immovable part of the body and, although the factory will tailor the seating position to meet the needs of each individual owner, there are also electrically-operated adjustable pedals to fine-tune the driving position.

The Mantara's interior can accurately be described as either cosy or cramped, depending on your size. There's an enormous transmission tunnel to nestle up to on one side and the door to bang up against on the other. The top of the low-raked windscreen frame also seemed perilously close to my forehead, and the all-too-cosy cockpit environment gets even more so when the hood is up.

Fortunately, by the time we'd finished with the drudgery of the M3 and were out onto the swooping tarmac of the A303, the sun had put his hat on. We were out to play. Down came the hoods (the Marcos' the most quickly by far) and on went the shades. Were it not for the inevitable dose of facial sunburn and the irksome, unseen threat of VASCAR, we could have been in Paradise.

All three cars were in their element and, as we motored past Thruxton a few miles on, I was tempted to drop in to try to wangle a few quick laps on the empty circuit – all in the cause of research, you understand. The driving position in the Mantara is as racy as you'll get in a road car and with such powerful brakes, ultra-quick steering, abundant grip and, not least, the raucous snarl of the exhaust, i

Down by the Riverside you'll find three road testers sharing a pint and a ploughman's. And three sports cars sharing a Range Rover-derived 3.9-litre V8 engine. The name on the top – and the level of tweaking inside – varies, but it's basically the same venerable old alloy thing to which Rover bought the rights from General Motors in 1964

seemed a pity to pass by. But we carried on without even slowing. Over the next few miles I consoled myself in the knowledge that an impromptu, spur-of-the-moment excursion on a race track with almost 700 horsepower to play with between us would quite probably have ended in tears.

Although the Mantara has a butch GT car persona, it does comes fairly well equipped as standard, with Wilton carpeting, central locking and a decent stereo. Our car also sported air-con, a heater of thermonuclear efficiency, a sophisticated alarm, power steering, a filament heated windscreen and a full leather interior.

This is all good, but we don't much favour the vast expanse of walnut veneer which covers the dash and giant central console. Black leather or maybe a bit of machine-patterned aluminium would be more in keeping with such a hairy-chested brute of a car. At the same time, the speedo and rev counter could also be moved from behind the steering wheel to a more visible position nearer the centre of the dash. Presumably Marcos' management know what their customers prefer, though.

We may have passed on an opportunity at Thruxton but we had no hesitation in pulling into the Hillside Cafe near Ilminster. As this is the last privately-owned eatery between London and Exeter and, as we discovered, soon to be demolished, it seemed like the ideal place to pause for a bite to eat and a couple of snaps. Pulling into the forecourt I managed to ground the low-slung Marcos on a protruding manhole cover, which reminded me of one traditional sportscar weakness: ground clearance.

Another trait which was becoming more apparent was the gymnastic level of suppleness required to get in and out of all these cars. The TVR is the easiest, though the doors don't open quite wide enough. Both the Morgan and Marcos are pretty tricky – especially when their hoods are raised. Full marks to the Marcos for its tiny turning circle, though. It's almost possible to slalom between petrol pumps.

A couple of hours later we were in sunny Torquay, where the liquorice-allsorts hotel frontages in the back streets reverberated to the sound of three throaty V8s held in a low gear. A bit antisocial maybe, but judging by the words and expressions of seaside strollers we chanced upon, our visual and aural display of British engineering appeared to enrich even this particularly pleasant Spring afternoon.

After a cool Grolsch or three and a large steak in the evening, a blissful time in the land of nod and a full English breakfast in a kitsch but most agreeable clifftop hotel, it was my turn to drive the TVR the next day.

On paper, the four-litre Chimaera is a little meatier than even our Sport Packed Mantara.

S E R I O U S S P O R T S S T A T S

	Marcos Mantara Spyder (Sport Pack)	Morgan Plus 8	TVR Chimaera 4.0
Performance			
0-30mph (secs)	2.2	2.3	2.2
0-60mph (secs)	5.6	6.6	5.8
0-70mph (secs)	7.6	8.4	8
0-100mph (secs)	15	17.9	15.6
0-120mph (secs)	23.2	–	23.7
Max Speed, mph	138.2	121.1	143.4
30-50mph in 3rd (secs)	3.7	3	4.1
50-70mph in 5th (secs)	8.3	6.9	10.1
30-70mph thro' gears (secs)	5.4	6.1	5.8
Braking 70-0mph (feet)	178.2	211	179.2
Standing quarter-mile	14.3	15	14.5
Terminal speed	98.2	92.9	96.7
Costs			
List price	£25,526 (+ £1,498 Sport Pack)	£25,936	£26,720
Test mpg	19.02	20.21	21.02
Insurance group	20	16	20
Service interval	every 6k miles	every 10k miles	every 6k miles
Warranty	1yr unltd miles	1yr or 12,000m	1yr unltd miles

What you get			
Central locking	yes	no	yes
Electric windows	yes	no	yes
Doorhandles	yes	option (really!)	not as such
Alarm	option	option	yes
Power steering	option	no	option
Alloy wheels	yes	yes (wire option)	yes
Technical			
Engine	90deg V8 ohv pushrod	90deg V8 ohv pushrod	90deg V8 ohv pushrod
Capacity	3,946cc	3,946cc	3,950cc
Max power	230bhp @ 4,750rpm	188bhp @ 4,750rpm	240bhp @ 5,250rpm
Max torque	270lb/ft @ 3,500rpm	230lb/ft @ 2,600rpm	270lb/ft @ 4,000rpm
Transmission	five-speed manual	five-speed manual	five-speed manual
Front brakes	10.4" vent discs	11" discs	10.6" vent discs
Rear brakes	9.9" discs	9x1.75" drums	9.9" discs
Front suspension	MacP struts,coil springs	indep coil springs	indep coil springs
Rear suspension	indep w/b, coil springs	Semi-elliptical springs	indep coil springs
Wheels (F/R)	15x7"	6.5x15"	15x7J/16x7.5J
Tyres (F/R)	205/55, 225/50 VR15	205/60 VR15	205/60, 225/55 ZR15/16
Dimensions (ins)	L157.5, W66.25	L156, W63	L158, W73.5

All the above statistics were taken at Millbrook test track. None of the cars quite achieved their manufacturer's claims, for some strange reason

TVR claim a potent 240bhp for this model. Our car, though, was just four days old when we took it to Millbrook and therefore by no means fully loosened up – for this trip at least, it was not quite a match for the Marcos. Having said that, none of this trio performed on the test track to anywhere near their manufacturer's claims. This showed up most noticeably over the 0-60mph sprint. Each of the three turned out to be around a second off the pace.

Still, 0-60 took well under seven seconds for the least rapid car (the Morgan) and this, coupled with a top speed capability of between 120mph (the Morgan) and 143mph (the TVR), was more than enough for our relaxed jaunt through the West Country.

The Chimaera certainly looks the business. It's beautifully finished in black paint a foot thick, with a tan half-leather interior. It sounds pretty special too; TVR has obviously taken great care to tune the exhaust for maximum musical stimulation. The Morgan rumbles and the Marcos growls like a racing car, but the TVR bellows its own distinctive melodic tune.

We spent the morning posing around Torquay (for the benefit of the camera, you understand) and then headed North for a few miles, round Babbacombe Bay and on towards Teignmouth. The traffic soon became heavy for some unaccountable reason, with the problem being compounded by having a huge road-worker's convention in the immediate area. So we headed inland and made for Bovey Tracey, for two reasons.

Firstly, it was on the edge of Dartmoor and so had some fine driving roads in the vicinity. And secondly, a place with a name like that was simply bound to have a pub which does a good lunch. Having rather stupidly allowed the only person without a map to lead the way, our ploughman's lunches were somewhat delayed, but driving round in circles is more fun in the Chimaera than in almost any other car, so what the heck.

But by now a few TVR niggles were appearing. Some were almost certainly because this particular car had undergone an exceptionally rushed pre-delivery inspection, and involved relatively simple bits and bobs which could have been easily remedied by a dealer There were some others, though, which seemed rather more permanent.

In that first section I'll mention one because it really got up my nose, and I'm not talking about the smell of fresh glass fibre either. All the instrument lights failed, which meant that I had to guess my speed and fuel reserve for many miles of unlit A-roads on the lengthy drive back to London.

The location of many of the switches and warning lights seems to have little to do with logic, either. Most switches aren't labelled, so unless you've memorised the diagram in the owner's manual, you just have to make do with guesswork. We also found that the rear screen folds uncomfortably when the hood is lowered, so the clear plastic window is likely to craze and split long before its time.

We also fail to see an advantage in any of TVR's oddball doorhandle mechanisms. The Griffith has its interior handles on the transmission tunnel, the Chimaera has an extra gearstick which you twist to open the doors, and there's more strangeness to come with the new Cerbera and its knock-to-open idea; just what is the point of it all?

These things aside, the Chimaera is huge fun and very capable when driven fast. The driving position is spot on, the gearbox is good, the brakes are strong and the tyres, chassis and suspension feel capable of handling just about anything you can throw at them.

TVRs have succeeded in crossing over to the mainstream market and are now selling in good numbers to non-enthusiasts, but there's nothing in the Chimaera's basic makeup which would disappoint a serious sports car freak.

By the time we left Dartmoor and headed for home, the sun was going down and once again there was a distinct chill in the air. We simply donned every coat, scarf, hat and glove we had and hacked back to London al fresco. The Chimaera's heater wasn't up to much but I managed to stay just about warm enough to reflect on these three thundering cars.

Normally at this point you'd get a verdict - the 'based on all the available information, this is the car should you buy' treatment. But not this time. The reason is that although they're all British-made, handbuilt, two-seater V8 sports cars, they have very different characters. For the most part, they will each appeal to a completely different type of customer.

The Morgan is for the purist, for the person who appreciates the grand traditions of motoring and who will savour every minute of the five-year wait before taking delivery of their bespoke motor car.

Among dozens of other decisions considered in that time, they will have pored over whether they want a walnut dash and an aluminium or steel body. They'll have selected which type of accelerator pedal they prefer, and they will have chosen from over fifty different grades and colours of leather trim. Chances are that once they finally achieve ownership they will love, honour and cherish their 'Moggy' till death us do part. They probably won't ever want to sell, either, even though depreciation is not a word normally used in association with Morgans.

The Marcos buyer won't be oblivious to tradition either. This marque has soldiered on successfully for 35 years now, but misty-eyed historical stuff won't be a primary motivation to buy. What's important here is looks, power, speed, noise and sheer, undiluted fun – all in equal proportions.

The Mantara makes the adrenalin flow like rainwater in a Manchester gutter. It's not for the faint-hearted or feeble-footed, but then no real sportscar ever was.

The TVR Chimaera provides much of the raw, tyre-squealing appeal of the Mantara, but it's packaged in smoother, more modern, more civilised clothing. Most commonly, a Chimaera buyer will be looking for a revitalising, youth-giving experience – and a completely different alternative to a run-of-the-mill executive saloon. A Porsche Cabriolet would do the trick but they're oh-so-much money compared with the TVR and, by George, the TVR is British.

The Morgan, Marcos and TVR simply don't compete with each other for sales. And before you even started to read this story, you probably already knew which one you'd prefer. So go on, treat yourself. Buy it! □

The Morgan Things Change

The map points of Land's End and John O'Groats have several things in common: They're both bleak, barren, windswept, uninspiring and just plain best avoided.

Some would say the same about a Morgan—a view with which I was beginning to concur as gale-force winds, ground-level clouds and a penetrating drizzle greeted my arrival at the ragged promontory of England's most westerly point. I couldn't imagine a less hospitable starting line for an old-fashioned "reliability trial:" It was madness to start a 1500-mile vintage rally from Land's End but, as more than one waggish fellow competitor pointed out, it was even crazier to have entered a Morgan.

It had been a good 6-hour drive from The Smoke to Penzance, capital of the "Cornish Riviera"—more than long enough to become acquainted with my 1953 Morgan Plus Four rallycar. Powered by a dowdy, tractor-derived Triumph TR engine and the famous/infamous 4-speed Moss gearbox it felt unbreakable, like a miniature Jaguar XK120 without the sweet sounds.

The last time I'd been foolish enough to enter a topless sportster in a winter endurance event it had been my own Jaguar on the Monte Carlo Challenge, in which—wholly by dint of careful teammate selection—we scooped top team honors. This Mog used the same oft-maligned Moss transmission and there was great similarity in the way both cars fit,

drove and handled. On poor surfaces the Jaguar and Morgan even quaked alike, their flexing ladder frames leading to a curious tendency to dart in directions unrelated to the one you'd intended.

Rally Heritage

So why were we doing it? At the height of the summer it had seemed like a jolly good wheeze—Morgans, we reasoned, had always performed well in traditional trials. Rugged, simple, reliable, agile and decently fit for torque, they were unstoppable from the sport's earliest days. H.F.S. Morgan's first 3-wheeler took a gold in its competition debut at the arduous Exeter Trial of 1910, and derivatives went on to wrest scores more.

Christopher Bibb gets to it with the Master's Plus Eight. Photography by Cymon Taylor.

When the advantages of four wheels over three became accepted at last, Morgan announced the first Plus Four. (Never in a rush to follow trends, the year was 1935.) Nevertheless, by the end of the interwar period the marque had already closed the gap on its 4-wheeled competitors, most notably with a class victory in the 1939 RAC Rally.

Our aged Plus Four started life as a rally-car, being the regular mount of a game and attractive duo from Lancashire, the Neil sisters. So what could be more appropriate, we wondered, than comparison of this old crock with the latest coming-to-America version of the car? During the ensuing 72 hours—only a handful of which were spent asleep—I learned little about the elderly Morgan I didn't already know; a long way from John

O'Groats, its pugnacious yet indomitable spirit had won my heart, even if my frozen brain became somewhat scrambled in the process. Additionally, my respect for Andy and Chrissie Neil came to know no bounds: Here was a car made for whizzing about English lanes in summer, not racing about Scotland in darkest winter, yet they'd carried on with genuine English pluck.

Déjà New

Luckily, it was almost six months later by the time Charles Morgan offered me his very own Plus Eight for a week of old-versus-new comparison. In the last 40 years Britain has changed irrevocably. While America and Russia indulged in the space race, British ineptitude allowed its

domestic car and motorcycle industries to implode on cue, with Healey, MG, Triumph and many other sporting marques disappearing in the melee. There were a couple of survivors, though, and the family-run Morgan concern is one. All set to celebrate its 60th anniversary at the close of 1995, new examples of the Rover-engined Plus Four and Ford-powered 4/4 models are still being churned out along with the Plus Eight; 4/4 and Plus Eight models are also still being brought to America by San Francisco's Isis Imports concern.

"New," of course, is only a relative term; Morgan's latest model was introduced in the same year that saw Russian tanks rumbling into Prague, Robert Kennedy's assassination and the beginning of the Tet offensive.

Listen to the dreaded bar-stool critic and you'll be told the ride is so damn atrocious that riding around the block warrants a trip to the dentist.

> *Its rear-end grip considerably overwhelmed by power, the 190-horse Plus Eight whips around at the rear just as soon as the front tires grab. Bibb (top) seems unconcerned that this is Peter Morgan's personal car.*

Perhaps Morgan's key attraction is that its cars remain utterly tied to their original concept—providing more go with less hardware. Visually, the only significant change came in the early '50s, with the adoption of a curved radiator cowl; as reminders of a bygone era, the sweeping running boards and long, louvered hood remain. While never a fashion item, owning a Morgan has never been passé, either—it never fails to impress and is always acceptable.

Or is it? Listen to the dreaded bar-stool critic and you'll be told the ride is so damn atrocious that riding around the block warrants a trip to the dentist. Well yes, the ride

is pretty poor: The cart-sprung rear with its lever-arm shocks hasn't changed appreciably since the first 4-wheeled device appeared from Morgan's doors. Worse still, the sliding-pillar front suspension is the same design that graced the first 3-wheeler of 1909. Being independent, it was pretty advanced at its introduction—the system was later copied and improved on by Lancia for the revolutionary Lambda of 1922—but any initial advantage had largely evaporated by the time of the War.

Clearly, the Plus Eight will fail anyone wanting a decent ride, and your average hot-shot used to cavorting around in a modern

tin-top will be appalled at the intransiger vintage-style handling. For either of the drivers, the current Morgans will feel antiquated to drive as they look.

To anyone with a taste for prew sports-car behavior, however, it's a car be cherished. Venerable Morganists reco nize every sensation, and truly there nothing else like it. The V8 version is st pure Morgan, even sharing the small cars' endearing low-speed behavior whe the nose jiggles like an eager puppy. It's much fun that it's almost possible to forg this trait is caused by a virtual absence suspension travel.

that this car does *all* of its business in a distinctly vintage manner. In that idiom—and especially now that it's been punched up to 3950cc and fit with Lucas EFI—the Rover engine provides all the woof and holler one associates with American V8s of the same bygone era to which the Morgan belongs. A modest (drag-limited) top speed of 125 mph is claimed by the factory, and while the car is probably capable of more I'll be damned if *I'd* try it.

It simply flies up to the ton, but thereafter wind lash renders progress unbearable. Consuming well-surfaced roads at relative speeds well above traffic's is this car's forte—it reels in slower objects with uncanny ease and whips around them much sooner than expected—but the golden rule is to never to race into corners. In fact, *never hustle the car.* It has plenty of power to make a fast exit, so why rush—if midcorner bumps lie in wait you'd truly have your hands full.

The wheel is heavy and often vague: Sometimes the nose tucks in instantly and obediently, other times it want to plow straight on. Yet once the tires bite–and it's only a question of time–the car corners as if on rails. With the masses set low and the rear axle only inches behind, you can plant the throttle, get the tail to lick around and hold it in check with the greatest of ease.

On the straights a rough patch is less of a problem; sitting so far back there are visible

After driving the earlier car the Plus Eight feels immensely wide and powerful, though both share an amazing clarity on turn-in. A 60% increase in footprint copes with more than double the horsepower (a fact reflected in the car's girth), yet under the hand-formed sheetmetal doubling the number of cylinders called for remarkably few other changes. The old Z-section chassis rails were opened by two inches and the wheelbase grew a similar amount.

In 1968 it all seemed a fairly radical bit of kit, but it was also a godsend; short, squat, not too wide and no heavier than most iron Fours, the 3.5-liter, ex-Buick, Rover-sourced aluminum V8 didn't even demand a bulge in the hood.

Family Characteristics

Viewed objectively, however, the current Rover V8 is just as tractorlike as the TR unit used in the 1950s. Smooth, responsive and effortless though it is, this OHV engine with hydraulic tappets and long-stroker crank feels downright lazy today. Peak power is developed at a mere 4750 rpm and there's little point pushing too far over 5500. By modern 4-cam standards it's less than inspiring, but the bottom line is

▶ *When new, the Neils' 1953 Morgan Plus Four...*

First the front fenders perform a little dance as the tires shoot up the bump. Milli-seconds later the tremors come through your forearms, warning you to brace yoursel

...got better treatment than Bibb gave it.

and audible warnings before the disturban reaches your bum. First the front fende and hood perform a little dance as the tir shoot up the bump. Milliseconds later th tremors come through your forearms, warn ing you to brace yourself before the re axle transmits the shock, unattenuated, int the base of your spine.

Heart and Soul

To get the most impressive perfo mance from the Plus Eight one mu use all the power, whereas the old car seemed to operate best at half throttle. first and second gears with the right fo firmly planted the bigger car screech away leaving twin black swatches of rubb on the tarmac. Traction is first-rate, and accelerates with more verve than a 9 Carrera. That this car has a power-to-weig ratio better than the Lotus Esprit S4 Turb is a matter of fact.

Voluptuous body is formed of steel on standard car, aluminum as a weight-saving option. Owner of 1953 Plus Four comparison car Martin Emisson (right) confirmed the new Plus Eight's ability to outrun his own Porsche 911 Carrera.

The first Plus Eights to leave the Malvern factory relied on the Moss 'box carried over from the Plus Four, as Rover (and certainly Buick) didn't have an appropriate manual transmission strong enough. Rover being Rover, they soon came up with a full-synchro (but equally recalcitrant) 4-speed before finally recognizing the advantages of a fifth gear, if still not a user-friendly shift action.

Playing tunes with the gearbox is perhaps the least rewarding aspect of piloting the Plus Eight. On the other hand, mere mortals can expect to be totally intoxicated by the way the Plus Eight streaks and thunders off the line: No way is it short on soul, a fact that essentially makes up for every inadequacy. Certainly, after experiencing its power one wonders why anyone would opt for the four-bangers.

The Plus Eight is a charming, anachronistic, wholly unacceptable monster of a car

that will leave most people scratching their heads in perplexion and a rare, lucky few clutching their hearts in swoon.

As a machine for the extrovert, the flagship Morgan simply wins hearts and minds. Even in blasé central London it had heads swirling, perhaps the most memorable comment coming from a rap-mouthing skateboarder.

"Wicked motor, guv," he murmured, weaving expertly through traffic. He had no idea how right he was.

GALE FORCE 8

TAKE A MORGAN PLUS 8, PLACE A SUPERCHARGER BETWEEN THE BANKS OF THE 3.9-LITRE V8, TURN THE KEY AND PREPARE TO BE BLOWN AWAY!

I f it's in the A to Z of engines it has probably powered a Morgan. Singles, twins, fours, sixes, V8s, two-strokes, four-strokes, side-valves, twin-cams, blowers, turbos.... Moggies, three- and four-wheelers, have cradled pretty well everything in the motive power book.

Such diversification, rooted in Morgan's dependence on proprietary engines, has led to many intriguing experiments. Works rejects include a Ford V8-powered four-wheeler decades before the Plus 8 was even a distant dream (it went hard but wouldn't stop), and supercharged 4/4s (Coventry Climax and side-valve Ford) that tended to self-destruct.

Taking their lead from the factory, many Morgan owners have replaced knackered old engines with alien new ones, especially during refurbishment – and sooner or later most Mogs get restored. Bet you've never heard of a straight-six BMW Plus 4. It exists. Another boasts a Daimler 2.5 V8.

There are, then, umpteen precedents, authentic and otherwise, for the snorting Plus 8 built by Brands Hatch Morgan for owner Colin Treble. You've heard of the Plus 4 Plus. What we have here, the progeny of Rover's ubiquitous V8 and a Swedish supercharger, is the Plus 8 Plus.

Forget the Mogadons at the other end of the performance spectrum. Welcome here to Mogalomania.

Although Colin Treble's lovely car was made BC (Before Cuprinol) in 1983, it had been upgraded to a later spec – four-pot discs, new suspension (still by archaic sliding pillar, of course), telescopic rear dampers, galvanised chassis and so on – during a ground-up rebuild by Brands Hatch Morgan, one of Morgan's 18 UK distributors, quaintly known as agents.

The SU-based blower kit, which includes pistons that lower the compression to 8.5 to one, is the outcome of a liaison between BHM and Dennis Priddle of drag-racing fame. Development originally centred on a Sprintex blower – a big, ribbed monster like those that crown dragster engines. Later it switched to the Stockholm-built, twin-screw Opcon Autorotor that's pictured here, elegantly mounted in the V8's valley. With a boost pressure of 0-45 bar, output is said to be 297bhp – up from 190, though BHM's special fabricated exhaust accounts for 25 of the extra horses. Peak torque leaps from 235lb ft to a mountainous 320lb ft.

And torque is what this blockbuster is all about. The 3.9-litre howitzer fires without temperament and settles into a lazy drumbeat burble. Blip the throttle – response is instant, clean, menacing – and you can *feel* the gentle giant flexing its pecs. Seated al fresco (how else?), twixt guttural business end and pulsing exhaust, you seem to be at the heart of some quadraphonic sound system that conveys but one message: power. It's ▷

'Blip the throttle – response is instant, clean, menacing – and you can _feel_ the gentle giant flexing its pecs'

What we have here is a 3.9-litre Rover V8, usual output 190bhp, with SU carburettors and Opcon supercharger piled on top. Result: 297bhp and a sound to make grown men weak

not false. Nor, thank goodness, is it offensively loud.

Rick Bourne, no longer based at Brands Hatch but at Borough Green just down the road, warned me to go easy on the clutch as there was enough torque to rip it apart given too much abuse. No matter. Bumbling along the A25, heading for Ashdown Forest, two outstanding qualities were immediately apparent: massive muscle and easy access to it. The great thing about a good supercharged engine, as Aston Martin (DB7), Jaguar (XJR) and Mercedes (2.3 Kompressor) amply demonstrate, is that it builds up power gently, progressively, not with an aggressive turbo-like kick that can catch you unawares.

Low down, Mighty Mog displays no loss of flexibility or punch. Far from it. Open the tap – any revs, any gear – and out flow raw slugs of oomph. Keep your foot buried and the exhaust note hardens from engaging burble to deep-chested roar as acceleration zaps from fast to fearsome. Drop a cog or three and you're on the rampage, surging forward on tidal torque that starts strong and progresses to virulent as the revs soar towards the modest five-five cutout.

If Morgan's pre-cat 3.9 – reckoned to be the swiftest of all production Plus 8s – can rocket to 60mph in 6secs, this car, further fettled by a competition gearbox (ex-racing Vitesse) with deliciously close ratios, must have the potential to do it in five or less. In deference to the clutch, we didn't put it to the test. Besides, it's the

You'd expect all the leather and wood; the good driving position comes as a pleasant surprise. Note the rev-counter – it's skewed round like that so that the bits that matter aren't obscured by the wheel. Call it character...

mid-range wallop, the ability to despatch short straights, gradients and flat-cap crawlers – even 911 Turbos, I wouldn't wonder – in a one-grin surge, that make BHM's supercharged Morgan such an endearing companion, not to mention an entertaining vocalist. Scorchingly quick though it is, there's nothing viciously

white-knuckle about the *coup de grace*, though the crude, mind-of-its-own chassis ensures there are no dull moments. When was it otherwise in a car with sliding pillars inherited from a 1910 three-wheeler? As one American wag has it, the suspension is not so much for riding on as oiling.

Despite its innate flaws – no, make ▷

GALE FORCE 8

that because of them – BHM's Plus 8 Plus is a hoot to drive. I adored it. Getting in is a squeeze, weather protection minimal, the driving position cramped, the steering so heavy that if you tried to adopt a long-arm stance you'd not be able to turn the wheel. Just as well, then, that the surprisingly comfortable and embracing seat is fixed in position.

Extend your fingers and you've found the column stalks, so close to the polished timber dash they almost brush it. The tacho has been twisted, so you can see the calibrations that matter, and the gearlever – like the clutch, heavy, meaty, precise – is a handspan away from the rim of the wheel, belying the charge that Morgans have lousy ergonomics. The fly-off handbrake, heater, supplementary switches and ignition key are not so handy. But if the view down the long louvred bonnet, flanked by headlight pods and sexy wings, doesn't evoke either nostalgia or passion, you're a very queer fish indeed.

Morgan's lexicon excludes certain words. Like suppleness and fluency. Although Colin Treble's car feels rattle-free solid – given such a primitive chassis, the integrity of the ash-framed aluminium body is quite remarkable – it rides on stiff, short-travel springs with the decorum of a bronco on steroids. The addition of a bracing rear cross-member carrying telescopic dampers (which replaced lever-arm ones in '92), has improved ride and handling no end, says Rick Bourne. Even so, pattering off-line on bumpy corners is still a characteristic that demands your attention and skill.

Morgans don't go round corners in the way that quicksilver flows through tubes. They're not Lotus Elises. You have to bully them into changing direction, with flashing elbows and straining muscles. A dash of throttle assists, too. That old

You'd never guess that this car has enough performance to leave a 911 or an NSX for dead. That's why we like it

cliché about helping the tail round really is apt. Mind you, in this blockbuster blower there's a fine dividing line between neutralising understeer and provoking tail-end breakaway. Roadholding is not just a matter of tyre grip – and there's no shortage of that on 205/60 Yokohamas – but of remaining in contact with terra firma. Morgans are consistent in their behaviour only on super-smooth roads. No wonder the Germans love them.

Supercharged slingshots of this calibre don't come cheap. BHM's Opcon blower kit (also available for injected cat-cleaned cars) costs £7000 installed, plus VAT. Provided it fits under the bonnet – the aim was to make the installation no taller than an injected engine's plenum chamber – the conversion works as well on MG V8s, TR8s, TVRs, even Range Rovers from whence the V8 came. As an antidote to modern motoring, though, nothing comes close to a blown Plus 8. ◑

Myths surround Morgans. People call them stark, when the truth is that most are sumptuously trimmed. Others insist that driving one is like flying a pre-war biplane, which only goes to show that they've not noticed the Morgan's far superior ergonomics – and probably never left the ground.

The biggest Morgan myth is that the four-cylinder models are as slow and stately in performance as the Plus Eight is fast. As somebody who drove his first four-pot Mog 30 years ago (shortly after assisting its student owner to heft its newly repaired body out through the sitting room window of a house we shared, onto its chassis), I know. That flat-radiator Plus Four was light, torquey and fast. So, I discover, is its descendant, the Ford-engined 4/4 of today.

A burning need for a good day out in a four-pot Morgan recently led me to rise early from the couch and head northward to Pickersleigh Road, Malvern Link, near Worcester, where Morgan sports cars have been made since 1909. I sought a cup of tea and chat with the company's proprietors, Charles and Peter Morgan, a stroll through the works (to see the more streamlined production process and new £250,000 paint shop, which will eventually build production

REVOLUTION STARTS HERE

Morgan has changes in the pipeline that are radical by its standards. But it won't abandon its traditional car building methods. Quite right too, say's Steve Cropley after driving today's 4/4

from 500 to 750 units a year) and then a chance to borrow a 4/4 for an afternoon's driving in the surrounding Malvern Hills. Hard to imagine a better day out.

Everything hung on the weather. I was hoping for one of those sunny, slightly cool May days with breeze enough to lift the scents from the fields, and clouds enough to dapple the sunny hillsides. Of course, you can get huge satisfaction from driving Morgans in the worst possible conditions, clothes drenched like dishrags, raindrops pinging off teeth which are still revealed in a smile. But today I sought the relaxation of

balmy weather, and the wish was granted. We talked, we walked, the sun shone, then I drove.

As I pointed the long nose of the 4/4 out of the Morgan factory and up Pickersleigh Avenue in the wake of Charles Morgan's grumbling yellow Plus Eight, heading for the photogenic green slopes of the Malverns, the view down the maroon bonnet really lifted my heart.

Frankly, it would have lifted any heart that wasn't chained to the floor. A Morgan is completely different from anything else that comes new from a showroom. The way you sit in the car and look down the bonnet is worth half the price, just on its own. You sit there, eyeline just above the long, louvred expanse that tapers almost to a point, six or seven feet ahead. Your backside is only a couple of inches above the carpet-covered wooden floor, and the little doors, radically cut away beneath your elbows, go hardly any higher than your hips. Reach out and down and you can touch the road.

The big steering wheel, close to the dash and almost vertical, is a lot less than a full arm's reach away, so in most driving modes you can tuck your elbows comfortably into your sides. The facia and screen are closer to your head than in anything modern, and so is the rolled forward edge of the cockpit. You don't reach out for a switch

Ash body frame surprisingly strong, crashworthy

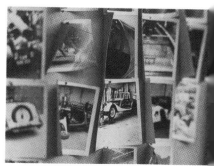

Definitely not the normal factory pin-up board

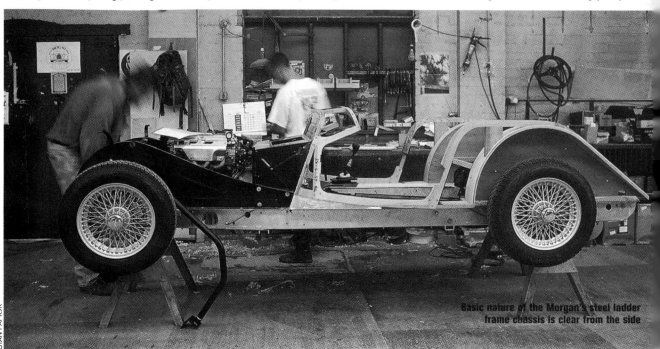

Basic nature of the Morgan's steel ladder frame chassis is clear from the side

STAN PAPIOR

on the dash so much as lift your hand to it.

The Morgan's flat screen protects you from turbulence far better than that of most roadsters, because you're so close to it. Other screens are as large, and more steeply raked, but they're invariably set further forward, allowing room for the wind to curl around their edges and smack you in the side of the head. The Morgan cockpit architecture is decidedly vintage in influence, but the facia itself has a surprisingly "designed" feel to it, with the simple, black-faced speedo and tacho sited sensibly straight ahead, and the four minor gauges, with rocker switches beneath, grouped in a neat panel in centre dash. It's

After almost 90 years, some things never change

"THE VIEW DOWN THE BONNET IS WORTH HALF THE PRICE ON ITS OWN"

Light nacelles will still be hand-made in future

just right for the character of the car, but works well in a modern context.

The 4/4 has a 121bhp version of Ford's Zetec 1.8-litre, 16-valve engine, a lusty enough power unit in the 1300kg Mondeo it usually inhabits, and therefore a sparkling performer in an 850kg sports two-seater. You have only to calculate the bhp/tonne figure – which comes out at 142.353 – to see why its straight-line performance is well ahead of the Mazda MX-5 and MGF. When we last ran performance figures on a Morgan 4/4, its 0-60mph time came out at 7.8sec, which undercuts the modern pair by

a full second. The Morgan has similar advantages for in-gear and passing acceleration times. The top speed of 110-115mph is hardly spectacular, limited by '30s aerodynamics, but it is more than enough for practical purposes. Only those who haven't tried it imagine that driving two-seater sports cars at three-figure speeds is something you can sustain in comfort.

It's not the thrust of the engine which strikes you when you begin to drive. It's the surprising refinement, the crisp response, the torque, the ability to pull onward in each higher gear with ease. Also the engine note. ◆

Perfect Morgan day: cool, bright, breezy, with the top down on an open, smooth stretch of tarmac

Reach out and the road is there for the touching.
Close screen protects from any wind buffeting

Building a Morgan is still a very hands-on job...

◆ To a large extent, Europe's latest noise regulations have dulled sporting exhausts, and this Morgan could never be called loud or fruity. But there is still a surprisingly pleasant thrum to the engine, quite enough to make its character and capabilities clear.

The clutch is light. The brakes bite well. The gearchange somehow feels better than it does in a Ford. In short, this 4/4 is all sports car, in the most traditional sense.

Any Morgan's underpinnings are its most controversial parts. The Malvern company's approach to chassis design divides families, causes rifts between lifelong friends, may even start wars. Traditionalists believe the sliding pillar front suspension and a leaf-sprung live rear axle are fine, for the good reasons that they work, and because that's the way HFS Morgan – Peter's father, Charles' grandfather – wanted it in the first place. The other faction believes the chassis/suspension is just not good enough in this day and age. Each is half right.

Don't think for a moment that Morgan is standing still, however. Its latest GT racer, which ran for the first time at Silverstone earlier this year, has all-independent,

STOP PRESS! NEW MORGAN FOR SEPTEMBER!

Even Morgans move on. In September the company will launch a developed version of the Plus Eight with a 4.6-litre version of the Range Rover V8 as its staple engine. Morgan's engineers have high hopes for the car's performance potential, already impressive, against more modern but generally heavier cars such as the TVR Chimaera.

The new model will have extra cockpit room, made available by providing more space between facia and seat backrests, and more footwell room. This is the frequently discussed "long door" model, aimed at accommodating today's taller drivers. At the same time, there will be modifications to other interior details, and to the hood mechanism.

Biggest manufacturing change will be the adoption of a new system of one-piece pressings for the front wings, which will reduce factory fabrication time, and thus cost. The headlight nacelles will still have to be hand made and fitted.

The move is a step towards Morgan's general aim of giving its cars all-alloy bodies over the next several years, a feature, it believes, of which buyers will approve.

A Plus Eight with an all-aluminium chassis and wishbone suspension front and rear, based on the current GT racer, is thought still to be several years away. The company is thought to be experimenting with prototypes, but no decision has been reached about either a form or a date for the new version's introduction. In any case, traditional Morgans will continue to be made alongside the new model, which would carry a premium price.

...although future plans include some automation

kept his family firm's fortunes shining as others have foundered.

There is no point in pretending the Morgan suspension is a match for the all-independent set-ups you'll find under more or less everything else of the 4/4's performance potential. In particular, the ride is disturbing when you begin to drive. You can plainly feel both the flexibility of the ladder frame chassis – a weird feeling in this day and age – and the lack of compliance in that idiosyncratic sliding pillar front end. The two things add up to a strangeness of response that cause you to distrust your Morgan until you've come to know it thoroughly. As far as ride comfort goes, the Morgan simply doesn't have much.

Yet the 4/4 and its gait do have a curious appeal. There's a robustness and a lack of complication about it. And a deep involvement with your actual progress: a Morgan is very far from being a capsule or a cocoon. On smooth roads, there's nothing much wrong with the handling. Body roll is zero, and at sane speeds the 4/4 corners close to neutrality, graduating to understeer as you get really energetic. A Plus Eight will oversteer with bootfuls of power, but a 4/4 doesn't have so much torque to spare. Short, sharp bumps often jolt you off line in

Vintage cockpit layout is still surprisingly effective

it. The knowledge that Charles Morgan and his team are working away on a modern chassis somehow frees you to enjoy the car the way HFS laid it down in the first place.

I drove on little Worcestershire roads for most of the sunny afternoon. By the end of the day I was full of the 4/4's vintage flatness in corners, the abundant flow of power from its engine, the subdued rumble of exhaust bouncing back off grassy banks, and the surprisingly decent levels of grip.

On the way back to Malvern Link it dawned on me that the key to enjoying a Morgan – as it is made now – is understanding that its simple steel chassis and strong ash body frame just don't *mind* being bounced about on bumps. They've been doing it together for 60 years, so they must love it. Realise this, and joining in their dance seems to make all the sense in the world. ☉

ar leaf springs are primitive, but do the job

Charles Morgan will not alienate old fans

MORGAN'S APPROACH TO CHASSIS DESIGN DIVIDES FAMILIES, STARTS WARS"

-sprung, double wishbone suspension, ng on a sophisticated, deep section ssis. The car has shown promise in a ple of races this year, and recent wind nel tests at Mira have confounded ectations that the car's aerodynamics ld be vastly inferior to those of its als. What it needs, says Charles Morgan, ore downforce and a decent engine. s for the road car, Morgan says he ldn't dream of breaking faith with the y sports car traditionalists who have

a way the driver of modern cars simply won't have experienced, but the nose or tail never goes far and correction is a mere flick of the wrists. Discomfort for your passenger is the main drawback.

The 4/4 steering loads up more in hard corners than is fashionable, and the car needs its big-diameter steering wheel because it is heavy at parking speeds, but it is direct at 2.7 turns lock to lock. Archaic the Morgan's dynamics may be, but you can still get sufficiently acclimatised to enjoy

As always, a blast from the past to look at and to drive, but Plus 8 has been extensively updated. Still built to last, as it should be; waiting list is six years

Something old, a lot is new

Morgan Plus 8 4.6
PRICE £28,000
ON SALE Now

It's very easy to be cynical about a new Morgan model. As often as not the only thing that has changed is the shape of the petrol cap or the size of the glovebox.

But this time the update is for real. The latest Plus 8 model has no less than 21 significant modifications, encompassing everything from a powerful new 4.6-litre engine to a redesigned cockpit and, incredibly, optional twin airbags.

Yes, you heard right the first time. You can now specify your new Morgan with the very latest in de-powered, progressively-inflating airbags, engineered and crash tested at the MIRA facility. Eat your heart out TVR.

Of course, you'd have to be a serious Moggie freak to spot the changes, because Morgan is still the master of disguise. To the untrained eye the basic style

and shape hasn't changed a bit. Our car didn't have the new airbags fitted, but taking a really good look at one in the factory didn't provide many more clues. The trick to incorporating this high technology in the car is a folding aluminium panel covered in a thin slice of walnut veneer, designed to blend in with the rest of the immaculately polished dashboard.

This is the kind of detailing which Morgan thrives on. This and the fact that the Plus 8 can still blast the tyres off any number of today's so-called super coupes.

Power comes from yet another version of Rover's long-standing V8, but because Land Rover is unable to supply the Range Rover's 4.6-litre engine with a manual gearbox, Morgan has its engine specially assembled by

Cockpit has extra room thanks to packaging changes; airbags now optional

PTP of Coventry, still using the block and internals from the 4.6 but incorporating the gearbox and crankcase from the older 3.9-litre powerplant.

Whatever the recipe, the end result is predictably spectacula Anything that weighs under a tonne but has 220bhp up front certainly going to shift, and th Morgan does not disappoint. It's not outrageously fast from standing start through the gea – there isn't enough top-end power for that – but for in-gea flexibility and smooth, effortle acceleration it's got the measu of any Porsche Boxster.

There is so much torque available (260lb ft at 3600rpm that changing gears becomes a matter of choice rather than necessity. It will pull from 20mph in fifth almost as quick as it will in third. All that changes is the soundtrack. In fifth it's a low, fruity burble in third it's a smooth, urgent thrum. Select your track and press the play pedal.

Creature comforts such as assisted steering and brakes

have not yet appeared on the Morgan options list, but then that isn't really the point. This car is meant to be a blast from the past, and that's exactly what you get. The antiquated sliding pillar front suspension and leaf-sprung live rear axle don't stand a chance of delivering a decent ride quality, but even that doesn't seem to matter.

The steering weights up dramatically in corners, the rear end hops and skips over bumps and squirms sideways under power, and the brakes require an almighty shove to get them to bite, followed by some gentle

Wings are now pressed aluminium

Rover-derived V8 uses new 4.6 internals with old 3.9 crankcase and gearbox

balancing to prevent locking up the front wheels over any road imperfections.

On the plus side, the pedals are beautifully positioned for heel and toeing, with a unique roller throttle that helps you to apply the power as precisely as the bucking chassis will allow. Driving a Morgan quickly is an

art that takes months – even years – to master, and even then it will remain a challenge.

Thankfully, the cockpit is now a more comfortable place in which to practise the black art. By changing the packaging of the battery and fuel system and redesigning the rear end, Morgan has found an extra two

inches of length in the cockpit without having to change the wheelbase and extend the doors to match.

A tilting steering column (albeit only by a few degrees) improves matters further, so that it is now possible to cater for both the lanky and the portly. A reprofiled hood and larger sidescreens make a big difference to visibility and reduce the cabin's claustrophobia, while an electrically-heated windscreen prevents the previous model's misting up problems. Unfortunately, you still won't be able to read any of the speedometer numbers between 20mph and 100mph, but the angle of the needle will give you a rough idea.

Finally, a stainless steel exhaust, fuel pipes, bumpers and cockpit brace (to help rigidity and side impact crash protection) have all been added to give the vulnerable metalwork a sporting chance of matching the life expectancy of the Morgan's extraordinarily resilient ash wood frame. All of which is intended to ensure you years of lasting pleasure.

And so it should. With the waiting list still stretching out to six years, despite the adoption of new high-tech superplastic pressed aluminium wings rather than the previous model's hand-beaten panels, you will want your new toy to last a year or two.

Oh, and in case you think they've overlooked something – the glovebox is larger, too. Some things never change.
Hugo Andreae

Morgan PLUS 8

MODEL TESTED 4.6 litre **LIST PRICE** £28,000
TOP SPEED 128mph **30-70MPH** 5.4sec
0-60MPH 6.0sec **60-0MPH** 4.1sec **MPG** 19.6
FOR Effortless performance, fine build, peerless character
AGAINST Old world handling, massive waiting list

Masters of deception or defenders of the faith? This is the question that has vexed Morgan critics since it stopped changing the basic design of its cars in the mid '30s and became frozen in a pre-war time warp. Over the intervening years, countless other car companies have come and gone, yet Morgan surges on.

Now, in 1997, it is embarking on the biggest raft of changes to the classic Plus 8 two-seat roadster since the Rover V8 engine was first installed under the bonnet nearly three decades ago. As ever, the basic exterior shape is retained, even though every panel has been subtly altered, but everything else from the size and style of the cockpit to the safety of its occupants and the power of its V8 engine have been uprated.

If Morgan has done its sums correctly, this promises to be the finest incarnation yet of one of motoring's strangest and most pleasurable phenomenons.

STAN PAPIOR

Latest Plus 8 is much more heavily revised than its familiar looks suggest

DESIGN & ENGINEERING

Morgan's V8-engined Plus 8 looks much older than it is. Its 4/4 ancestor dates back to 1935 and the current shape to 1955 but the Plus 8 was only born in 1968.

Naturally the Plus 8 has undergone a number of different changes during the intervening years, but none as substantial as this. The cramped cockpit and lack of modern safety features have forced Morgan into redesigning the cockpit. The dashboard has been move forward by one inch, the seat runners extended two inches backwards and the doors enlarged by a similar amount without altering the familiar 2489mm wheelbase. Cockpit width has also been slightly increased and the steering column changed for a rake-adjustable item. A stainless steel roll bar has been added under the dashboard to limit

deformation in side impacts and airbags (optional in Britain) have been fitted into the wheel and dashboard.

The new 4.6-litre Rover V8 (the 3.9 stays in the range as a separate model) is based on that of the top Range Rover. However, because the stock unit is only available with an automatic gearbox and an unfeasibly large MEMS ECU that wouldn't fit under the roadster's long bonnet, Morgan asked Rover subsidiary

Powertrain Projects Engineering of Hinckley to tailor-make a unique engine for the Plus 8. The Morgan engine has the same long-stroke 4.6-litre block but acquires the cylinder heads from the 3.9 (same bores) and Lucas 14 CUX distributor ignition. The Plus 8 4.6 now produces 220bhp at 5000rpm and 260lb ft at 3600rpm.

Underneath the classic aluminium-on-ash body sits the same cruciform-braced

Z-section steel chassis as before. The coil-sprung sliding pillar front suspension and half-elliptic leaf-sprung live axle rear make no concessions to modernity, although the unassisted steering changed from worm and nut to rack and pinion in 1982-83. The brakes are unassisted discs at the front and drums at the rear.

Technically outdated but still a glorious piece of design

Bonnet is a work of art in itself

PERFORMANCE/BRAKES

Part of the appeal of the Plus 8 is its knack of performing far better than its antiquated looks suggest. Now with more power than ever before beneath its louvred bonnet, it has the ability to surprise even a few of today's front-line supercars.

The statistic that will wow any bar room bore is that between 50 and 70mph in top, the Morgan is quicker than the Ferrari 550 Maranello, the Porsche 911 GT1 and the TVR Cerbera, covering this benchmark flexibility test in just 5.5sec. Of course, all of these cars are handicapped by taller gearing than the Plus 8 and would demolish the Morgan in a sprint through the gears, but it does give some idea of the effortless way in which the Morgan gathers speed.

The latest development of the 4.6-litre Rover V8 is torquier than ever, with a whopping 260lb ft at 3600rpm. But judging from the ease with which it pulls away from idle in fifth, most of this must be available from tickover

4.6-litre V8 churns out 260lb ft

onwards. The engine note drops an octave under the load, then the Morgan imperiously gathers speed until the aero-not-at-all-dynamics stop the needle at 128mph.

The only time the engine fails to deliver is at the top of its rev range. Above 5000rpm it is disappointingly flat compared with the harder-hitting TVR versions. This and the appalling axle tramp under full-bore standing starts prevent the Plus 8 from reaching 60mph quicker

Ride is better than that of previous Morgans – but that's not saying much

than six seconds dead.

The five-speed gearbox has the same chunky feel as all Rover V8 manuals, but the short, straight lever gives it a cleaner throw than the previous angled item. The floor-mounted brake pedal, by contrast, is heavy, prone to lock-up and difficult to modulate, hence the poor 60-0mph time of 4.1sec.

Effortless performance but brakes feel past it ★ ★ ★ ★

HANDLING & RIDE

There are two distinct ways to drive a Morgan. Either you can take off the side screens, fold back the hood and burble gently through the countryside revelling in the unique Morgan character, or you can tackle the beast head on and wrestle your way down the road fighting with the controls to squeeze every last drop of grip from its antiquated chassis.

Both approaches can be equally rewarding, depending on your mood. From a purely objective point of view, it cannot be described as a fine-handling car. The sliding pillar front suspension and live axle rear end stand no chance of delivering the standard of ride comfort or wheel control that you would expect of a modern car. It hops and skips over bumps (albeit without the appalling crashiness that used to characterise previous

Morgans), it latches on to unwanted ruts and cambers under braking, and when it does lose grip under power it is never as gentle or progressive as you would wish.

Part of the problem is the steering, which manages to combine the two faults of being both excessively heavy and worryingly slow (3.0 turns between locks), with a vastly oversized steering wheel to control it. As a result, you end up steering from the shoulders, leaning into the corners and bracing your weight against the wheel, feeling for all the world like a Bentley Boy on a qualifying lap at Brooklands. This is all very well until the power finally overwhelms the grip of the 205/55 ZR16 Pirellis and the back end steps out. You then have fractions of a second to unwind the steering, apply the corrective lock and slingshot out of the corner in a perfectly controlled power slide. Get it right and you will be congratulating yourself for years to come; get it wrong and you will be sweeping up wood splinters from the gutter.

Of course, any other lightweight special like a Caterham 7 or Lotus Elise would have long sinced disappeared over the horizon without so much as a wobble. We can't help feeling that a Morgan that handled more predictably would be no less desirable because of it, even if the driving experience wasn't quite as evocative.

Hopelessly outdated but strangely enjoyable chassis ★ ★

Optional mohair hood looks far better than standard PVC item

ENGINE

Layout 8cyl in 90deg vee, 4555cc
Max power 220bhp at 5000rpm
Max torque 260lb ft at 3600rpm
Specific output 48bhp per litre
Power to weight 221bhp per tonne
Torque to weight 261lb ft per tonne
Installation front, longitudinal, rear-wheel drive
Construction Aluminium alloy head and block
Bore/stroke 94/82mm
Valve gear 2 valves per cyl, ohv
Compression ratio 9.35:1
Ignition and fuel Lucas 14 CUX

GEARBOX

Type 5-speed manual
Ratios/mph per 1000rpm
1st 3.32/6.8 **2nd** 2.09/10.8
3rd 1.39/16.2 **4th** 1.00/22.5
5th 0.79/28.5 **Final drive** 3.23:1

MAXIMUM SPEEDS

5th gear 128mph/4500rpm
4th 128/5700 **3rd** 97/6000
2nd 65/6000 **1st** 41/6000

ACCELERATION FROM REST

True mph	sec	speedo mph
30	2.2	30
40	3.3	40
50	4.4	50
60	6.0	60
70	7.5	69
80	9.4	79
90	12.4	89
100	15.3	98
110	20.2	108
120	27.3	118

ACCELERATION IN GEARS

mph	5th	4th	3rd	2nd
10-30			3.0	2.0
20-40	5.5	4.0	2.8	1.9
30-50	5.7	3.9	2.7	2.0
40-60	5.6	3.8	2.7	2.6
50-70	5.5	3.9	2.9	–
60-80	5.7	4.0	3.6	–
70-90	6.3	4.4	5.1	–
80-100	7.2	5.3	–	–
90-110	8.6	7.8	–	–
100-120	12.5	17.1	–	–
110-130	–	–	–	–

30-70mph 5.4sec
Standing qtr mile 14.5sec/97mph
Standing kilometre 26.2sec/117mph

SUSPENSION

Front Sliding pillar, gas-filled dampers, coil springs
Rear Live axle, leaf springs, dampers

STEERING

Type Rack and pinion
Turns lock to lock 3.0

WHEELS & TYRES

Wheel size 7Jx16in
Made of Alloy
Tyres 205/55 ZR16 Pirelli P6000
Spare Full size

CONTROLS IN DETAIL

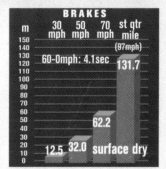

1 Rear-view mirror totally obscures apex of any left-hand corner 2 Five-speed gearbox has new, shorter, straighter gear lever. Makes shifting a faster and more pleasurable process 3 Larger glovebox or passenger's airbag – the choice is yours 4 New dials bunched together for better visibility 5 Speedometer is obscured between 20 and 100mph for tall drivers 6 Roller throttle feels odd but helps in heel-and-toe downchanges

BRAKES

Front 279mm discs
Rear 229mm drums
Anti-lock n/a

LAYOUT

BRAKES

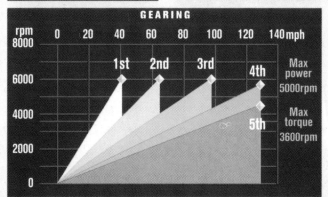

m	30 mph	50 mph	70 mph	st qtr mile
				(97mph)
60-0mph: 4.1sec	12.5	32.0	62.2	131.7

surface dry

GEARING

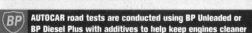

1st 2nd 3rd 4th — Max power 5000rpm
5th — Max torque 3600rpm

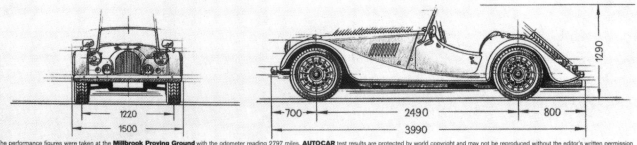

BP AUTOCAR road tests are conducted using BP Unleaded or BP Diesel Plus with additives to help keep engines cleaner

Body 2dr roadster **Cd** n/a **Front/rear tracks** 1350/1450mm **Turning circle** 10.0m **Min/max front leg room** 950/1080mm **Head room** 890mm **Interior width** 1195mm **Boot width** 1035mm **Boot height** 260mm **Boot length** 580mm **VDA boot volume** 100 litres/dm³ **Kerb weight** 975kg **Distribution f/r** 46/54 per cent **Max payload** 250kg **Max towing weight** 500kg

FUEL CONSUMPTION

TEST RESULTS

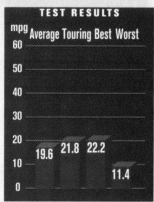

mpg — Average 19.6 Touring 21.8 Best 22.2 Worst 11.4

GOVERNMENT CLAIMS

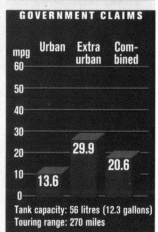

mpg	Urban	Extra urban	Combined
	13.6	29.9	20.6

Tank capacity: 56 litres (12.3 gallons)
Touring range: 270 miles

NOISE

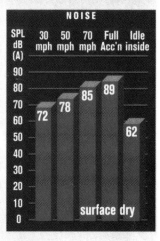

SPL dB (A)	30 mph	50 mph	70 mph	Full Acc'n	Idle inside
	72	78	85	89	62

surface dry

1220
1500

700 2490 800
3990
1290

Cabin may be an ergonomic nightmare but it looks and feels wonderful. Wood and leather are essential options

COMFORT, EQUIPMENT & SAFETY

Increasing the length of the cabin and doors by around two inches has done wonders for ease of access and comfort. The featherlight doors swing open on leather retaining straps and you can now ease yourself down the slim gap between steering wheel and seat cushion without too much trouble. Once installed, you sit almost on the floor with your legs outstretched and the oversized steering wheel sitting in your lap, but not nearly as close to your chest as was previously the case. It even tilts up and down – to a laughably small degree. The pedals look particularly special, sprouting from the leather-trimmed carpet, with a unique roller throttle for smoother heel-and-toe downchanges. All it lacks is a clutch rest for your left foot.

The redesigned facia is a useful improvement, although the steering wheel still obscures most of the speedometer's range. You will also have to splash out the best part of £3000 on leather, wood, sports seats and a mohair hood to match the superbly classy appearance of our test car.

A basic but powerful heater and a heated front windscreen should keep you reasonably snug in winter, although the sliding perspex side screens and and simple clip-on roof are

Chrome coach handles and mirrors

unlikely to hold the elements at bay for long. Worse still, the only place for luggage is a small well behind the seats and the facia-mounted glovebox.

Amazingly, Morgan has developed airbags to fit into the dashboard and steering wheel without spoiling the looks. The drawback is a record-breaking £2056 bill for the privilege. At least the new stainless steel roll bar fitted under the dashboard is included in the price. And don't expect any luxuries such as a stereo, air conditioning or an alarm. An immobiliser should be available from next year, but that's it.

Stylish and less cramped than usual, but short on equipment ★ ★ ★

Extra cabin length improves driving position and access, but luggage space is limited to the area behind seats

ECONOMY

No prizes for guessing that the Plus 8 is not the world's most economical car. An average fuel consumption of 19.6mpg is the inevitable consequence of combining brick-like aerodynamics with a thirsty V8 engine. The fact that this increases to around 22mpg on gentle cross-country runs and motorways is unlikely to provide much comfort.

Morgan claims that the Plus 8 has a 56-litre fuel tank, giving a theoretical touring range of 270 miles, but unless you're prepared to call the fuel guage's bluff you are effectively limited to 40 litres and 190 miles.

> Light kerb weight does little to quench Morgan's thirst ★★

MARKET & FINANCE

Volume car makers could learn a lot from Morgan. Like how to peg supply well behind demand. The reward, of course, is sky-high residuals. Morgans that cost between £10,000 and £20,000 as new cars just laugh at depreciation.

However, those that list at over £20,000 merely grimace. A 92J Plus 8 that cost £25,814 new retails today for £19,650 and has a trade value of about £17,000. It doesn't augur well for this new 4.6-litre version at £32,900.

Through specialist Morgan insurers Philip Bell General Insurance (01480 457570), a 37-year-old Surrey driver pays a stiff £545. Even if the annual mileage is limited to 5000, he still pays £515. A 50-year-old driver pays £450 and £400 respectively.

To get your Morgan, you have to pay £250 to join the waiting list and then, three months before production begins, another £2000 to buy the options you want.

Can't wait for your new Plus 8? One chap is selling his place on the waiting list for £1000.

> Not as depreciation-free as cheaper Morgans, stiff to insure ★★★

Triple wipers, exposed tail lights and spare wheel are Morgan trademarks

WHAT IT COSTS

On-the-road price	£32,900
Total as tested	£37,965
Cost per mile	n/a

EQUIPMENT
(**bold** = options fitted to test car)

Automatic transmission	–
Cruise control	–
Airbag driver/pass	**£2056**
Anti-lock brakes	–
Traction control	–
Aluminium wings	**£705**
Alarm/immobiliser	–
Centre-lock alloys	**£1704**
Metallic paint	**£423**
Rake column adjustment	●
Leather trim	**£1116**
Sports seats	**£470**
Mohair hood	**£1058**
Walnut dash	**£294**
Air conditioning	–
● standard – not available	
Insurance group	15

WARRANTY
12 months mechanical,
12 months anti-corrosion

SERVICING
5,000 miles, 5.0 hours

PART PRICES

Oil filter	£10.92
Air filter	£8.59
Brake pads/shoes	front £23.79
	rear £24.18
Set of sparkplugs (8)	£23.97
Exhaust (excluding cat)	£932.48
Door mirror glass	£34.66
Tyre (each typical, rear)	£152.16
Windscreen	£440.63
Headlamp unit	£61.10
Front wing	£462.66
Rear bumper	n/a

Order now and your Morgan could be delivered by the year 2004

THE AUTOCAR VERDICT

Hard cornering requires swift reactions and a keen eye for bumps

HOW THE RIVALS COMPARE

MAKE/MODEL	LIST PRICE	MPH/0-60	TEST DATE	
Marcos Mantara Spyder	£29,104	131/6.0sec	13.7.94	
Not a patch on new Mantis but striking to look at and drive			★★★	
TVR Chimaera 4.5	£32,950	154/5.1sec	13.8.97	OUR CHOICE
The best TVR yet. Fast, tidy, nicely built and great looking			★★★★	
Westfield SEiGHT	£25,950	140/4.3sec	5.6.91	
Lacks the class of the Morgan but considerably quicker			★★★	

However much you want to slam the Morgan for its outdated dynamics and chronic ergonomics, it is hard not to be won over by the skill of the craftsmanship and the undiluted character of the driving experience. You are not merely buying a car but a perfectly preserved piece of motoring history. We cannot imagine people seriously trying to decide between a Morgan and a TVR. They are two completely different machines designed to fulfil two totally different requirements. If anything, they are more likely to look at a genuine classic from another period, such as an E-type Jaguar or Austin Healey 3000.

Therefore, it seems fruitless to judge the Morgan by objective criteria alone. That's not to say that the Plus 8 is unable to compete on a facts and figures basis – it is extremely rapid by most standards and below most people's expectations of pricing – but there is a whole lot more to owning a Morgan than the usual list of pros and cons. For the full experience, you need to go to the factory itself and watch each ash wood frame being carefully cut, shaped and glued into place before having the hand-beaten aluminium bodywork made to measure.

Nor is it fair to describe the end result as an irrelevant anachronism. Morgan is not averse to change, so long as it does not affect the overall character of the car. The latest improvements have made it safer, more comfortable to live with and able to meet all the latest noise and emissions regulations. We have no doubt that it could also have engineered such comparatively simple items as power steering, assisted brakes and independent coil-sprung rear suspension. The point is that it chose not to for fear of veering too far from the Morgan experience.

Whether you agree with that standpoint is another matter. We don't. But until that fabled six-year waiting list starts to drop, there seems little point in arguing with the masters of survival.

> ### TEST NOTES
>
> Of the people we asked, most were surprised to find that the Plus 8 cost as little as £32,900. One person thought £70,000 sounded more appropriate.
>
> The view down the Morgan's long, louvred bonnet is to die for. You half expect to see a Messerschmitt ME109 fly into your sights as you play at being Biggles in full flying helmet and goggles.
>
> Lift up the carpet behind the rear seats and there is only a piece of plywood and a live axle between you and the road. It really is that basic.
>
> The fuel filler has an annoying habit of spitting petrol all over you and the car.

A unique driving experience ★★★

Morgan Plus 8, Plus 4, 4/4

Morgan new for 1998; driver's grimace remains the same

Grandad gets new teeth

Bigger engine and cabin mods give new life to the old man of soft-top motoring

YOU KNOW HOW IT IS. You wait for ages for one to turn up and then suddenly they all come along at once. Convertibles, that is. Now you can request-stop a Z3, an SLK, an MGF and a myriad other rag/auto-tintop pretenders. Yet the oldest charabanc of them all is still going strong – and, what's more, has been thoroughly updated to meet the challenge. Roll forward the latest 1898-model Morgan.

Sorry, couldn't resist that. Truth is, this is the most comprehensive overhaul of the Morgan range since the 1950s, although the good news is that you wouldn't know it. On the outside, it's the same old winged wonder: flat screen, long fluted bonnet and spare wheel bolted on the back. So what are the differences? Well, there's a new engine, getting in and out has got a bit easier, and it's much safer. On the production side, too, there have been changes, though the Malvern works hasn't quite gone over to robots yet.

Only a Morganologist would

New Moggie has a slightly curvier rear end, and longer doors

COLIN CURWOOD

Cabin comfier and safer, with optional airbags

be able to spot the slight curve to the rear body and the marginally longer doors. And once inside, they might just notice that there's an extra two inches in the cockpit and a rake-adjustable steering column. All of which makes it ergonomic ecstasy for a pint-sized pilot like me, while vertical over-achievers can at least get reasonably comfy. ('Comfort' and 'Morgan' are not words that have traditionally gone together.)

Bolted to the column is a new, but rather nondescript, 15in steering wheel. Also new is the switchgear. Morgan wouldn't reveal which mass-market product it came from (it looks Land Roverish) but it should have stayed there. In particular, the Tetris-like array of warning lights looks cheap whereas the rest of the car, including the veneer dash

that houses them, doesn't. At least they resisted the temptation to fit cup and saucer holders, opting instead for the much more useful heated screen. Yes, really.

As for safety, the Morgan has always done pretty well in crash testing, but this new version has got MIRA's thumbs-up as producing the least severe injuries of any car tested. There's now a

'Performance is notably more urgent'

Morgan Plus 8, Plus 4, 4/4

This is a bespoke motor, so your wheels can be bespoked or alloy

Evolutionary updates bring Morgan into the 20th century

Switchgear not entirely at home

stainless-steel internal roll-bar which runs behind the dashboard, the new seats are of the anti-submarine variety and there are even optional driver and passenger airbags.

One of the most radical changes is that a tool is now used to form the famous wings. Heresy to purists, perhaps, but the use of superplastic aluminium alloy makes for a more consistent and durable panel. And don't panic – the tin-bashers have to finish the return edge and fit the headlamp pod so there is still plenty of human input.

The factory has been thoroughly reorganised, but you wouldn't know it. Reducing work in progress and increasing quality hasn't made the place any less friendly, or any less like the

bespoke operation it always has been. Only the new paint-shop strikes a high-tech note: with 30,000 water-based combinations available, it can match your Mog to your wallpaper (it's happened).

Mechanically, the cars are much as before, though now they have a stainless steel exhaust and fuel pipes, plus a new fuel tank and internal pump. There's the narrow-bodied 1.8-litre Escort-engined 4/4 which doesn't feel as special as it should, the best-compromise Rover T-series Plus Four, and the slightly mad V8 Plus Eight. New to the range is a 4.6-litre version of the V8. The performance is noticeably more urgent than in the 3.9, with a welcome wodge of extra torque.

Morgan masochists will be pleased to hear that the driving experience is as spine-jarring and bladder-tingling as ever, although the new side-screens fail to flap like the old ones. If you've driven all the Zs, Fs and Ks of this brave

new convertible world you'll know how ordinary they can feel in traffic, or even pressing on sometimes. A Morgan, by contrast, never lets you forget that you are bowling along in a bespoke sports car. The Morgan experience is a unique one. It's an exclusive car built by real people at an incredibly reasonable price which turns every journey into an event. The only problem is that, unlike the mass-produced raggers, there's a six-year waiting list – though Charles Morgan has pledged to reduce this to around two (see page 164).

With this latest round of changes, Morgan has

demonstrated that it is not just a preservation society, but a forward-thinking company that is concerned about meeting Federal regulations in pursuit of exports. It even has a website.

If the appeal of the Morgan has to be explained to you, then you're never going to want one. All you really need to know is that the '98 Moggie is just as lovable/loathable as before. ★★★

MORGAN
PRICES: £19,999-£32,489
ENGINE: 4555cc dohc V8, 220bhp, 260lb ft
PERFORMANCE: na
ON SALE IN UK: Now (as long as you ordered one in 1992)

Torque-laden 4.6-litre V8 spices up performance

OLD MOG, NEW TRICKS

AFTER A GENERATION, THE MORGAN PLUS EIGHT HAS FINALLY GIVEN IN TO POLITICAL CORRECTNESS. HAS THE INSTITUTION BEEN THUS RUINED? NOT LIKELY, SAYS COLIN GOODWIN

I HAVE HAD TWO HUGELY ENJOYABLE DRIVES IN THE last few weeks. The first was in a new Nissan Skyline GT-R in Scotland, right through the Highlands, very rarely dropping under three figures. Blew all the cobwebs away and damned nearly my driving licence too. The second driver was on a sunny end-of-summer Sunday in Morgan's new and heavily revised Plus Eight. The roads were not as dramatic as those in Scotland, far from it. Surrey lanes, with no small amount of crawling Sunday traffic either. Never did I get near three figures; probably never went over 70mph, in fact.

The two cars could not be more different. The Skyline a laboratory on wheels with four-wheel drive, four-wheel steering, ABS and just a couple of turbochargers thrown in to make it work; complicated for sure, but also one of the finest high-performance cars in the world, and definitely among the fastest across country. The Morgan on the other hand is simplicity itself. There's a live axle at the back with drum brakes on its ends and sliding pillar suspension at the front. No power steering, no ABS, nothing that isn't absolutely necessary.

The drive in the Nissan was all adrenaline. Fun, but a bit hard on the nerves. The Morgan is the exact opposite. Driving it relaxes you, mentally if not physically. In so many modern performance cars the primary sensation is speed; take that away and you're not left with much. The Morgan Plus Eight is fast too, but it also sounds wonderful at low speeds and provides a fabulous view across the bonnet. But more importantly, it gives pleasure when you're not even driving it. Just looking at it is a pleasurable experience. So would be polishing it on a Sunday morning, perhaps after an early morning rumble for no reason other than the hell of it. In this age of clogged roads and speed cameras the arguments for Morgan ownership are stronger than ever.

Pop down to the Malvern factory and it looks as though time has stood still. Time doesn't, though, and Morgan has had to move with it. You'd be hard pressed to tell looking at it, but this Plus Eight has been radically changed; more than ever before in its 29-year life. Safety and emissions regulations have made it inevitable. Experienced Morganists will spot some of the changes as soon as they slide into the car. For starters, they'll have found the act of ingress easier than before as the doors are now two inches longer. There's more room inside because the seats have also moved back two inches and the dashboard forward one. You can't see it, but there's a stainless steel tube that runs around the dashboard to limit deformation in side impacts.

Our car is not fitted with them, but the Morgan is now available with air bags. With them out goes the glovebox, which is rather a loss as it's a big percentage of the available space gone west. I haven't seen the airbag wheel, but it's not likely to be a thing of beauty and it's certainly a thing of great cost – a cool £2056 for the full option. The standard wheel on this car has a nasty bit of padding stuck to its spokes. It would go in the bin straight away and be replaced by a wood-rimmed wheel. The Morgan now uses a Range Rover steering column and stalks. The column is adjustable for rake, but in such a small arc that it hardly makes a difference. The 15in wheel is still nearly in your lap. The stalks are ⟩⟩

Plus Eight interior (above) is more comfortable and easier to enter, thanks to longer doors. Twin airbags are a new and surprising option. Engine (below) is 4.6-litre unit, will take fourth gear from rest

SPECIFICATIONS

Morgan Plus Eight

ENGINE

Type	90deg V8 dohc, 2 valves per cyli
Capacity	4555cc
Bore/stroke ...	94 x 82mm
Compression ratio	9.4:1
Induction... ...	Lucas 14 CUX electronic ignitior fuel injection
Max power ...	220bhp at 5000 rpm
Max torque ...	261lb ft at 3600rpm
Specific output ...	48bhp/litre
Power to weight	221bhp/tonne
Transmission ...	5-speed manual
Ratios	1st, 3.32/6.8; 2nd, 2.09/10.8;
(mph/1000rpm)	3rd, 1.39/16.2; 4th, 1.00/22.5; Top, 0.79/28.5

CHASSIS

Steering	Unassisted rack and pinion
Brakes f/r... ...	Ventilated discs/drums
Front suspension	Sliding pillar, coil springs
Rear suspension	Live rear axle, leaf springs
Wheels	Cast alloy, 7x16in
Tyres	205/55 ZR 16, Pirelli P6000

DIMENSIONS

Length	157.1in
Width	59.1in
Height	50.8in
Wheelbase ...	98.0in
Track (f/r) ...	48.0in/48.0in
Kerb weight ...	2148lb

PERFORMANCE

0-60mph	6.0sec
Top speed... ...	128mph

KEY ENGINEERING POINTS

Concessions to modern safety standards have meant the dashbo moved forward an inch, a stainles steel roll bar concealed within it, a twin air-bags have also been mad available. While the 4.6-litre engin the largest ever to be offered in a Morgan, its true purpose is not mc power but reduced emissions

IN ONE SENTENCE

Safer and better, the Plus Eight ha lost none of its legendary charms

---

much better, though. They used to be so near the dash you grazed your knuckles using them.

That's safety out of the way, now it's emissions. Actually, it is the emission of noise that Morgan's engineers really had to address. To get the car to chug past the delicate ears of the noise meter in the drive-by test a 3.23 final drive was fitted instead of the previous 3.45 gears. Obviously that's taken some of the Plus Eight's sprinting ability away, so the chaps at Morgan have popped a 4.6-litre V8 under the car's louvred bonnet. Morgan always tries to use as many production parts as possible but the new 4.6 engine is not pulled straight from the Range Rover 4.6 HSE. It uses the block from that engine, but the 3.9's heads. The block has to be machined so that the 3.9's timing cover can be fitted. That's used

because Morgan puts an old fashioned distributor on the motor instead of the hugely complicated direct ignition system and mammoth ECU. The Range Rover is automatic only and the ECU gets so upset that the auto 'box has gone that it refuses to function with a manual gearbox. Good riddance to all that complicated electronics and welcome back the distributor, say I.

The new engine doesn't feel as responsive as the 3.9 or even the old 3.5-litre for that matter, but it does have huge torque. It is quite possible to pull away from a junction in fourth gear. Pulling off in first gear is really not worth doing. I found myself leaving in second gear and then going straight into fourth. It hardly hampers your progress. Besides, super-quick departures in first gear result in most

unpleasant axle tramp that gives the impression the whole tail end is going to destroy itself. The Plus Eight is at its most impressive when aske overtake from about 60mph. It'll blast past traf briskly as any supercar.

The new engine fits the Morgan's charact perfection. The last thing a car like this need motor that's all top end. Besides, if you start tr to thrash this car around the place the whole dri experience starts to become rather frantic. A yo colleague couldn't believe it when I told h thought this new Morgan rode quite a bit b than previous Plus Eights. And better it is, albei pretty appalling. The older cars used to crash potholes with such a bang that it was a toss u to whether the car's or the driver's backbon

Hard to believe this Morgan contains some of the most radical advances in the marque's long history. Mercifully it looks, feels and sounds exactly the same.

uld be the first to break. Trouble is, the roads that most enjoyable these days are often among the npiest. There you are, cracking along in the rgan at quite some pace, judging where to brake the upcoming corner, pressing hard on the brake al (no assistance), then suddenly you hit a bump the front end jumps, the brakes lock for a ment and it all gets a bit fraught. You have to t the heavy steering to get the car settled and on right track again. Some may say this is all part he challenge and fun of driving a car like this. not convinced.

You enjoy the Plus Eight much more when you e it in a more relaxed fashion. Top down, side ens in place, engine rumbling away gently. It sounds wonderful, this engine, despite the fact that it complies with the rules. You drive the Morgan hoping that around every corner you'll find a tunnel so that you can blip the throttle, sling the thing down a gear and bounce that lovely noise off the walls. I've never seen the attraction of a four-cylinder Morgan, and it's not just a matter of performance.

Ordering your Plus Eight without the optional leather, mohair hood and wood trim would almost be sacrilege, even if it does add almost £3000 to the Morgan's albeit reasonable £28,000 price. The Plus Eight's interior is very comfortable, at least while it's stationary. There's now plenty of legroom and even some extra elbow room. Sidescreens are a must, even on a warm day, as without them you are blown around rather too much. Cold days are no problem even with the roof down as the heater is nuclear in its output. Turn it on full blast and you'll be worried that there's a fire raging in the footwells. The stubby windscreen is now conveniently fitted with a heating element so that you no longer have to use your scarf to wipe away the mist. No Morgan has ever been easier to live with.

I was rather hoping not to take the car back to Malvern myself because I've had several narrow escapes from the place in the past. I'm usually fine until I step into the building where rows of Morgans await finishing off and then collection by their owners. It's a fabulous sight. This is when the cheque book starts to flutter in your pocket. There's a magic about the place that tempts you in. Owning a Morgan isn't like owning any other car; just as the car itself cannot be judged against others. It is unique. **M**

buyers guide
MORGAN 4/4, PLUS 4 & PLUS 8

Morgans simply scream traditional British sports car at you. Danny O'Driscoll hears some expert advice on how to buy one

HERITAGE. The one thing the British motor industry still does better than anyone else, which is why BMW just paid more than £40m for the right to build cars with Rolls Royce badges on them. Thankfully, there's still one British owned independent car maker that oozes heritage from its every grease nipple. Few car makers have the mystique of Malvern-based Morgan and in these days of mass-produced this, computer-designed that, it's reassuring to know that Morgan has refused to pander to fads and stuck with what it knows best, hand-building traditional sports cars for a discerning clientele.

Some writers criticise Morgan for retaining mechanical throwbacks like sliding pillar front suspension, but as far as Morgan is concerned it works, so why change it? Here's the rub: Morgans are built in such a traditional way a new approach is needed when it comes to buying one. That's why you need to talk to an expert like Phil Benfield, of long-time Morgan specialist Allon White and Sons, of Cranfield, Bedfordshire.

BODY AND CHASSIS

EVEN before poking beneath that curvaceous body, there are several areas to examine to get an overall impression of a Morgan, says Phil. Although the 4/4, Plus 4 and Plus 8 had different bodies and chassis, with variety in each, the same general rules apply.

A quick way to give you an idea of the state of the car, says Phil, is to check the wooden rocker member below each door, and the sill board that underlies it. With the door open, press your fingers into the cabin's side padding to feel for softness in the rocker, and look for loose tack pins in the threshold strip.

Another check is to look for cracks in the elbow panel because of the door being shut too hard, or problems in the wood behind. Doors also give you an idea of other problems and if the hinge pillar is flexing, the bottom joint will be weak.

The top part of the frame is long lasting. After 1986, wooden members were treated at the factory, but provided the wood is sound, there's no reason to reject a pre-1986 car out of hand.

That date is important because before then cars were spray painted with the wings on, while after '86, wings were

PHOTOGRAPHY BY JOHN COLLEY

Laying on of hands — Phil Benfield is showing how the brazing holding the headlamp pods cracks because of the way the body flexes.

'Morgans are built so traditionally, a new approach is needed when buying'

painted separately before being fixed in place. As the body is designed to flex, the paint cracks round the painted-over beading on pre-'86 cars, allowing moisture in, while it is not uncommon to find extensive rust behind the wing.

If you do need a replacement wing, they take a fair amount of work to get right as they are not pre-drilled by the factory: Phil reckons four hours is the minimum time it takes to get one to fit properly, but it can easily stretch to a day.

With the bonnet open, check for rust where the bulkhead joins the front wings. Once moisture has penetrated into the back of the toolbox, rust can

spread into the inner wings (valances).

On cars with aluminium wings, electrolytic reaction can occur along their edges, which are rolled over a steel wire and on the front wings where the steel support brackets attatch.

Underneath the car, refer to our pictures and look at where the bulkhead meets the valance. Stainless steel inner wings and bulkheads are now available from the factory. Examine chassis members for ripples or creases, which point to accident damage.

If you sniff petrol, check the corners of the tank for leaks — the mounting brackets are stressed when the chassis

Morgan 1955 to date Two- or four-seater sports car. Excellent spares availability, plenty of poke, easy to maintain and great to drive. Bit too harsh for motorways but fabulous for swooping along B-roads. Stand out from the crowd. £3000-£35,000

...es. Later cars' tanks are mounted on ...nks which reduce the stress and these ... be retro-fitted.

GINES AND GEARBOXES

A RULE of thumb, Series II and later ...s use Ford engines and gearboxes, ...s 4s have Triumph TR2–4A engines ... Moss 'boxes, and Plus 8s, Rover V8 ...ines and Moss 'boxes. Post-April 1972 ...s 8s generally have the four-speed ...nual from the P6 3500S saloon and ...t-'76 cars the five-speed Rover 'box. ...he 4/4 1600 replaced the Series V 4/4

in 1968 and was fitted with Ford's 1600 Kent engine until supplies dried up in 1981. Morgan then turned to Fiat's twin-cam 1600 and 2-litre engines and five-speed gearboxes, which they fitted in only 93 of the 4/4.

The Plus 4, whose name was revived in 1985 after disappearing with the last of the TR-engined cars in 1969, kept the 2-litre Fiat engine until 1988.

Fortunately, both Italian engines and the gearbox are tough units, but seem a little out of place in such a thoroughly British car. Check for cam and cam-belt wear. The 2-litre was never fitted in a

Fiat sold in Britain, parts are scarce here.

Alongside the usual checks for worn bores, valve guides and piston rings, as well as bottom-end rumblings, you will also need to consider the following.

Starting with 4/4s, the Ford sidevalve 1172cc engine used in the Series II will last only about 50,000 miles before its whitemetal bearings wear, creating a worrying rumbling — although it's possible to convert the engine to shell bearings with new con-rods. Coolant pipes break down with age and can lead to overheating. This engine, because of its long stroke, is also prone to wear in the rings

...the bonnet open, examine the strengthening plates ... front and rear of each bonnet half for corrosion.

The gaps around the bonnet should be even, if they are not, Phil warns the quality of the rebuild is suspect, or the car has been involved in an accident.

With his thigh lifting the door, Phil checks for flexing in the hinge pillar. Wear in the hinge itself is acceptable.

OUR SPECIALIST

PHIL BENFIELD graduated from the workshop at Allon White and Sons to become the approved Morgan agent's general manager. After an apprenticeship at a Vauxhall main dealer in Luton, Phil joined the Cranfield company, which offers every service a Morgan owner could think of, from MoTs to storage and complete restorations.

Because they make new cars, Morgan has had to keep pace with modern engineering under the bonnet, introducing ECUs and fuel-injection, so Phil, a member of the Institute of Automotive Engineering Assessors, has also made sure his own knowledge is up-to-date.

Allon White, which is still a family-run business, marked its 25th anniversary as a Morgan agent in 1991, although its involvement with Morgans dates back to the early Fifties. If you ever want to see how a garage should look, take a peek at the workshops behind the showroom, where Morgans are worked on by an array of craftsmen who have dedicated their working lives to just one marque.

As well as the traditional services, Allon White runs an efficient spares arm that can supply everything from suspension shims through to full body frames, chassis and wings. Not only can you buy the bits for your Morgan, but in return for just £250, Allon White will put your name down on the factory's waiting list for a new car. But be warned, the waiting list means it will be five to six years before your drive is graced with a slice of Malvern magic.

buyers guide
MORGAN 4/4, PLUS 4 & PLUS 8
continued

and bores. The 997cc Anglia 105E overhead valve four in the Series III can be difficult to start if compression has dropped because of wear.

The Series IV's Classic 109E three-main-bearing 1340cc is weak and suffers from bearing wear, timing chain rattles on high-milers, piston slap and broken piston rings, while the Series V's Kent 1600 shows its age first in the camshaft and followers, which can give off a clacking sound. It's not unusual to find a pre-1600 car running a 1600 Kent engine, as owners fitted the newer lump to overcome parts problems in the Seventies.

The CVH Ford from the XR3, fitted in the 4/4 1600, is prone to wear in its valve guides. If the bottom end is worn, it's usually cheaper to buy a short engine from a reconditioner than to rebuild one. Morgan replaced the CVH with Ford's 1.8 Zetec engine from 1993 on.

The timing chains in 1991cc TR2 and more powerful TR3/3A engines in Plus 4s wear, while emulsion in the oil points to the figure-of-eight gasket at the bottom of the liners rusting out in the 2.1-litre Vanguard engine fitted in dropheads until 1958. The larger TR4 and 4A engines fitted until the Plus 4 name was temporarily dropped, are equally robust.

Plus 4s were revived with the Fiat twin-cam, before gaining the Rover M16 2-litre, followed by the T16, both of which are unburstable.

Early Plus 8s overheated because the radiator couldn't cool the Rover V8 adequately. Oilways must be kept clean by using a quality oil and treating the car to regular changes to prevent wear in the cam. Duplex timing chains are stronger than the single chains, which stretch, throwing the timing out.

Early Plus 8s shared the Plus 4's Moss gearbox with either high or low ratios. Moss specialist John Smith, of Colchester, says it is possible to rebuild one at home, but it's unlikely you'll end up with a satisfying 'box — and there's the potential for some horrible mistakes.

'There aren't any special tools needed — you could strip one down in the middle of the Sahara, but it's not going to

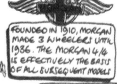

Both these are Eighties cars, but you'd be hard pressed to tell unless you're a Morgan expert. Note that even Morgans as young as these may need a rebuild if they have led a hard life.

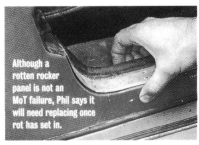

Although a rotten rocker panel is not an MoT failure, Phil says it will need replacing once rot has set in.

If the number plate panel flexes, it could be because the goal-post shaped wooden frame behind is rotten.

...r bottoms rust when water seeps past the glass seals, ...ch spreads to the wooden frame and rots them.

...e should only be one join in the panel below the ...; if it's missing, the car has been badly repaired.

'IT MADE me feel less selfish, as I have a family,' says Frank Orton to explain why his Morgan had to be a four-seater 4/4. But that is only the half of it, as Frank sums up the embodiment of what Morgan motoring is all about — not only does he have the practicality of a four-seater, but he also competes in it in hill-climbs and sprints and is an enthusiastic member of the Morgan Sports Car Club.

After owning a Turner which was forever undergoing restoration, Frank was determined that the next classic he had would never be off the road for more than six months at a time. And even after a bad crash while hillclimbing at Wiscombe, Frank's Morgan was back in action in time for the next meeting!

'It had already done 60,000 when I bought it, so it was pretty tired — Morgans do need rebuilding, as they don't stand up to years and years of hard use very well. So I rebuilt it.'

Despite systematically going through the car, replacing and repairing as required, Frank kept his word about the car not being off the road for more than six months at a time.

run sweetly — and there are bits you can put in the wrong way round,' he warns.

Overhauling a shot Moss 'box can easily cost up to £2500, while a straightforward overhaul is about £1000. But as John says: 'It might seem expensive, but people need to come to me only once.'

Another problem for Plus 8 owners is that parts for the Rover Vitesse gearbox, which replaced the SD1 unit when fuel injection arrived in 1985, are difficult to find — the same goes for Fiat 'boxes.

Worn synchromesh is the main worry with all gearboxes, but the Moss takes getting used to as it has straight-cut first and reverse. Plus 8 'boxes also leak, which is not too much of a problem, advises Phil Benfield, unless the quantity of oil is copious. Ford 'boxes are good but watch for the lever jumping out of gear, particularly in the Kent-engined cars, because of wear in the coupling dogs or selector fork rod, or because the selector fork has worked loose.

The limited-slip differential in Plus 8s should not make any graunching or cracking noises, and can leak, allowing oil to seep into the brakes, Phil says. The Series II to V 4/4 use a Salisbury rear differential, for which parts are unobtainable but axle specialists can

Turn the page for more buyers guide info →

PLUS FOUR PLUS (1963-66) MORGAN TOOK THE PLUS FOUR CHASSIS AND TR4 ENGINE, THEN WRAPPED THE RESULTS UP IN A GLASSFIBRE BODY AND SOLD JUST 26 OF THEM. INTERESTINGLY THE COUPE' WAS QUICKER (110 MPH, 60 MPH IN 12 SECS) THAN TRAD CAR.

PLUS 8 (1968 TO DATE)

ROVER 3.5 V8, 143 BHP, LIMITED SLIP DIFF, STEEL FLOOR, ALLOY WHEELS, 2" EXTRA WHEELBASE. OPTIONAL ALUMINIUM BODY IN '75, FIVE SPEED GEARBOX '77, FUEL INJECTION '85, 3.9 V8 '90 OPTIONAL 4.6 '97. UPRATES AS PLUS 4 FOR '97-98

1998 JAMES RUPPERT

READ THE BOOK

Original Morgan 4/4, Plus 4 and Plus 8, by John Worrall and Liz Turner. ISBN 1 870979 29 X. £19.95. Bayview Books
Completely Morgan: Four wheelers 1936 to 1968, by Ken Hill. ISBN 1 874105 33 2. £35. Veloce Publishing
Completely Morgan: Four wheelers from 1968, by Ken Hill. ISBN 1 874105 34 0. £30. Veloce Publishing

JOIN THE CLUB

Morgan Sports Car Club
£5 joining fee, £29 membership per year, bi-monthly 50-page A4 magazine, technical advisers for individual models, spares service, regalia, social and competitive events, regional and overseas groups, archivist (see Club Guide on p152 for contact details).

WHAT TO PAY

RESTORATION projects start at £3000 and go up to £7000. There's not a great deal of difference between two- and four-seater prices, although expect upwards of £10,000 for a good usable car.

Plus 8s start at the £10,000 mark and rise to a heady £30,000 for cars just a few years old. Mid-Eighties Plus 8s are £18–19,000 or more, for a good one.

SPECIALISTS

RESTORATION, PARTS, SERVICING, SALES, MOTS
Allon White and Sons,
Beds (01234 750205)
Brands Hatch Morgans,
Kent (01732 882017)
SALES AND PARTS
Morgan Motor Co,
Worcs (01684 573104)
GEARBOXES
John Smith, Essex (01376 570438)

There is also a network of factory-approved Morgan agents, including Allon White and Sons, throughout the country.

PRICES

When ordering parts always quote the chassis number.
Front wing: £288.66 (steel), £402.40 (aluminium)
Hood: £235.50 (two-seater Plus 4), £394.35 (four-seater). Both in black.
Clutch kit:£69 (Ford engine)
Wooden frame: £1407.95 (two-seater 4/4), £1681 (four-seater 4/4)
Kingpin: £12.50
Kingpin bush: £5.50
Chassis: £535 (standard), £630 (galvanised)
Disc brake: £36.55
All prices from Allon White and Sons (01234 750205) and are plus VAT.

INSURANCE QUOTE

£380 — 25yo, 2yrs NCB, 10,000, kept on the driveway, only car, clean licence
£198 — 42yo, full NCB, 3000 miles, second car, garaged, clean licence

Quote is for a 4/4 1600, from Lancaster (01480 484848)

buyers guide
MORGAN 4/4, PLUS 4 & PLUS 8

continued

rebuild them. Plus 4s, which have a Salisbury 7HA diff, can use the second generation Plus 4 diff.

SUSPENSION, STEERING AND BRAKING SYSTEM

THE FRONT suspension of the Morgan goes back to 1909. Although unusual, it's effective if looked after. Excessive play in the kingpin means it and its bushes need replacing, says Phil. Wheel wobble can be caused by worn kingpins or its pair of phosphor-bronze bushes, but can also be down to incorrect adjustment of the damper blades, which should only move in and out, not sideways.

There is a one-shot sliding pillar oiling system on all Morgans from 1951 onwards, which uses engine oil and has to be operated when the engine is cold. You'll need to grease the kingpins' grease nipples regularly — as well as the myriad of other nipples throughout the car — while also checking for cracks in the lugs at the bottom of the suspension pillar mounts. Phil reckons looked-after kingpins last about 18,000 miles.

Slack Burman steering boxes on four-cylinder cars can be adjusted but the pegs wear, although 0.5in play at the wheel is acceptable. It's possible to replace a worn out Burman box with the later Gemmer box, fitted from 1985, which costs £330. You may need to change the brake hoses and brackets, Phil advises, to prevent fouling when the steering is turned.

Lack of lubrication will kill the track rod ends, making the steering feel very heavy. They need greasing every 5000 miles. The UJs in the steering column also wear, Phil warns.

At the back, leaf springs sag and crack, while lever arm dampers can leak.

Some play in the kingpin is acceptable, says Phil, but test by grasping the bottom of the wheel and trying to move it in and out.

SPECIFICATIONS

	4/4	Plus 4	Plus 8	Plus 4
Engine	1172-1796cc	1991-2138cc	3529-3946cc	1995-1994cc
Power	36/4400-	90/4800-	160/5200-	122/5300-
(bhp@rpm)	89/6000	104/4700	190/4750	138/6000
Torque	54/2500-	115/2600-	210/2700-	129/3500-
(lb ft@rpm)	120/4500	131/4500	235/2600	131/4500
Top speed	70-114mph	100-110mph	125-122mph	112-110mph
0-60	30-8.9secs	13.3-9.3secs	6.7-6.1secs	8.8-7.7secs
Gearbox	3-spd/5-spd	4-spd/5-spd	4-spd/5-spd	5-spd
Length	12ft-12ft 9in	11ft 8in-12ft	12ft 8in-13ft	12ft 9in-13ft
	(3.658m-3.886m)	(3.556m-3.658m)	(3.861m-3.962m)	(3.886m-3.962m)
Width	4ft 4in-4ft 9in	4ft 8in-5ft 3in	4ft 9in-5ft 4in	4ft 9in
	(1.321m-1.449m)	(1.422m-1.6m)	(1.449m-1.626m)	(1.449m)
Weight	1540-1914lb	1800-1850lb	1900-2072lb	1870-1959lb
	(698kg-868kg)	(816kg-839kg)	(862kg-940kg)	(848kg-920kg)

Note: because of the wealth of different engine and gearbox combinations used, figures are approximate

ABOVE: power and torque of a Plus 8 gives it a sub-seven second 0-60mph time and 125mph top end. If you don't enjoy driving this, catch the bus.

LEFT: avoid the M25 and look for roads like this — there are still a few left — if you want to know what driving Morgans is really all about.

Kits to convert the rear suspension to telescopic dampers are readily available.

Lack of use — a perennial Morgan problem— leads to brake calipers seizing and possible master cylinder problems. The splines on the wire wheel hubs wear, while the spokes loosen with age.

HOODS AND INTERIOR

HOODS should always be put on from the back, Phil says, to prevent problems with overstretching the material and possibly cracking the screen. Hoods also suffer from fraying at the front and stitches rotting. As a hood is made for an individual car, fitting is laborious and best done by the factory or a trimmer.

Interior trim is hard wearing, but the stitching in the vinyl or optional leather seats splits and trim can be missing if the car has led a competitive life. Webbing underneath seat squabs on early- to late-Eighties cars deteriorates with age, allowing the squab to drop.

VERDICT

WHICHEVER Morgan you buy, you get a little bit of British history with it. Because each car is handbuilt it can also be hand rebuilt, but the individual nature of the cars means that many parts will have to be adjusted before they'll fit properly.

That said, the factory still supplies a lot of parts new, from chassis to hoods. So if, like BMW, you fancy a bit of pure British heritage, then the Morgan's for you. Picking one up for less than £40m should be no problem.

'Because each car is handbuilt, it can also be hand-rebuilt'

The suspension design dates back to 1909, but is effective if greased regularly.

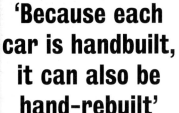

One key area for trouble, Phil warns, is where the inner wings bolt to the chassis.

derneath the car, look for corrosion where the assis crossmembers meet the longitudinal members.

They may look similar but there are plenty of differences between models. Plus 8s are wider than their four-cylinder cousins, while there was also the option of low or high bodies.

MANY THANKS TO

Phil Benfield of Allon White and Sons and **John Smith**, as well as the officers of the Morgan Sports Car club

Morgan Plus 8

Malvern Link leapfrogs past the 20th century—and just in time

BY DENNIS SIMANAITIS
PHOTOS BY ALLAN ROSENBERG

OUR MOST RECENT ROAD TEST of a Morgan Plus 8 was in August 1980. Our most recent First Drive of one was in September 1992. Yet here we are, not even a decade later, with the test of a significantly revamped Morgan.

The pace in Malvern Link, Worcestershire, where these wonderful examples of British sports car are built, has evidently been accelerating. In fact, in many ways the factory has leapt directly from Early Industrial Revolution into Post-modern Technoid, passing directly from Dickensonian soldering irons heated at the forge to manufacturing techniques as advanced as next year's SAE papers.

What ever did Morgan do?

But, first, for the benefit of those who have inexplicably missed any Morgan mutterings in R&T over the years, here's a one-paragraph history.

In 1909, H.F.S. Morgan built his first car, a 3-wheeler. Trikes continued in production until 1952. In 1936, sensing that 4-wheel motoring might be more than a passing fad, Morgan introduced the 4/4, its name identifying the number of cylinders and wheels. Since then, engines from one source or another have defined the Plus 4 (whose four cylinders were more powerful than a 4/4's—get it?) and Plus 8 (with a Rover V-8). The only anomaly was when H.F.S.'s son, Peter, got caught up in the Madcap Sixties and brought out the Plus Four Plus, a streamlined fiberglass coupe, only 26 of which were produced. Which brings us to Charles, H.F.S.'s grandson and the company's Operations Manager, and our Road Test of Morgan's new Plus 8.

In admiring our Plus 8's classic lines, you'd think that little has changed since 1936. And, in fact, the underslung Z-section steel ladder chassis is still there, albeit now galvanized. And still perched atop it is a framework of Cuprinol-treated ash wood to which body panels of aluminum and stainless steel are attached. With little nails and screws. Lots of them.

Just as cars used to be assembled.

But the aluminum front fenders—wings, our British pals call them—are no longer pounded out by hand; instead, they are made by an innovative vacuum-forming technique. It's not the first time this process has been used in the auto industry, but it's certainly the first time such technology reached as far as Malvern Link. And therein lies a tale: As fenders were previously hand-cut and formed to fit, Morgan had no drawings or patterns to offer its tooling supplier, Superform Aluminium. Instead, Superform digitized the fender shapes of three separate cars and used CATIA design software to produce a theoretical image of the typical Morgan front fender. From this, a one-quarter-scale model was formed and used to devise the tooling.

■ Rover (nee Buick) aluminum V-8 now has full 3.9 liters. Revamped cockpit features obligatory airbags—the passenger's artfully lurking behind matched burled walnut—and knee bolsters, the right-hand one doubling as a parcel shelf. Gizmo visible beyond flyoff handbrake is remote control for AM/FM/CD(!).

Thus, though other aspects of Morgan bodywork may still vary from car to car, a precise front fender shape is shared by them all.

As for these other variations, for example, Morgan cites that passenger compartments have now been lengthened by 2 inches. The doors are extended aft as well, still retaining their hand-formed inward curvature, top to bottom.

The reason for this lengthened passenger compartment is one of immense significance to Morgan and its sales around the world: A Morgan can now be had with driver and passenger airbags; indeed, in our market these passive restraints are standard equipment. The steering-wheel hub for the driver's bag is ungracefully large; the passenger's bag resides rather more artfully behind a flip-out panel of matched burled walnut. Knee bolsters

are part of the passive-safety scheme; though they look a bit clunky, they never actually get in the way and, in fact, the right-side one does double-duty as a parcel shelf.

It was no mean feat for a small company like Morgan to engineer airbags, especially within the confines of a classic cockpit renowned for its elbows-out driving position; hence that added 2 in. The rear deck is revised as well, though the wheelbase remains at 98.0 in. (or as Morgan prefers calling it, 8 ft. 2 in.).

The seating position is a tad lower now as well, to the benefit of head room—and the unlikely assumption that one might even erect the top. And, in classic sports-car fashion, "erect" is the correct word as well. You fiddle the frame into place, then affix the canvas with snaps and fasteners. If the weather's really inclement, there are side curtains as well, and the atmosphere becomes down-right cozy. All the better to enjoy our

Plus 8's AM/FM/CD.
AM/FM/CD?!

Isis Imports' Bill Fink knows my love of music, and I can't help accepting some responsibility/blame that such a device is fitted to our test car. As the controls are nestled quite far forward in the center console, the system has a remote control that's affixed with Velcro within easy reach.

But, after all, Morgans aren't about Mozart—or even Rasputina, for that matter. They're about driving, in an elemental manner that has attracted enthusiasts for nearly a century.

Here's where I might wax eloquent about donning stringback gloves, sighting along a louvered bonnet, blah, blah, blah. But, instead, I propose that a Morgan Plus 8 is one helluva neat sports car by *modern* standards. And, in substantiation of this, I cite the views of my colleagues—with nary a Morgan diehard among them.

About the engine, shared with the U.S.-specification Land Rover Discovery: "At first," said one staff member, "I was put off by not hearing the classic rasp of a British four or six. But the V-8 won me over in a big way. It really scoots this low roadster down the road!

"The gear ratios," he continued, "are perfectly matched for spirited acceleration runs."

Well, yes and no. In the real world, you're never at a loss for torque. However, in the rarefied realm of road tests, the gearing is tantalizingly short of reaching 60 mph at 2nd-gear redline, and this clearly played a role in our Plus 8's 6.7-second 0–60 run. In analysis, the leap from 50 to 60 mph (including that requisite 2–3 shift) takes longer than from 60 to 70, even though one is evidently on a steeper part of the acceleration curve.

The Plus 8's handling calls for no

1999 Morgan
Plus 8

Isis Imports Ltd.
P.O. Box 2290, Gateway Station
San Francisco, Calif. 94126
www.morgan-motor.co.uk

ROAD & TRACK ROAD TEST

At a Glance...

0–60 mph	6.7 sec
0–¼ mile	14.9 sec
Top speed	est 130 mph
Skidpad	0.86g
Slalom	61.0 mph
Brake rating	very good

List Price: $59,000
Price as Tested: $64,779

Price as tested incl std equip. (leather uphol-stery, rake-adj steering wheel), center-lock alloy wheels & wide fenders ($2500), AM/FM/CD w/remote ($650), gas-guzzler tax ($1000), luxu-ry tax ($1629), (delivery taken at Isis Imports).

SCALE: 10 IN.(254mm) DIVISIONS
DRAWING BY TIM BARKER

SPECIFICATIONS

Engine

Type......**aluminum block & heads, V-8**
Valvetrain......**ohv 2 valve/cyl**
Displacement......**241 cu in./3946 cc**
Bore x stroke......**3.70 x 2.80 in./ 94.0 x 71.1 mm**
Compression ratio......**9.3:1**
Horsepower (SAE)......**190 bhp @ 4750 rpm**
Bhp/liter......**48.2**
Torque......**235 lb-ft @ 2600 rpm**
Maximum engine speed......**6100 rpm**
Fuel injection......**sequential elect. port**
Fuel......**premium unleaded, 91 pump octane**

Warranty

Basic warranty......**1 yr/12,000 miles**
Powertrain......**1 yr/12,000 miles**
Rust-through......**none**

Chassis & Body

Layout......**front engine/rear drive**
Body/frame......**aluminum & stainless steel/ash & steel**
Brakes: Front......**11.0-in. vented discs**
Rear......**9 x 1.8-in. drums**
Assist type......**none**
Total swept area......**na**
Swept area/ton......**na**

Wheels

cast alloy, 16 x 7

Tires

Pirelli P6000, 205/55VR-16
Steering......**rack & pinion, non-assisted**
Overall ratio......**na**
Turns, lock to lock......**3.0**
Turning circle......**32.0 ft**

Suspension

Front: **ind sliding pillars, coil springs, tube shocks**
Rear: **live axle, semielliptic leaf springs, tube shocks**

General Data

Curb weight......**2250 lb**
Test weight......**2400 lb**
Weight dist (with driver), f/r, %......**50/50**
Wheelbase......**98.0 in.**
Track, f/r......**53.0 in./57.0 in.**
Length......**156.0 in.**
Width......**67.0 in.**
Height......**52.0 in. (top up)**
Ground clearance......**6.0 in.**
Trunk space......**3.0 cu ft**

Accommodations

Seating capacity......**2**
Head room......**34.0 in.**
Seat width......**2 x 16.0 in.**
Leg room......**46.0 in.**
Seatback adjustment......**5 deg**
Seat travel......**6.5 in.**

Drivetrain

Transmission: **5-speed manual**

Gear	Ratio	Overall ratio	(Rpm) Mph
1st	3.32:1	11.54:1	(6000) 36
2nd	2.09:1	7.21:1	(6000) 58
3rd	1.40:1	4.83:1	(6000) 87
4th	1.00:1	3.45:1	(6000) 121
5th	0.79:1	2.73:1	est (5100) 130

Final drive ratio......**3.45:1**
Engine rpm @ 60 mph in 5th......**2350**

Instrumentation

160-mph speedometer, 7000-rpm tachometer, oil press., coolant temp, fuel level

Safety

dual front airbags, knee bolsters (all standard equip.)

PERFORMANCE

Acceleration

Time to speed	Seconds
0–30 mph	**2.1**
0–40 mph	**3.7**
0–50 mph	**4.8**
0–60 mph	**6.7**
0–70 mph	**8.5**
0–80 mph	**10.7**
0–90 mph	**14.4**

Time to distance	
0–100 ft	**3.0**
0–500 ft	**8.1**
0–1320 ft (¼ mile)	**14.9 @ 91.1 mph**

[Graph: MPH vs SEC, ¼ mile marked at ~90 mph]

Braking

Minimum stopping distance
From 60 mph......**157 ft**
From 80 mph......**285 ft**
Control......**very good**
Brake feel......**very good**
Overall brake rating......**very good**

Fuel Economy

Normal driving......**17.7 mpg**
EPA city/highway......**18/30 mpg**
Cruise range......**244 miles**
Fuel capacity......**14.8 gal.**

Handling

Lateral acceleration (200-ft skidpad)......**0.86g**
Balance......**mild understeer**
Speed through 700-ft slalom......**61.0 mph**
Balance......**mild understeer**
Lateral seat support......**average**

Interior Noise

Idle in neutral......**68 dBA**
Maximum in 1st gear......**83 dBA**
Constant 50 mph......**80 dBA**
70 mph......**86 dBA**

Test Notes: The Plus 8 launches easily at around 2200 rpm; its shifter is precise but 60 mph being unobtainable in 2nd hampers the 0–60 time. With no ABS, it's easy to lock up the front tires and get re-sulting instability; brake pedal feel is good, however, so incipient lockup can be modulated. Mild under-steer and good grip characterize the handling, though bumps will upset the front wheels.

Test Conditions:

Temperature	Humidity	Elevation	Wind
70°F	21%	1010 ft	calm

Keeper of our Morganist faith

It's amazing that a company as small as Morgan has been able to keep up with the evolving complexities of U.S. emissions and safety regulations. In a very real sense, the folks at Malvern Link—and we—owe a great deal to a gentlemanly Anglophile named Bill Fink, whose Isis Imports is our usual source of Morgans here at R&T.

Bill got into all this back in the early Sixties through a love of collegiate rowing, practiced vigorously while ostensibly studying political history and business administration at Yale, Stanford and at Oxford, in England. While over there, he bought a Plus Four 4-Passenger Family Tourer (a green one, just like mine, come to think of it). Before long he found that he could turn a tidy little sum (I suspect, with the emphasis on "tidy" and "little") through buying Morgans in the U.K., converting them to left-hand drive and selling them over here. He got to know people at the factory, and a storehouse of spares got him into Morgan parts distribution here in the U.S.

With the onslaught of federal regulations came a phone call from the owner of an independently-imported Morgan stuck in U.S. Customs. Bill knew a little about what was required to legalize the car; and he has been learning the rest ever since. Anti-intrusion door beams, firewall hoop structures, propane power for a while (though cars are all gasoline-fueled now), cold-start emissions controls, cost-effective bumper designs, OBD-2 hardware—and, Bill's latest learning curve, airbags.

Bill and his wife, Judy, live in Bodega, California, with a menagerie of pets, including a pair of 17-year-old Himalayan cats waking them up each morning at 4:00 a.m. to rumble. The Isis digs at Pier 33, San Francisco, has its own cat contingent led by a lovely calico.

—Dennis Simanaitis

such hedge. On the other hand, here I should lapse ever so briefly into the engineering past tense. A Morgan's rear suspension is classic simplicity, a live axle on semielliptic leaf springs, the entire (and considerable) mass snubbed by gas-over tube shocks. In front are Morgan's legendary sliding pillars, an arrangement dating from H.F.S.'s very first car and later used by the likes of Lancia as well for years. An independent system (indeed, perhaps a bit too independent), the hubs slide on vertical pillars, their load carried by coil springs and their motion damped by a pair of tube shocks.

In theory, the front wheels are always parallel to the pillars; in practice, the pillars aren't necessarily parallel to anything else, yet the system evidently has its virtues. Our Plus 8 circled the skidpad at a highly respectable 0.86g and snaked around the slalom cones at 61.0 mph. Road Test Editor Patrick Hong reported that the car displayed good grip at both venues with only mild understeer.

Patrick also noted a Morgan oddity that's part of its period charm: If the surface is anything but smooth, its front suspension has a way of bobbing around minutely, this way and that, as the Morgan rounds a corner. Plus, you sit low and well aft of the car's center of gravity—it's about even with your shins, I'd guess. Hence, your perspective of all this is distinctly unlike that of other cars.

"I'd like more side support in the seat, though," said Patrick (and, in-

■ **No, its chassis isn't wood. It's galvanized steel, atop which wood, steel and aluminum are artfully (and classically) perched.**

deed, he can order the bolstered sport seat if he wants).

By contrast, Feature Editor Andy Bornhop, R&T's 6-ft.-4-in. linebacker candidate, said, "The flat seats are very comfortable. And, besides, I don't need any side bolstering as I'm already up against the door anyway."

I'm not as tall as Andy, but rather wider, and I too fit just fine. It's something of a circus act, however, to see me enter or exit with the top up (a bizarre and athletic display that's easily avoided by the simple expedient of leaving the top stowed).

Said Bert Swift, Assistant Art Director and evident aesthete, "Despite the addition of some unsightly equipment—the driver airbag, for instance—the Morgan is still drop-dead gorgeous. Friends who have no interest in cars fall all over themselves to compliment it."

In fact, this is an intangible characteristic of a Morgan (and one, alas, not shared by all enthusiast cars): It has a way of engendering good-hearted responses from everyone around you. If they're automotive enthusiasts, they likely already know something about Morgans and admire the car, at least in theory, for what it is. (I've had Ferrari owners give an acknowledging wave as we encounter each other.) And, as Bert learned, even if people aren't especially into cars themselves, they respond warmly to Morgan drivers because they assume that you're having fun. And, of course, they're absolutely correct in this assumption.

The Morgan Plus Eight doesn't know if it's Anne Hathaway's cottage or a Santa Pod dragster. Its raffish outline is pure thirties English, a car that would look perfectly at home – apart from its alloy wheels – in a film about WWII fighter aces: men with pipes, quiffs and square jaw lines dashing about the English countryside in sketchy sports cars.

The magic ingredient is Rover's all-purpose 3.5-litre V8 which Morgan first used to create the Plus Eight in 1968. Its still with us, 32 years on, and you'll still have to form an orderly line outside Morgan's Malvern factory to get your hands on a new one.

It'd be easy to dismiss the Morgan as a nasty retro car, like a Panther Lima, but its lineage gives it all the credibility it needs. Morgans have always looked this way and have always been built this way – alloy panels over a wooden frame.

This barely protected wooden frame is one of the car's weak spots – once it gets wet and stays wet, rot spreads quickly and can be expensive to sort.

Although it looks by far the oldest of our five, in some respects it feels the most contemporary to drive – in as much as sheer acceleration will never seem passé. Modern Caterham drivers would recognise its raw appeal as a car that can jerk your head back violently with every gearchange, spin its wheels with childish ease in first, second and maybe even third, and corner very flatly indeed. This flat cornering comes by

virtue of the fact that the Plus Eight doesn't really have any suspension.

Observed from a following car, the Plus Eight bounces along in a constant series of short, sharp vertical movements. The steering loads up heavily and kicks back strongly and you soon learn to control the car's attitude as much with your right foot as with the steering wheel. In the wet, lurid over-steer is a way of life, but lifting off soon gets everything straightened up again.

It all feels as bit loose, and on bumpy roads you'll think you've developed double-vision because the dashboard shakes around so much. It's a hand built car but, like so many handbuilt cars, it doesn't feel particularly well made or nicely detailed. Most of the dashboard furniture seems to have come from a Leyland parts bin labelled 'Marina rejects'.

The car we have here is an '81 with a five-speed Rover SD1 gearbox which is strong and positive, and it turns the car into a reasonable motorway cruiser.

Well, reasonable if you don't mind getting soaked: putting the hood and side-screens up is such a pain that you effectively drive around top down all the time. Boot space? You throw your luggage in a space behind the rear seats.

Buy one of these and you'd better be ready for some commitment, even if you only use it half the year. They thrill and tire you in equal measure, but on the right day, on the right road, its appeal as a machismo roadster for the real ale set isn't difficult to appreciate.

MORGAN	
MODEL	
Plus Eight	
ENGINE/PERFORMANCE	
3528cc V8, 190bhp	
0-60mph in 5.6secs, 126mph	
TYPICAL PRICES	
Condition 1 (great)	£15-17,000
Condition 2 (average)	£10-12,000
Condition 3 (crap)	£6.5-8,000
CONTACT	
Morgan Sports Car Club	01773 830281
THANKS TO	
Harpers Morgan	01923 260299
I BOUGHT ONE	
Michael Cooper	Internet consultant

‘ Ten years ago, I went looking for a car to have fun with. I fell in love with a Plus Eight in the final stages of re-assembly following a wings-off respray. It had started life in yellow with silver wings and a red interior. Ugh! Since then, the roof's only been on about 20 times over some 40,000 delicious miles of use. The car still gives me a buzz, even though I don't drive it every day. The best addition I made was a stainless steel exhaust that gave the car a proper V8 sound. I've had 10 years of fun, and that's spelled with a capital F. ,

WORCESTER

SAUCE

alvern-bred Aero 8. Steve Cropley drove it

By the time we hit top gear, a few hundred yards from the spot where Charles Morgan offered me the wheel of his new car for the first time, I understood why the world needs the Morgan Aero 8.

In the five months between the car's high-profile unveiling at the Geneva Motor Show and our rapid sprint across the foot of the Malvern hills, like many others I had imagined that this £50,000 newcomer might distract Morgan from what it does best: hand-building rugged roadsters from steel and wood.

In a few minutes, my mistake became clear. In fact, it was blindingly obvious. What you don't appreciate until you slip behind the new car's wheel are the consequences for the driver of its high-tech body, chassis and suspension design, its world-beating engine and its Ferrari-bashing power-to-weight ratio.

Initially, your eye simply falls on a coachbuilt shape with overtones of Plus 8, complete with leather seats, wood-trimmed cockpit, flat screen and a vintage-style arrowhead bonnet, and it doesn't see a supercar. But it should.

When you begin to drive, you realise that this Aero 8 is altogether too modern, too flat-riding, too well-damped, too *capable* to be some kind of carry-over from Morgan's old school.

It may still give you a Plus 8 driver's view of the world, but your hands and backside soon inform you, beyond doubt, that the entire mechanical package has been designed and developed at the Worcestershire factory over the past year or two using rigorous modern standards, rather than evolving from something penned before the war.

The Aero 8 is very much the brainchild of Charles Morgan, the family's third generation of Malvern Link management. He believes it has always been part of his destiny and has worked for the past four years with Morgan's stalwart engineering consultant, Chris Lawrence, ◗

All-new car, driven here by engineer Chris Lawrence, retains vintage styling inside and out; arrow-shaped bonnet hides BMW's superb 32-valve, 4.4-litre V8

Charles Morgan (left) explains how Aero 8's low weight was achieved by use of coachbuilt wooden frame in the style of more traditional Morgans

◆ to bring his ideas to life.

Only now is it clear what Charles Morgan was trying to achieve when he began an apparently fruitless GT2 racing campaign in 1996 and 1997, battling pure-bred, mega-buck racers with an unaerodynamic apparition that looked like a kind of tin-top Plus 8.

Gradually, details began to emerge: the car had a cleverly designed aluminium monocoque chassis, part bonded, part riveted, to be both stiff and light. That has been adopted wholesale for the Aero 8.

It also had an interesting all-independent, all-coil suspension (single top links with wide-based lower wishbones in front; double wishbones behind) whose spring/damper units were cantilever-mounted inside the main chassis members to cut unsprung weight and leave maximum room for a large engine. That turned out to be destined for production, too.

But the racing programme did much more than produce the Aero 8's hardware. It was instrumental in forging Morgan's relationship with BMW which allows the Aero 8 to use one of the world's finest V8 engines: the 32-valve, 4.4-litre all-alloy unit from the latest 540i, complete with double variable valve timing and 286bhp under the driver's right foot.

"We'd approached BMW back in '94 in the pre-Rover days," says Morgan. "Then we ran into BMW's engineers at the Nürburgring. We weren't nearly as quick as they were, so they were pretty surprised when we finished well up the order with an old Morgan that plainly wasn't very aerodynamic. We all got on well, and pretty soon they decided to help."

The BMW-Morgan co-operation has grown into something both companies value for more than its business consequences. In particular, the Bavarians admire the Aero 8's lightness: it weighs well under 1000kg at the kerb (a Plus 8 is around 950). The low weight has much to do with some of the core values the company has decided to stick to: a lightweight, coachbuilt body formed of alloy panels and supported by an ash body frame.

When you begin to drive the Aero 8, this light weight is not instantly obvious. The long nose and deep, well equipped cockpit give the impression of a big, substantial car (you tend to forget that the rear wheels are level with the small of your back), and the ride is so flat and well damped that there's a feeling of mass and rigidity as the car traverses broken bitumen in a straight line at speed. The pitching of the Plus 8 is completely gone.

Two things soon alert to you the new car's lightness. One is the alacrity with which it responds to steering inputs. True, this car has powered rack and-pinion steering, and rides on 225/40 ZR18 Dunlop tyres which have a very large

Aero 8's lightness helps make handling quick and accurate; 0-60mph takes under five seconds; cornering is excellent and six-speed 'box feels precise

Cropley examines all-independent suspension of Aero 8; Morgan lifts aluminium monocoque to show how light it is

FACTFILE

0-62mph	Below 5.0sec (est)
Top speed	160mph (est)
Chassis	Aluminium monocoque
Suspension	All-independent
Weight	Below 1000kg (est)

ENGINE

Type	32-valve, quad-cam V8, 4.4 litres
Max power	286bhp at 5500rpm
Max torque	322lb ft at 3700rpm

All figures are manufacturer's claims

VERDICT

New roadster with high-tech chassis and traditional look has supercar performance.

---

footprint. But there's no denying the impressive speed and accuracy of the Aero 8's response to the wheel, consistent with a light car with 50:50 weight distribution.

The other clue is the raw straight-line performance. Quite a few £50,000 sports cars have 286bhp – and more – but their acceleration is dulled by anything up to 500kg more body weight. The Mog has nearly 300bhp per tonne at its disposal, and engineers say it can sprint from standstill to 60mph in "well under five seconds" and will run well beyond 160mph. Top

(sixth) gearing is a relaxed 28.5mph per 1000rpm.

The Aero 8 feels both powerful and agile. It is an extremely flexible car, which can deliver instant, powerful performance in any gear but the tall sixth. Its steering is accurate and predictable, though not especially high geared at 3.0 turns lock to lock.

All the major controls – steering, clutch, gearchange, brakes – require pleasant, deliberate efforts but have a pleasant precision about them.

The Getrag six-slot gearbox is familiar from other applications:

fairly long of throw and heavy in supermini terms, but accurate and satisfying.

On our brief drive, cornering seemed close to ideal: bags of grip, very little body roll, a neutral stance even at pretty extreme road speeds, and a neatly controlled tightening of the line when you suddenly rolled off the throttle in mid bend. They tried prototypes with all kinds of stability controls fitted, says Charles Morgan, but that killed the car's ability to poke its tail out under power, which he didn't like.

Once you're cruising, the Aero 8's surprising aerodynamics come into play. The new car has a 0.39 drag coefficiency, low for any roadster, let alone a machine with traditionally

flowing wings like this one has. The new Mog may be around 40 per cent more slippery than a Plus 8, but it still has the age-old Morgan advantage of a screen fairly close to the occupants for top-class wind protection. Early indications are that this will be a top-down tourer par excellence.

The Morgan Aero 8 I drove is no production car, and only a general guide to what owners will buy. You should bear in mind that our test car had been built rapidly and driven hard, and some of its panels were glass fibre, not alloy.

Nonetheless, anyone who tries the car as I did will rapidly see that the Aero 8's ingredients make a fine mixture. This is going to be a different Morgan, but a very good one. ◎

AERO DYNAMIC

AMorgan in *BMW Car* magazine? What's the world coming to? You'd be amazed. In 1929 when the first car to bear the BMW badge appeared, the Morgan Motor Company, of Malvern Link, Worcestershire, had been building cars for almost 20 years. Seventy-odd years on, Morgan is still in Malvern Link, still in the same quaint factory where it had already been resident for 15 years before the first BMW 3/15 rolled out. It is still hand-building its famous sports cars.

But the latest Morgan is like nothing the company has built before, and it is powered by a BMW engine. What's more, the Aero 8 is easily the fastest and most accomplished Morgan ever.

In 71 years, BMW has built hundreds of different models, from bubble cars to supercars. In 90 years, Morgan had only

built four distinct types: tubular framed vee-twin powered three-wheelers, ladder framed four-cylinder three-wheelers, ladder framed four-cylinder four-wheelers and ladder framed V8-engined four-wheelers. The cars have evolved, but the basics have changed very little. They all had a traditional Morgan look, as does the latest, fifth generation Morgan, the BMW-powered Aero 8 – unveiled in Geneva in March and just reaching production now.

But looks apart, that's where the similarity with other Morgans ends. For 90 years all Morgans have had simple chassis with almost identical suspension layouts of cart springs and live axles (or just one driven wheel) at the back, and the infamous coil-sprung sliding pillars at the front. All have been clothed in a hand-formed body over a traditional wooden

frame, with looks that have survived in essence for over 60 years. Not any more.

And driving a Morgan wasn't like driving any other car. Morgans have always been unashamedly old-school sports cars, worshipping performance rather than conventional comfort and convenience. There haven't been any slow Morgans, but even the extremely rapid Rover V8-powered Plus 8 had the same flexible chassis and ultra-stiff suspension, which gave it great grip on a billiard-table smooth surface and a nerve testing, filling-removing nervousness on anything less than that. That was the Morgan way, you either loved it or hated it. But enough people loved it to make the length of its waiting lists the second most famous thing about Morgan.

Maybe the outside world doesn't understand Morgan as well as it thinks it

It has all the traditional British trappings, but underneath is pure Munich muscle. How does Morgan's BMW-powered Aero 8 stack up? Words: Brian Laban Photography: David Shepherd

does, because under the familiar skin, the cars have always evolved. No more than they had to, but as much as they needed to, keeping the company in business where others have failed, and satisfying a market that still clearly exists. Now, under the direction of Charles (the third family generation, and with father Peter regularly in the office next door), the aim is not only to evolve Morgan's products, but also to expand its markets.

Enter the Aero 8, the first ever BMW-powered Morgan production car. It is the first of a new generation with eye-open-ingly big-time credentials, plus a history rooted in Morgan motorsport. It may look like a Morgan – and may have attracted a lot of flak for doing so – but it's new from the ground up. And under the traditional body lies serious modern technology, and

massive performance. What's more, BMW's role was not on the fringes, it is at the heart of the Aero 8 story, which is worth retelling, starting in the 1990s, when Charles Morgan went GT racing.

In 1992 he had sketched his first ideas for a new chassis for the Plus 8 racer, working with former racing driver Chris Lawrence who had won the 2.0-litre class for Morgan at Le Mans in 1962. Lawrence, who is as clever a chassis man as you could wish to meet, became technical director for the Aero 8 project.

The original idea was to stiffen the Plus 8's bendy, pressed steel frame with strate-gically placed sheet aluminium structures, giving the suspension a chance to keep up with the Rover V8's ample power. When the the first version was raced late in 1994, it beat its previous best lap time

at Silverstone by 10 seconds. In 1995, it was superceded by a Plus 8 racer whose chassis used adhesively-bonded aluminium honeycomb sheet, and was twice as stiff as the production ladder.

This car had all independent suspension, with double wishbones at the front, trailing arms at the back, and coil springs all round – revised to all wishbones by the time the racing season started. Then, for 1996, there was a proper all-aluminium chassis, similar to the reinforced ladder – in effect the final link to the Aero 8.

Or almost. With the old Rover V8 finally nearing the end of its days, a new flagship production car would need a new engine, and that's where BMW came in.

Four and a half years ago Charles Morgan spoke to BMW and a deal was struck, with Munich becoming a partner in the development of the new car. BMW would help Morgan develop an installation package, delegating its engineers to the programme, providing access to BMW test facilities and Bosch ECU development, and eventually supporting the legislative sign-offs. The Aero 8 was on its way.

Morgan wanted a car weighing 1000kg, with 50/50 weight distribution, high-speed aerodynamic stability, good levels of comfort and a V8 with bucket-loads of torque. BMW's 4.4-litre four-cam 32-valve V8,

with double VANOS variable inlet timing sprang readily to mind.

Modified to suit Morgan's needs, the V8 is squeezed, without a centimetre of spare space, under the vast bonnet of the Aero 8. Although it has Morgan badges on its cam covers, it is a BMW through and through. It produces 286bhp and 322lb ft of torque. In 1000kg of car that makes for some interesting figures. BMW's Z8 has 400bhp and 369lb ft of torque, but it weighs 1585kg. Calculators out. The Aero 8 has a power to weight ratio of 286bhp per ton and a torque to weight ratio of 322lb ft per ton – according to Morgan, that's as much torque per ton as you can buy in a production car. Now things are getting interesting.

And the chassis is about as far removed as you can get from an old-style Morgan chassis. It is new and hugely impressive technology and design. Between the race cars and the road car, a super-stiff aluminium tub evolved, using innovative pre-coated, laser-cut aluminium panels and formed sections, bonded with high-performance adhesives and rivetted with specialised fasteners. This created a very light chassis that has unique detachable sections for easy accident repair.

The chassis carries an innovative suspension layout developed by Chris

It won't take a genius to figure out that the Aero 8 has oversteer for the asking

● The Aero 8 is an ingenious mixture of traditional and modern: lashings of handcrafted aluminium and leather adorn the cabin, while underneath lies BMW's latest technology giving staggering performance from the 4.4-litre V8

Lawrence. It uses lower front wishbones with long upper cantilever arms operating inboard coil springs and dampers. At the rear there are long wishbones and upper cantilevers with fully floating springs and dampers. It doesn't need anti-roll bars, and its geometry stays consistent over a large range of travel, so it promises comfort as well as exceptional control – and the Aero 8 delivers all it promises.

We are on the road in the middle of winter. It is cold, damp in places, with areas in the dappled light on twisting tarmac slick with fallen leaves – a thought-provoking recipe for a car with all that power and torque yet so little weight. But the conditions simply confirm what a stunning package the Morgan-BMW partnership has created.

In the flesh, the Aero 8 looks monumentally aggressive, almost malevolent, race-bred and every inch a Morgan. That, for better or worse, was another design parameter, and Morgan hasn't done too badly so far in giving people cars that look like Morgans. The order books for the Aero 8, at £49,950, are overflowing.

There are other Morgan traditions to be adhered to. The bodywork is aluminium over an ash frame, now with the largest panels hydro-formed, and with elements of the wooden structure neatly exposed in the cockpit. With a dash and other splashes of engine-turned aluminium, traditional round instruments and cleverly sourced switches that you won't find on any other car, and with the combination of low seats, high sides, tiny windscreen and thrusting bonnet, this is a unique place to be.

The snugly shaped seats only adjust for reach, but the column tilts and even for a tall, wide driver it's comfortable, because the Aero 8 is longer inside than any previous Morgan. The one bad bit is the lack of elbow room, because the inner door panels don't allow any, but Morgan is listening to its customers, so that may change.

The hood is best left down whenever possible because visibility is restricted with it up. It's fairly easy to put up with just two locking levers at the front and a couple of tensioning levers behind the seats.

In the flesh the Aero 8 looks monumentally aggressive, almost malevolent, race-bred and every inch a Morgan

Look out of the front and the view is wonderful. Although the car feels big initially, it soon falls into proportion. It goes, not surprisingly, like a rocket, but has a friendly and absolutely unique character.

The BMW V8 starts on a push button and sounds muted, but is clearly carrying a big stick. The six-speed gearshift has a familiar look and sits in just the right place. There's also a fly-off handbrake on the big centre tunnel and drilled alloy pedals buried close together, without much space around them, deep under the footwell.

But the Aero 8 is easy to drive gently, and apart from a fairly heavy clutch action is a pussycat at low speeds. The big advantages are all that torque and a remarkable degree of manoeuvrability. The Aero 8 has an amazingly compact turning circle and the option of sticking it in any mid- to high-range gear and burbling around as if you're in an automatic.

Drive harder and the combination of that wonderful torque, the tangibly light weight and linear throttle responses lay the foundations for a superbly balanced

and exploitable driver's car. The power that is so deceptively docile at low speeds arrives in torrents of acceleration when you ask, and the only traction or stability controls are a limited slip diff plus whatever you can muster on the ends of your arms and legs. The Aero 8 doesn't even have ABS, because no-one wanted to corrupt the pure sports car driving feel.

And they certainly haven't. With no more than a little tail end squirming, the

● The badge on the cam covers may be Morgan's, but the force behind this modern classic is BMW V8 power at its best

its balance of grip, suppleness and roll-free point-and-squirt agility are a revelation

Aero 8's big rear 225/40ZR18 run-flat Dunlops on the lightest available OZ Racing magnesium wheels, translate what BMW supplied into a sub-five-second zero to 62mph time and a 160mph maximum speed. Both of these times will give the more powerful but heavier Z8 a mighty run for its (considerably more) money, and the Morgan's mid-range punch – at any speed in any gear – will light up the broadest possible grin. It's huge.

In any earlier Morgan, this would be where the modern world ended, but the Aero 8's chassis is as good on the road as it is on paper. Even on damp B-roads its balance of grip, suppleness and roll-free point-and-squirt agility are a revelation. The body shimmies, but the chassis is stiff and suspension control is outstanding. The

brakes are staggeringly good, as ventilated discs the size of dustbin lids with four-pot AP Racing calipers on the front ought to be in a car that weighs this little. Like the throttle, their action is utterly progressive.

The steering is never light but always fantastically precise – the car goes where you point the nose, unless you want to adjust your line with the other obvious option, the throttle. It won't take a genius to figure out that the Aero 8 has oversteer for the asking, but with your bum so close to the rear wheels and with the car's co-operative throttle responsiveness, it's a joy rather than a threat. A real sports car.

When BMW's engineers first had their hands on the Aero 8 prototypes, they told Morgan this was something special. By any standards, they were very right ●

it promises comfort as well as exceptional control, and the Aero 8 delivers

first steer

Aero dynamics

I'm a Morgan virgin. I'm a Malvern virgin too. So I make no apologies for kicking off with the obligatory references to the 'sleepy' Worcestershire town where this 'quirky' car company continues to build its 'much-loved' but utterly geriatric 'motor cars'. Here we go, then. Malvern is sleepy. Morgan is quirky. Its cars are throwbacks to a gentler age.

But what's this? The man from Morgan is using the word 'revolution' more freely than Citizen Smith. There's a fax machine in his office. Heaven forfend, there's even a Morgan 'website' these days. Best of all – and the reason I'm losing my Morgan/Malvern cherry after all these years of celibacy – there's an all-new car, the Aero 8, the first such thing for 65 years. The snoozy denizens of this pretty English enclave don't know what's hit them.

Even my mum has a better grasp of Morgans than I do, because a man with a beard the size of Scotland and a fondness for real ale once took her for a spirited drive in one. That, in a nutshell, is Morgan's natural constituency. The Plus Four and Plus Eight have always been highly attractive cars, but largely irrelevant. The Aero 8, on the other hand, is largely unattractive, but highly relevant. It also has a power-to-weight ratio of 286bhp per tonne.

It's truly difficult to love the way it looks, though. Unless you don't mind getting involved in a bizarre boss-eyed face-off, squint while you're gawping

at it and it doesn't seem quite so bad. Nobody at Morgan gives a toss, happily admitting that the Aero 8's provocative appearance hasn't deterred customers. The waiting list is currently just under 600-strong – not bad for a 50 grand car – with about 20 per cent of Plus Eight customers transferring their order to the new model.

As demented as it might appear, the Aero 8 has actually been designed this way. And it works. Kansas farmyard barns slip through the air more efficiently than Morgans, but the new one manages a respectable 0.39 drag factor, flowing running boards and all. The in-set nose and flat under-tray keep the engine cool and assist underbody airflow. It also proves adept at scooping up autumn road detritus, much to the lensman's displeasure.

But at least it still looks like a Morgan, which is surely the whole point.

No visit is complete without a tour of the factory premises, and for all our host's revolutionary rhetoric there is still plenty of loving craftsmanship and traditional skill on display, not to say widespread evidence of builder's bum. And while we see both hacksaws and hammers being deployed in a way that defies the 'loving' bit, there's no getting away from the unusual truth that the Aero 8 is a genuinely radical creation.

Beneath the bonkers body lies an aluminium monocoque structure, bonded and riveted to provide the sort of torsional rigidity that low-volume British sports cars can usually only dream about. Not only is it strong, it's also light, and Morgan claims impressive crash-worthiness. A prototype

that survived a 40mph head-on collision with a Spanish truck offers visible proof. Perhaps the lorry driver was briefly paralysed by the Aero 8's boggle-eyed stare. Or maybe he was musing on why those crazy English persist in clothing their now state-of-the-art monocoques in wood. But persist they do.

Should you still be struggling to take it seriously, let me point you in the direction of Morgan's masterstroke: beneath the Aero 8's cartoon-car bonnet lies one of the world's best engines, BMW's 4.4-litre V8. The last time I experienced this engine was in an X5 off-roader and, despite tipping the scales at well over twice the weight of the Aero 8, it still had enough mumbo to blow my socks clean off. I admit to being hugely partial to BMW engines, but consider the facts: it has 32 valves, variable inlet-valve timing, a fly-by-wire throttle, a purpose-made Bosch engine management system, and it pumps out an easy 286bhp at a fairly lazy 5,500rpm and an even more mouthwatering 335lb ft of torque at 3,700rpm. Stick this in something that weighs 1,000kg and socks aren't the only underwear in jeopardy.

A Getrag six-speed manual transmission is charged with the task of getting it all cleanly onto the road, and traction control comes courtesy of your right foot. The massive AP Racing brakes – ventilated discs all-round with four-pot calipers – sound good; the absence of ABS sounds, er, interesting. The Aero 8 promises a sly blend of modern mechanical manners with explosive old-school performance. Apparently, some BMW people have been speculating that perhaps this is how the over-wrought Z8 should have finished up. Let's find out.

Whatever else has moved on, the Aero 8's doors haven't: they're still small and flimsy. Curiously, though, its cockpit isn't a million miles away from the exaggerated retro of BMW's pricey aluminium roadster. You sit low and snug, your arse-end only a few inches above the rear axle, facing a dash layout that has more than a hint of *Flash Gordon* rocket-ship about it, with big cream-faced dials nestling in engine-turned alloy. TVR-style rotary knobs take care of heating and demisting duties, while a motley bunch of nasty plastic switches operate lights and other ancillaries. These will be upgraded on final production cars, but the beautifully damped BMW indicator and wiper stalks will remain.

The driving position is exemplary and evocative, with enough legroom for even the lankiest of Morgan clientele. Chubbier customers might have some

trouble with the well upholstered seats, although a certain degree of masochism has always been part of Morgan's USP. As you'd expect, there's evidence of hand-built inconsistency in some of the trim but, again, that's surely part of the deal. So is the wood. It's everywhere.

Prod the green starter button and the Aero 8 wakes up with a surprisingly muffled woofle. Flex the throttle a bit and there isn't quite the amount of torque reaction you might expect when you drop a big V8 into a lightweight body, but it still feels very potent. The footwell is cramped for big feet and there's a racing-car abruptness and weight to the clutch and the accelerator. If it's high performance you're after, the Aero 8 sends out all the right signals.

Thank God its chassis is up to the job. Worcestershire in late autumn might be sleepy, but its roads are bloody

treacherous and even at modest speeds the Aero 8's rear Dunlops get well and truly duffed up by the laws of physics.

Morgan claims that the new car can pull 1g of lateral acceleration through dry corners and I don't doubt it, but take liberties on a greasy road and the only thing you'll be pulling is pieces of hedge out of your hair, believe me. But even as you're grappling with oversteer in the first three gears, at least you know when and where it's coming; a few hard seasons GT2 racing has clearly not gone to waste on the Aero 8, though I'd prefer even more sharpness in the steering.

Of course, you don't have to drive it that way, and fourth gear is where you'd be best advised to spend most of

your time if you really want to savour the Aero 8's immense performance. Racing genes or not, it does a grand job of grand touring, all that torque translating into a loping great stride on the road. If it wasn't for that outlandish body, it could almost pass for an Aston Martin (its switchgear is certainly better).

Central to this relatively genteel manner is a ride quality that is uncommonly good, especially for such a low-volume car. Morgan is rightly proud of the Aero 8's suspension, so much so that it has even applied for the patent on part of its design. Well, you can hardly patent wood, can you?

I'm no apologist for plucky British sports car manufacturers and would

generally plump for Porsche eff... over quirky, hand-built charm a... of the week. The beards (an... mother) are welcome to it.

The thing about the Aero 8 is... could have been absolutely dr... forcing Morgan to skulk back i... 1930s time-bubble while the res... fiddle with websites, queue up... PlayStation 2s and marvel at th... Middle Eastern meltdown.

But bizarrely – and quite poss... accident – the Aero 8 is a car... time. A very good one, as it ha... and much more focused than its... looks would suggest □

Story Jason
Photography Simon

FACT FILE	
Model	two-seater sports conv...
Engine	4398cc 32v V8, 2...
Performance	0-62mph in under 5...
	max speed 16...
Price	£4...
On sale in the UK	
Rivals	Marcos Mantis 4.6 S...
	BMW M Roadster, Corvette, TVR T...
Likes	engine, performance, ha...
Dislikes	styling, some interior de...